# CANADIAN SOCIAL POLICY FOR SOCIAL WORKERS

# CANADIAN SOCIAL POLICY FOR SOCIAL WORKERS

Edited by
**Robert Harding
& Daphne Jeyapal**

OXFORD
UNIVERSITY PRESS

# OXFORD
## UNIVERSITY PRESS

Oxford University Press is a department of the University of Oxford.
It furthers the University's objective of excellence in research, scholarship,
and education by publishing worldwide. Oxford is a registered trade mark of
Oxford University Press in the UK and in certain other countries.

Published in Canada by
Oxford University Press
8 Sampson Mews, Suite 204,
Don Mills, Ontario M3C 0H5 Canada

www.oupcanada.com

**Library and Archives Canada Cataloguing in Publication**

Canadian social policy for social workers / edited by
Robert Harding & Daphne Jeyapal.

Includes bibliographical references and index.
ISBN 978-0-19-902684-5 (softcover)

1. Canada—Social policy—Textbooks.  2. Social
service—Canada—Textbooks.  3. Textbooks.  I. Harding, Robert
(Robert Leonard) editor II. Jeyapal, Daphne editor

HN107.C36 2019            361.6'10971            C2018-906668-7

Cover image: @AlenaK/Shutterstock
Cover and interior design: Sherill Chapman

Oxford University Press is committed to our environment.
This book is printed on Forest Stewardship Council® certified paper
and comes from responsible sources.

Printed and bound in the United States of America
1 2 3 4 — 22 21 20 19

# Contents

# III • Social Policy for Social Issues   219

# Preface

This book grew out of a desire to create an introductory social policy textbook that is engaging, comprehensive, and relevant to the lives of social work and human services students. Both of us teach social policy and, over the years, have concluded that a fresh approach to the subject is desperately needed. Students often come into our social policy courses believing that social policy is boring and unnecessarily complicated, irrelevant to their lives, disconnected to the actual practice of social work, and impossible to influence. To address these myths we have included realistic, but in most instances fictional, "Case Examples" to illustrate how the lives of people, including social work students, are affected by their unique social locations and are impacted—sometimes enhanced, other times diminished—by numerous policies. The book also features "Social Policy Change in Action" boxes that describe actual policy changes brought about by social workers and social work students, as well as "International Comparisons" boxes to provide a broader context for the policy issues being discussed.

But perhaps what most clearly distinguishes *Canadian Social Policy for Social Workers* from other undergraduate social policy textbooks is our emphasis on public discourse, which we argue plays a decisive role in determining who and who is not "deserving," setting the limits of what social policy can and cannot achieve, and defining concepts such as inequality, need, citizenship, and community. Since social policy may function as a regulatory force, we feel it is important to explore how inclusionary and exclusionary discourses construct those who are raced, classed, and gendered as "less than" or in opposition to those Canadians "normalized" as citizens. Too often social policy serves as a means to colonize, racialize, or marginalize.

Canadian policy discourse is delimited by what has been tried before and what we are doing today, or through comparisons with our southern neighbour's more modest social policy landscape. To furnish a fuller context for policy discussions, we incorporate examples of international social policies that represent dramatically different approaches to many issues and populations, such as poverty, criminal justice, and Indigenous peoples. Our aim is to expand the definition of what is possible for social policy to achieve, and to provide examples of innovative and effective policies being applied in other jurisdictions. We are grateful that our vision was shared by a diverse and talented set of contributing chapter authors, each of whom wrote accessible, informative, and engaging chapters on key policy topics. These authors bring with them a wealth of social policy expertise and experience to their respective areas.

This book comes at an important juncture in the evolution of Canadian policy. The 2015 federal election signalled a change in direction in Canadian politics, with the new government vowing to create policies with an emphasis on gender equality and social justice, among other things. While the Liberal government has certainly not delivered on all of its election promises, it has put in place some promising new policies and has implemented, or is considering implementing, some of the progressive policy changes promoted in this book, including the indexation of benefits, such as the Canada Child Benefit. Hopefully, *Canadian Social Policy for Social Workers* will demystify social policy for social work and human services students; equip them with the knowledge, skills, and confidence to actively engage in policy discussions and processes; and imbue them with a sense of the transformative potential of social policy.

## Acknowledgements

As with most successful projects, *Canadian Social Policy for Social Workers* is the product of numerous collaborations and contributions from many people. We start by thanking Dr Christopher Walmsley, who in autumn 2015 approached us with an idea for a social policy textbook that would be comprehensive, practical, and relevant to today's social work and human services students. We are indebted to him for providing the initial spark for this book, and for bringing the two of us together and making our writing/editing partnership possible.

As well, we thank our contributing authors for producing exceptional chapters and for being wonderful collaborators who were always receptive to new ideas and demands. We also owe a debt of gratitude to our external reviewers, both named and anonymous, for providing us with meticulous, constructive feedback, including Samantha Clarke, Wilfrid Laurier University; Darrell Fox, University of the Fraser Valley; Cynthia Gallop, Mount Royal University; Susan Noakes, University of Victoria; Cristine Rego, Sir Sanford Fleming College; Akin Taiwo, Western University; and Mary Pat Thompson, North Island College. Their efforts helped make our book much stronger!

Others who made important contributions along the way include our research assistants, Kathryn Schultz and Sabrina Beattie. A special shout-out goes to Dr Eldon Yellowhorn for not only taking the lead on writing a crucial chapter on Indigenous peoples and social policy, but also for reviewing all Indigenous content in the book to ensure accuracy and consistency. We also extend our appreciation to our copy editor, Richard Tallman; OUP acquisitions editor, Stephen Kotowych; and our development editor, Leah-Ann Lymer, who was always patient, resourceful, and supportive, yet able to give us a gentle nudge when we needed it the most.

We would like to thank our partners, Anna McMurtry and Dominic Green, who supported us throughout the intensive writing and editing process that spanned nearly three years. Above all, this book is dedicated to our students—especially those taking our social policy courses—whose practical questions and critical inquiries pushed us continually to reassess and improve our social policy courses. Ultimately, they are the ones who inspired us to write this book.

Robert Harding and Daphne Jeyapal
November 2018

# Contributors

**Sarah Natalie Cooper**, MSW, is a research assistant at the School of Social Work, Dalhousie University, and has been practising social work with refugee resettlement for 10 years. Research/practice interests include intersection between refugee experience and (dis)Ability, international (dis)Ability policy, cross-cultural interpretation in social work and health settings, and program evaluation for non-profit organizations.

**Michele Fairbairn** is a PhD candidate teaching social work at the University of Victoria on unceded territories of the Coast Salish peoples. Michele has completed narrative research about child welfare workers formerly in state care as children or who were investigated as mothers. Her doctoral research is a post-structuralist policy analysis of social work regulation.

**Robert Harding** is an associate professor teaching in the BSW and MSW programs in the School of Social Work and Human Services at the University of the Fraser Valley. In the late 1990s, Robert led the university in partnering with the Stó:lō Nation to develop an Indigenous social services program based on traditional principles of healing and helping. He has presented his research in Canada, the US, Costa Rica, Scotland, Finland, Italy, Austria, and Germany, and has published in journals such as the *Canadian Review of Social Policy, Discourse and Society, Canadian Journal of Native Studies*, and *American Indian Culture and Research Journal.*

**Daphne Jeyapal** is an assistant professor in the Faculty of Education and Social Work at Thompson Rivers University. Dr Jeyapal earned her PhD in social work from the University of Toronto in 2014. Her research centres on challenging racial discrimination in social activism, social work, and Canadian social policy. She is the principal investigator for a SSHRC Insight Development Grant on "Anti-terrorism or anti-activism? Examining public and policy discourses on the criminalization of diasporic resistance in Canada." At present, she lives and works on Tk'emlupste Secwepemc territory, the unceded traditional lands of the Secwepemc Nation.

**Marjorie Johnstone** is an assistant professor at the School of Social Work, Dalhousie University. Her research interests are critical approaches to the history of social work, feminisms, and practice.

**Terry Kading** is an associate professor of political science at Thompson Rivers University. He teaches in the areas of comparative politics, Canadian politics, and local government. He is the editor of *No Straight Lines: Local Leadership and the Path from Government to Governance*, and (with Christopher Walmsley) editor of *Small Cities, Big Issues: Reconceiving Community in a Neoliberal Era.*

**Tamara Krawchenko** is a policy analyst at the Organization for Economic Co-operation and Development in Paris. Her multidisciplinary research has covered a wide range of topics—from rural development and the governance of land use to public finance. She has authored over 40 articles, books, and reports. Tamara holds a PhD in Public Policy from Carleton University and degrees in public administration, history, and political science from Dalhousie University.

**Judy E. MacDonald,** PhD, is Director of the School of Social Work and Assistant Dean of Equity and Inclusion in the Faculty of Health, Dalhousie University. Research areas include (dis)Ability access, inclusion, and accommodations within post-secondary education, along with anti-oppressive and critical practice. She supports (dis)Abled students bringing their stories forward through autoethnographic research methods.

**Nick J. Mulé**, PhD, is an associate professor at York University's School of Social Work. He researches the inclusion/exclusion of LGBTQ populations in social policy and service provision and their recognition as distinct communities in cultural, systemic, and structural contexts. In critically analyzing the LGBTQ movement he is working on the development of queer liberation theory.

**Jennifer Murphy,** PhD (University of Essex, UK), is a lecturer in the Faculty of Education and Social Work at Thompson Rivers University. Her research interests include critical criminology, in particular penal policy and reintegration issues; feminist/AOP perspectives; and social work pedagogy.

**Melita Ptashnick** is currently affiliated with the Factor-Inwentash Faculty of Social Work at the University of Toronto. She holds an MA from the University of British Columbia. Her research interests focus on inequality, health care, immigrant settlement, and education.

**Susan Strega** teaches social work at the University of Victoria. She is the co-editor, with Sohki Aski Esquao (Jeannine Carriere), of *Walking This Path Together: Anti-Racist and Anti-Oppressive Child Welfare Practice* (Fernwood, 2015) and the co-editor, with Leslie Brown, of *Research as Resistance: Revisiting Critical, Indigenous, and Anti-Oppressive Approaches* (CSPI, 2015).

**Christopher Walmsley** is professor emeritus at Thompson Rivers University. He is the author of *Protecting Aboriginal Children* (UBC Press, 2005), co-editor of *Child and Family Welfare in British Columbia* (Detselig, 2005), and co-editor of *Small Cities, Big Issues: Reconceiving Community in a Neoliberal Era* (Athabasca University Press, 2018). In 2013, he received TRU's Master Scholar Award.

**Juliana West** is an assistant professor in social work at Thompson Rivers University. She is the co-author (with Bob Mullaly) of *Challenging Oppression and Confronting Privilege: A Critical Approach to Anti-Oppressive and Anti-Privilege Theory and Practice,* third edition (Oxford University Press, 2018). Dr West's research areas include processes of criminalization and contemporary colonialism. She is the recipient of three teaching awards.

**Nettie Wiebe** farms near Delisle, Saskatchewan, growing organic grains and pulse crops and raising cattle. She held leadership positions in the National Farmers Union and the global La Vía Campesina movement. A professor emerita of St Andrews College, University of Saskatchewan, her recent publications include co-editing two volumes on food sovereignty and articles on investor landownership in Saskatchewan.

**Eldon Yellowhorn** is from the Piikani Nation, where he conducts historical archaeology research. He completed his PhD at McGill University in 2002, served as president of the Canadian Archaeological Association in 2010–12, and was the founding chair of the Department of First Nations Studies at Simon Fraser University.

**Daniyal Zuberi** is RBC Chair and a professor of social policy at the Factor-Inwentash Faculty of Social Work and School of Public Policy and Governance at the University of Toronto. His research interests include poverty, social policy, inequality, health, education, social welfare, work, and immigration.

# 1    A Critical Perspective on Canadian Social Policy

*Robert Harding and Daphne Jeyapal*

From our experience of teaching Canadian social policy to social work students, we have learned that students often think of the study of "social policy" as either intimidating or irrelevant. Removed from day-to-day life, it is seen as vast, boring, and difficult. The goal of this book is to demystify Canadian social policy for undergraduate social work students by addressing these assumptions. We will show that the study of social policy is a critical dimension to all social work practice, it is "real" and tangible, and it is an important window illuminating the values, cultures, and approaches to welfare in our society. In this chapter, we explore four central components that underpin our conception of **social policy**: (1) social policy results from value-based choices; (2) social policy affects everyone; (3) social policy is an instrument of social justice; and (4) a critical approach is necessary for understanding how social policy impacts social work practice. The chapter concludes with a summary of how the book is organized.

## Social Policy Results from Value-Based Choices

Scholars have created unique definitions to understand the realm of social policy and what it does, and does not, constitute. Chappell (2014, p. 477) offers a basic definition, describing social policy as "a plan or guideline developed and used by government to create, maintain or change living conditions to make them conducive to people's health and well-being." However, social policy is not the exclusive domain of governments. Graham, Shier, and Delaney (2017, p. 8) observe that the private sector is also involved in creating "policies that shape investments in Canada's social economy and in the creation of employee assistance programs." In addition to government and the private sector, voluntary organizations are also engaged in policy-making. Lightman and Lightman (2017, p. 64) point out that, not only is social policy a "form of charitable giving," it can also be seen as a form of "self-help on a grand scale—a community coming together to address common and shared needs and concerns."

Social policy is closely connected to people's values and beliefs. Indeed, Graham, Shier, and Delaney (2017, p. 9) believe that values are so deeply embedded "in every aspect of social, economic, and public policies that many social policy theorists . . . warn that a major role of policy-makers is to learn to control their own values and prejudices."

Policies result from deliberate choices made by policy-makers, and those choices have the potential to dramatically improve people's lives. Depending on one's perspective, they can either "act as insurance against capitalist exploitation" or they "can lock people into lives of dependency" (Lightman & Lightman, 2017, p. 64). Furthermore, as individual citizens, all of us have the capacity to make choices that influence policy development through our active citizenship—by joining political parties, participating in community development initiatives, engaging in civil disobedience to pressure governments to reform policy, and exercising our right to vote at the municipal, provincial, and federal levels.

We presume a broad and inclusive definition of social policy in this text, although we recognize little consensus exists about its definition. We view it as a regulatory force that constructs, maintains, and challenges social welfare and the state. Social policy is inextricably linked to economic policy and constructed through political processes within a context of interconnected systems and structures of power. In Canada, an examination of social policy reveals the social divisions of society and the unequal distribution of wealth and power in an increasingly neo-liberal environment.

Definitions are significant as they influence the topics often considered relevant—or not relevant—for study. Some regard income security, housing, health, and personal social services as key areas, whereas others approach social policy from the vantage point of social groups and discuss the old, the young, the disabled, the poor, the Indigenous person, and the immigrant. A historical analysis of Canadian social policy scholarship finds race and racialization, sexual diversity, criminal justice, and food security and sovereignty only infrequently within the purview of social policy. However, we believe these are important areas today. Race and racialization are central to understanding the logics and politics of a white settler society like Canada. Sexual diversity is an important site of contested rights and views. Criminal justice services sit at the intersection of poverty, race, and inequality. And food is both a basic necessity of life and an arena where Indigenous communities and grassroots social movements are confronting the environmental challenges of our times.

We define social policy as a regulatory force that constructs, maintains, and challenges social welfare and the state. To understand today's social policy outcomes, we situate this field in the reality that Canada is deeply divided along social, economic, regional, linguistic, and political lines, and these divisions impact the discourse, development, and implementation of social policy. Furthermore, we recognize that social policy-making in Canada is complex due to the differing federal and provincial powers defined by the Constitution, the role of the Supreme Court, the separate policy-making structures for Indigenous peoples regulated by the Indian Act, and the significant role privatization plays through non-profit and commercial provision of benefits and services. Benefit distribution systems and tax collection systems further mitigate and augment inequality in complex ways. Regardless of this complexity, at the end of the day, we locate policy-making as a human process based in power relations, and this process reveals the social divisions of society and the distribution of wealth and power in an increasingly neo-liberal environment.

## Social Policy Affects Everyone

All our lives are influenced by social policy to some degree. Social policies regulate how and whether we afford tuition for post-secondary education, where our children attend daycare, how we access health care, and the quality of the food we eat. It influences where we live, the conditions of our workplaces, and our income. It shapes and regulates our daily lives. Depending on our social location, social policy can be experienced differently: it may be experienced as a just right of citizenship based on the egalitarian foundation of a democracy, or as a form of social control that subjugates, oppresses, and colonizes us in society. As social workers, we also work within the context of social policy. Whether at a grassroots agency, a school, a hospital, an NGO, or within the government itself, the parameters and conditions of our work are determined by policy. As social workers, we have discretion about how policies are implemented and experienced, and we have a responsibility to use policy to mobilize access to people's social, political, economic, and civil rights. This requires us to develop a critical understanding of policy to recognize when policies do not meet people's needs and when they function as barriers to social justice.

As social policies are intended to address social inequities (though not always), social workers often explore policy areas from the entry point of the oppressed. This means that we typically attend to issues relating to one-dimensional figures: the "person who lives in poverty," the "woman," the "immigrant," the "Indigenous person," among others. While this serves the purpose of categorizing key areas of study, framing people and their experiences this way is problematic. First, it implies that an essentialized view of such a social identity category is accurate. It is not. Not all people who experience poverty experience it in the same way. Not all women are impacted by their gender unilaterally. Some are more vulnerable to the social forces regulating their lives and others are less, depending on their race, sexual orientation, social supports, income levels, health, housing, and marital status, among other factors. Second, categorizing people by a realm of oppression diffuses the reality that people's lives are multi-faceted. People's privileges and oppressions are also much more complex and intersecting.

Realizing the intersectionality of social identities and systems of oppression and discrimination is key to understanding the scope of social policy's reach. **Intersectionality** is a term first coined by Kimberlé Crenshaw in 1989. She, along with other Black feminist scholars, demonstrated that forms of oppression, such as race, gender, sexuality, and age, are shaped by one another. Therefore, to better understand the lived experience of a Black woman, for example, one must examine how her racialization and her experience of social systems and social structures are also shaped by her gender, sexuality, age, and socio-economic status. Attention to her race alone, or her gender alone, would not convey a complete picture of her oppression. Furthermore, scholars suggest that we incorporate a paradigm that recognizes that all social classifications, while understood to be distinct, are interconnected. Social systems and cultural patterns are not only interrelated but bound together and further influenced by the intersectional systems of society, a phenomenon called a "matrix of domination" or a "matrix of oppression" (Hill Collins, 2000).

## Social Policy Is an Instrument of Social Justice

According to the Canadian Association of Social Workers' (2008, p. 1) *Scope of Practice Statement*, "The profession of social work is uniquely founded on altruistic values respecting the inherent dignity of every individual and the obligation of societal systems to provide equitable structural resources for all their members." It encourages us to focus primarily on "the relationships between individuals, their natural support resources, the formal structures in their communities, and the societal norms and expectations that shape these relationships." Our *Code of Ethics* (2006, p. 3) further enshrines our profession as one "dedicated to the welfare and self-realization of all people," "the achievement of social justice for all," and the "needs and empowerment of people who are vulnerable, oppressed, and/or living in poverty." We do not tolerate discrimination on any grounds, and are committed to human rights protected through Canadian law, as well as to international conventions such as those established by the United Nations. Approaching social policy as the dominant lens with which to understand the social organization of Canadian society locates the intentionality of our work. In order to change society, we must first understand it and how it operates. We must know what social structures and systems are, and their limitations; who they value and who they ignore; who they benefit and who they marginalize. Only then can we locate ourselves as agents of advocacy to work alongside communities and colleagues to organize and advocate to better meet people's needs.

## A Critical Approach to Social Policy

In this book, we examine social policy from a critical analytical perspective. Critical theory relates to an approach within the social sciences that recognizes that we live in a world organized through great inequalities. Critical theory aims to confront and challenge this status quo. Critical approaches critique and theorize social injustice by unpacking the structures and systems of power that create conditions of inclusion for some at the expense of the exclusion of others. They aim to create the understanding necessary to transform our social context and promote justice for all. As such, our critical approach through this book centres on understanding how social policy provides the regulatory context to our lives as citizens and social workers. We view social policies as embedded within the social struggles, inequalities, and values that underpin Canadian society. We also unpack societal views about responsibility to others in various situations and stages of the life cycle, unpacking social policy as responses to the social pressures of a divided, unequal society. Social policy is not a neutral force but gendered, racialized, and classed. In essence, then, critical theory constructs and confronts the "matrix of oppression" in today's society. Our critical analytic perspective to the study of social policy examines the historical and institutional forces underlying social phenomena, the moral considerations framing policy shifts, and the role of ideological, economic, and discursive forces that lend coherence to the intersecting inclusions/exclusions of categories of people. Specifically, we explore who benefits through social policy, who is marginalized through social policy, and how.

Our approach is also unique in our emphasis on the social realm of discourse. Discourse analysis is the study of the social relations of language. It is based on an understanding that the rhetoric surrounding social issues not only informs public consciousness of a topic, but also forms the social structures informing it. For a study of social policy, examining political and media discourse allows us to unpack the parameters of how social issues and solutions are defined in Canadian society. It enables us to think critically about concepts such as need, risk, welfare, inequality, citizenship, and democracy—how they are understood both in our field and in society as a whole. Thus, the following chapter considers how people, politicians, and journalists talk about a subject, and the subsequent ways in which government policies are established, developed, and implemented. Through this book, we will show how policy discourses of social inclusion/exclusion organize social hierarchies of those normalized as the "citizen" against Indigenous peoples and those who are racialized, gendered, classed, or otherwise othered, to unpack how social policy has, and continues to be, a force of colonization, racialization, and marginalization in present-day Canada.

# How This Book Is Organized

This book is organized into three sections. In Part 1, we introduce you to ways of approaching policy and understanding policy processes, contexts, and functions. Chapter 2 introduces the role that media and discourse play in shaping our thinking about social issues and influencing how policies are conceived and implemented. Chapter 3 provides a historical account of how ideas about social welfare have changed over time, while Chapter 4 explores the political, legal, and social factors that shape our policy responses. Chapter 5 explains how fiscal policy—decisions made by government about how (and how much) to raise revenue, and from whom—may enhance, or detract from, our governments' ability to develop effective social policy.

Part 2 presents areas of social policy through various marginalized social identity categories. Chapter 6 examines the impacts of colonial and racist policies on Indigenous peoples, and describes how they been actively defining new relationships with settler society based on mutual respect. Many other groups have also experienced racism and oppression in Canada's white settler society. Chapter 7 explores how race, racialization, and racism are discursively constructed through social policy. Social policy also plays a role in regulating and controlling the lives of other people and groups. Chapters 8 and 9 address the effects of policy on the lives of women and LGBTQ populations. Chapter 10 examines how policy affects people with disabilities, while Chapter 11 focuses on children and youth.

In Part 3, we examine social issues that dominate the field of policy. Chapter 12 discusses post-secondary education policy—how we conceptualize and value it as a society, and how policy may facilitate access or create barriers to post-secondary education. Chapters 13 and 14 outline policy approaches to two areas of fundamental human need—housing and food. These two chapters examine the role that policy plays in addressing homelessness and hunger, and in supporting food security and food sovereignty. Chapter 15 assesses the effectiveness of policy in addressing the health care needs of Canadians, and identifies gaps and inequities in the health care system. Chapter 16 critiques criminal justice policy, highlighting some of the damaging impacts of our criminal justice system on marginalized and vulnerable populations.

Chapter 17 situates immigration as a highly contested area of social policy that is heavily influenced by neo-liberal discourses of nationalism, securitization, and criminalization. A common theme throughout our analysis of social categories and social issues is how poverty impacts the lives of many Canadians and exacerbates other social problems. Chapter 18 examines how myriad policies affect the lives of the poor, and proposes practical policies to ameliorate poverty. Finally, Chapter 19 summarizes the lessons we can learn from other countries' innovative policies, as well what we can take away from our own policy successes, including the traditional approaches and practices of Indigenous peoples. Social policy carries with it the potential for transformative social change.

While we categorize chapters by social categories and social issues to promote the readability of this text, we realize that our categorization of oppressed groups, by its very nature, is incomplete and problematic. We attempt to address this limitation through the anecdotes introduced in each chapter that highlight the complexities of people's lives. We also incorporate a framework of intersecting and interlocking matrices as we explore the dominations and oppressions underlying each social issue and social category. Through creative education strategies across chapters, including the use of features such as Case Examples boxes (at the start of chapters), International Comparisons boxes, and Social Policy Change in Action case studies from the perspective of social workers, we encourage you to engage with each chapter as an entry point to a complex area. These chapters, like the social identities and issues we present, overlap and complement each other. As such, we hope by the end of this book you recognize that social policy, while vast and complex, is an area filled with possibility and potential for social justice. In the concluding chapter, we consider ways we can actively engage with social policy as an arena of social work practice that offers resistance, social change, and social transformation.

## References

Canadian Association of Social Workers (CASW). (2006). *Code of ethics*. Ottawa: CASW.

———. (2008). *Social work scope of practice statement*. Retrieved from https://casw-acts.ca/sites/casw-acts.ca/files/attachements/scope_of_practice_august_08_e_final_17.pdf

Chappell, R. (2014). *Social welfare in Canadian society* (5th edn). Toronto: Nelson Education.

Graham, J. R., Shier, M. L., & Delaney, R. (2017). *Canadian social policy: A new introduction*. Don Mills, ON: Pearson.

Hill Collins, P. (2000). *Black feminist thought: Knowledge, consciousness, and the politics of empowerment*. New York: Routledge.

Lightman, E., & Lightman, N. (2017). *Social policy in Canada* (2nd edn). Toronto: Oxford University Press.

# I Social Policy Processes, Issues, and Realities

# 2 Media and Public Discourse

## Their Roles in Policy-Making

*Robert Harding and Daphne Jeyapal*

---

### Chapter Objectives

*This chapter will help you to develop an understanding of:*
- what discourse means and how it is constructed through multiple forms of text and talk;
- the culturally and historically specific nature of discourse;
- how dominant discourses are embedded in power relations;
- how discourse categorizes meaning and creates categories of people;
- how to perform basic discourse analysis of media texts.

---

## Introduction

Social issues and how we understand them and their solutions are constructed through media and public discourse. The roles of the media and the public are most critical, as they create the parameters of what is made possible and necessary within the Canadian socio-political context. In this chapter, we begin with an introduction to what we mean by discourse, and explain how discourse operates, circulates, and shapes conversations on social policy. The study of discourse cuts across numerous disciplines, and several theories of discourse and discourse analysis exist. We introduce the reader to some foundational concepts, and explore how media and public discourse inform social policy.

## Contextualizing Language

Language is never neutral because it is an expression of our personal and social contexts (van Dijk, 1988a). Consider the words "victim" and "survivor." Both are used to describe people who have experienced violence, but each word emphasizes a different aspect or degree of individual agency. These two words also can be construed to suggest temporality or a continuum of time: one becomes a "survivor" after having been a "victim" in the immediate moment and its aftermath. Words matter, beyond simply being politically correct. Reflect on some of the language used to describe migrants: "immigrant," "foreigner," "illegal," "undocumented," and "alien." Each word is political as it signals different dimensions and levels of belonging within the country. Each also points to the significance of the speaker: Who gets to define these categories? How do they come into being? When and how did some words become more popular than others? Language is never "detached" or "objective." By attending to some aspects of belonging and not others, the implicit ideological underpinnings of language highlight some dimensions of belonging and marginalize others. The additional element of identifying as any kind of migrant and not a settler, or simply as a "Canadian" and not a "settler," points to the significance and imagery of language. As Canada is a settler society, aren't all settlers migrants and all migrants settlers? Who is entitled to make these claims? Language is embedded in the socio-economic, political, and cultural interests through which it emerges and circulates.

# Understanding Discourse

You are likely familiar with the everyday definition of discourse that refers to written or spoken communication or debate. In this chapter, we introduce you to a theoretical approach to discourse. This approach includes an understanding of how power operates through language to inform knowledge and people's identities to create culturally and historically located meanings. In this context, all language (referred to as **text** by scholars who study discourse) includes written words, spoken words, body movements, gestures, dressing, accents, smells, codes, and conventions—basically any communicative act. **Discourse** is "a system of communicative practices that are integrally related to wider social and cultural practices, and that help construct specific frameworks of thinking" (MacDonald, 2003, p. 1). Put simply, discourse refers to anything written, spoken, or communicated to describe a way of thinking about and understanding the world around us.

A theoretical understanding of discourse allows us to consider how power is produced and circulates, how meaning is made, and how people are understood. It challenges us to consider how there is no single, objective "truth," that everything we know is constructed through our own cultural lens, and that dominant groups determine the "norm."[1] It allows us to examine how we privilege some conversations while marginalizing others. It permits us to unpack how we define people in certain ways while marginalizing other aspects of their identities. Over the past several decades, scholars from various disciplines have been dedicated to understanding the significance of discourse. In the following sections, we provide a brief summary of some of their important contributions, and share a few key definitions as we explore how discourse is produced by power (and produces power) and how it categorizes meaning and creates subjectivities.

## Discourse and Power

For critical social workers invested in social justice, understanding discourse is particularly important as it provides insight into the power relations underpinning our social context. Michel Foucault was a French theorist whose work focused on unpacking the saying "Knowledge is power." In his seminal work, *Power/Knowledge* (1980), he proposed that creating an objective truth on anything is impossible, but that people, typically a group of powerful people, create what is considered the truth. Since physical force is less frequently used in Western societies to enforce power, social forces do this work. Now a powerful few create and impose their idea of what is true, right, and good onto the majority of people.

Foucault claimed that statements about the political and social world are rarely right or wrong. Rather, "the question of whether discourse is true or false is less important than whether it is effective in practice. When it is effective—organizing and regulating relations of power—it is called a '**regime of truth**'" (1980, p. 131). His work suggests that it may be more relevant and necessary to consider how power creates these dominant understandings of the truth than it is to understand what objective truth may exist on any particular issue. While physical force may still be a component of how power operates, Foucault argues that the work of knowledge/power is achieved through language.

Foucault's many works examine the ways people are categorized as "normal" and "abnormal" through regimes of truth. By analyzing numerous historical records, he demonstrated that human behaviours of "criminality" (1975), "madness" (1988), "illness" (1973), and "sexuality" (1979) were favoured at some times in history and demonized at others. He also argued that contemporary society has increasingly regulated the lives of those considered "abnormal." During some historical periods, sick people were cared for at home and criminals were held accountable to and by their communities. In contrast, today, those who are not "normal" are increasingly examined, excluded, or incarcerated. Yet, Foucault argued that those who are "abnormal" still hold a critical place in society, because it is often in contrast to them that "normal" people are defined.

People with power construct the differences between those who are considered "normal" and "abnormal," and define what are considered to be objective criteria to differentiate the two. What most people know about "criminals" is based on the knowledge and perspectives of lawyers, politicians, and criminologists. What most people know about "patients" is based on physicians' perspectives. What most people know about "social service users" is based on social workers' perspectives. What criminals, patients, and the people that social workers serve have to say is not typically considered as relevant because it is assumed that they have no knowledge, or that their knowledge is less valuable. Without assumed knowledge, they also have limited power in society. Furthermore, specialists establish their fields based on dominant ideas of what they believe to be true. For example, the discourse of "criminality" produced by the criminal justice system, lawyers, psychiatrics, social workers, and others defines "abnormal" based on what is "deviant," "dangerous," or "dysfunctional" at the time. In doing so, they also construct the "normal" person who is functional, adaptive, and non-threatening. While critiques on Foucault's work are widespread, he provides a useful lens to understand how, as a society, we know who we are based on who we are not. These dichotomies inform the suppression and exclusion of the "other," as well as broader conditions and structures of power in Western societies.

## Discourse Categorizes Meaning

The meanings discourses create are never neutral. Discourses are politicized, as they reflect political interests, often of the political elite. **Dominant discourses** provide a singular interpretation of political, social, and economic events. Karim (1993, p. 197) explains: "dominant discourse maintains its superiority by being dynamic, continually co-opting and transmuting the words, images and symbols of other discursive modes that threaten its propaganda efforts. In this way it corresponds to the maneuverings of elites by whom it is produced and whose position it reinforces." Consider one of the dominant discourses of this country: "Canada is not a racist society" (Henry & Tator, 2006). Most people vehemently believe this to be true. It is a discourse that is strengthened intertextually. **Intertextuality** is a concept that refers to how discursive texts shape each other, based on the reader's prior knowledge and frameworks. While it may not be clearly apparent, other texts and voices are potentially relevant and incorporated in any given text. For example, the dominant discourse that Canada is not racist is created by multiple speakers—government, media, and politicians—building on the others to form a complex web of understanding. It is incorporated through our equity policies and immigration policies and in our emphasis on multiculturalism and human rights. Public and media discourses often use this dominant discourse of inclusivity to compare ourselves to other nations, particularly the US, to differentiate Canada as different and implicitly better. Dominant discourses permeate how we think and feel about particular issues, and they shape what we believe to be true—they establish cultural meanings.

A **discursive formulation** describes a way of understanding the social boundaries that define what can be said about a specific topic. It creates the parameters of the language, social relations, and social identities considered true, relevant, and appropriate for a particular topic. By constructing these parameters, a discursive formulation also signifies a range of social guidelines: "'is's' and 'oughts,' 'do's' and 'don'ts,' 'cans' and 'cannots,' 'thou shalts' and 'thou shalt nots'" (Goldberg, 1993, p. 26). Applying this concept to the above example allows us to consider the efficacy of the dominant discourse that "Canada is not a racist society." Its prevalence ensures that what we are exposed to through mainstream media and public discourse creates a coherent and consistent message. Events, histories, and people contradicting this message are viewed as "outside" this discursive formulation, and therefore they are not as easily understood or accepted as those that espouse it.

Recurring dominant discourses construct **systems of representations** to convey meanings (Hall, 1997). They provide readily understandable ways of interpreting events, histories, and people. As cultural theorist Stuart Hall (1997, p. 258) argued, such **stereotyping** "is part of the maintenance of social and symbolic order. It sets up a symbolic frontier between the 'normal' and the 'deviant', the 'normal' and the 'pathological', the 'acceptable' and the 'unacceptable', what belongs and what does not or is 'Other', between 'insiders and 'outsiders', us and Them." As social work students in Canada, you are already familiar with those who are considered "deviant," "pathological," "unacceptable," or "outsiders" within our multicultural society. We see "them" on TV, read about "them" on social media, and hear about "them" on the news. "They" are not like us. "They" need our help because "they" cannot help themselves. "They" appear different, threatening, even dangerous.

Representations are political and personal:

[These representations] sometimes call our very identities into question. We struggle over them because they matter—and these are contests from which serious consequences can flow. They define what is "normal," who belongs—and therefore, who is excluded. They are deeply inscribed in relations of power. Think of how profoundly our lives are shaped, depending on which meanings of male/female, black/white, rich/poor, gay/straight, young/old, citizen/alien, are in play in which circumstances. (Hall, 1997, p. 10)

The process of **othering** relies on a binary that divides a group into "us" (who belong) and "them" (who do not belong). Othering creates power relationships and hierarchies of superiority and inferiority among groups of people: men and women, white and racial-ized, able-bodied and differently abled, heterosexual and LGBTQ people. More insidiously, it assumes the dominant group is the "norm" that sets the standard that other groups are judged by and must conform to.

## Discourse and Subjectivity

Discourses create the social boundary that defines what can be said about a specific topic and specific categories of people. Discursive practices involve "ways of being in the world" that signify specific and recognizable social identities. As meanings are organ-ized through discourses, **subjectivities** refer to how identities are made possible within a given discourse. In other words, individuals are asked to occupy or must occupy certain subject positions to be recognized. A simple example of this is to reconsider the many binaries through which people are created, such as male/female, Black/white, rich/poor, gay/straight, young/old, citizen/non-citizen. Each binary pair is made possible by the rela-tion between the two terms, as well as through dominant discourses that construct what each term or category means. The binary of male/female is easy to unpack. Most people in Canadian society have some sense of what a "man" and a "woman" look like and how they are supposed to act. These ideas are informed by discourses of masculinity and fem-ininity that construct people's physical traits, styles of dress, mannerisms, behaviours, roles within the family, and even their occupations, thereby providing meaning to gender. Those that do not conform to traditional gender norms are typically not included in this dominant discourse. Dominant discourses also define what is desirable and undesirable within these parameters, for example, who are "good men" versus "bad men" and who are "good women" versus "bad women."

Despite their dominance these categories aren't fixed, as cultural identity "is a matter of 'becoming' as well as 'being'. It belongs to the future as much as to the past" (Hall, 1991, p. 225). Thus, identities carry signifiers of the past and present as they continue to evolve. Discourses are produced, reproduced, responded to, negotiated, rejected, and discarded. As subjectivities are informed through discourse and discourses are informed through power, changing social contexts bring shifts, change, and possibilities. For example, con-sider how the notion of the "desirable migrant" has changed over the decades. At one point, Canada prioritized migrants from certain parts of Europe to foster its colonial pro-ject and indoctrinate an Anglocentric moral and social fabric for society. It then priori-tized the manual labour involved in building the infrastructure of Canada. From there, it has embraced immigration to diversify the country and provide the skills, expertise, and population growth it required. In turn, both "citizens" and "migrants" know to regulate themselves and each other to perform what is acceptable, in order to be acceptable. The discourse, and thereby the subjectivity of the "desirable migrant," has changed through the decades based on what is economically, politically, and socially dominant. Policy changes alongside these discursive changes transform our social contexts.

# Social Policy and Discourse

Social policies are framed through dominant discourses. Dominant discourses provide the context for which social issues are considered urgent and necessary, and to what degree. They inform what is knowable and possible. Let's return to our example of the dominant discourse of "Canada is not a racist society." As Henry and Tator (2006, p. 1) argue, this discourse has "cast an illusory spell that has allowed Canadians to ignore the harsh reality of a society divided by colour and ethnicity. Canada suffers from historical amnesia. Its citizens and institutions function in a state of collective denial." The discourse that Canadians are not racist builds a specific national identity that ensures that Canadians feel good about themselves. However, in the face of centuries of colonial oppression and the enactment of racist laws, social policies, politics, and economics, the power of this discourse has effectively marginalized and ignored the experiences of Indigenous and racialized peoples. When some Canadians hear of racism, they assume it is something else, often the deficit of the othered person in question. This "blame the victim" mentality has allowed and enforced the implementation of laws, policies, and practices that don't address racism within institutions like the criminal justice system, hospitals, schools, workplaces, and public spaces. Instead, these environments can further criminalize and demonize Indigenous and racialized people.

Social policy informs, and is informed by, discourse. Through dominant discourses, social policies, alongside other legislation and state institutions, construct social issues and define their parameters. Consider, for example, missing and murdered Indigenous women and girls. For decades, activists, victims' families, and Indigenous communities across the country have been vocal and active in calling public attention to this nationwide crisis of violence targeting Indigenous women, girls, transgender, and two-spirit people. However, as recently as August 2014, Prime Minister Stephen Harper stated that this was simply a matter of "crime" and "not a sociological phenomenon" or systemic issue that required a policy response. However, when Justin Trudeau promised to establish a federal inquiry into missing and murdered Indigenous women during the 2015 election campaign, the issue was identified as a national crisis. The crisis did not take place over the span of these few months; nearly 1,200 Indigenous women and girls have been murdered or have gone missing in Canada over the past three decades. Yet, the shift of political power and public discourse altered the national consciousness on this issue, along with Trudeau's promise for a "total renewal" of the country's relationship with its Indigenous peoples (Murphy, 2015). We now have a national inquiry to address what is framed as one of the most urgent issues of our time.

Discourses create the labels we use to understand social issues and groups of people implicated in social policy. It informs who we consider at-risk, risky, wounded, angry, vulnerable, and poor. These are usually taken-for-granted categories that seem commonsensical and "true" until we start unpacking them. These subjectivities and social identities are informed and regulated through social policy. See the "Terminology" list created by the Indigenous Foundation at the University of British Columbia (http://indigenousfoundations.arts.ubc.ca/home/identity/terminology.html). The terms used to describe Indigenous peoples in Canada, such as "First Nations," "Inuit," "Métis," "Indian," "Indigenous," and "Native," reflect the complex relationship of discourse, subjectivity, power, and social policy. For instance, "Aboriginal" gained popularity by being entrenched in section 35 of the Constitution Act, 1982; "First Nations" describes Aboriginal people who are not Métis or Inuit, but does not have a legal definition; "Inuit" people are not considered "Indian" under the law; "Métis" is an identity that generally refers to people of mixed ancestry, but in a legal context has been restricted to refer to the descendants and members of specific Indigenous communities; "Indian" was legalized to refer to people registered under the

"Indian Act"; "Indigenous" is a term endorsed by the United Nations; and "Native" does not refer to a specific Indigenous ethnicity. All these definitions are contested as they signal complex power dynamics, colonial histories, inclusions, and exclusions. Some terms were imposed on Indigenous peoples by colonizers who have misrepresented them and controlled their identity, and other terms were fought for and claimed by Indigenous peoples to identify themselves. There are many other terms as well, including "treaty" versus "non-treaty," "registered" versus "unregistered," "status" versus "non-status," as well as a plethora of derogatory and slang terms, some of which have been used by Canadian government officials over the years. An understanding of subjectivities allows us to interpret social identities through histories of oppression and privilege.

Social policies, in explicit or subtle ways, for better or for worse, regulate people based on these categories of good/bad, normal/abnormal, deserving/undeserving, and desirable/undesirable. People's construction within these binaries elicit and justify different state responses. Edward Said's (1978) study on "Orientalism" explains the significance of this regulation and the ways in which it benefits those in power. Said examined historical documents especially emanating from European colonial powers in the Middle East, which was referred to as "the Orient" at the time, and demonstrated that Western discourses on "the Orient" constructed the stereotype of the "other" as savage, exotic, subservient. In fact, he argued that "the Orient" itself was a figment of Western imagination, as no homogeneous culture existed across the Middle East. Instead, its construction was "a political vision of reality whose structure promoted the difference between the familiar (Europe, the West, 'us') and the strange (the Orient, the East, 'them')" (Said, 1978, p. 43). Orientalism not only defined the Middle East in a dehumanizing light, but also allowed the West to construct itself in relation to this dehumanized "other." In contrast to Orientals who were "savage," those from the West were "civilized." Instead of being naturally "subservient" and in need of Western intervention, Europeans were naturally "dominant" and "superior." This was a fruitful strategy, and one that followed the paths of colonialism around the globe. The discourse Europeans created allowed them to produce the colonial logics and systems that justified the subjugation of people and the extraction of wealth and resources for European consumption.

Similar processes of othering have been used to justify the slave trade of Africans across the Atlantic (Césaire, 1972) and the colonization of Indigenous peoples and land in Canada (de Leeuw, 2009) and other countries. Over time, new stereotypes perpetuate the dispossession for previously colonized peoples (Larocque, 1989), frequently to continue to fuel capitalist economic enterprise. As Amadahy and Lawrence (2010) explain, the rhetoric of Indigenous peoples as "vanished" through physical and cultural destruction effectively erases their histories and their claim to lands as "there for the taking." Similarly, Black diasporic communities in Canada are racialized in relation to slavery to create an ongoing anti-Black discourse that constructs their deviance and criminality, among numerous other constructed socio-political traits. This ensures the marginalization of Black people in Canada, as well as Western interventions that create the poverty and political disenfranchisement of Black-led nation-states around the world (Amadahy & Lawrence, 2010, p. 106). How society frames people, their knowledges, their humanity, and their personhood undeniably influences who is seen to be worthy and have rights. The contradictions of how Western notions of "progress" are projected onto "others," who are imagined to be "savage," "inferior," or "abnormal" through social policy, are explored throughout this book.

# Identifying and Analyzing Discourse

As critical social workers invested in disrupting and dismantling power, we must first understand it. Power is typically invisible and normalized, and discourses often don't seem to have meaning or power until you unravel them. However, where dominant discourse can be exclusionary and destructive, it can also be contested. As the renowned bell hooks (1990) explains:

> Language is also a place of struggle. We are wedded in language, have our being in words. Language is also a place of struggle. Dare I speak to oppressed and oppressor in the same voice? Dare I speak to you in a language that will move beyond the boundaries of domination—a language that will not bind you, fence you in, or hold you? Language is also a place of struggle. The oppressed struggle in language to recover ourselves, to reconcile, to reunite, to renew. Our words are not without meaning, they are an action, a resistance. Language is also a place of struggle.

Our aim in this chapter is provide the analytic tools to unpack discourse and domination, to create strength, social justice, resistance, and revolution. Although discourse can be analyzed from various perspectives, in this book we take a critical approach, which emphasizes the relationship between language and power.

---

**Case Examples**  Contextualizing Critical Discourse Analysis

---

Scholars have approached **critical discourse analysis** (CDA) differently despite analyzing similar issues invested in power, such as racism, gender, political discourses, media discourses, and the construction and negotiation of identities. For example, van Dijk's (1988b) interdisciplinary system of critical discourse analysis "is heavily reliant on contemporary cognitive psychology in its concern with the 'social cognition' (van Dijk, 1988b, p. 181) of news production and audience interpretation" (Harding, 2007, p. 343). That is, his approach focuses on how people may perceive news reports based on a variety of cognitive factors including their "personal memories and experiences of events" as well as shared knowledge, values, norms, and attitudes (van Dijk, 1997, p. 31). However, similarities among these approaches emerge. An important emphasis of CDA is its attention to power. As Blommaert (2005, pp. 1–2; emphasis in original) argues, this approach does not merely "criticise power" but also includes "an analysis of power *effects*, of the outcome of power, of what power does to people, groups, and societies, and of *how* this impact comes about. The deepest effect of power everywhere is *inequality*, as power differentiates and selects, includes and excludes."

CDA does not approach the power of discourse and inequality as a singular force of any one person. Rather, it asserts that texts are often sites of struggle that provide insight into different ideologies and discourses that are negotiated for dominance. Therefore, close

*continued*

attention is paid to the significance of power in discourse, but also in how that power flows, circulates, and is negotiated through discourse. As Hall (1997, p. 228) has put it, "meaning floats. It cannot be finally fixed." Critical discourse analysis allows us to examine how language operates as a social practice, and to understand how discourses shape events, situations, institutions, and social structures and how they are also shaped by them. When we unpack and challenge dominant discourses and practices through discourse analysis (by disclosing cultural and historical forces underlying ideas, beliefs, and norms), when we reject them and choose not to collude with these discourses and their outcomes for individuals, and when we ensure the inclusion of otherwise excluded or marginalized subjectivities and perspectives, we unleash the transformative power of discourse analysis.

## Media, Public Discourse, and Policy-Making

Prior to the rise of modern media, local citizens would gather in the town square to socialize, catch up on the latest news, and discuss politics and current affairs (Habermas, 1993). Today's public squares are, in effect, the mass media, which represent the "essential lifeblood of a healthy democratic society" (Taras, 2001, p. 5). However, by the end of the twentieth century, the Canadian news media were already getting dangerously "out of kilter" (Taras, 2001, p. 240), partly due to the increased concentration of ownership. This conglomeration of media ownership coincided with a dramatic narrowing of the bounds of debate, resulting in a "right wing information infrastructure" (Taras, 2001, p. 210). Today, one huge corporation, Postmedia Network, owns the majority of mainstream print media outlets in the country (Gutstein, 2014), and ownership of media in all other areas has become more concentrated. Even Canada's public broadcaster, Canadian Broadcasting Corporation/Société d'État Radio-Canada (CBC/SRC), once a trusted alternative to commercial news media, has been underfunded and undermined, most recently through the "crippling" cuts inflicted by the Harper government from 2006 to 2015 (Tremblay, 2016, p. 192). Indeed, in many Western countries, including Canada, communications researchers have observed a trend towards "the gradual and calculated suffocation of public media" (Tremblay, 2016, p. 192). Even though, in its 2016 budget, the Liberal government promised to invest additional resources and revitalize the CBC/SRC, "the logic of neoliberalism continues to threaten the CBC and specifically how Canadians think about the role and merit of the public broadcaster" (McCurdy & DeCillia, 2016, p. 548).

Aside from the CBC/SRC, media outlets are owned by large corporations; therefore, it is unsurprising that much mainstream news content reflects and supports corporate values. News coverage is dominated by neo-liberal discourses that promote policies of low tax, small government, "economic freedom" for individuals and corporations, and a residual approach to social welfare. Media theorists Herman and Chomsky (1988) argue that the symbiotic relationship between corporate and political elites and the mass media has resulted in news coverage that simply "reproduces" the public's consent in the service of the interests of powerful individuals and corporations. Nonetheless, while corporate and political elites enjoy obvious advantages in getting their messages across in the media, news media also represent **contested space**. What becomes news is influenced and shaped by a wide variety of forces, processes, and actors, including journalists themselves.

## The Profession of Journalism, Objectivity, and "Truth-Telling"

The profession of journalism, which has its own set of professional values, operates within this highly corporatized environment. In spite of the subjectivities of individual journalists, historically, the profession itself has long aspired to reflect objectivity in news reporting. However, in recent years, professional journalist associations have largely stopped referring to objectivity; instead, they emphasize journalists' obligation to pursue the "truth" or "tell our stories," a popular line on the CBC. Still, news stories are cast in the language of objectivity and constructed as class-neutral, colour-blind, and impartial representations of *what is*, or what has transpired, by reporters who are only looking at "the facts" or the "truth."

The emphasis on seeking the truth represents a slight modification to the profession's traditional quest for objectivity in news reporting. While contemporary journalists accept the importance of *making every effort to achieve objectivity*, they have adapted a more pragmatic and flexible view of how to implement it in the everyday practice of journalism. Yet the term "objective reality" may have little practical application to journalism today. At the very least, the notion of the existence of an objective reality is highly contested and many would argue it is unattainable for journalists since journalism is not "objective . . . cannot be objective . . . [and] should not be objective" (Lichtenberg, 2000, p. 238). If one accepts the view that journalism is not objective and that multiple "truths" are possible, then all representations in the news media and popular culture must be regarded as social and cultural constructions that people interrelate to on a daily basis by either assimilating or defying them (Williams, 2003). Through this lens, reporters are akin to storytellers: they reflect and reiterate existing discourses.

Even so, there is little doubt that many journalists strive to report the "facts," attain objectivity, and make a conscious effort to separate their own beliefs and views from their reporting. Producing "balanced" news reports is one way that journalists protect themselves against accusations of bias. Balance, itself a prime value of contemporary journalism, requires that journalists are even-handed in their attempts to present different sides to a story. But what is balance? In many news reports, the term seems to be synonymous with the *two sides to every story* format. In fact, many reporters are so focused on finding "polarities" in news stories that when they don't find them, they abandon the story (Russell, 2006). News coverage of many social policy matters fits this two-pronged profile. Yet social issues are always multi-faceted, suggest diverse responses based on ideology and other factors, and impact myriad individuals and groups in innumerable ways. Furthermore, once published, stories are often dismissed or challenged by politicians and those in power because they are incongruent with their own ideological positions and platforms. A well-known example of this phenomenon is US President Donald Trump's dismissal of media reports as "fake news," a tactic intended to highlight perceived biases of journalists and media sources. By dismissing narratives as "fake news," he effectively reframes news stories based on the parameters he chooses to address, marginalizing the mainstream news that challenges the corruption of his presidency and inner circle.

# How to Identify and Analyze Discourse: Sample Analysis of a Headline

## Context

Early in the new millennium, the province of British Columbia, along with the cities of Vancouver and Whistler, collaborated on a proposal to the International Olympic Committee to host the 2010 Winter Olympics. The provincial and national news media closely followed this campaign and were generally supportive of the bid. Some British Columbians were enthusiastic about the bid, others less so, and some protested. Reasons for protest included concerns about social justice, such as the potential displacement of low-income residents of downtown Vancouver. Others felt it was inappropriate to spend vast sums of money on a sporting event given the high rates of poverty and social problems affecting Vancouver and the province generally. BC's over 50 First Nations also reflected various positions on the Olympics, ranging from collaboration and support to outright protest. On 2 July 2003, the IOC awarded the games to Vancouver.

## Lexical Choices

When applying discourse analysis to news texts, one of the first steps is to consider the **lexical choices** of the writer. The words used by journalists in stories and headlines are carefully selected based on conscious decision-making processes designed to convey particular meanings and definitions of events. Words have power, especially in the press where tens of thousands or even millions of people may read them. A simple word choice can influence the way readers understand an issue, define solutions to a problem, or view an entire population or group of people. A single word can access a whole string of associations, mobilize long-standing stereotypes, and evoke powerful emotions in readers. Consider the differences between describing someone as a "terrorist" as opposed to a "freedom fighter," or as "progressive" versus "left-wing." Verbs are particularly important as they convey the degree to which actors have agency or free will. Actors positioned as *subjects* of sentences—usually signified by proper nouns or subject

**Figure 2.1**  Front-page news

pronouns—have agency because they are taking action and can be constructed as "heroes" or "villains," whereas *objects* lack agency because they are the recipients of the actions of others and are often cast as "victims" or "survivors."

## Conflation

In this case, in order to describe the actor(s) carrying out the action in the headline, the headline writer chose the proper noun "Natives," which was, even at the time, an outdated referent signifying Indigenous peoples. Thus, the first word of the headline, which exemplifies subjectivity in discourse, has already delimited the possible identities of Indigenous peoples. Indigenous peoples are defined in relation to the long-established binary of Natives/non-Natives.

Furthermore, the writer made another significant lexical choice—in this case by *not placing* an adjectival modifier, such as "some," in front of the subject noun. A decision was also made not to mention the specific First Nation(s) described as trying to obstruct the bid. Since the question of *which Natives?* is not addressed, "Natives" connotes that *all* Indigenous peoples or Indigenous peoples generally were attempting to block the Olympic bid. This is known as **conflation**, wherein diverse groups and perspectives are subsumed into a single monolithic label. Conflation is a problematic feature of much *racialized* news coverage, especially when specific sets of behaviours or motivations are ascribed to all members of a particular racial group, such as African Canadians or Muslims, and significant variations and differences are glossed over.

## Us versus Them

However, this headline is remarkable not only for its conflation of diverse Indigenous peoples into "Natives," but also in its undisguised construction of the issue as one involving *us versus them* through the use of the possessive pronoun "our." This brings us to ask: *Who is included in "our"*? Clearly, not "Natives," the ones doing the "blocking." Given the racialized nature of the headline, readers might assume that it refers exclusively to white or Euro-Canadian British Columbians. The use of "our" establishes non-Natives as the "norm" and others as Natives. *Where do racialized and migrant communities fit into this?*

Not only are multiple Indigenous communities conflated into "Natives," but the headline also conflates a number of distinct Indigenous perspectives on the Olympics, which included protest, collaboration, support, and indifference. Only a minority of Indigenous people were protesting the Olympic bid, yet all Indigenous peoples were represented as trying to "thwart" it.

## Binary Oppositions

It is in the context of this **binary opposition** of Natives versus "us" that we can best make sense of verb use in this headline. Natives are willing to "go" all the way to Europe in order to harm "our" interests. "Block" connotes that Natives are trying to obstruct or prevent something someone else is trying to achieve. The idea that protesting the Olympics may be a valid exercise of one's democratic right to engage in civil disobedience in support of a just cause was not included in the agenda of mainstream media. Instead, in this newspaper, and in the press generally, the prospect of the Olympics "coming" to the province was portrayed as something intrinsically good for British Columbians, in particular, and for Canadians generally—a boon for the economy as well as for the international reputation of "our" city, province, and, indeed, the "imagined community" of Canada. This idealized, nationalistic vision of Canada's greatness exists alongside a great deal of inequality, and as Benedict Anderson (1983) has written, the newspaper has played a critical role in forging the "imagined community" of nation-states. In Canada, news coverage of Indigenous peoples and racialized migrants sometimes constructs them as "existing outside the symbolic borders of the imagined community of Canada" (Henry & Tator, 2002, p. 224).

Binary representations of issues in the press are ideological in that the audiences are being persuaded to support one position over another. In this case, the headline constructs Indigenous peoples as causing harm to non-Indigenous peoples, by obstructing something—the Olympics—denoted as positive for "us." Having this representation on the front page of the second largest circulation daily newspaper in western Canada privileged this interpretation of events, situated non-Indigenous British Columbians as victims of Indigenous aggression, and may have influenced public perceptions of Indigenous peoples. This discursive formulation of Indigeneity resonates with perhaps the most enduring trope about Indigenous peoples rooted in the Canadian consciousness—that of Indigenous peoples as "Warriors."

*Why would this newspaper in particular, and the news media in general, take this position on the Olympics and characterize Indigenous peoples in this way?* First, major international sporting events of this nature are seen as good for business for news organizations. After all, such events generate heightened public interest not only in the sporting events themselves, but also in the financing, buildup, and promotion in the months and years leading up to them. In the case of the print media, this means more work for journalists, higher sales, and more advertising revenue. Second, corporate media owners have holdings in other sectors, such as retail, finance, and manufacturing, and these enterprises may benefit economically from the additional spending in the local economy stimulated by the Olympics. Finally, the implicit representation of "Natives"-as-obstructionist is part of a larger neo-liberal policy discourse in which Indigenous peoples are seen as threatening the economic vitality of the province through treaty negotiation and land claims. Indeed, much contemporary news discourse about treaties is anchored in cautionary tales about the dire threat posed by increased Indigenous control of the land to British Columbia's elite business interests and to neo-liberal conceptions of "democracy" and "equality." These are just a few of the elements of intertextuality that shape the interpretative framework that readers may bring to bear in making sense of this single headline.

## Student Exercise

The headline "Natives go to Europe to block our Olympic bid" on the 27 June 2002 front page of the Vancouver tabloid newspaper, *The Province* (see Figure 2.1) strongly reinforces an image of Indigenous people as contentious and standing in the way of progress and economic opportunity.

1.  What impact would this type of headline have on relations between Indigenous and non-Indigenous British Columbians? How might this story have been different if it had been written from an Indigenous person's perspective?

2. What options did the headline writer/editor have?
3. Based on what you now know about the issue, rewrite the headline. How would your headline have changed how readers might have interpreted the story? What impact might this have had on how British Columbians viewed Indigenous peoples?
4. Considering the time that has passed since this headline, how have dominant discourses evolved or stayed the same? Which current social issues illicit similar discourses?

# Features of the News

## Ownership and News Content

In Canada, as in other countries, very large corporations, often transnational in nature, own the majority of newspapers, television and radio stations, and Internet providers. For example, the Postmedia Network Canada Corporation is the largest publisher of English-language publications in the country. In addition to the *National Post*, its holdings include eight broadsheet dailies, six tabloid dailies, *24 Hours* (a free daily distributed in Toronto and Vancouver), dozens of community newspapers, and several magazines. Fifty-eight per cent of this huge corporation is owned by a consortium of investment and asset management companies, including two American hedge funds, Silver Point Capital and Golden Tree Asset Management (Gutstein, 2014).

How could the ownership of a media corporation affect news content? Consider news coverage of poverty. Clearly, reducing poverty rates through government intervention is expensive, at least in the short term, and has implications for taxation levels. It is in the best interests of media corporations to favour commentary that discredits government-funded social services and frames poverty as an individual problem, one best left to market forces. Indeed, the regime of truth about poverty in the news media includes the idea that poor people ought not to rely on government programs, but should instead fend for themselves and "pull themselves up by their bootstraps." As Foucault pointed out, the veracity of a dominant discourse is less important than its "effectiveness," and, in this case, the dominant discourse about reducing social services has been reflected in government policy through cuts to programs and the erosion of the real value of income support benefits due to inflation.

A study of *National Post* poverty reportage supports this hypothesis. This national newspaper offered a simple neo-liberal prescription to the problem of poverty: *leave it to "market forces" and individual initiative* (Harding, in press). The efforts of anti-poverty campaigners were constructed as inimical to the economic health of the country as a whole and poor people in particular. Anti-poverty advocates were constructed as being outside the normative base of Canadian politics. Descriptors such as "leftist," "left-leaning," "left-wing," or "on the left" were routinely employed to delegitimize them. Their efforts were characterized as costly, ineffective, and even counterproductive in that their actions actually made things worse for the poor. On the other hand, business people and pro–free market economists were constructed as the sole experts on poverty reduction. The newspaper's portrayal of anti-poverty advocates and poverty reduction policy is an example of Foucault's concept of the "practical exercise of power" discussed earlier in this chapter.

Indeed, Postmedia, the parent corporation of the *National Post*, has shown a willingness to vigorously represent its corporate interests through its media strategies. For example, the corporation gave a presentation to the Canadian Association of Petroleum

Producers enthusiastically offering to collaborate with the oil and gas industry to "'bring energy to the forefront of the national conversation,' and 'engage executives, the business community, and the Canadian public to underscore the ways in which the energy sector powers Canada'" (Gunster & Saurette, 2014, p. 335).

## Media and Framing[2]

In *The Whole World Is Watching: Mass Media in the Making and Unmaking of the New Left*, Todd Gitlin (1980, p. 6) advances his classic definition of a news frame as "principles of selection, emphasis and presentation composed of tacit little theories of what exists, what happens, and what matters . . . that routinely organize the news." In effect, news **framing** singles out certain themes or *storylines* for attention while de-emphasizing or ignoring others. Related to news frames is the concept of **scripts**. While news frames exemplify themes or topics in news stories, scripts refer to the specific sets of behaviours ascribed to certain types of actors. In *Language and Power* (1989), Fairclough writes that scripts "typify the ways in which specific classes of subjects behave in social activities, and how members of specific classes of subjects behave towards each other—how they conduct relationships" (Fairclough, 1989, pp. 158–9). Some scripts are culturally based. For example, in news discourse about sports in the United States, a popular script is that of the African-American athlete from the urban ghetto who rises above an environment of poverty and crime by parlaying a strong work ethic and athletic prowess into fame and fortune as a professional athlete in a sport such as basketball, football, or boxing. There are strict social expectations about how these actors must behave in a range of situations.

## The Power of Headlines

Headlines direct audiences' attention to prominent semantic features of news texts. While some headlines summarize content, others are more likely to represent selected aspects of news stories as more important than others. Headlines, along with lead paragraphs, are the "most likely" feature of news texts to be remembered by audiences when defining issues and events later on (Lambertus, 2004). Headlines are usually written by editors and not by the reporters who write the news stories. They direct attention to what those editors consider the main meanings of news stories. Even readers who have not read a particular article may form images and opinions of events and groups solely based on that story's headline.

Headlines may have connotations and implications that are distinct from the news texts associated with them and may be analyzed separately. Because they contain potent and highly compressed information that cue audience interpretation of issues and events, an analysis of them may yield important clues about news frames, semantic strategies, linguistic techniques, and other features of discourse, as we saw above in the discussion of a headline from a British Columbia newspaper.

## Stereotyping

The phenomenon of stereotyping—how it arises, what function it performs, and its impact—has an interesting history that might provide insight into contemporary manifestations. While it may have harmful consequences for those subjected to it, in fact, stereotyping is a feature of basic cognition. In today's digital media universe, stereotyping enables people to efficiently sort and interpret large amounts of data by affixing specific labels to particular aspects. However, when people attach labels to entire groups or broad classes of individuals (e.g., Indigenous people, the LGBTQ "community," or single mothers), whole patterns of behaviour and constellations of personality traits are ascribed to individuals. Yet stereotyping performs a useful function for busy reporters who must quickly fashion compelling stories about people, issues, and events. By invoking stereotypes, journalists avail themselves of a ready-made structure that will support their stories.

Technological advances in news production in the early to mid-twentieth century may have made the use of stereotypes almost unavoidable since the brief amount of time available to produce enormous quantities of news text and other media materials required the use of specialized "formulas" (Adorno, 1957). By the end of the twentieth century, journalists were required to produce twice as much copy as they did in the 1960s (Goldsmiths Media Group, 2000). Other factors, in addition to convenience, efficiency, and technological innovation, also account for the routine use of stereotypes by reporters. Journalists may not derive their stereotypes from direct contact with those people who are the object of them. Instead, their stereotypical ideas are shaped by discursive influences such as family, people within their social networks, and the institutional environment of the corporate media, including sources, reporters, editors, and news reports from the large, trend-setting news outlets (Gitlin, 1980). In developing their ideas about social issues, journalists may depend more on these secondary sources of information than they do on direct contact with the groups and individuals about whom their stories are written, and this can lead to stereotyping.

Furthermore, it is important to note that very little diversity exists in Canadian newsrooms. Research has demonstrated that more than three-quarters of all English-language national columnists, and two-thirds of all editors, are men (Smith, 2015). A 2010 study based in the Greater Toronto Area demonstrated that even in one of the most diverse cities in Canada, those involved in media production are still predominantly white: only 5.9 per cent of "newsroom decision makers" (i.e., editors and producers) are from visible minorities, and the proportion drops to 3.6 per cent among senior management (Cukier, Miller, Aspevig, & Carl, 2012). The lack of diversity matters beyond the representation of newsrooms: as journalists create subjective knowledges, their contacts, interests, and world views are informed by their social locations. As such, the news media ultimately represent only a partial segment of Canada's population, but create dominant discourses that purport to represent everyone.

## Agenda-Setting and Priming

While the news media may not be able to dictate what audiences think, they are able to set the menu of topics for discussion. Their power to set the agenda results in *selected* issues being put before the public for discussion, and **priming** is the process by which news media influence the *criteria* the public use to evaluate matters of social policy. Indeed, audiences may not be able to bring all of their knowledge to bear in assessing political situations and "rely on what comes to mind, 'those bits and pieces of political memory that are accessible'" (Williams, 2003, p. 182). For example, the evaluative criteria for the policy debate about universal child care in Canada's news media include *how much of a subsidy* (if any) governments should provide for child care, but do not include *the viability of a no-cost universal option*. Since the news media furnish scant coverage of international examples of free, universal daycare—such as those programs available in many European countries—the public has no opportunity to consider this option. Thus, the media play a critical role in foregrounding what is important about social policy and providing the public with tools with which to navigate those issues, such as "common sense."

## Ideological Construction of Common Sense

**Agenda-setting**, priming, and stereotyping lay the foundation for the media's construction of the "common sense" that audiences use to interpret the news. Once entrenched in the public idiom, common-sense understandings of our social realities are very difficult to shift even when clear evidence to the contrary is available. Common-sense definitions offer specific yet "partial reading[s] of the world, while appearing to be universal and uncontroversial" (Nesbitt-Larking, 2001, p. 87). However, these definitions have very real implications for progressive policy change and new program development, and for the people who rely on such policies and programs. Consider the following common-sense assessments:

> **Assessments of policy**
> *Canada can't afford free universal child care.*
> *Generous social programs sap people's incentive to work.*
> *Indigenous peoples aren't ready for self-governance.*

As well, common-sense characterizations of various groups and classes of people constrain individuals' free will and limit their potential for self-fulfillment.

> **Characterizations of people**
> *Able-bodied people who aren't working are lazy and unmotivated.*
> *Violent youth crime is increasing.*
> *Muslim people are more inclined to engage in terrorist acts than "us."*

While common-sense notions in the news media may appear natural and value-free, in fact, they are part of a larger process of presenting a hegemonic understanding of the world to audiences, what Gramsci (1980) refers to as the "production of consent."

## Hypervisibility and Invisibility

Related to its agenda-setting function, **hypervisibility** refers to the news media's ability to draw intense attention to certain groups and populations, or to highlight some features of the news over others. The reporting of crime has always been one of news media's most visible tasks. Whether routine or sensational, criminal activity and criminals are constructed through media attention to certain issues at the expense of others. Stuart Hall and his colleagues were among the first scholars to unpack how the issue of hypervisibility in crime related to social policy—in this case, how Caribbean young people were connected to the mugging phenomenon of the 1970s in the United Kingdom (Hall, Critcher, Jefferson, Clarke, & Roberts, 1978). They demonstrated how the weaving together of news and police discourses on crime, unemployment, and sexuality constructed Caribbean youth as a symbol of threat, crime, and other undesirable economic, social, and political changes. The ensuing **moral panic**—the disproportionate attention and exaggerated public response over an issue constructed as a threat to society's social and moral order—resulted in dramatic policy changes based on unexamined racial profiling. The image of the Black criminal became further entrenched as a dominant discourse in the UK. Henry and Tator (2000, p. 166) demonstrate that this construction continues to thrive in Canada, where Black youth continue to be over-represented in reports on crime, and are used as a marker for the dominant Canadian public to re-evaluate their strategies for policing, controlling, and managing race.

Conversely, when one aspect of a group or class of individuals is emphasized, other aspects are rendered invisible. This phenomenon has been observed in news coverage of Indigenous child welfare policy. In recent decades, partial control over child welfare has been returned to Indigenous peoples through the implementation of delegated Indigenous child welfare agencies. Unfortunately, in the news these agencies are hypervisible as wasteful and incompetent, yet they remain invisible as underfunded, resourceful, and innovative institutions (Harding, 2010). Since Indigenous agencies are only reported on when bad things happen, such as the injury or death of a child in care, some members of the public may conclude that Indigenous people are "not ready" to manage their own institutions. Because delegated Indigenous child welfare agencies are relatively new institutions, about which little is known by the public, news audiences may have few other interpretive options available to them.

## How Do Social Media Complicate the Field of Public and Policy Discourse?

In the digital age, alternative news sites flourish. People are now able to create their own content and engage with a range of otherwise marginalized discourses to make sense of their own identities and social issues around the world. Like past town hall meetings or print news debates, online spaces allow the development of new **imagined communities** through interactive comments sections and in contexts that dominant news media may not represent or support. They provide spaces of inclusion and activism that may not be readily accessible in person. Indeed, the strategic use of social media has played a significant role in the rise of recent social justice movements such as Idle No More and Black Lives Matter, using what has become known as **hashtag activism**. It has even helped topple undemocratic governments, such as in Tunisia in the "Arab Spring," a series of protests and uprisings that occurred in the Middle East and North Africa beginning in 2010.

In addition, social media transform how people access their news. No longer is a print newspaper the only option or the norm. Growing numbers of people access their news via their Facebook feeds or their networks on Twitter, Instagram, or other social media platforms. Notably, this shift creates a reliance on platform programs and friends or followers that limit the issues and opinions to which we are exposed.

Despite these trends, corporate online news sites still provide the most news to the largest number of people, and dominant discourses continue to permeate how we think about social issues. While alternative understandings are possible, scholars suggest that when we access the virtual, we are more likely to affirm our identities and ideological positions than we are to create new ones (Nakamura & Chow-White, 2012). In addition, the anonymity of online spaces provides the context for opinions and "isms" that are not condoned in real spaces. This has led to mainstream news sites finding new strategies to control debates following certain issues. For example, in 2015 the online arm of CBC decided to temporarily shut down all commentary on news articles covering issues related to Indigenous peoples in an attempt to control the virulence of public discourse. Brodie Fenlon, acting director of digital news at CBC, explained:

> We've noticed over many months that these stories draw a disproportionate number of comments that cross the line and violate our guidelines. Some of the violations are obvious, some not so obvious; some comments are clearly hateful and vitriolic, some are simply ignorant. And some appear to be hate disguised as ignorance (i.e., racist sentiments expressed in benign language). (Fenlon, 2015)

This trend highlights some of the ways in which public policy debates are complicated online. As the editors of the book *Race in Cyberspace* argue, "race matters in cyberspace precisely because all of us who spend time online are already shaped by the ways in which race matters offline, and we can't help but bring our own knowledge, experiences, and values with us when we log on" (Kolko, Nakamura, & Rodman, 2000, p. 5). In essence, the inclusions and exclusions of "real space" (i.e., our three-dimensional world) are translated to "cyberspace," not necessarily transformed. Social media provide possibilities, but also new limitations, for public and policy discourse. And, as Brodie Fenlon has suggested, the anonymity of cyberspace can exaggerate the exclusions and increase the volume of vitriol.

## Chapter Summary

In this chapter we have examined what discourse means, how it operates through power relations, and how it comes to define groups of people and social issues. Critical discourse analysis unpacks lexical choices, strategies of conflation, binary opposition, ideological leanings, sources, and headlines to explore how social issues are framed to create and perpetuate dominant discourses. Dominant discourses tend to favour and protect the interests of the dominant groups, at the expense of others. Despite further marginalizing already marginalized peoples, journalists and media gatekeepers use patterns of stereotyping, agenda-setting, priming, "common sense," hypervisibility, and invisibility to create the illusion of objectivity. As public and media discourse plays an important role in how social policy is constructed and negotiated, the role of identifying and challenging discourse offers a critical entry point to disrupt power and create social policy change.

# Discussion Questions

Select a news story about an issue related to social work from a major Canadian news provider (e.g., *National Post, Globe and Mail, Toronto Star,* or CTV) and answer the following questions about it.

1.  What lexical choices did the writer make and how did they affect the overall meaning of the text?

2.  Are issues represented in a binary fashion (i.e., good versus bad) or are readers given multiple and nuanced options for understanding the news story?

3.  Who is quoted in the news story? Whose voices are excluded? Are those most affected by the events in the news story given voice (e.g., social work clients, welfare recipients, Indigenous people, single mothers)?

4.  If the news text references statistics, numbers, or quantitative measures, can you think of other statistics, numbers, and facts that, if included, would have given readers other interpretive choices?

5.  Is the meaning conveyed by the headline consistent with the substance of the story? If not, how does this impact readers' understanding of the issue? Who is most affected by that?

6.  If you wrote the story, how would it be different?

7.  How is this social issue mediated through social media? How is it similar, and how it is different?

# Notes

1.  Objectivity is knowledge assumed to be based only on "evidence" or "facts and figures." This approach implies that it is possible to remove personal and cultural biases and norms from what we understand to be accurate and "true" knowledge. On the other hand, subjectivity challenges the notion that any "evidence" can be impartial, or that a single version of a knowledge exists. Instead, subjectivity implies that one's values, beliefs, ideologies, experiences, and social positioning influence the "truth," even when they are constructed through "evidence." Knowledge, and perspectives on knowledge, therefore varies from person to person, based on their unique social and lived realities and interpretations.

2.  This section and the following three sections in this chapter are based on Robert Harding's "Re/framing Aboriginal social policy issues in the news: Old stereotypes and new opportunities" (doctoral dissertation, 2007).

# References

Adorno, T. (1957). Television and the pattern of mass culture. In B. Rosen & D. M. White (Eds), *Mass culture: The popular arts in America* (pp. 474–88). Glencoe, IL: Free Press.

Amadahy, Z., & Lawrence, B. (2010). Indigenous peoples and Black people in Canada: Settlers or allies? In A. Kempf (Ed.), *Breaching the colonial contract: Anti-colonialism in the US and Canada* (pp. 105–36). New York: Springer Publishing.

Anderson, B. (1983). *Imagined communities*. London & New York: Verso.

Blommaert, J. (2005). *Discourse: A critical introduction*. New York: Cambridge University Press.

Boutilier, A. (2014, 21 Aug.). Native teen's slaying a "crime" not a "sociological phenomenon,"

Stephen Harper says. *Toronto Star.* Retrieved from https://www.thestar.com/news/canada/2014/08/21/native_teens_slaying_a_crime_not_a_sociological_phenomenon_stephen_harper_says.html

Canadian Association of Journalists. (n.d.). *Principles of ethical journalism.* Retrieved from http://www.caj.ca/wp-content/uploads/2011/09/Principles.pdf

———. (2011). *Ethics guidelines.* Retrieved from http://www.caj.ca/ethics-guidelines/

Césaire, A. (1972). *Discourse on colonialism.* (J. Pinkham, Trans.). New York: Monthly Review Press (originally published 1950).

Cross, K. (2006). *Elections without politics: Television coverage of the 2001 BC provincial election.* Unpublished doctoral dissertation, Simon Fraser University, Burnaby, BC.

Cukier, W., Miller, J., Aspevig, K., & Carl, D. (2012). Diversity in leadership and media: A multi-perspective analysis of the Greater Toronto Area, 2010. *International Journal of Diversity in Organizations, Communities and Nations, 11*(6), 63–78.

de Leeuw, S. (2009). "If anything is to be done with the Indian, we must catch him very young": Colonial constructions of Aboriginal children and the geographies of Indian residential schooling in British Columbia, Canada. *Children's Geographies, 7*(2), 123–40.

Fairclough, N. (1989). *Language and power.* London: Longman.

——— & Wodak, R. (1997). Critical discourse analysis. In T. van Dijk (Ed.), *Discourse studies: A multidisciplinary introduction,* vol. 2 (pp. 258–84). London: Sage.

Fenlon, B. (2015, 30 Nov.). CBC News Canada—Editor's Blog: Uncivil dialogue: Commenting and stories about indigenous people. Retrieved from http://www.cbc.ca/newsblogs/community/editorsblog/2015/11/uncivil-dialogue-commenting-and-stories-about-indigenous-people.html

Foucault, M. (1972). *The archaeology of knowledge.* (A. Sheridan Smith, Trans.). London: Routledge.

———. (1973). *The birth of the clinic: An archaeology of medical perception.* (A. Sheridan Smith, Trans.). New York: Pantheon Books (originally published 1963).

———. (1975). *Discipline and punish: The birth of the prison.* New York: Random House.

———. (1979). *The history of sexuality. Volume 1: An introduction.* London: Allen Lane (French publication 1976).

———. (1980). Two lectures. In *Power/Knowledge: Selected interviews and other writings, 1972–1977.* Colin Gordon (Ed.). New York: Pantheon.

———. (1988). *Madness and civilization: A history of insanity in the age of reason.* (R. Howard, Trans.). New York: Vintage-Random House (originally published 1965).

Gee, P. J. (2005). *Discourse analysis: An introduction to theory and method.* New York and London: Routledge.

Gitlin, T. (1980). *The whole world is watching: Mass media in the making and unmaking of the new left.* Berkeley: University of California Press.

Goldberg. D. T. (1993). *Racist culture: Philosophy and the politics of meaning.* Oxford: Blackwell.

Goldsmiths Media Group. (2000). Media organisations in society: Central issues. In J. Curran (Ed.), *Media organisations in society* (pp. 19–68). London: Arnold.

Gramsci, A. (1980). *Selections from the prison notebooks.* New York: International.

Gunster, S., & Saurette, P. (2014). Storylines in the sands: News, narrative, and ideology in the *Calgary Herald. Canadian Journal of Communication, 39*(3), 333–59.

Gutstein, D. (2014, 17 Apr.). Follow the money, part 4: Who owns the *National Post*? Donald Gutstein's blog. Retrieved from http://rabble.ca/blogs/bloggers/donald-gutstein/2014/04/follow-money-part-4-who-owns-national-post

Habermas, J. (1993). *The structural transformation of the public sphere: An inquiry into a category of bourgeois society.* Cambridge, MA: MIT Press.

Hall, S. (1991). Old and new identities; old and new ethnicities. In A. D. King (Ed.), *Culture, globalisation and the world-system: Contemporary conditions for the representation of identity.* Basingstoke: Macmillan.

———. (1997). *Representation: Cultural representations and signifying practices.* London: Sage.

———, Critcher, S., Jefferson, T., Clarke, J., & Roberts, B. (1978). *Policing the crisis: Mugging, the state and law and order.* London: Macmillan.

Harding, R. (2007). *Re/framing Aboriginal social policy issues in the news: Old stereotypes and new opportunities.* Doctoral dissertation, Simon Fraser University, Burnaby, BC. Retrieved from http://summit.sfu.ca/item/2681

———. (2010). The demonization of Aboriginal child welfare authorities in the news. *Canadian Journal of Communication, 35*(1), 85–108.

———. (In press). The *National Post*'s campaign against anti-poverty advocates: A war in words with real casualties. *Intersectionalities: A Global*

*Journal of Social Work Analysis, Research, Polity, and Practice.*

Henry, F., & Tator, C. (2000). *Racist discourse in Canada's English print Media.* Toronto: Canadian Race Relations Foundation. Retrieved from http://www.crr.ca/divers-files/en/pub/rep/ePubRepRacDisMedia.pdf

———— & ————. (2002). *Discourses of domination: Racial bias in the Canadian English-language press.* Toronto: University of Toronto Press.

———— & ————. (2006). *The colour of democracy: Racism in Canadian society* (3rd edn). Toronto: Nelson Educational.

Herman, E., & Chomsky, N. (1988). *Manufacturing consent: The political economy of the mass media.* New York: Pantheon Books.

hooks, bell. (1990). *Yearning: Race, gender, and cultural politics.* Boston: South End Press.

Jullian, P. M. (2011). Appraising through someone else's words: The evaluative power of quotations in news reports. *Discourse and Society, 22*(6), 766–80.

Karim, K. H. (1993). Constructions, deconstructions and reconstructions: Competing Canadian discourses on ethnocultural terminology. *Canadian Journal of Communication, 18*(2), 197–218.

Kolko, B., Nakamura, L., & Rodman, G. (2000). *Race in cyberspace.* New York: Routledge.

Larocque, E. (1989). Racism runs through Canadian society. In O. McKague (Ed.), *Racism in Canada* (pp. 73–76). Saskatoon: Fifth House Publishers.

Lambertus, S. (2004). *Wartime images, peacetime wounds: The media and the Gustafsen Lake standoff.* Toronto: University of Toronto Press.

Lichtenberg, J. (2000). In defense of objectivity revisited. In J. Curran & M. Gurevitch (Eds), *Mass media and society* (pp. 238–54). London: Arnold.

MacDonald, M. (2003). *Exploring media discourse.* New York: Bloomsbury Publishing.

McCurdy, P., & DeCillia, D. (2016). The sound of silence: The absence of public service values in Canadian media discourse about the CBC.

*Canadian Journal of Communication, 41*(4), 547–67.

Murphy, J. (2015, 8 Dec.). Canada launches inquiry into murdered and missing indigenous women. *The Guardian.* Retrieved from https://www.theguardian.com/world/2015/dec/08/canada-40m-inquiry-violence-indigenous-women-justin-trudeau

Nakamura, L., & Chow-White, P. (Eds.). (2012). *Race after the Internet.* New York: Routledge.

Nesbitt-Larking, P. (2001). *Politics, society and the media: Canadian perspectives.* Peterborough, ON: Broadview Press.

Pritchard, D., & Sauvageau, F. (1999). *Les journalistes Canadiens: Un portrait de fin de siècle.* Québec: Presses de l'Université Laval.

Russell, N. (2006). *Morals and the media: Ethics in Canadian journalism* (2nd edn). Vancouver: University of British Columbia Press.

Said, E. W. (1978). *Orientalism.* New York: Pantheon Books.

Smith, V. (2015). *Outsiders still: Why women journalists love—and leave—their newspaper careers.* Toronto: University of Toronto Press.

Taras, D. (2001). *Power and betrayal in the Canadian media* (updated edn). Peterborough, ON: Broadview Press.

Tremblay, G. (2016). Public service media in the age of digital networks. *Canadian Journal of Communication, 41*(1), 191–206.

van Dijk, T. (1988a). News as discourse. In G. Smitherman-Donaldson & T. van Dijk (Eds), *Discourse and discrimination.* Detroit: Wayne State University Press.

————. (1988b). *News as discourse.* Hillsdale, NJ: L. Erlbaum.

————. (1997). The study of discourse. In T. van Dijk (Ed.), *Discourse as structure and process* (pp. 1–34). London: Sage.

Ward, S. (2004). *The invention of journalism ethics: The path to objectivity and beyond.* Montreal & Kingston: McGill-Queen's University Press.

Williams, K. (2003). *Understanding media theory.* London: Arnold.

# 3 Ideas and Social Policy

*Christopher Walmsley*

---

### Chapter Objectives

*This chapter will help you to develop an understanding of:*
- the differences between charity, mutual aid, and social regulation;
- how Indigenous welfare differs from social insurance;
- the major programs of the Canadian welfare state;
- liberalism, conservatism, socialism, and their variations;
- how social citizenship differs from social investment.

---

## Introduction

> *"Ideas shape the course of history."*
>
> —John Maynard Keynes (n.d.)

This chapter explores ideas about welfare to better understand Canadians' customary ways of giving to others. The chapter begins by looking back, before the era of European settlers, to the communities of Indigenous peoples to understand continuity and change in ideas about helping. Then, those policies and practices of everyday life in Britain and France transplanted to New France and British North America during the seventeenth to nineteenth centuries are explored. Next, the nineteenth-century ideas of mutual aid and social insurance, emerging as Euro-Canadians began to recognize a mutual dependence on one another, are examined. Finally, "new" ideas such as social citizenship and social investment, emerging in the twentieth century with the welfare state, are considered. These ideas, sometimes thought to be "just common sense," express ways of being in society with others. They emerge in conversation between friends and family, but are also found in government reports, political speeches, news stories, and circulating on the Internet. At one time, they might have been presented at an academic conference or published in a journal or scholarly book. Today, they take a thousand forms quite separate from their origin. Capable of informing thought and guiding action, their exploration is the focus of this chapter.

Social welfare has been described as "help given to the stranger," and is recognized as an integral part of modern industrial societies (Wilensky & Lebeaux, 1965, p. 141). It is a complex system of pensions, benefits, grants, fees, services, entitlements, and tax credits engaging all three levels of Canadian government, and represents about three-quarters of the spending of federal and provincial governments (Department of Finance Canada, 2017). It is a labyrinthine network of contributions, obligations, transfers, and rights usually summed up in the phrase the **welfare state**. It was not always this way.

# Indigenous Welfare

Before Europeans explored and colonized the territory now known as Canada, Indigenous communities cared for the old, young, sick, and disabled—those members of society most often the focus of social policy—in their own ways. The earliest Europeans in contact with Indigenous peoples were explorers, missionaries, whalers, and fur traders. Although they were in an ideal position to observe Indigenous cultures before colonization, many were infused with European preconceptions of the "Indian": they did not speak Indigenous languages, and were uninterested, biased, or merely superficial observers of the communities with which they were in contact (Lutz, 2007; Fisher, 1992). Understandably, many Indigenous people were reluctant to reveal private information, and "tended to tell the European inquirer what they thought he wanted to hear rather than what was actually true" (Fisher, 1992, p. 76). A better way to understand Indigenous ways of helping might have been through the oral histories of Elders passed down from generation to generation. But how reliable can "memory" be as a source of knowledge across generations and centuries? The Royal Commission on Aboriginal Peoples (RCAP, 1996, p. 62), confronting this dilemma in its work, argued that "applying insights from contemporary accounts of Aboriginal persons knowledgeable in their culture, along with documentary records that are fragmentary and sometimes blatantly biased by the political or economic motives of the colonial participants," is the best way to achieve "an in-depth understanding of early relations." However, it cautioned that Indigenous nations "were as different from each other as the European countries . . . . [and] the use of a term such as Aboriginal obscures real differences among the various indigenous nations" (RCAP, 1996, p. 49). In addition, the period

---

### Case Examples    Panhandling in the Street

A young man in faded jeans and a grey hoodie makes his way between two lanes of cars that wait to turn left onto the freeway at the edge of Vancouver. In one hand is a squeegee and tucked under the other arm is a small dog. The passenger window of a black SUV rolls down and a woman's hand can be seen with a $20 bill. He simultaneously takes the money, acknowledges it with a brief nod, and moves on. The SUV window rolls up, the light changes, and the car disappears into freeway traffic. A transitory encounter between strangers in one Canadian city, repeated many times a day in cities large and small across the country. One has a squeegee, a guitar, a cardboard placard, a paper cup, or an outstretched hand, and the other makes a donation or averts eyes and crosses the street. How should Canadians respond to those in need?

of contact, and thereby the length of the colonization process, varied considerably—over 400 years in Quebec and the Atlantic provinces, 200 years in parts of western Canada, and just 75 years in the northern territories. Against this background, Indigenous ideas about caring and helping are explored.

The Iroquois Confederacy—comprising the Mohawk, Seneca, Oneida, Cayuga, and Onondaga[1]—provided for those in need through village-based mutual aid and medicine societies, and "the rules of hospitality that bound biological relatives and clan members to share food and shelter with kin ensured that no one was destitute" (RCAP, 1996, p. 61). The Blackfoot Confederacy considered the land "a mother, a giver of life, and the provider of all things necessary to sustain life" (p. 64). The deep reverence and respect for Mother Earth was "reflected in the Blackfoot practice of referring to the land, water, plants, animals and their fellow human beings as 'all my relations'" (p. 64). This bond of mutuality "entrusted them with the responsibility of caring for the land and all their relations," including the young, the old, the sick, and the needy (p. 64). In the Pacific Northwest, a symbol of Indigenous peoples' generosity to others was the **potlatch**, a ceremonial practice "convened to mourn deaths, bestow names, erase the shame of accidents or ceremonial errors, recognize succession to titles and economic rights, and acknowledge marriages and divorces. . . . Being a good host and showing generosity brought respect not only for the chief but also for the members of his clan" (pp. 75–6). The gifts distributed at potlatches usually included utensils, blankets, boxes, canoes, and copper plates.

Indigenous ways of honouring each life stage suggest how life itself is valued. In a study of northern Algonquian women, Anderson (2011) found children bring hope and happiness as they represent the future; youth start to assume adult caring responsibilities for the young and old; adults take responsibility for caring and providing; young to middle-aged women are the keepers of relationships whose extra hard work manages the limited resources; and Elders are the teachers and keepers of knowledge, law, and ceremony, with female Elders focusing their attention on kinship, health, well-being, and spirit connections in their communities (Anderson, 2011, pp. 8–12).

Taken together, an Indigenous approach to welfare values the contribution of each community member, expresses an ethic of mutual caring, is grounded in an interconnectedness between all living things, recognizes generosity to others, and leaves no one behind.

## Welfare as Charity

The oldest idea informing Western societies' approach to giving is the Judeo-Christian ethic of charity. Often expressed by the maxims "love thy neighbour as thyself" and "'do unto others as you would have them do unto you," it has provided the intellectual foundation and activist momentum to help the less fortunate for centuries. Whether one was a beggar in early New France, an orphan in nineteenth-century British North America, an unemployed worker during a twentieth-century economic depression (Finkel, 2006), or a homeless person struggling with addictions in the twenty-first century, charitable acts have given rise to orphanages, hospitals, thrift stores, soup kitchens, women's shelters, seniors' residences, and food banks. Historically, the wealthy and socially advantaged citizenry took the lead because they saw charity as their preferred response to the poverty and destitution wrought by capitalist economic cycles, industrialization, and urbanization. Today, 82 per cent of Canadians give money to charities (or non-profit organizations), with an average household donation of $652 amounting to total annual giving of $12.8 billion (Statistics Canada, 2015, 2017). The Canadian government encourages Canadians' generosity through tax credits[2] and periodically matching donations in times of humanitarian crisis. These figures appear to testify to Canadians' generosity, but charitable giving has fundamental flaws as a mechanism to ensure the well-being of society.

First, charity is inefficient. A significant disconnect occurs between the interests of charitable givers and society's most pressing needs. Canadians give first to their church and then to health charities before making gifts to food banks, women's shelters, street youth, or persons with addictions (Statistics Canada, 2015). Donations to the opera, symphony, and nature conservation soar while fundamental needs for food, clothing, and shelter remain unmet. When charitable gifts are given for basic needs, there is no guarantee they are evenly and equitably distributed. Charitable giving follows givers' interests and not receivers' needs. It develops haphazardly and becomes available in some geographic areas but not in others. This leads to a patchwork of responses that depends on where one lives and what others choose to donate (Lightman & Lightman, 2017). This mismatch becomes particularly evident in times of natural disaster when there can be an overwhelming level of donations. The donated goods may not match at all the urgent needs of those in crisis. In effect, such charitable giving is a poorly focused type of redistribution from the "haves" to the "have-nots."

Second, charity is insufficient. Canadians' total charitable giving represents only about 30 per cent of the Canadian government's present spending on programs for the elderly (Statistics Canada, 2014). This is clearly not enough to meet the basic needs of poorer Canadians for food, clothing, and shelter. Nor would it cover today's seniors' needs for a basic income, as pointed out above. It is also inadequate to respond to a host of other social concerns ranging from the opioid crisis to refugee resettlement. Some assert that if government did less, citizens would do more based on an unleashing of the "altruistic spirit." Yet, it is hard to imagine an increase in charitable giving so great that government spending on pensions, health care, child benefits, and housing could be replaced.

Charitable giving and voluntary action have considerable value as mechanisms through which those sharing a common interest, heritage, culture, or concern can act collectively to respond to a need they perceive in the community. Viewed positively, they are an "early warning system" about emerging social needs that "allow needs to be met which may otherwise go unrecognized" (Kennedy, 2013, p. 100). Children's aid societies, seniors' housing, immigrant social services, mental patients' associations, transition houses, sexual assault centres, and AIDS services are examples of voluntary action responses to emerging needs in different time periods. Today there are over 19,000 charitable organizations in the Canadian social service sector. But they receive only 11 per cent of their income from gifts and donations; by contrast, 66 per cent came from government contracts and 20 per cent from earned income or fees for services (Imagine Canada, 2006, p. 1). Government is the largest actor in the social policy field, but it has not always been this way.

## Welfare as Mutual Aid

Violet learned that life on a debt-ridden farm fifteen miles from the village and the railway was not easy, but because the people of the district believed in co-operating with one another they were able to overcome some of their hardships. Their co-operative efforts to cut ice, build the school-house, and take care of a big family who were all ill with typhoid, helped to create a close-knit, vibrant community. (Fairbairn, MacPherson, & Russell, 2000, p. 63)

The idea of **mutual aid**—that those who share a common bond work together to help one another in good times and bad—is deeply embedded in the Canadian psyche. Mutual aid, encompassing the activities above, also includes building a barn, harvesting a crop, establishing a co-operative, or fighting a fire. It can be a response to the illness, disability, death, or natural disaster of an individual or community. In the late nineteenth and early twentieth centuries, this informal helping began to take a more formal turn as farmers' and fishers' co-operatives, credit unions, fraternal insurance programs, and the social service organizations of religious and cultural communities were established.

Fraternal insurance became a means for many Ontario workers in the last quarter of the nineteenth century "to protect themselves and their families from the financial devastation of permanent injury, sickness, or death" (Galer, 2010, p. 9). The International Order of Odd Fellows, the Ancient Order of Foresters, and the Ancient Order of United Workmen became the three largest insurers in Ontario and dominated the insurance industry before 1900. These were multi-class associations of white men providing the "ritualized means to define one another as brothers" and recreating the kinship network, extended family, or village life one had in Europe before immigrating to North America (Beito, 2000, p. 8). The voluntary insurance programs of fraternal societies were primarily focused on sickness, permanent injury, and death benefits, although some provided periodic support to orphans and in response to natural disasters, fires, and epidemics (Beito, 2000, p. 10). During the Victorian era in Ontario, "fraternal insurance was attractive because it provided benefits as a matter of *right* and was a way for injured members to retain their dignity and independence without resorting to charitable relief" (Galer, 2010, p. 17). Although it provided benefits to a worker at the time of injury or illness, if these resulted in a permanent disability the benefits were terminated because such programs did not have the capacity to support members on an ongoing basis. Fraternal insurance excluded those who could not afford the annual dues, as well as women and the racialized.

Co-operatives, another form of mutual aid, were similarly inspired by British and European models. In the late nineteenth and early twentieth centuries, farmers' co-operatives developed on the prairies, as did fishers' co-operatives in the Atlantic provinces and savings and credit co-operatives (caisses populaires) in Quebec (Fairbairn, MacPherson, & Russell, 2000). Agriculture, consumer, financial, housing, fishery, energy, health, child care, and production co-operatives are now active across Canada. Perhaps the most significant innovation in the co-operative sector since World War II has been the growth of non-profit co-operative housing. Today, there are 2,220 housing co-operatives in Canada with 91,846 units (Co-operative Housing Federation of Canada, 2017).

The idea of mutual aid was not restricted to early anglophone and francophone settlers of Canada. "Jewish migrants . . . brought a tradition of establishing a communal body, called a 'kehillah' to look after their social welfare needs. The first . . . in Canada was the Young Men's Hebrew Benevolent Society, founded in Montreal in 1863" (Schoenfeld, 2015). In the late nineteenth and early twentieth centuries, Jewish people fleeing persecution in Europe migrated to Montreal, Toronto, Winnipeg, and Vancouver. They developed a wide range of mutual aid organizations to meet their religious, cultural, educational, and social needs, to replicate the extended family network available in pre-World War I Europe, and to create "a sense of belonging in a strange and often hostile environment" (Giberovitch, 1994, p. 76).

Today, the idea of mutual aid has grown to incorporate parent-run daycare centres, community health centres, and self-help groups such as Alcoholics Anonymous, mental patients' associations, women's resource centres, and men's groups. Some are structured as non-profit associations and include professional staff to animate support groups and programs. Others retain a more informal status, with those sharing similar challenges forming a social network to help one another.

Mutual aid is not a new idea: it has been integral to the survival and well-being of Indigenous peoples for thousands of years. The idea of living interdependently with members of your community, sharing resources, and living life in balance with nature are integral to Indigenous ways of knowing and being. But there was likely not much opportunity to share these insights with the new settlers, who brought their own ideas about mutual aid from Europe.

Has the idea of mutual aid been successful in eliminating poverty, homelessness, and hunger in Canada? Although countless Canadians are clearly better off today due to the idea of mutual aid, it still is insufficient to meet the social challenges of our times. Mutual aid implies a level of communitarianism—an obligation to help those with whom one shares a common bond. Yet, if some are part of a community, others, by extension, are not. Who will be there for "the excluded" in their time of need? When a catastrophic economic, social, or natural disaster occurs affecting many across a society, the limits of mutual aid become glaringly apparent. The Great Depression of the 1930s was the most striking example.

# Welfare as Social Regulation

The beginning of state welfare in Britain can be traced to Elizabeth I's reign and the Poor Law of 1601. For the first time, the hand of the state was visible in regulating the behaviour of those who were out of work, ill, elderly, and disabled, as well as those children whose families were either unavailable or an insufficient resource. The Poor Law stipulated that towns and counties appoint an "overseer of the poor" and create two types of institutions—the poorhouse, for destitute unemployables (mothers with young children, the ill, the elderly), and the workhouse, for those deemed employable. The aid provided in these two institutions was called "indoor relief," and aid provided to individuals and families in their own homes was termed "outdoor relief."

## Houses of Industry

During the late eighteenth and early nineteenth centuries, outdoor relief became more and more common in Britain until the Poor Law Amendment Act of 1834. This act essentially eliminated outdoor relief; integrated the elderly, infirm, insane, and alcoholics into "mixed workhouses" with those who were employable; and forced everyone capable of doing so to engage in casual labour at substandard wages. "The New Poor Law had an almost instant effect on social policy in British North America" (Finkel, 2006, p. 48). Between 1835 and 1840, Houses of Industry, the Canadian name for the poorhouse and workhouse, opened in Kingston, Saint John, Montreal, Quebec, and Toronto. During this time, public works at wage rates below the private sector were used to create employment for employable men. The work involved agricultural labour, canal building, shipbuilding, and road improvement. Women and children worked as knitters, spinners, domestic servants, and washers. As the twentieth century progressed, Houses of Industry were replaced by stigmatizing forms of financial aid for specific groups—veterans, seniors, mothers with children, and "employables." In Nova Scotia and New Brunswick, though, Houses of Industry continued as virtually the only form of state welfare until the 1950s.

## State-Funded Charities

Canada was changing from an agricultural to an industrial economy between 1867 and 1914, the years between Confederation and the beginning of World War I. Towns and cities, home to more than half the Canadian population by the 1920s, grew rapidly as many left the farm to become industrial workers. Workhouses, orphanages, hospitals, asylums, and other institutions proliferated to house those newly marginalized by the wage economy, and the state worked actively with these new charities to financially subsidize their work. In the years between 1871 and 1921 the Canadian government's social welfare expenditures increased from 1.2 per cent to 13.1 per cent of the federal budget, and provincial expenditures on health and social welfare increased from 9.5 per cent to 12.5 per cent of the total (Moscovitch & Drover, 1987, pp. 21–2). The expenditures, directed to public works programs for the unemployed, veterans' pensions, and the support of the new institutions listed above, also gave rise to the fields of psychiatry, social work, probation, and public health. Government and charity organization leaders, drawn from Canada's business, professional, and religious elites, had strong views about the lives charity recipients should lead. Indigenous children were to attend religious residential schools to convert to Christianity and become socialized to Canadian society (Finkel, 2006, p. 72). Poor mothers who breastfed their babies were to be rewarded with a financial allowance. Widows, who were deemed "moral" mothers, were to receive a state "pension" to support themselves and their children, whereas unwed mothers, who were characterized as "immoral," would not (Little, 2005, p. 333). "Wayward" girls, through their incarceration in juvenile jails, would develop "the stamina and courage to maintain life on a higher level" through the staff's instruction (Matters, 2005, p. 83). As the twentieth century progressed, the state, through its funding of charities and institutions, assumed a new role—the moral regulator of the poor and marginalized.

## The Great Depression

Canada confronted an unemployment crisis of unprecedented proportions during the Great Depression of the 1930s. In the winter of 1932, an estimated 26 per cent of the labour force was unemployed, not counting youth, farmers, fishers, and wives not previously employed. Only one-third to one-half of the unemployed received relief, and young single people were generally ignored. Where public works programs were provided, these only offered work at substandard wages. Public protests about the treatment of the destitute were increasing across the country as the Conservative government of Prime Minister R.B. Bennett moved to institute a system of work camps in remote locations. Over 100,000 single men passed through the camps between 1932 and 1936, where they received only 25 cents per day for their work (Finkel, 2006, pp. 110–12).

## Family Allowances

In 1945, Canada took a step towards the welfare state by implementing a universal program of family allowances, but this also became a new way to regulate parental behaviour. The federal government began issuing a monthly cheque to each mother with a child under 15 to support the cost of raising children. However, in Quebec, many large families relied on older siblings leaving school and entering the workforce to help support the family. Compulsory schooling legislation, implemented in 1943, was not being enforced. The Roman Catholic Church, recognizing Quebec needed a well-educated citizenry to move from an agrarian past to an industrial future, wanted children to stay in school until the age of 15. Having control of the local Catholic school boards, it effectively tied receipt of the family allowance to school attendance by reporting children who had withdrawn from school to the federal bureaucracy managing the family allowance program. They were not the only ones who used a social program to change parental behaviour. "In the Northwest Territories and the Yukon, administrators decreed that parents who took their children with them as they hunted rather than sending them to school on a regular basis would be deprived of family allowances" (Finkel, 2006, p. 134). This increased the threat that children would be removed from the family if not in school, and meant many families abandoned traditional lifestyles and moved to settlements to be close to school.

## Social Regulation by the State

Today, a vast army of state and quasi-state workers[3] supports the state's regulatory role. From child protection workers to those who enforce maintenance orders, from psychiatric nurses to family justice counsellors, from income assistance clerks to mental health police constables—all are a part of a **tutelary complex**, that is, state agents who apply the new knowledge claims, educative techniques, and social practices of psychiatry, psychology, and criminology to the poor and working classes (Donzelot, 1997). It is "the iron fist of the state with a velvet glove" (Abbott & Meerabeau, 2003, p. 13) that polices, monitors, advises, and directs. It ensures there are consequences for poor choices and bad behaviour while "good choices" are rewarded with admission to treatment and support programs and the approval of discretionary financial allowances. Some have argued the state's regulatory power is most evident in income assistance programs (Piven & Cloward, 1993), but today social regulation takes many forms.

# Welfare as Social Insurance

Workers' compensation, the earliest form of state social insurance in Canada, began in the early twentieth century. "The notion of a no-fault workmen's compensation fund into which all employers would make contributions and from which injured workers or the families of workers who died on the job could draw, appeared a better solution to many employers in industries where accidents were common" (Finkel, 2006, p. 83). It relieved employers of the unpredictability of large legal awards due to workplace accidents, and relieved workers of the delays of a long trial with its costs and effects. With support from both management and labour, workplace injury and death were now risks to be shared and administered through a government fund. In relatively short order, several Canadian provinces implemented workmen's[4] compensation acts, beginning with Quebec (1909) and followed by Ontario (1914), Nova Scotia (1915), British Columbia (1915), and New Brunswick (1918). Although this was a significant advance, farm and domestic workers were excluded, and a significant length of time would pass before social insurance was expanded to include unemployment, disability, and illness.

Canada's first Unemployment Insurance Act passed Parliament in 1940 with the Liberal government of Prime Minister Mackenzie King. The legislation required the consent of nine provinces and the British Parliament to make a constitutional amendment. Under Canada's Constitution at the time, the British North America Act (1867), the proposed federal Unemployment Insurance Commission was a clear intrusion into an area of provincial jurisdiction. However, this was not controversial. World War II meant a full employment economy virtually wiped out unemployment, and payroll deductions of workers as well as employers' contributions during the war ensured a fund at war's end for those involuntarily unemployed. Nevertheless, the fund was limited in scope: married women, seasonal workers, farmers, forestry workers, and fishers were all excluded. Only 42 per cent of Canadian workers in 1940 qualified for unemployment insurance. Yet, this was the first national program to provide "recognition that unemployment was generally not voluntary and that at least some segments of the unemployed had a social right to state aid" (Finkel, 2006, p. 117). It also enshrined in national legislation that unemployment was a risk to be shared by all.

# The Welfare State in Canada

Canada, Britain, and the United States, while engaged in World War II (1939–45), were planning for life at war's end. Memories of the Great Depression of the 1930s, still alive in the minds of citizens, politicians, and government officials, meant no one wanted a return to the pre-war days of massive unemployment and social chaos in the transition to a peacetime economy. The war had created a full-employment economy where everyone was working in the armed forces, in war industries, or in support of both. Men who left high-paying industrial jobs to enlist in the armed forces were replaced by women, which created a need for daycare for children so that women could contribute to the war effort on the home front. But what would happen when the men returned home at war's end?

## Planning the Welfare State

During the war, public support was high for a comprehensive program of state welfare. Eighty per cent of Canadians supported a national health insurance plan and universal pensions for seniors, and a majority favoured a planned economy (Finkel, 2006, p. 125). In 1941, Canada established an Advisory Committee on Reconstruction with subcommittees on housing, social security, and women. The most publicized committee's report, the *Report on Social Security for Canada*, known as the Marsh Report, was published in 1943. It "provided a blueprint for a comprehensive social-security system built upon a foundation of full employment" (*Canadian Encyclopedia*, 2017a). This was to include contributory social insurance and universal health insurance. However, the Liberal government of Prime Minister Mackenzie King found the Marsh Report too radical and proceeded to bury it. All that was achieved by war's end was Marsh's proposal for universal family allowances and a generous program of veterans' benefits. Veterans now had the right to return to their former position and employer (or its equivalent), could receive free university or vocation training, had preference for civil service jobs, were eligible for a year's unemployment insurance, and could obtain low-interest loans to go into business (Finkel, 2006, pp. 127–8). A post-war recession didn't materialize, economic prosperity continued, and Canadians appeared to lose interest in comprehensive social security. Twenty years would pass before universal health insurance and old age pensions became part of the Canadian welfare state.

## National Health Care

Canada's progress towards a national health care plan grew incrementally between the 1940s and 1960s. The Saskatchewan Co-operative Commonwealth Federation (CCF) government of T.C. Douglas implemented the first tax-funded province-wide system of hospitalization insurance in North America in 1947. About the same time, the Liberal/Conservative coalition in British Columbia implemented a universal hospital insurance program with user fees and a 3 per cent sales tax, and Alberta negotiated a plan to jointly fund hospital care through municipalities, the province, and voluntary subscriptions. After considerable pressure from the provinces, the federal government passed the Hospital Insurance and Diagnostic Services Act in 1957. It provided for a 50 per cent contribution from the federal government to provincial hospital programs. In 1961, Conservative Prime Minister John Diefenbaker appointed Justice Emmett Hall to head the Royal Commission on Health Services. Justice Hall's report, released in 1964, recommended comprehensive universal health services including physician services, hospital costs, prescription drugs, home care, prosthetic services, dental care for children, expectant mothers, and those on income assistance, and vision care for children and those on low income (Finkel, 2006, p. 183). After a four-year period of delay and negotiation between the provinces and the federal government, the Medical Services Act passed Parliament in 1968 under the Liberal government of Prime Minister Lester Pearson. It provided federal funding to those provinces that respected four criteria: comprehensive physician service coverage, universality of coverage, public administration, and portability of services (coverage outside one's home province). In effect, it made the federal government a major contributor to provincial costs for physician services, diagnostic services, and hospital care. By 1969, nine provinces met the federal criteria, and with Quebec joining in 1972 a coast-to-coast universal health service limited to physician care, hospital care, and diagnostic services had been created.

## Pensions for Seniors

Like health care, pensions for seniors had a long, slow implementation period. Although Canada had had a form of senior's pension since 1927 jointly funded with the provinces, it was restricted to those over 70 whose annual income was less than $125 and required a means test to determine eligibility. Seniors might have to sell all their assets and demonstrate their families were unable to provide care before being eligible for a pension. Public attitudes were changing in the twentieth century, and more and more Canadians believed a lifetime of hard work entitled one to a public pension in senior years. Provincial organizations of pensioners, beginning in the 1930s, advocated for a "citizen's wage" or universal old age pension. They were supported by such diverse organizations as the Canadian Congress of Labour, the Canadian Chamber of Commerce, and the Canadian Association of Social Workers. The first government proposal for a national universal old age pension was contained in the 1945 Green Book of Mackenzie King's government, but it wasn't until 1951 that the federal government passed the Old Age Security Act. It provided a modest universal pension to seniors over 70, but was totally inadequate to meet most seniors' living costs. A means-tested provincially administered program for seniors aged 65 to 69 was also available, but seniors considered it invasive and stigmatizing (*Canadian Encyclopedia*, 2017b). During the 1950s and early 1960s, debate about seniors' pensions focused on whether to eliminate the means test, how generous the pension should be, what should be its relationship to private pension plans, whether the plan should be contribution-based, and how to work with the provinces. Quebec was developing its own plan during this time, and Ontario was considering the same. In the end, a modest contribution-based pension plan was introduced by the Liberal government of Prime Minister Pearson in 1965, about the same time that a similar plan began in Quebec. It rewarded those with high salaries and a long history in the labour force. It disadvantaged part-time workers, minimum-wage workers, and women who had lower wages and whose unwaged caring work with children and elders was not recognized (Finkel, 2006).

As the 1970s began, Canada's welfare state now looked remarkably like Britain's in 1950. Soon, these achievements would be questioned, and by the 1980s they would be under attack.

## Theorizing the Welfare State

A common feature of liberal democracies in the post–World War II era was the state's new and sometimes extensive engagement in the provision of health, education, income, and social services. Known euphemistically as "the welfare state," it has been defined as "state responsibility for securing some basic modicum of welfare for its citizens" (Esping-Andersen, 1990, pp. 18–19). It gave rise to new ways of articulating the difference in approach from earlier periods. T.H. Marshall (1950), one of the earliest welfare state theorists, argued that the creation of the British welfare state in the twentieth century represented an extension of a citizen's rights from the civil rights attained in the eighteenth century to the political rights developed in the nineteenth century, to the social rights of the twentieth century. He provided a rationale for the various entitlement programs of the post-war welfare state by suggesting they represented an expansion of the idea of citizenship. Marshall's analysis provided the language to view social programs as a right of citizenship and had some applicability to developments in Britain, but it lacked applicability to Canada. Groups such as women, Indigenous peoples, and persons of Asian origin were disenfranchised politically well into the twentieth century in Canada (Courtenay, 2015). Canadians did not talk about social programs using a "rights" discourse. Medicare, regarded as the singular greatest achievement of the Canadian welfare state, was more often described as a "sacred trust" rather than a right of citizenship.

During the 1960s a second approach, from American scholars H.L. Wilensky and C.N. Lebeaux (1965, pp. 138–40), conceptualized two models of social welfare—the residual and the institutional. The residual model assumes an individual's needs are primarily met through the market and the family. Only when these are unable to respond should social welfare institutions come into play, and then only on an emergency or short-term basis. Once the market economy and the family are functioning "properly" and can meet an individual's needs, social welfare institutions should withdraw. An example of a residual service today is temporary income assistance for employable persons. The institutional model, by contrast, views social welfare as an integral part of modern society. It aims to assist individuals and groups "attain satisfying standards of life and health" (Wilensky & Lebeaux, 1965, p. 139). There is no stigma, emergency, or abnormality implied in the receipt of health care, education, and social services. Provided on a non-market universalist basis, institutional services respond to categorical needs such as childhood, old age, illness, and disability. Contemporary Canadian examples are old age security and medicare.

In the early 1970s, Richard Titmuss, a British theorist, identified a third model of social policy[5] called the industrial achievement performance model (Titmuss, 1974, p. 31). In this model, the market is dominant in meeting social needs, and social policy functions as an adjunct. Social benefits are provided based on merit, work performance, occupational achievement, and employment-based productivity. Today, employers often provide extended health benefits and access to a company pension plan when one passes from temporary, on-call, or probationary status to full-time or permanent status. As one's pay grade increases with promotions and years of service, one's pension at retirement also increases. This model places the focus on the extensive unrecognized system of welfare tied to employment. Believed to be a reward for loyalty and hard work, it is generally not seen as social policy. Titmuss also delineated the extensive hidden "occupational welfare" that exists alongside state welfare. **Occupational welfare** refers to non-wage benefits provided by an employer to enhance the work environment and maintain good employee relations. In unionized environments, these normally include extended health benefits and pensions, but can also include counselling services, transit passes, and retirement payouts of unused sick leave. Depending on the position and the employer, occupational welfare might also include: housing (university presidents), boats and automobiles (corporate executives), university tuition fees (faculty), flight passes (airline employees), season's sports tickets (corporate executives), subsidized meals (parliamentarians, oil patch workers, restaurant workers), and work clothing (fast-food employees, emergency responders). This list demonstrates that employers, in certain environments, are meeting some of the most basic needs of their employees—for food, clothing, and shelter—through an unrecognized system of occupational welfare.

In Canada, the virtues of universal welfare state programs such as family allowances, old age security, and medicare were often praised because they were provided without stigma or assessment of need to everyone within a category (parents with children, seniors). By contrast, selective programs targeted to a group, need, or income level stigmatized the recipient as "needy" or "poor." However, these distinctions have become blurred with time. During the 1980s, many began to question whether a retired bank president[6] should receive a universal old age security cheque. At the same time, others realized a tax system could become more than just a collection system. It could also provide information for a confidential assessment of need and, partnered with Service Canada, become a "distribution" system. The Child Tax Credit (now discontinued) and the Guaranteed Income Supplement for seniors targeted income to poorer Canadians, particularly women, without stigmatizing them in the process. In recent years, the Liberal government of Prime Minister Justin Trudeau combined the Child Tax Credit and the Universal Child Care Benefit (UCCB) to create a universal-like program with the Canada Child Benefit where the benefit decreases as one's income rises (see Chapter 11 for more on the Canada Child Benefit).

In the 1990s, welfare state research examining the relationship among the state, the market, and the family began to identify qualitative differences across different nation-states. This approach, known as **welfare state regimes**, recognized "the relation between state and economy (as) a complex of legal and organizational features . . . systematically interwoven" (Esping-Andersen, 1990, p. 2). One cluster is described as the "liberal" Anglo-American welfare state, and includes the United Kingdom, the United States, Canada, and Australia. Here "means-tested assistance, modest universal transfers or modest social insurance plans predominate" (Esping-Andersen, 1990, p. 26). Benefits are small, often stigmatizing, and geared primarily to low-income or working-class individuals with the aim of encouraging their rapid return to the market economy.

A second regime-cluster, described as "corporatist-conservative" welfare states, includes Austria, France, Germany, and Italy. These countries emphasize the preservation of status differentials, and benefits are attached to employment and uphold one's status and class. There is a strong commitment to preserve the traditional family, social insurance excludes non-working wives, daycare and other family services are underdeveloped, and there is a minimal redistribution of benefits. This regime privileges the male breadwinner as well as the family's resources, and the state only intervenes when the family's resources are exhausted.

A third regime-cluster, the social democratic, represents the Nordic countries of Finland, Denmark, Sweden, Iceland, and Norway. In these countries, the welfare state is grounded in the principles of universalism, equality, and full employment. All social classes enjoy equal rights and everyone is incorporated into one universal insurance system. The differences in the three regimes can be explained by "the pattern of working class political formation," the "political coalition-building in the transition from a rural economy to a middle-class society," and "the institutionalization of class preferences and political behavior" in past reforms (Esping-Andersen, 1990, p. 32). In the welfare regimes approach, distinct ideologies or political theories begin to become visible. These are explored in the next section.

# Political Theory, Ideology, and Social Policy

The three most visible ideologies on the Canadian political landscape during the twentieth century have been liberalism, conservatism, and socialism.

**Liberalism** is "associated with freedom of religious choice and practice, free enterprise and free trade in the realm of economics, and freedom of expression and association in politics" (Brooks, 2012, p. 37). The cornerstone of this tradition is the individual's freedom to express views as well as religious convictions, and to freely associate with those she chooses without state interference. The British philosophers Adam Smith and John Stuart Mill provided the intellectual foundations for liberalism through their eighteenth- and nineteenth-century works.

**Classical conservatism**, by contrast, "accepted human inequality—social, political, and economic—as part of the natural order of things" (Brooks, 2012, p. 38). It stressed the importance of tradition, continuity with the past, the maintenance of law and order, and support for the monarchy. It also believed the wealthy had an obligation to assist the poor, as all are members of the same society. Conservatism tended to support an established church, for example, the Anglican Church in English Canada or the Roman Catholic Church in Quebec. Edmund Burke is the intellectual most associated with this tradition in Britain.

**Classical socialism**, the most recent of these three ideologies, argues that when individuals have roughly equivalent levels of wealth, power, and status they will be better able achieve their full potential. It is based on the principle of equality of condition. It supports "a vastly greater role for the state in directing the economy, better working conditions and greater rights for workers vis-à-vis their employers, and reforms like public health care, unemployment insurance, income assistance for the indigent, public pensions, and universal access to public education" (Brooks, 2012, p. 38). Socialism, by definition, is critical of capitalism and the economic and social relations it creates. Its ideas are informed by the work of such nineteenth-century intellectuals as Karl Marx and the Fabian socialists Sidney and Beatrice Webb.

These three ideologies inform Canada's political life and social policy and propose different relationships and roles for the state, the individual, and society. They suggest "what needs to be done" in social policy, but are not static unchanging entities. They grow, change, and mutate, retaining some dimensions and adding new ones as Canadian society evolves. Liberal ideas are now widely infused in Canadian society and politics, are found across the political spectrum, and are arguably Canada's dominant ideology (Marchak, 2011). Whether in the wording of the Constitution Act, 1982, political party platforms, or informal discussions, ideas such as freedom of the individual or equality of opportunity are taken for granted. However, other ideas also form part of Canadians' political discourse. These include neo-conservatism, neo-liberalism, social conservatism, "red Toryism," and social democracy.

**Neo-conservatism**, a variant of traditional conservatism, had its beginning in the 1970s. It stood for "political individualism and a qualified endorsement of free markets" (Ball & Dagger, n.d.), and was a label given to Margaret Thatcher's Conservative government in Great Britain (1979–90), Ronald Reagan's Republican presidency in the United States (1981–9), and Brian Mulroney's Progressive Conservative government in Canada (1984–93). Neo-conservatives argue current social programs are too generous, create dependency, reduce individual initiative, and make the state rather than the individual responsible for welfare. While not opposed to some welfare state programs, they argued for a rollback of social expenditures, often in relation to "employables," and advocate the introduction of "workfare" to move people from income assistance to the workforce. Today, it is more common to apply the term "neo-liberalism" to many of the same beliefs.

**Neo-liberalism** is usually associated with a strong belief in a free-market economy, minimal state intervention in economic and social affairs, the free movement of capital, and free trade between nations (Smith, n.d.). It emerged as a contrasting view to Keynesian economics in the 1970s and its belief that the state should play a more active role in economic and social affairs. Keynesianism[7] aimed to lessen the effects of a capitalist market economy on individuals and families through government intervention in the economy. During the 1980s, neo-liberal ideas "took hold in all of Canada's major political parties" (Finkel, 2006, p. 285). Provincial governments elected in the 1990s influenced by neo-liberal ideas included the Alberta Progressive Conservatives (1993), the Ontario Progressive Conservatives (1995), the British Columbia Liberals (2001), and the Quebec Liberals (2003). These governments limited welfare state expenditures in such popular areas as health care and education, and reduced them in areas without broad public support, such as services to transients, unemployed youth, and lone mothers. Neo-liberalism inspired a major rethinking of the state's role in welfare provision, with one outcome being an interest in the "social investment state," discussed below.

**Social conservatism** focuses on promoting non-fiscal conservative values in political life, such as heterosexual lifelong marriage, a traditional role for women in the family, promotion of Christian values, and opposition to divorce, abortion, LGBTQ rights, and same-sex marriage (Conservapedia, 2017). These views were commonly found in Canada among members of the Roman Catholic and evangelical Christian churches, and in the policies of the Reform Party of Canada (1987–2000) and its successor, the Canadian Alliance (2000–3). When the Canadian Alliance and the Progressive Conservative Party merged in 2003 to create the Conservative Party of Canada, these views appeared to decline in prominence. However, they may be resurfacing with the 2017 election of Andrew Scheer as the leader of the Conservative Party of Canada.

**Red Tories**, by contrast, "are conservatives who believe that government has a responsibility to act as an agent for the collective good, and that this responsibility goes far beyond maintaining law and order" (Brooks, 2012, p. 68). The wealthy and privileged have an obligation towards the poor and less privileged, according to red Tories, and government's responsibility is to express that obligation through welfare state programs. This implies a communitarian dimension to conservative thought that is traceable back to conservative thinking in Britain. A more positive and nationalistic view of the state is also implied. Its role is to bind society together, to support Canadian culture, and to protect the poor—albeit in a paternalistic way. George Grant (1918–88) is the intellectual most associated with this tradition in Canada.

**Social democracy** refers to the gradual movement towards socialism achieved through social reform in a parliamentary democracy. There is a favourable attitude towards state intervention to achieve greater equality in society, to fairly distribute economic rewards, and to manage capitalism's economic cycles. Social democrats generally favour a mixed and full employment economy, some nationalization of key industries, and an active role for government to ensure stable economic growth. They support a comprehensive public education system to enable individuals to reach their full potential, and a comprehensive welfare state including health, housing, education, and social services available to all on a universal basis (Miller, 2000). In Canada, the League for Social Reconstruction, a group of 75 intellectuals formed in 1932 by F.R. Scott and Frank Underhill, is the group most associated with this philosophy. It was instrumental in the founding of the CCF, which three decades later became the New Democratic Party.

# The Mixed Economy of Welfare

Since Canada's beginning as a white settler society, state and charitable sectors have coexisted in Canadian social policy. Starting in the nineteenth century, homes for the elderly, hospitals, shelters for destitute women, and orphanages, often under Catholic or Protestant religious auspices, operated with substantial subsidies from the state (Finkel, 2006). At the same time, those with the financial means obtained services privately by engaging a physician to treat their family, hiring a nanny to mind their children, paying a nurse to care for aging parents, or entering the private wing of a local hospital reserved for fee-paying patients. In effect, a small commercial sector existed alongside the charitable and state sectors. Throughout the twentieth century, the range of services available for purchase increased substantially and now includes: dental care, vision care, child care, home care, physiotherapy, nursing care, counselling, marital therapy, and addiction treatment. At times, these services are subsidized by the state or made available without charge to individuals with low income. At other times, they become available as part of an employment-based extended benefit package paid through employee and employer contributions. Sometimes services are available on a sliding scale, with the client paying a small fee and a charitable organization picking up the rest. Whether the area is health care, social services, education, housing, or a service focused on the care of children, the elderly, or the disabled, Canada has evolved into a complex **mixed economy of welfare**. It includes a non-profit or charitable sector, a co-operative sector, a fee-for-service/commercial sector, and a state/public sector. Determining the balance between these sectors at any point in time is a matter of political discourse and public debate.

At the beginning of the neo-liberal era in the early 1980s, a dramatic rethinking of the state's role in welfare occurred. This rethinking favoured a significant reduction in the role of the state, a widespread privatization of public services, and an overall widening of the space available for private/commercial operators in health, education, housing, and social services. One writer described this as "the new mixed economy of welfare" (Kammerman, 1983). Anglo-American nations favoured a diminished role for the state, but this was not the approach taken in most European countries, as the social democratic and conservative-corporatist welfare regimes discussed above indicate.

## The Social Investment State

Over the past three decades, welfare states of varying theoretical and ideological persuasion have implemented policies known as the **social investment strategy**. This strategy ensures maximum returns on social expenditures through active labour force employment and social participation: "welfare states are expected to help non-working people back into employment, to complement income from employment for the working poor, to enable parents reconcile career and family life, to promote gender equality, to support child development and to provide social services for an ageing society" (Van Kersbergen & Hemerijck, 2012, p. 476). Most European Union member states have implemented a range of policies that transform their welfare systems from "passive benefit machines" to ones that actively emphasize the employment of women, the disabled, older workers, and those with low skills. As Van Kersbergen and Hemerijck (2012, p. 478) note: "The greater the number of people participating in the labour market, the greater the contribution they make to the affordability of adequate levels of social protection. The novelty of the new approach lies in the combination of investment in human capital and stronger work incentives."

Across various European countries, programs have several common themes:

- reduction in the duration of social assistance and unemployment benefits and levels;
- provision of various forms of assistance to obtain employment: personalized support, core skills training, and individual guidance;
- expansion of child-care and parental leave options;
- pressure to either accept suitable job offers or participate in education;
- provision of wage subsidies to employers in the private sector;
- financial support for education and training.

In simple terms, the social investment strategy relies on a mix of carrots and sticks to activate labour force participation. It encourages all to become wage-earning, taxpaying citizens and participate in the nation's competitiveness and economic growth. It thereby helps to ensure a healthy national financial reserve to fund programs for others during times of dependency such as illness, old age, and new motherhood.

In Canada, the idea of social investment is visible in the federal government's policies with respect to post-secondary education (Chapter 12) and children (Chapter 11). A mix of grants and loans, with larger grants to Indigenous and disabled students, encourages young adults to pursue education and achieve a stable middle-class income. The new Canada Child Benefit program supports a significant number of poor families to move out of poverty and provides financial support to single mothers, among others, to re-enter the labour force.

## Chapter Summary

This chapter has introduced foundational ideas that inform Canada's approaches to social policy. Indigenous ways of caring for community members predate the first French colony and Canada's formation as a nation, but other ideas have been part of white settler society since its inception. Charity, mutual aid, and social regulation continue in various forms today. The welfare state, social citizenship, and social investment now actively inform how Canadians think about and respond to others' needs.

To return to the young man in the case example at the beginning of this chapter, how might he fare in different historical periods? As an Indigenous man, he would arrive at adulthood knowing he had a responsibility to provide and care for others. If he was a street beggar in Quebec City in the seventeenth century, and didn't have a licence for begging, he might have been imprisoned. During the nineteenth century in British North America, he likely would have been sent to a House of Industry, and would have been put to work breaking stone or sent to a farm to work as a labourer to cover his meagre rations and upkeep at the workhouse.

In the Great Depression of the 1930s, he likely would have been refused municipal relief. He might have spent many long days standing in line for a bowl of soup, and would have been sent to an isolated work camp to work for a pittance per day. If he joined others to protest his conditions and the rising unemployment, he might have become part of the "On to Ottawa" trek. When the trekkers arrived in Regina, and the "Regina Riot" occurred, he would have been arrested and sent to prison.

When World War II began, he might have joined the army and found himself on a battlefield in Europe. If he wasn't either killed in battle or badly disabled at war's end, he would have become eligible for an education allowance, a year's unemployment insurance, and priority at civil service jobs.

If he found himself unemployed during the 1970s, he might have stumbled upon a Guaranteed Annual Income experiment (see Chapter 18), which would have provided a stable basic income without stigma or means tests. By the 1990s, though, all that was available was a shelter and food allowance insufficient for a month of either, and he would have been pressured to enrol in a work-for-welfare scheme.

In the twenty-first century, he might have been homeless, forgotten, and living on the edge of society. Alternatively, if an employment counsellor took an interest in him, he might have enrolled in an apprentice program where he received a living allowance while training and a job with a solid "middle-class" income on completion.

## Discussion Questions

1. List the social groups, in order of priority, from most deserving of your help today to least deserving. Discuss your ranking and rationale with your group. What ideas inform your thinking? Is your list similar to or different from those of other members of your group?

2. Beside each group in your list, describe the basis on which you think they should be given help. Draw upon words like: charity, mutual aid, social regulation, social insurance, social right, and social investment. Discuss your thinking with others.

## Notes

1. Whose traditional territory is found today in upper New York State and southern Ontario.
2. Under $200 a year, 15 per cent is returned on federal taxes; over $200 a year, 29 per cent is returned.
3. Those employed by non-profit organizations supported by government grants.
4. Its name at the time.
5. Social welfare and social policy sometimes appear to be synonyms. Wilensky and Lebeaux refer to "residual" and "institutional" as "conceptions of social welfare," whereas Titmuss called these "models of social policy" (Titmuss, 1974, pp. 30–1).
6. A symbol, in media discourse, of an economically advantaged pensioner.
7. Named for the theories of the twentieth-century British economist and civil servant, John Maynard Keynes.

## References

Abbott, P., & Meerabeau, L. (2003). *The sociology of the caring professions* (2nd edn). London & New York: Routledge.

Anderson, K. (2011). *Life stages and native women: Memory, teachings and story medicine.* Winnipeg: University of Manitoba Press.

Ball, T., & Dagger, R. (n.d.). Neoconservatism. *Encyclopedia Britannica.* Retrieved from https://www.britannica.com/topic/neoconservatism

Beito, D. (2000). *From mutual aid to welfare state: Fraternal societies and social services, 1890–1967.* Chapel Hill: University of North Carolina Press.

Brooks, S. (2012). *Canadian democracy* (7th edn). Toronto: Oxford University Press.

*Canadian Encyclopedia.* (2017a). Social security. Retrieved from http://www.thecanadian encyclopedia.ca/en/article/social-security/

———. (2017b). Old age pension. Retrieved from http://www.thecanadianencyclopedia.ca/en/article/old-age-pension/

Conservapedia. (2017). Social conservatism. *Conservapedia.* Retrieved from http://www.conservapedia.com/Social_conservatism

Courtenay, J. (2015). Right to vote in Canada. *Canadian Encyclopedia.* Retrieved from http://www.thecanadianencyclopedia.ca/en/article/franchise/

Department of Finance Canada. (2017). Your tax dollar. Retrieved from https://www.fin.gc.ca/tax-impot/2014/2013-14-e.pdf

Donzelot, J. (1997). *The policing of families.* Baltimore: Johns Hopkins University Press.

Esping-Andersen, G. (1990). *The three worlds of welfare capitalism.* Princeton, NJ: Princeton University Press.

Fairbairn, B., MacPherson, I., & Russell, N. (Eds.). (2000). *Canadian co-operatives in the year 2000: Memory, mutual aid and the millennium.* Saskatoon: Centre for the Study of Co-operatives, University of Saskatchewan.

Finkel, A. (2006). *Social policy and practice in Canada: A history.* Waterloo, ON: Wilfrid Laurier University Press.

Fisher, R. (1992). *Contact and conflict: Indian–European relations in British Columbia, 1774–1890* (2nd edn). Vancouver: University of British Columbia Press.

Galer, D. (2010). A friend in need or a business indeed? Disabled bodies and fraternalism in Victorian Ontario. *Labour/Le Travail, 66,* 9–36.

Giberovitch, M. (1994).The contributions of Holocaust survivors to Montreal Jewish communal life. *Canadian Ethnic Studies, 26*(1), 74–85.

Imagine Canada. (2006). *Social service organizations in Canada.* Retrieved from www.imaginecanada.ca/sites/default/files/www/en/.../j_social_services_factsheet.pdf

Kammerman, S. (1983). The new mixed economy of welfare: Public and private. *Social Work,* (Jan./Feb.), 5–10.

Kennedy, P. (2013). *Key themes in social policy.* London & New York: Routledge.

Keynes, J.M. (n.d). *John Maynard Keynes quotes.* Good Reads. Retrieved from https://www.goodreads.com/author/quotes/159357.John_Maynard_Keynes

Lightman, E., & Lightman, N. (2017). *Social policy in Canada* (2nd edn). Toronto: Oxford University Press.

Little, M. (2005). Claiming a unique place: The introduction of mothers' pension in B.C. In D. Purvey & C. Walmsley (Eds.), *Child and family welfare in British Columbia: A history* (pp. 327–48). Calgary: Detselig.

Lutz, J. (2007). *Myth and memory: Stories of Indigenous–European contact.* Vancouver: University of British Columbia Press.

Marchak, P. (2011). *Ideological perspectives on Canada.* Montreal & Kingston: McGill-Queen's University Press.

Marshall, T. H. (1950). *Citizenship and social class and other essays.* London: Cambridge University Press.

Matters, I. (2005). Sinners or sinned against? Historical aspects of female juvenile delinquency in British Columbia. In D. Purvey & C. Walmsley (Eds.), *Child and family welfare in British Columbia: A History* (pp. 77–90). Calgary: Detselig.

Miller, D. (Ed.). (2000). *The Blackwell encyclopedia of political thought.* Oxford: John Wiley & Sons.

Moscovitch, A., & Drover, G. (1987). Social expenditures and the welfare state: The Canadian experience in historical perspective. In A. Moscovitch & J. Albert (Eds.), *The benevolent state: The growth of welfare in Canada* (pp. 13–43).Toronto: Garamond Press.

National Archives. (2017). The Beveridge Report and child benefit. Retrieved from http://www.nationalarchives.gov.uk/cabinetpapers/themes/beveridge-report-child-benefit.htm

Piven, F., & Cloward, R. (1993). *Regulating the poor: The functions of public welfare.* New York: Vintage Books.

Royal Commission on Aboriginal Peoples. (1996). *Report of the Royal Commission on Aboriginal Peoples. Volume 1: Looking forward, looking back.* Ottawa: Minister of Supply and Services Canada. Retrieved from http://data2.archives.ca/e/e448/e011188230-01.pdf

Schoenfeld, S. (2015). Jewish Canadians. *Canadian Encyclopedia.* Retrieved from http://www.thecanadianencyclopedia.ca/en/article/jewish-canadians/

Smith, N. (n.d.). Neoliberalism. Retrieved from https://www.britannica.com/topic/neoliberalism

Statistics Canada. (2014, 19 Dec.). Your tax dollar: 2013–2014 fiscal year.

———. (2015, 16 Dec.). Infographic: Charitable giving in Canada.

———. (2017, 27 Jan.). Infographic: 2015 household spending in Canada.

Sullivan, M. (1996). *The development of the British welfare state.* London: Prentice-Hall.

Titmuss, R. (1974). *Social policy: An introduction.* London: George Allen & Unwin.

Van Kersbergen, K., & Hemerijck, A. (2012). Two decades of change in Europe: The emergence of the social investment state. *Journal of Social Policy, 41*(3), 475–92.

Wilensky, H. L., & Lebeaux, C. N. (1965). *Industrial society and social welfare: The impact of industrialization on the supply and organization of social welfare services in the United States.* New York: Free Press.

# 4

# The Ideals and Realities of Policy-Making Processes and Structures in Canada

*Jennifer Murphy and Juliana West*

---

### Chapter Objectives

*This chapter will help you to develop an understanding of:*
- the complexity of the Canadian federal state, including federal, provincial, and municipal responsibilities and powers;
- the political divisions that drive policy development and change;
- how policy-making is constructed within a political, legal, and social framework;
- the political discourses that frame policy-making;
- how social workers can influence social policy using a critical lens for analysis.

---

## Introduction

This chapter focuses on the development of social policy within a political, legal, and social framework that privileges some discourses or explanations for social problems and how to "fix" them. One example of this is the discourse of substance use/addiction as a criminal matter rather than a health issue. Within social work direct practice, these discourses influence not only funding and the prioritization of resources, but also the determination of who is the more "deserving" of help. Using a critical framework for analysis of policies and policy-making, students will learn how to deconstruct dominant narratives in the Canadian neo-liberal state that entrench privilege within policy at all levels of government and political parties.

The complexity of the Canadian federal state and its relationship to policy development is discussed, as it is critical for social workers to develop a clear understanding of the processes that lead to policy-making so that they can individually and collectively advocate for change. The series of steps that lead to policy development and implementation will be delineated using a critical perspective that questions how political parties are influenced in a variety of ways, including by sections of the electorate, pressure groups, and the media. The ideal of a rational and straightforward approach to developing policy is challenged in this chapter to demonstrate to the readers that policy-making is an action replete with compromise, contradictions, and failure. The examples used throughout the chapter to highlight some of the complexities of policy-making include a case study focused on the issue of substance use and the establishment of Insite, a safe injection site, in Vancouver's Downtown Eastside (DTES) in 2003. Under the Conservative federal government, Insite was defined as an illegal drug site through the lens of the Criminal Code, while the provincial government considered Insite to be an essential component of a harm reduction approach to drug use within a medical model. The province's position was supported by the city of Vancouver, the provincial health authority, social workers working in the field of substance misuse, and ultimately the courts. The oppositional discourses around this issue will be examined and discussed.

In addition, the federal Liberals campaigned in 2015 on a policy platform that promised the legalization of marijuana, in contrast with the Conservative Harper federal government, which advocated continued criminalization, and the federal NDP, whose policies included decriminalization but not legalization (as discussed further below). The Liberals formed the government in 2015 and introduced a bill in the spring of 2017 to legalize marijuana in 2018, concomitantly with tougher impaired driving penalties. The Senate passed Bill C-45 at second reading in March 2018 and sent it to committee for further study. A final vote in the Senate passed on 19 June 2018, with implementation of the law announced to take effect on 17 October (Sapra, 2018; Scotti & Cain, 2018). Current discourses on the issue have now shifted into a discussion of the logistics of regulating cannabis. Kristy Kirkup (2017), for example, details the provincial role: the provinces and territories will have to develop rules around the regulation and distribution of the drug, including how it will be packaged and sold in retail outlets. The distribution of marijuana will also have a significant effect on municipalities, which will be expected to regulate the industry through zoning laws, bylaws, and enforcement.

## Case Examples   The Complexity of Drug Dependence

*As you read this chapter, you may want to consider these profiles of people involved in substance use to aid in your discussion of the political realities of policy-making and its effects on individuals, families, and communities. The profiles are fictitious but representative of service users struggling with substance use and addiction.*

**Marie** is an Indigenous woman in her thirties living in the Downtown Eastside of Vancouver (DTES). She has been diagnosed with PTSD as a result of intergenerational trauma from residential school, which three generations of her family attended. Her two children have been removed from her care and placed in non-Indigenous foster homes. She lives with **Manny**, also in his thirties, who arrived in Canada as a teenage refugee claimant from El Salvador. His refugee claim was successful and he is now a Canadian citizen. He has also been diagnosed with PTSD after witnessing significant violence, including the murder of family members, before leaving El Salvador. Marie has a criminal record involving shoplifting and solicitation offences, mostly to raise money for street drugs. Both Marie and Manny are heroin users and use the services at Insite to access counselling as well as clean needles and a safe place to inject heroin. Neither Marie nor Manny has ever voted in a provincial or federal election, and they do not view politics as part of their everyday lives.

> **James** is a delivery truck driver in his forties who lives in Surrey, BC, a suburb close to Vancouver. He is a white male who considers himself to be a social and fiscal conservative, and he always votes in provincial and federal elections. He struggles with lifting heavy objects since he injured his spine in a car accident five years ago. His doctor has prescribed opioids in ever-increasing doses, as James has developed a significant tolerance for painkillers over the last five years. He describes his prescription drugs as a "cure" for his chronic pain, and both he and his doctor view his condition as a medical issue rather than a dependency on prescription drugs. James's doctor has warned him, however, that he is in danger of impaired driving if his dose is increased further.

# Political Parties in Canada

A key question to bear in mind when reading this chapter is how political parties in the municipal, provincial, and federal arenas could welcome marginalized and criminalized community members, who may feel excluded from political power and consequently disenfranchised. While all political parties in Canada focus on getting "their" voters to the polls on election day, they also draft policies that will appeal to discrete categories of voters, in terms of class, race, and gender. For example, all three major federal political parties consistently focus on addressing middle-class concerns, often with a vague description of what "middle class" actually means (as an example, see the federal Liberal Party website, https://www.liberal.ca). In addition, while some political parties advocate for building more social housing and adding resources to the health care budget to tackle mental health issues, for example, which may not necessarily be seen as middle-class concerns, failures of collaboration and co-operation between the federal and provincial governments may prevent a joint reallocation of budget and resources to tackle these significant issues. The result then becomes a shifting of blame from provincial to federal government and vice versa rather than a call to action.

To differentiate between political parties in the Canadian landscape it is necessary to understand the different ideological underpinnings of each party, both historically and currently. While all political parties have adapted over time to significant changes within Canadian society, readers may want to reflect on the process of political change: should political parties lead change (for example, in Canada's relationship with Indigenous peoples) or should they simply reflect changing public opinion as it emerges? While these questions are difficult to answer definitively, and political change often involves a combination of both approaches, as social workers who work with marginalized groups in society we need to understand how political processes are influenced by many factors, including the media, lobby groups, court decisions, think-tanks, and party members.

The main political parties fit more or less into three categories: conservatism, liberalism, and social democracy (see Chapter 3). These parties correspond in the federal system to the Conservatives, the Liberals, and the New Democratic Party (NDP). However, as Graham, Shier, and Delaney (2017) point out, political parties are held together in a complex interaction that includes differing and sometimes opposing viewpoints within each party so that no federal or provincial party in Canada represents an ideal or pure ideological standpoint. All parties regularly compromise on policy issues (Graham, Shier, & Delaney, 2017, p. 74). Variants of these parties, sometimes with different names, are also represented provincially; for example, the current BC government (from June 2017) consists of a coalition between the provincial NDP and Green Party, with the former governing party, the Liberals (a neo-conservative party), in opposition after 16 years in power. This chapter will concentrate, however, on the federal parties in Canada and their policies and party platforms, particularly as they relate to drug policies, to uncover the discourses that frame their approaches to policy development.

## The Conservative Party of Canada

The Conservative Party of Canada (https://www.conservative.ca) has undergone a series of transformations over the last 30 years, from the Progressive Conservative era (1942 to 2003), which included John Diefenbaker (1957–63), Joe Clark (1979), and Brian Mulroney (1984–93) as prime ministers, to its merger with the Alliance Party (formerly the Reform Party) to form the Conservative Party of Canada in 2003 under the leadership of Stephen Harper (Graham et al., 2017, p. 75). The Conservative Party formed government in 2006 with Harper as Prime Minister, first as a minority government then a majority, until its defeat in October 2015, when the federal Liberal Party regained power with a majority government. In the last election, the Conservative Party focused on its core message: lower taxes and self-reliance rather than investment in social programs, with marketization, free trade, and capitalism as the foundation for public welfare (Chappell, 2014, p. 107), nuclear families as the foundation of society, and a "Tough on Crime" approach to law and order (Conservative Party of Canada, 2015). Their election platform promised increased resources for law enforcement (p. 105) and stated that the Liberals wanted to make marijuana available for sale in corner stores, "thereby making it accessible to our children" (p. 119). In addition, the Conservatives under Harper argued that "the Liberals and NDP would establish so-called 'safe' injection sites in our communities, bringing serious drugs into our neighbourhoods and closer to our children" (p. 119). The law-and-order approach taken by the Conservative Party fits with their core message that individuals are wholly responsible for their actions and that previous Liberal governments had created a system that focused only on "criminals" and ignored "victims" (p. 115).[1] The Conservatives also proposed toughening penalties for drug crimes in the Protecting Communities from the Evolving Dangerous Drugs Trade Act and continuing the criminalization of marijuana (p. 113). The Conservative Party platform, therefore, positioned drug use firmly within the Criminal Code and within an ideology that associated drug use with deviance. In this scenario, society (particularly children) needs to be protected from the risk of exposure to illegal drugs. Legal drugs, for example, prescription drugs, were only added by the Conservatives to the mandate of the National Anti-Drug Strategy in 2014 (p. 105), and the opioid crisis, which places drug use within a more complex scenario, was overlooked in the party platform.

The Conservative's National Anti-Drug Strategy focused on three areas: prevention, treatment, and enforcement (p. 105). This approach included tougher penalties for drug dealers, legislation to prevent drug trafficking in prison, increased resources for law enforcement to investigate and prosecute drug crimes, increasing awareness around the dangers of drug use, and "significant support for treatment, to help people who've fallen prey to addiction" (p. 105). The terminology used by the Conservatives includes "addiction," "addicts," "drug gangs," "drug crimes," and "drug abuse" and reflects a discourse around substance use that assumes it is at best illicit and at worst criminal. Within this discourse, safe injection sites, harm reduction approaches, and a medical approach to substance use are seen as ineffective and indeed immoral. The moral imperative, in contrast, is to continue to demand abstinence from those struggling with substance use, including continued criminalization in a "war on drugs" mandate. The abstinence approach places substance use within a narrative of individual failure and weakness rather than within systemic issues that marginalize individuals, groups, and communities in an analysis of race, class, and gender. This approach, of course, is reflected in the policies and legislation proposed by the Conservative Party. Going back to the case examples at the start of this chapter, the lens of intersectionality that social workers use to analyze societal issues would view the situations of Marie and Manny very differently from a Conservative Party approach that situates problems within the person rather than the structures of society, and emphasizes individual over societal responsibility.

## The Liberal Party of Canada

The federal Liberal Party (www.liberal.ca), in contrast, focuses on "the middle class and those working hard to join it" (Liberal Party of Canada, 2015, p. 4), without defining who belongs to the middle class (for example, in terms of income, educational level, or job/career). Its website aims to appeal to a broad section of the Canadian voting public, including women, immigrants, and young voters. However, former federal Liberal governments in the 1990s and early 2000s under Jean Chrétien and Paul Martin, rather than maintaining social programs, continued with the 1980s Progressive Conservative approach to reduce the social safety net by clawing back benefits, reducing federal transfer payments to provinces, and effectively eroding the principles of a universal welfare state (Chappell, 2014). The Liberals became what Chappell defines as "*business* Liberals" rather than "*social* Liberals (Chappell, 2014, p. 95; emphasis in original). In other words, faced with the effects of globalization, disappearing full-time permanent work, and an economy in recession, the Liberal government focused first and foremost on reducing the federal deficit and the national debt. The result was to decentralize government by reducing transfer payments and downloading responsibilities for funding post-secondary education, health care, and social programs to the provinces and/or the private sector (Chappell, 2014, p. 93). The impacts of these reductions are still felt today.

After almost 10 years in opposition, the Liberal leader, Justin Trudeau, ran the 2015 election campaign on a platform of optimism, focusing on inclusivity and caring (https://www.liberal.ca/files/2015/10/New-plan-for-a-strong-middle-class.pdf) in contrast to the Conservative Party's "Get Tough on Crime" approach and the Conservatives' promise to set up a "barbaric cultural practices hotline" for the Canadian public to contact the Royal Canadian Mounted Police (RCMP) to report crimes, such as so-called "honour killings." Aujla and Gill (2014) argue that the very term "honour killing" places domestic violence within the concept of the "exotic other," that is, within immigrant and specifically racialized communities, usually Muslim. They prefer the use of the term "femicide," which they state places the crime within the context of mainstream communities and emphasizes that the murder of women by family members is an extreme form of domestic violence. The divisiveness of the Conservative Party platform had an impact on voters across a number of demographics, including young and first-time voters, many of whom voted Liberal rather than Conservative or NDP (Grenier, 2015). The Liberal Party platform focused on appealing to a broad range of voters: women (every new policy would be viewed through a "gender lens"); families (promise to increase daycare affordability and spaces); seniors (promise to assist veterans and protect health care); and immigrants (promise to increase numbers of family reunification immigrants).[2] These programs would be paid for by planning for deficits rather than balanced budgets until 2019.

For young voters, in particular, the Liberals promised more assistance for federal student loans and the legalization of marijuana. In contrast to the Conservative "Get Tough on Crime" approach, the Liberals promised tougher criminal penalties for those convicted of domestic violence, which fitted with their women-focused approach, but no other new criminal sanctions (Liberal Party of Canada, 2015, p. 52). However, their promise to legalize marijuana use was widely discussed: "We will legalize, regulate and restrict access to marijuana" (p. 55). The preamble to this election promise was that prohibition was ineffective, costly to administer, provided funds for traffickers to finance other illegal activities, and left many Canadians with criminal records for a non-violent offence. This appeared to be a pragmatic approach to drug use rather than a moral imperative that supported Conservative prohibition measures. Legalization of other drugs was not mentioned in the party platform.

## The New Democratic Party of Canada

The third party in the three-way race to form government in the 2015 federal election was the New Democratic Party. The Co-operative Commonwealth Federation (CCF), the forerunner to the federal NDP, was founded as an alliance of trade unions and farmers' co-operatives in the Great Depression of the 1930s (Graham et al., p. 75). The CCF became the NDP in 1961 under the leadership of Tommy Douglas, who stepped down from his position as premier of Saskatchewan to lead the new party, which continued its allegiance to social democratic principles and policies. The NDP has never formed government federally, but it has held the balance of power, from 1972 to 1974 in the minority government of Liberal Prime Minister Pierre Trudeau, and during that time influenced the passage of a national affordable housing strategy and pension indexing (NDP, 2017). In 2011, the NDP under the leadership of Jack Layton became the official opposition for the first time after winning 103 seats, but the party, led by Tom Mulcair, was reduced again to third-party status after the 2015 election, winning just 44 seats.

In 2015, the NDP campaign focused not so much on social democratic principles but rather on centrist policies that appeared at times to be to the right of Justin Trudeau's Liberals. For example, the NDP platform, *Building the Country of Our Dreams*, focused on "fiscal sustainability" and balanced budgets without cuts in service (NDP, 2015, p. 62), in contrast to the Liberal platform that promised infrastructure spending to create jobs, which they acknowledged would lead to deficit budgets. Like the Liberals, however, Mulcair also stated that his upbringing had instilled in him the core middle-class values of helping others, working together, and putting principles into action (NDP, 2017). Social democratic values were not discussed: terms such as "the working class" and "the class struggle" were absent from the platform. Instead, the NDP focused on the promise to reduce poverty, remake relationships with Indigenous peoples, sustain the public health system, create good jobs, enhance environmental protections, and introduce $15-a-day daycare.

The NDP discussion of crime and security issues is similarly positioned as centrist or steeped in liberal values rather than leftist in approach. Graham, Shier, and Delaney (2017, p. 72) argue that classic social democratic ideals are no longer represented in the policy pronouncements of the NDP. For example, the 2015 platform addressed community safety issues by promising to add 2,500 new RCMP officers to the national force while concomitantly funding crime prevention programs and victim assistance programs (NDP, 2015, p. 40). In addition, the NDP promised to decriminalize the possession of marijuana for personal use (p. 40). This policy was quite different from the Liberal Party's election pledge to legalize marijuana. The NDP would leave marijuana as a prohibited drug in the Criminal Code, while the Liberals aimed to remove marijuana from criminal sanction. The NDP platform did not address safe injection sites, treatment facilities, or the relaxation of criminal sanctions for drugs other than marijuana. The underlying premise is that illicit drug use should continue to be regulated through the Criminal Code and criminal sanctions rather than through the health care system, which focuses on harm reduction and treatment options.

## Policy Implications of the 2015 Federal Election

Overall, the Conservatives in 2015 ran on a very different and opposing platform to those of the Liberals and NDP in terms of social issues. The Liberal and NDP platforms were fairly closely aligned, mainly because the NDP moved further towards the centre rather than maintaining a classic social democratic manifesto, which would focus on full employment, market regulation through government intervention, and supporting the social safety net so that greater social and economic equality can be achieved

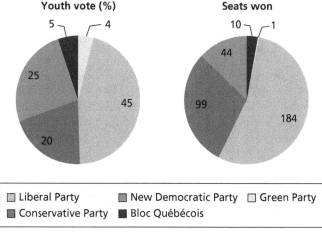

**Figure 4.1** Federal Election Youth Voter Turnout by Party by Seats Won

Source: Data compiled from http://www.cbc.ca/news2/interactives/results-2015; Coletto (2016).

(Graham et al., 2017, p. 72). In addition, the Conservatives seemed less interested in gaining new voters and more interested in ensuring that their base support (around 40 per cent of Canadian voters) would get out and vote in enough numbers to ensure at least a minority Conservative government. However, according to Kashani (2016) in an analysis of voting strategies, there were five million unaligned voters in Canada in 2015, including voters who did not vote in 2011 and new voters. This large section of the electorate can change the outcome of an election, and when the impact of strategic voting is added into a volatile election campaign, that is, voter choice determined by an "Anybody but Harper" approach, there was a significant shift in outcomes. Overall, the Liberals were elected in a shift of 1.4 million votes from the NDP to Liberal candidates (Kashani, 2016).[3] This shift in voting preference led to the formation of a majority Liberal government, with the Conservatives moving to official opposition and the NDP reduced to third-party status.

# Major Influences on Policy Development

As the section above outlines, political party platforms differ substantially in terms of priorities, approaches to social problems, and ideas about how to solve them. These differences lie at the heart of the ideological distinctions among the Conservatives, Liberals, and NDP. The party manifestos, which include policy processes, are developed in conjunction with party members, party politicians, think-tanks, experts, research, Royal Commissions, public opinion, and other formal and informal influences. However, Westhues and Kenny-Sherber (2012) argue that the party leader has the most significant influence on policy development within the political process, although cabinet ministers and MPs also contribute to policy. One question to consider again is what influence Marie and Manny or, for that matter, James (in the case examples at the start of the chapter) could have on the development of policy within a party political framework. Also, you might want to consider the possible influence of social workers on policy development, as experts in a particular field as either practitioners or researchers.

## Think-Tanks

Most writers in the field of policy development describe a number of groups that influence policy (Chappell, 2014; Graham et al., 2017; McKenzie & Wharf, 2015; Westhues & Wharf, 2012). For example, McKenzie and Wharf (2015) detail the different approaches to policy formation, from think-tanks (over 100 in Canada) to social movements and advocacy groups. There is a great deal of variety in the ideological approaches of think-tanks in Canada, from neo-conservative (e.g., the Fraser Institute) to left of centre (e.g., the Canadian Centre for Policy Alternatives). These groups are generally aligned with political parties, and they provide research and policy briefs to the public as well as to politicians. In addition, some think-tanks, such as the Caledon Institute on Social Policy and Canadian Policy Research Networks, influence policy through their deep connections with the federal government and knowledge of how government operates (McKenzie & Wharf, 2015). This knowledge ensures that they can influence policy through the identification of emerging issues and offer possible solutions.

## Royal Commissions

Other formal avenues that influence policy development include Royal Commissions, which can have a significant impact on government funding and policies. McKenzie and Wharf (2015) discuss the impact of the Royal Commission on Aboriginal Peoples (1996), which heard evidence from Elders, experts, researchers, and others to develop an understanding of the effects of government policies on Indigenous groups through a lens of colonization. More recently, the Truth and Reconciliation Commission of Canada (2015), which came out of the Indian Residential School Settlement Agreement, made 94 Calls to Action to change the relationship of Indigenous peoples with the federal government, and many of these Calls to Action involve areas of concern to social workers (see Chapter 6 for further discussion of the historical and modern policies of colonization).[4]

## Lobby Groups

Aspiring or retired politicians often work for lobby groups and think-tanks, where they build up their credentials and public awareness of their positions. Stephen Harper, for example, was the president of the National Citizens Coalition (NCC) from 1997 to 2002 after he resigned his parliamentary seat as a Reform MP. He returned to federal politics to lead the Reform Party, then the Alliance Party, and finally the merged Progressive Conservative Party and Alliance Party, renamed the Conservative Party. The NCC is a right-wing lobby group, founded in 1967 by Colin Brown in opposition to medicare (Harper Index, 2015). According to the NCC website (http://nationalcitizens.ca), the organization was "founded in 1967 with the express goal to stand up for Canadian taxpayers and to champion small-c conservative values. The National Citizens Coalition is made up of a dedicated group of people working together to ensure the continued success of Canada's largest non-partisan organization." However, a more accurate description of its mandate is that it champions right-wing causes through its opposition to the funding of what it calls "special interest groups," for example, women's groups, social science research, and the arts. Right-wing ideological approaches deny that systemic injustice based on race, ethnicity, sexual identity, or gender exists. Instead, the emphasis on individualism versus collectivism positions responsibility for poverty, racism, and misogyny within individual failure to compete successfully in a capitalist society.[5]

## Social Movements

More informal approaches to policy development include social movements, particularly when they gain momentum through broad public support, for example, Campaign 2000 (McKenzie & Wharf, 2015). The Campaign 2000 policy started in 1989 after widespread public concern about the numbers of children in Canada living in poverty brought politicians together to pass an all-party resolution to end child poverty by the year 2000 (Campaign 2000, 2017). Although the goal has not been met to date, the organization that grew out of the campaign continues to raise awareness of the issue (according to the Campaign 2000 website, 1.34 million children are currently living in poverty), including asking voters to lobby their MPs and releasing an annual report card on the progress (or lack of it) in eradicating child poverty. The organization has over 120 partners at all levels of government who assist in raising awareness of the issue locally, provincially, and nationally.

### The Role of the Media

Finally, the media disseminate policy information through news stories, editorials, and opinion pieces in newspapers, at online sites, and on television. While the influence of media on policy formation may not be direct, politicians and political parties are careful to include media briefings when releasing new policies. Given the concentration of media ownership in Canada, a plurality of political views is more often found on the Internet than in newspapers, which tend to endorse either the Liberal or Conservative Party in general elections (see Chapter 2 for further discussion of news discourse about social policy).

# The Process of Policy Development

Policy development within the political context is a complex process that, although often delineated in stages (Chappell, 2014; McKenzie & Wharf, 2015; Westhues & Kenny-Sherber, 2012), is rather a fluid and reflexive exercise in determining what constitutes a problem and whether or how it should be addressed through public policy. Chappell (2014) lists the process as starting with the identification of a problem, then developing an understanding of it, followed by consultation processes with stakeholders, and then formulation, implementation, and evaluation of the new policy. Within the stages approach, however, a number of questions arise. In the first instance, the identification and naming of a problem needs to be deconstructed in terms of language and the concepts used to name an issue. In the Conservative Party manifesto, the perceived problem of "drug addiction" would be met with criminal sanctions as a means not only to punish "criminals" but also to act as a deterrent to illegal drug users in general. The NDP approach shifted the narrative to one of decriminalization, which would still not address the issue of drug use within a medical model. The Liberal Party focused on legalization, which would shift the discussion back to harm reduction within a medical model, but the only drug to be removed from the Criminal Code is marijuana. In all these examples, the issues of drug dependency, substance use, harm reduction, and safety for intravenous drug users are not addressed.

Similarly, when formulating and implementing policy, the initial definition and language used to name the problem shape the eventual determination of the political process to develop a specific policy to address the problem. Within the ideological confines of political parties, it is difficult to challenge fundamental principles about the relationship of individuals, groups, and communities to the state. Using an intersectional approach to the analysis of social problems and policy-making, and using drug policy as an example, the individualistic approach of the Conservatives led to the development of a policy in the Conservative platform that placed drug use firmly within the purview of the Criminal Code, regardless of considerations of race, gender, and class. However, as the case study of Insite (below) illustrates, drug policies and prohibitions have been developed directly along these lines, as illegal drug users (often poor, racialized, and female) end up criminalized in the sex trade in order to afford to buy illegal substances. The NDP and Liberal parties had more nuanced approaches to the criminalization of substance users, and their policy proposals appeared less punitive and more concerned with not subjecting large segments of the Canadian public to criminal sanctions over marijuana use. The decriminalization of other drugs has been rejected as a possible policy development by the three main federal political parties, which illustrates that none of these parties use the lens of gender, race, and class in analyzing this complex issue. The difference between the approaches of the three parties in their policy manifestos, while substantive, is also an indication of the difficulty in taking a truly innovative policy stance to substance use within a mainstream political party, for example, the decriminalization of all drugs.

# Governing in Parliament

Once a political party has won sufficient seats to form a majority federal government (currently 170 of 338 seats), the realities of governing influence which policies from the party manifesto are prioritized and which will be delayed (or eventually dropped) from the government's agenda. As Canada is a federal state, powers are shared and divided with the 10 provinces and three territories, and the two levels of government have separate and distinct powers, which do, however, overlap at times (Graham et al., 2017, p. 46). Jurisdiction over criminal matters rests with the federal government, for example, but federal transfers and equalization payments from the federal government provide funding to the provinces for social welfare programs, including health care. When federal transfers are reduced in the name of deficit reduction, as they have been since the 1980s, provincial governments face budget restraints and tend to download the reductions to municipal governments, which are consequently limited in the responses they can make to address social issues within their communities (p. 47).[6]

Canada relies on the Westminster model of government in which the Prime Minister and cabinet constitute the executive branch, the House of Commons and the Senate make up the legislative branch, and federal and provincial courts make up the judicial branch of government (McKenzie & Wharf, 2015). Canada is a constitutional monarchy, with the monarch (at present 92-year-old Queen Elizabeth II) as head of state, and the Queen's representative in Canada, the Governor-General, provides royal assent to legislation passed by the House of Commons and the Senate. Although governments can be defeated on confidence votes (usually those involving finance, for example, the budget), majority governments are rarely at risk of losing confidence votes because MPs are obliged to vote along party lines. Minority governments may have to make agreements with other parties in the House of Commons to pass legislation and move ahead with the government's policy agenda.

Policy implementation through the political process includes a number of steps that, when successful, lead to the enactment of policy through legislation. McKenzie and Wharf (2015) document the stages of policy development in Parliament, from initial development by a department tasked with putting political policy into action to ministerial and cabinet approval before the bill is drafted.

- At first reading, the name of the bill, with a short introduction, is introduced by the relevant cabinet minister to the House of Commons.
- At the second reading, the bill may be sent to committee for review and revision after debate on its merits in the House.

- The third reading takes place and a vote is held when the committee (which involves representation from all parties) makes its report to the House.
- The bill receives royal assent and becomes law when it has been passed by the House and Senate.

The final act may be substantially different from the original draft, as amendments and changes may have been made after debate and at the committee stage. As this demonstrates, there are a number of checks and balances involved in enacting policy, including both political and bureaucratic processes, which should allow for a thorough review of the implementation and effects of a new policy. In addition, the Liberal government of Justin Trudeau made a policy promise in the Liberal election platform to include a gender lens for analysis of policies and legislation: "Public policies affect women and men in different ways. We will take these differences into account when making decisions in Cabinet. We will also ensure that federal departments are conducting the gender-based impact analyses that have been required of them for the past 20 years" (https://www.liberal.ca/realchange/gender-impacts/). According to the Status of Women Canada website, "all policies, programs and legislation will include consideration of the differential impacts on diverse groups of women and men" (www.swc.cfc.gc.ca/gba-acs/index-en-html). This policy follows the Action Plan on Gender-based Analysis (2016–2020) recommendations, but it was originally developed in 1995 to advance gender equality in Canada.

# Case Study: Insite

This case study provides readers with an example of how critical policy initiatives are developed in a complex collaboration between all levels of government, with proponents and opponents using legislative approaches and the court system to fulfill or overturn policy directives. The overarching federal Conservative Party ideology that places Insite within a criminal discourse is set against the federal Liberal Party, the BC provincial government, the city of Vancouver, health professionals, researchers, and others who view substance use within a medical discourse of harm reduction. Use of the "deserving/undeserving" trope, however, still dominates public discussion of social policy throughout Canada and on all social welfare topics.

## Background

Insite, North America's first supervised injection site, has been operating in the Vancouver Downtown Eastside (DTES) since 2003. No official sites exist in the United States or Mexico, but 92 such sites are located in 61 cities around the world (Jozaghi, 2016). Insite's history has been one of support and opposition involving all levels of government, and this safe injection site has relied on the work of community activists and researchers, legislation, and successful court challenges. Located in one of the poorest postal codes in Canada and home to a high number of street-involved individuals living with illegal drug use, Insite has offered a safe site for injection drug use and has operated from a harm reduction approach. This approach involves connecting users to resources and a continuum of care for coexisting health and mental health issues, including detox and recovery.[7] Insite does not supply people with illegal drugs—individuals bring the drugs they need for their personal use (Vancouver Coastal Health, 2017a).

Since its opening, Insite has been the focus of more than 50 peer-reviewed studies—all of which noted only favourable effects. These effects include cost-saving service delivery, reduction in drug overdoses and emergency service utilization, decline in the number of publicly discarded syringes and syringe-sharing occurrences, no increase in drug trafficking or drug-related crime, increased follow-up with treatment referrals, reductions in public drug use, and enhanced public awareness (Jozaghi, 2016). In addition, Insite has also facilitated its service users in participating in community advocacy and transformation processes, thus becoming "safety and educational ambassadors within their own communities" (Jozaghi, 2012, p. 1159). Over its 15-year history, over 3.6 million injection visits were supervised at Insite with more than 6,400 overdoses prevented, resulting in zero deaths (Vancouver Coastal Health, 2017b).[8]

Insite's existence has evolved through three general phases: initial coalition-building and emulation of successful harm reduction policy; research generation and dissemination; and political strategizing (Fafard, 2012). In the decade preceding Insite's inception, public health officials, community groups, and politicians at various jurisdictional levels sought to shift public opinion to the benefits of harm reduction and, in the DTES, emulate strategies used in several European cities that reduced deaths due to injection drug use. Once operational, Insite became a site for harm reduction services, and due to its exemption from the Controlled Drugs and Substances Act it became the focus of ongoing research led by the British Columbia Centre of Excellence for HIV/AIDS. Despite its documented efficacy, opposition based on "'politics' and 'ideology' rather than science" from the then federal Conservative government required Insite to focus on political strategizing and to pursue court challenges (Fafard, 2012, p. 907).

## Levels of Decision-Making and Policy-Making Processes: Municipal, Provincial, and Federal

In the late 1990s, public health officials noted the increased rate of HIV and heroin-related deaths in the DTES. In 1995, the Chief Coroner for British Columbia headed a task force looking into the deaths due to heroin use and released a report calling the war on drugs "an expensive failure" (British Columbia, 1994, p. vi). The Chief Coroner called for an anti-drug strategy framing drug use as a social and health issue rather than one of crime, and called for the decriminalization and legalization of drug use. As the number of people dying from overdoses increased, the Vancouver Chief Medical Health Officer declared a public health emergency in the DTES in 1997, and the following year the British Columbia Provincial Health Officer called for harm reduction strategies. In 2000, and following the lead of Vancouver, the provincial and federal governments signed on to the Vancouver Agreement, making harm reduction one of the four pillars (harm reduction, prevention, treatment/rehabilitation, and enforcement) of its new anti-drug strategy. The support for harm reduction increased later in 2000 when the federal Liberal Party, which signed the Vancouver Agreement, won a second term, and again in 2002, when the newly elected Mayor of Vancouver and British Columbia's most recent Chief Coroner won on a platform highlighting the need for a supervised injection site (Dooling & Rachlis, 2010; Fafard, 2012).

In addition to the multi-level governmental support, community initiatives were instrumental in the years leading up to 2003 in raising public awareness and leveraging government support. The Vancouver Area Network of Drug Users (VANDU) formed in 1997 as an advocacy group for drug users as well as for the establishment of a supervised injection site. In addition, the Vancouver health authority—Vancouver Coastal Health— funded VANDU and a number of community service organizations involved in reducing health risks to drugs users, helping to establish the harm reduction coalition. The coalition grew to include academics, journalists, citizen groups, and numerous police officers. In 2000, a conference brought coalition members and politicians together to discuss new approaches and strategies in harm reduction (Dooling & Rachlis, 2010).

The government and community support for a supervised injection site was not, however, without opposition. A business and police coalition hosted their own conference challenging harm reduction as a strategy and, while many Vancouver police officers supported harm reduction initiatives, the Royal Canadian Mounted Police (RCMP) were staunchly opposed (Dooling & Rachlis, 2010). Despite this opposition, the federal government granted Vancouver Coastal Health a three-year exemption from the Controlled Drugs and Substances Act, to run and evaluate a pilot supervised injection facility. Insite opened in September 2003 and within weeks was running at near capacity (Dooling & Rachlis, 2010; Fafard, 2012).

Opposition to Insite that began in Vancouver increased once the federal Conservative Party took power in 2006. The Harper government promised a tougher stance on drug use, eliminated harm reduction as a pillar from its new National Anti-Drug Strategy, and threatened to close Insite. Consequently, Insite's exemption was only temporarily renewed for 15 months, to the end of 2007 (Fafard, 2012). At the same time, the RCMP and the Canadian Police Association called for a halt of all research on Insite with the then federal Health Minister, claiming that existing Insite research left critical new questions unanswered. Funding to the Insite research cohort stopped and a new advisory committee was struck, excluding many university research groups, including the British Columbia Centre of Excellence for HIV/AIDS, from participating.[9] Amid the ongoing threats to close Insite, in October 2007 a second renewal extended Insite's temporary exemption to June 2008 (Small, 2010).

## Legislation

The 1996 Canadian Controlled Drugs and Substances Act is the federal drug statute controlling the possession and use of illegal substances. Section 56 allows the federal Minister of Health to grant an exemption "necessary for a medical or scientific purpose or [that] is otherwise in the public interest" (Canada, 2017, p. 53). The 2002 exemption placed restrictions on Insite's operations, including limiting its capacity and prolonging wait times, but protected Insite staff and drug users from being criminally prosecuted for possessing and administering drugs (Small et al., 2011). The exemption contained the condition that rigorous scientific evaluation of Insite's effect be ongoing (Jozaghi, 2016). Section 56.1, referring specifically to the exemption for supervised consumption sites, was added in 2016.

## Court Challenges

Facing the threat of imminent closure, proponents of Insite took the federal government to the British Columbia Supreme Court in late 2007. In 2008, and one month before Insite's final exemption was to expire, the BC Supreme Court ruled that the closure of Insite, under the Controlled Drugs and Substances Act, was unconstitutional—the closure would undermine the right of drug users to life-saving health care under section 7 of the Charter of Rights and Freedoms (Jozaghi, 2016; Small, 2010). Whereas health care is designated as under provincial jurisdiction in the Constitution Act, 1867 (formerly known as the British North America Act), and the Controlled Drugs and Substances Act is federal, the 1982 Charter of Rights and Freedoms was ruled to give users of Insite, as a provincial health facility, the right to life-saving health care (Dooling & Rachlis, 2010; Small, 2010). British Columbia Supreme Court Judge Ian Pitfield stated, "I cannot agree with the submission that an addict must feed his addiction in an unsafe environment when a safe environment that may lead to rehabilitation is the alternative" (Dooling & Rachlis, 2010, p. 1443).

The federal government appealed the BC Supreme Court's ruling, and in 2010 the BC Court of Appeal upheld the 2008 ruling (Jozaghi, 2016; Small, 2010). The federal government appealed to the Supreme Court of Canada in 2011 and lost again, with the Court ordering the Health Minister to grant the waiver for Insite to remain open. The ruling stated: "On future applications, the Minister must exercise that discretion within the constraints imposed by the law and the Charter, aiming to strike the appropriate balance between achieving public health and public safety" (Jozaghi, 2016, p. 226). Having lost a third time, the Harper government responded by introducing Bill C-65, now Bill C-2. The 2015 bill posed a significant barrier for the approval of any additional sites. Bill C-2 amended the Controlled Drugs and Substances Act by adding the adherence to 26 conditions before any new site could be granted an exemption (Jozaghi, 2016). After the federal Liberal Party won in 2015, a significantly streamlined Bill C-37 amended section 56.1 of the Controlled Drugs and Substances Act. Bill C-37 allowed the opening of additional safe injection sites across Canada and reduced the conditions from 26 to five: evidence of effect on crime rates, assessment of local needs, outline of regulatory structure, resources for sustainability, and evidence of support and opposition (Pacey, 2016).

## Current Situation

Even with the more accessible conditions, advocates for safe injection sites are concerned that Bill C-37 does not include mechanisms to accelerate approvals in times of crisis, and that the bill is framed under law enforcement rather than a harm reduction approach. Significant time and resources will still need to go into gathering evidence for the five criteria, resources that could provide desperately needed services that community groups without legal protection are currently covering (Pacey, 2016). In response to the burgeoning fentanyl crisis, British Columbia declared a public health emergency in April 2016, stating the numbers of people dying from overdoses had accelerated (Vancouver Coastal Health, 2017b). In 2015, 151 fentanyl-detected deaths were identified in the province, in 2016 the number ballooned to 657, and in 2017, 1,210 died from fentanyl-related overdoses (British Columbia Coroners Service, 2018). Even with the addition of five unofficial community-run pop-up injection tents appearing in the DTES, Insite was not able to meet the escalating crisis. As a result, in July 2017, a second supervised injection site opened in the DTES. Across Canada, the fentanyl crisis has put pressure on Health Canada to respond. As of July 2018, Health Canada (2017a) had approved 30 additional supervised consumption sites[10] in Kamloops, Kelowna, Surrey, Victoria, Edmonton, Lethbridge, Ottawa, Toronto, and Montreal. An additional 10 applications to expand services to Grand Prairie, Medicine Hat, Hamilton, London, and Thunder Bay were pending approval (Health Canada, 2018) at the time of writing, but Manitoba, Saskatchewan, Nunavut, Yukon, NWT, PEI, New Brunswick, Nova Scotia, and Newfoundland

and Labrador still do not offer supervised consumption sites. In addition, Health Canada listed seven applications awaiting approval for sites in Vancouver, Victoria, Calgary, and Ottawa. All sites continue to require obtaining exemptions from the federal Controlled Drug and Substances Act (Health Canada, 2017a; Hutchinson, 2017). How the Cannabis Act (2018) or the legal control over the "production, distribution, sale and possession of cannabis across Canada" will affect supervised consumption sites remains to be seen.

# Challenges and Opportunities for Social Workers to Become Agents for Change

The role of social workers in a variety of practice areas, for example, health care, family support, and child welfare, opens up opportunities, along with challenges for them to advocate for social change. Social work practitioners have critical insight from their front-line work, and their experience in working with substance use, for example, gives them knowledge, training, and an in-depth understanding of the issues. In addition, the Canadian Association of Social Workers *Code of Ethics* defines social work values of supporting self-determination of service users and working towards social change. One of the ways to do this is to forge alliances with service users to support changes to policy in grassroots action campaigns. The lived experiences of service users and the practice experience of social workers can be valuable means of supporting changes to social service policies. In a political climate in which substance use is deemed to be a criminal matter as opposed to a health care issue, there is a need for distinct voices to reframe the discourse to one that is anti-oppressive and multi-faceted in its approach.

## Social Policy Change in Action

### Profile of a Social Worker Involved in the Political Process

Margaret Mitchell (1925–2017) was an NDP MP from 1979 to 1993. Before entering politics, she was a social worker in Vancouver, working with abused women and children living in poverty. In 1982, with Pierre Trudeau as Prime Minister leading a majority Liberal government, she rose in the House of Commons to raise an issue of national importance and urgency:

"The parliamentary report states that one in ten Canadian husbands beat their wives regularly", I began. Before I could continue, an uproar of male shouts and laughter erupted, making it impossible for me to be heard. . . . My angry questions topped the TV news that evening. Women's groups across the country rallied. They mounted a major protest, helping to raise awareness of violence against women among politicians and the general public. In the months to come, both federal and provincial politicians responded with progressive change. RCMP and local police forces trained officers to respond to domestic violence, and more charges were laid. More funds were allocated to establish transition houses for women to escape violent partners and find new circumstances. Educational programs made the public more aware that violence was not to be tolerated. (Mitchell, 2008, p. xiii)

## Chapter Summary

This chapter has introduced the reader to the complexities of policy-making, from initial discussions of policy "gaps" identified by a variety of mechanisms (for example, public opinion, experts and researchers, social workers, social service agencies, interest groups, and politicians) through to drafting legislation and implementing policy. The mechanisms of policy development within a legislative framework were also detailed. The political dimensions of policy-making were analyzed through a critical framework that positions political discourse within the ideologies of federal political parties.

Insite, the Vancouver safe injection site, exemplifies the complexities of policy development. Lengthy struggles occurred to keep Insite open and operating in the face of changes in the federal government from a Liberal majority to a Conservative majority and then back to a Liberal majority again in 2015. The Conservatives' unsuccessfully pursued court challenges to Insite, and used legislation (subsequently revised) to attempt to block new safe injection sites from being developed across Canada. The history of Insite demonstrates the connections among social policy, political discourses, and the lives of people who are the users of social services. This direct relationship between service users and the political realities of decision-making is one that social workers need to bear in mind when working and advocating in collaboration with marginalized individuals, groups, and communities to make changes that will improve and even save lives.

## Discussion Questions

1.  Reflecting on the processes of policy development, what role(s) do you think social workers can and should play in the advancement of social policy?

2.  Discuss the difference between the discourse of crime and the discourse of health as it impacts substance use policy, using the profiles of Marie, Manny, and James (see the case examples at the start of the chapter).

3.  Discuss some of the political, legal, and social frameworks that influence policy-making decisions, from identifying a "gap" in service to enacting legislation to "solve" a problem.

## Notes

1.  This simplistic approach, that "criminals" and "victims" are two diametrically opposed groups, led to an increase in punitive criminal laws that, for example, followed the American penal system in establishing a whole-life term in Bill C-53, Life Means Life Act, which the Conservatives promised to enact immediately upon re-election (Conservative Party of Canada, 2015, p. 112).

2.  The core principles in the election platform included a new relationship with Indigenous peoples, a poverty reduction plan, support for families, support for new environmental policies, infrastructure investment, and a new health care plan (Liberal Party of Canada, 2015).

3.  Eric Grenier (2015), in a further breakdown of the vote, stated that the Liberals won the votes

of people who did not vote in 2011, particularly in Ontario and British Columbia, and it came at the expense of the Conservatives. In Quebec, the Liberals took votes at the expense of the NDP.

4. For example, the first Call to Action addresses child welfare and the need for child welfare social workers to be educated about the history and impact of residential schools on Indigenous families and communities (Truth and Reconciliation Commission, 2015, p. 1). All political parties have promised to address the Calls to Action and promised to improve the federal government's relationship with Indigenous peoples.

5. In addition, it runs media campaigns against politicians it considers to be left-wing or centrist, and has challenged government policies in court that restrict third-party advertising during elections (Harper Index, 2015).

6. For example, in regard to this downloading of responsibilities, the Canadian Public Health Association (2016) put out a position paper in December 2016 calling on provincial and territorial governments across Canada to declare the opioid crisis a public health emergency so that funding and resources could be allocated to the problem, and the position paper called on municipalities to focus on providing harm reduction strategies and increased health resources within their jurisdictions to help mitigate the effects of the crisis.

7. Insite offers 12 supervised booths and the materials needed to inject safely (including syringes, water, tourniquets, alcohol swabs, spoons),

supervision and care by nursing and health care staff (overdose prevention and revivals, wound care), and referrals (housing, health, social services).

8. In 2016, Insite saw over 8,000 individuals with an average of over 500 injection room and 75 needle exchange visits per day. Most of the visits were for individuals using heroin (60 per cent), with 27 per cent of service users identifying as women and 18 per cent as Indigenous persons. In addition to the nearly 215,000 visits that year, there were almost 1,800 interventions preventing overdose, 4,500 clinical treatment interventions, and over 5,300 social service and drug treatment referrals made.

9. The non-peer-reviewed findings from the advisory group, as well as research commissioned from the RCMP, challenged the validity of Insite's efficacy (Dooling & Rachlis, 2010) and alleged, in contrast to the existing scientific research, that Insite fostered substance dependence, a claim frequently cited by the new federal government (Jozaghi, 2016).

10. Health Canada (2017b) now uses the term "supervised consumption sites" to refer to locations where "people can bring their own illicit substances (substances obtained in an unauthorized manner) to consume under hygienic conditions with the supervision of trained workers, thereby reducing health risks such as overdose, infections and increasing access to other health and social services including treatment."

# References

Aujla, W., & Gill, A. K. (2014). Conceptualizing "honour'" killings in Canada: An extreme form of domestic violence. *International Journal of Criminal Justice Sciences, 9*(1), 153–66. Retrieved from http://www.sascv.org/ijcjs/pdfs/aujlagillijcjs2004vol9issue1.pdf

British Columbia. (1994). *Report of the Task Force into Illicit Narcotic Overdose Deaths in British Columbia.* Burnaby, BC: Ministry of Attorney General. Retrieved from http://drugpolicy.ca/wp-content/uploads/2016/11/Cain-Report.pdf

British Columbia Coroners Service. (2018). *BC Coroners Service statistical report—Fentanyl-detected illicit drug overdose deaths January 1, 2012 to March 31, 2018.* Retrieved from https://www2.gov.bc.ca/[...]/death-investigation/statistical/fentanyl-detected-overdose.pdf

Campaign 2000. (2017). Retrieved from https://www.campaign2000.ca

Cannabis Act. (2018). Ottawa. Retrieved from https://laws-lois.justice.gc.ca/eng/acts/C-24.5/

Canada. (2017). Legalizing and strictly regulating cannabis: The facts. Retrieved from https://www.canada.ca/content/dam/hc-sc/documents/services/campaigns/27-16-1808-Factsheet-The-Facts-eng-03.pdf

Canadian Public Health Association. (2016). Retrieved from https:www//cpha.ca/sites/default/files/uploads/policy/positionstatements

*CBC News.* (2018, 23 Mar.). Trudeau government avoids defeat on key pot bill vote. Retrieved from www.cbc.ca/news/politics/government-cannabis-bill-senate-vote-1.4588560

Chappell, R. (2014). *Social welfare in Canadian society* (5th edn). Toronto: Nelson.

Coletto, D. (2016). *The next Canada: Politics, political engagement, and priorities of Canada's next electoral powerhouse: Young Canadians.*

Retrieved from http://abacusdata.ca/the-next-canada-politics-political-engagement-and-priorities-of-canadas-next-electoral-powerhouse-young-canadians/

Conservative Party of Canada. (2015). *Protect our economy: Our Conservative plan to protect the economy.* Retrieved from https://www.poltext.org/sites/poltext.org/files/plateformes/conservative-platform-2015.pdf

———. (2017). Retrieved from https://www.conservative.ca

Controlled Drugs and Substances Act. (2017). Ottawa. Retrieved from http://laws-lois.justice.gc.ca/PDF/C-38.8.pdf

Dooling, K., & Rachlis, M. (2010). Vancouver's supervised injection facility challenges Canada's drug laws. *Canadian Medical Association Journal, 182*(13), 1440–4.

Fafard, P. (2012). Public health understandings of policy and power: Lessons from INSITE. *Journal of Urban Health, 89*(6), 905–14.

Graham, J. R., Shier, M. L., & Delaney, R. (2017). *Canadian social policy: A new introduction* (5th edn). Don Mills, ON: Pearson.

Grenier, E. (2015, 22 Oct.). Why the polls called it, but seat projections missed. *CBC News.* Retrieved from www.cbc.ca/news/politics/canada-election-2015-grenier-projections-oct22-1.3282596

Harper Index. (2015). Retrieved from www.harperindex.ca

Health Canada. (2017a). Supervised consumption sites: Status of applications. Retrieved from https://www.canada.ca/en/health-canada/services/substance-abuse/supervised-consumption-sites/status-application.html

———. (2017b). Supervised consumption site: Guidance for application form. Retrieved from https://www.canada.ca/en/health-canada/services/substance-abuse/supervised-consumption-sites/guidance-document.html

———. (2018). Supervised consumption sites: Status of applications. Retrieved from https://www.canada.ca/en/health-canada/services/substance-abuse/supervised-consumption-sites/status-application.html#open

Hutchinson, B. (2017, 1 Sept.). Canada's first safe injection site struggles with the rise of fentanyl. *Maclean's.* Retrieved from http://www.macleans.ca/news/canada/canadas-first-safe-injection-site-struggles-with-the-rise-of-fentanyl/

Jozaghi, E. (2012). "A little heaven in hell": The role of a supervised injection facility in transforming

place. *Urban Geography, 33*(8), 1144–62. doi:10.2747/0272-3638.33.8.1144

———. (2016). Morality versus the scientific evidence: The story behind Bill C-2. *Journal of Substance Use, 21*(3), 225–7.

Kashani, A. (2016, 22 Oct.). Strategic voting for Justin Trudeau. *Huffington Post.* Retrieved from www.huffingtonpost.ca/ali-kashani/strategic-voting-justin-trudeau_b_835796.html

Kirkup, K. (2017, 13 Apr.). Liberals' marijuana legislation bills introduced in the House of Commons. Retrieved from www.huffingtonpost.ca/2017/04/13/marijuana-legalization-bill-liberals_n_15991856.html

Liberal Party of Canada. (2015). *New plan for a strong middle class.* Retrieved from https://www.liberal.ca/files/2015/10/New-plan-for-a-strong-middle-class.pdf

———. (2017). Retrieved from https://www.liberal.ca

McKenzie, B., & Wharf, B. (2015). *Connecting policy to practice in the human services.* (4th edn). Toronto: Oxford University Press.

Mitchell, M. (2008). *No laughing matter.* Vancouver: Granville Island Publishing.

National Citizens Coalition. (2017). Retrieved from http://nationalcitizens.ca

New Democratic Party of Canada. (2015). *Building the country of our dreams: Tom Mulcair's plan to bring change to Ottawa.* Retrieved from http://xfer.ndp.ca/2015/2015-Full-Platform-EN.pdf

New Democratic Party of Canada. (2017). Retrieved from https://www.ndp.ca

Pacey, K. (2016). *Federal drug laws under Bill C-37: Lives on the line.* Vancouver: Pivot Legal Society. Retrieved from http://www.pivotlegal.org/c_37_lives_on_the_line

Royal Commission on Aboriginal Peoples. (1996). *Final Report,* Volumes 1–5. Ottawa: Government of Canada, Canada Communications Group.

Sapra, B. (2018, 20 June). Canada becomes second nation in the world to legalize marijuana. *CNN.* Retrieved from https://www.cnn.com/2018/06/20/health/canada-legalizes-marijuana/index.html

Scotti, M., & Cain, P. (2018, 20 June). Who wins, who loses from later-than-expected marijuana legalization date. *Global News.* Retrieved from https://globalnews.ca/news/4286507/legal-marijuana-winners-losers-timeline-date/

Small, D. (2010). An appeal to humanity: Legal victory in favour of North America's only supervised injection facility: Insite. *Harm Reduction Journal, 7*(1), 23.

Small, W., Shoveller, J., Moore, D., Tyndall, M., Wood, E., & Kerr, T. (2011). Injection drug users' access to a supervised injection facility in Vancouver, Canada: The influence of operating policies and local drug culture. *Qualitative Health Research, 21*(6), 743–56.

Status of Women Canada. (n.d.). Retrieved from www.swc.cfc.gc.ca/gba-acs/index-en-html

Truth and Reconciliation Commission of Canada. (2015). *Calls to action*. Retrieved from http://www.trc.ca/websites/trcinstitution/File/2015/Findings/Calls_to_Action_English2.pdf

Vancouver Coastal Health. (2017a). Insite—supervised injection site. Retrieved from http://www.vch.ca/public-health/harm-reduction/supervised-injection-sites/insite-usstatistics

———. (2017b). Insite user statistics. Retrieved from http://www.vch.ca/locations-services/result?res_id=964

Westhues, A., & Kenny-Sherber, C. (2012). The policy-making process. In A. Westhues & B. Wharf (Eds.), *Canadian social policy: Issues and perspectives* (5th edn) (pp. 23–42). Waterloo, ON: Wilfrid Laurier University Press.

———, & Wharf, B. (2012). *Canadian social policy: Issues and Perspectives* (5th edn.). Waterloo, ON: Wilfrid Laurier University Press.

# 5 Making Canadians Richer and Poorer

## Taxation, Spending, and Budgeting

*Tamara Krawchenko\**

---

### Chapter Objectives

*This chapter will help you to develop an understanding of:*

- the relationship between the size of the economy, decisions about raising public revenues, and the role and scope for public/governmental action in a country;
- the difference between the revenue-raising capacities of each level of government—federal, provincial, and territorial;
- the manner in which revenues, including taxes and transfers from one level of government to the other, are structured, and how this impacts the programs and services that citizens receive.

---

## Introduction

The capacity of governments to *act*, in the social policy sphere or any other, is in large measure determined by their fiscal policies—that is, by the amount of money they take in from types of taxation or other forms of revenue (e.g., fees, royalties). The nature of how government revenues are structured and how the redistribution occurs matters a great deal. In some countries, governments pursue **progressively redistributive taxation**—i.e., those with lower incomes are taxed proportionally less than those with higher incomes.[1] In other countries, government revenue comes from **regressive taxation** where lower-income individuals are taxed the same or even greater than those with higher incomes. This is more common than you might think because taxes from wages (labour) tend to be much higher than taxes on capital (economic rents), a system that benefits the wealthy. In many countries, some taxes are progressive and others are regressive. A key point is that it is important to think of government finance and spending from a variety of angles. Choices about how to raise revenues and how to spend, and whether to go into debt or to save for the future, are *political choices* with real impacts on people, both now and in the future.

---

\* The opinions of the author do not necessarily represent the official views of the OECD or of its member countries. The opinions expressed and arguments employed are those of the author.

---

**Box 5.1**   Public Discourse about Public Finance

---

Discussions about public finance are highly politicized. The manner in which budgets and public finances are reported and discussed in the news and by political parties and think-tanks, among others, is often framed from a particular perspective that is fundamentally grounded in an idea about what the role of government is and should be.

For example, during the 2015 federal election, both the NDP and the Conservatives campaigned on balancing the budget. Politicians regularly use the analogy of the family budget—"you can't spend what you don't have" and "I don't want my grandchildren to have to pay for us going into debt and overspending today." The Fraser Institute—a conservative think-tank—has promoted the idea of a "Tax Freedom Day" that measures the total yearly **tax burden** imposed on Canadian families by all levels of government. This highlights how much taxes people pay, but it does not speak to what individuals receive in lieu of taxes or what it means to live in a society that is more equal and where those who are more vulnerable are provided some supports. As a media consumer, it is important to digest such discourse with a critical eye and think about the underlying judgements guiding each perspective.

---

The political rhetoric around these policy decisions can be intense and confusing (see Box 5.1, Public Discourse about Public Finance). One side may argue that taxes are way too high and are stifling economic growth while another group will argue that they aren't high enough and that far more needs to be spent on investments, education, and infra-structure for the very same reason—to spur economic growth and well-being. One group will argue that we need to cut back on public spending to pay off government debt while others call for deficit spending at the same time. Public finance—taxation and spending—requires balance. You don't want to spend too much or too little, tax too much or too little. A big grey area in the middle, in terms of how to achieve this balance, ultimately comes down to what you think the role of the government should be and how the resources in society should be distributed.

This chapter examines these issues in three parts. It first looks at how Canada compares internationally in terms of government revenue and spending. Second, the pattern and structure of Canadian revenue and spending over time are discussed. Finally, the policy implications of these decisions for social policy are examined, including debates about how to better structure both taxation and redistribution.

## Government Finance: Canada in International Perspective

Governments generally collect revenue for two reasons: (1) to *redistribute wealth and income* from those who have a great deal to those who have less and (2) to *pay for goods and services* that are used by businesses and residents. How does Canada stand in terms of the amount of revenue collected compared to other similar countries? One way to determine this is to compare the level of government revenue in a country as a share of its gross domestic product (GDP)—i.e., the measure of the market value of all final goods and services produced in a year. This includes the amount of money spent constructing new buildings and houses, public investments in such things as new roads and hospitals, the private consumption of consumer goods, and the money businesses invest in their capital stock, such as new machines, among other expenditures. GDP is an indicator of the size of an economy and so this ratio provides an idea of the scope and importance of the public revenue in a country as well, though, as will be discussed, it is not always so straightforward.

**OECD (Organisation for Economic Co-operation and Development)** countries (a group of 35 like-minded market democracies) offer a useful comparison for Canada. As can be seen in Figure 5.1, general government revenue as a percentage of GDP in Canada falls *below* the OECD average (the black line) and is similar to that of Poland and Estonia.[2] That means that, compared to the average of all OECD countries, the amount of money that the Canadian government takes in is lower in proportion to the size of its economy. In contrast, the Nordic countries of Denmark, Finland, and Norway show the highest share of general revenue as a percentage of GDP—they are strong social welfare states with high and progressive rates of taxation. This, combined with public social benefits (e.g., education and health care), has led to these countries having among the lowest rates of income inequality and poverty among OECD countries.

The size of the respective economies of OECD countries differs greatly. What is interesting about Figure 5.1 is that economies with a high level of GDP do not necessarily have higher government revenue (and spending). It is very much a political choice. Consider, for example, the two countries at the very bottom end of the scale in terms of government

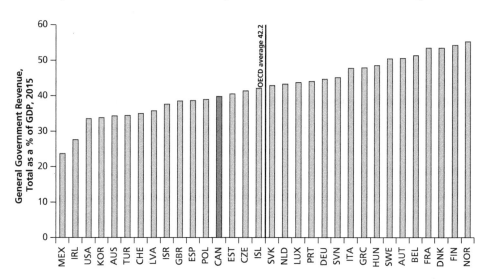

**Figure 5.1** General government revenue, total as a percentage of GDP, Canada and OECD countries, 2015

Note: This indicator is measured in terms of US$1,000 per capita and as a percentage of GDP. Data are under System of National Accounts (SNA, 1993) for all countries except for Australia and United States (SNA, 2008).

Source: Data from OECD (2017a). General government revenue (indicator). doi: 10.1787/b68b04ae-en (Accessed on 14 April 2017).

revenue as a proportion of GDP—Mexico and Ireland. Among OECD countries, Mexico has the lowest level of GDP per capita but Ireland has the third highest.[3] Ireland has instituted a policy of low tax rates to attract businesses and government revenue is smaller in part because of this—meanwhile, companies have flocked to Ireland and GDP has increased. In contrast, Canada ranks 24 out of 35 among OECD countries in terms of per capita GDP; this is lower than Norway and Denmark, but it is *higher than* Finland—which stands near the top in terms of government revenue as a proportion of GDP.[4] So, it cannot be said that wealthier countries necessarily have higher government revenue than less wealthy countries. Among other considerations, the size of the population and its characteristics are also important. Luxembourg (a very small country with a large financial services sector) has by far the highest GDP per capita of any OECD country—but its government revenue as a proportion of GDP is only slightly above the OECD average. With a small population, Luxembourg has fewer demands on its public goods and services. Thus, it makes sense that government revenue would be proportionally smaller.

## Changes in Government Revenue over Time

Decisions about government revenue are generally "sticky"—they are influenced by past decisions and present-day politics, and as a result, large-scale changes can be difficult to make. There are a few reasons why this is the case. First, taxes are generally unpopular and so it is usually much easier to reduce taxes than to increase them. Balancing this, people become used to a certain quality of goods and services, and if government revenue were to decline sharply the "knock-on" effect would likely prove unpopular. For example, if cuts are made to health care, wait times increase and people suffer poorer health outcomes as a result of reduced access to quality and timely health care. So, how has government revenue changed in recent decades? General government revenue as a percentage of GDP in Canada today is around the same as in the 1980s.[5] It peaked in the late 1990s and has been falling since then. In the mid-1990s, Canada sought to cut the federal deficit and reduce the amount of federal debt. This was achieved by increasing some taxes; on the flip side, government spending decreased significantly. More recently, the stimulus spending in the wake of the 2008 economic crisis is not particularly evident in Figure 5.2 because the economy was contracting at the same time (Box 5.2). Figure 5.2 shows the average for OECD countries over time, given available data; data from 1981 include seven countries, while those from 1991 include 31.

## Redistributing Wealth

Trends in government revenue give a general picture, but it is also important to consider how taxes and transfers impact the *redistribution of wealth in society*. Without such redistribution, countries would have far higher levels of income inequality. Across OECD countries it is estimated that income taxes and cash transfers such as unemployment benefits reduce income inequality by around 27 per cent on average in 2014 (OECD, 2016b: 3). However, since the 2008 economic crisis, this redistribution has been weakening. In general, across OECD countries it is found that higher-income households benefited more from the economic recovery than those with middle and lower incomes and that income inequality remains at record highs in many countries despite an improving situation for employment and declining unemployment rates (OECD, 2016b).

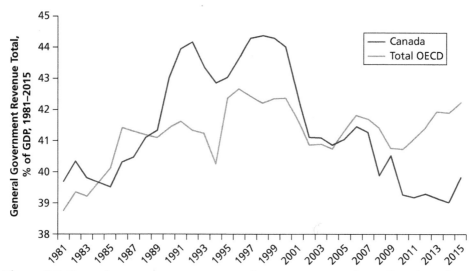

**Figure 5.2** General government revenue, total as a percentage of GDP, Canada and OECD countries, 1981–2015

Note: This indicator is measured in terms of US$1,000 per capita and as a percentage of GDP. Data are under System of National Accounts, 1993 (SNA 1993) for all countries except for Australia and United States (SNA 2008). The data start date differs by country due to data availability.

Source: Data from OECD (2017b). General government revenue (indicator). doi: 10.1787/b68b04ae-en (Accessed on 14 April 2017).

In Canada, the percentage reduction of income inequality due to taxes and transfers is lower than the OECD average, at around 21 per cent. Further, the extent of this reduction is lower now than it was in 2007 (the triangles versus the vertical bars in Figure 5.3). This weakening of income redistribution may be due, in part, to the phasing out of fiscal stimulus measures introduced in 2008 as a result of the economic crisis. It could also be a

**Box 5.2**   Economic Stimulus

In times of economic crisis, governments generally act to stimulate the economy by cutting interest rates (making it easier to borrow money and spend it) and by increasing government spending to drive employment growth and consumption. For example, in the wake of the 2008 economic crisis, Canada decided to cut interest rates and embarked on a major program of spending on infrastructure across the country. Rather than raise taxes, which would have reduced disposable income for consumption just when the economy was contracting (a bad idea), the government borrowed money to achieve its goal.

Governments borrow money to spend when they do not have enough in a given year (the budget deficit), and this contributes to a country's national debt (the total amount of outstanding borrowed money from the current and previous fiscal years). This in turn has a generational impact—borrowing today can leave future generations in debt. There is always a balance that needs to be struck, and decisions about how much debt is acceptable are not always as clear as one might suppose.

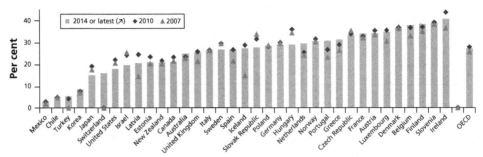

**Figure 5.3** Percentage reduction of market income inequality due to taxes and transfers, 2007–2014

Note: Redistribution is defined as the difference between market income and disposable income inequality, expressed as a percentage of market income inequality. Market incomes are net of taxes in Hungary, Mexico, and Turkey.

Source: Data from OECD Income Distribution Database, at http://oe.cd/idd.

result of the tightening of unemployment benefits (e.g., limits placed on eligibility), as was seen in Canada under the Harper Conservative government (Porter, 2015; Grundy et al., 2016). It bears noting that while Ireland was at the bottom of the pack in terms of the share of government revenue to GDP, its rate of reducing market inequalities through taxes and transfers is the highest among OECD countries.

## Government Spending

The final piece of the puzzle is government spending. Canada's general government spending as a percentage of GDP varies year by year.[6] It stood at a two-decade high in 2010, at 8.29 per cent, in large measure due to stimulus spending in the wake of the 2008 economic crisis. In 2016 it stood at approximately 8.03 per cent of GDP, which places it among the middle of the pack of OECD countries (Figure 5.4).

The revenues taken in by governments may not in fact match closely to the revenues that are spent. For example, countries that see a boom in revenues due to the gains of natural resource extraction, may save this public revenue for future generations instead of spending it all now. Norway has pursued such a prudent strategy through its Sovereign Wealth Fund. Alternatively, governments may run large budget deficits such that the revenue they take in annually does not match government expenditures. For example, budget deficits peaked in 2010 across the OECD due to the need to spend money in the wake of the 2008 economic crisis (stimulus spending). It can generally be said that this spending was needed and it helped to boost consumption and employment. A much bigger question, however, involves the best way to design stimulus measures for the greatest long-term positive impact (Stoney & Krawchenko, 2012). Long-standing debates also continue about the impact of fiscal policies, particularly government deficits on aggregate demand in an economy. Canada's general government *debt* as a ratio of GDP was around 116 per cent in 2015; this is similar to that of the United Kingdom (at 113 per cent), but much below that of Japan, which had a debt-to-GDP ratio of 234 per cent in 2015—the highest among OECD countries (OECD, 2017d).

The amount of money going to social expenditures is an important indicator of social policy in a country. Social expenditures generally include spending on old age, survivor

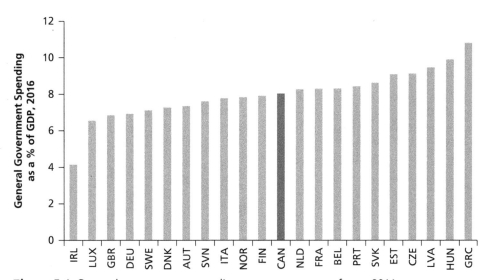

**Figure 5.4** General government spending as a percentage of GDP, 2016

Source: Data from OECD (2017c). General government spending by destination (indicator). doi: 10.1787/d853db3b-en (Accessed on 29 April 2017).

and incapacity-related benefits, health, family and active labour market programs, unemployment benefits, housing, and other social policy areas. Figure 5.5 shows social expenditures as a percentage of GDP for Canada and OECD countries between 1980 and 2016. These figures include public, voluntary, and **mandatory private social expenditure** at a program level. In 2015 (the last available year for data in the case of Canada), social expenditures in Canada as a percentage of GDP were 17.2 per cent, which was below the average for all OECD countries of 21 per cent for that year. Social expenditures in Canada increased from the 1980s to the mid-1990s before declining thereafter. Spending on health care and pensions account for the vast majority of social spending in the OECD—around two-thirds (OECD, 2016a). Public social spending for Canada amounted to approximately

## Case Examples    Spend Now or Save for Later?

It is often said that politics discounts the future. After all, politicians are elected by people today, and in no more than four-year cycles at that! Given this, there are important time considerations in the structure of public finance. When governments have windfall gains, for example, from the royalties collected from extractive industries, should they spend that money now or invest it for future generations? And if they do spend it now, what should they spend it on?

In 2005, the province of Alberta faced just such a decision. Windfall gains from oil sands royalties led to a budget surplus. The Progressive Conservative government of

*continued*

the day decided to give every resident of the province a cheque for $400. The "prosperity bonuses" were nicknamed "Ralph Bucks" after the Premier, Ralph Klein. However, Alberta has also saved for the future. Like many oil-rich governments, Alberta has a fund where the proceeds from non-renewable resources are invested. The Alberta Heritage Savings Trust Fund was established in 1976 with three objectives: "to save for the future, to strengthen or diversify the economy, and to improve the quality of life of Albertans." But contributions to the fund were short-lived; after the late 1980s contributions dropped off significantly.

What do you think of these policy choices? What should governments that see a boon in revenue do with that revenue? What are our fiscal obligations to present and future generations?

US$332,348.2 million in 2014, while mandatory private and voluntary social spending amounted to US$87,309.4 million (OECD, 2017b).

Overall, across the OECD, general trends paint a troubling picture. Since the 1980s, most OECD counties have experienced "rising inequality, challenging budget conditions, and a reduction in the income tax share" (Islam, Madsen, & Doucouliagos, 2017, p. 2). This has real and tangible impacts on people's lives. Rising inequalities lead to diminished opportunities and lower quality of life. Further, such inequalities can be cemented over time and can have multi-generational impacts. The fiscal system is an important part of this policy puzzle. The following section looks at Canada's fiscal policies in greater detail with a focus on social spending.

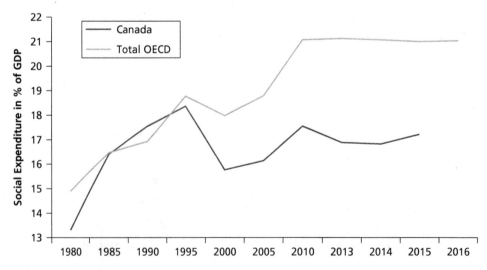

**Figure 5.5** Social expenditure as a percentage of GDP, Canada and OECD, 1980–2016
Source: Data from OECD (2017b).

# Fiscal Policies and Government Revenue in Canada

Fiscal policies (revenue and spending) are different in every country. Canada—as a federal country—has some unique characteristics.[7] For example, there are mechanisms for sharing wealth across the country, such as the Canada Health Transfer and Canada Social Transfer, so that all Canadians can have equal access to high-quality health care and education. In terms of who spends what, the lower levels of government in Canada (provinces, territories, and municipalities) do the bulk of government spending, accounting for around 70 per cent of all government spending (OECD, 2016c). They are particularly important in such areas as health care, where they account for 80 per cent of all government spending (OECD, 2016c, p. 138). The following section outlines how government revenues are raised and shared in Canada and how they are spent with a focus on social spending.

## Federal Government Revenue

The federal government in Canada has several ways to raise money. The most important source of revenue is *income taxes* for individuals and corporations (see Box 5.3). There are also consumption taxes (such as the government sales tax, GST), contributions to social security plans, revenue from the sales of goods and services, investment incomes, and revenues from other sources including other taxes. The federal government also receives revenue from general and specific-purpose transfers.

   The nature of these taxes and contributions has changed over time. For instance, the GST was introduced in 1991 under the Progressive Conservative government of Brian

---

### Box 5.3   Canadian Federal Income Tax Rates, 2018

Canada has a progressive federal personal income tax rate with five tax brackets:

- 15 per cent on the first $46,605 of taxable income;
- 20.5 per cent on the next $46,603 of taxable income (on the portion of taxable income over $46,605 up to $93,208);
- 26 per cent on the next $51,281 of taxable income (on the portion of taxable income over $93,208 up to $144,489);
- 29 per cent on the next $61,353 of taxable income (on the portion of taxable income over $144,489 up to $205,842);
- 33 per cent of taxable income over $205,842.

Corporate federal income tax rates differ depending on deduction eligibilities. The basic corporate income tax rate was 38 per cent in 2018 before deductions but falls to 10 per cent, for example, for small businesses.

Sources: CRA (2018a, 2018b).

Mulroney to replace the hidden manufacturers' sales tax. The visibility of this tax on everyday purchases has made it quite unpopular and there have been ongoing discussions about whether it should be repealed altogether. In 2006 it was reduced by 1 per cent under the Conservative government and then by another 1 per cent in 2008. The GST currently stands at 5 per cent in Canada. Discussions about reducing or eliminating the GST are in part based on the fact that it is a regressive tax. That is, this type of tax consumes a larger share of the disposable incomes of lower-income individuals. However, this feature of the tax is in part mediated by tax credits provided to individuals based on income and household size and also by not taxing basic food products and residential rents. Another counter to the prospect of eliminating the GST is that it is an important source of money for social funds and other spending—it has become important for the stability of government revenues over time. This debate illustrates the dynamics at play with choices about just one revenue source. For each revenue source multiple mechanisms are at play, and potential impacts include incentives or disincentives for individual behaviour.

## Provincial and Territorial Revenue

Revenues raised by subnational governments are referred to as "own-source revenue." This term is used to convey the fact that these revenue-raising powers are decentralized to them.[8] Own-source revenues of provincial and territorial governments in Canada are similar to those of the federal government. Each province sets its own corporate and personal income tax rates. Provincial corporate income taxes range from an effective tax rate of zero in the case of Manitoba for small businesses to a high of 16 per cent for larger businesses in the case of Nova Scotia. Income taxes also differ considerably by province and territory, in terms of both the overall rates and the number of tax brackets. For example, the lowest bracket of Nova Scotia's personal income tax is 8.79 per cent on the first $29,590 of taxable income while British Columbia's lowest tax bracket is set at 5.06 per cent on the first $38,898 of taxable income (2017 figures). Alberta's lowest tax bracket starts at 10 per cent on the first $126,625 of taxable income; that means that everyone making lower than this amount is taxed the same provincial rate (2017 figures). The province's top tax bracket is now 15 per cent on any amount over $303,900. Until recently Alberta had a **flat tax** rate of 10 per cent for all incomes; low-income and high-income individuals were taxed the same amount. There are ongoing debates about what types of tax rates and threshold amounts are appropriate, fair, or equitable—depending on how one defines those criteria. Should individuals making $30,000 or less be taxed the same as those making $100,000? What are the repercussions of this type of tax compared to the more progressive taxation of other provinces? What about the impacts of differing provincial tax rates on the concentration of wealth across Canada? Will lower effective income tax rates for high-income earners in some provinces (e.g., Alberta) lead to a concentration of the wealthy individuals there? Will this heighten regional disparities? A recent study of this phenomenon by Milligan and Smart (2015) finds that "higher income concentration in Canada is largely unrelated to taxes" and that "the long-run changes in tax rates are not large enough to explain the big changes in income concentration." Tax rates, of course, are not the only considerations for locational choices of individuals and businesses—one must also consider the impact of family benefits and other transfers—and so this can be a complex matter to assess (see International Comparisons box).

## International Comparisons

### Taxes and Transfers by Family Type in Canada

Given the different tax rates and tax brackets for individuals across Canada and the transfers that individuals receive for various benefits, it can be hard to have a picture of the effective tax rates for individuals. The table below shows combined central and sub-central government income tax plus employee **social security contributions**, less family benefits (in respect of dependent children) paid by general government as universal cash transfers, as a percentage of gross wage earnings. The estimates are based on average wages in Canada. This shows that single people with no children pay the highest rate (23.1 per cent) while a married couple with one income earner and two children pays the lowest rate overall (even lower than a single person with two children).

Compared to other OECD countries, Canada has a low average personal income tax rate (**all-in less cash transfers**) for single persons with two children—only Iceland's is lower at 1.2 per cent (OECD, 2017e). Belgium has the highest such rate at 29 per cent. In almost all OECD countries, a married couple with one income earner and two children pays a lower personal income tax rate after accounting for cash transfers. The exception is Chile, where the rates are the same for all family types (at 7 per cent). In Ireland the effective tax rate is in fact negative for this type of family—standing at –1.6 per cent in 2016. The design of the tax and transfer system can either advantage or disadvantage different family types. In some instances, countries facing demographic decline create special incentives to boost fertility rates, as Poland has done with its new 500+ program—a monthly cash transfer for each additional child born. The impact of these types of transfers on fertility rates has been mixed and may depend more on such factors as cultural traditions and female labour market participation (Hoem, 1993; Castles , 2003).

Taxes and transfers are important to the redistribution of wealth in society. Beyond their impacts on family types, it is also important to recognize that they have age cohort effects. Taxes and transfers reduce the degree of income inequality significantly for all ages, but substantially more so for the elderly due to age-related features of the tax and transfer system (Crisan, McKenzie, & Mintz, 2015).

**Table 5.1**  All-in Average Personal Income Tax Rates at Average Wage by Family Type, Canada, 2016

| All-in Rate | | | | All-in Less Cash Transfers | | |
| Single Person | | One-Earner Married Couple | | Single Person | One-Earner Married Couple | |
| No Child | Two Children | No Child | Two Children | Two Children | No Child | Two Children |
|---|---|---|---|---|---|---|
| 23.1 | 18.3 | 18.9 | 18.3 | 1.7 | 18.9 | 1.2 |

Source: Data from OECD (2017e).

Federal, provincial, and territorial governments can also levy consumption taxes.[9] However, not all choose to do so. For example, Alberta and the three territories do not levy provincial tax rates, so individuals in these jurisdictions pay only the federal GST. In contrast, the Atlantic provinces in Canada have all levied 10 per cent provincial **sales tax** for a total tax rate (provincial and federal, also known as the harmonized sales tax or HST) of 15 per cent. As in the case of the federal GST, this consumption tax can be very difficult to bear for low-income earners. Provinces have designed rebates to lessen the effect—for instance, there are tax rebate programs for the purchase of energy sources. However, one may question whether this is enough.

Provinces and territories across Canada are endowed with different fiscal capacities. Some provinces, such as Alberta, have benefited from natural resource exploitation and, consequently, have had much higher fiscal capacities to fund goods and services.[10] The fiscal provisions of subnational governments in Canada are not very detailed in Canada's Constitution. For example, there is no prescription for intergovernmental transfers or tax-sharing between levels of government. However, the idea of equalization payments among provinces has been enshrined in Canada's Constitution since 1982. (Territories are treated separately and receive federal funding through the Territorial Formula Financing [TFF] Program).[11] Equalization payments are made to provinces via the federal treasury and are calculated on the basis of ensuring that all 10 provinces have equal access to the average of per capita revenues for all provinces. Some provinces (the "haves") are net contributors to net equalization payments because they have high per capita revenues, while other provinces (the "have-nots") are net receivers. As such, equalization payments do not go to all provinces; it is a zero-sum formula. Equalization payments have been a source of contention for the "have" provinces, and from time to time new ways of calculating the equalization formula are proposed. However, reforms to the system prove politically challenging and divisive, and the Trudeau government has recently announced that it will keep the current formula for payment calculations in place to 2024—thus putting off this debate for another day. It is important here to note that equalization payments only consider the revenue side of the equation and not the demand side—i.e., the cost of providing services in respective provinces. For example, provinces with larger elderly populations or provinces with more dispersed and remote communities may have much higher costs in delivering services than others where this is not the case. The system of equalization is important in reducing regional disparities across Canada, but disparities remain despite such mechanisms. Equalization payments are non-conditional transfers, meaning that the federal government does not tell provinces and territories how they should spend the money.

In contrast to equalization and territorial payments, the Canada Health Transfer (CHT) and the Canada Social Transfer (CST) are conditional payments. For example, the Canada Health Transfer, which is the largest transfer payment, must be used to "maintain national criteria" set out in the Canada Health Act. These criteria are related to public administration, comprehensiveness, universality, portability, and accessibility. The health and social transfer payments used to be one block transfer for health, post-secondary education, and welfare, but they were split into two separate transfer payments in 2004 to provide greater accountability for the health spending portion of the funds. The Canada Health Transfer is made up of both a cash transfer and a tax transfer; the tax transfers are done on a per capita basis while the cash transfers account for the different fiscal capacities of provinces and territories. The nature of the Canada Health Transfer is negotiated between the federal and provincial governments through the Canada Health Accord (though provinces have disputed the collaborative nature of these negotiations and some feel that the federal government simply imposes its will). Finance and health ministers meet every 10 years to negotiate regarding both the level at which the transfers should be set and the conditions attached to them (e.g., reducing wait times in hospitals). Provinces have very different health care needs, and a key issue for provinces like Nova Scotia, with a large elderly population, is that the Canada Health Transfer does not account for health care consumption based on demography. There are ongoing calls for a needs-based funding model that takes such considerations into account (Aiken, 2015).

The smaller of the two transfers, the Canada Social Transfer, provides funding to provinces to support post-secondary education, social assistance and social services, and early childhood development, early learning, and child care. Like the CHT, it is calculated on an equal per capita cash basis, has a tax transfer component, and is negotiated every 10 years. Conditions under the 2011 agreement set priority funding for children, post-secondary education, and social programs. A main condition of the CST is that provinces and territories must continue to provide social assistance to all residents without imposing minimum residency requirements. If they did not do this, it could provide a real disincentive for people to be able to move from one part of Canada to another. It is important to note that, beyond the CST, the federal government also supports post-secondary education and social assistance and other such services through transfers to persons such as payments to the elderly, children, the working poor, and unemployed Canadians.[12]

## Municipal Finance

The financing powers of local governments in Canada are at the discretion of provinces and territories. This includes rules about what kinds of taxes they can levy, whether they can operate a deficit, and how they can borrow, along with broader decisions about what municipalities are responsible for and their standards for service provision. Municipal revenues differ by province and territory in part because of these differences in their roles and responsibilities. In general, municipalities receive a combination of unconditional transfers based on per capita equalization and conditional transfers for transportation, the environment, and, in the case of Ontario, social services. Though the federal government bears no direct responsibility for municipalities, some federal funding programs and transfers support municipalities, such as the gas transfer tax, infrastructure grants, homeless grants, and economic stimulus grants.

Beyond funds from other levels of government, municipal own-source revenue is largely composed of property and related taxes. This makes up around half of their total revenue. The second most common source of municipal revenue is **user fees** (at around one-fifth of total revenue). **Property taxes** in Canada are based on the assessed value of a home, including its location—the more valuable a home, the higher the property tax. Property taxes can be considered a fair tax in that those who pay the taxes benefit from the goods and services provided in their locale. In the case of renters, the cost of property taxes to owners is passed on to them through their rental fees. However, myriad details must be considered in relation to the impacts of property taxes on individuals. One issue is that property taxes can increase greatly in neighbourhoods that become desirable. As a result, these tax increases may have the effect of pushing out long-time residents who find them unaffordable. This is particularly the case for retired individuals on fixed incomes. On the one hand, these individuals benefit from having their asset appreciate in value. They could use this appreciation to sell their house and move to a more affordable neighbourhood. But what if people are tied to their neighbourhood and community? What if they have social ties there that are important to their quality of life? One way to address this is to provide tax relief or other measures for individuals who find themselves in this situation.

Another revenue source for municipalities, user fees, may seem to be fair because such fees mean that people are paying to access the goods or services they are using. Again, however, the details matter. A user fee—for instance, a yearly membership for access to a municipal library, municipal swimming pool, or ice hockey arena—may be a real disincentive to using that service for low-income individuals. Indeed, all user fees are a form of regressive tax in that lower-income people pay a higher proportion of their income on user fees than do those with higher incomes. To reduce barriers to access or other negative effects, these issues need careful attention when decisions about how to fund public goods and services are made.

## Key Fiscal Principles in Canada

This discussion of government revenues in Canada demonstrates that some fundamental principles underlie our federation—a key one is that subnational governments should be able to provide a level of goods and services to their citizens that is similar across the country. For instance, people living in one part of the country should not be disadvantaged in terms of their access to health care and education relative to any other part of Canada. Also, different regions in Canada have varying approaches to public finance. Thus, the income tax in Alberta is very flat compared that in Nova Scotia. The varying fiscal capacities of Canada's provincial and territorial governments lead them to rely to a greater or lesser extent on their own-source revenues—hence, some provinces do not need to levy a provincial sales tax while others very much rely on this revenue to provide goods and services. These differences can lead to very different outcomes despite the underlying goal of equality in our federation.

Regional politics and policies also play a role. There are different views across the Canadian federation about the size, purpose, and role of government and these views change over time. The differences in terms of what this means for people depends on the policy area in question. In some cases the difference between provinces and territories is not so great, but in others it is. As one example, tuition fees for undergraduate students are highest in Ontario and lowest in Newfoundland and Labrador, with a difference of more than $5,000 in 2017 (Statistics Canada, 2017) (see Chapter 12 for more on tuition fees).

How the various choices about public revenues play out at regional and local levels will differ and these interact with myriad other policies in terms of how they make a difference in people's lives. Because of this, it is important to think of the place-based impacts of policies and to try and understand effects both in isolation and in tandem with other policies and interventions. It is a complex system. With this caveat in mind, Figure 5.6 gives an overview of spending on all public health and social service institutions by

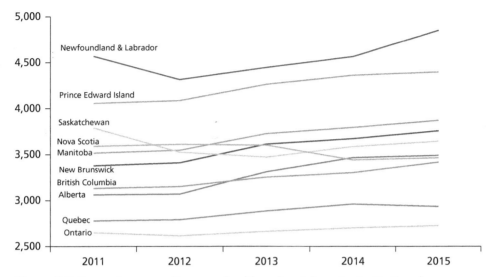

**Figure 5.6** Per capita expenditures on health and social service institutions by province, 2011–2015

Note: This figure includes all expenditures—including capital expenditures and debt obligations.

Source: Data from Statistics Canada (2017b).

province. This figure includes spending by all health boards, hospitals, residential care facilities, and social services organizations controlled by each respective provincial government. It shows quite significant differences and year-to-year fluctuations in the amount of spending, with Ontario having the lowest per capita spending and Newfoundland and Labrador the highest. These differences in expenditures can be due to a number of different factors. As already mentioned, it can be more cost-effective to provide social and health care services in more densely populated places. Further, population demographics can impact social and particularly health care spending; places with a rapidly growing population may require major capital investments in new facilities. Also, regions with proportionally larger senior populations experience greater demand on health care consumption.

# Fiscal Policy in Canada—Policy Implications

All countries make numerous decisions at each level of government about how to raise money, how to spend it, and whether to borrow now or save for the future. These decisions have a very real impact on people's lives. They can lead to either growing or shrinking regional and individual inequalities. They can make the difference in access to affordable housing and high-quality health care and education for all or, alternatively, systems can be designed so that costs are individualized as opposed to shared. Comparisons across OECD countries demonstrate very different approaches to these issues. Some fiscal systems are more redistributive and some are less so. Some countries have a much larger role for the public sector, while in others many goods and services are provided by the private sector and the costs are borne by the individual rather than the state.

Comparative policy analysis points to some of the merits of these different approaches. For instance, investing in education is crucial for reversing inequality across OECD countries, and higher education in particular is "one of the most important elements to foster economic growth in the long run" (OECD, 2015, p. 44). The work of Piketty (2014) emphasizes that education expenditure particularly benefits those on low incomes, and such investments play an important role in reducing income inequality. Nordic countries have the most inclusive educational systems across the OECD countries—and these investments are made possible through substantial public financing (Atkinson, 2015, p. 486). Decisions about public finance thus have a very important role to play in reducing inequalities.

Across OECD countries there are worrying trends that policies are headed in the opposite direction, as income inequalities have been growing since the 1980s (McKnight, Duque, & Rucci, 2016). This relates to a much bigger point—what is the objective of public policy? Should the objective be to reduce inequalities or should it be economic growth? Are these two objectives interrelated? What are the core objectives of public policy across Canada and are they the same by region? What are the implications of this for people's lives?

This review of revenue and expenditure across our federation has shown that fundamental principles of universality are realized through equalization and the Canada health and social transfer system, and yet, very different fiscal capacities remain. Several key trends may exacerbate these regional differences over time. Health care is the largest expenditure of provincial governments. Rapid population aging is leading to ballooning health care costs in some provinces—most notably the Maritime provinces, where, at the same time, the share of the working-age population is declining. These trends present real risks in terms of the ability to deliver high-quality goods and services in these provinces. The variability of natural resources revenue presents another fiscal and public policy challenge, particularly for provinces such as Alberta and Newfoundland and Labrador, which are highly dependent on resource revenues. The impacts of climate change should also be considered, the consequences of which are likely wide-ranging—from the loss of agricultural production, rising sea levels, and more frequent and unpredictable storms, all of which impact **fiscal policy**. All of these issues test our federation.

## Chapter Summary

Overall, decisions about taxation and spending are *never policy-neutral*. They are fundamentally grounded in a view about the overarching role of the state and the goals of public policy. It is hoped that you take away from this chapter a critical lens on these issues so that, when you think about decisions such as levying user fees for services or paying off the deficit through austerity budgets—you link these to broader political considerations and the impacts on people's lives both now and for future generations.

## Discussion Questions

1. Should individuals making $30,000 or less be taxed the same as those making $100,000? What are the repercussions of this type of tax compared to more progressive taxation (i.e., where those with higher incomes are taxed at a higher rate)?

2. Should provinces with proportionally larger elderly populations or those with more dispersed populations receive some kind of additional sums due to the higher demand on their health care systems? In other words, should Canada's health and social transfers take account of a province/territory's unique demographic character-istics that create additional costs of providing services?

3. To what extent should governments rely on corporate and personal income taxa-tion to fund goods and services and to what extent should they rely on user fees? What are the benefits and drawbacks of these different approaches? Is one approach fairer? If so, why? To illustrate your choice, draw a pie diagram and indicate the percentages that should be derived from income, corporate taxes, and user fees. Compare the chart with those of classmates and discuss the rationale for the choices.

# Notes

1. See, for example, Bird and Smart (2016) for an analysis of the redistribution effect of Canadian value-added taxes (VATs)—i.e., consumption and excise taxes.

2. General government revenue includes four sub-sectors: central/federal government and related public entities; federated government ("states") and related public entities; local government (i.e., regional and local governments and re-lated public entities); and social security funds. Data are consolidated within this grouping and within each subsector to neutralize financial cross-flows.

3. GDP per capita in Mexico was US$16,448 in 2015 while in Ireland it stood at US$58,117.

4. GDP per capita in Canada was US$42,270 in 2015 while in Norway it was US$59,274, Finland US$37,973, and Denmark US$44,549.

5. General government revenue as a percentage of GDP was 39.7 per cent in 1981; in 2015 it stood at 39.8 per cent.

6. The OECD's measure of general government final consumption can be broken down into two distinct groups: (1) expenditures for collective consumption (defence, justice, etc.) that benefit society as a whole, or large parts of society, and are often known as public goods and services; and (2) expenditures for individual consump-tion (health care, housing, education, etc.) that reflect expenditures incurred by government on behalf of individual households. This cat-egory of expenditure is equal to social transfers in kind from government to households and so includes expenditure by government on market goods and services provided to households. As goods and services produced by government usually do not have a market price, the relevant

products are valued at the sum of costs needed to produce these goods and services. These costs mainly consist of compensation of employees, intermediate consumption, and depreciation. Final consumption of government can then be estimated as the difference between, on the one hand, government output, and, on the other hand, payments made for goods and servi-ces produced by government and the relevant output that is used for fixed capital formation. This indicator is measured as percentage of gross domestic product. Data are under System of National Accounts, 1993 (SNA 1993) for all countries except for Australia and United States (SNA 2008).

7. The Constitution Act, 1867 (originally called the British North America Act) and Constitu-tion Act, 1982, which includes the Charter of Rights and Freedoms, define a federal system of shared powers in which the federal government and the provinces have equal status. Provinces and territories have their own and some shared responsibilities with the federal government. Provinces and territories are responsible for providing education, health care (including hos-pitals), highways, prisons, and natural resour-ces, and have purview over municipal affairs. Provinces and territories together with the fed-eral government have shared responsibility for pensions, energy, water, agriculture, and immi-gration. Because municipalities are "creatures of the provinces," their scope and functions can differ considerably (e.g., in Ontario muni-cipalities have shared responsibility for social assistance). Typically, municipalities in Canada are responsible for: roads and transit; police and fire protection; water, sewerage, and waste;

recreation and culture; land-use planning; and social housing. Independently elected school boards are responsible for primary and secondary education (and are directly answerable to provinces and territories).

8. In contrast, the federal government, under the Constitution Act, 1867, has unlimited taxing powers.

9. These are the provincial sales tax and the harmonized tax in the case of Ontario and the four Atlantic provinces. The HST is a blended combination of the provincial sales tax and the federal sales tax; the HST is collected by Revenue Canada, which then remits the appropriate amounts to the participating provinces.

10. It is important, however, to recognize that royalty fees based on natural resource revenue can be volatile and are linked to prices set on international markets. For a discussion of how this applies to Alberta's royalty regime, see Dobson (2015).

11. Equalization enables less prosperous provincial governments to provide their residents with public services that are reasonably comparable to those in other provinces, at reasonably comparable levels of taxation. TFF provides territorial governments with funding to support public services, in recognition of the higher cost of providing programs and services in the North (Department of Finance Canada, 2017).

12. Major income security programs financed by the federal government are: Old Age Security, Guaranteed Income Supplement, the Allowance (an income support program for older Canadians), Canada Child Benefit, Universal Child Care Benefit, Working Income Tax Benefit, and Employment Insurance. Ottawa also administers the Canada Pension Plan, which is paid for by employer and employee contributions. Quebec operates the analogous Quebec Pension Plan.

# References

Aiken, M. (2015). Payment where payment is due: Canada's federal transfer system and a needs-based solution to health transfer spending. *Health Tomorrow: Interdisciplinarity and Internationality, 3*(1).

Atkinson, A. B. (2015). *Inequality: What can be done?* Cambridge, MA: Harvard University Press.

Bird, R. M., & Smart, M. (2016, 14 Mar.). Taxing consumption in Canada: Rates, revenues, and redistribution. Retrieved from https://ssrn.com/abstract=2747459

Canada Revenue Agency. (CRA). (2018a). Canadian income tax rates for individuals—current and previous years. Retrieved from https://www.canada.ca/en/revenue-agency/services/tax/individuals/frequently-asked-questions-individuals/canadian-income-tax-rates-individuals-current-previous-years.html

———. (2018b). Corporation tax rates. Retrieved from https://www.canada.ca/en/revenue-agency/services/tax/businesses/topics/corporations/corporation-tax-rates.html

Castles, F. G. (2003). The world turned upside down: Below replacement fertility, changing preferences and family-friendly public policy in 21 OECD countries. *Journal of European Social Policy, 13*(3), 209–27.

Crisan, D., McKenzie, K. J., & Mintz, J. (2015, 10 Feb.). The distribution of income and taxes/transfers in Canada: A cohort analysis.

SPP Research Paper No. 8, Issue 5. Retrieved from https://ssrn.com/abstract=2563152

Department of Finance Canada (2017). Federal support to provinces and territories. Retrieved from https://www.fin.gc.ca/access/fedprov-eng.asp

Dobson, S. (2015, Mar.). *Peering into Alberta's darkening future: How oil prices impact Alberta's royalty revenues.* Calgary: University of Calgary School of Public Policy, SPP Research Papers, vol. 8, no. 14. Retrieved from https://www.policy school.ca/wp-content/uploads/2016/03/alberta's-oil-prices-dobson.pdf

Grundy, J., & Laliberte Rudman, D. (2016). Deciphering deservedness: Canadian employment insurance reforms in historical perspective. *Social Policy & Administration, 53*(30), 809–25.

Hoem, J. M. (1993). Public policy as the fuel of fertility: Effects of a policy reform on the pace of childbearing in Sweden in the 1980s. *Acta Sociologica, 36*(1), 19–31.

Islam, M. R., Madsen, J. B., & Doucouliagos, H. (2017). Does inequality constrain the power to tax? Evidence from the OECD. *European Journal of Political Economy, 52*, 1–17.

McKnight, A., Duque, M., & Rucci, M. (2016). *Creating more equal societies: What works?* Brussels: European Commission. Retrieved from http://www.lse.ac.uk/business-and-consultancy/consulting/assets/documents/Creating-More-Equal-Societies.pdf

Milligan, K., & Smart, M. (2015). Taxation and top incomes in Canada. *Canadian Journal of Economics/Revue canadienne d'économique, 48*(2), 655–81.

OECD (2015). *In it together: Why less inequality benefits us all.* Paris: OECD.

———. (2016a). Economic Outlook 99 database; Statistics Canada, Table 378-0119.

———. (2016b). Income inequality remains high in the face of recovery. Income inequality update, Centre for Opportunity and Equity. Retrieved from https://www.oecd.org/social/OECD2016-Income-Inequality-Update.pdf

———. (2016c). Spending power of sub-central governments. In *Fiscal federalism 2016: Making decentralisation work.* Paris: OECD. doi:http://dx.doi.org/10.1787/9789264254053-8-en

———. (2016d). Social spending stays at historically high levels in many OECD countries. *Social expenditure update 2016.* Retrieved from http://www.oecd.org/els/soc/OECD2016-Social-Expenditure-Update.pdf

———. (2017a). General government revenue (indicator). doi:10.1787/b68b04ae-en

———. (2017b). Social expenditure database (SOCX). Retrieved from http://stats.oecd.org/Index.aspx?DataSetCode=SOCX_DET

———. (2017c). Glossary of tax terms, Centre for Tax Policy and Administration. Retrieved from http://www.oecd.org/ctp/glossaryoftaxterms.htm

———. (2017d). General government debt (indicator). doi:10.1787/a0528cc2-en

———. (2017e). All-in average personal income tax rates at average wage by family type. Retrieved from http://stats.oecd.org/index.aspx?DataSetCode=TABLE_I6#

Piketty, T. (2014). *Capital in the twenty-first century.* Cambridge, MA: The Belknap Press of Harvard University Press.

Porter, A. (2015). Austerity, social program restructuring, and the erosion of democracy: Examining the 2012 Employment Insurance reforms. *Canadian Review of Social Policy, 71,* 21–52.

Statistics Canada. (2017). Tuition fees for degree programs, 2016/2017. Retrieved from http://www.statcan.gc.ca/dai-quo/special-eng.htm

———. (2017b). Table 385-0035, Canadian government finance statistics (CGFS), statement of operations and balance sheet for health and social service institutions annual (dollars x 1,000,000). Retrieved from http://www5.statcan.gc.ca/cansim/a26

Stoney, C., & Krawchenko, T. (2012). Transparency and accountability in infrastructure stimulus spending: A comparison of Canadian, Australian and US programs. *Canadian Public Administration, 55*(4), 481–503.

# II Social Policy for Social Categories

# 6 Social Policy and Indigeneity

## Internal Colonization and the Canadian State

*Eldon Yellowhorn and Robert Harding*

---

### Chapter Objectives

*This chapter will help you to develop an understanding of:*
- Indigenous social systems, ways of doing, and policies that govern community life, including child and family welfare, health, and poverty;
- Canada's legacy of colonial policies and practices and their impacts on Indigenous peoples;
- how current policies affect Indigenous peoples;
- influences on policy, the social work profession, news discourse, the court system, and jurisdictional issues, specifically the former Department of Indigenous and Northern Affairs, which has since been divided into the Department of Indigenous Services Canada and the Department of Crown–Indigenous Relations and Northern Affairs Canada;
- community-led policies and programs, and how Indigenous resilience, resistance, and activism influence policy.

---

## Introduction

As European settlers and then the Canadian state engulfed **Indigenous peoples**, Canada adopted policies to control their lives and determine their destiny. Settler governments imposed a role of guardianship over Indigenous peoples, and created legislation, such as the Indian Act (1876), to define their respective roles. Well into the twentieth century, Canadian governments continued to enforce disastrous colonial policies and practices on Indigenous peoples in all areas of their lives, including child welfare, education, and governance of traditional territory. Without power and marginalized on reserves, Indigenous peoples had few choices beyond living under the whims of successive political parties and their policies. They have always resisted the arcane ward–guardian relationship that has defined their identity under Canadian law, and are actively defining a new relationship with settler society based on mutual respect.

## Case Examples   Some Social Issues Facing Indigenous People

*The following three fictional biographical sketches suggest some of the issues that Indigenous people confront in a white settler society such as Canada.*

**Danielle**, a member of the Piikani Nation in Alberta and a residential school survivor, married a white man in 1973 at the age of 18 and lost her Indian status and band membership. Shortly after she gave birth to a daughter, Tina, the couple separated. Many years later, her daughter, a sex trade worker in Vancouver's Downtown Eastside, disappeared. At age 57, Danielle moved to the Vancouver area to search for Tina and look after her three grandchildren. She spoke to the police several times, but they did not take her concerns seriously, telling her that perhaps she had run away with one of her johns. Although she and her family regained status under Bill C-31, she discovered that her family did not have band membership restored. She learned that Tina's children would not inherit her status because their father was white. They would be status Indians only if Tina had married a status Indian; otherwise they would have no recognition. Moreover, her brothers' families did not face this peril. Their identity would not diminish even if their children were to marry outside their community. She wondered how official discrimination could continue even with amendments to the Indian Act.

When he was a baby with a single mom, social workers apprehended **Chester**, a Cree from Nichisawayasihk First Nation at Nelson House, Manitoba. A white family adopted him, but after some years in Canada they returned to their homeland of Scotland, where he grew up feeling alienated. Although he finished school and apprenticed to be a welder he never felt connected to his environment. Despite his having a wife and children he always thought of himself as an outsider. On his forty-fifth birthday his curiosity led him to seek out his birth family and to learn of the circumstances of his adoption. He learned he was a status Indian with a large group of relatives, including siblings, who were surprised to learn of his existence. Once Chester made the connections with his ancestry he grew eager to learn as much as he could about the life that was hidden from him.

**Billy's** grandparents took custody of him shortly after his birth in 1983 and raised him on a Mi'kmaw reserve in Nova Scotia. He and his five siblings were exposed to domestic violence and drug and alcohol abuse. When he self-identified as two-spirit at the age of 13, he was bullied by other kids. His grandfather, who had gone to a residential school where homophobia was deeply entrenched through Biblical teachings, inflicted shame and physical abuse on him until, at 15, Billy ran away from home. The toll of a negative life led to drug and alcohol abuse. He soon began working in the sex trade and committing petty crime to support his addiction. After being diagnosed with HIV/AIDS at 18, he met his social worker through a care program. She had little understanding of Indigenous peoples or of the unique discrimination that two-spirit people face. Billy moved to Toronto, where he connected with Two-Spirited People of the First Nations, an organization providing targeted support, including for those living with HIV/AIDS. They referred him to Poundmaker's Lodge in Alberta, where he received culturally appropriate support. His home reserve in Nova Scotia committed funds to his 42-day treatment program there. Afterward he got his addiction under control and his life back on track.

## Social Lives of Ancient Peoples

Mortuary research provides the best insights for social relations because ancient peoples put a particular emphasis on rituals associated with death. **Paleopathology** sheds light on the afflictions and ailments that affected the health and personal integrity of ancient peoples, and ancient burial sites provide rich evidence of the life and death of those who have gone before. By studying human remains physical anthropologists can determine age, gender, and cause of death from skeletal tissue, and the manner of burial alludes to abstractions such as status, class, and ideology. Discoveries from burial sites located across Canada reveal the actions of people from what they have left. About 7,500 years ago at the L'Anse Amour site on the south coast of Labrador overlooking the Strait of Belle Isle, a boy about 12 years old was interred with elaborate ceremony. Ochre paint and grave goods typically associated with an older hunter were laid beside him and then buried under a mound of earth and fieldstones. These burial artifacts indicate he was important to his family and that perhaps his family was important to his community.

Along the west coast in the Nisga'a village of Greenville, a large cemetery was unearthed during construction of a subdivision. Fifty-seven individuals were excavated—a cross-section of males and females in all age groups, including one fetus. Accidents and violence caused injuries that healed, and in a number of cases were the cause of death. One individual showed signs of congenital scoliosis, a crippling condition that led to severe twisting of the spine and fusing of several vertebrae. However, this person died in adulthood. This means that there was a social system in place that cared for this person through childhood and into maturity (Cybulski, 1992). On Gabriola Island in present-day British Columbia people began burying their kin in a cave around 2,800 years ago. Archaeologists excavated 121 individuals and their funerary offerings from a matrix of shellfish that indicated ritual feasting for the dead. Trauma and injury pointed to hazardous activities for young adults, but degenerative joint diseases typical for the aged were also common (Curtin, 2002).

Together these cases teach us that ancient people were not immune to suffering and injury, sometimes from ailments that modern people recognize. Their pharmacopoeia of plant-based medicines indicates that they actively sought out treatments for their aches and pains. Thus, our understanding of belonging, empathy, and compassion connect us to our ancestors. They demonstrate how our caring professions begin with kinship and cultural affinity that is comparable to a social safety net in larger, more anonymous, groups.

---

### Box 6.1   Who Are Canada's Indigenous Peoples?

Canada's Constitution Act, 1982 (section 35[2]) defines "aboriginal peoples" as "the Indian, Inuit and Métis peoples of Canada." However, "Indian" is a misnomer rarely used in Canada except in reference to the Indian Act, its definitions of status and **non-status Indians**, and Indian reserves, and in some legal and bureaucratic discourse. Terms such as "Native," "Aboriginal," and "Indigenous" seek to encompass a broad group of people who inhabited present-day Canada prior to European "discovery" and settlement. "Native" simply means to be born in a certain place. "Aboriginal" has roots in Latin, meaning "from the beginning": the prefix "ab-" (from) is attached to the stem "origene" (origin). "Indigenous" emphasizes place of origin, as in the news story that scientists had discovered indigenous water beneath the moon's surface, although some might claim it to be inappropriate because of the cognate words "indigence" and "indigent," which signify poverty. In Canada, "Indigenous" has become the preferred term in recent years since the federal ministry overseeing the affairs of those who first inhabited this land was renamed Indigenous and Northern Affairs Canada in 2015 (more recently divided into two separate Indigenous ministries) by the new Liberal government. For most of the department's history the term "Indian" was attached to its name, and before the recent name change it had been the Department of Aboriginal Affairs and Northern Development. The change to "Indigenous" reflected the wishes of client groups and usage by the United Nations, as in its Declaration on the Rights of Indigenous Peoples. "First Nations" are political designations that originate with Indian reserves and the Indian Act, and the term was adopted for political reasons, notably with the formation of the Assembly of First Nations in 1982 out of what had been the National Indian Brotherhood. "Inuit," meaning "the people" in Inuktitut, were historically and formally known as "Eskimos" or "Esquimaux," an exogenous term of disputed meaning. And finally, "Métis" are those of mixed Indigenous and European descent whose culture and lifeways reflect their dual ancestry.

The takeaway message is that attempting to capture diversity with generic terms is a futile endeavour.

## Contemporary Demographic Trends

In 2016, Indigenous peoples comprised over 1.67 million people, or about 4.9 per cent of the Canadian population (Statistics Canada, 2017). The total **status Indian** population, those Indians registered under the Indian Act, makes up the largest portion. As a group they cross many linguistic and cultural boundaries, but together they form one demographic minority. The **Métis** constitute the second largest population, followed by **Inuit**. Indigenous cultures and communities are located in all the provinces and territories, but their proportion of the population varies by jurisdiction. Inuit men and women have the shortest life expectancy, at 64 and 68 years respectively, whereas the figures for the overall Canadian population are 79 and 83. Métis men and women can expect to live to 74 and 80 years, while Indian men typically reach 73 years and women 78 years. By population, the northern territories have small populations, though a large proportion of Inuit live in Nunavut. Median age for Canadians is 40, compared to 27 for Indigenous peoples.

When Canadians were celebrating their centennial in 1967, Indigenous peoples were more associated with rural life than the inner city. Most lived on reserves or in remote communities, but choosing civic citizenship is now a prominent narrative. When the 1970s began, Indigenous peoples were the absent citizens of urban Canada, but by 2006 over half their number had joined the diaspora from their reserves and remote villages to metropolitan settlements. City life has meant adapting cultural and social institutions for an amorphous, porous identity that absorbs the symbols and teachings from an amalgam of traditions. Some social movements, such as friendship centres, started in the early 1960s as a way to overcome the isolation that accompanied moving to the city. These centres, besides being gathering places, offer a wide range of social services. Organizations such as Luma Native Housing in Vancouver provide affordable housing to individuals and families with low or middle incomes.

Crossing the rural/urban divide invariably requires some trade-offs. Status Indians who leave their reserves are often politically disenfranchised because they can no longer participate in the governance of their natal communities, especially if geographic distance is a factor. Estrangement from reserve politics has fostered a new generation of urban politicians who are more engaged in municipal, provincial, and federal government. Urban Indigenous people have access to better services, education, and life choices, which translate to economic security and social mobility. Although they may be remote from their ancestral cultures, the cosmopolitan blending of customs has led to new modes of cultural and artistic expression.

## Historical Policies of Regulation and Control

Throughout the global era, when humanity had encircled the globe, encounters between peoples naive of each other created the discipline of anthropology. Searching for explanation to the puzzle of human existence occupied anthropological thought since its early days. Initial attempts to explain the myriad cultures, languages, rituals, and customs posited a single path for humanity starting with mobile hunters, moving to sedentary farmers, and culminating with urban industrialists. Anthropologists conceived of stages, subdivided by rankings of lower, middle, and upper depending on their material culture, governance, and lifestyle, which began in "savagery" and transited to "barbarism". Progression to civilization, based on European notions of racial hierarchy, modernity, and social organization, required no subdivision (see Table 6.1).

Early anthropologists surmised that Europe dominated global politics and economy because Europeans had gone out and encountered the world. Moreover, nobody they met had anything like the Industrial Revolution, which was, for them, more evidence of European superiority. This perspective created a conventional wisdom that people practising "savage

**Table 6.1** Mid- to Late Nineteenth-Century Racist Interpretation of Hierarchies of Civilization

| Civilization | | Defined by the presence of writing<br>State-level societies organized by kingdoms |
| --- | --- | --- |
| Barbarism | Upper<br>Middle<br>Lower | Defined by the appearance of farming<br>Chiefdoms tolerate hierarchy and social inequality |
| Savagery | Upper<br>Middle<br>Lower | Mobile hunting/gathering people<br>Egalitarian societies led by tribal chiefs |

Source: Adapted from Lewis Henry Morgan, *Ancient Society* (1878).

ways and barbarous customs" completed the hierarchy of this artificial and arbitrary spectrum. Flawed though it was, this attempt at a unifying theory of human culture had a powerful influence on the politicians and technocrats who had the task of designing social policy to incorporate many distinct peoples into the empires of European states, most notably the British Empire. Thus, when the Province of Canada (present-day Ontario and Quebec) enacted the Gradual Civilization Act (1857) its vocabulary exhibited ethnocentric ideas of progress prominent in nineteenth-century anthropology. When legislators decided on the education policy that established the residential school system, they found their rationale in the idea conveyed in the **White Man's burden**. The ideology is explicit in Canada's foundational law, the Constitution Act, 1867 (the British North America [BNA] Act), wherein section 91(24) treats Indians and their lands as wards of the Crown. By infantilizing them, making them equivalent to children, the government gave itself the power to manipulate the lives of Indigenous people to suit its own objectives. Subsequent public laws, such as the Indian Act (1876) and the Indian Advancement Act (1884), preserve and entrench this colonial superiority complex. Moreover, in that era women generally were regarded as inferior to men in Europe so the provisions in the Indian Act that embedded gender discrimination simply followed the social convention extant in Canada. Although cultural relativism eventually replaced **unilinear evolutionism** as the guiding paradigm for anthropological thought, Canadian public policy crystallized around the original Eurocentric assumptions of the discipline, which may explain the many policy failures through the twentieth century. Nevertheless, because of their mission as students of the human condition, anthropologists would play a substantial role in designing public policy.

## Indigenous People and Canada's Second Century

As Canada's centennial approached, one of the gnawing questions among the political class involved the status of Indians. Indeed, in 1964 that question motivated Prime Minister Lester Pearson to create a Royal Commission. His Minister of Indian Affairs, Arthur Laing, turned to the Department of Anthropology at the University of British Columbia and recruited Harold Bertram Hawthorn to lead the Commission. He tabled his report, titled *A Survey of the Contemporary Indians of Canada*, in the House of Commons in 1966. Unofficially known as the Hawthorn Report, it contained 91 recommendations. Of these, two are most commonly cited because together they offered a remedy for the systemic oppression of Indigenous people. Hawthorn proposed an end to restrictions on their mobility rights and argued for no longer apprehending Indigenous children to advance a discredited policy of assimilation. The Hawthorn Report also introduced the concept of **citizens plus**, suggesting that, besides the regular rights of citizenship, Indigenous people had additional rights as a result of their having been here first and, for many, having signed binding treaties with the Canadian state and its pre-Confederation precursors. After the centennial celebrations abated, Pearson retired and the subsequent Liberal Party leadership vote elevated Pierre Trudeau to the Prime Minister's Office. At the outset, his idea of Indian policy was very different.

As Canada's second century started, expressions of discord through direct action made public the political and social turmoil festering among Indigenous people. Then in June 1969, the federal government issued its preferred option in its White Paper, the Statement of the Government of Canada on Indian Policy. Its proposals, such as abolishing the

Indian Act, Indian status, and dividing Indian reserves among members of each Indian band, stirred outrage among Indian leaders and served only to foment a national consensus opposing it. Harold Cardinal, the young Cree leader of the Indian Association of Alberta, gave voice to the discontent in his book *The Unjust Society*. He dissected the grating optimism in each phrase of the policy statement and disputed its content and objectives. Indigenous peoples wanted a better deal but not the one prescribed in the White Paper. Crowning an eventful year was the decision handed down in November by the Supreme Court of Canada in the case of **Regina v. Drybones**. Ostensibly it challenged a clause in the revised 1951 Indian Act banning Indians from possessing or consuming alcoholic beverages. Among the precedents it set was activating the Canadian Bill of Rights (1960). However, its impact was profound and the rights gained from it continue to affect Indigenous peoples across the country. This era of change began to disrupt a century-old bond with modern social mores.

When Indigenous peoples began to question the source of power that dictated their lives, they directed their activism towards demanding a better deal from Canada. The federal government, too, was looking for new initiatives to replace the White Paper it had abandoned. Politicians searched for a new vocabulary to meet the novel challenges of the 1970s. When the Cree and Inuit of northern Quebec sought a legal injunction to halt planned hydroelectric developments on their ancestral lands, the concept of Indian title was back on the public agenda. Adding to the tension, *Calder v. Attorney General of British Columbia* reached the Supreme Court of Canada. Commonly known as the *Calder* decision (1973), this landmark case was a non-victory for the Nisga'a because they did not get the declaration they sought—that title to their Nass Valley homeland survived colonial rule. However, the case rehabilitated the common-law doctrine of Indian title, first articulated in the Royal Proclamation of 1763, as six of the seven justices hearing the case affirmed an existence of Aboriginal title. Out of this turmoil a federal Office of Native Claims was set up in 1974, which launched the land claims era. The James Bay and Northern Quebec Agreement of 1975, negotiated by the James Bay Cree, Inuit of northern Quebec, and the federal and Quebec governments, known as the first modern land claim agreement, served as the template for subsequent modern treaties such as the Nunavut Final Agreement. Despite an intransigent BC government, the Nisga'a plaintiffs concluded their search for justice in 2000 when their agreement was enacted by the federal Parliament. Afterward, the BC government created the BC Treaty Commission to negotiate land claim settlements in that province, where, except in the northeast (Treaty 8 of 1899) and on southern Vancouver Island (the Douglas treaties of the 1850s), no land-cession treaties had ever been negotiated.

Outstanding claims prompted radical activism among young Indigenous people, but just as many were motivated by pragmatic activism. Direct action meant confronting the state at protest rallies and blockades to advance a cause, but it also created a way to grapple with the social impact of Canadian policies. Evident discord between Canadians and Indigenous peoples owed much to the long-held government view that "Indians and lands reserved for Indians" were federal wards. The British North America Act was written when the conventional wisdom held that the "benefits" of civilization had not yet landed on the Indians. The **Fathers of Confederation** believed that until Indigenous peoples adopted European notions of cultural advancement, there was no point to including them in the division of governing powers. Therefore, the state accepted a duty to advocate for its wards, yet often made decisions adversarial to them. Ignoring its trust relationship while surrendering Indian lands and amending the Constitution to advance provincial rights to the detriment of its fiduciary obligations were among the most egregious examples. In Canada's second century, Indigenous peoples pushed back against government action because they were tired of the outmoded and discredited policies that were supposed to improve their quality of life. A century of oppression had not quelled their desire for autonomy, to make their own decisions, and to receive compensation for losses and injuries. Many Indigenous leaders saw patriation of the BNA Act, with Pierre Trudeau's desire to add a new Charter of Rights and Freedoms, as their opportunity for the better deal they sought. When provincial governments attempted to exclude Aboriginal rights from the text, they only invited protest marches and rallies across the country. After a series of meetings between the Prime Minister, provincial premiers, and Indigenous organizations representing status Indians, Métis, and Inuit, section 35 was added to the Constitution Act, 1982, immediately following the new Charter.

# The Charter Era

In the nineteenth century, almost all mixed marriages occurred between white men and Indian women. Marriages of white women and Indian men were rare, at least in part because they resulted in a situation where neither the husband nor the wife enjoyed personhood under Canadian law. The architects of the Indian Act in 1876 accepted that women were the property of their husbands so a white woman who married a status Indian fell into his orbit and shared his status, as did their children. When the federal government updated the Indian Act in 1951, it left in place many of the features of the original legislation. Hence, by the late twentieth century, Indigenous women who married non-Indigenous men still lost their Indian status because of the gender discrimination of section 12.1.b of the Indian Act.

However, once the Charter of Rights and Freedoms was added to the existing Constitution at the time of the 1982 patriation of the BNA Act, it soon began to have an important influence on public policy. Section 15 of the Charter, which protects Canadians' equality rights, required the federal government to amend all laws that discriminated against Canadians on the basis of gender. Thus, Bill C-31, or An Act to Amend the Indian Act (1985), nullified section 11 of the Indian Act, which had defined Indians in terms that ensured Indian status flowed through the male line. Section 12 (which described who was not an Indian and mainly referred to women, as either daughters, wives, widows, and unwed mothers and their children) also disappeared.

## Bill C-31, An Act to Amend the Indian Act (1985)

When the Indian Act came into existence in 1876, it had to be determined who was within its ambit. Given that Canada's first legislators were all white men who were accustomed to treating women as property, their cultural baggage meant that Indian women would receive scant consideration. With the enactment of the 1982 Charter of Rights and Freedoms, which guaranteed all laws would apply equally to men and women, the government had to amend all acts of Parliament to bring them into accord with that provision. This triggered an automatic review of the Indian Act and led to Bill C-31 in 1985. Nobody gained or lost status through marriage, bands would develop their own membership codes, and women who lost their status now had a remedy for themselves and their children. One consequence, however, was to sever Indian status from band membership because not all Indian bands were willing to accept the women and their children who had their status restored. Thus, some women, like Danielle in the Case Examples box at the beginning of the Chapter, lost band membership as a result of this aspect of the bill, and their grandchildren faced the prospect of losing their Indian status.

More than 30 years later, controversy still appears in its wake. Early in 2017, Senator Marilou McPhedran introduced amendments to Bill S-3, through which the Liberal government intended to remove any remaining discrimination against the descendants of men and women who did not marry status Indians. Her amendment has the potential to make its effect retroactive to 1876 when the first Indian Act appeared, whereas the government supports such measures only to 1951 (Galloway, 2017a). Indian status still matters, even in our age of non-traditional planning of parenthood. One sign was the personal advertisement on Craigslist wherein two status Indian women sought potential full-status sperm donors (Monkman, 2017).

## Royal Commission on Aboriginal Peoples (1991–1996)

Harry B. Hawthorn was one of the many anthropologists to make Indigenous peoples the most studied in Canadian history. Commissions and public inquiries to investigate urgent or controversial issues are standard means that successive governments have used to inform policy. Since the Hawthorn Report, several commissions, as well as parliamentary committees, have received mandates to gather evidence about Indigenous peoples and issues. While they may produce useful findings and recommend changes in policy, they often take years to conduct their work. Governments sometimes call for inquiries as a way of managing thorny political issues or social problems or to delay taking action. Thereafter, they exercise their option to pick and choose the recommendations to implement and which to ignore. One example of this was the 1991 Royal Commission on Aboriginal Peoples (RCAP) set up by Prime Minister Brian Mulroney in the wake of the 78-day standoff at Oka, Quebec, that started on 11 July 1990 when Mohawk people defended their traditional territory against the Sûreté du Québec and the Canadian army. The seven commissioners held hearings at dozens of communities across the country and consulted extensively over a five-year period. In 1996, the RCAP delivered a five-volume report that made 440 recommendations to the federal government about urgent changes needed in funding, policy, and programs over the short, middle, and long term (RCAP, 1996). By the time the report reached Parliament, a general election had brought Jean Chrétien and the Liberal Party to power. Prime Minister Chrétien, the architect of the White Paper in 1969, felt no loyalty to his predecessor's initiative and dismissed many of its proposals, some of which, admittedly, were sweeping and aspirational, as they involved a total restructuring of Indigenous and mainstream Canadian institutions ranging from Indian bands to Parliament. Like the Hawthorn Report before it, the RCAP report, arguably, became another example of government inaction. Importantly, however, the RCAP added a loud voice to a changing conversation.

## Truth and Reconciliation Commission (2008–2015)

South Africa instituted the first Truth and Reconciliation Commission in the early 1990s as a means of moving past the harms and crimes of the apartheid era. Canada adopted this model of inquiry in 2008, along with a formal apology read in Parliament, as part of the Indian Residential Schools Settlement Agreement (IRSSA). It was the culmination of a class action lawsuit brought by 86,000 plaintiffs who sought damages and compensation for psychological and physical injuries suffered at these schools. Resolving this litigation included a clause that funds would be set aside to support an inquiry to create a public record of their experiences. The Truth and Reconciliation Commission of Canada (TRC), first formed in 2008 and then reconstituted in 2009, held hearings, conducted extensive interviews, and organized ceremonies of remembrance and reconciliation across Canada, and in 2015 presented its final report, *Honouring the Truth: Reconciling for the Future*, and issued 94 "Calls to Action" designed to address the legacy of residential schools and facilitate reconciliation between Indigenous peoples and other Canadians, with an emphasis on their shared history. The first five "Calls to Action" challenge social workers—both practitioners and social work educators—and child welfare organizations to establish national standards for apprehension and child custody cases and to commit to reducing the number of children in care. They emphasize the importance of child welfare social workers being well educated about the history and impact of the residential school system and the **Sixties Scoop** (discussed below), and also about the ability of affected communities and families to provide culturally appropriate "solutions to family healing." In the Case Examples, the lives of both Danielle and Billy bear the scars of the residential school system. Danielle was taken from her family when she was five years old, so she lost her connections to Blackfoot culture, forgot how to speak her language, and suffered severe trauma as a result of the abuse and cruel treatment inflicted on her. While Billy was not a residential school student, his grandfather suffered harms that then reverberated across generations. (See Chapter 11 for more about Indigenous child welfare issues.)

## National Inquiry into Murdered and Missing Indigenous Women and Girls (MMIWG)

During the general election in 2015 Justin Trudeau made a promise to launch a National Inquiry into Missing and Murdered Indigenous Women and Girls. Many Indigenous leaders and organizations, as well as social justice advocates and organizations in Canada and abroad, have long advocated for such an investigation into the murder and disappearance of more than a thousand Indigenous women and girls in recent decades. An Amnesty International publication, *Stolen Sisters* (2004), emphasized the importance of addressing systemic issues of gender and racism. The report's authors concluded that all levels of government have "a clear and inescapable obligation to ensure the safety of Indigenous women" (Amnesty International, 2004, p. 35), and recommended that they recognize the seriousness of the problem and take immediate action to deal with it. A year later the Native Women's Association of Canada (NWAC, 2007) launched its Sisters in Spirit initiative, which documented the cases of 582 Indigenous women who disappeared or were murdered over a 20-year period. Through a story on the Al Jazeera news network

(O'Toole, 2014), the international community learned about this injustice under the headline, "Seeking Justice for Canada's Murdered Women."

Rather than addressing this crisis, former Conservative Prime Minister Stephen Harper cut federal government funding for the NWAC initiative after its first five years and downplayed the seriousness of the murders and disappearances. He repeatedly dismissed calls from organizations advocating for immediate action to address the structural and systemic nature of the underlying causes and conditions of the problem. Instead, he argued that the issue was a criminal matter best left to the police rather than a crisis derived from colonialism, institutional racism, sexism, and indifference. Yet the scale and nature of the problem clearly warranted a comprehensive and organized investigation. While a 2014 RCMP report estimated that 1,181 Indigenous women were murdered or disappeared between 1980 and 2012, many people believed the actual number was much higher. Indeed, in 2016, the federal Indigenous Affairs Minister asserted the number was "way bigger" than the official record (Kirkup, 2016). Going back to the Case Examples box, Danielle's daughter Tina was one of these victims. The experience of losing her daughter and the dismissive attitude of the police left Danielle emotionally scarred, and she lost her trust of authority figures, especially police officers.

As with all national commissions and inquiries, the MMIWG inquiry is designed to operate at arm's length from the federal government. While the Inquiries Act empowers the inquiry to compel people to give testimony and present evidence in the same way that any civil court could, it has no authority to prosecute criminal wrongdoing or investigate past problematic actions and practices in agencies such as police departments or government bureaus. It is to examine this national tragedy, identify the root causes, and make recommendations to improve the quality of justice for Indigenous women and girls. The purpose of the MMIWG, as defined on its website, is to (1) find the truth; (2) honour the truth; and (3) give life to the truth as a path to healing. Unfortunately, the inquiry is embroiled in controversy, its leadership is in question, and resignations threaten to hamper its effectiveness. Adding to the jeopardy was the resignation of one of the original commissioners, who cited flaws in the process to explain why she had lost confidence in the inquiry (www.mmiwg-ffada.ca). Similar problems beset the TRC at its outset. (See Chapter 8 for more about MMIWG and other issues affecting Indigenous women.)

## Discourse about Indigenous Peoples and Policy

Through discursive, cognitive, environmental, and social influences people gain an understanding of the world around them. Hence, Canadians hone their views of Indigenous people and policy issues by contact with families, social and religious institutions, political parties, workplaces, and countless other formal and informal social settings. In particular, the public education system is a powerful social institution that plays a pivotal role as young people assimilate new knowledge, values, and attitudes about Indigenous people and issues affecting them. Schools in Canada have the potential to play a significant role in giving Canadians the opportunity to develop a greater understanding of historical factors and contemporary contexts that led to residential schools, healing and reconciliation, land claims, treaties, and child welfare and self-governance issues. Yet Canada's public education system has historically failed to inform Canadians about those topics or foster a critique of colonialism. In recent years there has definitely been progress, although it has been slow to come and uneven across the country.

Similarly, the news media too often promote colonial discourses that obscure and erase historical context, exclude diverse voices and perspectives, and rely on racist logics. Impressions formed by television audiences have caught the attention of government agencies such as the Canadian Radio-television and Telecommunications Commission (CRTC). A 2017 CRTC study examining the representation of ethnic and cultural minorities on publicly accessible channels concluded that Indigenous peoples are virtually invisible on Canadian airwaves, and that, except for the Aboriginal Peoples' Television Network, most Canadians had difficulty finding examples where they are represented at all.

Public understanding of Indigenous peoples and policy issues is forged in Canada's news media, which are at the centre of a political, economic, institutional status quo carrying out the production of official communications (Foucault, 1984). Thus, news media promote national interests at the expense of Indigenous people, and convey their message using the vernacular of stereotypes such as wise Elders, drunks, angry warriors, Indian princesses, and pathetic victims (RCAP, 1996). One remedy to counter these stereotypes and challenge colonial ideas is to teach Canadians a critical history of their country and its treatment of Indigenous people.

Unfortunately, much news discourse focuses either on the tragic consequences of the social and environmental conditions Indigenous people experience or on "wrong-minded" social policies and the vast resources "squandered" on or by them. The editorial pages of some major daily newspapers have featured critiques of "lucrative" treaty settlements, "expensive" residential school healing programs, and the large sums of government money "handed" to Indian reserves, Indigenous child welfare agencies, and similar sponsor organizations. Furthermore, while sensationalistic stories sell news, rarely do these accounts connect to any analysis of the impact of settler society and colonization on the current lives of Indigenous people. Colonial amnesia about the past is not unique to Canada; rather, it is a feature of journalistic writing in settler societies around the world (Spurr, 1993). For example, in 2015, the CBC, a public corporation, demonstrated its capacity to sanitize the virtual news sphere and obscure the extent of settler racism. Rather than proactively filtering out hateful, racist comments on Indigenous stories on its website or insisting that those wishing to comment identify themselves, it simply disabled online commentary on these stories due the sheer number of virulent, racist posts (Fenlon, 2015).

Dominant discourses have a powerful influence over how Canadians view critical social policy issues. For example, someone's "common-sense" conclusion may be that in settling long-standing land claims and addressing community concerns about poverty, addictions, homelessness, and other issues, governments encourage dependency on the state, and thus exacerbate the social problems highlighted in the press. In fact, the themes of such reactionary critiques of state policy are deliberately provocative and incendiary (see, e.g., Flanagan, 2000; Widdowson & Howard, 2008). Rarely is there any acknowledgement that this culture of dependency is the legacy of public policy gone awry, which has placed a heavy burden on Indigenous peoples. Nor do these authors consider that once the British North America Act gave the federal government fiduciary powers for Indians and lands reserved for Indians, it then used those powers to thwart the aspirations of its wards.

Such biased assertions limit the interpretive choices available to Canadians about important public policy issues. Misconceptions and a lack of knowledge about the historical contexts of significant, and detrimental, policies can impede public acceptance of reconciliation initiatives. They also can make Canadians less receptive to vital policy initiatives in areas such as First Nations self-governance over child welfare.

While such declarations find expression in the news media, they are influenced by a variety of organizations outside their ambit. Neo-conservative, privately funded think-tanks, such as the Fraser Institute, have long taken an interest in government policy towards Indigenous peoples and attempted to influence public discourse. They devote resources to research "Aboriginal policy," which they point to as an area that holds profound implications for Canadians' quality of life. Their lists of "experts" who readily find space in editorial pages and television airtime on current affairs programming include the likes of Tom Flanagan, professor of political science at the University of Calgary, and Gordon Gibson, former leader of the BC Liberal Party. Their conservative politics are persuasive enough to sway public opinion on official policy statements, which then take on the aura of fact because they go unchallenged.

Less government being the right-wing mantra, this position tilts towards minimizing the state's obligations to Indigenous peoples: less dependency would stimulate a desire among them for economic independence, thus diminishing the need to spend money on expensive programs and services. The prescription offered by these think-tanks is that Indigenous peoples need to embrace private landownership, and they argue that being unfettered from government funding could cultivate a sustainable self-sufficiency. The basic goals of this argumentation are to erode government services, slash programming, and force people to be more "competitive." In other words, a neo-liberal "Aboriginal policy" advances the settler perspective in ways that rationalize the benefits accruing to wealthy Canadians and corporations, while simultaneously hindering the desire of Indigenous peoples to exercise the elements of governance that foster their autonomy. (See Chapter 2 for more about news discourse and Indigenous peoples and issues.)

## Racism and Social Policy

Social institutions such as the public education system and the news media have long advanced a discourse of denial about the existence of racism in contemporary Canada. Many citizens may believe the widely promoted fiction of our egalitarian country, a just and free society wherein racial prejudice is a remnant of the past. Yet, a succession of high-profile inquiries and commissions, such as Manitoba's Aboriginal Justice Inquiry (1991), the RCAP (1996), and the TRC (2015), have refuted the notion of a colour-blind Canada and concluded that eliminating racism and creating equality for Indigenous people is a far-off goal.

Indeed, public policy about Indigenous peoples grew in a colonial matrix that saw them as inferior. These policies were designed to control their lives, repress their cultures, and contain their aspirations. Today, as in the past, the Indian Act is the most influential piece of legislation that carries on this statutory lineage, through the former Department of Indigenous and Northern Affairs, which has since been divided into the Department of Indigenous Services Canada and the Department of Crown–Indigenous Relations and Northern Affairs Canada. The existence of modern policies and practices embodying racist or ethnocentric ideology is not surprising, and one result is substandard and inferior programs and services. Policies in areas such as health, education, and child welfare provide lower funding levels far below national standards, afford Indigenous peoples little or no control over their administration and design, and are imposed on communities with negligible consultation. The notion of the White Man's burden still appears among public officials who think that Indigenous peoples are incapable of looking after themselves. While Prime Minister Justin Trudeau has spoken about his desire to nurture a relationship of reconciliation, he too displays this cultural chauvinism. He argued in 2017 that Indigenous peoples "do not yet know how they would spend additional funds for child welfare and health services" (Galloway, 2017b).

Poorly conceived and unfair policies shape systems and programs in ways that have profoundly destructive consequences for Indigenous people. A short list includes the criminal justice system, health, child welfare, housing, and income security. Compared to Canadian averages, Indigenous people have fewer opportunities in education and employment. They experience higher rates of poverty, violent crime, child welfare placements, homelessness, incarceration, unemployment, and substance abuse. Living on a reserve might mean going without clean water, basic sanitation, and adequate housing, and experiencing food insecurity. (See Chapter 14 for more about Indigenous peoples' and food security issues.) While Canada is a wealthy country with an enviable standard of living, Indigenous people do not share that quality of life. They face a situation akin to a developing country. According to the United Nations Human Development Index (HDI), Canada ranked ninth in the world in 2015, whereas AFN National Chief Perry Bellegarde noted that Indigenous people ranked sixty-third on that scale (Wiart, 2016).

Implicit racism invariably accompanies child welfare, which is manifested in a disproportionate number of placements of Indigenous children relative to their percentage of the total population. A significant cause of this over-representation is consistent underfunding of Indigenous child protection agencies. For example, BC's Representative for Children and Youth has found this to be the leading cause for their removal from their homes and placement in care (Richard, 2017).

Inadequate health care policy and funding also lead to higher rates of preventable diseases such as diabetes and heart disease, resulting in higher mortality rates and the shortest life expectancy of all Canadians. Yet they often lack any control over the design and delivery of health care services and policies for their people. This may be beginning to change in some parts of Canada. Since 2013, BC has had a First Nations Health Authority that works in partnership with the province's First Nations. (See Chapter 15 for more about Indigenous initiatives to gain more control of health care.) In 2017, Ontario and the Nishnawbe Aski Nation signed a deal on health care that will hopefully "begin the process of decolonizing the provision of care in the province's north" (Tasker, 2017). Despite such efforts, a 2016 human rights tribunal ruled the federal government discriminated against Indigenous children by underfunding services for them (FNCFCS, 2017). It concluded that "Health Canada documents reveal the department knew it faced serious shortfalls in the level of health services provided to First Nations children and was unprepared to implement changes prescribed by the human rights ruling" (Barrera, 2017). (See Chapter 7 for more about the impact of racist social policy on Indigenous peoples.)

---

**Box 6.2**   Innovative Indigenous Policy: The *Gladue* Decision

---

In December 1999 the Supreme Court of Canada (SCC) rendered its judgement in the case of Jamie Tanis Gladue, who had appealed her sentence for second-degree murder. Although the appeal was dismissed (she had received probation after serving six months of a three-year sentence for stabbing to death her common-law partner), the court ruling was made in light of the historic over-representation of Indigenous people in custody. Therefore, sentencing judges were directed to consider available alternatives to incarceration and to give special attention to offenders' personal backgrounds. Since then provincial and federal courts have responded to this judgement by accepting "Gladue reports," which detail the special circumstances for Indigenous offenders who plead guilty and are awaiting a sentence. "Gladue courts," such as the Toronto Aboriginal Persons Court, also play a role in responding to the SCC judgement. However, 18 years after this landmark decision, "Gladue rights for Indigenous offenders are being ignored, underfunded or flat-out denied" (Edwards, 2017). (For more about the *Gladue* decision, see Chapter 16; also see, e.g., www.thecanadianencyclopedia.ca/en/article/r-v-gladue.)

---

# Role of Social Work

Governments as well as business interests, social institutions, churches, and other organizations benefited greatly from colonialism. The same is true of the profession of social work and some of the social workers who worked with Indigenous peoples in the past. Cindy Blackstock (2009) described their destructive impacts as the "occasional evil of angels." Ironically, they, and the organizations representing them, were rarely bright lights in the treatment of Indigenous people. For example, in 1946, the Canadian Association of Social Workers (CASW), in concert with the Canadian Welfare Council (CWC), recommended to the House of Commons that Indigenous people be assimilated into mainstream society and stated that residential schools "have a place in a well-rounded system of Indian Education" (Blackstock, 2009). Well into the 1960s, social workers routinely moved Indigenous children into residential schools. Later on, they were seizing children from their homes and placing them with white foster or adoptive families, even when there were opportunities to place them with extended family members in their natal communities.

However, the profession did acknowledge its mistakes and has worked to develop practices that offer different options. Today, the Canadian Association of Social Work Educators (CASWE) directs schools of social work to have specific curriculum requirements for cultural content and to teach about residential schools and Indigenous peoples from the perspective of social justice. Furthermore, in 2015, the TRC called for professional educators to ensure that social work students learn about the "history and impacts of residential schools" as well as the "potential for Aboriginal communities and families to provide more appropriate solutions to family healing." In 2017, the CASWE issued a

Statement of Complicity and a Commitment to Change in which it apologized and acknowledged that "colonizing narratives, policies, and practices have been, and continue to be, embedded in social work education, research, and practice." Clearly, a growing awareness of social work's historical and contemporary role in colonialism supports a strong desire to improve the situation. Good intention, however, is not enough. Only dramatically improved outcomes for Indigenous children, families, and communities working with social workers will demonstrate the success of efforts to extricate social work from its colonial roots.

# Key Policy Areas and Issues

## Child Welfare Policy

Child welfare policy illustrates the destructive effects of colonialism on Indigenous peoples. As the residential school system wound down in the 1960s and 1970s, provincial child welfare agencies and social workers picked up where Indian agents, residential schools, and missionaries left off in undermining the integrity of the family. Like the old policy, thousands of children were "scooped up" from their homes and placed in adoptive and foster homes far removed from their cultures, traditions, and languages. Even Jean Chrétien, while Minister of Indian Affairs, adopted a Dene baby boy and raised him as a member of the family.

With the phasing out of residential schools, provincial governments began to legislate the provision of Indigenous child welfare services and the campaign to control Indigenous peoples assumed a different form. Across Canada, the 1960s and 1970s were known as the Sixties Scoop, a term that refers to the aggressive adoption practices of provincial child welfare agencies. During these two decades, approximately 15,000 children were placed in white middle-class homes in Canada and the United States based on the "assumption that these couples would make better parents than low-income families on Indian reserves and in Métis communities. . . . [These children] were submerged in another culture, and their native identity soon disappeared. They became a lost generation" (York, 1992, pp. 202–6).

Indigenous parents had little say in the wholesale "abduction" (Fournier & Crey, 1997) of their children by social workers acting on behalf of provincial child welfare authorities. Former Stó:lō social worker Ernie Crey observed that "no turn of the century missionary pursued his work among the Indians with greater vigour than the freshly scrubbed young social workers assigned to inquire into the welfare of Indian children newly returned from the residential schools" (Fournier & Crey, 1997, p. 155). Chester, in our Case Examples, was one of these children that Fournier and Crey described as "abducted" from their birth families. Instead of putting supports and services in place for his birth family or looking at possibilities for adoption within his extended family or Indigenous community, social workers apprehended him as an infant and placed him with a white family in another province based on fallacious and ethnocentric assumptions about the superiority of white home environments to Indigenous ones. Eventually, his adoptive family left the country and Chester lost all connection to his family, band, culture, and Indigenous roots.

Since that era, the over-representation of Indigenous children in Canada's child welfare system has actually increased. In 2007, while only one Canadian child out of every 200 was in care, fully 10 per cent of First Nations children were in the system (NationTalk, 2007). This means that First Nations children were 20 times more likely to be in the custody of child welfare authorities than other children. The 27,000 First Nations children in care is three times the number of children that were housed in residential schools at the peak of that system's operation (NationTalk, 2007). Today, Indigenous Services Minister Jane Philpot describes the "overrepresentation of Indigenous children and youth in government care [as] a 'humanitarian Crisis'" (Hyslop, 2018).

### Jurisdiction for Indigenous Child Welfare

Disputes about responsibility for services to Indigenous peoples are a recurrent feature of federal–provincial relations. Under the Constitution, the provinces are responsible for child welfare, while the federal government is responsible for Indigenous peoples. Until the early 1950s, provincial governments rarely provided child welfare services to status Indians as they regarded this as federal government jurisdiction. Even after section 88 of the Indian Act was passed in 1951, which extended the general applicability of provincial laws to on-reserve Indians, most child welfare agencies intervened only in "life and death" situations, usually by apprehending Indigenous children and placing them in white homes and institutions (Sinclair, Bala, Lilles, & Blackstock, 2004). Finally, in 1975, the Supreme Court ruled, in the *Natural Parents* case, that provincial legislation applied to Indigenous children just as it did to other provincial residents, and provincial governments "grudgingly" extended child welfare services to Indigenous children (Sinclair et al., 2004, p. 218).

### Delegated Indigenous Child Welfare Agencies

In 1981, Manitoba established the first delegated Indigenous child welfare agency. Since then, dozens of similar agencies were negotiated into existence. Under this model, provincial or territorial governments authorize local representatives to offer comprehensive child protection services (fully delegated agencies) or are partially delegated and empowered to offer family support and guardianship services (Sinclair et al., 2004, p. 222). Delegated Aboriginal agencies (DAAs) operate under statutory frameworks defined by provincial/territorial ministries. Paradoxically, these same governments regularly underfund these agencies, a charge confirmed by the Canadian Human Rights Commission (CHRC) in 2016. As we can see in the case of Chester, had these agencies been an option when he was born in the 1970s, Indigenous social workers would have supported his mother in caring for him, thus maintaining his connection to his community and Cree culture, or if that was not possible, they may have facilitated adoption by a relative or local Cree family.

### Jordan's Principle

Jordan Anderson, a young Cree boy, passed away in 2005 while the Canadian and Manitoba governments argued about who should pay the cost of urgent medical care. In response to public pressure, the federal government established Jordan's Principle, which legally obliged governments to immediately act in the best interests of Indigenous children before resolving jurisdictional disputes. This much-needed, well-intended policy appeared in 2007, but in 2017 the CHRC found that the federal government failed to adhere to it consistently, often with tragic results.

## Social Policy Change in Action

### Spallumcheen Indian Band Bylaw for Children in Care

The Spallumcheen Band in British Columbia's Okanagan region invoked the powers of the band council to enact bylaws as stated in section 81 of the Indian Act, without provincial supervision. In 1980, shortly after the enactment of the Family and Child Services Act, band members staged massive protests against the government in response to the removal of at least 150 children from their community. Provincial child welfare authorities then placed them with white families (Metallic, 2016). Eventually, BC's Minister of Human Resources signed an agreement giving the band exclusive jurisdiction over child welfare issues, including child removal, which thereafter followed local Indigenous traditions.

The Chief and band council assumed significant responsibility over child and family services, which was their right to make bylaws for purposes such as providing for reserve residents' health (Sinclair et al., 2004). Splatsin Stsmamlt Services now oversees the community's child welfare services alongside social workers and family support workers. The bylaw applies to all Splatsin children, whether they live on reserve or not. The long-term goal is to return these children to the community and eliminate the need for foster care while maintaining preventative services (Splatsin, 2017; for a timeline of the Spallumcheen's campaign to gain control over child welfare, see http://caravan.ubcic.bc.ca/sites/caravan.ubcic.bc.ca/files/Child.Caravan.Timeline.pdf).

## Education

For all Canadians, delivery of education services from primary to post-secondary is a provincial responsibility. Only Indigenous peoples who live on reserves receive their instruction in federally run and financed schools. From the nineteenth century and into much of the twentieth century the partnership of churches and government created the residential school system that caused destruction and harm for Indigenous children, families, and communities. By 1967, this denominational education could not keep up with the modern education systems in provincial schools. Superintendents in the Department of Indian Affairs tried a number of approaches, such as on-reserve day schools and outsourcing delivery to public schools in neighbouring towns, as alternatives to the church-run residential schools. The secular education meant students no longer spent their school years in religious institutions that placed a higher emphasis on catechism than on science or math. While progress has been slow there are some bright spots in that individuals have made great strides in demonstrating the potency of education in breaking the cycle of poverty. (See Chapter 18 for more about the impact of poverty on Indigenous peoples.) Post-secondary education programs routinely graduate teachers who bring their experience back to their communities, but the strongest trend is that the gender ratio of this profession is heavily skewed in favour of women.

## Chronic Underfunding

Chronic underfunding is one factor implicated in the higher rate of social problems and lower quality-of-life indicators Indigenous people experience. For a variety of reasons, many programs and services for them (including health care, education, and child welfare) are funded at lower levels than for other Canadians. There are also discrepancies between the types and level of services and programs available in rural areas, on reserves, and in urban areas, where an increasing majority of Indigenous people live. Whereas the provinces are responsible for delivering services to Canadians such as health care, education, and child welfare, the federal government delivers these to Indian reserves.

While section 35(2) of the 1982 Constitution Act defines "aboriginal peoples" as "Indians, Inuit and Métis," only status Indians met the federal government's definition of "Indian." Federally funded services and programs available through the Indian Act did not apply to Métis and Inuit. To further complicate matters, the federal government and the provinces are involved in a protracted constitutional dispute about the jurisdiction responsible for Métis people and non-status Indians. Thus, large numbers of Indigenous peoples cannot access the same level of services and entitlements as status Indians. However, in 2016, a unanimous Supreme Court decision affirmed that the federal government has the same fiduciary relationship with the 700,000 strong Métis and non-status Indian population because they qualify as "Indians" within the context of Canada's Constitution. This decision has significant implications for policy and funding, and exemplifies the important role played by the court system in policy-making.

## Social Policy Change in Action

### Justice as Peacemaking

Mohawk scholar Patricia Monture-Angus (1995) writes that in the Navajo system an offender is a person acting as if he or she has no relatives. The idea that offenders are people alienated from their families and communities and who act out by harming others suggests a very different path for dispute resolution. Indeed, restorative justice or "peacemaking" contrasts sharply with adversarial, "objective," and "neutral" systems of justice in Canada and other Western countries. Traditionally, Indigenous peoples employed peacemaking processes in their communities as a way to resolve disputes, deal with cultural infractions, and maintain harmony and balance in their communities.

Indigenous governments and agencies are developing formal policies and programs that embody these traditional cultural practices. For example, in BC, the Stó:lō Nation developed the Qwí:qwelstóm Justice Program, a peacemaking process that uses traditional methods and involves Elders. Qwí:qwelstóm is the Halq'eméylem word for "justice," which focuses on repairing relationships and restoring harmony to the community through consensus-based decision-making. People can refer themselves to Qwí:qwelstóm or can be referred by the court system, the RCMP, the Stó:lō fisheries department, or a community agency. Referrals are only accepted if the person accepts responsibility for the harm done. The plaintiff is also fully informed about the process and has the option to participate (Stó:lō Service Agency, n.d.; for more information, see http://www.stolonation.bc.ca/justice).

# Creating Policy for Indigenous People

## The First Nations Child and Family Caring Society of Canada

Founded in 1998, the First Nations Child and Family Caring Society of Canada (FNCFCSC) is a national organization devoted to supporting service agencies across the country through the provision of professional development, research, and policy. Fully independent from the federal government, this non-profit society has worked tirelessly to educate the Canadian public, giving over 300 public presentations between 2010 and 2017. Through its journal, *First Peoples Child and Family Review*, the organization also promotes research by scholars and practitioners into "innovative, preventive, and traditional or healing approaches to child, family and community related research, practice and policy" (*First Peoples Child and Family Review*, n.d.).

In addition to its educational work, FNCFCSC advocates for better child welfare policies such as Shannen's Dream. Shannen Koostachin was a young activist from the Attawapiskat First Nation in northern Ontario and the author of this initiative. She drew attention to the appalling conditions and culturally inappropriate curriculum of reserve schools and demanded that the federal government provide safer and better-quality education for Indigenous children living on reserves. Tragically, she died in a car accident at the age of 15 in 2010, but her efforts led to a campaign to bring better schools to northern reserves. By supporting and advocating for more effective and culturally appropriate policy, FNCFCSC helps to strengthen Indigenous families, and restore healthy and independent Indigenous communities (for more information, see https://fncaringsociety.com/).

## Aboriginal Healing Foundation

By 1950, a vibrant healing movement had emerged, which coincided with a growing political awakening focused on reversing "the damaging effects of colonial policies" (Degagné, 2014, p. 425). Advocates for mental health services got a boost from the 1996 RCAP report when public attention turned to the destructive impacts of policies such as the residential school system. In the wake of the Canadian government's first apology for past actions, the Aboriginal Healing Foundation (AHF) was launched in 1998. With funds from the federal government, the AHF's nationally representative board of directors supported Indigenous peoples in "building and reinforcing sustainable healing processes" designed to address the legacy of residential schools. The AHF fostered healing initiatives that emphasized health and wellness, and used traditional beliefs and rituals, such as **sweat lodges**, pipe ceremonies, and smudging.

During more than 15 years of operation it funded over 1,500 projects. After the federal Conservative government cut funding to the AHF, the Foundation closed in 2014, but its legacy includes many programs across the country. For example, the Eyaa-Keen Healing Centre in Winnipeg provides a variety of programs and services to help its clients deal with trauma and become "better parents, workers, leaders and mentors" within their families and communities. In Charlottetown, the Aboriginal Survivors for Healing Program provides "counselling, traditional healing methods, men's and women's eight week healing groups, and training of support workers to assist survivors of residential schools, and of subsequent abuses" (Degagné, 2014, p. 436). For the full story about AHF,

---

**Box 6.3**    Indigenous Harm Reduction

---

Harm reduction policies and practices have a lot in common with traditional approaches to health and wellness. They are holistic, involve respecting the uniqueness of individuals, and emphasize the importance of community. Indeed, a number of these principles are relevant when working with Indigenous people, including "the importance of not imposing one's own values, recognizing strengths, encouraging empowerment and autonomy and appreciating the role of socio-economic factors in harmful substance abuse" (Wardman, 2014, p. 102).

The Western Aboriginal Harm Reduction Society (http://wahrs.ca/) is located in Vancouver's Downtown Eastside. It is a collective of Indigenous people who formerly struggled with addiction. It is a grassroots movement dedicated to improving the quality of life for those whose dependency on drugs and alcohol continues. Its mission is to provide education, material support, and training programs that reflect Indigenous culture. The society's members employ direct action to protest the impact of unfettered development in their urban neighbourhood. They partner with local agencies and organizations that advance their mission, but they emphasize the needs of their members.

---

see "Full Circle: The Aboriginal Healing Foundation & the Unfinished Work of Hope, Healing & Reconciliation" (2014), at http://www.ahf.ca/.

## Political Action Organizations

Organizing political action on a national scale always proved problematic, due mostly to the challenge of overcoming geography in the second largest country in the world. Regional organizations, such as the Indian Association of Alberta, advocated for their constituencies and pursued specific goals, but no national voice emerged until 1968 when the federal government created the National Indian Brotherhood (NIB). Ostensibly an initiative to have an interlocutor to inform regional groups of policy changes, the NIB opposed the first government proposal following its formation—the 1969 White Paper. With this precedent, the NIB evolved into its role of representing all First Nations, advocating for its constituency, and co-operating with government when possible.

During the period when patriation of the BNA Act was on the public agenda the NIB undertook its own reorganization and emerged in its current iteration as the Assembly of First Nations (AFN). It remains the principal collective for articulating a national perspective for most Indigenous people. Among the early actions of the NIB was opposing Jeanette Corbiere-Lavell in her 1971 challenge to that section of the Indian Act that penalized women and rewarded men for marrying white partners. Since its stand in this case directly supported the status quo, Indian women determined their need for an association that advanced their concerns. In 1974 the Native Women's Association of Canada (NWAC) incorporated as a non-profit organization and became the national advocate for a constituency of women. Its president was one of the four national leaders invited to witness and respond to Prime Minister Stephen Harper's 2008 apology in the House of Commons for the residential school system.

## Indian Summer of 1990

After 1967, the frequency of crises in the relationship between Indigenous peoples and other Canadians began to escalate. The 1990 Oka Crisis, sometimes referred to as Canada's "Indian summer," proved to be one such flashpoint that strained this relationship. This standoff between the Mohawk Warrior Society and the Quebec provincial police, the Canadian Army, and the municipal government in Oka, a small town 60 kilometres west of Montreal, attracted intense scrutiny in the local, national, and even international press. When the municipality of Oka announced its plans to expand a golf course onto lands under dispute since the eighteenth century, the Mohawk protested the move and erected a blockade on a road leading to the proposed development. When the Quebec police stormed the barricade one officer was shot and killed. In a show of solidarity, other Mohawks blocked access to a major bridge connecting the island of Montreal, via the Kahnawake reserve, and the suburb of Chateauguay, and some sympathy protests and blockades of roads and rail lines occurred in other parts of the country. Canada's actions, including deploying several thousand military personnel with helicopters, tanks, and other vehicles, caused embarrassment in front of the international community and led to harsh critiques of government actions, and the Mohawks' defence of their traditional territory gained attention and support in other countries.

In 1991, in the aftermath of the failed Meech Lake Accord and still reeling from criticisms it received for its handling of the Oka Crisis, the federal government established the RCAP. To no surprise, the RCAP found that Canadian news media did little to shed light on the complex issues surrounding these events. Instead, most news reports were organized around one central image—that of "bandanna-masked, khaki-clad, gun-toting" warriors, a stereotypical image that bears a remarkable resemblance to the "war-bonneted warrior—the dominant . . . media image of Aboriginal men in the last [19th] century" (Roth, Nelson, & Kasennahawi, 1995, p. 6; see also CBC, 2018).

Among other tense standoffs in recent memory have been those at Gustafsen Lake, BC, and Ipperwash, Ontario, in 1995, and at Caledonia, Ontario, in 2006.

## Idle No More

In November 2014, four women (three of whom were First Nations women) in Saskatoon, Saskatchewan, held a workshop on the potentially destructive consequences of new federal legislation aimed to cut back environmental protections on Canadian waterways and forests. A simple tweet from one of the workshop organizers, Tanya Kappo, with the hashtag "#IdleNoMore" ignited a unique Indigenous rights movement. Before long, Indigenous people from across the country came together using social media and employed civil disobedience tactics to pressure the federal government into action. They also used creative strategies to educate their fellow citizens about the intolerable conditions that are a fact of life for Indigenous peoples in Canada. Simultaneous with Chief Theresa Spence's 44-day hunger strike protesting the federal government's inaction over an appalling housing crisis on the Attawapiskat First Nation in northern Ontario, Idle No More (INM) became a protest against the federal government's indifference to their plight. While the strategy of direct action seemed to come out of nowhere, the roots of this protest went straight to the political culture of this country. (See Chapter 13 for more about the housing issues affecting Indigenous peoples.)

In the 2006 election Canadians voted for change when they rejected the Liberals under Paul Martin and brought in a minority Conservative government under Stephen Harper. In June 2008, Prime Minister Harper stood up in the House of Commons and accepted responsibility for the harm caused to Indigenous peoples by the residential school system. At the time this apology seemed to augur a welcomed change in approach. Yet on 25 September 2009, barely a year later, Harper announced to an international audience at a G20 Summit: "[Canadians] have no history of colonialism." His apparent amnesia about the country's legacy of colonialism and oppression seemed to confirm what many Indigenous peoples suspected. Frustration with government inaction on self-governance initiatives, education, poverty, and land claims finally culminated in Idle No More. Participants obstructed roads, slowed down traffic, blocked rail lines, and organized flash mob round dances, traditional feasts, benefit conferences, teach-ins, workshops, and much more. The name of this new movement summed up all the discontent with the status quo, exasperation with delays in dealing with chronic problems, and weariness with watching Canada grow wealthy while First Nations live with boil-water advisories.

Although there is a direct line of occupations, protests, and civil disobedience back to the early days of Canada, Idle No More was different as it was the first to go viral and to trend on social media. It had no front line and its leadership grew more indistinct the farther the movement expanded from its epicentre. Its goals were amorphous—at best they could be described as aspirational—and it had no end game or clear path to a resolution or outcome. It truly was a sociological phenomenon, and it was unique to our time because it generated recognizable traffic on electronic platforms that translated to feet on the street in record time. Within days there were people holding solidarity demonstrations in other countries. Ultimately, though, activism is difficult to sustain because of the same elements that make it successful. Like "the wave" that moves through a crowd at a sporting event, there is much enthusiasm at first but then the next trend comes along and captures the electronic audience.

Perhaps the more important feature of Idle No More is the legacy it leaves to motivate its advocates. Working on the premise that "knowledge is power," organizers empower youth by providing education about historical treaties, treaty rights, and contemporary interpretations of them. The movement's vision statement invites all Canadians to participate in a "peaceful revolution, to honour Indigenous sovereignty, and to protect the land and water" (Idle No More, n.d.). The movement maintains an online presence (www .idlenomore.ca), which links to its Facebook page and Twitter account to keep the membership informed about activities taking place. So while feet may no longer beat the street, Idle No More persists as a collective of social activists whose protest is evolving with the times and technology.

## Box 6.4   The Medicine Wheel

The medicine wheels discussed in healing and recovery conversations are not to be confused with the archaeological manifestations built in antiquity by people on the northern Plains. Rather, they are the malleable heuristics, such as a pie chart, that organize the cultural teachings intended to aid people struggling with issues of trauma, cycles of violence, and addiction. Indigenous people today must contend with the violent narrative of dispossession that is their history. Their path to self-discovery must traverse a chaotic terrain of injury, hurt, and pain, so the medicine wheel charts a course through life's journey. It is an Indigenous model for inner therapy wherein the spirit, mind, body, and heart form a culture of healing.

This holistic approach finds its archetype in the circle, subdivided into quadrants that are vessels for the teachings and ceremonies that support the person embarking on this psychological crossing. Natural phenomena such as the seasons, totemic animals, colours, and geographical directions are the metaphors that inspire the therapeutic messages in the medicine wheel (Storm, 1972; see Figure 6.1). Rites of passage once played the role of preparing a person for the cognitive dissonance that accompanies maturation, and their absence does not negate their value to inner peace. Thus, this concept of the medicine wheel is both a psychological and literary device because it puts into words the teachings that help a person find a way to a healthy lifestyle (Chansonneuve, 2007).

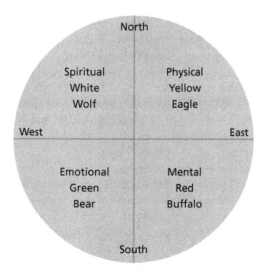

**Figure 6.1** Medicine wheel
Source: Adapted from *Seven Arrows* (1972) by Heymeyohsts Storm.

## Self-Determination, Indigenization, and Decolonization

When Europeans colonized and settled North America, Indigenous peoples were already present, living in the communities they built in the homelands of their ancestors. However, the introduction of colonial laws and policies usurping lands and resources eroded severely their ability to govern themselves in their customary mode. With mixed success, Indigenous peoples often tried to assert their own agenda in spite of the government's attempts to control them or impose decisions or systems of decision-making on them. Indigenous peoples have "consistently defended their nationhood as best they could; and they have sheltered and nurtured their cultures, keeping the core alive despite all manner of hostility and degradation" (Alfred, 1999, p. 3). While Indigenous peoples have demonstrated remarkable resistance and resilience in the face of colonialism, they were constrained by national boundaries. With no status outside the nations that claim their homelands they could not successfully use the shield of international law to defend their inherent rights and traditional territories. Since the creation of the United Nations, there has been increasing recognition that non-state actors, such as Indigenous peoples, possess the right to self-determination, as proclaimed in the UN's 2007 Declaration on the Rights of Indigenous Peoples. However, subnational entities, such as First Nations, must rely on the will of the body politic to secure such rights in the pursuit of self-determination.

*Decolonization* is the ***Zeitgeist*** of the early twenty-first century and it involves becoming educated in the ways of the Elders by unmasking colonized patterns of thinking because even Indigenous people raised in traditional ways may internalize patterns of colonial thought. While colonialism is inherently destructive, it may provide "a certain security" for factions in their communities. The obverse side argues that decolonization misappropriates a strategy deployed after World War II by former colonial powers, such as Belgium, France, and England, to grant independence to their former colonies. Large populations in Africa and Asia became autonomous again, but North America, Australia, and New Zealand were exempt from the United Nations resolution supporting decolonization. Thus, while Indigenous peoples in Africa and Asia can experience political decolonization, those in the **anglosphere** of nations must settle for an abstraction of it. While Indigenous peoples in Canada have initiated numerous innovative decolonizing policies and practices, other countries' Indigenous populations have also developed decolonizing policies that strengthen Indigenous culture and language. Table 6.2 summarizes four examples of such policies.

*Indigenization* is an option that has gained some traction with Canadians who wish to support Indigenous peoples in "decolonizing" their country. It is most visible when challenging and transforming colonial institutions such as universities, child welfare agencies, and the justice system. There is a movement within Canadian educational institutions to indigenize the workplace in response to the Calls to Action contained in the TRC final report. To this end, many universities have adopted indigenization as a strategic objective and have launched efforts to "indigenize the academy." Indigenization is a multi-faceted endeavour that pursues an agenda of ensuring that Indigenous peoples are represented among all positions of administrators, faculty, and staff. It might consist of attracting and retaining students from target communities, and creating programming and curricula germane to them.

**Table 6.2**   Innovative Indigenous Social Policy Initiatives from around the World

| Indigenous Social Policy Initiative | Details |
|---|---|
| Indigenous self-governance: Kichwa passport Kichwa Ecuador | On 12 October 2015, Carlos Pérez Guartambel entered Ecuador on the first Kichwa passport issued by that country's Indigenous authorities. After initial confusion, border personnel allow him to enter the country. While the government eventually reversed its position and declared such passports invalid, Indigenous peoples celebrated this because issuing and holding a passport is a "core dimension of Indigenous peoples' right to self-governance and self-determination" (Woons & Picq, 2015). |
| Language and cultural preservation: Kōhanga Reo Māori Aotearoa (New Zealand) | In 1982, Māori leaders initiated Kōhanga Reo ("language nest"), a community-managed program that immersed children in the Māori language from infancy to school age. The program's success led to the establishment of Kura Kaupapa Māori, which designated Māori as the primary language of instruction in some primary and secondary schools. Further strengthening the position of the language was the Māori Language Act of 1987, which gave it official language status (Cram, Phillips, Sauni, & Tuagalu, 2014). |
| Crime prevention: Community Night Patrols Aborigines Australia | Community Night Patrols, a form of holistic crime prevention organized by Aborigine women in the late 1980s, are now used in Indigenous communities throughout Australia. Not only do these patrols improve safety and reduce crime and victimization in under-policed areas, they also foster community involvement, ownership, empowerment, and collaboration in Aborigine communities (Closing the Gap Clearinghouse, 2013). |
| Higher education: Indigenous curricula Mohawks Akwesasne, which straddles Ontario, Quebec, and New York State | Iohahi:io Akwesasne Adult Education Centre (IAAEC) is a Mohawk post-secondary institution that provides culturally appropriate post-secondary education for Indigenous people by partnering with colleges and universities to offer degree programs, apprenticeships, certificate programs, and diploma programs to Indigenous students. Educational curricula are adapted to ensure they reflect community needs, cultural heritage, and identity, and meet the needs of Indigenous learners (Mohawk Council of Akwesasne, 2017). |

## Social Policy Change in Action

### Students Create Stó:lō Traditional Territorial Acknowledgement Video

*by Taylor Nicholls, on behalf of SOWK 380: Social Work and Community Development students at the University of the Fraser Valley, Winter 2017*

In 2017, as part of SOWK 380: Social Work and Community Development, a group of students created a video so that students, faculty, staff, and visitors can acknowledge that the University of the Fraser Valley is located on traditional unceded Stó:lō territory. While none

*continued*

of us identify as Indigenous, we wanted to contribute something towards reconciliation. In working with Elders and other Indigenous people on this video, all of us learned important lessons about respect and reconciliation.

This video is designed to address any questions that may come up about the university's location on traditional Indigenous territory. *Who are the Stó:lō? What does Stó:lō territory include? What does unceded territory mean? Why is it important to know this?* Our goal was to educate the university community and, more importantly, help them understand why they should care about this. For us, caring about and honouring the traditional Indigenous territory where we live, work, and study is an important step towards reconciliation. All of us were able to think of reasons why this mattered: *we live and go to school on this land; my family has farmed this land; and we believe in correcting injustice and honouring the truth.*

We needed to go about this project in a good way, especially since none of us were Indigenous. Our group held meetings with key people from the university and worked collaboratively with Elders and other Indigenous people to decide on what would be appropriate content for the video. We also put up poster boards in the Indigenous Student Centre so that Indigenous students could offer their ideas for this video, which we also included. We wrote a script and, with the university's help, produced the territorial acknowledgement video, which was then adjusted based on feedback from Stó:lō Elders, leaders, and community members. Two Stó:lō people played key roles in producing this video: one provided the narration, while another performed traditional drumming in the background. The video was approved by the university and by university Elders, and is available at https://ufv.ca/indigenous/territory-acknowledgment/.

## Chapter Summary

Since 1867, Canadian government policies have reflected the colonial, gendered, and racist thinking that caused enormous hardship for, and damage to, Indigenous peoples. Today, they are still recovering from the effects of these policies and trying to heal their families, communities, and nations. Because the social work profession is implicated in many of these policies and practices, it must acknowledge its responsibility for the harm caused. More importantly, social workers must demonstrate, by collaborating and allying with families and communities, that they have learned from past mistakes.

Indigenous peoples have consistently resisted colonial policies, shown incredible resilience, influenced government policy in creative ways, and adopted innovative new policies and practices of healing and helping that embody traditional principles. While today's discourse of reconciliation between Canadians and Indigenous peoples represents a hopeful view of the future, for that relationship to be truly transformative, children, families, and communities should not face obstacles because of their Indigeneity. Public policy must be based on collaboration and respect. Only when Indigenous peoples have control over all aspects of their lives—and enjoy the same benefits and quality of life as all other Canadians—can we confidently speak of reconciliation.

# Discussion Questions

1.  In the Navajo justice system, why is an offender thought of as someone who is acting as if he had no family? How do the benefits of this approach to justice compare to Western approaches emphasizing punishment and segregation for offenders?

2.  Why do you think it is important for all Canadians to be educated about the residential school system and the Sixties Scoop? Why is it particularly important for social workers to know about these destructive policies and practices?

3.  How do stereotypes affect our thinking about Indigenous peoples? What do you think some of the impacts of stereotyping are on Indigenous people? Why is it important for diverse images of Indigenous peoples, cultures, and perspectives to emerge in the media?

4.  How can all of us—Indigenous and non-Indigenous people alike—work together to overcome the damaging impacts of colonial policies and practices on the relationship between Indigenous peoples and other Canadians?

# References

Alfred, T. (1999). *Peace, power and righteousness: An Indigenous manifesto*. Toronto: Oxford University Press.

Amnesty International. (2004). *Stolen sisters: A human rights response to discrimination and violence against Indigenous women in Canada*. Retrieved from https://www.amnesty.ca/sites/amnesty/files/amr200032004enstolensisters.pdf

Bala, N., Zapf, M. K., Williams, R. J., Vogl, R., & Hornick, J. P. (Eds.). (2004). *Canadian child welfare law* (2nd edn). Toronto: Thompson Educational Publishing.

Barrera, J. (2017, 24 Oct.). Health Canada knew of massive gaps in First Nations child health care, documents show. *CBC News*. Retrieved from http://www.cbc.ca/news/indigenous/health-canada-ruling-children-1.4368393

Blackstock, C. (2009). The occasional evil of angels: Learning about the experiences of Aboriginal Peoples and social work. *First Peoples Child & Family Review, 4*(1), 28–37.

Canadian Association of Social Work Educators (CASWE). (2017, 26 June). Board of directors media release: Statement of complicity and commitment to change. Retrieved from https://caswe-acfts.ca/media-release-board-of-directors-endorses-a-statement-of-complicity-and-commits-to-change/

Canadian Broadcasting Corporation (CBC). (2018). Oka timeline: An unresolved land claim hundreds of years in the making. Retrieved from http://www.cbc.ca/firsthand/features/oka-timeline-an-unresolved-land-claim-hundreds-of-years-in-the-making

Canadian Radio-television and Telecommunications Commission (CRTC). (2017, 22 June). *Cultural diversity in Canadian media*. Report prepared for the CRTC.

Chansonneuve, D. (2007). *Addictive behaviours among Aboriginal people in Canada*. Ottawa: Aboriginal Healing Foundation.

Closing the Gap Clearinghouse. (2013). The role of community patrols in improving safety in Indigenous communities. Resource sheet no. 20. Canberra: Australian Institute of Health and Welfare and Melbourne: Australian Institute of Family Studies. Retrieved from https://www.aihw.gov.au/reports/indigenous-australians/the-role-of-community-patrols-in-improving-safety/

Cram, F., Phillips, H., Sauni, P., & Tuagalu, C. (Eds). (2014). *Maori and Pasifika higher education horizons*. Bingley, UK: Emerald Books.

Curtin, A. J. (2002). *Prehistoric mortuary variability on Gabriola Island, British Columbia*. Burnaby, BC: Archaeology Press.

Cybulski, J. S. (1992). *A Greenville burial ground: Human remains and mortuary elements in British Columbia coast prehistory*. Mercury Series Paper No. 146. Ottawa: Archaeological Survey of Canada.

Degagné, M. (2014). The story of the Aboriginal Healing Foundation. In P. Menzies & L. Lavallee

(Eds.), *Journey to healing: Aboriginal people with addiction and mental health issues* (pp. 425-39). Toronto: Centre for Addiction and Mental Health.

Edwards, K. (2017, 18 Oct.). Why *Gladue* has not lived up to its promise for Indigenous justice. *Maclean's*. Retrieved from http://www .macleans.ca/news/canada/why-gladue-has-not-lived-up-to-its-promise-for-indigenous-justice/

Fenlon, B. (2015, 30 Nov.). Editor's Blog: Uncivil dialogue: Commenting and stories about in-digenous people. *CBC News*. Retrieved from http://www.cbc.ca/newsblogs/community/editorsblog/2015/11/uncivil-dialogue-commenting-and-stories-about-indigenous-people.html

First Peoples Child and Family Review. (n.d.). Re-trieved from: https://fncaringsociety.com/first-peoples-child-family-review

First Nations Child & Family Caring Society (FNCFCS). (2017). I am a witness: Canadian Human Rights Tribunal decision. Retrieved from https://fncaringsociety.com/i-am-witness

Flanagan, T. (2000). *First Nations? Second thoughts*. Montreal & Kingston: McGill-Queen's University Press.

Foucault, M. (1984). Truth and method. In P. Rabinow (Ed.), *The Foucault reader* (pp. 31–100). New York: Pantheon Books.

Fournier, E., & Crey, E. (1997). *Stolen from our em-brace: The abduction of First Nations children and the restoration of Aboriginal communities*. Vancouver: Douglas & McIntyre.

Galloway, G. (2017a, 25 May). Senators amend legis-lation aimed at removing sexism from Indian Act. *Globe and Mail*, A4.

———. (2017b, 28 June). Indigenous leaders call out Trudeau over funds for social services. *Globe and Mail*. Retrieved from https://www.theglobeandmail.com/news/politics/indigenous-leaders-call-out-trudeau-over-funds-for-social-services/article35496813/

Hyslop, K. (2018, May 9). How Canada created a crisis in Indigenous child welfare. *The Tyee.ca*. Retrieved from https://thetyee.ca/News/2018/05/09/Canada-Crisis-Indignenous-Welfare/

Idle No More. (n.d.). Vision. Retrieved from http://www.idlenomore.ca/vision

Kirkup, K. (2016, 15 Feb.). Carolyn Bennett says there are more than 1,200 missing or murdered Indigenous women. *Huffington Post*. Retrieved

from http://www.huffingtonpost.ca/2016/02/15/carolyn-bennett-missing-m_n_9238846.html

Metallic, N. (2016). Indian Act by-laws: A viable means for First Nations to (re)assert control over local matters now and not later. *University of New Brunswick Law Journal, 67*, 211–34.

Mohawk Council of Akwesasne. (2017). *Iohahi:io Education & Training Centre*. Retrieved from http://www.akwesasne.ca/Iohahiio

Monkman, L. (2017, 28 Feb.). Native "sisters" post Craiglist ad looking for "full status sperm donor." *CBC News*. Retrieved from http://www.cbc.ca/news/indigenous/craigslist-full-status-sperm-donor-1.3997963

Monture-Angus, P. (1995). *Thunder in my soul: A Mohawk woman speaks*. Halifax: Fernwood.

Morgan, L. H. (1878). *Ancient society: Or, researches in the line of human progress from savagery through barbarism to civilization*. New York: Henry Holt & Company.

NationTalk. (2007, Feb. 23). First Nations Child and Family Services—Questions and Answers. Retrieved from http://nationtalk.ca/story/first-nations-child-and-family-services-questions-and-answers

Native Women's Association of Canada (NWAC). (2007). Missing and murdered Indigenous women and girls: A national crisis. Retrieved from https://www.nwac.ca/mmiwg/

O'Toole, M. (2014, 7 Mar.). Seeking justice for Canada's murdered women. *Al Jazeera*. Retrieved from http://www.aljazeera.com/indepth/features/2014/03/seeking-justice-canada-murdered-women-2014338655968569.html

Richard, B. (2017, Mar.). *Delegated Aboriginal agen-cies: How resourcing affects service delivery*. BC Representative for Children and Youth. Re-trieved from http://www.rcybc.ca/sites/default/files/documents/pdf/reports_publications/rcy-daa-2017.pdf

Roth, L., Nelson, B., & Kasennahawi, M. D. (1995). Three women, a mouse, a microphone and a telephone: Information (mis)management during the Mohawk/Canadian governments' conflict. In A. N. Valdivia (Ed.), *Feminism, multiculturalism and the media: Global diversi-ties* (pp. 48–81). Thousand Oaks, CA: Sage.

Royal Commission on Aboriginal Peoples (RCAP). (1996). *Final report*, vol. 3, *Gathering strength*. Ottawa: Government of Canada, Department of Indian and Northern Affairs. Retrieved from http://data2.archives.ca/e/e448/e011188230-03.pdf

Sinclair, M., Bala, N., Lilles, H., & Blackstock, C. (2004). Aboriginal child welfare. In N. Bala,

M. K. Zapf, R. J. Williams, R. Vogl, & J. P.
    Hornick, (Eds), *Canadian child welfare law*.
    Toronto: Thompson Educational Publishing.

Splatsin. (2017). Splatsin Stsmamlt Services.
    Retrieved from: https://www.splatsin.ca/
    departments/splatsin-stsmamlt-services

Spurr, D. (1993). *The rhetoric of empire: Colonial
    discourse in journalism, travel writing and
    imperial administration*. Durham, NC: Duke
    University Press.

Statistics Canada. (2017, 25 Oct.). Aboriginal peoples
    in Canada: Key results from the 2016 census.
    *The Daily*. Retrieved from http://www.statcan
    .gc.ca/daily-quotidien/171025/dq171025a-eng
    .htm

Stó:lō Service Agency. (n.d.). Justice. Retrieved from
    http://www.stolonation.bc.ca/justice

Storm, H. (1972). *Seven arrows*. New York: Harper
    & Row.

Tasker, J. P. (2017, 24 June). Government, Indigen-
    ous leaders herald health agreement that
    will dismantle "colonial" system. *CBC News*.
    Retrieved from http://www.cbc.ca/news/
    politics/nan-health-deal-colonial-1.4219620

Truth and Reconciliation Commission (2015).
    *Honouring the truth, reconciling for the future*.
    Final Report of the Truth and Reconciliation
    Commission of Canada. Retrieved from http://
    www.myrobust.com/websites/trcinstitution/File/
    Reports/Executive_Summary_English_Web.pdf

Wardman, D. (2014). Harm reduction. In P. Menzies &
    L. Lavallée (Eds.), *Journey to healing: Aboriginal
    people with addiction and mental health issues*
    (pp. 101–14). Toronto: Centre for Addiction and
    Mental Health.

Wiart, N. (2016, 12 Oct.). Perry Bellegarde makes
    his pitch for a developed, respectful Canada.
    *Maclean's*.

Widdowson, F., & Howard, A. (2008). *Disrobing the
    Aboriginal industry*. Montreal & Kingston:
    McGill-Queen's University Press.

Woons, M., & Picq, M. (2015, 23 Oct.). Indigenous
    passports assert self-determination in Ecuador.
    *IC Magazine*. Retrieved from https://
    intercontinentalcry.org/indigenous-passports-
    assert-self-determination-in-ecuador/

York, G. (1992). *The dispossessed: Life and death in
    Native Canada*. Toronto: Little, Brown & Co.

# 7 Race, Racialization, and Racism

## Social Policy and the Making of a White Settler Society

*Daphne Jeyapal*

---

### Chapter Objectives

*This chapter will help you develop an understanding of:*
- concepts of race, racialization, and systemic racism;
- the historical and contemporary context of Canada's white settler society;
- current state policies that paradoxically institutionalize racial diversity while maintaining racial logics;
- how discourses of racialization support and maintain "democratic racism" within social policies and political debate.

---

## Introduction

This chapter explores how race, racialization, and racism are discursively constructed through social policy in Canada's white settler society. For this analysis, I consider how race operates through the construction and implementation of policy, as well as how policy functions as a regulatory process that organizes social hierarchies of race. Through a review of the history of White Canada and its intolerance of racialized groups enacted through policy, we arrive at the present context where diversity is institutionalized as state policy. I pay special attention to key policies—the Multiculturalism Act (1972, 1988), the Charter of Rights and Freedoms (1982), the Canadian Human Rights Act (1985), and the Employment Equity Act (1986)—to examine the potentials and paradoxes of racial diversity as Canadian state policy and national identity. As critical race scholars have demonstrated, these public policies, which were intended to ameliorate inequality, play a role in maintaining the virulence of racism over 30 years later. As the Case Examples box below highlights, while Canada continues to grapple with the quest for equity in its social welfare system, the persistence of institutional, systemic, and democratic racism remains a central point of reference and difference within its socio-political and economic context.

---

## Case Examples  Being Racialized

---

**Keith**, 45, immigrated to Canada as a "skilled immigrant." In Jamaica, Keith earned his undergraduate and graduate degrees in Library and Information Science and worked as a senior librarian for 15 years. Hearing much about Canada's international reputation of opportunity and inclusion, he believed it would provide an ideal new home for him and his family. However, upon arrival, Keith realized his credentials and skills were not recognized and he could get no interviews for a comparable job, let alone a job in the field of library technology. To make ends meet, Keith worked for four years at a call centre that paid minimum wage. Unlike other call centres, at this place he was not asked about his lack of "Canadian experience" to qualify. However, a year ago, the call centre shut down and began outsourcing its operations. He has been unemployed since then.

**Rohan**, 21, was born and raised in Toronto after his family fled Sri Lanka in 1983, following the genocide directed at the country's Tamil minority. He attends a community college, and works part-time at McDonald's after school and on weekends. Walking home one day after work, Rohan was approached by two police officers who demanded to see the contents of his backpack. Afraid, Rohan handed his bag over. When they found the pamphlets he had picked up from a recent community event, he overheard the officers refer to him as a "terrorist." He stood at the side of the road as one of them ran a background check on him. Rohan knows that "carding" is a controversial practice, but is unsure of what his rights are now.

**Naomi**, 38, is a new professor, hired through affirmative action in a designated position for a "racialized scholar." As the only racialized person in her faculty, Naomi experiences racism from both her peers and her students. Her anonymous student evaluations regularly comment on her body, her style of dress, her hair, and her accent (despite English being her first and only language). She recently found out that she is paid significantly less than her colleagues hired with the same qualifications and years of experience. At a recent faculty event at her university, Naomi was approached by a professor from another faculty and told that students were not allowed to attend the event. When Naomi looked around the room, she realized that she was the only racialized faculty member in the room.

# Understanding Race, Racialization, and Racism

## Key Concepts

The concept of **race** has evolved over time. People have always compared themselves to other groups based on geography, religions, and ethnicities. For example, early global references to the German race or Italian race were commonplace, and in early Canada the differences and conflicts between the French and English often were cast in terms of race. However, the history of European colonialism around the world changed how the concept of race was understood. At their core, European colonial projects were based on the acquisition of material wealth alongside religious conversion. But once material relations were established and colonized groups were religiously converted, new ways became necessary to distinguish the colonizer from the colonized to ensure power relations between the two groups. Some of this was achieved through the work of **scientific racism**—the scientific study of supposed biological or constitutional racial differences that aimed to classify racial superiority and inferiority. Between the seventeenth century and the mid-twentieth century, numerous writers—in the name of science—established new ways of identifying so-called superiority and inferiority through physical traits: skull size implied intelligence; dark skin colour suggested savagery. Europe now had a new way to distinguish itself from the "other."

Today, scholars recognize that concept of race is limited. Recent studies highlight the ambiguity and complexity of biological and physical differences among people and groups. While constructed physical traits may distinguish us from each other visually, social theorists now understand that the meaning-making process behind these physical traits is more significant than any real biological or physical difference. The social processes that make meaning of race are referred to as racialization. **Racialization** is the social and discursive practice that denotes some people as "different" or "inferior" and marks them for unequal treatment based on these perceived biological or physiological differences. Discourses that construct racialized people as somehow more dangerous, criminal, primitive, untrustworthy, violent, subservient, or in need of saving perpetuate their racialization. A study of racialization highlights society's role in assigning meaning to difference and treating people differently based on these assumptions. Racialized qualities are not innate characteristics of people themselves but are social understandings that are culturally and historically specific. They evolve over space and time. For example, groups that were at one time highly racialized within Europe, such as people with Irish or Jewish ancestry, are now (for the most part) considered white in the West.

Racialization operates in relation to whiteness and white privilege. In **white settler society**—a society that has been, and continues to be, constructed through colonial processes and policies—whiteness is socially, politically, and economically enforced as the norm that other groups are compared to. **White privilege** refers to the unconscious bias of those of European descent who accept their experience as normative and, therefore, superior. Like the United States, Australia, New Zealand, and other nations where European settlers established their colonies—based on the displacement and marginalization of Indigenous peoples—Canada was made by and operates through settler social policies embedded with whiteness. This context creates complex racial hierarchies that construct the social groups within it. Systemic racism is one of the ways that these power differentials manifest. The study of **systemic racism** examines the disenfranchisement of racialized groups at a structural level. Unlike individual racism, or micro-aggressions that operate on a person-to-person level, these are macro societal structures that disadvantage racialized people.

## The Study of Race, Racialization, and Racism

Critical race theory can help us to unpack the central role that social policy plays in managing racialization and institutional racism in Canada. **Critical race theory** is a field of study that emerged in law in response to growing dissent in the United States. While the law is often assumed to be objective and impartial, legal scholars began disrupting this assumption in the 1970s by demonstrating that the law, like other social forces, was entrenched in social and discursive processes of racialization. As a result, even the law implicitly valued and benefited white people to the disadvantage of Indigenous and racialized others. Critical race theory as a movement and an analytical perspective has now spread across other white settler societies, including Canada. Looking through its lens allows us to unpack the insidious nature of racialization, its entrenchment in social policy, and its different impacts. Conditions of racialization intersect with other categories of social location such as gender, sexuality, age, and social status. These conditions are in stark contrast to an analytic approach that claims to be colour-blind. Such a presumed "neutral" approach is actually problematic, if not dangerous.

## The Intersection of Social Policy and Racialization

Social policy plays a significant role in managing and negotiating racialization and institutional racism in Canada. In fact, social policy constructs racialized groups legally and formally as **visible minorities**. Statistics Canada and the federal Employment Equity Act define categories of visible minorities, in contrast to Caucasian people, and in contrast to Indigenous people. However, because "visible minority" implies the permanence of minority status, it is loaded with connotations of inferiority and disempowerment (Galabuzi, 2006), and may not represent the actual demographics of a geographical space based on Canada's increasing diversification, particularly in major cities. It is an ambiguous term that generally refers to people with physical features that mark them as members of racial minority groups. The following groups are included among visible minorities in the Employment Equity Act: Chinese, South Asians, Blacks, Arabs, Central/West Asians, Filipinos, Southeast Asians, Latin Americans, Japanese, Koreans, and Pacific Islanders. These categories promote distinct ways of understanding, studying, and marking groups of people; however, they emphasize these differences as biological and not socially constructed. As you see, some of these categories refer to specific countries and others generalize vast regions and **diasporas**. In contrast, "Blacks" in this list is the only category that explicitly refers to racial markers. An emphasis on racialization shifts the focus to understand the role that society plays in making meaning of people's differences and similarities. While Indigenous groups are racialized, in that people's physical and biological traits are marked differently, they are not categorized as "racialized" in Canadian policy and thereby cannot be conflated into the same group as racialized groups. Indigenous peoples' claims to the land and relation to the state are uniquely marked when compared to racialized groups, who are themselves settlers within the Canadian state. (For more on how social policy specifically constructs Indigeneity and Indigenous peoples, see Chapter 6.)

## International Comparisons

### "Race" in Public and Policy Discourse: The Case of the United States

While Canada refers to racialized people (except for its Indigenous peoples) as "visible minorities," the United States offers a vastly different approach, categorizing groups by race based largely on ancestry. In 1790, there were three categories of race, but now there are 19. In the 1800s, only "colour" was referred to, not "race." Between 1880 and 1940, census forms included both the terms "colour" and "race." In 1950, the word "colour" was removed

*continued*

from the form, but it returned again in 1970. Furthermore, until 1960, people were not able to identify their own race; instead, census enumerators performed this task on their behalf. Only in 2016 were the terms "Negro," "American Indian," "Oriental," "Eskimo," "Aleut," and "a Spanish-speaking individual of Spanish descent" replaced with "African American," "Native American," "Asian American," "Alaska Native," "Native Hawaiian," "Pacific Islander," and "Hispanic" within anti-discrimination subsections of the US Code. Notably, current debates on the 2020 census challenge whether the census should move away from using the words "race" or "origin" at all. Instead, people may be asked to pick "categories" that best describe themselves, and may select more than one group. According to the US Census Bureau, respondents may have other options: white; Hispanic, Latino, or Spanish origin; Black or African American; Asian; American Indian or Alaska Native; Middle Eastern or North African; Native Hawaiian or other Pacific Islander; or some other race ethnicity or origin. The different ways that countries discuss and document racial characteristics highlight how race evolves and is socially constructed. Society's biases and limitations on how we understand and interpret difference further influence social, structural, and political contexts.

## Social Policy and the Making of White Canada

To understand the significance of the role of racial discourse in Canadian social policy, one must first understand something of Canada's history of race relations and how intolerance of racialized groups has been enacted through policy. As a white settler society, Canada's race-based colonial practices had the earliest and most virulent effects on Indigenous people. Social policy dictated every aspect of Indigenous people's lives—their identities, geographies, claims to the land, access to resources, ability to travel off-reserve for First Nations people, and basic living conditions—and it continues to do so. Specific policies like the Indian Act enforced systemic racism across numerous social and political realms to ensure the oppression of Indigenous groups and individuals. The irreparable violence committed against generations of Indigenous people continues today.

While the Canadian state marginalized and murdered Indigenous peoples, it simultaneously engaged in the process of building the nation. Indeed, that marginalization was central to the nation-building project. Nation-building for a settler colony ensures a unique identity for a newly possessed nation. Canada's nation-building project was centralized through immigration policy alongside other social policies. Until the 1960s, ensuring the supremacy and privilege of white people was critical to Canada's identity. These explicitly racist roots, enforced through "a strict hierarchy of preferred racial groups for immigration" (Mackey, 2002, p. 33), formed the origins of White Canada. As Hawkins (1991, p. 16) explains, restrictive immigration policies that first targeted Chinese immigrants were later expanded to restrict the entry of all "potential non-white immigrants . . . the power to exclude would-be immigrants in certain categories and of certain origins, on which the White Canada policy was based, was laid down in the Immigration Act of 1910."

While early immigration policy openly preferred white people from Europe (initially also excluding those from Western Europe who were considered racialized), racialized people from around the world were part of the fabric of Canadian society as early as the 1600s. However, their place in society was negotiated and challenged: discourses have framed them as inferior, dangerous, and criminal, at times alongside contradictory discourses that mark them as subservient and in need of "saving." While racial groups have experienced unique histories of oppression, the following case studies provide insight into how social policy and discourses of racialization converge through Canada's history.

## Canada's Invisible History of Slavery

While the legacy of the transatlantic trade of enslaved Africans is often associated with the United States, a lesser-known reality is Canada's own shrouded history of complicity. Records indicate that by 1759, 1,509 slave owners—most owning two or three slaves—purchased slaves who were sold, "often side by side with livestock, since no public market was set apart expressly for their sale" (Winks, 1997, p. 15). As Afua Cooper (2007a) explains, the seventeenth, eighteenth, and nineteenth centuries were marked by European acquisition and the maintenance of slave colonies to ensure their own modernity and progress at the expense of African nations and other countries around the world. She describes the relationship interconnected through colonial relations, economies, and self-interest. What would later become Canada entered the slave trade by relation and by proximity to Britain and France, the world's largest slave traffickers. At least 60 slave ships were built in British North America to be used for the transportation of slaves (Cooper, 2007a), and the British colonies were also connected to the slave trade through a complex web of economies, particularly between the elite in the Maritimes and Newfoundland and slaveholders in Caribbean countries. Salt cod from the Atlantic coast was exported to feed the enslaved people in the West Indies, with the return cargo comprising slave-grown and manufactured products like sugar, molasses, coffee, rum, and tobacco purchased by Canadian merchants. Slavery was institutionalized in New France and later in the British colonies from 1628 to 1834 (Cooper, 2007a). During this time, enslaved Black people were considered property. However, following the Act for the Abolition of Slavery throughout the British colonies that took effect 1 August 1834, the general model of servitude remained across the British Empire. Historians have documented how girls as young as 11 years old were sold in Halifax and New Brunswick for indentured service as late as 1852 (Thompson, 1979; Walker, 1985).

In addition to the economic benefits of slavery for merchants, slavery was justified, rationalized, and implemented through racism. White supremacy and the racial construction of Black people as inferior, subhuman, and savages ensured the prevalence and practice of treating people as chattel to be bought and sold for profit. They were "reduced to the category of animal or thing," which allowed the brutalization and dehumanization of their bodies. These cultural and material practices reinforced values of white superiority and Black inferiority. While countries like Britain have expressed "regret" for slavery, the Canadian government has yet to officially recognize its role within the transatlantic slave trade. This colonial erasure and national amnesia sustain continuing oppressions. As Cooper (2007b) writes:

> Institutionalized racist practices, anti-black racism, the colour line, colonialism, African underdevelopment, and also that of former slave societies in the New World, duplicity of western governments, white supremacy, economic disadvantage, racialization of black peoples, and psychic distance between black and white have all been identified as legacies of the slave trade and slavery.

## The Internment of Japanese Canadians during World War II

The case of Japanese Canadians during the World War II highlights the precariousness of Canadian citizenship and the racialized conditions of being an "enemy alien." Since Japanese began arriving in Canada in 1877, they faced a range of racist policies and practices. For decades, anti-Asian racism constructed Japanese as unassimilable social, racial, and economic threats to White Canada through fear-based logics: fear of economic competition, fear of intermarriage and social disruption, and fear of national security (Sunahara, 1981). However, this racism gained virulence during World War II when the Japanese attack on Pearl Harbor in December 1941 escalated dominant discourses of threat to Canada. Scholars have shown that no evidence of real threat existed, but racist politicians and journalists at the time emphatically constructed the Japanese in Canada as secret spies with no true allegiance to Canada. Many people in BC believed that they were part of a long-term conspiracy by Japan to possess British Columbia and incite an interracial world war (Sunahara, 1981).

In response to this growing public perception, on 24 February 1942 Prime Minister Mackenzie King ordered the evacuation and internment of all Japanese Canadians. Kelley and Trebilcock argue that the internment of Japanese Canadians was largely a discriminatory response to public pressure against a community long considered an "alien and undesirable race" (2010, p. 313). Japanese Canadians' right to a fair trial was waived through the implementation of the War Measures Act and, as Sunahara (1981, p. 2) explains, "each Order-In-Council under the War Measures Act that affected Japanese Canadians—uprooting, confinement, dispossession, deportation and dispersal—was motivated by political considerations rooted in racist traditions accepted, and indeed encouraged by persons within the government of the day." Men were separated from women and children and forced to build railways and roads and work on farms. People were stripped of their property and confined in crowded detention camps surrounded by barbed wire, with no electricity or running water. The federal government sold their property, in part to pay for their own internment, unlike prisoners of war who were expected to be protected by international "rules" of war. Nearly 22,000 Japanese Canadians faced this fate, despite the fact that at no point during their seven-year exile was the Japanese community an actual threat to Canada's national security (Sunahara, 1981) and not a single Japanese Canadian was legally charged with an act of disloyalty.

The majority of younger Japanese Canadians had been born in Canada. Among the older generation, many had lived in Canada for over two decades. Yet, they were constructed as "outsiders" based on their country of origin and potential saboteurs and spies based on the relationship the Canadian state had with Japan at the time (Kelley & Trebilcock, 2010; Robinson, 2010; Sunahara, 1981). The logic of racialization determined those who belonged and those who did not belong.

This reality has become increasingly relevant in the post-9/11 context, with the threat of terrorism represented as ever-present and with "foreigners"—now Muslims and people of colour representing the potential terrorist (Razack, 2007; Thobani, 2007)—marked as "different," "dangerous," and "threatening" to the nation-state. Again, we live in a context where dominant discourses challenge whether the civil liberties of "others" may be stripped to ensure the safety and national security (based on real or, more often, imagined threat) of the majority, as is evident in the story of Rohan (see Case Examples box at the start of the chapter). In 1988, over 40 years after the internment of Japanese Canadians, Prime Minister Brian Mulroney signed an agreement to compensate Japanese-Canadian survivors and their families for their internment and the expropriation of their property. He also apologized: "We cannot change the past. But we must, as a nation, have the courage to face up to these historical facts."

## The Destruction of Africville

The case of Africville highlights the interconnected social and economic violence of colonialism, slavery, and white settler social policy. Africville was a town across the bay from Halifax that was first inhabited by Indigenous people. It was sold by white landlords to Black families—many who were Black Loyalists freed by the British during the American Revolution and the War of 1812 or who were escaped slaves. The community experienced poverty and racism. People had little access to education, and the majority (estimates of up to 65 per cent) worked as domestic servants (AGS, 1992). Despite paying municipal taxes to Halifax, the people of Africville did not have the basic necessities of Halifax—running water, sewage lines, roads, electricity, garbage collection, fire protection, or building permits to maintain homes. As a growing desire for urban renewal and revitalization spread within the province, in 1961 the city of Halifax established a Development Department. In the following years, the municipal government unanimously voted to evict all of Africville's residents despite protests against this initiative. The eviction was framed as being in the best interests of the people—who were constructed as unable to know what was best for themselves. This discourse was furthered by social workers and city officials. Notably, the person responsible for implementing the relocation was Peter MacDonald, a social worker and graduate of St Francis Xavier University and the Maritime School of Social Work at Dalhousie. That one person held the power to perform property assessments (undeniably biased through character assumptions and assessments of those he interacted with) to implement this eviction highlights social welfare processes at the municipal level, where "power was neither anonymous nor, it seems, particularly extensive" (Loo, 2010, para 31). The discretionary power and racial biases of social workers have tangible racist outcomes.

Jennifer Nelson's study of planning documents on Africville highlights the role of discourses of racial inferiority, criminality, and the social deviance of the poor that constructed the community as a problematic slum in need of containment and destruction. Through all these documents, race and poverty discourses intersect and "are rarely distinguishable from one another; both elements are deeply infused with particular judgements about respectable family life, gender and moral codes, and the need for discipline and regulation" (Nelson, 2011, p. 129). The mainstream media at the time also reiterated racist tropes. Edna Staebler, a *Maclean's* magazine journalist, described Africville as "almost as obscure and sinister as a village in an African jungle" (Staebler cited in Nelson, 2008, p. 30). Despite the formation of the Halifax Human Rights Advisory Committee, which unanimously voted for the residents of Africville to remain in their homes, 400 residents were evicted and the city began demolishing homes one at a time. On 2 January 1970, the last house was destroyed.

Today, a highway runs through the land where Africville once stood. The activism of past residents and their descendants brought renewed attention to the community in the 1980s when a small park was built on the site in spite of the city's denial of wrongdoing for the forced eviction of residents and its attempt to silence protest (Nelson, 2002, 2008). In 2010, this park was renamed "Africville." In recent years the Canadian government has admitted its wrongdoing: in 2002, Africville was named a national historical site. In 2005, NDP MPP Maureen MacDonald introduced the Africville Act in the Nova Scotia legislature, which included a formal apology as part of a compensation package to Africville residents. The bill did not pass.

Some historical wrongs have received official apologies from the Canadian state in recent years—the *Komagata Maru* incident of 1914, when a ship carrying hundreds of Sikh immigrants was turned back at Vancouver harbour; the MS *St Louis* affair of 1939, when a ship from Germany with over 900 Jewish refugees was forced to return to Europe; the hanging of six Tsilhqot'in chiefs in 1864. Other historical instances of state-sanctioned racism are yet to be acknowledged. These stories of Canada's overtly racist past are important because they contradict Canadian national identity today. Now, Canada is known as a multicultural haven that is diverse, equal, and inclusive to all. How did this come to be? Is this an accurate representation of our present-day race relations?

# The Potentials and Paradoxes of Race, Racialization, and Racism in Canadian State Policy

The decades of the 1960s, 1970s, and 1980s were marked with social and racial unrest. During this period, new legislation and social policies addressed the growing turmoil underscoring Canada's pluralism. For the first time, in 1967 immigration policy eliminated explicitly racial criteria for admission into the country, and crucial legislation sought to negotiate Canada's increasingly diverse demographics. Four key legislative actions are important, not just because of what they officially claim to do but also for what they *discursively* do in practice: (1) the Multiculturalism Act (1972, 1988); (2) the Charter of Rights and Freedoms (1982); (3) the Canadian Human Rights Act (1985); and (4) the Employment Equity Act (1986). Existing law, however, continues to create growing gaps between policy and practice. Gaps emerge through the lack of accountability structures to address racial discrimination, the existence of institutional racism even within institutions attempting to address it, and the persistence and denial of racism among that those who interpret policy.

## The Multiculturalism Act (1972, 1988)

The Multiculturalism Act, passed in 1972 by the government of Prime Minister Pierre Trudeau in 1972 and revised under Prime Minister Brian Mulroney in 1988, solidified a new brand of Canadian politics and national identity that altered the rhetoric of two "founding nations" to that of a multicultural nation. The implementation of this policy ushered in a new era of "celebrating" diversity, and thereby initiated the entrenchment of race-neutral and racism-denying logic. However, the reality is that racialization and racism were important factors in the development and implementation of the policy. Not only did racist discourse frame the parliamentary discussion at the time, but politicians also failed to address the issue of compensation for racialized people who had previously faced racial discrimination (Wood & Gilbert, 2005).

As the first country to implement multiculturalism as official state policy, Canada is "routinely cited as a world leader in Multiculturalism, exuding a discourse of relatively peaceful coexistence of multiple ethnicities, religions, and so on" (Wood & Gilbert, 2005, p. 680). Multiculturalism is a brand that operates as "an influential, liberal cosmopolitan component of 'bourgeois urbanism'"(Goonewardena & Kipfer, 2005, p. 2): it interweaves assumptions and strategies along with dominant practices and socio-political goals that benefit the middle class and the elite.

However, scholars argue that multiculturalism was a manifestation of a much more urgent battle involving Quebec's separatists, Indigenous peoples, and the federal government. They suggest that this legislation played a special role in reframing and reconstituting Canada's relationship with Indigenous and racialized peoples, along with those from Quebec. In effect, it silenced the resistance from all sides by providing a new, singular framework through which people were to be recognized by and could make claims to the state. While the brand of multiculturalism aligned with previous Liberal rhetoric and initiatives for citizenship and inclusion, this policy also ensured the neutralization of growing dissent. Simultaneously, racialized others are indoctrinated into a fragile narrative of inclusion through the discourse of multiculturalism that emphasizes a celebration of cultural practices and ceremonies but makes no mention of or commitment to structural racial inclusion, racial equity, or the eradication of racial discrimination. As Sunera Thobani (2007, p. 159) argues, "the success of multiculturalism lies in its facilitation of the integration of immigrants on the nation's terms; it remains dependent on the derailment of the struggles of people of colour against the racism of the nation-state."

## The Canadian Charter of Rights and Freedoms (1982)

The Canadian Charter of Rights and Freedoms (commonly referred to as "the Charter"), which guarantees the rights and freedoms of individuals, is one of the most significant and, for some, controversial sections of the Canadian Constitution. It includes the freedom of expression, the right to a democratic government, the right to live and seek work anywhere in Canada, the legal rights of people accused of crimes, Aboriginal peoples' rights, the right to equality including gender equality, the right to use either of Canada's official languages in communication to or from the government, and the right of French or English minorities to an education in their language, among others (Government of Canada, 2017). Article 15 specifically emphasizes that every individual, regardless of race, national or ethnic origin, colour, religion, sex, age, or mental or physical disability, is equal by law. In effect, it grants courts the power to create judicial reform based on their interpretation of the principles and parameters of the Charter. Before a new law is made, substantive equality must be considered. That is, social oppressions and disadvantages must be taken into account to ensure that biases within the law are addressed.

While the constitutional document has made significant victories possible for some equity-seeking groups (such as the right to same-sex marriage and the right to reproductive choice, as well as linguistic rights for francophones outside Quebec), racial justice and justice for Indigenous peoples have not faired nearly as well. In fact, in a study reflecting on the Charter's effectiveness in addressing racialization, David Tanovich (2008) argues that this legislation has not interrupted the reality that many people hold racist views or that our criminal justice system perpetuates these stereotypes. He says that Canada continues to "incarcerate Aboriginals and African Canadians at alarming rates, racial profiling at our borders and in our streets continues to flourish, and the federal government continues to propose legislation that will further entrench the problem" (Tanovich, 2008, pp. 656–7). In this context, the courts and the judiciary have failed to adopt the necessary critical race standards to disrupt the logics of white supremacy, claiming lack of knowledge, silence in naming race, or outright hostility in response to race-based arguments. He argues that the problem is "not with the Charter but those who argue and interpret it," overwhelmingly white judges and lawyers. This allows it to be a "Charter of Whiteness."

## The Canadian Human Rights Act (1985)

The Canadian Human Rights Act (CHRA, the Act) was established to extend the laws in Canada through:

> the principle that all individuals should have an opportunity equal with other in- dividuals to make for themselves the lives that they are able and wish to have and to have their needs accommodated, consistent with their duties and obligations as members of society, without being hindered in or prevented from doing so by discriminatory practices based on race, national or ethnic origin, colour, reli- gion, age, sex, sexual orientation, marital status, family status, disability or con- viction for an offence for which a pardon has been granted or in respect of which a record suspension has been ordered. (Canadian Human Rights Act, 1985)

While the Act reiterates the discourse of equality across multiple social demographics, ac- cording to Delores Mullings race-based discrimination continues to be reproduced by the Canadian Human Rights Tribunal (which enforces the CHRA). Mullings describes how race, racialization, and racism are complicated through organizational processes and are repro- duced by the tribunal through institutional practices and institutional discourses to legit- imize existing power relations. Analyzing the "discourse of language the adjudicators and respondents used to describe the complainants, the normalization of racist behaviour that occurred in both the workplace and the Tribunal; and the arguments adjudicators used to rationalize their decisions" (Mullings, 2009, p. 147), she identifies six elements that "can con- tribute to the paradox of inequality being reproduced through the structures that have been created to reduce power imbalances and discrimination in Canadian society" (pp. 253–4). She defines these elements as: (1) claiming neutrality and objectivity; (2) affirming organiz- ational norms, values, and expectations; (3) accepting negative descriptions and categoriz- ations of complainants; (4) constructing a guilty complainant; (5) normalizing racism; and (6) failing to recognize the possibility of everyday racist practices in the workplace.

Again, the gap between policy and the structural context is evident. The biases of the in- stitutional context that claim race neutrality operate to the disadvantage of racialized people: "Institutional discourses embedded in the complaint process allowed adjudicators to use their position of power to continually reject the complainants' experiences while legitimizing the respondents' claims" (p. 259). Despite the importance and intention of the formal policy, people's own biases become determining factors. In this case, the role of tribunal adjudica- tors is paramount because their perspectives, knowledges, and practices come to represent the Act. Despite the rhetoric of equality, discursive practices inform implementation.

## The Employment Equity Act (1986)

In 1984, the report of the Royal Commission on Equality in Employment urged Canada to adopt policies and practices for four designated groups: women, Aboriginal people, persons with disabilities, and visible minorities after concluding "that voluntary measures are an unsatisfactory response to the pervasiveness of systemic discrimination in Canadian workplaces." The Employment Equity Act (EEA) that followed pertains to industries federally regulated under the Canadian Constitution. It requires employers to use proactive processes to increase the representation of employees belonging to the designated groups. It focuses on "the principle that employment equity means more than treating persons in the same way but also requires special measures and the accommodation of differences" (Employment Equity Act, 1995). While the Act aims to achieve equality in the workplace, its lack of formal accountability and consequence places the onus on racialized people to demonstrate the existence of racism through an adversarial process. Again, we find "a structural disconnection between the legislation and the program" (Mullings, 2009) because employers are not fined for violations and decision-makers interpret the intent of the policy with varying degrees of understanding of their biases in choosing how or whether they proceed with employment equity programs (EEPs). Employees who believe their rights have been violated under the EEA have no opportunity to seek redress unless they file a complaint with the Canadian Human Rights Commission (Mullings, 2009). The problem with this is that "complainant" workers who experience discrimination as an everyday practice have to become adversaries, making their case and using evidence just as they would in court. An adversarial system doesn't promote social justice (Mullings, 2009, p. 261). This reality highlights the structural disconnect between a policy that claims equity as an aim but, in effect, continues to operate through race-neutral logics that disadvantage racialized people facing discrimination.

Recent studies indicate that employment equity policies have not resulted in much progress in ensuring equitable racial diversity within the federally regulated sector, which amounts to 6 per cent of Canada's workforce and includes Canada-wide industries that operate beyond the provincial level and thereby are governed by the Canada Labour Code. According to the 2016 census, visible minorities numbered 7.7 million or 22.3 per cent of Canada's population, of which 30 per cent were born in Canada, yet white people still represent 96 per cent of judges (Griffith, 2016) and just over 86 per cent of MPs (Tolley, 2015). Most Canadian universities remain "largely white and male" (CAUT, 2010). A groundbreaking study of research-intensive universities (U15) and several other major universities by Malinda Smith uncovers how this pervasive trend includes the leadership of Canadian universities. She examined the 142 senior administrators on the leadership teams at 24 major universities in Canada and found that "in 2016, the majority of the U15 institutions—73.3 per cent (11)—have an all-white leadership team. More, of the 99 individuals on these teams, an astonishing 96 per cent are white. Notably, of the 4 per cent (5) who are visible minority men, 3 are university presidents . . . . not a single university had a visible minority woman or Aboriginal man or woman on their presidential leadership teams" (AWA, 2016, p. 1). The inclusion of racialized faculty has garnered increasing attention over the past few decades—as more racialized faculty demand equity within the walls of the ivory tower, racial representation isn't the only consideration. How people are treated, how their knowledges are valued, and how they experience inclusion must be examined. Also very troubling is the fact that racialized faculty members earn 10 per cent less than their white counterparts (CAUT, 2010). These findings reflect Naomi's experience in the Case Examples box: while racialized faculty are just as qualified, inequities related to hiring, pay, inclusion, and retention rates uncover more insidious racist realities.

## The Current State of Racialization in Canada

As we have seen, Canadian policies create the illusion of a racially inclusive nation where racism is not tolerated and is criminalized. However, the implementation of the policies provides little institutional accountability and/or structural opportunity to address racial discrimination, and consequently the policies achieve very little true racial inclusion. The discourse of Canada's inclusivity appears firmly in place: we represent ourselves as being more inclusive and more welcoming than other Western nations. Of course, comparisons to the more overtly racist politics of the United States stand in stark contrast to our own polite forms of covert racism. However, our national identity based on narratives within these policies also complicates how these very forms of racialization and racism manifest and circulate. As Henry and Tator (2009) argue, instead of a multicultural nation free of racism, we now have a nation based on what they refer to as "democratic racism." This racism is invisible precisely because it exists in contrast to Canada's national identity. In this context, Canada's history of racial oppression enacted through centuries of social policies and laws, and the current lived realities of racialized peoples, are silenced. Instead, where narratives of racism emerge, as in "driving while Black," or when racialized peoples share their experiences of racism in public forums, public discourse assumes it is anything but the logics of racism at work. Instead, dominant discourses frame racist actions, behaviours, and outcomes as aberrations or exceptions that prove the rule (i.e., Canada is not racist), and dismiss any notion that racism is a factor in "modern" Canada. Racist acts are always individualized, and racist logics are never even acknowledged, let alone debated. Sometimes, such arguments seems appears commonsensical, but they validate practices that exclude racialized peoples. For example, in our earlier Case Examples box, requiring "Canadian experience" as a prerequisite for employment in Canada limited Keith's ability to find work.

## Social Policy Change in Action

### A Human Rights Policy to Address the Canadian Experience Barrier for Newcomers

*by Dr Shaheen Azmi, Director of Policy, Education, Monitoring and Outreach, Ontario Human Rights Commission*

After completing my studies in social work in 1996 one of the first major areas of research I was recruited to support involved access to professions and trades for foreign-trained immigrants to Ontario. The issue of immigration exclusion in employment practices was emerging in the public conscious and my research was conducted in Ontario's Ministry of Citizenship. In these early days the issue was seen largely as immigration barriers, which, while frustrating, were not rooted in discrimination. Efforts to address these concerns identified many employment barriers, including the pernicious one of lack of "Canadian experience" that many employers and professional regulatory bodies established as requirements for accreditation. Efforts to address these barriers focused on ways to help newcomers obtain experience in Canada.

Many years later, when I became the Director of Policy, Education, Monitoring, and Outreach at the Ontario Human Rights Commission (OHRC), the issue of Canadian experience came back to me for consideration. OHRC commissioners indicated that Canadian experience requirements continued to be a major barrier for newcomers obtaining accreditation and employment, and asked our Policy Branch to consider ways to help address this. When we looked at the whole issue from a human rights angle what quickly became apparent was that Canadian experience requirements generally could not pass the discrimination test. Under the Ontario Human Rights Code discrimination is prohibited in relation to grounds including race, colour, ancestry, citizenship, place of origin, and ethnic origin. Canadian experience requirements were fundamentally a type of discrimination related to these grounds because, in essence, having relevant experience is more pertinent than where that experience is obtained. Although, people had long suspected that Canadian experience requirements were proxies for subtle racism, no one in the community or government had advocated for change based on the idea that such requirements were illegal. The OHRC took the first step in this direction by developing its "Policy on Removing the Canadian Experience Barrier," which was released in 2013. This made clear the link between discrimination and Canadian experience requirements and provided a new tool to those struggling to remove this barrier for newcomers.

In other instances, racialized people are blamed for their own oppression (the "blame the victim" narrative), or they are criminalized to justify extreme state responses to "manage" "them." The combined national rhetoric of inclusion, alongside a lack of redress through legislation, fosters the conditions of "democratic racism" in Canada (Henry & Tator, 2009). Discourses of racialization allow racism to continue and reproduce racism and hierarchies of race. In effect, these public policies, which were intended to ameliorate inequality, play a role in maintaining its virulence over 30 years later. The current state of racialization and the lived realities of racialized groups reveal significant contradictions. Paradoxically, the current state of racialization in Canada others and criminalizes racialized people.

The persistence of systemic and democratic racism remains a central point of reference and difference within our socio-political and economic context. According to the 2009 General Social Survey (GSS), a quarter of all visible minorities reported discrimination or unfair treatment during the five years preceding the survey, compared to 13 per cent for the non-visible minority. The Environics Institute for Survey Research (2016) conducted research in late 2015 and early 2016 with a representative sample of 600 self-identified Muslims across Canada who were 18 years and older. One in three Canadian Muslims reported having experienced discrimination as a result of their religion or ethnicity in the past five years. These experiences most commonly took place in the workplace, in public spaces, in retail establishments, and in schools and universities.

Racism also affects people's experiences within the social service and health care sectors. For example, despite universal access to health care, racialized patients experience racism within the health care system. A study conducted by Women's Health in Women's Hands, a health care clinic that serves racialized women in Toronto, uncovered racial discrimination as a health risk among young women of colour. This study—which included individual interviews with 81 women, focus groups with 14 women, and nine interviews with self-defined "anti-racist" health care practitioners—found that 29 per cent of the women interviewed described their experience in the health care system as quite negative (Women's Health in Women's Hands, 2003). One in five women reported encountering explicit racism in the form of "cultural insensitivity or ignorance from doctors, name calling or racial slurs, receiving an inferior quality of care and being overcharged for services" (p. 31). Epidemiologist Nancy Krieger (2011) has demonstrated that experiencing racism further harms health. Research also indicates that racism impacts people within the employment sector. The 2016 Labour Force Status Data shows that all racialized groups—except those who identify as Japanese or Filipino—had higher unemployment rates than non-racialized people. Significant variations among racialized communities exist. For example, in comparison to their non-racialized counterparts who have an unemployment rate of 7.3 percent, those who identify as Black and Arab have unemployment rates of 12.5 and 13.5 percent—that's 71 and 85 percent higher than non-racialized Canadians (Statistics Canada, 2016).

This brief snapshot paints a grim picture. The following three case studies—two from Ontario, the most racially diverse province in the country, and one from the federal Parliament—help us to understand more fully how the management of race underlies the logic of Canadian policy. How do "invisible" logics of racialization and racism operate through these policies and political debates? How can the framework of "democratic racism" enrich your analysis?

## Case #1: The Safe Schools Act

In 2001, the Ontario government, led by Conservative Premier Mike Harris, passed the Safe Schools Act (SSA). This Act implemented a policy of "zero tolerance" to violence in schools and formalized a provision for mandatory suspension, mandatory expulsion, and police involvement, with some clauses for mitigating factors. On the surface, the policy depicts "zero tolerance" as a neutral, colour-blind, and fair principle to discipline all students involved in all forms of violence within the schools. Arguably, the public appeal for this Act comes from its no-nonsense approach—it implies that there are no compromises and no tolerance for bad behaviour.

Since its implementation, the policy has come under intense scrutiny for standardizing an approach in addressing the complexities of violence. Critics have questioned whether overall security and safety for students is ensured, and whether the policy has a disproportionate impact on racialized students and students with disabilities. Racialized males, in particular, receive much harsher penalties for their transgressions. In addition, "there is a perception that students from certain racial groups, particularly Black, Tamil, Aboriginal and Latino students, are treated more harshly than other students in the application of discipline for the same offence" (Bhattacharjee, 2003, p. viii). Professionals who implement the Act disagree. In a study involving 16 school personnel in five Ontario public schools, Daniel and Bondy (2008, p. 9) found that those implementing the Act believed "the SSA brought consistency which they equated with fairness although they had some misgivings." They drew upon a discourse of colour-blindness to defend the policy and its impacts.

The Ontario Human Rights Commission (OHRC) found that the implementation of the SSA correlated with an increased number of students with disabilities who were suspended or expelled for their behaviour. The Commission filed complaints against the Ministry of Education and the Toronto School Board, insisting that the Act failed to provide a fair trial or equal rights for all students. In 2007, a landmark settlement was reached with the Ministry of Education to "promote school safety while ensuring that all students, including students with disabilities and racialized students, are given the opportunity to reach their full potential" (OHRC, 2007). In doing so, the ministry confirmed that the concept of "zero tolerance" had no place in educational policy, and committed to a shift towards corrective and supportive discipline.

## Case #2: Carding in Ontario

The Toronto Police Service, specifically its specialized Anti-Violence Intervention Strategy (TAVIS), records information about people that police consider to be of interest in cases of pedestrian and traffic stops. Carding refers to the process of filling out a "208" card with information about the individual who has been stopped. Police defend this carding policy as a valuable documentation and investigation tool that allows them to make crucial connections between people, places, and cases. It implies equality through the process: anyone can be stopped, questioned, and documented. Yet, the nature of this process dictates that carding is a matter of police discretion: "suspicious activity" is subjectively defined.

Residents and critics argue that this practice is a form of racial profiling that allows some racialized communities to be targeted more than others. A *Toronto Star* investigation into race, policing, and crime revealed significant disparity and bias in carding (Rankin, Winsa, Bailey, & Ng, 2013). Proportionately, Toronto police implemented carding at a higher frequency than the stop-and-frisk policies of the New York City police, a similar policy that received immense public outcry and ushered in numerous lawsuits and settlements until it was deemed unconstitutional and an indirect form of racial profiling by a US court.

The *Toronto Star* investigation found that:

- In each of the city's 70-plus patrol zones, Blacks—and to a lesser extent people with "brown" skin—remained more likely than white people to be subjected to police stops that result in no arrest or charges being laid. The likelihood increases for Blacks in areas of the city that are predominantly white.
- The proportion of Blacks stopped and carded in Toronto is three times greater than their share of the city population. In New York, the proportion of Blacks stopped and frisked was 2.3 times greater than their share of that city's population.
- More than half of the people documented between 2008 and 2012 lived in or near the patrol zone where they were stopped. That number increases in at-risk neighbourhoods, where incomes are lower and people less mobile. (Rankin et al., 2013)

Despite public outcry against carding from a range of human rights groups and racialized activists and several lawsuits by individuals and by the Black Action Defence Committee, on 17 November 2016 the Toronto Police Services Board again voted to continue the practice (in a revised form). According to an open letter to the city of Toronto and province of Ontario from Black intellectuals, writers, and organizers, "the decision by the TPSB represents a significant impact on the rights of Black, Indigenous, and Brown people, as well as homeless people and other marginalized people in our Toronto community" (Walcott et al., 2016). They argued that the practice is unconstitutional because it illegally gathers and stores information for an unspecified use. It robs targeted people of their Charter rights and their dignity, freedom of movement, freedom of assembly, and bodily integrity.

## Case #3: Anti-Islamophobia Motion in Parliament

In a Quebec City mosque in January 2017, six Canadian Muslims were murdered and 19 were injured as they worshipped. Dominant discourses debated whether this constituted a terrorist act or a hate crime, and the extent to which this reflected growing anti-Muslim hate. In the wake of this massacre, Liberal MP Iqra Khalid tabled a motion (M-103) to address Islamophobia. This motion called on the federal government to commit to three tasks: recognize the need to "quell the rising public climate of hate and fear; condemn Islamophobia and all forms of systemic racism and religious discrimination;" and "request that the Standing Committee on Canadian Heritage undertake a study" to propose recommendations to address the issue. Because this is not a bill but a motion, it will not change or infringe on existing Canadian laws. It is not the first of its kind: in 2015, a parliamentary motion condemning anti-Semitism was unanimously supported by the federal government to "advance the combating of anti-Semitism as a domestic and international priority."

This anti-Islamophobia motion initiated divisive debates from its opponents. Some called it a "modern-day blasphemy law." Some Conservative politicians, such as MP Maxime Bernier, warned that it will erode free speech. Others have argued that it is the first step towards sharia law. Critics like MP Kellie Leitch also questioned why Islamophobia needs to be named or even mentioned at all. In response, MP David Anderson tabled a motion to instead condemn "all forms of racism, religious intolerance, and discrimination," specifically erasing Islamophobia from the conversation. These actions operate alongside a context where hate crimes against Muslims have doubled over the last three years—the most significant increase of all racialized groups (Statistics Canada cited in Paperny, 2016). Recent polling conducted by the Forum Poll (2016) through random sampling of 1,304 Canadian adults indicates that more Canadians hold biased views of Muslims than of any other group in society.

As a consequence of her motion, Khalid received an onslaught of hate mail and death threats. To contextualize a few of the 50,000 e-mails, many overtly racist messages, she read some in the House of Commons. The following are some of the messages the MP received:

- "Kill her and be done with it. I agree she is here to kill us. She is sick and she needs to be deported."
- "We will burn down your mosques, draper head Muslim."
- "Why did Canadians let her in? Ship her back."
- "Why don't you get out of my country? You're a disgusting piece of trash and you are definitely not wanted here by the majority of actual Canadians." (Harris, 2017).

In March 2017, the motion passed by a vote of 201–91.

# Chapter Summary

This chapter examines how the making of Canada as a white settler society requires constant negotiation of racialization through policy and political debate: who is racialized and how they are included or excluded through policy are political decisions. An overview of key historical examples and key state policies highlights the current context of what Henry and Tator (2009) call "democratic racism," which dominates the potentials and limitations of Canadian social and state policy. When people and institutions assume that they are "colour-blind," the exact opposite is the case. Implicit racist biases disproportionately target racialized people.

Looking again at the case examples at the start of the chapter helps to uncover important dimensions of how these biases operate. Regardless of being welcomed through immigration policy, Keith's credentials and qualifications are not considered equivalent to Canadian credentials and are not recognized. He continually experiences the barrier of "Canadian experience" in the workplace, and ultimately loses his employment due to outsourcing—a growing trend of exporting work to poorer countries with fewer regulations that allow employers to pay "others" around the world less, for the same work, while accruing profit for themselves in Canada. Rohan's ethnicity and the socio-political relationship between Canada and countries marked as exporting potential "terrorists" inform how police view and treat him. He is racially marked as dangerous, and such stereotyping is so ingrained in Canadian culture that it justifies treating him as a threat without any evidence beyond the subjective meanings assigned to his physical characteristics. And the case of Naomi, employed within the university through affirmative action policies, exposes how policies do not necessarily address practices in public or professional contexts. While "whites only" spaces are no longer official policy, in certain contexts they continue to operate implicitly in practice: some are the expected bearers of status and inclusion, and others are not. In the final section of the chapter, case studies highlighting provincial policy and political debates reveal how the discourse of meritocracy, equality, fairness, and other liberal principles cloaks the underlying logic and overwhelming tendency towards racialization and racism in Canadian society.

# Discussion Questions

1. How might "zero-tolerance" policies appear colour-blind but produce racialized effects in practice? What are the structural conditions that might influence this outcome?

2. Whose "safety" and "security" did the Safe Schools Act in Ontario emphasize? Who is excluded from these discourses?

3. How do processes of racial profiling underlie who society has historically and discursively marked as criminal, deviant, risky, and at-risk? Who is the victim and who is the perpetrator?

4. Is an explicit motion denouncing Islamophobia necessary? Why, or why not? How can we interpret Parliament's and the public's hesitancy to support this motion? What are

the broader implications of this public backlash for Muslim people in Canada? For MP Iqra Khalid? For Canada's parliamentary system?

# References

Academic Women's Association, University of Alberta (AWA). (2016, 18 Aug.). The diversity gaps in Canadian university leadership. Retrieved from https://uofaawa.files.wordpress.com/2016/08/awa_diversitygap_cdnuniversityleadership_18aug16fin.pdf

Africville Genealogy Society (AGS). (1992). *The spirit of Africville.* Halifax: Formac Publishing.

Bhattacharjee, K. (2003). *The Ontario Safe Schools Act: School discipline and discrimination.* Retrieved from http://www.ohrc.on.ca/sites/default/files/attachments/The_Ontario_Safe_Schools_Act%3A_School_discipline_and_discrimination.pdf

Canadian Association of University Teachers (CAUT). (2010). The changing academy? *CAUT Education Review, 12,* 1–8. Retrieved from https://www.caut.ca/docs/education-review/the-changing-academy-a-portrait-of-canada-rsquo-s-university-teachers-(jan-2010).pdf?sfvrsn=14

Cooper, A. (2007a). Editorial commentary. *Directions: Research and Policy on Eliminating Racism, 4,* 1 (Summer). Canada Race Relations Foundation.

———. (2007b, 25 Mar.). The invisible history of the slave trade. *Toronto Star.* Retrieved from https://www.thestar.com/opinion/2007/03/25/the_invisible_history_of_the_slave_trade.html

Daniel, Y., & Bondy, K. (2008). Safe schools and zero tolerance: Policy, program and practice in Ontario. *Canadian Journal of Educational Administration and Policy, 70.* Retrieved from https://www.umanitoba.ca/publications/cjeap/pdf_files/daniel.pdf

Environics Institute for Survey Research. (2016). *Survey of Muslims in Canada, 2016.* Retrieved from http://www.environicsinstitute.org/uploads/institute-projects/survey%20of%20muslims%20in%20canada%202016%20-%20final%20report.pdf

Forum Research Inc. (2016). Muslims the target of most racial bias. Retrieved from http://poll.forumresearch.com/data/d54592bb-24e1-46df-bfd2-3d6e28710839Fed%20Racism%20Release%202016%2012%2008%20(AM).pdf

Galabuzi, G. E. (2006). *Canada's economic apartheid: The social exclusion of racialized groups in the new century.* Toronto: Canadian Scholars' Press.

Goonewardena, K., & Kipfer, S. (2005). Spaces of difference: Reflections from Toronto on multiculturalism, bourgeois urbanism and the possibility of radical urban politics. *International Journal of Urban and Regional Research, 29*(3), 670–8.

Government of Canada. (2017). Your guide to the Canadian Charter of Rights and Freedoms. Retrieved from https://www.canada.ca/en/canadian-heritage/services/how-rights-protected/guide-canadian-charter-rights-freedoms.html

Griffith, A. (2016). Diversity among federal and provincial judges. *Policy Options.* Retrieved from http://policyoptions.irpp.org/2016/05/04/diversity-among-federal-provincial-judges/

Harris, K. (2017, 6 Feb.). "Kill her and be done with it": MP behind Islamophobia motion reads out hate mail. *CBC News.* Retrieved from http://www.cbc.ca/news/politics/threats-hate-islamophobia-khalid-1.398656

Hawkins, F. (1991). *Critical years in immigration: Canada and Australia compared* (2nd edn). Montreal & Kingston: McGill-Queen's University Press.

Henry, F., & Tator, C. (2009). *The colour of democracy: Racism in Canadian society* (4th edn). Toronto: Nelson Thomson.

Kelley, N., & Trebilcock, M. J. (2010). *The making of a mosaic: A history of Canadian immigration policy.* Toronto: University of Toronto Press.

Krieger, N. (2011). *Epidemiology and the people's health.* Oxford: Oxford University Press.

Loo, T. (2010). Africville and the dynamics of state power in postwar Canada. *Acadiensis, 39*(2), 23–47.

Mackey, E. (2002). *The house of difference: Cultural politics and national identity in Canada.* Toronto: University of Toronto Press.

Mullings, D. (2009). The paradox exclusion within equity: Interrogating discourse at the Canadian Human Rights Tribunal. *Theses and Dissertations (Comprehensive).* Paper 1069.

Nelson, J. J. (2002). The space of Africville: Creating, regulating and remembering the urban "slum."

In S. Razack (Ed.), *Race, space, and the law: Unmapping a white settler society* (pp. 211–31). Toronto: Between the Lines.

———. (2008). *Razing Africville: A geography of racism.* Toronto: University of Toronto Press.

———. (2011). "Panthers or thieves": Racialized knowledge and the regulation of Africville. *Journal of Canadian Studies, 45*(1), 121–42.

Ontario Human Rights Commission (OHRC). (2007, 13 Apr.). Human rights settlement reached with the Ministry of Education on safe schools. Retrieved from http://www.ohrc.on.ca/en/ resources/news/backgroundedsettlement

Paperny, A. M. (2016, 13 Apr.). Hate crimes against Muslim-Canadians more than doubled in 3 years. *Global News.* Retrieved from http:// globalnews.ca/news/2634032/hate-crimes-against-muslim-canadians-more-than-doubled-in-3-years/

Rankin, J., Winsa, P., Bailey, A., & Ng, H. (2013, 27 Sept.). As criticism piles up, so do the police cards. *Toronto Star.* Retrieved from https:// www.thestar.com/news/gta/knowntopo-lice2013/2013/09/27/as_criticism_piles_up_so_do_the_police_cards.html

Razack, S. (2007). "Your client has a profile": Race and national security in Canada after 9/11. *Studies in Law, Politics and Society, 40,* 3–40.

Robinson, G. (2010). A tragedy of democracy: Japanese confinement in North America. *Journal of Transnational American Studies, 2*(1).

Statistics Canada. (2016). Labour Force Status. Statistics Canada Catalogue number 98-400-X2016286. Ottawa. Retrieved from: https://www12.statcan.gc.ca/census-recensement/2016/dp-pd/dt-td/Rp-eng.cfm? TABID=1&LANG= E&A=R&APATH=3& DETAIL=0&DIM=0&FL=A&FREE=0& GC=01&GL=-1&GID=1341679&GK=1& GRP=1&O=D&PID=110692&PRID=10& PTYPE=109445&S=0&SHOWALL=0& SUB=0&Temporal=2017&THEME=124&

VID=0&VNAMEE=&VNAMEF=&D1=0& D2=0&D3=0&D4=0&D5=0&D6=0

Sunahara, A. G. (1981). *The politics of racism: The uprooting of Japanese Canadians during the Second World War.* Toronto: James Lorimer.

Tanovich, D. (2008). The Charter of whiteness: Twenty-five years of maintaining racial injustice in the Canadian criminal justice system. *Supreme Court Law Review, 40,* 655–86.

Thobani, S. (2007). *Exalted subjects: Studies in the making of race and nation in Canada.* Toronto: University of Toronto Press.

Thompson, C. A. (1979). *Blacks in deep snow: Black pioneers in Canada.* Don Mills, ON: J. M. Dent & Sons (Canada) Limited.

Tolley, E. (2015, 26 Nov.). Visible minority and Indigenous members of Parliament. *The Samara Blog: Political News.* Retrieved from http://www.samaracanada.com/samarablog/ blog-post/samara-main-blog/2015/11/26/ visible-minority-and-indigenous-members-of-parliament

Walcott, R., et al. (2016, 23 Nov.). Carding: An open letter to the City of Toronto and Province of Ontario from Black intellectuals, writers and organizers. *The Rabble.* Retrieved from http://rabble.ca/blogs/bloggers/views-expressed/2016/11/carding-open-letter-to-city-toronto-and-province-ontario-blac

Walker, J. W. S. (1985). *Racial discrimination in Canada: The Black experience.* Historical booklet no. 41. Ottawa: Canadian Historical Association.

Winks, R. (1997). *The Blacks in Canada: A history.* Montreal & Kingston: McGill-Queen's University Press.

Women's Health in Women's Hands. (2003). *Racial discrimination as a health risk for female youth.* Toronto: Canadian Race Relations Foundation.

Wood, P. K., & Gilbert, L. (2005). Multiculturalism in Canada: Accidental discourse, alternate vision, urban practice. *International Journal of Urban and Regional Research, 29*(3), 679–91.

# 8 Women, Intersecting Oppressions, and Social Policy in Canada

*Marjorie Johnstone and Daphne Jeyapal*

---

### Chapter Objectives

*This chapter will help you to develop an understanding of:*
- dominant discourses, social realities, and material constraints constructing the fight for and against women's equality;
- a gender-based analysis of the intersecting oppressions women experience in Canadian society;
- historical and contemporary social policies impeding and addressing women's fight for equality and equity;
- the context of women's struggles through a detailed examination of the conditions of child care, reproductive justice, and violence against women.

---

## Introduction

In contrast to nations around the world, dominant public discourses construct Canada as a country where women and men are equal. Prime Minister Justin Trudeau has identified as a feminist and has introduced visible symbols of this position. At the 2016 World Economic Forum in Davos, Switzerland, he identified poverty as a feminist issue; he has launched an inquiry into missing and murdered Indigenous women and girls (MMIWG); he promoted acceptance of the burkini following a ban declared by 15 towns in France; he appointed women to half of his cabinet and announced that the next series of Canadian banknotes in 2018 will feature a woman (Sathish, 2016). Why is his position notable? Does feminism still matter? Moreover, have we achieved the state of equality that dominant discourses and our PM's rhetoric lead us to believe?

As this chapter explores the role of social policy in Canadian women's lives, we define what we mean by the term "woman." **Essentialism** is the idea that any individual can be identified by characteristics of the group. In the context of distinguishing between a man and woman this means that having common genitalia makes us the same. To move beyond essentialism, it is useful to consider *sex* and *gender*. **Sex** refers to the biological differences between men and women—the assumption used to be that this was fixed at birth, but variants within this constructed dichotomy are possible and common. On the other hand, **gender** expresses what is socially and culturally constructed about the nature of femininity and masculinity. It refers to the social expectations around what it means to be a woman or a man—how a woman or a man should perform at work, as a parent, in politics, religion, relationships, and education. These gendered assumptions underpin the complexities of people's lived experiences, regardless of their biological or identified gender.

For the discourse of equality to be accurate, the social status between genders, including their treatment by law and custom, must be the same. For sociologists, **equality** is defined as equal status in measurements of population data in areas such as life expectancy, income, education, and employment opportunities. Yet, many important aspects of women's lives are controlled by law and regulation. For example, laws regarding marriage, divorce, property rights, and political rights shape the lives of women (Marsden, 2012).

Furthermore, women's lives intersect with multiple systems of social inequality. **Intersectionality** is a conceptual tool that allows us to consider how identities can be connected in complex ways. For example, a single identity might include such social categories as queer, Indigenous, trans, able-bodied, racialized, immigrant, educated, poor, and young. But as Kimberlé Crenshaw highlighted when she coined the term "intersectionality," no one has a single identity, and no one lives a single-issue life. Black women, for example, are oppressed because of both their gender and their race, among a myriad of other social factors; this creates complex social realities. The term **positionality** is often used to describe our location in a community and this might include class, nationality, citizenship, gender, religion, level of education, and employment status. Drawing upon the theory of intersectionality allows us to forefront that "the multiplicity and diversity of experiences and social locations, or positionalities is central to analysis" (Bromley, 2012, p. 49). This chapter incorporates an intersectional analysis of discourses, experiences, and categories of women, including Indigenous, racialized, trans, queer, disabled, and poor women to unpack where women stand in Canadian society and the role social policy plays in their lives.

---

## Case Examples    The Intersectionality of Women's Lived Experience

These brief snapshots show how policies can have different consequences for different segments of the population, and in these cases we show how some policies particularly influence the quality of women's lives.

**Joann**, 50, is the mother of three children aged 5, 8, and 14. She is the first woman in her family in four generations who has not been forced to attend a residential school, and has raised her own children. However, like many women at some point in their lives, Joann is in an abusive relationship. She has sustained permanent injuries from physical abuse, and has attempted to leave her violent husband on several occasions. Joann's sister feared for Joann's life and encouraged her to call the RCMP for protection after the last violent incident, but based on previous interactions Joann decided she was more fearful of the RCMP

*continued*

than her husband. Now, Joann is trying to access a shelter but because she wants to leave with her children—one of whom is a teenage boy—she is unable to find a space that will provide them with temporary shelter. She faces the choice of separating from her children, separating her children, or remaining in her increasingly violent relationship.

**Suzanne**, 36, raises two children in a major metropolitan city and is a manager at a recruitment company. Despite working there for 12 years, her employers have consistently overlooked her for promotions, and she earns substantially less than her male counterparts at the same location. As the only lesbian at her job, she is often the only person not invited to work parties and networking after hours. As a lone mother, Suzanne often finds herself going into debt to cover her monthly child-care costs along with her other bills. She lives paycheque to paycheque, and worries constantly about making ends meet.

**Melissa**, 25, lives in New Brunswick in a religious and conservative family. Melissa recently found out from a home pregnancy test that she is pregnant. She is terrified to inform her family as she knows they will insist she have the child, although she does not want to. Melissa knows she will need to leave the province to access a safe abortion without fear of ostracism or shame, but as a student she does not have the money to cover the cost of the trip and the procedure. Out of desperation and lack of support, she accesses unlicensed and unsafe termination options herself using online resources.

# Where Are We Today?

After centuries of struggle, women today have the right to vote, and have rights to education, political representation, property, and health, including reproductive health. Yet, we know there are ongoing discrepancies. **Discrepancies** are the differences between the ratio of a particular group to the total population and the representation of that group (in this case, women) in an identified circumstance, such as poverty, victims of assault, or victims of domestic homicide, that suggests inequality. Table 8.1 highlights existing gender discrepancies across a spectrum of social, economic, and political markers. While the authors acknowledge that more than two genders exist, we are limited to this binary analysis due to limitations on how national statistics are collected and compiled.

As this table indicates, despite dominant discourses suggesting that men and women are equal, significant gender discrepancies exist between men and women in Canada. Women earn less, have lower rates of representation in politics, occupy fewer political leadership positions, are over-represented in low-paying occupations, and face more precarious employment.

Paradoxically, dominant discourses state otherwise. Popular false beliefs that women are equal in Canadian society have resulted in **backlash**. You recognize backlash when you hear that "if you haven't made it it's because you weren't good enough or you didn't try hard enough"—in other words, it's your fault. This discourse of meritocracy suggests that there is nothing structural or systemic holding you back. Backlash is built on myths such as: there is no more racism now (Barack Obama, after all, became the President of the United States); and women and men have equal opportunity in politics, and women

**Table 8.1**  Gender Discrepancies between Men and Women in Canada

|  | Men | Women |
| --- | --- | --- |
| Average earnings | In 2008, average total income was $47,000 (Statistics Canada, 2011). In 2008, male lone parents made an average of $60,400 (Statistics Canada, 2011). In 2015, men made $29.86 per hour (*The Daily*, 2017) | In 2008, average total income was $30,100 (Statistics Canada, 2011). In 2008, female lone parents made, on average, $42,300 (Statistics Canada, 2011). In 2015, women made $26.11 per hour (*The Daily*, 2017) |
| Participation in politics | In 2013, 24 per cent of men were interested in politics (Turcotte, 2015). In 2013, just as likely to vote in federal election (Turcotte, 2015). In 2013, just as likely to protest (Turcotte, 2015). In 2013, 17 per cent of men attended a public meeting (Turcotte, 2015). | In 2013, 16 per cent of women were interested in politics (Turcotte, 2015). In 2013, just as likely to vote in federal election (Turcotte, 2015). In 2013, just as likely to protest (Turcotte, 2015). In 2013, 13 per cent of women attended a public meeting (Turcotte, 2015). |
| Political leadership roles | In 2011, total number of seats in House of Commons was 308. Seats occupied were 232 (*CBC News*, 2015). In 2015, total number of seats in House of Commons was 338. Seats occupied were 250 (*CBC News*, 2015). | In 2011, total number of seats in House of Commons was 308. Seats occupied were 76 (*CBC News*, 2015). In 2015, total number of seats in House of Commons was 338. Seats occupied were 88 (*CBC News*, 2015). |
| Representation in the professions | In 2015, 17.1 per cent of men occupied positions in teaching, nursing and related health occupations, social work, clerical or other administrative positions, or sales and services (*The Daily*, 2017). In 2015, 75.6 per cent of men were employed in science, technology, engineering, and math (STEM) occupations (*The Daily*, 2017). Over-represented in high-paying occupations, under-represented in low-paying occupations (*The Daily*, 2017). | In 2015, 56.1 per cent of women occupied positions in teaching, nursing and related health occupations, social work, clerical or other administrative positions, or sales and services (*The Daily*, 2017). In 2015, 24.4 per cent of women were employed in science, technology, engineering, and math (STEM) occupations (*The Daily*, 2017). Over-represented in low-paying occupations, under-represented in high-paying occupations (*The Daily*, 2017). |
| Part-time employment | In 2012, representation (per thousands) was 1,082.3 (Statistics Canada, n.d.A). In 2016, representation (per thousands) was 1,191.8 (Statistics Canada, n.d.A). In 2016, part-time work for "Goods Producing Sector" $21.32 (Statistics Canada, n.d.B). In 2016, part-time work for "Services Producing Sector" was $16.52 (Statistics Canada, n.d.B). | In 2012, representation (per thousands) was 2,222.4 (Statistics Canada, n.d.A). In 2016, representation (per thousands) was 2,275.9 (Statistics Canada, n.d.A). In 2016, part-time work for "Goods Producing Sector" $19.12 (Statistics Canada, n.d.B). In 2016, part-time work for "Services Producing Sector" was $18.33 (Statistics Canada, n.d.B). |
| Life expectancy | 2009–11, adult mortality (average age) is 79 (Martel, 2013). | 2009–11, adult mortality (average age) is 84 (Martel, 2013). |

can hold top political office if they are good enough (Kim Campbell was Prime Minister of Canada, and numerous women have been provincial premiers). These arguments are constructed to prove that feminism is founded on falsehoods, and that feminists persist in striving for equality that has already happened (Bromley, 2012).

Backlash alerts us to social resistance to change. For some, backlash represents a wish to maintain the status quo and complacency about current power relations. For others, it is an indicator of patriarchal and misogynist resistance—women gaining true equality means sharing power with people who have held it as an unquestioned right for a long time. Even the term "feminist" has been disparaged through this backlash and is now often represented as a woman who is deviant. Backlash is sustained through discourses of female inferiority, male superiority, racism, homophobia, victim blaming, slut shaming, and fat shaming, all of which construct women as responsible for their own oppression in a world of equality. These discourses must be contextualized within women's centuries-long struggle for social, economic, and political inclusion.

## A Brief Review of the Successes and Failures of Canada's Gender Inclusion

Patriarchy was dominant at the time of Confederation in 1867. This included the prevalent belief that women did not have the intellectual capacity to reason, learn, or benefit from education, were unfit to participate in political life, and were unable to own property; thus, when the law referred to "persons" it did not include women. This public discourse influenced the policies put in place. Only men were eligible to vote, own property, or go to university, and only men could become lawyers, doctors, ministers, or politicians and attend post-secondary institutions (Bromley, 2012; Marsden, 2012; Prentice et al., 1988). Women began to challenge patriarchy as early as the 1600s but collective resistance began in the late nineteenth and early twentieth centuries. Scholars categorize the progression of this movement in three waves.

First-wave feminism (1900–46) was characterized by a fight for political rights—the right to vote, pursue higher education, own property, and hold political office. Second-wave feminism (1960–90), which became known as the women's liberation movement, was characterized by a fight for equal rights in all areas of public and private life—gender roles at home, the sexual division of labour in the workplace, and control over their bodies (Bromley, 2012; Tong, 2014).

The belief that "the personal is political" was central to second-wave feminism and marked a shift in women's consciousness from seeing the problem as individual and discrete to seeing it as political. Women's activism resulted in the Royal Commission on the Status of Women (RCSW) of 1970, which documented women's economic, social, and political oppression and thus made it part of the public record. The Commission reported that only 3 per cent of managers were women and that although there were equal pay laws in eight of the 10 provinces, women were paid less than men for doing the same work. In addition, two-thirds of people on welfare were women. The RCSW made 167 wide-ranging recommendations to give women and men equal opportunities, including maternity leave, equal training opportunities, birth control, pensions, daycare, and educational opportunities (Prentice et al., 1988). In 1971, the federal government appointed a Minister for the Status of Women. The Canadian Advisory Council on the Status of Women (CACSW) was set up in 1973, and in 1976 this organization became the government-funded advisory council to the Minister for the Status of Women.

Beginning in the 1980s, women who were not white, heterosexual, middle class, and able challenged the relevance of the women's liberation movement to their lives; this began third-wave feminism. Intersectionality and the understanding of difference through class, ethnicity, sexual orientation, age, and ability became central parts of the movement (Bromley, 2012; Tong, 2014). Many of the achievements of the women's movement were earned by and for white women. Indigenous and racialized women have had a much longer struggle to be recognized within state and social policy.

Despite dominant discourses of gender equality, women are still disadvantaged in Canada, and the role of social policy is central to their marginalization. The following case studies examine three areas of social policy, as they construct the complexity of women's lived experience at home, at work, and within society more broadly. We consider how the politics of neo-liberalism, class, race, and sexuality intersect through each case study.

---

## Box 8.1  Timeline of Canadian Women's Fight for Equality

| | |
|---|---|
| **1825** | Ladies Coloured Fugitive Association (Black women helping refugee slaves). |
| **1893** | National Council of Women (predominantly Caucasian membership) founded in Toronto. |
| **1916–19** | Women win the vote in Manitoba, Alberta, Saskatchewan, BC, Ontario, Nova Scotia, New Brunswick, and Yukon. |
| **1918** | Federal government granted the right to vote to Caucasian women. |
| **1921** | First white woman elected to House of Commons (Agnes Macphail). |
| **1929** | Women were ruled legally persons by the Supreme Court of Canada. |
| **1945** | Canada signed and ratified the United Nations Charter. |
| **1947** | Chinese Canadians and Indo-Canadian women gain the vote; Canada signs the UN Charter of Rights. |
| **1948** | Canada signed the Universal Declaration of Human Rights (which was drafted by a Canadian). |
| **1948** | Japanese-Canadian women gain the right to vote. |
| **1960** | Status Indigenous women gain the right to vote. |
| **1972** | National Action Committee on the Status of Women (SWC) formed. |
| **1972** | First Canadian Black woman elected to political office (Rosemary Brown, who served 14 years as an NDP MLA in the BC provincial legislature). |
| **1973** | Canadian Women's Negro Association held first National Conference of Black Women. |
| **1973** | Native Women's Association of Canada founded. |
| **1987** | Canadian Armed Forces dropped its prohibition on women in active service. |
| **1988** | Federal law on abortion was invalidated by section 7 of the Charter. |
| **2006** | Prime Minister Harper's Conservative government shut down 12 of 16 regional offices of the Status of Women Canada and reduced the budget by $5 million. |

# Case #1: The Crisis in Child Care: Redefining Family and Equity in the Labour Market

Over the past few decades, women's part-time, contract, and service-sector employment has increased and more women are working multiple jobs to try to make ends meet. Today, only one in five mothers with children under five years old does not work outside the home. Few women can afford stay-at-home mother/parenting and this has created a crisis for affordable, high-quality, non-parental child care, and yet there is no federal discussion about a national public child-care strategy (Albanese & Rauhala, 2015; Friendly, 1994; Mahon, 2009). The Canadian government instead frames it as an issue of "choice" or a private matter. The lack of affordable, accessible child care is particularly pertinent to women.

Feminists use the term **social reproduction**, originated by the nineteenth-century theorist Karl Marx, to separate the physiological process of bearing children from the social, physical, emotional, and material processes involved in caring for children. A related concept is **social provisioning**, which describes caring work as rearing children and also caring for those who are sick, disabled, elderly, or dying. This unpaid work is primarily done by women, and while it's a crucial part of the economy it is not recognized as such (Neysmith et al., 2012; Rice & Prince, 2013). Classical economics only discusses paid labour (Waring, 1988). The gendered idea that families (i.e., women) are best suited to caring for children and other dependants is widespread in Canadian social policies and this is particularly clear in the case of child care.

The prevalence of dual-earning families is steadily increasing. In 2014, 69 per cent of couple families with at least one child under 16 were dual-earner families compared to only 36 per cent in 1976. In this same period the percentage of lone-parent families doubled and the majority of these were lone-mother families (Uppal, 2015). The median after-tax income for lone-mother families is $27,554 (Milan, 2015), and Ferns and Friendly (2014) report that the average cost of parent fees for child care is $9,132 annually. While this amount varies among provinces and territories and according to the age and needs of the children, common sense suggests this is an enormous sum of money for a dual-income family to pay, never mind a lone-mother family. Child-care space is also a significant problem. In 2012, there were full- or part-time centre-based child-care spaces for only 22.5 per cent of Canadian children aged 0–5 years. The labour force participation rate for women in 2012 was 69.7 per cent for mothers whose youngest child was 0–2 years, 76.6 per cent for mothers with a child 3–5 years, and 84 per cent for those whose youngest child was 6–15 years (Ferns & Friendly, 2014). Thus there are long waiting lists for child care and many families must confront the problem of the unavailability of regulated child care. Women are primarily responsible for managing the care of their children, making daily sacrifices to balance work and child care. They have to skip lunch, lose wages, take on challenging shifts, and reduce the number of hours they work to juggle paid work and child care (Albanese & Rauhala, 2015). If women across Canada are confronting these issues daily, why haven't we addressed this pressing, but surely solvable, social problem?

A glimpse into our history provides context to this issue. Historically, child care has been viewed as a private responsibility and not part of the public good, i.e., the responsibility of families, not the government. Child-care policies have been formulated using the *male breadwinner model*, which assumes that families have heterosexual parents and the father supports the family through earnings from paid employment, while women/wives are full-time mothers and homemakers. However, even at the turn of the twentieth century, poor working-class women contributed to the family economy through home-based work such as washing laundry, sewing, and taking in boarders so they could supervise their children and earn money simultaneously. In the absence of government programs, charitable services established crèches to provide child care for less affluent women who engaged in domestic service or factory work, and many of the settlement programs offered child care for newly arrived immigrants (Prentice et al., 1988).

During World War II, in the absence of men, women entered the workforce and this created a child-care crisis. For the first time, the federal government created public child care with the 1943 Dominion–Provincial Day Nurseries Agreement. After the war, the federal government terminated that funding agreement in 1946, arguing that child care was not a peacetime concern. Women, including social workers such as Bessie Touzel, protested this cut to child-care services and they were condemned as being socialist agitators (Johnstone, 2015; Prentice, 1992).

A patchwork of provincial child-care programs, which do not meet the needs of children or of working parents, particularly working mothers, has operated since the end of the federal child-care program. In 1945 universal family allowances, which still fell short of covering the expense of child care, were introduced. Through the 1966 Canada Assistance Plan (CAP) the federal government contributed to the provinces half of the funding to support social service delivery, but in 1996 CAP was replaced with Canada Health and Social Transfer (CHST), which reduced funding from the federal government to the provinces.

The Royal Commission on the Status of Women (1970) recommended that the federal government set up and manage a universal system of child care but these recommendations were never acted on, and so in the 1980s a well-organized pan-Canadian child-care advocacy movement developed to continue pushing for public child care (Friendly, 1994). In the 1990s there was a discursive shift from viewing child care as a woman's issue to an exclusive focus on the child. Ending child poverty (ignoring the fact that poor children have poor mothers) and providing early education became the focus. Women's needs were discursively written out of the child-care debate (Dobrowolsky & Jenson, 2004). The universal family allowance benefit was replaced with the Child Tax Benefit (1993), an income tax claim for child-care expenses. This meant that those who were poor and paid little income tax were disadvantaged as they didn't have the income tax dollars to claim exemption (Mahon, 2009). In the early 2000s, resulting from advocacy work led by the Childcare Advocacy Association of Canada and more moderate social inclusivity policy approaches, three federal/provincial/territorial agreements were passed: the Early Childhood Development Agreement (ECDA) (2000); the Multilateral Framework Agreement on Early Learning and Child Care (2003); and the Bilateral Agreements-in-Principle on Early Learning and Childcare (2005).

These agreements provided optimism that some child-care issues would be addressed. However, in 2006, the Conservative government of Prime Minister Stephen Harper cancelled the agreements and introduced the Universal Child Care Benefit (UCCB) and the Child Care Spaces Initiative (CCSI). The UCCB provided $100 per month per child as a taxable benefit to families with children under the age of six, and the CCSI provided financial incentives for the creation of 25,000 new child-care spaces (Findlay, 2015).

The UCCB returns Canada to the male breadwinner/stay-at-home-mother family model. Yet, it was framed through the neo-liberal discourse of "choice" for women: using the $100 to allow choice between paying for child care or providing it themselves. The CCSI began as a plan to provide financial incentives to business to build 25,000 new spaces, but when this was critiqued by universal child-care activists, the funds were rolled into the Canada Social Transfer, where no accountability exists for the provinces and territories to allocate the funds to child care. For mothers, particularly single mothers such as Suzanne in the Case Examples box, providing trustworthy child care is financially prohibitive and further widens the inequity between women and men. Suzanne, after all, is unable to do overtime or "be flexible" and is thus less likely to be promoted or advanced in her career. Neither the UCCB nor the CCSI has improved the availability of regulated child care, lowered fees for parents, or improved wages for early childhood educators (Findlay, 2015). These policies have collectively led to the child-care crisis. In a 25-country study by UNICEF that ranked early childhood education and care (ECEC) access and quality, Canada was tied with Ireland for last place, achieving only one of 10 benchmarks (Adamson, 2008).

---

**Box 8.2**    Canada's Live-in Caregiver Program (LCP):
An Exploitative "Solution" to the Child-Care Crisis?

---

Soon after Confederation, Canada began recruiting British women as live-in domestic servants, but after World War I demand exceeded supply and Canada turned to non-preferred countries in Eastern Europe and the Caribbean. Black women from the Caribbean were paid half as much as their white counterparts and had no possibility of citizenship. After World War II, as more white women entered the workforce (racialized women had always been in the workforce), the demand for nannies increased and a second domestic scheme was negotiated by Canada with Jamaica and Barbados that allowed landed immigrant status. In 1973 the Temporary Employment Authorization Program replaced citizenship status with a temporary work visa. This precipitated feminist and LCP activism, and in 1981 the Foreign Domestic Movement allowed landed immigrant status after two years of domestic service. In 1992 this was amended again to the Live-in-Caregiver Program, which conditionally allows some an application for landed immigrant status after two years of indentured service. The live-in requirement was repealed in 2014, following much critique from advocates on the prevalence of economic, physical, and sexual abuse women were facing from their employers. Currently over half of live-in caregivers come from the Philippines.

The shortage of child-care options in Canada makes the LCP program attractive to middle- and upper-class Canadian women who can employ racialized women to provide child care and social provisioning services. Economic insecurity motivates migrant women to accept low-wage precarious labour so they can have the opportunity to compete for permanent citizenship and earn remittances. The social policies in sending and receiving countries foster and regulate this migration through application processes, entry requirements, duration, and types of stay (Lee & Johnstone, 2013). This program is an example of the neo-liberal push to privatize child care as a personal responsibility and highlights the inequity of gender, citizenship, race, and class.

# Case #2: Reproductive Justice

Is abortion an issue of a women's right to decide what happens to her body? Is it an issue of social justice? Or is it a medical issue? The United Nations organized the International Conference on Population and Development in Cairo in 1994, and 20,000 delegates from governments, UN agencies, and NGOs discussed a range of population issues including reproductive health and rights. Their benchmark declaration stated that "all couples and individuals have the basic right to decide freely and responsibly the number and spacing of their children and to have the information, education and means to do so" (International Conference on Population and Development, 1994, p. 12). We adopt the term "reproductive justice" since it puts activism for reproductive rights within broader social justice movements and recognizes the intersecting identities women have in relation to class, race, sexual orientation, ability, language, religion, relationship status, age, immigration status, and national origin and the inequality that exists in access to reproductive health care programs (Chrisler, 2014).

## Social Policy Change in Action

### A Social Work Narrative

*by Notisha Massaquoi*

*Notisha Massaquoi is currently the Executive Director of Women's Health in Women's Hands Community Health Centre for Black Women and Women of Colour in Toronto. In 2012 Notisha Massaquoi was awarded the Amina Malko Award for women who have made a significant contribution in policy, advocacy, and settlement services for newcomers. This is her story in her own words.*

I am currently the Executive Director of Women's Health in Women's Hands Community Health Centre (WHIWH-CHC) in Toronto, which has the distinction of being the only health centre in Canada specializing in primary health care for racialized women. As a child I immigrated with my family from Sierra Leone to a small community in Newfoundland, where my parents were recruited to work as medical professionals. Ironically, while they were providing medical care to underserviced communities in Newfoundland, as the first Black immigrants to the area we were provided no supports as we navigated our settlement process. From this experience I have always been committed to work that improves access to health care for immigrant, refugee, and racialized communities in Canada.

Shortly after completing my MSW in 1997 at the University of Toronto Inwentash Faculty of Social Work, I joined WHIWH-CHC as a Program Manager in 1998 and later, in 2006, became the Executive Director. From my 20 years at the centre it is clear that the women with the most pressing health care needs are those who are undocumented (living in Canada without immigration status, precarious immigration status, or caught in different stages of the immigration or refugee process without status) and, therefore, not afforded the same rights to universal health care that Canadian citizens enjoy. Prior to 2009 their Canadian-born children were also denied universal health coverage—these children did

*continued*

not receive Canadian citizenship at birth because their mothers were undocumented and most often afraid to challenge the system for fear of deportation.

WHIWH-CHC has a long history of working with communities to effect policy change and I was able to draw on our collective organizational experience. A strategy was developed with a legal aid clinic to educate our undocumented clients as part of their prenatal care. When you give birth in Canada the hospital opens a file and assigns the baby a number. Women were educated to ask for this number and told it could not be withheld due to their lack of immigration status, which had been a standard practice. With this number, women were then instructed on how to register the birth of the baby, which enabled them to get a birth certificate and then a social insurance number and Canadian passport for the baby. If women experienced any challenges our staff would advocate to ensure the process went smoothly. We did this for hundreds of women while we lobbied MPs and MPPs, city councillors, and hospitals. We educated other community health centres to ensure that all children of undocumented mothers were being registered at hospitals, which meant they could receive health care and all other services and benefits of Canadian citizenship.

After nine years of intense work, the Citizenship Act was amended and children born in Canada, regardless of the immigration status of their parents, could receive Canadian citizenship. In 2012 I was very proud to be awarded the Amina Malko Award for women who have made a significant contribution in policy, advocacy, and settlement services for newcomers, but I am even prouder of the many undocumented women who, despite the risks, lobbied and advocated collectively with our CHC for their Canadian-born children to be treated simply as if they mattered in our country.

Currently, much of the activism for reproductive justice centres on the pro-choice movement, which demands that women should have full control of decisions regarding their reproductive health and function. The pro-life position revolves around the issue of fetal rights and supports the criminalization of abortion. Indigenous activist-academic Andrea Smith (2005, p. 125) asserts that the criminalization of abortion marginalizes poor women, racialized women, women with disabilities, and other groups of marginalized women: "given the disproportionate impact of criminalization on communities of color, support for criminalization as public policy also implicitly supports racism." Smith argues that the criminalization of abortion is a flawed approach to address a social problem by pointing out that abortion is a difficult decision for women (confronted more often by poor women), who must weigh what's best for the child now and in the future.

### When Was Abortion Illegal?

Abortion has not been a criminal offence in Canada since 1988 (Siobhan-Reid, Kieran, Cawthorne & Arthur, 2016). In 2014 there were 81,897 abortions performed in Canada, 33,931 in hospitals and 47,966 in clinics (Canadian Institute for Health Information, 2014). Although there is no legal limit on the age a fetus may be aborted, it is medically advised that abortion be completed before 20 or 22 weeks. Thus, 89.4 per cent were completed within the first 12 weeks of gestation and only a small number (<.86 per cent) were provided after 20 weeks of gestation (Siobhan-Reid et al., 2016).

In the nineteenth century, a pregnancy was not confirmed until the fetus had "quickened"—meaning there had been movement in the womb, which usually occurs in the fourth month. Until that time, women believed they were experiencing irregular periods and would seek medication available in pharmaceutical stores to regulate their periods. Following Confederation, scattered anti-abortion provincial laws became national criminal law. Despite this, white middle-class women limited the number of children they had through birth control measures (coitus interruptus, douches, sheaths, abstinence, and abortion) but feminists did not take a public position on birth control until the 1920s (Backhouse, 1991).

In 1969 a Criminal Law Amendment Act was passed to allow abortions when the health of a woman was in danger, as determined by a three-doctor therapeutic abortion committee (TAC). The TAC process proved to be a hornet's nest of inconsistencies, as there were variations in provincial requirements, hospitals were not mandated to have a committee, and the concept of health was not defined. Race and class biases among medical professionals were also rampant. Women sought psychiatric support to meet gatekeeping health requirements and Catholic hospitals opted out (Sethna & Doull, 2012).

In 1970, the women's movement organized their first national action—the abortion caravan—to protest these inequities. Beginning in Vancouver, they travelled to Ottawa and marched on Parliament Hill. At Prime Minister Pierre Elliott Trudeau's residence they left a coffin draped in the Canadian flag on his doorstep. The coffin represented all women who had died from illegal abortions. The following day they returned to the House of Commons and chained themselves to chairs in the galleries. The police took 10 women to the police station and later released them without charges. Following media coverage of the incident, the Vancouver Women's Caucus met with Trudeau and demanded (unsuccessfully) that the 1969 abortion law be repealed (Rebick, 2005). In 1975, the Badgley Committee was appointed to investigate the process for getting a therapeutic abortion. It reported that only 20.1 per cent of accredited hospitals had TACs. The average wait time was eight weeks, and in the year 1974, 11,194 Canadian women had abortions in the US. Wide discrepancies between the provinces revealed some TACs had requirements such as parental notification, and some refused requests while others accepted many. This resulted in abortion tourism within Canada as well as to more liberal countries (Sethna & Doull, 2012).

## The Decriminalization of Abortion

In defiance of the law, Dr Henry Morgentaler began performing abortions in his Montreal clinic without TAC approvals. On two occasions, the Quebec government took Morgentaler to court but he was acquitted, despite his public announcement that he had performed 5,000 abortions. After 15 years of operating private abortion clinics, in 1984 Morgentaler appealed to the Supreme Court of Canada. In 1988 the Court ruled that the anti-abortion law was unconstitutional as it violated the Canadian Charter of Rights and Freedoms.

Since decriminalization, abortion is categorized as a medical procedure and as such it is governed by the Canada Health Act, which states that medically necessary physicians and health services must be funded. However, the legislation does not define the terms "medically necessary" and "medically required." Thus, there is latitude for a wide variation between provinces and hospitals on responding to a request for abortion. Negotiations between the provincial ministries of health and physicians determine which services will be available through public funding. These discussions occur out of the public domain and justifications guiding their decisions are not subject to scrutiny (Kaposy, 2009). Geographical discrepancies quickly surfaced throughout the country. For example, Indigenous women in the Northwest Territories were forced to travel at their own expense, as were women from Prince Edward Island (Sethna & Doull, 2012). Presently, Alberta and Manitoba have two abortion clinics, British Columbia has six, Ontario has 11, and Quebec has 36; Saskatchewan, Nova Scotia, PEI, Yukon, Northwest Territories, and Nunavut have none (Siobhan-Reid et al., 2016). The federal government has not asserted its authority over provinces where abortion access is problematic. As can be seen in Case Examples box with Melissa, this uneven availability of services is a serious health threat for women as it promotes the use of unsafe illegal measures and means that Canada as a nation fails to provide the universal health coverage it purports to implement.

---

## Box 8.3    Extra-Legal Impediments: The Case of PEI

Pro-life/right-to-life groups opposing abortion became active across Canada in the wake of the 1969 criminal law amendment. They were very successful in PEI, where the activists lobbied the medical community, politicians, neighbours, friends, and families. In Prince Edward Island, it is in part a faith-based movement as almost 50 per cent of the population are Roman Catholic. However, it is also a reflection of increasing divisions in the international medical community as physicians and scientists who oppose abortion adopt scientific and religious arguments to "prove" that abortion is immoral. Even though Canadian law states that a fetus has no rights, Canadian medical societies do not have indisputable scientific guidelines to determine when life begins.

Advancements in neonatal medicine highlighting embryological development complicate this issue. Physicians and scientists who are convinced that life begins at conception have developed anti-abortion positions, and their testament has been disseminated by the right-to-life movement globally. The Canadian Medical Association (CMA) policy of 1970 in support of abortions for socio-economic or mental health reasons polarized the medical community. Fierce debates raged in the CMA throughout the 1970s. Doctors were not required to perform abortions and hospitals were not required to set up TACs or provide abortion services, resulting in limited availability in the province. In 1978 PEI's abortion rate was the lowest in Canada. When abortion was decriminalized in 1988, 30 physicians at Charlottetown's Queen Elizabeth Hospital opposed offering abortions. Citizens packed the legislature when the Liberal government passed Resolution 17, declaring that the Legislative Assembly of PEI opposed abortion. Following approval, an anti-abortion resolution was sent to the federal government proclaiming PEI as a pro-life province (Ackerman, 2014). Recently, under the threat of a constitutional challenge to its long-standing anti-abortion policy, the PEI government announced that medical and surgical abortions would be available by the end of 2016. In response, Prime Minister Justin Trudeau stated: "The Government of Canada reaffirms its belief that a woman should have access to reproductive health services, no matter where they live in our country" (Moulton, 2016, p. 171).

# Case #3: Violence against Women

Research on violent victimization shows that violence varies according to the gender of the victim (Table 8.2). Men are more likely to be victims of homicide, aggravated assault, and robbery; women are more likely to be victims of rape, sexual assault, and domestic violence (Hunnicutt, 2009). How can we interpret this difference?

Before the 1970s there was no name for violence against women by their partners (now called "intimate partner violence") and no studies had been done on the subject (DeKeseredy & Dragiewicz, 2014). Early research on violence against women was largely empirical and sought to establish the extent of the problem. It quickly became clear that the phenomenon was pervasive and defied class, race, age, and ability (Brinkerhoff & Lupri, 1988; DeKeseredy, 1988). Feminist activism brought this aspect of social violence into public awareness. The Canadian Advisory Council on the Status of Women (CACSW) was one of the funded partners in the 1988 federal Family Violence Initiative, and new knowledge on violence against women and the impact on children witnessing such violence was publicly debated. Intervention tools such as training manuals, safety audits, and a network of women's shelters and victim services were developed (Mann, 2008).

In the 1990s, the knowledge became more refined, with growing awareness of post-separation woman abuse and intimate femicide, for example, which established that separated women have a heightened risk of being killed (Brownridge, 2006). A surge of funding for research on physical and sexual assault against women occurred after the 1989 murder of 14 female students at École Polytechnique in Montreal by a man raging against "feminists." The Canadian Panel on Violence against Women (VAW) was formed and Health Canada funded a nationwide survey (DeKeseredy & Dragiewicz, 2014). These

**Table 8.2**  Reported Rates of Victims of Violence by Gender in Canada

|  | Women | Men |
|---|---|---|
| Rates of violence | In 2015, police reported 175,414 violent crimes against women (Burczycka & Conroy, 2015). In 2014, there were 206 police-reported human trafficking incidents, 93 per cent of which involved women (Karam, 2014). In 2015, there were 2,658 reported sexual assaults and 53,023 physical assaults against women (Statistics Canada, 2015). In 2015, there were 73 cases of attempted murder against women (Statistics Canada, 2015). | In 2015, police reported 159,276 violent crimes against men (Burczycka & Conroy, 2015). In 2014, there were 206 police-reported human trafficking incidents, 7 per cent of which involved men (Karam, 2014). In 2015, there were 72 reported sexual assaults and 16,541 physical assaults against men (Statistics Canada, 2015). In 2015, there were 34 cases of attempted murder against men (Statistics Canada, 2015). |
| Intimate partner violence (IVP) | In 2015, 79 per cent of 92,000 victims were women (Burczycka & Conroy, 2015). In 2011, there were 75 spousal homicides and 76 attempted spousal homicides of women (Sinha, 2013). | In 2015, 21 per cent of 92,000 victims were men (Burczycka & Conroy, 2015). In 2011, there were 13 spousal homicides and 30 attempted spousal homicides of men (Sinha, 2013). |

initiatives played a pivotal role in shaping institutional arrangements, and domestic violence legislation was introduced in a number of Canadian provinces to complement the federal Criminal Code (Girard, 2009).

# Changes in Canadian Discourses: Men's Rights Backlash and Violence against Women Research

## Wife Beating and Wife Battering

Early feminist anti-violence activists used the terms "wife beating" and "wife battering" to emphasize the severity of the problem and arouse public support. More recently, the term "woman abuse" has been adopted (Dragiewicz & DeKeseredy, 2012). However, there is a call for the use of gender-neutral terms, particularly by men's rights groups who claim that there is no gender difference in intimate partner violence.

## Men's Rights Backlash

General Social Survey data have been widely used by men's rights groups to argue that there is no gender difference in intimate partner violence and they have demanded that gender-neutral terms such as "domestic violence" and "intimate partner violence" replace the feminist term of "violence against women." To support this argument men's rights groups have used a 1999 study by Statistics Canada called the General Social Survey on Victimization (GSS). This study used the Conflict Tactics Scale (CTS), which does not record context—a very relevant factor in the issue of gender and violence. A common cause of women's violence is self-defence and a common cause of men's violence is power and control. Also, sexual assault and homicide were not calculated into the statistic (DeKeseredy, 2011). Thus this study concluded that 8 per cent of women and 7 per cent of men reported at least one incident of intimate partner violence between 1994 and 1999, but this suggests no difference in severity or meaning. Statistics Canada produced similar findings again for 1999–2004, with 6 per cent of men and 7 per cent of women reporting intimate partner violence. The shortcoming in gender-neutral language is that it obscures women's needs, interests, and experiences (Dragiewicz & DeKeseredy, 2012). It is widely recognized that violence in a domestic setting is grossly under-reported, and research exclusively using police and court reports only provides information bounded by those restrictions. For example, in 1993 the number of reports of physical assaults perpetrated by a spouse recorded by the police was 46,800, by the GSS 107,500, and by a VAW survey 201,000 (Dragiewicz & DeKeseredy, 2012).

## Men's Rights Backlash Changes the Legislation

Between 1983 and 1986, the federal and provincial Solicitors General implemented new policy directives requiring police to charge in cases of domestic violence. This was framed as a move to "protect" women, but one of the results was an unexpected increase in the number of women charged and an increase in dual-charging of both the man and the woman in cases of domestic violence (Poon, Dawson, & Morton, 2014).

Since then, criminal justice policies such as the Domestic Violence Court Program in Ontario (1997) funnel victims and offenders into mandated programs run by probation officers and social workers (Fong, 2010). These initiatives fit with the neo-liberal "get tough on crime" agenda and reduce the social problem of domestic violence to an individual problem, rather than a structural problem.

## Changes in the Women's Shelter Movement

Social work scholar Kim (2013) points out that in the early days of the women's shelter movement, "experts" were the graduates of the program—women who had been through the experience themselves—but the court-mandated programs mandate treatment with professional social workers (i.e., social work graduates with research-based academic expertise) have created a new kind of "expert" as the primary individual responder. This shift has resulted in social workers building an alliance with the criminal justice system and has inhibited social work activism in the anti-violence movement, where challenging inequities in the criminal justice system, such as over-representation, racial profiling, and police bias, would be important aspects of macro practice.

## Neo-Liberalism and Women's Equality

Similar to other policy areas, neo-liberal trends have deeply affected women's equality. When Prime Minister Harper took office in 2006 he cemented previous governments' neo-liberal policy decisions. This included unprecedented cuts to Status of Women Canada—a 40 per cent reduction in the operating budget, the closure of 12 regional offices (from 16 to 4), and the elimination of all funding for research on women's issues by any women's organizations advocating or lobbying governments. Subsequent cuts to funding for women's organizations include Canadian Research Institute for the Advancement of Women (CRIAW), Native Women's Association of Canada (NWAC), Alberta Network of Immigrant Women, Ontario Association of Interval and Transition Houses (OAITH), National Association of Women and the Law (NAML), and Sisters in Spirit, an Indigenous women's project that led the way in research on missing and murdered Indigenous women.

Notably, the Harper government refused to launch a national inquiry to investigate the more than 1,000 missing and murdered Indigenous women and girls documented by families, advocates, and the RCMP (Strumm, 2015; Ready, 2016). He argued that it was not a "sociological issue" that pointed to the systemic violence in Indigenous women's lives, but an individualized issue of "crime." In this context, it is understandable why the current Prime Minister identifying as a "feminist" has made national and international headlines. Yet, while Prime Minister Justin Trudeau's decision to initiate a National Inquiry on MMIWG was welcomed by Indigenous activists, the Liberal government's rhetoric and the process around the inquiry have received much criticism. The NWAC has set up a quarterly report card on the progress of the inquiry as a way of monitoring and evaluating its progress. Their report on the last quarter of 2016 noted five areas where further action was required: providing timelines, transparency regarding progress and information, developing community relations with stakeholders, providing funding to ensure the participation of stakeholders, and setting up a trauma-informed inquiry process. The report of April 2017 noted 10 areas graded as failing and three where further action was required.

This is not a positive report for the ongoing inquiry as no categories have yet been graded as a pass. In June 2018 the NWAC voiced its frustration that the inquiry had been given only a six-month extension, not the two years it had called for so all involved families could testify, "a sustaining aftercare initiative" could be pursued, and time could be given for further written submissions, among other issues (NWAC, 2018).

The crisis of missing and murdered Indigenous women was identified by the Truth and Reconciliation Commission of Canada as one of the intergenerational legacies of the residential school system. More broadly, racism within the police force is an ongoing problem with roots in the historical role the RCMP played in enforcing the Indian Act. The force was created to assist European settlement by preventing Indigenous resistance to colonization, and modern activists call attention to the parallel circumstance of Vancouver's Downtown Eastside, where fewer Indigenous people enhances real estate value (Pinto, 2013). Indigenous children are grossly over-represented in foster care, which is the current heritage of a history of abduction into residential schools, followed by the "Sixties Scoop" when social workers apprehended children from their families and communities and placed them in white foster homes. Indigenous people are over-represented in the criminal justice system and this means that for an Indigenous woman like Joann experiencing domestic violence (see Case Examples box), calling the police not only may seem a "betrayal" of her people, but she may not be taken seriously, is at risk of being charged herself, and places her children at risk of apprehension (Fong, 2010). The full force of colonial trauma is just entering mainstream politics as the Calls to Action of the Truth and Reconciliation Commission are operationalized. Since the terrorist attacks in the US of 11 September 2001 there has also been an increasing alliance between the criminal justice system and immigration services in Canada. This means that undocumented women are fearful of authorities and may not seek help, and women with precarious immigration status are vulnerable to threats of deportation from abusers. This creates a situation of increased isolation added to cultural and language differences, financial hardship, and systemic racism (Fong, 2010; Kim, 2013).

In the practice field of violence against women, what began as collective community-based services such as peer counselling, consciousness-raising, and group support have become professionally based services where specific credentials are required and the services are individually based with funding for shelters, law enforcement, and targeted interventions such as separate counselling for men and women. Underwriting these services is the presumption that physical safety is paramount and contact between the victim and victimizer is viewed as failure. Meanwhile, more complex changes that might interrupt the conditions supporting violence, such as unemployment, poverty, and dismantling the social welfare system, remain unaddressed.

## International Comparisons

### The Status of Women in Cuba

According to Article 44 of the Cuban Constitution, "Women and men enjoy equal economic, political, cultural, social, and familial rights. The State guarantees that women will be offered the same opportunities and possibilities as men to achieve their full participation in the development of the country." In addition, it lists social supports, such as child centres, semi-boarding and boarding schools, residences for care of the aged, and services to aid the working family. The government commits to granting working women paid maternity leave before and after childbirth, and temporary work options if they require them, "to create all the conditions that will lead to the implementation of the principle of equality."

Women—such as Vilma Espín, Tete Puebla, Celia Sánchez, Melba Hernández, and Haydée Santamaría—were among the leaders who fought for freedom alongside Fidel Castro, and women were at the forefront of state planning following the Revolution. They played a central role in the literacy brigades teaching people to write and read to combat a widespread literacy problem that disproportionately affected women.

Today, Cuba has one of the highest rates of women's political representation in the world. According to a report by the Center for Democracy in the Americas (2013), six policies have produced the most significant results: programs to increase female workforce participation; commitments to education and health care; establishment of a constitutional and legal architecture that protects women's rights; the articulation of women's equality and rights as a core part of the revolution's political project; establishment of women's organizations to serve as advocates for change; and a successful, early campaign to address illiteracy in Cuba. This report suggests that these and other policy interventions allow Cuba to not only fulfill the Millennium Development Goals for primary education, gender equality, and reducing infant mortality, but also score first among developing countries in maternal mortality, live births attended by health care personnel, and female life expectancy at birth. Yet, like nations elsewhere, Cuban women's fight for equality is incomplete. Discriminatory social relations, continuing sexism within workplaces, and unfair division of labour within the private sphere underscore women's struggle—often referred to as the "revolution within the revolution."

# Chapter Summary

Backlash from men's rights movements and dominant discourses of meritocracy would lead us to believe that Canadian society treats men and women equally. However, almost five decades after the Commission on the Status of Women, gender relations continue to be unequal and dominant discourses are fraught with contradictions and inconsistencies. The national crisis framing the lack of child care, limited access to reproductive justice, and the prevalence of violence against women indicate that patriarchal discourses and policies remain. Restrictive social policies affected by neoliberalism and criminalization further challenge women's freedom, equality, and equity. In this context, backlash against feminism signals a more urgent underlying problem: women's rights, and the lack thereof, have been made invisible or normalized within national discourse. Confronting gender inequality requires addressing the inaccurate and problematic dominant discourses that mask women's oppression through Canadian social policy.

## Discussion Questions

1. What social, economic, and political factors contribute to dominant discomforts and backlash against "feminism"?

2. Quebec's child-care model indicates that comprehensive and accessible child care is possible. Investigate this child-care model and discuss why you think the rest of Canada has not followed this approach.

3. Locate recent media reports on the National Inquiry into MMIWG. What are the dominant discourses representing the investigation, Indigenous women, and the issue of violence against women?

4. What social policy challenges do intersectional feminists face in confronting the gender biases and social, moral, and economic regulation of women's lives?

## References

Ackerman, K. (2014). In defence of reason: Religion, science, and the Prince Edward Island anti-abortion movement, 1969–1988. *Canadian Bulletin of Medical History, 31*(2), 21.

Adamson, P. (2008). *The child care transition: A league table of early childhood education and care in economically advantaged countries.* Report Card 8. Florence, Italy: UNICEF Innocenti Research Centre. Retrieved from https://www.unicef-irc.org/publications/pdf/rc8_eng.pdf

Albanese, P., & Rauhala, A. (2015). A decade of disconnection: Child care policies in changing economic times in the Canadian context. *International Journal of Child, Youth and Family Studies, 6*(2), 22.

Backhouse, C. (1991). The celebrated abortion trial of Dr. Emily Stowe, Toronto, 1897. *Canadian Bulletin of Medical History, 8*, 28.

Brinkerhoff, M., & Lupri, E. (1988). Interpersonal violence. *Canadian Journal of Sociology, 13*, 17.

Bromley, V. L. (2012). *Feminisms matter: Debates, theories, activism.* Toronto: University of Toronto Press.

Brownridge, D. (2006). Violence against women post-separation. *Aggression and Violent Behaviour, 11*, 16.

Burczycka, M., & Conroy, S. (2015). Family violence in Canada: A statistical profile (Catalogue No. 85-002-X). Canadian Centre for Justice Statistics. Retrieved from http://www.statcan.gc.ca/pub/85-002-x/2017001/article/14698/03-eng.htm

Canadian Institute for Health Information. (2014). *Induced abortions reported in Canada.* Ottawa, Canada. Retrieved from: https://www.cihi.ca/sites/default/files/document/induced_abortion_can_2014_en_web.xlsx

CBC News. (2015, 13 Oct.). Works cited: 50% population, 25% representation: Why the parliamentary gender gap? Retrieved from http://www.cbc.ca/news/works-cited-50-population-25-representation-1.3268921

Center for Democracy in the Americas. (2013). *Women's work: Gender equality in Cuba and the role of women in building Cuba's future.* Washington, DC. Retrieved from: http://democracyinamericas.org/wp-content/uploads/2016/06/CDA_Womens_Work.pdf

Chrisler, J. (2014). A reproductive justice approach to women's health. *Analyses of Social Issues and Public Policy ASAP, 14*(1), 205–9.

Cool, J. (2011). Government, parliament and politics. *Parliamentary Information and Research Service.* Retrieved from http://www.lop.parl.gc.ca/content/lop/ResearchPublications/2011-56-e.pdf

DeKeseredy, W. (1988). Woman abuse in dating relationships: The relevance of social support theory. *Journal of Family Violence, 3*, 13.

———. (2011). *Violence against women: Myths, facts, controversies.* Toronto: University of Toronto Press.

——— & Dragiewicz, M. (2014). Woman abuse in Canada: Sociological reflections on the past, suggestions for the future. *Violence Against Women, 20*(2), 16. doi:10.1177/1077801214521325

Dobrowolsky, A., & Jenson, J. (2004). Shifting representations of citizenship: Canadian politics of "women" and "children". *Social Politics: International Studies in Gender, State & Society, 11(2)*, 154–80.

Dragiewicz, M., & DeKeseredy,W. (2012). Claims about women's use of non-fatal force in intimate relationships: A contextual review of Canadian research. *Violence Against Women, 18*(9), 18.

Ferns, C., & Friendly, M. (2014). *The state of early childhood education and childcare in Canada 2012*. Retrieved from http://childcarecanada .org/sites/default/files/StateofECEC2012.pdf

Findlay, T. (2015). Child care and the Harper agenda: Transforming Canada's social policy regime. *Canadian Review of Social Policy/Revue canadienne de politique sociale, 71*(1), 20.

Fong, J. (Ed.). (2010). *Out of the shadows. Woman abuse in ethnic, immigrant and Aboriginal communities*. Toronto: Woman's Press.

Friendly, M. (1994). *Child care policy in Canada. Putting the pieces together*. Don Mills, ON: Addison-Wesley.

Girard, A. (2009). Backlash or equality? The influence of men's and women's rights discourses on domestic violence legislation in Ontario. *Violence Against Women, 15*(1), 18.

Hunnicutt, G. (2009). Varieties of patriarchy and violence against women: Resurrecting "patriarchy" as a theoretical tool. *Violence Against Women, 15*(5), 20.

International Conference on Population and Development. (1994). *Report of the International Conference on Population and Development*. New York: United Nations. Retrieved from https://www.ipci2014.org/fr/node/64

Johnstone, M. (2015). Don't take the social out of social work: The social work career of Bessie Touzel (1904–1997). *Affilia, Journal of Women and Social Work, 30*(3), 12.

Kaposy, C. (2009). The public funding of abortion in Canada: Going beyond the concept of medical necessity. *Medical Health Care and Philosophy, 12*, 10.

Karam, M. (2014). Trafficking in persons in Canada, 2014. *Canadian Centre for Justice Statistics*. Retrieved from http://www.statcan.gc.ca/ pub/85-002-x/2016001/article/14641-eng.pdf

Kim, M. E. (2013). Challenging the pursuit of criminalization in an era of mass incarceration: The limitations of social work responses to domestic violence. *British Journal of Social Work, 43*, 17.

Lee, E., & Johnstone, M. (2013). Global inequities: A gender based analysis of the live-in caregiver program and the kirogi phenomenon in Canada. *Affilia, 28*(4), 401–14.

Mahon, R. (2009). Childcare and varieties of liberalism in Canada. In A. Dobrowolsky (Ed.), *Women and public policy in Canada: Neoliberalism and after* (pp. 65–86). Toronto: Oxford University Press.

Mann, R. (2008). Men's rights and feminist advocacy in Canadian domestic violence policy arenas. *Feminist Criminology, 3*(1), 44–75.

Marsden, L. (2012). *Canadian women and the struggle for equality*. Toronto: Oxford University Press.

Martel, L. (2013). Mortality: Overview, 2010 and 2011. *Report on the demographic situation in Canada*. Retrieved from http://www.statcan .gc.ca/pub/91-209-x/2013001/article/11867-eng.pdf

Milan, A. (2015). *Families and living arrangements*. Ottawa: Statistics Canada. Retrieved from http://www.statcan.gc.ca

Moulton, D. (2016). PEI to finally offer abortions on the island. *Canadian Medical Association Journal, 188*(9). doi:10.1503/cmaj.109-5274

Native Women's Association of Canada (NWAC). (2018, 5 June). Media release—NWAC frustrated & disagrees with six month extension at MMIWG. Retrieved from https://www.nwac .ca/2018/06/05/media-release-nwac-frustrated-disagrees-with-six-month-extension-at-mmiwg/

Neysmith, S., Reitsma-Street, M., Baker Collins, S., & Porter, E. (2012). *Beyond caring labour to provisioning work*. Toronto: University of Toronto Press.

Pinto, M. (2013). Pamela Masik and *The Forgotten* exhibition: Controversy and cancellation at the Museum of Anthropology. *Museum Anthropology, 36*(1), 13.

Poon, J., Dawson, M., & Morton, M.(2014). Factors increasing the likelihood of sole and dual charging of women for intimate partner violence. *Violence Against Women, 20*(4), 1447–72.

Prentice, A., Bourne, P., Brandt, G. C., Light, B., Mitchinson, W., & Black, N. (1988). *Canadian women: A history*. Toronto: Harcourt Brace Jovanovich.

Prentice, S. (1992). Workers, mothers, reds: Toronto's postwar daycare fight. In P.A. Connelly (Ed.), *Feminism in action. Studies in political economy*. Toronto: Canadian Scholars' Press.

Ready, C. (2016). *Shelter in a storm: Revitalizing feminism in neoliberal Ontario*. Vancouver: University of British Columbia Press.

Rebick, J. (2005). *Ten thousand roses: The making of feminist revolution*. Toronto: Penguin.

Rice, J., & Prince, M. (2013). *Changing politics of Canadian social policy*. Toronto: University of Toronto Press.

Royal Commission on the Status of Women in Canada. (1970). *Report of the Royal Commission on the Status of Women in Canada.* The Commission. Retrieved from: http://publications.gc.ca/site/eng/9.699583/publication.html

Sathish, M. (2016). Justin Trudeau's 7 most wonderfully feminist moments will make you love the Canadian leader even more. Retrieved from http://www.bustle.com/articles/180958-justin-trudeaus-7-most-wonderfully

Sethna, C., & Doull, M. (2012). Accidental tourists: Canadian women, abortion tourism, and travel. *Women's Studies, 41,* 18.

Sinha, M. (2013). *Family violence in Canada: A statistical profile, 2011.* Ottawa: Statistics Canada. Retrieved from http://www.statcan.gc.ca/pub/85-002-x/2013001/article/11805-eng.pdf

Siobhan-Reid, M., Kieran, S., Cawthorne, J., & Arthur, J. (2016). Access after 1988. Retrieved from: http://www.morgentaler25years.ca/the-struggle-for-abortion-rights/access-after-1988/

Smith, A. (2005). Native American feminism, sovereignty and social change. *Feminist Studies, 31*(1), 116–32.

Statistics Canada. (n.d.A). Table 282-0002: Full-time and part-time employment by sex and age group. *CANSIM database.* Retrieved from http://www.statcan.gc.ca/tables-tableaux/sum-som/l01/cst01/labor12-eng.htm

———. (n.d.B). Table 282-0072: Labour force survey estimates (LFS), wages of employees by type of work, North American Industry Classification System (NAICS), sex and age group, annual (current dollars unless otherwise noted). *CANSIM database.* Retrieved from https://docs .google.com/document/d/1tr0LiabMK G6wESAnM-fJuVkxaIfy6sk9poPsndsx M1A/edit#

———. (2011). *Women in Canada: A gender-based statistical report* (Catalogue no. 89-503-X). Ottawa: Statistics Canada. Retrieved from http://www.statcan.gc.ca/pub/89-503-x/89-503-x2010001-eng.pdf

———. (2015). Table 3.4: Victims of police-reported intimate partner violence for selected violent offences, by sex of victim and type of offence, Canada, 2009 to 2015. Retrieved from http://www.statcan.gc.ca/pub/85-002-x/2017001/article/14698/tbl/tbl3.7-eng.htm

Strumm, B. (2015). Women in Harperland: A critical look at gender inequality in Canada since 2006. *Canadian Review of Social Policy/Revue canadienne de politique sociale, 70,* 12.

*The Daily.* (2017, 8 Mar.). Study: Women in Canada: Women and paid work. Retrieved from http://www.statcan.gc.ca/daily-quotidien/170308/dq170308b-eng.pdf

Tong, R. (2014). *Feminist thought.* Boulder, CO: Westview Press.

Turcotte, M. (2015). Civic engagement and political participation in Canada. *Spotlight on Canadians: Results from the General Social Survey.* Retrieved from http://www.statcan.gc.ca/pub/89-652-x/89-652-x2015006-eng.pdf

Uppal, S. (2015). Employment patterns of families with children. Ottawa: Statistics Canada. Retrieved from https://www150.statcan.gc.ca/n1/pub/75-006-x/2015001/article/14202-eng.htm

Waring, M. (1988). *Counting for nothing. What men value and what women are worth.* Cambridge, MA: Allen & Unwin.

# 9 Sexual and Gender Diversity

*Nick J. Mulé*

---

### Chapter Objectives

*This chapter will help you to develop an understanding of:*

- the historical and contemporary oppression experienced by LGBTQ people;
- the specific needs of LGBTQ populations and the importance of their representation in social policy;
- what current social policies exist for LGBTQs in Canada and the degree to which they are benefiting these communities;
- the paradoxical implications of LGBTQ social policies on these communities and mainstream Canadian society;
- how the human rights and social policy protections of LGBTQ Canadians compare to those of LGBTQ people around the world.

---

## Introduction

Sexuality and gender identity and expression are characteristics and identity markers that are often collectively grouped as those who are **lesbian**, **gay**, **bisexual**, **transsexual**, **transgender**, **two-spirit**, **intersex**, **queer**, and **questioning** (LGBTQ). The LGBTQ acronym is a commonly used one that for the purposes of this chapter is meant to capture the varying identities in the broad gender and sexually diverse communities outside of **cisgenderism** and heterosexuality. It also avoids turning into an excessively long acronym and provides opportunity for intersex communities to determine the extent of their connection to these broader communities. This chapter will look at the realities and experiences of these populations and how they have historically been defined as oppressed. This oppression is partly due to the lack of formal recognition of LGBTQ people in social policy, leaving them vulnerable to discrimination, social exclusion, and marginalization. Through the work of the LGBTQ movement and demands for equal rights protections, social policy in Canada has shifted, positioning Canada today in the distinct category of the few countries in the world with progressive policies regarding LGBTQs. Yet, to what extent is this considered progress? When acknowledging that the LGBTQ communities are far from monolithic based on their varied issues, needs, and concerns—coupled with

---

**Case Examples**   Sketches of Prejudice

---

A homophobic verbal attack in her high school on **Jessica**, 15, results in the suspension of a fellow student in accordance with the school's equity policy. Yet Jessica is now further stigmatized and resented by her attacker's friends and supporters.

Upon entering the prison system on an assault conviction, **Paula**, 34, is defined as a male based on her male genitalia and not on her female gender identity. She is given male prison clothes, housed in a men's prison, and restricted from continuing hormone therapy.

**Queer Action** is a progressive, critical, direct action community group of activists whose mission is to critique and challenge **heterosexism**, cisgenderism, and **homo-bi-transphobia**. The group's attempt to attain charitable status is rejected because of the political nature of their advocacy.

---

intersections of race, ethnicity, age, (dis)abilities, religion, and socio-economic status—the rights-claim approach has benefited some while further marginalizing others. The rights-claim approach refers to the development of formal social policy through legislation at various levels of government, which becomes a basis or source for legal justice. This will be counterbalanced with on-the-ground social justice and how the two can influence each other, sometimes positively, sometimes negatively. Throughout this chapter are sensitized lessons in the work of policy-making, given the paradoxical dynamic of social policy regarding gender and sexually diverse populations.

This chapter begins with a look at the present state of social policy in Canada regarding LGBTQ people. Such a review will include an overview of the history of social policy development as instigated by the LGBTQ movement. What policies have been attained? Who is benefiting from them and who is not? The roles of the three levels of government as well as the Supreme Court of Canada in making changes to social policy will also be examined. In addition to these structural sectors, the non-profit sector and how it is regulated will also be considered. Canadian society's shifting values, norms, and morals have contributed to shaping an ever-changing discourse, particularly with regard to sexuality and gender identity and expression. How Canada fares compared to the rest of the world on LGBTQ social policy is reflected on, as well as the implications for social work and the role social workers can play.

## The Present State of LGBTQ Social Policy in Canada

Before delving into the many aspects of social policy in Canada for LGBTQs, a review of the three case examples at the start of this chapter is warranted. Each scenario presents challenges to social policy and how it is designed regarding the LGBTQ population. Such challenges should be kept in mind when reading this chapter. In the Case Examples box, the scenario regarding Jessica is an example of a policy with good intentions that can have deleterious effects. Although the high school she attends can be commended for having an equity policy inclusive of LGBTQs, the penalty of suspension for the offending student in the absence of sensitivity training and follow-up supports for both students creates new problems. Therefore, the good intention of this policy is based on its restrictiveness as a response to a homophobic scenario, but it fails to address systemic homophobia in the high school setting.

In the second example, the policy circumstance that Paula is placed in is one of omission. Federal policy regarding trans prison inmates is currently being revised to recognize the inmate's chosen gender identity rather than biological genitalia (Harris, 2017). At present, however, Paula's personal gender identity is overruled by prison policy that determines gender on biological assignment only. This policy is too restrictive because abiding by traditional binary notions of sex and gender has detrimental effects on trans prison inmates who are housed with inmates whose gender they do not identify with.

In the third example, regarding Queer Action, policy is deliberately delineated between those organizations that undertake extensive political activities (non-profits) and those that do far less of it (charities). Although Queer Action was hoping to reap the benefits of becoming a charity (such as issuing tax receipts for donations received), the policy defines the political activities they engage in as non-charitable. Such rigid definitions, in turn, raise questions as to the minimal support politicized non-profits get and the regulatory restrictions on charities regarding political action and the dual effect on Canada's democracy. (For more on this topic, see Box 9.1.)

## How LGBTQ Issues Have Developed Historically

LGBTQ social policy issues have developed in Canada from the bottom up. The late 1960s, when homosexuality was decriminalized in Canada and the Stonewall riots took place in New York City, marked the beginning of what would be a burgeoning gay liberation movement. This movement followed closely on the heels of, and was influenced by, the Black civil rights movement, the women's liberation movement, and the peace movement. Not only did the gay liberation movement assert itself for public recognition, it was also the beginning of developing a community with its own sensibilities and culture. In a pre-Internet era this included the establishment of publications such as newsletters and magazines, consciousness-raising and support groups, phone lines and informal counselling services, all of which provided outlets and spaces for those with same-sex attractions and gender variance to meet others who felt the same to establish friendships, relationships, and ultimately community (Warner, 2002).

As the LGBTQ communities continued to grow and develop, so did a rights-claim sentiment that called for the inclusion of "sexual orientation" as a recognized characteristic for protection against discrimination. Between 1977 and 1998 virtually every province and territory in Canada added sexual orientation to their respective human rights codes (CUPE, 2009). In 1995, the Canadian Charter of Rights and Freedoms began to be interpreted by the courts as including sexual orientation (Carroll & Ramon Mendos, 2017), and this was added to the Canadian Human Rights Act in 1996 (Canadian Human Rights Commission, n.d.; Ontario Human Rights Commission, n.d.).

More recently, demands for inclusion of "gender identity" and in many cases "gender expression" have arisen. "Gender identity" refers to those trans individuals who identify with a gender that was not biologically assigned at birth. This identification may be female or male, a variation, or no gender at all. "Gender expression" refers to individuals whose expression of their gender varies, as driven by their feelings at given times rather than committing themselves to a fixed gender. Most provinces and territories have now enacted gender identity and/or expression legislation, while others have yet to do so. Trans recognition at the federal level passed in 2017 with Bill C-16, which amends the Canadian Human Rights Act to include gender identity and expression as prohibited grounds for discrimination. It also amends the Criminal Code to extend protection against hate propaganda as well as hate crimes based on gender identity or expression (Parliament of Canada, 2017) (see Table 9.1).

## Current LGBTQ Social Policy

These initial rights claims were achieved mostly through the courts due to the Charter's section 15 recognition of rights being extended to all Canadian citizens without discrimination or disadvantage "based on race, national or ethnic origin, colour, religion, sex, age or mental or physical disability." The Court Challenges Program, which existed from 1994 until 2006, was an independent non-profit organization receiving federal funding that provided financial assistance to noteworthy court cases towards the advancement of language and/or equality rights (Court Challenges Program, n.d.). This Program assisted LGBTQ communities greatly in challenging existing laws through a sexual orientation and gender identity and expression lens. The Harper federal government cancelled it in 2006, but the Trudeau federal government announced in February 2017 it will provide

**Table 9.1**   LGBTQ Human Rights Protections in Canada

| Canada and Provinces/ Territories | Sexual Orientation | Gender Identity | Gender Expression |
|---|---|---|---|
| Canada | 1996 | 2017 | 2017 |
| Alberta | 2009 | 2015 | 2015 |
| British Columbia | 1992 | 2016 | 2016 |
| Manitoba | 1987 | 2012 | none |
| New Brunswick | 1992 | Bill 51 Pending | Bill 51 Pending |
| Newfoundland & Labrador | 1995 | 2013 | 2013 |
| Northwest Territories | 2002 | 2002 | none |
| Nova Scotia | 1991 | 2012 | 2012 |
| Nunavut | 1999 | 2017 | 2017 |
| Ontario | 1986 | 2012 | 2012 |
| Prince Edward Island | 1998 | 2013 | 2013 |
| Quebec | 1977 | 2016 | 2016 |
| Saskatchewan | 1993 | 2014 | none |
| Yukon | 1987 | under review | under review |

Note: This table provides the years in which human rights legislation passed federally and in Canada's provinces and territories regarding sexual orientation, gender identity, and gender expression.
Source: Compiled from the Canadian Bar Association (2016); Equaldex (2017); Wikipedia (2017).

$12 million over five years to reinstate a modernized version of the Court Challenges Program. If acted upon, it will provide financial assistance to Canadians with important constitutional or quasi-constitutional court cases (Government of Canada, 2017). Beyond the basic recognition of LGBTQs in human rights legislation, numerous other social policies have addressed the needs of these populations. These include same-sex couples adopting, same-sex marriage, protection for those living with HIV, pensions and benefits for widow(er)s of same-sex partners, and the right to establish gay–straight alliances (GSAs) in high schools.

# Strengths and Limitations of Social Policy

The strength of such inclusion in social policy is state-legitimized recognition of LGBTQs as a population with particular needs. Hence, such recognition simultaneously provides formal sanctioning of LGBTQs, which contrasts greatly from these populations historically having been deemed as sick, immoral, or perverted. Human rights legislation seeks to protect LGBTQs from being fired from their jobs, thrown out of housing, or denied services, all of which regularly happened before legislative protections existed (Smith, 1999; Warner, 2002). Yet, a limitation to these developments is that policy tends to reflect mainstream norms, in effect homonormalizing LGBTQ communities. LGBTQs who most mimic straight people (i.e., marrying their same-sex partner, then adopting children) tend to benefit most from these kinds of policies (Mulé, 2015). Those who live outside these homonormative models of existence are not equally sanctioned. For example, a same-sex married couple and their children are far better accommodated by social policy than a family constituted of three or more parents. Independent LGBTQs who opt not to be in relationships are not as sanctioned as those who are in relationships. Furthermore, settlers have long colonized the Indigenous populations of our land, thus positioning two-spirit people in particularly vulnerable circumstances. On the one hand, settler-dominant Canada imposes white **heteronormative** values on Indigenous communities, while on the other hand, due to the pervasive effects of colonization, two-spirit people are not necessarily assured support by their Elders or peers within Indigenous communities.

### Which LGBTQs Are Included, and Which Are Excluded?

At the outset, extending social policy to recognize LGBTQs is meant to be inclusive across these communities, but in reality this is not the case because power differentials, intersectionalities, and social positioning play a role. Generally speaking, white, middle-class, able-bodied, and cisgendered LGBTQs—especially males—tend to be most represented and benefit the most from these social policies. Racialized, ethnicized, lower-class, disabled, and trans LGBTQs tend to be excluded, which is further compounded for those who identify as women. They tend to have less education, are of lower-class status, earn a low income, and thus face greater challenges in accessing the resources needed when faced with discrimination. Systemically, LGBTQs tend not to be distinctly recognized in social policy. Such lack of recognition can be further complicated, depending on how individuals assemble their social location and how this intersects with their LGBTQ status. Indigenous people are often overlooked or not included in policy development, which then lacks Indigenous cultural perspectives (McNeil-Seymour, 2015).

Quebec is the most progressive province in the country on LGBTQ issues (via its anti-homophobia policy perspective and initiatives) (Justice Quebec, 2017), setting itself apart from the other provinces and territories. Not only was Quebec the first province in the country to recognize sexual orientation as an enumerated ground for human rights protection in its Human Rights Code, it set the tone early on by addressing the needs of LGBTQ communities from the perspective that Quebec needed to address its own homophobia. Therefore, in order to honour this human rights recognition, the Quebec government established an anti-homophobia policy perspective in collaboration with LGBTQ activists.

## Roles of the Federal, Provincial, Municipal Governments and the Supreme Court in LGBTQ Social Policy

While formal human rights protections based on sexual orientation have been en-acted as formal legislation by all provincial and territorial governments and federally, the recognition of gender identity (and expression) at the federal level has not been matched across all the provinces and territories. Recognition for LGBTQs varies across municipal governments, with larger urban centres being the first to provide inclusive equity policies due to pressure from organized LGBTQ movements in those locales. In addition to formal legislation, the LGBTQ movement has also brought challenges through the courts. The 1995 landmark ruling of *Egan v. Canada* by the Supreme Court of Canada (SCC) recognized sexual orientation as an "analogous ground," implicitly included in section 15 of the Charter, and hence a prohibited ground for discrimina-tion (Smith, 1999). Beyond basic human rights protections, the LGBTQ movement in Canada continues to fight for rights and recognition in policy on numerous issues, from sexual activity to various forms of anti-discrimination protections and from same-sex relationship recognition to parenting rights and depathologization of LGBTQs (see Table 9.2).

**Table 9.2**   LGBTQ Issue-Based Rights in Canada

| Issue | Rights | Notations |
| --- | --- | --- |
| Same-sex sexual activity legal | ✓ | 1969 |
| Equal age of consent | ✗ | Unequal age of consent for anal sex regardless of sexual orientation. In AB, BC, NS, ON, and QC this law is not applied. (Change pending.) |
| Anti-discrimination laws in employment | ✓/✗ | 1996 for sexual orientation only. |
| Anti-discrimination laws in the provision of goods and services | ✓/✗ | 1996 for sexual orientation only. |

| | | |
|---|---|---|
| Anti-discrimination laws in all other areas (including indirect discrimination, hate speech) | ✓/✗ | 1996 for sexual orientation only. |
| Anti-discrimination laws in housing | ✓/✗ | Sexual orientation and gender identity: QC, NWT (2017); BC, NB (2016); ON (2012); MB, NL, NS, NU, PEI, SK, YT (n.d.) Sexual orientation only: AB (2009) |
| Recognition of same-sex couples | ✓ | Financial and immigration benefits granted to same-sex couples since 2000. |
| Same-sex marriage | ✓ | Legalized in Canada in 2005; previously legalized by 8 of 10 provinces (BC and ON in 2003; MB, QC, NS, SK, and NL in 2004; NB in 2005) and 1 out of 3 territories (YT in 2004). |
| Stepchild adoption by same-sex couples | ✓ | Legal in all provinces and territories, yet rules vary (rulings and legislation passed from 1996 to 2011). |
| Joint adoption by same-sex couples | ✓ | |
| Access to IVF and IUI for lesbians | ✓ | Lesbians and same-sex attracted female couples have access to in vitro fertilization (IVF) and intrauterine insemination (IUI). |
| Equal access to surrogacy for all couples | ✓ | Since 2004, the Assisted Human Reproduction Act has prohibited commercial surrogacy for all couples (regardless of sexual orientation). However, altruistic surrogacy is permitted and surrogate mothers may be reimbursed for some expenses. Quebec law allows neither altruistic nor commercial surrogacy (but doesn't explicitly forbid it, and Quebec has reimbursed gay men for surrogacy costs). |
| Coverage for gender confirmation surgery | ✓ | In several provinces (to a variable extent), but none of the territories. |
| Transgender identity declassified as an illness | ✗ | All Canadian provinces are still using *Diagnostic and Statistical Manual* (DSM 5). |
| Sexual orientation conversion therapy banned on minors | ✓/✗/~ | Banned in MB and ON (both in 2015) only. Not banned in AB, NB, NL, NS, NWT, and SK. Uncertain in BC, NU, PEI, QC, and YT. |
| Men who have sex with men (MSM) allowed to donate blood | ✓/✗ | Since 2016, one-year-deferral period. |

Notes: ✓ denotes existing rights and policy. ✗ denotes rights and policy does not exist. ~ denotes uncertainty regarding interpretation of rights and policy.
Source: Compiled from Equaldex (2017); My Big Gay Family (2015); Wikipedia (2017).

# Roles of Family, Market, Charity, and Non-Profit Sector in LGBTQ Social Policy

Beyond formal legal rights, other segments of society, such as family, the market, and the non-profit sector, play a role in the level of tolerance and acceptance accorded the LGBTQ populations. Over time, families have increasingly become supportive of LGBTQ members. For example, Parents and Friends of Lesbians and Gays (PFLAG) has successfully advocated over the years that their loved ones be recognized with supportive policies. However, LGBTQ communities have also become commodified within the mainstream market. Part of this commodification is due to the LGBTQ communities being seen as having large amounts of disposable income, which ignores impoverished members, and the corporatization of Pride events in large urban centres. The LGBTQ communities' own commercialization (LGBTQ-owned bars, bookstores, bathhouses, clothing stores, card shops) has also contributed to this commodification as part of its community development. The role of LGBTQ groups that fall into the charity and non-profit sector is somewhat minimized due to regulatory limitations (see Box 9.1).

---

**Box 9.1** The Non-Profit Sector and LGBTQ Communities

---

Canada's non-profit sector is divided into charities, incorporated non-profit organizations, and non-incorporated non-profit organizations (Canada Revenue Agency, 2016b). Additionally, "social enterprises" combine aspects of the non-profit and private sectors, yet not-for-profit gain (Liao, 2017).

Via the Canada Revenue Agency (CRA) the non-profit sector is regulated on a number of fronts, including political activity, which translates to advocacy. Charities have the advantages of being recognized by government, qualifying for both government and foundation-based funding, and issuing tax receipts for donations received. Their disadvantage is that they must operate under strict limits regarding ambiguously defined "political activities," with resources devoted to advocacy limited to 10–20 per cent depending on the size of the charity's budget (Canada Revenue Agency, 2016a).

The advantages for incorporated non-profits are that they qualify for limited government and foundation funding and have no limits placed on their political activity. The same lack of restrictions on political activity applies for non-incorporated non-profit organizations, yet their disadvantage is that they do not generally qualify for government or foundation funding. A major disadvantage for non-profit organizations, whether incorporated or not, is that they cannot issue tax receipts for any donations they receive (Canada Revenue Agency, 2016b). This latter point can have a major impact on their budget and sustainability.

As the LGBTQ communities have developed and grown in Canada, many have opted to seek charitable status and to function accordingly. In response to the 1980s AIDS crisis, LGBTQ communities mobilized to develop much-needed grassroots resources, leading to the emergence of numerous non-profit organizations dedicated to the needs of LGBTQ people. These organizations demanded state support from the government, which resulted in the formation of a series of AIDS service organizations (ASOs) across the country. (For more about services for people with HIV/AIDS, hepatitis C, and other sexually and blood-borne diseases, see Chapter 18.) Beyond ASOs, numerous LGBTQ organizations have obtained charitable status to gain legitimacy in the eyes of government and foundations and for a degree of financial sustainability (Mulé, 2011).

Yet, what are the implications of LGBTQ groups attaining charitable status with regard to the LGBTQ movement? Groups such as Queer Action do not qualify for charitable status and thus an application would be rejected by CRA because of their politicized mission (see Case Examples box). Do they depoliticize their mission, and hence their work, to gain the financial sustainability of being a charity? Do they forfeit their plan to be a charity and remain a non-profit (possibly incorporated) organization in order to maintain their political voice? These are the very questions organizations within the LGBTQ communities (as well as other social change-seeking communities) have to face (Mulé, 2011). Because Canada's non-profit sector is regulated in this way, their voices are restricted, which has wider implications on democracy in this country (Mulé & DeSantis, 2017; Parachin, 2017).

# External Influences on LGBTQ Social Policy

The media play a powerful role in how LGBTQ people are depicted, thereby influencing public discourse in the process. Over time, a shift in media representations and public discourses has taken place: dominant coverage has gone from "scandalous" reportage of same-sex couples dancing together in certain bars to positive portrayals of Pride celebrations that emphasize diversity. All the same, LGBTQs who most resemble straight people, such as those who enter into same-sex marriages, receive more favourable news coverage than those who do not, such as men who seek out other men for sex in washrooms and parks. In addition, the media have not fully embraced intersectionality as expressed through groups such as Black Lives Matter–Toronto (BLM–TO) and segments of the community that identify as LGBTQ Muslims. When BLM–TO, in its status of "Honoured Group," halted the 2016 Pride Parade in Toronto to outline a set of demands for better recognition of Black queer issues along with Indigenous and disabled concerns, the mainstream media framed them as disrespectful, disruptive interlopers who should take up "their" (read: Black) issues elsewhere. The media were incapable of recognizing that many, if not most, members of BLM–TO identified as queer. Similarly, LGBTQ Muslims get little media attention, as the two identities are seen as completely unlinked.

Representations and discourses that hold up and value white, middle-class, able-bodied, cisgendered LGBTQs (especially males) over racialized, ethnicized, lower-class, disabled, trans LGBTQs (women in particular) go on to inform policy that becomes shaped according to homonormative expectations. Coupled relationships, traditional notions of family constitutions, and family-unit parenting heavily influence social policy (i.e., same-sex marriage and same-sex parental adoptions). By upholding such values, social policy replicates such discourses, serving to benefit those who ascribe to a homonormative existence over those who live their lives outside such narrowed depictions. By doing so, policy then contributes to what mainstream society generally considers "acceptable" and "respectable" LGBTQ people, based on relative resemblance to straight society, while marginalizing those who are comparably queer.

# Recent LGBTQ Social Policy Achievements and Debates

The growth of representation and recognition of all members of LGBTQ populations has not happened in a parallel process. Trans members of the LGBTQ communities are a prime example of this process, given the harsh realities many of them face. Data from the Ontario-based Trans PULSE Health Survey, one of the few studies of its kind in Canada, reveals that trans Ontarians are disproportionately impoverished, with over 40 per cent unemployed, underemployed, or unable to work. Fifty per cent of trans Ontarians reported an annual income of $15,000 or less, with one-fifth living in assisted or unstable housing (Trans PULSE E-Bulletin, 2010). Trans Ontarians consistently experience discrimination from landlords and health care providers (with 43 per cent of these providers lacking formal training on trans issues), including denial of access to shelters, mental health, and rape crisis services (Trans PULSE, 2007).

The prevalence of depression among male-to-female transgender Ontarians is 61 per cent (Rotondi et al., 2011a), and 66 per cent among female-to-male transgender Ontarians (Rotondi et al., 2011b). Forty-three per cent of trans Ontarians are using hormones, with 14 participants (out of 402) taking non-prescriptive hormones and five participants having either attempted or performed surgical procedures on themselves (Rotondi et al., 2013). Suicidal thoughts affect 77 per cent of trans Ontarians and 43 per cent have attempted suicide (Bauer, Pyne, Francino, & Hammond, 2013). Approximately half of the 83 per cent of trans Ontarians who have a physician are uncomfortable discussing trans issues with them, while 37 per cent of transmasculine and 38 per cent of transfeminine persons have had a trans-specific negative experience (Bauer, Scheim, Pyne, Travers, & Hammond, 2015; Bauer, Zong, Scheim, Hammond, & Thind, 2015). Thirty-three per cent engage in heavy episodic drinking (Scheim, Bauer, & Shokoohi, 2016) while 12 per cent engage in illicit drug use (Scheim, Bauer, & Shokoohi, 2017). The statistics in this paragraph and the one above indicate that the social determinants of health for trans people are inextricably linked to their social (stigmatized) and economic status.

Most recently, an increasing number of trans policies have been achieved, for transgender people represent one of the most marginalized and vulnerable segments of the LGBTQ communities. It is estimated that one in 200 adults may be transgender (Scheim & Bauer, 2015). The important inclusion of gender identity and expression in human rights legislation has spawned other trans-related policies, including health care access to hormones and gender confirmation surgery; sex on ID as defined by the individual rather than by biological assignment at birth; gender-neutral washrooms; education and recognition at border crossings such as airports; federal prison protections; and inclusion in the national census (Queer Ontario, 2016). Because the trans segment of LGBTQ communities has advocated for and activated the development of such policies, they have been at the forefront of a nuanced policy debate on gender. These debates are raising important questions as to who/what defines gender, how it is labelled, and the extent to which we collect such data and for what purposes.

Another choice Canada has been faced with is the inclusion of same-sex couples in the institution of marriage. Same-sex marriage was intensely debated at the time of its proposal, but the media gave minimal coverage to internal debates that took place and continue within LGBTQ communities. These debates look at the kinds of relationships that get state-sanctioned recognition and those that do not, as well as the homonormative implications for these communities (see Box 9.2).

**Box 9.2**  Same-Sex Marriage: A Status of Equality or Homonormativity?

Same-sex marriage was legalized in Canada in 2005, making it the fourth country in the world to do so. This recognition extends the full benefits associated with marriage to same-sex married couples. Before this recognition was attained, dominant debates centred on whether same-sex couples should be permitted access to the institution of marriage (Historica Canada, 2016). The media's depiction of the debates positioned the LGBTQ communities as in favour of same-sex marriage. The argument was that limiting marriage to a union between a man and a woman was a clear example of discrimination, for same-sex couples did not have access to the benefits—e.g., tax benefits and rights related to pensions, hospital visitation and health information, and inheritance—accorded to opposite-sex married couples. Opponents were depicted by the media as being moral (often religious) traditionalists, who argued same-sex couples did not warrant access to the institution of marriage. The notion here is that marriage was traditionally recognized as a union between one man and one woman and that same-sex couples were not recognized as equal to opposite-sex couples.

From an equality perspective, restricting marriage to opposite-sex couples is indeed discriminatory, delegitimizing the relationship between same-sex couples in the process. Yet, when looked at from a queer liberation position (Polikoff, 2008), which draws from a feminist perspective (Mossman, 1994; Phelan, 2001), the institution of marriage itself is questioned. Mulé (2010, p. 86) poses a series of questions that deconstruct notions of the institution of marriage, types of relationships, and this policy itself:

- How do we justify legal recognition of same-sex marriage as a human right to the exclusion of the myriad of relationships that exist in gender and sexually diverse communities and society in general?
- Are we aware that the pursuance of such an initiative contributes to a hierarchy of human rights with regard to relationship recognition?
- What message is being communicated to non-assimilationist sexually diverse individuals in light of married same-sex couples being elevated to the same level as a heteronormative construct?
- What impact will the **homonormalizing** of relationships have on queer culture?

"In essence," then, as I have argued (Mulé, 2010, p. 86), "why is society structured so that conjugal relationships warrant social and legal recognition over all other kinds of relationships?"

The media gave scant attention to the internal debates that took place and continue within LGBTQ communities. Queer liberationist segments of the LGBTQ movement raise critical questions such as the ones listed above. One implication of legalizing same-sex marriage for LGBTQ communities is that it exposes an ideological divide between those who buy into a homonormative model of couple-based relationships and those who do not. Benefits and social sanctioning are accorded the former, whereas the latter are further marginalized (Ettelbrick, 1997). Legalizing same-sex marriage in Canada may have achieved a form of couple-based equality, but this policy falls short of addressing equity with the myriad relationships outside of conjugality, whether LGBTQ or not.

# Future Directions for LGBTQ Social Policy in Canada

Although the equality-based approach to social policy development has benefited some LGBTQ people, the less privileged within these communities have been further marginalized. A queer liberationist perspective calls for a far less homonormative approach to policy that truly respects a diversity of lifestyles. That diversity must also capture intersectionalities that address far more nuanced issues that social policy needs to respond to. Ultimately, Canadian social policy needs to shift from the heavy legal influence of focusing on the individual to a more efficacious approach of focusing on systemic issues. For LGBTQ Canadians, it would mean developing social policy that shifts binary systemic approaches to sex, sexuality, and gender to address the diversified reality of their lives and the lives of all Canadians.

## International Comparisons

### LGBTQs in Canada Compared to Other Countries

When comparing the status of LGBTQs with regard to legal recognition and social protections internationally, Canada provides some of the most extensive legislation for its LGBTQ citizens. Legal recognition and social policy for LGBTQ Canadians include: decriminalization of same-sex sexual acts (1969); constitutional prohibition of discrimination based on sexual orientation (1995); prohibited grounds for discrimination based on sexual orientation (1996); hate crimes in which sexual orientation is considered an aggravating circumstance (1996); incitement to hatred based on sexual orientation prohibited (1996); same-sex marriage (2005); joint adoption by same-sex couples (provincially and territorially legislated between 1996 and 2009); and second-parent adoption (2005) (Carroll & Ramon Mendos, 2017; Equaldex, 2017).

Federally, trans populations received human rights protection when Bill C-31 passed in the Senate in June 2017. Such protections at provincial and territorial levels with regard to gender identity and/or expression vary. According to their respective vital statistics legislation, all provinces now permit name changes on birth certificates and driver's licences without the individual having gender confirmation surgery. This policy is similar in regard to gender markers on documentation in all provinces, with some variable conditions in Alberta and Quebec (Chiam, Duffy, & González Gil, 2016).

At the United Nations (UN), Canada has made repeated recommendations in Universal Periodic Reviews (UPRs) of other nation-states with regard to the decriminalization of same-sex acts and relations; threats of violence and persecuting of perpetrators; and anti-discrimination legislation. Canada has gathered some of this information through its Immigration and Refugee Board regarding LGBTQ-identified asylum seekers or refugee applicants seeking status in Canada. In addition, initiatives are undertaken in Canada to train and sensitize law enforcement officials regarding the human rights of LGBTQs. With regard to physical and mental health, conversion therapy (attempting to turn LGBTQs straight) has been banned in both Ontario and Manitoba (Carroll & Ramon Mendos, 2017; Equaldex, 2017). Nevertheless, Canada continues to have unequal age of consent for same- and different-sex sexual acts.

In the international rights arena of LGBTQs and sexual orientation, gender identity and expression, and sex characteristics, the UPRs are a place to express concerns, which it is hoped over time will lead to recommendations that can be followed up on to see if they have been implemented. Over the past eight years, there has been a noted increase in recommendations brought forth by LGBTQ advocates regarding these rights.

Internationally, Canada is considered one of the most progressive countries in the world with regard to its recognition and treatment of LGBTQs. The human rights laws and protective policies that provide recognition and affirmation in Canada are in stark contrast to other countries. The death penalty is imposed on same-sex sexual activity in 13 countries or in regions within these countries: Afghanistan, Iran, Iraq, Mauritania, Nigeria, Pakistan, Qatar, Saudi Arabia, Somalia, Sudan, Syria, United Arab Emirates, and Yemen (Carroll & Ramon Mendos, 2017). In another 12 countries same-sex sexual activity can result in imprisonment from 15 years to life, with 53 states (or parts of countries) having prison sentences of up to 14 years. (The terms "countries" and "states" are used interchangeably at the UN.) The criminalization of same-sex relationships includes 45 states that deem relationships between females illegal and 72 states that deem the same for relationships between males. Maximum sentencing can be generated by "promotion propaganda" laws (3 states), sexual act (15 states), sodomy (11 states), against nature (30 states), buggery (13 states), and morality laws that prohibit LGB expression (19 countries and some provinces) (ILGA, 2017a).

By contrast, Canada is counted among protectionist states for prohibiting discrimination against sexual orientation. Nine states explicitly name sexual orientation as grounds for protection against discrimination in their constitutions. In Canada, as noted earlier, it took the Supreme Court's 1995 *Egan v. Canada* decision to affirm that the general prohibition in section 15 of the Charter against discrimination based on sex includes sexual orientation. Canada is one of 43 states where "hate crimes based on sexual orientation" are "considered an aggravating circumstance." Similarly, Canada is among 39 states where "incitement to hatred based on sexual orientation" is "prohibited," and is also one of 86 states with a national human rights institution that includes sexual orientation within its mandate (ILGA, 2017c). In addition, Canada recognizes same-sex unions (as do 46 other countries and 50 other entities, i.e., geographical areas without state or provincial status) (ILGA, 2017b), legalized same-sex marriage (22 countries) (ILGA, 2017d), joint adoption (26 states), and second-parent adoption (27 states) (ILGA, 2017b). Canada is seen by many persecuted LGBTQ people as a safe haven to seek asylum or refugee status, as it is one of 44 countries in the world to recognize persecution based on sexual orientation and gender identity and expression (UN, 2011).

On the surface, Canada appears accepting given its national track record of policy protections for LGBTQs, not to mention our federal leaders raising concerns in the international arena regarding LGBTQ human rights violations in other countries. Yet, Canada's

*continued*

protectionist policies for LGBTQs can be the "homonationalist" veneer that distracts from its poor attention to Indigenous, racialized, disabled, and impoverished populations, all of which include LGBTQs. Canada is also implicated in pinkwashing, that is, campaigns that support other countries that hold up respectful treatment of LGBTQs on the surface, while covertly continuing to oppress subgroups of LGBTQs within. LGBTQ recognition in the political world is not solely about social justice, but in fact, about money and power (McCaskell, 2016).

# Role(s) for Social Workers in LGBTQ Social Policy Development

Social workers can work at all levels—micro (within the setting of their employer), mezzo (within the community of service recipients they are serving), and macro (any of the governmental levels and/or with social movements)—in addressing LGBTQ policy issues. Social workers can apply their skills by working within the system (sometimes as policy-makers) or by transferring their skills outside the system (participation in social movements) or both. As our profession's advocating voice, the Canadian Association of Social Workers (CASW) and/or its member provincial/territorial bodies can be urged to take up LGBTQ issues more actively. Through social work's commitment to social justice and to advocate for those who are disenfranchised and marginalized, social workers can assist both individually and collectively in addressing the needs of LGBTQ communities (see Social Policy Change in Action box).

## Social Policy Change in Action

### LGBTQ Proactive Social Work

Beginning at the most micro level, all social workers are well served to engage in personal reflexive practice regarding their own comfort level with diverse sexual orientations and gender identities and expressions. Developing knowledge and understanding of LGBTQ issues and concerns and learning how best to respond to them can assist greatly in providing services. Being familiar with existing rights, laws, and policies regarding LGBTQ communities provides a proactive lens with which to approach doing social work with these populations.

Also at the micro level, approaching all aspects of our work with an awareness of LGBTQ issues creates a sensitized gaze that allows us to determine whether the services we offer are inclusive. LGBTQ-aware approaches include welcoming environmental settings, intake forms, assessment forms, services, and programming that can accommodate and respond to the realities of LGBTQ lives.

At the mezzo level, social workers can often have a direct hand in developing and writing policy or, at minimum, providing feedback. Similarly, social workers can facilitate input from service recipients via focus groups and public forums to ensure they have a direct say in the shaping of agency policy and programming. It is also at this level that the knowledgeable social worker can apply her or his understanding of human rights and legal justice policy in settings where such voices are less likely to be heard. After all, not only do heteronormative and cisnormative policies make agencies vulnerable to human rights complaints, but such policies are not in keeping with social work ethics and values.

The larger macro level offers social workers the opportunity to contribute to the voice of the profession via one's professional association, whether at the local, provincial/territorial, or national level. Social workers can also assert their voices directly with politicians, civil servants, and policy-makers via letters, deputations, or meetings. Once again, asserting an LGBTQ-sensitized perspective is a means of holding these policy actors to account regarding the policy to be addressed. Finally, social workers have an enormous amount of transferable skills that can be applied outside formal social work and in the world of social movements. From analyzing critical policy to writing, from facilitating issue-based discussions to organizing events and actions, from educating the public to lobbying politicians and policy-makers, social workers can continue to contribute to the work of social movements and ultimately to social change.

# Chapter Summary

This chapter began by examining the present state of social policy in Canada regarding LGBTQ people. A cursory overview of the history of social policy development driven by the LGBTQ movement was then provided. The LGBTQ movement's prioritizing of anti-discrimination human rights protections has resulted in sexual orientation being recognized as a protected ground at all levels across the country. Gender identity/expression is increasingly becoming an enumerated ground for protection. Structurally, Canada's three levels of government and the Supreme Court of Canada have been the settings in which many social policy changes for LGBTQs have taken place.

Yet, despite these developments, a critical intersectional analysis reveals that within these communities some people benefit while others do not. The complexities of social policy for LGBTQs were highlighted in three areas: how advocacy is regulated within charities and non-profits in Canada affecting LGBTQ organizing; the recognition of same-sex marriage and its divisional effects on the LGBTQ communities; and how Canadian LGBTQs compare to LGBTQs around the world. Although Canadian society's values, norms, and morals have certainly shifted towards greater acceptance of LGBTQ people, the LGBTQ communities themselves have their own ever-changing discourse that policy may not fully reflect. Finally, the role social workers can play in contributing to the positive development of social policy for LGBTQ populations was outlined.

# Discussion Questions

1. To what extent are sexual orientation and gender identity and expression formally recognized in human rights legislation in Canada?

2. Beyond basic anti-discrimination human rights protections for LGBTQ Canadians, what other human rights protections are unique to them as opposed to other Canadians?

3. Human rights legislation and social policy are often seen as beneficial to LGBTQs, but can they also have a detrimental effect? If so, how?

4. What roles can social workers play to ensure that LGBTQs are equally and equitably recognized in practice?

5. How does Canada's recognition of LGBTQs compare to that of other countries around the world?

# References

Bauer, G. R., Pyne, J, Francino, M. C., & Hammond, R. (2013). Suicidality among trans people in Ontario: Implications for social work and social justice. *Social Services, 59*(1), 35–62.

———, Scheim, A. I., Pyne, J., Travers, R., & Hammond, R. (2015). Intervenable factors associated with suicide risk in transgender persons: A respondent driven sampling study in Ontario, Canada. *BMC Public Health, 15*, 525.

———, Zong, X., Scheim, A. I., Hammond, R., & Thind, A. (2015). Factors impacting transgender patients' discomfort with their family physicians: A respondent driven sampling study. PLoS ONE, 10(12), e0145046.

Canada Revenue Agency. (2016a). Political activities. Retrieved from http://www.cra-arc.gc.ca/chrts-gvng/chrts/plcy/cps/cps-022-eng.html

———. (2016b). What is the difference between a registered charity and a non-profit organization? Retrieved from http://www.cra-arc.gc.ca/chrts-gvng/dnrs/rgltn/dffrnc-rc-np-eng.html

Canadian Bar Association. (2016). Letter: Inclusion of gender identity and gender expression in Nunavut Human Rights Act. Retrieved from https://www.cba.org/CMSPages/GetFile.aspx?guid=32ed971e-7e3a-42e8-9190-10c231179c85

Canadian Human Rights Commission. (n.d.). Milestones. Retrieved from https://www.chrc-ccdp.gc.ca/eng/milestones-timeline

Canadian Union of Public Employees (CUPE). (2009). Timeline on Canada's queer rights. Retrieved from https://cupe.on.ca/wp-content/uploads/2015/03/LGBT-TIMELINE-CANADA1.pdf

Carroll, A., & Ramon Mendos, L. (2017). *State-sponsored homophobia: A world survey of sexual orientation laws. Criminalisation, protection and recognition* (12th edn). Geneva: International Lesbian, Gay, Bisexual, Trans and Intersex Association (ILGA). Retrieved from http://ilga.org/downloads/2017/ILGA_State_Sponsored_Homophobia_2017_WEB.pdf

Chiam, Z., Duffy, S., & González Gil, M. (2016). *Trans legal mapping report 2016: Recognition before the law.* Geneva: ILGA. Retrieved from http://ilga.org/downloads/TLMR_ENG.pdf

Court Challenges Program. (n.d.). About CCP. Retrieved from http://www.ccppcj.ca/en/about.php

Equaldex. (2017). LGBT rights in Canada. Retrieved from http://www.equaldex.com/region/canada

Ettelbrick, P. L. (1997). Since when is marriage a path to liberation? In R. M. Baird & S. E. Rosenbaum (Eds), *Same-sex marriage: The moral and legal debate* (pp. 164–8). New York: Prometheus Books.

Government of Canada. (2017). Overview—Court Challenges Program. Retrieved from http://canada.pch.gc.ca/eng/1485454544282/1485789535473

Harris, K. (2017, 13 Jan.). Correctional Service flip-flops on transgender inmate placement policy. *CBC News.* Retrieved from http://www.cbc.ca/news/politics/transgender-inmates-placement-policy-1.3934796

Historica Canada. (2016). Same-sex marriage in Canada. Retrieved from http://www.thecanadianencyclopedia.ca/en/article/same-sex-marriage-in-canada/

Hurley, M. C. (2005). *Sexual orientation and legal rights: A chronological overview.* Ottawa: Parliament of Canada. Retrieved from http://www.lop.parl.gc.ca/content/lop/research publications/prb0413-e.htm

International Lesbian, Gay, Bisexual, Trans and Intersex Association (ILGA). (2017a). Sexual orientation laws in the world—Criminalisation. Retrieved from http://ilga.org/downloads/2017/ILGA_WorldMap_ENGLISH_Criminalisation_2017.pdf

———. (2017b). Sexual orientation laws in the world—Overview. Retrieved from http://ilga.org/downloads/2017/ILGA_WorldMap_ENGLISH_Overview_2017.pdf

———. (2017c). Sexual orientation laws in the world—Protection. Retrieved from http://ilga.org/downloads/2017/ILGA_WorldMap_ENGLISH_Protection_2017.pdf

———. (2017d). Sexual orientation laws in the world—Recognition. Retrieved from http://ilga.org/downloads/2017/ILGA_WorldMap_ENGLISH_Recognition_2017.pdf

Justice Quebec. (2017). The fight against homophobia. Government of Quebec. Retrieved from http://www.justice.gouv.qc.ca/english/ministere/dossiers/homophobie/homophobie-a.htm

Liao, C. (2017). The changing face of the nonprofit sector: Social enterprise legislation in British Columbia. In N. J. Mulé & G. C. DeSantis (Eds), *The shifting terrain: Nonprofit sector public policy advocacy in Canada.* Montreal & Kingston: McGill-Queen's University Press.

McCaskell, T. (2016). *Queer progress: From homophobia to homonationalism.* Toronto: Between the Lines Press.

McNeil-Seymour, J. (2015). Cross-dancing as culturally restorative practice. In B. J. O'Neill, T. A. Swan, & N. J. Mulé (Eds), *LGBTQ people and social work: Intersectional perspectives* (pp. 87–105). Toronto: Canadian Scholars' Press.

Mossman, M. J. (1994). Running hard to stand still: The paradox of family law reform. *Dalhousie Law Journal, 17,* 5–34.

Mulé, N. J. (2010). Same-sex marriage and Canadian relationship recognition—One step forward, two steps back: A critical liberationist perspective. *Journal of Gay and Lesbian Social Services, 22*(1–2), 74–90.

———. (2011). Advocacy limitations on gender and sexually diverse activist organizations in Canada's voluntary sector. *Canadian Journal of Nonprofit and Social Economy Research, 2*(1), 5–23. Retrieved from http://www.anserj.ca/index.php/cjnser/article/viewFile/52/18

———. (2015). The politicized queer, the informed social worker: Dis/re-ordering the social order. In B. J. O'Neill, T. A. Swan, & N. J. Mulé (Eds), *LGBTQ people and social work: Intersectional perspectives* (pp. 17–35). Toronto: Canadian Scholars' Press.

——— & DeSantis, G. C. (2017). A "political activity": The inherent politicization of advocacy. In N. J. Mulé & G. C. DeSantis (Eds), *The shifting terrain: Nonprofit sector public policy advocacy in Canada.* Montreal & Kingston: McGill-Queen's University Press.

My Big Gay Family. (2015). Lesbian access to IVF and IUI in Canada. Retrieved from http://www.mybiggayfamily.com/lesbian-access-to-ivf-and-iui-in-canada/

Ontario Human Rights Commission. (n.d.). Part 1: The context: Sexual orientation, human rights protections, case law and legislation. Toronto: OHRC. Retrieved from http://www.ohrc.on.ca/en/policy-discrimination-and-harassment-because-sexual-orientation/part-i-%E2%80%93-context-sexual-orientation-human-rights-protections-case-law-and-legislation

Parachin, A. (2017). Shifting legal terrain: Legal and regulatory restrictions on political advocacy by charities. In N. J. Mulé & G.C. DeSantis (Eds), *The shifting terrain: Nonprofit sector public policy advocacy in Canada.* Montreal & Kingston: McGill-Queen's University Press.

Parliament of Canada. (2017). *Bill C-16,* Royal Assent. Retrieved from http://www.parl.ca/DocumentViewer/en/42-1/bill/C-16/royal-assent

Phelan, S. (2001). *Sexual strangers: Gays, lesbians and dilemmas of citizenship.* Philadelphia: Temple University Press.

Polikoff, N. (2008). *Beyond (straight and gay) marriage: Valuing all families under the law.* Boston: Beacon Press.

Queer Ontario. (2016). Queer Ontario applauds federal government's proposed Bill C-16: Urges responsible follow up. Retrieved from http://queerontario.org/page/3/

Rotondi, N. K., Bauer, G. R, Travers, R., Travers, A., Scanlon, K., & Kaay, M. (2011a). Depression in male-to-female transgender Ontarians: Results from the Trans PULSE Project. Canadian Journal of Community Mental Health, 30(2), 113–33.

———, ———, Scanlon, K., Kaay, M., Travers, R., & Travers, A. (2011b). Prevalence of and risk and protective factors for depression in female-to-male transgender Ontarians: Trans PULSE Project. *Canadian Journal of Community Mental Health, 30*(2), 135–55.

————, ————, ————, ————, ————, & ————. (2013). Nonprescribed hormone use and self-performed surgeries: "Do-it-yourself" transitions in transgender communities in Ontario, Canada. *American Journal of Public Health, 103*(10), 1830–6.

Scheim, A. I., & Bauer, G. R. (2015). Sex and gender diversity among transgender persons in Ontario, Canada: Results from a respondent-driven sampling survey. *Journal of Sex Research, 52*(1), 1–14.

————, ————, & Shokoohi, M. (2016). Heavy episodic drinking among transgender persons: Disparities and predictors. *Drug and Alcohol Dependence, 167,* 156–62. doi:http://dx.doi.org/10.1016/j.drugalcdep.2016.08.011

————, ————, & ————. (2017). Drug use among transgender people in Ontario, Canada: Disparities and associations with social exclusion. *Addictive Behaviors, 72,* 151–8. doi:http://doi.org/10.1016/j.addbeh.2017.03.022

Smith, M. (1999). *Lesbian and gay rights in Canada: Social movements and equality-seeking, 1971–1995.* Toronto: University of Toronto Press.

Trans PULSE. (2007). *Trans Pulse: Report on Phase I & plans for Phases II and III.* London, ON: University of Western Ontario. Retrieved from http://www.transpulse.ca/documents/Trans_PULSE_Phase_I_Report.pdf

Trans PULSE E-Bulletin. (2010). Who are trans people in Ontario? Vol. 1, 1. London: University of Western Ontario. Retrieved from http://transpulse.ca/documents/E1English.pdf

United Nations, Human Rights Council. (2011). *Discriminatory laws and practices and acts of violence against individuals based on their sexual orientation and gender identity.* Report of the United Nations High Commissioner for Human Rights. Retrieved from http://www.ohchr.org/Documents/Issues/Discrimination/A.HRC.19.41_English.pdf

Warner, T. (2002). *Never going back: A history of queer activism in Canada.* Toronto: University of Toronto Press.

Wikipedia. (2017). LGBT rights in Canada. Retrieved from https://en.wikipedia.org/wiki/LGBT_rights_in_Canada

# 10 (dis)Ability Policy

## A Tangled Web of Complexity

*Judy E. MacDonald with Sarah Natalie Cooper*

---

### Chapter Objectives

*This chapter will help you to develop an understanding of:*
- the social positioning of (dis)Abled persons as it pertains to historical and current marginalization;
- (dis)Ability policies at the federal, provincial, and post-secondary levels;
- the strengths and limitations of (dis)Ability policies;
- advocacy for (dis)Ability rights to support (dis)Abled persons' claim (or right) to equitable services and income;
- links between social work and social policy to (dis)Ability rights and services.

---

## Introduction

In Canada, 13.7 per cent of the population live with a (dis)Ability. Specifically, 30 per cent of Indigenous people (Rioux, 2014) and 42.5 per cent of people 75 and older report living with a (dis)Ability (Statistics Canada, 2015). Within a global context, 15.3 per cent of the world's population are estimated to live with a (dis)Ability, with 3 per cent living with a severe (dis)Ability (i.e., blindness, quadriplegia) (WHO, 2011). Geographical location, age, and gender all have a bearing on the rates of (dis)Ability: "across all countries, vulnerable groups such as women, those in the poorest wealth quintile, and older people had higher prevalences of disability" (WHO, 2011, p. 27). According to the United Nations (2006), 20 per cent of the poorest people in the world are (dis)Abled.

Within this chapter, a rights-based anti-oppressive perspective is used to critique (dis)Ability policy to specifically acknowledge (dis)Abled persons as socially marginalized; to centre their voices in decision-making processes; to deconstruct the impacts of **ableism**; and to support an inclusive, accessible culture (Carter, Hanes, & MacDonald, 2017). Case stories are shared throughout to illustrate the impact of (dis)Ability policies on the lived experiences of (dis)Abled persons. Readers are challenged to examine their own biases and assumptions about (dis)Abled persons as they consider the cases and envision practising as social workers. While the social focus and media portrayal of (dis)Abled persons in recent years have shifted to a more inclusive paradigm, decades of judgement, dismissal,

## Case Examples   Issues Facing the (dis)Abled

**Evelyn**, 57, a psychiatric nurse, singularly raised three children while living with chronic pain, rheumatoid arthritis, and severe asthma (MacDonald, 2006). Her afternoons were spent packed in ice in the physiotherapy department. The stiffness and pain were immobilizing. Her immune system was compromised. The simplest of tasks, like doing the dishes, were exhausting. After 36 years of nursing, she applied for the Canada Pension Plan Disability benefit. The application form consisted of 27 pages of questions, with the same question posed in at least three different ways. Exhausted and in pain, she had to collect medical documents from her family physician, rheumatologist, and physiotherapist. Further, she had to have the mental clarity and physical energy to fill out detailed medical information. Evelyn's application was denied. She had worked for more than three decades and now her body was saying "no more." Yet the government of Canada claimed that she was ineligible for this benefit. (See the section titled "The Quebec/Canada Pension Plan" later in this chapter for more about this case.)

In 2016, **Felipe Montoya**, a Costa Rican–born tenured professor at York University, was denied application for permanent residence in Canada because his 13-year-old son, **Nico**, who lives with Down syndrome, could place "excessive demands" on the Canadian health care system (*CBC News*, 2016a), aligning with section 38(1) of the Immigration and Refugee Protection Act (Government of Canada, 2001), which states that "a foreign national is inadmissible on health grounds if their health condition (c) might reasonably be expected to cause excessive demand on health or social services." A series of special medical examinations found Nico to be in good physical health, yet it was decided Nico's genetic condition could put an undue strain on Canada's health and social services. Nico's father and several supporters launched a public campaign, which eventually resulted in the decision being overturned on humanitarian and compassionate grounds. (See the section titled "Division Four of Canada's Immigration and Refugee Protection Act" later in this chapter for more about this case.)

and oppression continue to cloud how people with (dis)Abilities are viewed and subsequently treated. Therefore, a historical lens to (dis)Ability and (dis)Ability-related policies is highlighted, followed by a sketch of contemporary (dis)Ability policy and their related critiques. The ultimate objective is to guide the reader towards envisioning a communal society that embraces all abilities in their varied forms, with social policies designed for full participation.

## Perspective on (dis)Ability

**(dis)Ability** is socially, politically, and economically constructed (Mackelprang & Salsgiver, 2015). According to Oliver (1996, p. 33), "disability is something imposed on top of our impairments by the way we are unnecessarily isolated and excluded from full participation in society." "No more about us, without us" became the mantra for (dis)Ability organizations mobilizing for political change. The Independent Living Movement, formed in the early 1970s in the United States, followed by the Canadian Association of Independent Living in 1986, brought the voices of people with intellectual (dis)Abilities to public and government attention. Canadian members advocated for de-institutionalization by filming the stories of those institutionalized with the "Freedom Tour" project (MacDonald, Cooper, & Myers, forthcoming). People with "like experiences" came together to create a force and sense of power greater than what can be achieved through one person. Problem areas were "redefined as those of structural inequality rather than of personal inadequacy" (Hanes, 2016, p. 75).

The Independent Living Movement is based on the premise that (dis)Abled people and their supporters are best positioned to identify their needs, including the supports and policies necessary to strengthen their citizenship participation. An anti-oppressive practice lens that centres (dis)Abled persons' voices and knowledges, coupled with the Canadian Disability Policy Alliance (Bond & McColl, 2013, p. 10) principles—"a) equity – freedom from discrimination, b) access – ability to participate, and c) support – resources to address . . . needs"—forms the theoretical and applied perspective taken in this chapter.

Throughout history, people with (dis)Abilities have occupied different social and cultural spaces. Before colonialism, Indigenous communities considered (dis)Abled people to be part of their community, collectively responding to their needs (Dunn & Langdon, 2016). However, with European conquest, dominant European stereotypes of (dis)Ability carried over to Canadian culture. For example, the term "normal" versus "abnormal" stemmed from a Belgian statistician's use of the bell curve and normal distribution to identify the average human. "Normal became a standard to strive for, providing justification for systematic efforts to fix those considered abnormal" (Mackelprang & Salsgiver, 2015, p. 6). The biomedical model of (dis)Ability established medical professionals as the authorities to judge

---

## Box 10.1   Explaining "(dis)Ability"

Language is powerful. Shifting (dis)Ability discourse to inclusive, respectful identifiers is a critical aspect of anti-oppressive work.

Disability results from the interaction between persons with impairments and attitudinal and environmental barriers that hinders their full and effective participation in society on an equal basis with others. (UN, 2008)

In this chapter, the term "(dis)Ability" is presented with a capital "A" for "Ability" to acknowledge the multiple "Abilities" of people with (dis)Ability. The "(dis)" is in brackets with a small "d" to respect their social location as (dis)Abled individuals without over-emphasizing their impairment or *lack* of ability. (MacDonald & Friars, 2010).

"People-first language" emphasizes the person over the (dis)Ability re "people with (dis)Abilities," whereas "(dis)Abled persons" centres disability. The authors respect both language locations as demonstrations of the fluidity and complexity of (dis)Ability.

who was "normal." Today, (dis)Ability benefits still rely on medical evaluations, and many accommodation policies require physician verification of (dis)Ability and subsequent needs.

## Institutionalization

Institutional care for people with (dis)Abilities dates back to the mid-1800s, beginning with asylums for the insane. Centracare, originally called the Provincial Lunatic Asylum (1835) in Saint John, New Brunswick, housed up to 1,500 *patients* at its peak (Asylum Project, 2016). Legislation gave the provinces the right to build large institutions for the insane where people were involuntarily admitted and given no treatment options or voice in their own care (L'Arche Canada, 2014). Specialized schools or institutions for (dis)Ability-specific impairments were also created. For example, the first school for the deaf in Canada was in Quebec City (1831). The Institute for the Deaf and Dumb (later renamed The School for the Deaf) in Halifax, Nova Scotia, opened in 1856 in a house in the north end of the city with 12 students. A year later, through an annual grant of $1,200, it became the first school in the British colonies to secure government support, thereby acknowledging the government's responsibility to educate deaf children.

Another form of institutionalization came with the development of sanatoriums for tuberculosis, beginning with the Toronto Hospital for Consumptives (1904), followed by Queen Mary's Sanatorium for children in the same city in 1913 (Asylum Project, 2016). The development of antibiotics and vaccinations eventually eliminated the need for sanatoriums with the last TB sanatorium patient in Canada being discharged in 1970. Some institutions were then converted to facilities for people with developmental (dis)Abilities and/or mental health illnesses, including the Jordan Memorial Sanatorium in River Glade, New Brunswick (Hamilton, 1995).

Centracare closed in 1998 and the asylum in Orillia in 2009. Over time, "institutionalization of people with disabilities had become so widespread that it was commonly believed to be the natural order of things" (Hanes, 2017, p. 408). The stigmatization of (dis)Ability led families to hide (dis)Abled members in their attics or basements (MacDonald & Friars, 2010), as the perceived "defect" would devalue the family's social status.

Conditions within institutions for the (dis)Abled were inhumane. Parents were convinced to institutionalize their (dis)Abled children; physicians told them their children would be simplistic at best—that is, never able to participate fully in society. Dr Seana Kozar, writer, director, and producer of the documentary *Almost Normal*, about five (dis)Abled women, could have grown up in an institution. Seana's parents, after receiving the news their child was born with cerebral palsy, were advised to have her institutionalized. However, Seana, at the age of 19, was offered fully funded entrance into a PhD program (Kozar, 2004). As Seana argued, "Not bad for an invalid."

Many accounts of physical, emotional, and sexual abuse have been recounted from (dis)Abled children and adults who were institutionalized, as evident in the class action lawsuit against Ontario's institutions for people with mental health (dis)Abilities (*CBC News*, 2016d) in which a court approved $36 million in compensation for ex-residents. These children and adults described how institutionalized residents often had to work for very little pay (if they were paid at all), were given no privacy, with rows of beds lining the halls (L'Arche, 2014), and were abused as a means of control. For example, deaf children would be strapped for using sign language (MacDonald, 2016a).

## The Eugenics Movement in the Twentieth Century

The **eugenics movement** was ignited through the work of Francis Galton, an English academic, who explored genetics for the purpose of improving the human race (Bouche & Rivard, 2014). "Eugenicists implemented draconian social engineering measures to promote the survival of the fittest and to discourage the reproduction of undesirables in an attempt to purify society" (Mackelprang & Salsgiver, 2015, p. 7). People with (dis)Abilities were considered weak and vulnerable, a defect in human reproduction that needed to be hidden away from society and preferably euthanized. Adolf Hitler's T4 program (1939–45) saw people with (dis)Abilities in Germany sent to the gas chambers, including approximately 100,000 people taken from mental institutions (Withers, 2012). In fact, (dis)Abled persons were used experimentally to *perfect* the gassing process (Mackelprang & Salsgiver, 2015). Up to a quarter of a million (dis)Abled people are believed to have been murdered through the T4 program, including children and elders. Little attention was paid to what was happening to the (dis)Abled. The Nazis had one agenda—purification of the race—and people with (dis)Abilities did not fit this agenda. The T4 program was known as "Lebensunwertes Leben," meaning "life unworthy of life" (Mann, 2014).

The eugenicist philosophy emerged in North America through the sterilization of the (dis)Abled aimed at the prevention of procreation. Sterilization legislation in both Alberta (1928) and British Columbia (1933) created eugenics boards to approve sterilization of those deemed unfit for procreation (Withers, 2012). *Muir v. The Queen in right of Alberta* (1996) was filed after Leilani Muir discovered the appendectomy she had at age 15 was actually a hysterectomy. She had been admitted to the Provincial Training School for Mental Defectives when she was 10 years old, primarily because she came from a poor family, was a girl, and had a "habit" of stealing lunches from other children at school (*Muir v. Alberta*). The Eugenics Board application for sterilization from the school's physician noted Muir's diagnosis as "mental defective—moron" (*Muir v. Alberta*, p. 10). Leilani was awarded close to $750,000 for the damages inflicted upon her life and the pain and suffering she endured as a result of her forced sterilization and wrongful confinement in the Provincial Training School.

As (dis)Ability, in large part, is socially constructed, societal attitudes (such as purification of the race) direct legislation that then impacts the lives of citizens. The intersection of race and ability heightened one's exposure to oppression and abuse (MacDonald, 2016b). Stote (2015) has uncovered that Indigenous women in Canada were disproportionately sterilized without their consent until the 1970s. She ascertains sterilization was used to directly impact social policy, including reducing the size of houses needed on reserves if families were kept smaller. Sterilizing (dis)Abled women would limit the need for (dis)Ability services, including financial benefits. These policies were in direct opposition to (dis)Ability rights and Indigenous rights, that is, the right to autonomy and self-direction of (dis)Abled and Indigenous women.

Today, ableism is evident through modern-day eugenics infiltrating health and social services. Parents of severely (dis)Abled children have to advocate to have a "please resuscitate" order placed on their child's hospital chart upon admission (Beagan et al., 2006). Parents have been asked by pediatricians about a DNR (do not resuscitate) order being placed on the (dis)Abled child's chart whereby life-saving interventions would be withheld and the child would be allowed to die should a life-threatening situation arise—a form of passive euthanasia. Further, people with (dis)Abilities have been denied transplants. MacDonald and

Friars (2010) presented a case where a 17-year-old needing a heart/lung transplant was deemed too high risk to be placed on a transplant list. Her assessment was based on her being poor and having an intellectual (dis)Ability, as it was believed she would not have the emotional or financial supports to follow through with the strict post-operative transplant protocol. These examples involve professionals placing value judgements on the lives of (dis)Abled persons, judgements that relate back to eugenics—life unworthy of life (Mann, 2014).

## Deinstitutionalization

With the rise of the civil rights movement in the 1960s coupled with the return of injured veterans from World War II, the Korean War, and the Vietnam War, people with (dis)Abilities began to explore alternatives to institutionalization and push for access and inclusion within society (Carter, 2016; Stienstra, 2012). Women's rights, trade unionism, and the civil rights movements were creating an atmosphere of equity, non-discrimination, and fundamental human rights that carried over into (dis)Abilities communities (Pierre, 2014). The "Ugly Laws" were challenged (Eugenics Archive, 2015). These were municipal laws in the United States that prohibited people deemed to be "diseased, maimed, mutilated, or in any way deformed, so as to be an unsightly or disgusting object" (Coco, 2010, p. 23) from occupying public space. (dis)Ability activists were mobilizing: "The onus had shifted from the state and medical authorities to consumers, patients, and families who needed to navigate the contours of a patchwork of services, supports, and gaps in a modern health system" (Eugenics Archive, 2015, deinstitutionalization).

However, it is taking decades for large institutions warehousing people with (dis)Abilities to close, partly due to the need to create community service infrastructure. Some residents of large institutions had been incarcerated for 30 years, under constant surveillance and with no discretion to make their own decisions. Therefore, upon release they need support in adjusting to the community where their self-identity and self-worth must be redefined. The supports needed within the community are not always forthcoming, resulting in a service breakdown and even homelessness for the (dis)Abled, particularly people with mental health (dis)Abilities (Crichton & Jongbloed, 1998). Organizations like Independent Living, with 25 offices across Canada, seek to give voice to people with (dis)Abilities through consumer control. The primary focus is on people's ability, not their impairments. L'Arche Canada, another progressive organization, offers community living for people with developmental and intellectual (dis)Abilities based on the belief that "community forms when we discover we are interdependent and that every person has gifts to contribute to us and we to them" (L'Arche Canada, 2015). While these organizations are critically important in the support and services they provide, they do not begin to meet the need. Across the country 100,000 people with intellectual/developmental (dis)Abilities have "core" housing needs (Canadian Association for Community Living, 2016), meaning they have significant difficulty in finding affordable, suitable housing.

## (dis)Ability Rights

Following the eugenics and biomedical influences on (dis)Abilities, a rights-based emphasis on (dis)Ability emerged. Globally, the United Nations began with its Declaration on the Rights of Disabled Persons (1975), based on the self-worth and dignity of all persons and the principle of non-discrimination. The Canadian Charter of Rights and Freedoms (1982) brought a new mode of opportunity and organization to (dis)Abled Canadians. Notably, in an early draft of the Charter, section 15 (the non-discrimination clause) did not include "disability" (Murphy, 2016). It read, "Everyone has the right to equality before the law and to equal protection of the law without discrimination because of race, national or ethnic origin, colour, religion, age or sex" (Murphy, 2016, p. 87). (dis)Ability groups lobbied for months and mobilized a massive demonstration on Parliament Hill in November 1980. They pressured the government to include them in the Charter, arguing that to exclude people with (dis)Abilities would mean the overarching law of Canada would be based on a stratified system of rights, valuing some rights over others. Following their activism, the Charter does include disability in section 15. The non-discrimination clause has meant that (dis)Abled people in Canada cannot be discriminated against.

However, "do not discriminate against" does not necessarily equate with supporting (dis)Abled persons. Many critics believe the rights-based movements do not go far enough in advocating for supports and dismantling barriers for the (dis)Abled (Stienstra & Wight-Felske, 2003; Withers, 2012). Internationally, a number of (dis)Ability initiatives were taken up by the United Nations, including the International Year of Disabled Persons (1981), which focused on full citizen participation and increased public awareness of ableist barriers and mobilization of (dis)Abled persons (UN, 2006). This initiative was followed by the UN Declaration of the Decade of Disabled Persons (1983–92), which focused on education and employment of (dis)Abled persons. The United Nations Convention on the Rights of Persons with Disabilities (2008) asked all nations to work together in eliminating (dis)Ability oppression and promoting access and inclusion. In 2010, Canada joined countries around the world when they ratified this UN Convention and thereby committed to "combat stereotypes and prejudices and promote awareness of the capabilities of persons with disabilities" (Article 8). These efforts helped solidify (dis)Ability as a rights-based issue, as opposed to a medical or illness issue.

# (dis)Ability Policy

Canada does not have a national (dis)Ability) policy. Rather, (dis)Ability policy is a patchwork of federal (i.e., Canada/Quebec Pension Plan disability benefits) and provincial (e.g., Ontarians with Disabilities Act) legislation and municipal (e.g., Halifax's Access-A-Bus service for the (dis)Abled) programs (Prince, 2016). No structured framework of policy development strategically addresses the social, political, and economic conditions upon which (dis)Abled persons live.

Some policies come in the form of legislation. Some legislation is specific to (dis)Ability, such as the Canada Disability Savings Act, a registered (dis)Ability savings plan aimed at securing financial stability for (dis)Abled persons. The Act has three components: Registered Disability Savings Plan (RDSP), Canada Disability Savings Grant, and a Canada Disability Savings Bond. The RDSP through the Canada Revenue Agency is a tax-free saving plan for people who have been approved for the Disability Tax Credit. The federal government will match contributions up to $3,500 annually, with a 2/1 or 3/1 match depending on family income. The bond is $1,000/year from the federal government in an RDSP for families of low and modest income (Government of Canada, 2016). However, access is restricted in two substantive ways:

1. Those who have more money to contribute will receive the largest tax break and hence the greatest benefit. For example, the maximum lifetime grant cap if you are able to make contributions to an RDSP is $70,000, while the maximum lifetime bond cap for those with low income who cannot make RDSP contributions is $20,000.
2. Qualification is dependent on being approved for a Disability Tax Credit, which is a rigorous process with a high rate of denial (RDSP Plan Institute, 2008).

Assessments vary across Canada Revenue Agency jurisdictions and largely depend on how well the (dis)Abled person's physician can describe the day-to-day impact of the (dis)Ability on the person's life. A heavy reliance on biomedical expertise is valued over the lived experiences and self-knowledge of the (dis)Abled. People with (dis)Abilities are among the poorest of the poor, with high rates of unemployment and underemployment, along with inadequate accommodations within public and post-secondary education (MacDonald, 2016b). This brings into question the chance of people with (dis)Abilities having disposable income to contribute to an RDSP.

Other legislation has an impact on (dis)Abled Canadians but is not specific to (dis)Ability, such as the Canada Health Act, which provides health services for all Canadians. Universal health care means (dis)Abled persons have access to health care without the added pressure of paying for private health insurance or being means-tested for charitable access. The more society can be accessible and universal in design, the more inclusive we become as a culture respecting (dis)Abled people for their contributions. Also, the Canadian Human Rights Act (1985) prohibits discrimination based on several criteria, including (dis)Ability. Prohibiting discrimination is a critical first step in legislating that people cannot be denied employment based on their (dis)Ability or refused admission to an academic post-secondary program because they have a (dis)Ability. But not discriminating against does not mean the employer will be supportive of the employee with a (dis)Ability or that the educational institution will welcome and embrace students with (dis)Abilities. The Act addresses equity, but more needs to be done with respect to access and support. (See the "Social Policy Change in Action" box later in this chapter for Melissa Myers's policy change story.)

Ontario has shown leadership by passing the first provincial accessibility Act in Canada. The Accessibility for Ontarians with Disabilities Act of 2005 is a rights-based model whereby public institutions and businesses are compelled to respect the "dignity and independence" of persons with (dis)Abilities (Reg. 429/07, Accessibility Standards, s. 3[1]).The legislation, however, also has remnants of the medical model when verification by a physician or nurse is needed to solidify the use of a service animal (s. 9[b]). Standards also conflict with one another. For example, section 3(1) refers to respecting and valuing self-knowledge of the person with a (dis)Ability, yet s. 9(b) situates expert knowledge with medical personnel over that of the person with a (dis)Ability. Accessibility policies are only as strong as their standards and the enforcement of those standards.

This Accessibility Act has a targeted date of 2025 for Ontario's goods, services, buildings and facilities, and employment to be accessible for 1.8 million (dis)Abled people in the province. Fifty per cent of the membership of the committee tasked with developing the

Act's standards identify as (dis)Abled (Barrier-Free Manitoba, 2017). This clearly speaks to the respect of (dis)Abled persons' voices and their inclusion in policies that directly impact their lives. Other provinces are following Ontario's example to adopt similar legislation. Nova Scotia's Accessibility Act received royal assent on 28 April 2017.

## Regulations

Policies also come in the form of regulations, such as those created by the Standards Council of Canada. This body sets accessibility standards for (dis)Abled persons in respect to customer service, accessible transportation, and barrier-free design. The Council also oversees services, such as the Enabling Accessibility Fund (2007), which supports community projects to improve accessibility (McColl, Schaub, Sampson, & Hong, 2010).

Policies related to dis(Ability) extend across a number of social service areas, for example, health, income security, transportation, and education. Historically, the first (dis)Ability-related policies in Canada came at the end of World War I (with federally funded compensation for (dis)Abled soldiers) and provincially through Worker's Compensation, a government-backed insurance program that originated in Quebec (1909) and Ontario (1914) for workers injured on the job (Crichton & Jongbloed, 1998). The Ontario policy brought a theoretical shift away from a charity model of assistance to a rights-based model.

(dis)Ability advocacy groups have played a significant role in promoting (dis)Ability equity and inclusion. Organizations such as the Council of Canadians with Disabilities (CCD), founded in 1976 by (dis)Abled Canadians, lobbied politicians, met with business leaders, and consistently challenged policy-makers to respond to the needs of the (dis)Abled in securing participatory citizenship (D'Aubin, 2003).

## The Quebec/Canada Pension Plan

The Quebec/Canada Pension Plan (1966) is social insurance legislation funded by compulsory contributions from all employers and employees between the ages of 18 and 65 (where benefits are based on the applicant's contribution to CPP). CPP Disability is "a taxable monthly payment that is available to people who have contributed to the CPP and who are not able to work regularly because of a disability" (Government of Canada, 2016). For both QPP and CPP, the disability needs to be severe and prolonged. "Severe" is defined as a mental or physical disability that prevents the applicant "from doing any type of substantially gainful work," and prolonged is defined as a long-term disability "of indefinite duration or is likely to result in death" (Government of Canada, 2016). This benefit is not universal, as it is only *potentially accessible* to working people who have become disabled and can no longer work or to working disabled people whose disability has progressed to a point they can no longer work. Disability benefits are converted to CPP when a participant reaches the age of 65.

Going back to Evelyn in the Case Examples at the start of the chapter, the government collected CPP through payroll deductions on every paycheque during Evelyn's working life, yet she was faced with this cumbersome application process in order to possibly be considered for benefits. Upon denial of claim the applicant has the choice to appeal the decision. An appeal can require an appearance in front of a tribunal. Only 6 per cent of cases are approved through file review in preparation for the tribunal (Brannen, 2017).

The Registered Nurses Association of Ontario has requested that the federal government give nurses and nurse practitioners the authority to file medical documentation on behalf of applicants, thus cutting down of the demand placed on physicians while streamlining the process for applicants (RNAO, 2016). Arguably, this authority should be extended to allied health professionals, such as occupational therapists and social workers. In order for this inter-professional shift to occur, there would need to be a shift from a biomedical approach to (dis)Ability to a rights-based approach. Further, no one knows the impact of a (dis)Ability on an individual's life more than the person living with the (dis)Ability. Determining who is eligible and what documentation is required in making that assessment needs to be revisited.

CPP Disability has the reputation of being difficult to get, as it has "among the highest rejection rates in the world" for a benefit of its kind (Goodman, 2014). The tribunal, in its first year of operation, conducted 461 hearings for either CPP Disability or Old Age Security, resulting in 158 appeal applicants being successful (Goodman, 2014) and leaving 303 (dis)Abled or elderly persons without benefits. Due to the strict entry protocol, numerous (dis)Abled people in the community cannot access this benefits program. Brannen (2017) broke down the statistics: in 2014–15, 69,075 Canadians applied for CPP Disability and 39,707 or 57 per cent of applicants were denied benefits. Brannen found that 66 per cent of those who were denied stopped trying to convince the federal government they were (dis)Abled. Perhaps they were tired of always having to prove their reality. Perhaps they were not clear on how to appeal, or perhaps they did not even realize that they had a right to appeal. People who have been oppressed do not always have the resources and abilities to challenge the bureaucracy. Perhaps their impairment makes wading through the appeal process more complicated. Those who make it through the reconsideration appeal encounter an even higher denial rate of 65 per cent. Sixty per cent of applicants who received denial letters stop trying to change the minds of government officials. Of those who continue with a notice of appeal with the Social Security Tribunal, 40 per cent are denied following a tribunal hearing (Brannen, 2017).

All of this clearly demonstrates the inaccessibility of one of Canada's primary income supports for people with (dis)Abilities. Networking with (dis)Ability agencies in the community, including provincial (dis)Abled persons commissions to host information sessions on applying for CPP Disability and offering to help advocate for applicants who might be struggling with the process, would help decrease applicants' stress and improve success rates. Businesses exist to help applicants deal with the application process but they do not do this for free. Ads asking "Can We Win Your Case? Find Out Now" and proclaiming "No Fees Unless We Win" elicit (dis)Abled clients who feel trapped, unable to work, and fearful of how they will support themselves. Making the process so complicated and cumbersome leaves (dis)Abled persons vulnerable to companies that offer assistance at a profit. Paying for a lawyer or advocate will tax the (dis)Abled person's already limited financial resources.

Addressing vulnerability begins with bringing people together to create a space for shared knowledge while promoting a sense of empowerment. If the Coalition of Provincial Organizations of the Handicapped had not mobilized with other (dis)Ability organizations in 1980, (dis)Ability might not have become a protective clause under the Canadian Charter (Murphy, 2016). As such, the Council of Canadians with Disabilities and the provincial commissions/organizations (e.g., the Premier's Council on the Status of

Disabled Persons in New Brunswick) need to form a collective voice and challenge the federal government to make CPP and QPP Disability more accessible for (dis)Abled persons. CPP is a federal plan, yet it has tremendous impact on the provinces, especially provinces like Nova Scotia where 20 per cent of the population identify as (dis)Abled (Disabled Persons Commission, 2010).

Stereotypes and dominant discourses of people trying to "cheat" the system have influenced disability insurance companies conducting surveillance on claimants. Titles fill the Internet, such as "Disability Claims? You're Not Paranoid . . . They Are Watching You?" (Newfield & Frankel, 2011) and "Disability insurance: More delay and deny benefits tactics" (Shanoff, 2013). Chronic pain sufferers have shared stories of being harassed, demoralized, and disrespected by insurance investigators (MacDonald, 2006). One research participant shared a story of working with a pain sufferer who had a terminally ill child. The insurance investigator filmed the client carrying the dying child into the hospital, resulting in the company refusing to file his (dis)Ability claim. Advocates threatened to make headline news of the company's poor judgement, which resulted in the decision being overturned.

What is not understood is that (dis)Ability is not fixed; people have good days and difficult days. Living with a (dis)Ability means you may choose to garden for an hour on Monday realizing you'll not be able to move on Tuesday. Sometimes your actions are calculated, other times spontaneous. Indeed, the father in the above story probably did not stop and think of his back before he carried his child into the hospital.

Further, it can take people time to accept that they have a (dis)Ability and people do not come to a (dis)Ability identity needlessly (MacDonald, 2016b). Due to the stereotypes and stigma assigned to (dis)Abled persons, people with invisible (dis)Abilities often pass as able-bodied. People living with chronic health conditions, learning (dis)Abilities, or mental health (dis)Abilities often do not announce to the public or employers that they live with a (dis)Ability for fear of repercussions. People with (dis)Abilities have a long history of being considered "less than," always recognizing the limitation that their (dis)Ability presents, not the value-added of a lived experience in navigating an ableist world.

A detailed critique of CPP Disability assessment criteria needs to be conducted, bringing forward (dis)Abled people's experiences. With such a high denial rate for CPP Disability, what are we saying as a country about the value we place on the lives of (dis)Abled people? CPP Disability is the primary income maintenance program for people with (dis)Abilities in Canada, with an annual budget of more than $3 billion (Prince, 2009). Yet, (dis)Abled people are being denied, which impacts their health and livelihood.

## Division Four of Canada's Immigration and Refugee Protection Act

Division Four of Canada's Immigration and Refugee Protection Act (IRPA, 2001) addresses the conditions of inadmissibility to Canada. Among these conditions is health status. Section 38(c) makes it difficult, if not impossible, for persons with (dis)Ability to apply to immigrate to Canada under many immigration categories as there is a fear that the potential costs associated with their condition would drain our health and social services systems. Referring back to the Case Examples box, Felipe Montoya and his supporters argued that this policy was in conflict with the Canadian Charter of Rights and Freedoms, which prohibits discrimination on the basis of (dis)Ability (*CBC News*, 2016c). A child who had been living in Canada for several years and who had made connections in his community was now being told the country did not want him simply because of his genetic makeup. This example highlights how policies not originally intended to address issues of (dis)Ability (in this case the overlying issue was immigration) can unjustly impact those living with (dis)Ability. The message is that persons with (dis)Ability consume resources rather than enhance their communities. While the Montoya family was able to get the decision in their case overturned, the policy itself remains.

In a similar case in 2017, a family from Colorado who moved to Canada in 2013 to establish a hunting and fishing lodge were denied permanent residency because their six-year-old daughter, who had been diagnosed with epilepsy and global developmental delay, could put an undue strain on Canada's health and social services (*CBC News*, 2017). Putting dollar signs on the value and worth of a (dis)Abled child, applications such as the one by this family are turned down if the health costs of the (dis)Abled person are expected to exceed $6,655 annually (*CBC News*, 2017). Between 2014 and 2016, 1,100 applicants found themselves in this position (Russell & Hill, 2017). The federal Minister of Persons with Disabilities, Carla Qualtrough, claims her mandate is to create a national (dis)Ability law "so that it's not presumed that a disability will impede someone's ability to achieve anything, whether it be citizenship or employment" (*CBC News*, 2017), yet Immigration, Refugees and Citizenship claims it is "tasked, by way of the Immigration and Refugee Protection Act, with protecting Canada's publicly-funded health and social services" (*CBC News*, 2017). Two federal departments are at odds with each other, both claiming to represent the best interests of Canadians. Until this policy is changed so that persons with (dis)Abilities wanting to come to Canada are considered to be assets rather than liabilities, many people will continue to be precluded from immigrating to Canada with their families on the basis of (dis)Ability. Further, the federal government enables a dominant discourse that (dis)Abled persons drain the social welfare and health systems, again devaluing the worth of persons with (dis)Abilities.

## Intersections of (dis)Ability

(dis)Ability is complex. Variables of race, class, gender, age, and geographical location all influence the probability of living a portion of one's life with a (dis)Ability. Having access to clean drinking water, food security, adequate housing, public health programs such as immunizations, and accessible health care, education, and employment all have an influence on rates of (dis)Ability (Mackelprang & Salsgiver, 2015). In Canada, Indigenous reserves face many of these problems, as they contend with high rates of (dis)Ability.

Gallagher (reported by Vallas & Fremstad, 2014) states that "disability is both a cause and a consequence of poverty." As a cause, (dis)Ability can lead to unemployment or underemployment, educational access can be compromised, transportation might be non-existent or restricted, and housing, along with additional health care or equipment costs, can be inaccessible. As a consequence, poverty can create unhealthy living and working conditions, substandard housing, and food deficiency (costs of fresh fruit and vegetables in comparison to starch and processed foods), plus restricted access to extended health care such as prescription or over-the-counter medications.

Going back to the Case Examples box at the start of the chapter, Evelyn could no longer work; if her claim had been denied at the tribunal, she would be living well below the poverty line. And if Nico and his family had to return to Costa Rica, who knows what their financial fate would be or what services would be available. Governments, public institutions, and private service providers all need to be addressing issues of ableism, developing policies that are inclusive and accessible to people with (dis)Abilities.

## The Need for a National Disability Policy

Laws are in place to prevent discrimination, but that does not mean people with (dis)Abilities are fully supported through social policies and practices. As we saw earlier, Canada does not have a national disability policy. According to Bond and McColl (2013), Canadian (dis)Ability policy is a patchwork consisting of the following:

- Charter of Rights and Freedoms (1982)—do not discriminate against;
- Canadian Human Rights Act (1985)—protection of the rights of the (dis)Abled;
- Canada Health Act (1985)—universal benefits for health care.

Beginning in 2004 under the federal Ministry of Employment and Social Development, bilateral labour market agreements with each province and territory were developed for persons with (dis)Abilities. The primary goal of the agreements is employment-oriented, focused on increasing employability and job opportunities for persons with (dis)Abilities. Many (dis)Ability organizations are calling for a Canadians with Disability Act that would bring a co-ordinated, proactive approach to systemic change compared to the current reactive, complaints-based protocols that exist under human rights legislation (Hanes, 2017).

## International Comparisons

### A Global Perspective on (dis)Ability Rights in Canada

A unified Disability Act would be in keeping with countries such as the United States (Americans with Disabilities Act, 1990, amended 2008), Norway (Antidiscrimination and Accessibility Act, 2008), and, most recently, Japan (Law to Eliminate Discrimination against People with Disabilities, 2016). In reviewing eight countries (Canada, Argentina, Australia, Japan, Norway, South Africa, the UK, and the US), Canada was the only country that did not have targeted legislation on (dis)Ability.

Within the Charter of Rights and Freedoms, discriminating against people with (dis)Abilities is prohibited but it does not address accessibility and accommodations for (dis)Abled persons. The Americans with Disabilities Act and Japan's Law to Eliminate Discrimination Against People with Disabilities mandate businesses and public services to move towards inclusive practices and to dismantle ableist barriers (Mackelprang & Salsgiver, 2015; Otake, 2016). On its own, legislation is not enough; there must be the compliance standards and services to support full citizenship of (dis)Abled persons. Advocates recognized this with the Americans with Disabilities Act, motivating the 2008 amendments that included

*continued*

examples of reasonable accommodations in an effort to tighten up expectations (Mackelprang & Salsgiver, 2015). On the other hand, the new law in Japan has been criticized for its weak language pertaining to the private sector, which is asked to "strive" towards access and inclusion (Otake, 2016).

Internationally, the purpose of the UN Convention on the Rights of Persons with Disabilities is to advance the "human rights and inclusion of persons with disabilities" throughout the world. The Convention challenges countries to examine their own biases and to work actively towards dismantling discriminatory barriers, while increasing societal access and rights to citizenship. (dis)Ability policies are complex and vary in purpose, degree, and application from country to country.

## Policy Barriers

Even with an increased international focus, many (dis)Abled people still get left behind because they do not meet the specific qualification for a particular benefit or because barrier after barrier is presented to deny access. The Disability Tax Credit is for (dis)Abled Canadians (with a severe and prolonged (dis)Ability) who have been approved for this benefit through the Canada Revenue Agency. Approved taxpayers living with a (dis)Ability can save up to $1,200 on their federal taxes. CTV News (2016) reported that "Six in 10 adults with disabilities can't benefit from Disability Tax Credit" because persons have to be paying taxes in order to benefit. In other words, this tax benefit is not helping the most vulnerable (those with (dis)Abilities living in poverty). The (dis)Ability pension benefit is also not helping the most vulnerable. People with (dis)Abilities who have not paid into the Canada Pension Plan, because they have not been able to work in the traditional sense of the word, have to rely on provincial income assistance programs instead of the Canada Pension Plan.

Provinces have their own income assistance legislation and subsequent programs. The Employment Support and Income Assistance Act in Nova Scotia provides financial aid to people who cannot meet their basic needs. Basic needs are usually defined as housing, heat, food, and clothing. The program may also help with emergency dental care, eyeglasses, and prescription drugs. The operative words here are "may provide." Living with a (dis)Ability costs money, specialized diets, over-the-counter medications, and remedial aids such as canes, braces, transportation, furniture adaptations, and assistive technologies—the list goes on. The basic income assistance rate in most provinces is below the poverty line, and while many provinces will help out with additional costs, for example $110 for bifocals, it does little to address the true financial impact of life as a (dis)Abled person.

If the (dis)Ability is severe, requiring a level of care, the person would be directed to the Disability Support Program, under the mandate of the Social Assistance Act. A (dis)Abled individual seeking financial support has to go through an eligibility requirement regime, consisting of a medical assessment, functional assessment regarding level of support needed, and a financial assessment. The program ranges from supporting a (dis)Abled person living with her or his own family to 24-hour residential care placements. Eligibility, however, relies on medical expertise, a care co-ordinator's assessment of the (dis)Abled person's ability, and a neo-liberal financial examination into the individual's monetary worth. The Disability Support Program is a welfare policy meant to support the most vulnerable of the vulnerable, yet numerous barriers are in the way of direct access. For example, it is very difficult to get social assistance in most provinces unless you have a permanent address (Government of Nova Scotia, 2017). Someone living with a significant (dis)Ability could be forced to live on the streets or move from shelter to shelter, potentially complicating her/his impairments.

## Social Policy Change in Action

### Melissa's Story of Policy Change

*by Melissa Myers*

I was born with cerebral palsy, am an electric wheelchair user, and live with mobility and learning (dis)Abilities. Through perseverance and sheer determination I was able to get through undergraduate and graduate post-secondary education (see Myers, MacDonald, Jacquard, & McNeil, 2014). I struggled tremendously with issues of accessibility as I navigated the brick and mortar of universities built in the 1800s. The first day of class in a professional undergraduate program, I arrived 15 minutes early only to find an "out of order" sign on the door of the only elevator in the building—my class was on the second floor. The solution proposed was to carry me in my wheelchair up two flights of stairs.

From the moment I entered university, I was a strong advocate networking and politically lobbying for changes, including changes to the (dis)Ability benefits related to post-secondary education provided by the Nova Scotia Department of Community Services (DCS). When I began my post-secondary education I assumed I would be eligible for (dis)Ability benefits; however, (dis)Abled students were only approved for community college funding. I could receive benefits if I stayed home or if I went to community college, but I could not receive benefits for going to university. Committed to educational equity and (dis)Ability rights, I sought to have the DCS policy changed. I thought "very little was expected of me as a young (dis)Abled woman and I wanted to prove them wrong" (Myers et al., 2014, p. 80). I appealed the original decision, which denied access to university courses. I lobbied members of the provincial legislature and federal Parliament, spoke with departmental ministers, and talked to the media. Eventually, I won the right to take university courses, as did other (dis)Abled students.

Then, when I began my social work degree I found myself cut off from DCS assistance because post-secondary support covered only the first degree. Newspaper headings read: "Social work student's funding cut" (Lambie, 2007), "Province's advice: Get a job" (Jackson, 2007a), and finally, after I lobbied extensively—and successfully: "University welfare rules will help about 300 students: Province makes it easier for people on social assistance to improve their education" (Jackson, 2007b).

*continued*

The DCS policy change stated that "assistance for a second degree will be provided only in cases where the first degree may be considered a pre-requisite to further study (e.g., B.A. for a B.S.W.), or a student is enrolled in a concurrent degree program (e.g., B.A. and B. Ed.)" (para. 6). This change would apply to undergraduate degrees only. Sadly, I would not qualify for the benefit because it was for students who were about to begin their second degree, not those already working on their second degree.

I completed my BSW, followed by my MSW, during which I had successfully passed three field practicums. However, finding career-appropriate employment was proving to be my greatest challenge yet, as application after application yielded no results. Through progressive networking I found a program that supported (dis)Abled people transitioning to the job market. The program, however, only paid a baseline salary. I would be making well below my market value as a master's educated social worker, but I had little choice as access the job market was extremely limited for (dis)Abled people.

During my post-secondary education, I had an **academic attendant** as part of my accommodations paid for through the Department of Labour and Advanced Education, but this funding stopped when I graduated. Yet, an academic attendant was a crucial accommodation for me to be able to work. But what employer is going to hire two people in place of one? I knew I was up against a huge barrier given my physical and learning (dis)Abilities, yet this could not be the end of the road because I had worked too hard to get my education and professional designation.

I put my lobbying and negotiation skills to work yet again and designed a **Workplace Attendant Policy** with DCS and the Labour Market Agreement for Persons with Disabilities (Government of Canada, 2014). Today I am able to work because of this policy.

## Inaccessibility

As you have read in the Social Policy Change in Action box, Melissa Myers was born a social advocate, as she consciously and consistently pushes the normative boundaries of society, daring to envision a progressively inclusive world that values (dis)Abled people for the sincere and genuine contributions they are positioned to make in an equitable social order. She is an articulate, determined young woman who knows (dis)Ability needs and policies from a lived and studied perspective. Yet, she gets tired of always having to "fight" for a place in society.

The emotional and cognitive energy it takes to navigate an ableist world is truly exhausting. Melissa has to continuously be "on," thinking three steps ahead. (dis)Abled people need to be organized and plan their day; they are not allowed to be spontaneous. For example, in Nova Scotia you need to book Access-A-Bus in advance, up to seven days prior to the scheduled need (Halifax Access-A-Bus, 2013). You cannot wake up one morning, see it is a beautiful day, and decide to go out for dinner that night. These are privileges afforded to able-bodied persons.

Drawing a correlation between able-bodied and the (dis)Abled, Wendell (1996) highlights able-bodied dependence on societal infrastructures for education (public school system), transportation (metro or underground), and communications (radio, TV, social media). The social construction of (dis)Ability creates a discourse that identifies (dis)Abled persons as the "help seeker" and able-bodied persons, in contrast, as the "helper," when in essence we are both. For example, it is not Melissa, the (dis)Abled woman with cerebral palsy using a 300-pound wheelchair, that is (dis)Abling but rather the 26 stairs to her classroom. The social construction of (dis)Ability in this situation is housed in the physical layout of the university building. Melissa suggests moving the class, which is what finally took place. The Social Model of (dis)Ability (Oliver, 1996) views the structural barriers within society as the (dis)Abling aspect, because it is not Melissa's impairments that (dis)Able her, but, rather, the inaccessible structures—physical, attitudinal, or administrative—that limit her full participation.

Titchkosky (2011) takes accessibility within the academy further, by questioning how we perceive access and inclusion within universities in the first place. Traditionally, (dis)Abled persons are not understood to be occupying space within the academy. If you were (dis)Abled you were hidden from society, certainly not occupying space within the think-tanks of tomorrow. As society progressed towards a liberal notion of inclusion, universities had automatic doors installed and wider washroom stalls constructed, but do these minimalistic alterations truly make universities a welcoming and accepting place for (dis)Abled students? Melissa would suggest not, particularly as it relates to learning (dis)Abilities. Having universities embrace multiple ways of learning and knowing, including creative ways of meeting learning outcomes, would reduce the need for accessibility services and specific accommodations. This would help to eliminate the need for (dis)Abled students to constantly point to how they are different, inadvertently identifying how they do not belong.

In addition, university is at a minimum three to four years of undergraduate study, often followed by graduate work in a specialized field. Community college programs are usually one or two years, with a price tag significantly lower than university tuition, student fees, and so on. (Community college at $3,220 a year x 2 years = $6,440; whereas university at $6,667 per year x 4 years = $26, 668.) Was limiting (dis)Abled students access to post-secondary education simply a financial decision on the part of the provincial government, or was it fuelled by stereotypes and judgements that devalued the perceived worth of (dis)Abled people in society?

Carter, Hanes, and MacDonald (2012) found that access to social work education for students with (dis)Abilities declines with advanced degrees; specifically, in Canadian schools of social work (dis)Abled students represented 5.5 per cent of undergraduates, 4.1 per cent of master's students, and 1.3 per cent of doctoral students. The construction of (dis)Ability as "a negative and limiting condition of the individual—one that requires medical and wider professional attention to get disabled people closer to the world of normality, economic opportunity and the position of citizenship" (Roulstone, 2012, p. 217) consists of stereotypes influencing access to post-secondary education. The biomedical definition of normalcy defines who deserves to have access to full employment and societal participation. Melissa Myers continues to battle for full citizenship, as she refuses to retreat to the shadows outlined by society as her natural space and place.

The Workplace Attendant Policy, a provincial policy supported in part by federal money, is a creative solution that facilitates employability of (dis)Abled persons, but it is not without its flaws. For example, access to the policy requires a monthly co-pay by the participant, which is on a sliding income-based scale, meaning if the participant makes more money, then she must contribute more to the cost of the attendant. Does an executive director of an agency pay part of the administrative assistant's salary? Of course not. So why should a (dis)Abled employee have to contribute to her attendant's wage? The participant is responsible for advertising the attendant position, interviewing applicants, and making the subsequent hiring arrangements. This gives more control to the (dis)Abled person, but it also puts more stress and onus on that person as well.

Complicating matters further, the hourly fee for the attendant is just slightly above minimum wage. The program pays $20,000 per year for a full-time attendant, which works out to an hourly rate that is about the same as Nova Scotia's minimum wage ($10.88/hour in 2017). An hourly rate this low makes hiring a qualified academic attendant extremely difficult and contributes to high turnover, leaving the (dis)Abled employee in a vulnerable position, without an attendant or having to go through the entire hiring process again. The Workplace Attendant Policy began because of Melissa's advocacy skills and determination to secure employment. If she hadn't articulated her need, she would be unemployed; her years of schooling and professional education would be sidelined. One wonders how many (dis)Abled persons are denied opportunities because they are unaware of policies like the Workplace Attendant Policy or because no policy exists at all.

## Chapter Summary

Social policy in the area of (dis)Ability is emergent, divergent, perhaps embryonic yet historical. Ironically, as depicted through the case stories, (dis)Ability social policy, with the aim of breaking down barriers so as to move (dis)Abled persons towards full citizenship, is inaccessible in itself. According to Prince (2016, p. 110), "the effect of disability policy on people range[s] from supportive resources to restrictive laws, minimal interventions to oppressive conditions, and from experiencing a positive status to struggling with a spoiled identity of stigma." Policies might look promising on paper, yet their application reveals complications or omissions.

(dis)Ability social policies need to be read from a critical perspective, always looking for the loopholes that restrict full citizenship participation for (dis)Abled Canadians, access to meaningful and career-appropriate employment, equitable education, and accessible transportation and housing. For example, accommodation policies aim to support (dis)Abled students or employees so that they have a fair and equitable means to meet their objectives, whether in education or work. However, some accommodation policy is also written so that the request for accommodation cannot create "undue hardship" to the employer or learning institution. Undue hardship is based primarily on a financial assessment, but it is surprising how an educational institution, such as a university with total revenue in the hundreds of millions, can claim undue hardship for relatively inexpensive accommodations:

> Stigma, social exclusion and negative attitudes toward those with disabilities have become so engrained in modern society that most citizens, laws and policies, organizational structures, and indeed even social programs, actively discriminate against those with disabilities without even knowing they are doing so. (Robertson & Larson, 2016, p. 2)

"Do not discriminate against" does not guarantee actively supporting people with (dis)Abilities. Laws must move beyond this to include progressive engagement of (dis)Abled persons—where their value and worth are not measured against their health care costs or the limitations of their impairments but rather by what they can contribute to society and how society can be made more accessible in receiving those contributions. Social workers have an obligation to advocate for (dis)Abled persons' full citizenship participation in society. The social justice lens of our profession provides a necessary foundation for critical analysis of existing policies, and for advocacy and action for policy changes. Working with (dis)Ability communities, social workers are in the best position to effect (dis)Ability policy change.

# Discussion Questions

1. (dis)Ability policy is complex, involving many layers of government and social organization. For example, policies can be federal, provincial, municipal, and organizational. In thinking about issues of (dis)Ability access and inclusion, list a (dis)Ability policy within each of the areas noted above.

2. How does (dis)Ability policy fit within social work practice? Why is it important for a practising social worker to be familiar with (dis)Ability policies at all levels of intervention? How would the social worker's knowledge of (dis)Ability policy potentially impact a (dis)Abled client?

3. How can the historical positioning and dominant discourses of people with (dis)Abilities be challenged today? What can we do as a society to ensure the full participation of (dis)Abled persons' citizenship?

# References

Accessibility for Ontarians with Disability Act. (2005). O. Reg. 429/07: Accessibility standards for customer service. Retrieved from https://www.ontario.ca/laws/regulation/070429

Asylum Project. (2016). Provincial lunatic asylum in Saint John. Retrieved from http://www.asylumprojects.org/index.php?title=Provincial_Lunatic_Asylum_at_St._John

Barrier-Free Manitoba. (2017).The Accessibility for Ontarians with Disabilities Act (2005) Ontario. Retrieved from http://www.barrierfreemb.com/resourceaoda

Beagan, B., Stadnyk, R., Loppie, C., MacDonald, N., Hamilton-Hinch, B., & MacDonald, J. (2006). *Snapshots of the lives of caregivers: "I do it because I love her and care."* Halifax: Healthy Balance Research Program.

Bond, R., & McColl, M. (2013). *A review of disability policy in Canada* (2nd edn). Canadian Disability Policy Alliance. Retrieved from http://www.disabilitypolicyalliance.ca/latest-news/2013-review-of-disability-policy-in-canada.html

Bouche, T., & Rivard, L. (2014). America's hidden history: The eugenics movement. *Scitable*. Retrieved from https://www.nature.com/scitable/forums/genetics-generation/america-s-hidden-history-the-eugenics-movement-123919444

Brannen, D. (2017). CPP disability approval rates explained. Resolute Legal. Retrieved from https://resolutelegal.ca/cpp-disability-approval-rates-2015/

Canadian Association for Community Living. (2016). My Home My Community initiative informs national housing strategy. Retrieved from http://www.cacl.ca/news-stories/blog/my-home-my-community-initiative-informs-national-housing-strategy

Carter, I. (2016). Empowering strategies for change: Advocacy by and for people with disabilities. In J. Robertson & G. Larson (Eds), *Disability and social change: A progressive Canadian approach* (pp. 205–26). Halifax: Fernwood.

———, Hanes, R., & MacDonald, J. (2012). The inaccessible road not taken: The trials, tribulations and successes of disability inclusion within social work post-secondary education. *Canadian Journal of Disability Studies, 1*(1), 109–42.

———, ———, & ———. (2017). Beyond the social model of disability: Engaging in anti-oppressive social work practice. In D. Baines (Ed.), *Doing anti-oppressive practice: Social justice social work* (3rd edn, pp. 153–71). Black Point, NS: Fernwood Publishing.

*CBC News*. (2016a, 14 Mar.). York university prof denied permanent residency over son's Down syndrome. Retrieved from http://www.cbc.ca/news/canada/toronto/programs/metromorning/costa-rica-down-syndrome-1.3489120

———. (2016b, 15 Mar.). Canadian immigration rules "cold-hearted" but fair, expert says. Retrieved from http://www.cbc.ca/news/canada/toronto/programs/metromorning/immigration-down-syndrome-consultant-1.3492666

———. (2016c, 16 Mar.). Family whose son has Down syndrome can appeal "inadmissibility," Ottawa says. Retrieved from http://www.cbc.ca/news/canada/toronto/down-syndrome-immigration-1.3492810

———. (2016d, 27 Apr.). Court approves $36M for ex-residents in class action against Ontario institutions. Retrieved from http://www.cbc.ca/news/canada/toronto/ontario-class-action-settlement-adult-mental-disabilities-1.3555337

———. (2017, 28 July). Federal disabilities minister "frustrated" after family denied residency over daughter's health needs. Retrieved from http://www.cbc.ca/news/canada/manitoba/disabilities-minister-family-denied-residency-1.4227313

Coco, A.P. (2010). Diseased, maimed, mutiliated: Categorizations of disability and an ugly law in late nineteenth-century Chicago. *Journal of Social History, 44(1)*, 23–37.

Crichton, A., & Jongbloed, L. (1998). *Disability and social policy in Canada*. North York, ON: Captus Press.

*CTV News*. (2016). Six in 10 adults with disabilities can't benefit from Disability Tax Credit: study. Retrieved from http://www.ctvnews.ca/canada/six-in-10-adults-with-disabilities-can-t-benefit-from-disability-tax-credit-study-1.2970258

D'Aubin, A. (2003). We will ride: A showcase of CCD advocacy strategies in support of accessible transportation. In D. Stienstra & A. Wight-Felske, *Making equity: History of advocacy and persons with disabilities in Canada* (pp. 87–118). Concord, ON: Captus Press.

Department of Community Services. (2012). *Disability support program*. Halifax: Province of Nova Scotia. Retrieved from http://novascotia.ca/coms/disabilities/documents/Disability_Support_Program_Policies.pdf

Department of Labour and Advanced Education. (2017). Minimum wage. Retrieved from https://novascotia.ca/lae/employmentrights/minimumwage.asp

Disabled Persons Commission. (2010). *Persons with disabilities in Nova Scotia: A statistical report*. Halifax: Province of Nova Scotia.

Dunn, P., & Langdon, T. (2016). Looking back, rethinking historical perspectives and reflecting upon emerging trends. In J. Robertson & G. Larson (Eds), *Disability and social change: A progressive Canadian approach* (pp. 27–44). Halifax: Fernwood.

Eugenics Archive. (2015). Eugenics archives: What sorts of people should there be? Social Science and Humanities Research Council of Canada. Retrieved from www.eugenicsarchive.ca

Goodman, L. (2014). CPP disability benefits denied to 60% of applicants, among highest rejection rates in world. *Huffington Post*. Retrieved from http://www.huffingtonpost.ca/2014/12/03/cpp-disability-benefits-denied_n_6257988.html

Government of Canada. (2001). Immigration and Refugee Protection Act [2001, c. 27]. Retrieved from http://laws.justice.gc.ca/eng/acts/i-2.5/

———. (2014). Canada–Nova Scotia Labour Market Agreement for Persons with Disabilities. Retrieved from https://www.canada.ca/en/employment-social-development/programs/training-agreements/lma-disabilities/ns.html

———. (2016). Canada Pension Plan Disability Benefit—overview. Retrieved from https://www.canada.ca/en/services/benefits/publicpensions/cpp/cpp-disability-benefit.html

Government of Nova Scotia. (2017). Employment support and income assistance. Retrieved from https://novascotia.ca/coms/employment/income_assistance/HowtoApply.html

Halifax Access-A-Bus. (2013). Access to travel. Retrieved from http://www.accesstotravel.gc.ca/19.aspx?CarrierCd=441&CityCd=145&lang=en

Hamilton, E. (1995). *Tuberculosis in New Brunswick: The establishment of the Jordan Memorial Sanatorium* (Unpublished MA thesis). University of New Brunswick, Fredericton.

Hanes, R. (2016). Critical disability theory: Developing a post-social model of disability. In J. Robertson & G. Larson (Eds), *Disability and social change: A progressive Canadian approach* (pp. 65–79). Halifax: Fernwood.

——. (2017). Social work and persons with disabilities: From individual support to social change. In S. Hicks & J. Stokes (Eds), *Social work in Canada: An Introduction* (4th edn, pp. 404–31). Toronto: Thompson Educational Publishing.

Jackson, D. (2007a, 20 Oct.). Province's advice: Get a job. *Chronicle Herald*, p. A2.

Jackson, D. (2007b, 5 Dec.). University welfare rules will help about 300 students: Province makes it easier for people on social assistance to improve their education. *Chronicle Herald*, p. B3.

Kozar, S. (2004). *Almost Normal* [film]. Halifax: Healing Ground Productions.

Lambie, C. (2007, 20 Oct.). Social work student's funding cut. *Chronicle Herald*, pp. A1–A2.

L'Arche Canada. (2014). Institutions and de-institutionalization. Retrieved from http://www.larche.ca/education/Institutions_and_the_Deinstitutionalization_Movement.pdf

——. (2015). L'Arche. Retrieved from http://www.larche.ca

MacDonald, J. (2006). *Untold stories: Women, in the helping professions, as sufferers of chronic pain (Re)Storying (dis)Ability* (Unpublished doctoral dissertation). Memorial University of Newfoundland, St John's.

——. (2016a). *Report on School for the Deaf: Richard Robert Martell and Michael Harry Gerald Perrier and the Attorney General of Nova Scotia.* Halifax.

——. (2016b). Intersectionality and (dis)Ability. In J. Robertson & G. Larson (Eds), *Disability, society and social change* (pp. 136–66). Halifax: Fernwood.

——, Cooper, S., & Myers, M. (Forthcoming). "Nothing about us, without us": (dis)Ability Community Development in Nova Scotia. In S. Todd & S. Savard (Eds), *Canadian community work: From theory to practice.* Ottawa: University of Ottawa Press.

——& Friars, G. (2010). Structural social work from a (dis)Ability perspective. In S. Hicks, H. Peters, T. Corner, & T. London (Eds), *Structural social work in action* (pp. 138–56). Toronto: Canadian Scholars' Press.

Mackelprang, R., & Salsgiver, R. (2015). *Disability: A diversity model approach in human service practice* (3rd edn). Chicago: Lyceum Books.

Mann, P. (2014). Holocaust online. Retrieved from http://www.holocaustonline.org/medical-system/euthanasia-eugenics/

McColl, M. A., Schaub, M., Sampson, L, & Hong, K. (2010). *A Canadians with Disability Act?* Kingston, ON: Canadian Disability Policy Alliance Secretariat.

*Muir v. The Queen in Right of Alberta.* (1996). *Muir v. Alberta* – 132 D.L.R. (4th) 695 Court File No. 8903 20759. Edmonton. Retrieved from aix1.uottawa.ca/~srodgers/3375/muir.rtf

Murphy, J. (2016). Human rights, disability and the law in Canada. In J. Robertson & G. Larson (Eds), *Disability and social change: A progressive Canadian approach* (pp. 80–98). Halifax: Fernwood.

Myers, M., MacDonald, J., Jacquard, S., & McNeil, M. (2014). (dis)Ability and postsecondary education: One women's experience. *Journal of Postsecondary Education and Disability, 27*(1), 73–87.

Newfield, J., & Frankel, J. (2011). Disability claim? You're not paranoid . . . they really are watching you. ProHealth. Retrieved from http://www.prohealth.com/library/showarticle.cfm?libid=16124

Oliver, M. (1996). *Understanding disability: From theory to practice.* Basingstoke, Hampshire, UK: Palgrave MacMillan.

Otake, T. (2016, 2 May). New law bans bias against people with disabilities, but shortcomings exist, say experts. *Japan Times.* Retrieved from https://www.japantimes.co.jp/news/2016/05/02/reference/new-law-bans-bias-against-people-with-disabilities-but-shortcomings-exist-say-experts/#.WdEhhq3Myqk

Pierre, J. (2014, 28 Apr.). Disability rights. Retrieved from http://eugenicsarchive.ca/discover/encyclopedia/535eeb377095aa000000021b

Prince, M. (2009). *Absent citizens: Disability politics and policy in Canada.* Toronto: University of Toronto Press.

——. (2016). Disability policy in Canada: Fragments of inclusion and exclusion. In J. Robertson & G. Larson (Eds), *Disability and social change: A progressive Canadian approach* (pp. 99–114). Halifax: Fernwood.

RDSP Plan Institute. (2008). The grey list: Facing the challenges of qualifying for Disability Tax Credit. Retrieved from http://www.rdsp.com/2008/11/17/the-grey-list-facing-the-challenges-of-qualifying-for-disability-tax-credits/

Registered Nurses Association of Ontario (RNAO). (2016). Improving access to Canada Pension Plan Disability Benefits. Retrieved from http://rnao.ca/policy/letters/improving-access-canada-pension-plan-disability-benefits

Rioux, M. (2014). *Expanding the circle: Aboriginal people with disabilities know their rights.* Toronto: York University, Disability Rights Promotion International.

Robertson, J., & Larson, G. (Eds). (2016). *Disability and social change: A progressive Canadian approach.* Halifax: Fernwood.

Roulstone, A. (2012). Disabled people, work and employment: A global perspective. In N. Watson, A. Roulstone and C. Thomas, *Routledge Handbook of Disability Studies* (pp. 211–24). London: Routledge.

Russell, A., & Hill, B. (2017, 4 July). Inadmissible: Canada rejects hundreds of immigrants, Global News investigation finds. *Global News.* Retrieved from https://globalnews.ca/news/3551772/inadmissible-canada-rejects-hundreds-of-immigrants-based-on-incomplete-data-global-investigation-finds/

Shanoff, A. (2013, 25 May). Disability insurance: More delay and deny benefits tactics. *Toronto Sun.* Retrieved from http://www.torontosun.com/2013/05/25/disability-insurance-more-delay-and-deny-benefits-tactics

Statistics Canada. (2015). Canadian survey on disability, 2012. Retrieved from http://www5.statcan.gc.ca/olc-cel/olc.action?objId=89-654-X&objType=2&lang=en&limit=0

Stienstra, D. (2012). *Disability rights.* About Canada series. Halifax: Fernwood.

———— & Wight-Felske, A. (2003). *Making equality: History of advocacy and persons with disabilities in Canada.* Concord, ON: Captus Press.

Stote, K. (2015). *An act of genocide: Colonialism and the sterilization of Aboriginal women.* Halifax: Fernwood.

Titchkosky, T. (2011). *The question of access: Disability, space, meaning.* Toronto: University of Toronto Press.

United Nations. (1975). UN Declaration on the Rights of Disabled Persons. Retrieved from http://www.ohchr.org/EN/ProfessionalInterest/Pages/RightsOfDisabledPersons.aspx

————. (2006). World Programme of Action concerning Disabled Persons. Retrieved from https://www.un.org/development/desa/disabilities/resources/world-programme-of-action-concerning-disabled-persons.html

————. (2008). UN Convention on the Rights of Persons with Disabilities. Retrieved from https://www.un.org/development/desa/disabilities/convention-on-the-rights-of-persons-with-disabilities.html

United Nations Convention on the Rights of Persons with Disabilities. (2016). Infographic on the CRPS and the COSP. Retrieved from www.un.org/disabilities/documents/COP/cosp9_infographic.pdf

Vallas, R., & Fremstad, S. (2014). Disability is a cause and consequence of poverty. *Talk Poverty.* Retrieved from https://talkpoverty.org/2014/09/19/disability-cause-consequence-poverty/

Wendell, S. (1996). *The rejected body: Feminist philosophical reflections on disability.* New York: Routledge.

Withers, A. J. (2012). *Disability politics & theory.* Halifax: Fernwood.

World Health Organization (WHO). (2011). *World report on disability.* Geneva: WHO. Retrieved from http://www.who.int/disabilities/world_report/2011/report.pdf

# 11 Child and Youth Policy

## Building Equality or Buttressing Inequities?

*Michele Fairbairn, Susan Strega,*
*and Christopher Walmsley*

---

### Chapter Objectives

*This chapter will help you to develop an understanding of:*
- the historical context of Canada's child and youth policy;
- relevant research and the political, social, and economic ideas that inform child and youth policy;
- Canadian child and youth policy in an international context;
- some of the ways policy buttresses or dismantles inequalities;
- the possibilities for socially just policy change for children and youth.

---

## Introduction

Asked to name child and youth policies in Canada, many people will struggle to think of any—other than child protection policies. Disproportionately impacting those who are Indigenous, poor, and racialized, child protection policies touch only about 2 per cent of the child and youth population. Yet many other policies affect the well-being of children and youth—some support and benefit children's lives, others restrict and compromise those same lives. In this chapter, we demonstrate how policies optimize the lives of some while further marginalizing others. We show how children's welfare is entangled with policies that impact their families and communities, such as affordable child care, wage policies, immigration and refugee policies, and housing policies.

Child and youth policy is complex because the Canadian Constitution transfers most policy in health, education, and social services to the provinces and territories. Yet, the federal government retains control of policy with respect to Indigenous children and families, as it has constitutional authority under the Indian Act for services to Indigenous people that live on Indian reserves. Canada's treaty obligations in some instances extend to Indigenous people living on and off reserves. The most significant means by which the federal government shapes the lives of Indigenous people is by retaining the right under the Indian Act to define who is and who is not Indigenous. The net result is a patchwork of highly variable policies not unified by any coherent framework. They differ markedly from one province/territory, region, and constitutional mandate to another. While policies can be found on a continuum from child-focused to family-focused, all affect

---

**Case Examples**   Different Lives, Different Outcomes?

---

**Theresa**, 13, speaks Cree and English fluently. Her home in northern Ontario is a reserve community with a population of 1,000 that has had a boil-water advisory for the past decade. She lives with her grandparents, who are residential school survivors, her parents, and three younger siblings in a two-bedroom house provided by the band. It has ongoing mould problems. Since there is no secondary school in the community, she will start attending a public high school in Thunder Bay in September, boarding with another Indigenous family 10 months of the year. She hopes to play on the school volleyball team.

**Noah**, 13, came to Canada as a refugee from Liberia with his mother and younger brother when he was 10. His mother works as a chambermaid at a Vancouver hotel, and they live in a two-bedroom public housing apartment in Burnaby. He attends the local middle school, has two part-time jobs (delivering newspapers and stocking grocery shelves), and is responsible for his younger brother until his mother gets home from work. He loves basketball, but is not on any school or community teams.

**Nicole**, 15, attends a private girl's school in Montreal near her home in Outremount. She speaks French and English fluently, skis at Mont-Tremblant on weekends, and takes flute and ballet classes during the week. Her father, an anglophone, is a surgeon, and her mother, a francophone, is a social worker. Her parents met while attending McGill University, which is where Nicole intends to study.

**Robert**, 14, lives in a group home in Winnipeg, attends a special school program for children with learning disabilities, and has not had contact with either birth parent since the age of one. Initially placed in care at birth due to his mother's drug addiction, he spent several months with his paternal grandparents, but when they were unable to continue caregiving due to their own health issues, he was placed in foster care. He lived in a series of foster homes until the age of 12, when he was placed in the group home. He is not interested in sports, but loves video games.

---

children's welfare. In this chapter, we argue that policy shapes young people's lives as it intersects with Indigeneity and other social locators such as race, class, gender, dis/ability, and sexual orientation. You will be introduced to Theresa, Noah, Nicole, and Robert in the fictitious case examples below. We show how, sometimes, the lives of young people are impacted by policy to build equality, but more often, how policy reinforces existing inequities. We begin with a brief history of Canadian child and youth policy development, and then provide an examination of policy in specific areas.

# Brief History of Canadian Child and Youth Policy

Policy for children and youth initially focused on three areas—"correction" for those breaking the law, education, and substitute care for children deemed by authorities in need of protection. These policies all began in the second half of the nineteenth century and the early twentieth century. The federal government legislated An Act for the Establishment of Prisons for Young Offenders in 1857 in Upper Canada (present-day Ontario), which established reformatories; prior to this, young offenders were not differentiated from adult offenders. The Juvenile Delinquents Act (JDA), introduced in 1908 and in force for more than seven decades, was applied to any case in which a child under 18 and at least seven years of age violated any law, as well as to children who were truant or exhibited sexual immorality or any form of vice. Framed by the principle of **parens patriae**, literally, the state as parent of the nation, the JDA prioritized guidance over punishment of young people or the protection of society.

During the 1870s, most provinces introduced mandatory education for children under 14 and provided limited access to publicly funded education, although this did not occur in Quebec until 1943. Public education brought "unprecedented opportunities" for some children, but most poor or working-class children were steered to domestic and industrial training that prepared them for menial, poorly paid employment (Strong-Boag, 2002, p. 42). However, Indigenous children were prohibited from attending public schools. Canada constructed Indigenous peoples as "wards of the Crown" though the Indian Act in 1876, and an 1884 amendment required Indigenous children to attend church-run residential schools far from their home communities in order to become "civilized." The last residential school was not closed until 1996. (See Chapter 6 for more on residential schools.)

Since 1737 the Montreal order of Soeurs Grises (the Grey Nuns), churches, religious, and non-sectarian charities have cared for the abandoned children of settlers (Finkel, 2006). Following Britain's defeat of France in 1760, British Poor Law practices such as workhouses and poorhouses were introduced to "care" for children and their parents, and the system began of "apprenticing" children from poor families to work for others (Finkel, 2006). In the 1890s, beginning with Ontario, provinces passed child protection laws giving the state power to intervene in families in cases of neglect (primarily poverty-based) and to make children state wards and residents of orphanages run by the Catholic Church and non-sectarian Protestant organizations. Canada was an eager recipient of British "home children," as over 100,000 children without their parents were forcibly emigrated from the late 1860s to 1948 to be unpaid domestics and farm workers for Canadian families (Boucher, 2014). "Mother's allowance" policies began in Ontario in 1888, then in Manitoba, BC, and Saskatchewan between 1910 and 1913—shortly before women gained the right to vote. These were cash transfers provided to "good" mothers to support their children. A good mother was deemed to be a married British subject now single due to the death or desertion of a husband. All Indigenous and Asian mothers were excluded (Boucher, 2014).

The first step towards the post-war welfare state occurred in 1945 when Canada implemented the universal Family Allowance program, a monthly tax-free cash benefit for every child regardless of household income. It represented a move from the residual and stigmatizing "mother's allowance," available at the provincial level, to a more rights-based institutional form of social welfare available to all families. While it never offset the costs of raising a child, it was the first national measure to recognize the state as a partner with parents in children's well-being. Benefits were tied to children's attendance at school. In Quebec, when children left school to financially support their families, or in the Northwest Territories and Yukon, when Indigenous children left school to support their families through hunting or trapping, benefits were discontinued (Finkel, 2006). The universality of this program ended in 1989 when upper-income earners were required to claim the allowance as a taxable benefit, and in 1992 the Progressive Conservative government introduced the Child Tax Benefit. This program, although targeted to lower-income families, was only based on the previous year's tax return, not current income, and benefits were reduced as income increased. This policy change shifted Canada from a welfare state vision of family support to a neo-liberal employability agenda that transformed single mothers into poverty-level workers (Lessa, 2012).

Canada has generally supported the principle of parental autonomy in child-rearing (albeit not for Indigenous families) alongside a recognition that state measures are sometimes needed to ensure the health, safety, and well-being of the nation's young people—its future citizens and workers. The tension between these two principles of enabling parental autonomy while attending to children's needs as "citizens in the making" has underscored much policy-making involving Canadian children. In the following section, we describe how the neo-liberal social investment state envisions "a partnership with parents, one in which the community and the parents are responsible for investing in children" (Saint-Martin, 2007, p. 290).

## The Neo-Liberal Era

Neo-liberalism shifts the role of the state away from ensuring a social minimum for all citizens to the elimination or reduction of social expenditures in order to ensure the ability to compete in deregulated global markets. While entitlements to income security and public goods like education and medical care have not entirely disappeared, they are eroded to pave the way for privatization in the name of "efficiency" and "choice." The state believes its role should be limited, which consequently holds parents primarily responsible. Coinciding with the implementation of neo-liberal political and economic reforms in Canada in the 1980s, restructuring of the welfare state also began. Under these new relations, the state and parents are redefined as co-financiers investing in children as (future) human capital. Parents transmit not only financial but also cultural and social capital to their children; everyone is an economic stakeholder in the market, participating as beneficiaries and consumers. But, as we demonstrate, the neo-liberal logics inherent within these child-focused policies have the effect of optimizing the lives of only some children as good investments. While it may appear that all children have access to the education, housing, and health services required to facilitate their well-being and futures, social goods are not evenly distributed, particularly in quality. Going back to the Case Examples box at the start of the chapter, Nicole's private school, supported by the Quebec government and fees paid by her parents, is vastly superior to Theresa's non-existent reserve school or the Thunder Bay public school, where her attendance is supported by Indigenous and Northern Affairs Canada. Theresa's ongoing health care is provided by a nurse; Nicole's health care is provided by a leading Montreal pediatrician, a friend of Nicole's father. The geographical distribution of social goods, including access to and quality of K–12 education and health care, reflects income, class, race, and gender in a white settler society.

## The UNCRC and Children's Rights in Canada

The United Nations Convention on the Rights of the Child (UNCRC), ratified in Canada in 1991, upholds the idea that children are entitled to certain rights and to participate in decisions that affect them. The notion that children are rights-bearing individuals is closely aligned with neo-liberal ideas about the primacy of the individual and the investment and economization of children's lives. The UNCRC monitors several basic children's rights: the right to survival; to develop to the fullest; to protection from harmful influences, abuse, and exploitation; and to participate fully in family, cultural and social life. It also sets standards for the provision of children's health care, education, and legal, civil, and social services.

While the UNCRC has been ratified by every UN member state except the United States, in Canada and most other countries it exists primarily as a philosophical statement rather than directing child and youth policy development. The "best interests of the child" principle (UNCRC, Article 3) includes taking children's views seriously; emphasizing preventive and collaborative rather than adversarial decision-making; and developing the capacity of young people to decide what is in their best interests. The UN requested in 2003 that Canada integrate this principle into all its laws, policies, administrative processes, and programs for children, but aside from the incorporation of this principle into child protection statutes, little action has been taken. While the "best interests" principle has been partially incorporated into the refugee determination process (CCRC, 2011), the UN Committee on the Rights of the Child has repeatedly criticized Canada for taking years to process many family reunification applications (Gabriel, 2017).

Some progress has been made in ensuring children's participation in hearings on disciplinary measures in some provincial/territorial education systems and in certain child welfare and custody processes. But research continues to demonstrate that most young people (between 67 per cent and 75 per cent in different surveys) do not know their rights or how to exercise them (CCRC, 2011). In 2007, a Senate report on children's rights, *Children: The Silenced Citizens*, recommended that the federal government use child impact assessments of proposed policies and laws to support the implementation of the UNCRC. The Conservative government of the time responded that the current policy development process was adequate. Since then, bills that clearly violate the Convention have been passed, leading the National Alliance for Children and Youth (NACY), a coalition of Canadian organizations that work with children, youth, and their families, to recommend that Canada establish a uniform approach to children's rights that can account for jurisdictional variations (NACY, 2014).

## Universal and Targeted Policies

Canada has universal and targeted social policies for children and youth, which operate in tandem with federal and provincial legislation, and are mainly administered through the tax, income security, health, and education systems. A **universal policy** refers to a benefit or program equally available to all within a category (e.g., children 0 to 17). **Targeted or selective benefits and programs** are available to some but not others, and require applicants to meet a range of specific criteria that include need, program participation (e.g., Employment Insurance), condition (e.g., disability), or income level (see Box 11.1). Canada also has a significant non-profit sector with a wide range of child and family organizations. These organizations do not develop legislation though they may advocate for specific reforms. They often act as contractors to government and create internal policies to administer the programs, services, and benefits that flow from federal, provincial, and municipal legislation. Local municipalities also have bylaws, policies, and programs that benefit children and families within their communities, such as the development and maintenance of playgrounds, parks and greenways, bikeways, water and sewage systems, libraries, and recreation facilities.

## Box 11.1   Universal and Targeted Policies/Programs/Services

*Universal*
- Publicly funded education from K–12 (provincial/territorial; universal).
- Basic medical and health care, including child and maternal health provided through public health.
- Federal tax deductions for some child-related expenses such as private school and child care (though a family must have the means to pay for the expenses).
- Federal tax credits for dependent children and/or children with a disability.
- Tax exemptions on children's clothing (universal in some provinces and territories but others have no exemptions).

*Targeted*
- Maternity and parental leave (restricted to new parents who have made financial contributions to the federal or Quebec Employment Insurance [EI] program, and who meet minimum hours criteria).
- Parental child support and child support enforcement policies (child support payment schedules are based on contributors' incomes and vary depending on province/territory where the children reside).
- Subsidized child care (provincial/territorial; means-tested except Quebec).
- Subsidized prescription drugs and medical devices (provincial/territorial; means tested, unless child/youth qualifies based on age thresholds in some jurisdictions or as First Nations or Inuit under the federal Non-Insured Health Benefits [NIHB] Program).
- Subsidized rental and/or social housing (provincial/territorial, and/or municipal; means-tested).
- Subsidized recreation programs and facilities access (municipal; means-tested).
- Employment and income assistance (social assistance) or other forms of cash benefits (e.g., GST credit) intended to alleviate family financial distress (provincial/territorial; means-tested).
- Canada Child Benefit: monthly cash benefit for families with children under 18 (federal; means-tested).
- Disability Child Tax Benefit: monthly cash benefit for families with children with severe and prolonged physical or mental disabilities (federal; means-tested).
- Canada Pension Plan (CPP) disability benefits: monthly cash benefit for all children under 18 (or 25 if in full-time attendance at school or university), provided their parent made the required CPP contributions and that at least one parent meets program disability criteria (in receipt of CPP disability themselves), or at least one parent is deceased (federal; not means-tested).
- Respite care for caregivers parenting a child with a disability (provincial/territorial; means-tested in some jurisdictions).

# Family/Child/Youth Poverty

Women, Indigenous people, and new immigrants experience the highest levels of poverty in Canada, and almost 20 per cent of children now live in poverty (Campaign 2000, 2015). A child's poverty is also a family's poverty, and one strategy to reduce their poverty is to ensure parents have access to secure and well-paid employment. Minimum wage levels, which are set by provinces and territories except for federal workers, designate the lowest wage that can be paid to a worker.

Canada has flirted with the idea of a guaranteed annual income, initiating experiments in the 1970s and currently (see Chapter 18 for a fuller discussion), but unlike Finland, it has no minimum income policy for all Canadians. Instead, the provinces, territories, and Indigenous and Northern Affairs Canada offer stigmatizing income assistance programs to those able to demonstrate acute financial need. The amounts vary considerably across jurisdictions, do not meet basic living costs, and are not indexed to inflation.

In 2016, the Liberal government of Prime Minister Justin Trudeau replaced most of the child-focused benefits initiated by the former Conservative government with the Canada Child Benefit (CCB). It provides for low-income families a maximum monthly benefit of $533 for each child under six years old and $450 per child for children six years old and over. It is indexed to inflation, with the benefit slowly decreasing as family income rises. A family with an annual income of $90,000 receives $270 per child, whereas a family with an income over $160,000 does not receive any benefit (Battle & Torjman, 2015). By targeting lower-income families, it is anticipated the CCB will lift as many as 300,000 children out of poverty (*CBC News*, 2016), but not everyone knows about the program or has applied to

## International Comparisons

### Poverty Impacting Children and Youth

Canada has one of the highest levels of children's inequality internationally, falling behind 25 other countries with a ranking of 26 out of the 35 richest nations (UNICEF, 2016). The 2017 UNICEF Report Card 14, which assesses the status of children in 41 rich countries on 17 goals related to a healthy environment for children while meeting sustainable development goals (SDGs), ranks Canada 25th out of 41 countries (Figure 11.1).

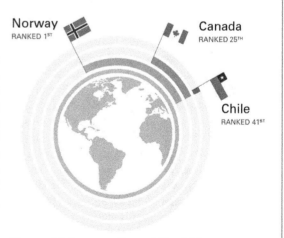

**Figure 11.1 UNICEF Report Card 14**
Source: http://www.unicef.ca/en/unicef-report-card-14-child-well-being-sustainable-world

receive the benefit (*CBC News*, 2017). In our Case Examples, Theresa's parents are not apply-ing for the program because the requirement of filing a tax return to determine eligibility means giving the government more information than they believe it should have. Noah's mother hasn't heard about the program, and so hasn't applied. Nicole's father discussed the program with his accountant, but determined Nicole is not eligible. All provincial and territorial child welfare organizations receive this benefit to assist with maintenance costs when children like Robert are in their care, even when care arrangements are temporary.

## Non-Citizen Children and Youth

In recent years, Canada has accepted about 200,000 to 250,000 immigrants annually (Ferrer, Picot, & Riddell, 2014), including those who initially arrive as refugees or asylum seekers. Between 2008 and 2012, about 17 per cent of accepted immigrants were youth aged 15 to 24 years (Citizenship and Immigration Canada, 2012). It is estimated that there are somewhere between 200,000 and 500,000 non-status migrants with precarious legal status in Canada, many of whom have dependent children (Hudson, Atak, Manocchi, & Hannan, 2017). This figure includes those with rejected refugee applications, immigration sponsorship agreement breakdowns, or those who have overstayed a work or student visa (Goldring & Landolt, 2013). It is unknown how many of those are children. While the Canada Border Services Agency (CBSA) reports significant numbers of youth (17 years of age or younger) are seeking asylum in Canada (2,011 in 2015 and 3,400 in 2016), "nei-ther the CBSA nor the Department of Immigration, Refugees and Citizenship are able to provide clear data on the number of unaccompanied or separated minors who arrive per year" (Kalaichandran, 2017).

Although almost half of all refugees accepted into Canada on humanitarian grounds are children and youth (CIC, 2012), no comprehensive national policy on unaccompanied minors (refugee and asylum-seeking children) exists. Since 1996, a "loose set of protocols" has guided the process of determining whether, and on what basis, they might be allowed to remain (Denov & Bryan, 2012, p. 68). Children and youth might be placed with relatives or in a temporary group residence, or put into detention when, for example, authorities have questions about their identity or background. If an asylum claim is made, the government designates a representative to assist the child or youth with the process, which can take sev-eral years (Denov & Bryan, 2010). Children and youth not granted asylum may appeal on compassionate and/or humanitarian grounds; deportation is rare but does occur.

Provincial or even local authorities have the responsibility to integrate and resource newcomers and provide them with education and health services. At present, five prov-inces have policies and processes in place for unaccompanied minors (BC, Manitoba, On-tario, Quebec, Newfoundland and Labrador), while five do not (Alberta, Saskatchewan, New Brunswick, Nova Scotia, PEI) (Canadian Council on Refugees, n.d.). The Toronto District School Board adopted a "Don't Ask Don't Tell Policy" in 2007 so that those chil-dren with precarious status or without status can access schooling without the fear of being reported to authorities. Similarly, three cities have designated themselves "sanctu-ary cities" (Toronto 2013, Hamilton 2014, Vancouver 2015), where all residents can access city services without revealing their immigration status (Hudson et al., 2017).

Most newcomer support and settlement needs are addressed through non-profit im-migrant and/or refugee serving agencies. While these agencies are required to transmit government policies to immigrants and refugees, their core funding was replaced in 1995 by competitive and unstable purchase-of-service contract funding (Mukhtar, Dean, Wilson, Ghassemi, & Wilson, 2016). In practical terms, this means that even though Canada is a signatory to the Optional Protocol of the Convention on the Rights of the Child on the involvement of children in armed conflict, which obligates it to assist and support war-affected children's recovery as well as their social reintegration (UN, 2010), few reliable resources exist to help these children and youth meet the challenges of resettlement (Rossiter, Hatami, Ripley, & Rossiter, 2015).

# Education

Educational attainment within Canada is increasing; high school non-completion rates dropped from 16.6 per cent in 1990–1 to 8.5 per cent in 2009–10 (Franke, 2010, cited in NACY, 2014). Even so, high school completion rates are lower for immigrant and refugee youth than for children born in Canada, except for Indigenous children (Corak, 2011). Hou and Bonikowska (2016) demonstrate the relationship between parental immigration class and educational outcome. While children of business and skilled-worker class immigrants have high secondary school and university completion rates, children of live-in caregiver and family-class immigrants, and refugees have much lower completion rates. One factor may be poverty. To supplement family income or support themselves, most youth work while attending school; Noah's story (see Case Examples box) is not the exception but the rule.

When parents living in poverty are blamed for their children's educational achievement through "deficit ideology" (Gorski, 2012), policy responses may focus on correcting these supposed deficiencies within parents or poor communities rather than on addressing problems of access to resources such as quality daycare and preschool, safe housing and neighbourhoods, and well-equipped and funded schools. Under the Indian Act the federal government has responsibility to fund education for children living on reserve. Indigenous children on reserve are thereby allocated $2,000 to $3,000 less per child per year for education funding than all other children in Canada, and often the schools have fewer education resources (e.g., libraries, computers) or supports for children with special needs (NACY, 2014).

# Health

There are notable health disparities among Canadian children and youth. For example, in the period between 1990 and 2014 Canada's infant mortality increased; rankings fell from sixth to 43rd, placing Canada at the top of the tier usually reserved for the world's poorest nations (CIA, 2014). Economically advantaged children benefit the most from publicly funded universal medical care because their families differentially access healthy food, safe, contaminant-free drinking water, adequate housing, and other health-promoting resources that are less available or unavailable to poor children and children living on reserve. As of August 2011, almost one out of five Indigenous communities in Canada was living under ongoing boil-water advisories (Auditor General of Canada, 2011); from 2004 to 2014, almost two-thirds of Indigenous communities had at least one advisory (Levasseur & Marcoux, 2015). Despite the Safe Drinking Water for First Nations Act of 2013, the federal government projects that it will be the year 2021 before it can end long-term drinking water advisories. Updated reports can be viewed on the Indigenous Services Canada website (https://www.canada.ca/en/indigenous-services-canada.html). Poor water quality, substandard housing, and limited access to culturally appropriate health care contribute to disproportionate rates of infant and child mortality, low birth weights, respiratory illnesses, diabetes, and developmental disabilities amongst Indigenous children (CCRC, 2011). The gap between children with access to essential health-supporting resources and children who lack the most basic resources, identified as a public health priority by provincial/territorial health ministers in 2007 and by Canada's Chief Public Health Officer in 2009 (CCRC, 2011), has yet to be addressed.

Other social policies indirectly impact children's health. For example, income assistance rates are implicated in one in six children experiencing food insecurity, with higher rates in Indigenous communities (Findlay, Langlois, & Kohen, 2013). Deficiencies in essential nutrients such as iron impair infant and toddler development and compromise learning in school-age children (Rose-Jacobs et al., 2008). Longitudinal studies in Quebec confirm that children living in poverty are more likely to develop health problems (Séguin, Nikiéma, Gauvin, Zunzunegui, & Xu, 2007). Hunger increases the likelihood that children will develop chronic health conditions, and elevates the risk of mental health difficulties such as suicide and depression among adolescents (Ke & Ford-Jones, 2015). While anyone might face mental health challenges, structural factors associated with poverty, such as unsafe neighbourhoods, substandard housing, and lack of access to essential services, place some young people at elevated risk of a mental health disorder (Kutcher & McLuckie, 2011).

## Mental Health

Although most youth and young adults in Canada (77 per cent) describe their mental health as very good or excellent, mental "disorders" are the most prevalent health conditions linked to disability among young people, and less than 20 per cent of those affected by mental illness receive appropriate treatment (Freeman et al., 2011). A British Columbia inquiry showed death by suicide is the second leading cause of youth mortality, surpassed only by motor vehicle accidents (White, 2009).

Risk of suicide is higher for Indigenous and LGBTQ youth, but policy responses do little to address social determinants such as racism, transphobia, and homophobia that are linked to elevated rates of suicidal behaviours (White, 2009). Historical and ongoing colonialism is an additional determinant of mental health for Indigenous young people. Indigenous youth in Canada take their own lives five to seven times more frequently than other youth, and the suicide rate for Inuit youth, at 11 times the national average, is among the highest in the world (Government of Canada, 2018a). Even when a social analysis is factored into youth suicide, school and community policy predominantly takes an anti-bullying focus, which represents the problem as being one of individual acts of bullying (Public Health Agency of Canada, 2008). Youth bullying and cyberbullying have been studied through a public health lens with co-occurrences to discrimination (Garnett et al., 2014), and in relation to marginalized identities and subsequent youth mental disorders and suicides (Abreu, Black, Mosley, & Fedewa, 2016). Clear links exist between completed youth suicides and the impacts of colonial violence and socio-economic inequalities, but policies targeting individual acts of youth bullying take a narrowly defined focus with desired outcomes being increased inclusion and physical, psychological, and emotional safety within schools for marginalized youth, despite social injustices.

Policy approaches focused on mental health intervention are also aligned with brain science theories to argue for pharmacological interventions. Although the safety and effectiveness of psychiatric medication for children and youth has yet to be clearly established, prescribing rates have risen steadily since the early 1990s (Brenner, Southerland, Burns, Wagner, & Farmer, 2014). Differentials in prescribing rates suggest that the medicalization of individuals, which fits neatly within neo-liberal policy approaches, is replacing a more robust social policy response to the compromised mental health of some children and youth. As a newly emerging area of legal and policy development, legalization of the non-medical use and sale of cannabis in Canada has prominently featured concerns about subsequent harmful health and neurodevelopmental effects for a greater number of young people. There is ample research suggesting that the developing bodies and brains of youth make them particularly vulnerable to adverse health effects, including implications for mental health and cognitive capacities (Kalant, 2015; Porath-Waller, Brown, Frigon, & Clark, 2013). Youth from affluent Western countries such as Canada have been less likely than youth from poorer European countries to consume cannabis—a trend reflected in family affluence and youth cannabis usage within all Western countries (Bogt et al., 2014). However, critics of legalization cite concerns that young people will equate legalization with safety, consequently encouraging a greater number of youth to try cannabis and increasing consumption rates among youth already using it (Kalant, 2015).

# Youth Justice

Youth justice is governed by federal statutes, though provinces and territories are responsible for detention facilities and justice-related programs. The Juvenile Delinquents Act was replaced by the Young Offenders Act (YOA) in 1984 to provide a more robust legal framework for youth crime, including due process and defendants' rights. While the YOA contained some diversion options, these were rarely used and incarceration was common; under the YOA Canada's youth imprisonment rate soared to among the highest in the world (Minkes, 2007). The Youth Criminal Justice Act (YCJA), introduced in 2003 and still in force, attempted to strike a balance between concerns about being either too "soft" or too "tough" on youth crime.

YCJA jurisdiction is limited to youth 12 to 18 years of age, with custody sentences reserved for youth 14 and older. Youth aged 14 or older charged with serious offences (e.g., murder, aggravated sexual assault) can be moved to adult court. Crimes committed by those under 12 years of age are dealt with under provincial or territorial family/child welfare laws and programs. While the YCJA mandates diversion for all first-time and non-serious offenders and a restorative approach to crime, for example by encouraging victim involvement, it also emphasizes the "responsibilization" of youth and in some cases their parents. Sentencing options under the YCJA (reprimands, discharge [with or without conditions], fines, compensation or restitution, community service, probation, referral to a support/supervision program, custody) are intended to provide accountability through "meaningful consequences" (Allen & Superle, 2016).

The YCJA has been successful in reducing the rate and number of young offenders in custody: between 2000–1 and 2013–14, the proportion of guilty youth sentenced to custody fell from 28 per cent to 15 per cent (Allen & Superle, 2016). While in this way the YCJA reflects the principles of the UNCRC, which advocates alternative sentencing and reintegration programs, with custody as a last resort, there is still a disproportionately high remand and custody rate for Indigenous and racialized youth (Bateman, 2011). For example, Indigenous youth account for 30 per cent of the youth custody population while they make up only 6 per cent of the Canadian youth population (Corrado, Kuehn, & Margaritescu, 2014). The highest rates of incarceration are in northern and central Canada; in Saskatchewan, Indigenous youth are more likely to go to prison than finish high school (Assembly of First Nations, 2012, cited in Dhillon, 2015). These regional variations remind us that although federal statutes frame youth justice, law is administered through provincial/ territorial policies.

Youth crime is continuing to trend downward (Silcox, 2016). In fact, more young people experience violence than perpetrate it: in 2009, youth aged 14 to 24 were nearly 15 times more likely than seniors to be victimized and Indigenous youth were victimized at twice the rate of their non-Indigenous peers (National Crime Prevention Centre, 2012). Only a small number of youth are repeat offenders or commit serious crimes such as drug trafficking or aggravated assault, and even these numbers are decreasing. But media coverage of youth crime presents an alternative discourse, creating a moral panic about youth crime that fuels policies out of step with the facts. Schissel (2008), Faucher (2009), and Silcox (2016) all show how frequency (the number of crimes) and severity (the type of crime) are exaggerated in media accounts of youth crime, despite the availability of crime statistics. Additionally, they demonstrate that racist and classist stereotypes dominate media coverage; for example, the race of accused youth is routinely included in crime stories except when offenders are white (Faucher, 2009).

Because Canada does not yet collect data on the race of criminalized youth (aside from Indigenous youth), it is challenging to provide statistical evidence of racial disproportionality. Fitzgerald and Carrington (2011, p. 472) use data from the National Longitudinal Study of Children and Youth to demonstrate that racialized youth in Canada were about "three times more likely than other youth to report having had contact with the police in the past year." Marginalized youth (particularly those who are Indigenous, Black, or poor) are more likely to be stopped by police and targeted during investigations (Silcox, 2016), more likely to be charged and to be convicted (Bell, 2015), and as much as eight times more likely to receive a custodial (as opposed to a community) sentence (Bateman, 2011). Youth in care of the state are also over-represented in the youth criminal justice system, though the extent varies across jurisdictions (Corrado, Freedman, & Blatier, 2011). For example, British Columbia reported in 2009 that one in six youth in care had been incarcerated, compared to fewer than one in 50 youth not in state care (British Columbia, 2009).

Alongside disproportionate incarceration and criminalization, Indigenous youth and girls in particular experience vastly disproportionate levels of violence. In her intersectional policy analysis of violence against Indigenous girls, Clark (2012) demonstrates the failure of state policies to protect them. Dhillon (2015) relates disproportionality directly to the ongoing settler/colonial context; she cites Butler's (2015, para. 2) observation that "some lives matter more than others, that some lives matter so much that they need to be protected at all costs, and that other lives matter less, or not at all." Continued disproportionality mandates the development of new strategies. As Corrado et al. (2014, p. 56) note, one major challenge is to mitigate the ongoing impact of colonial laws and policies on Indigenous youth, families, and communities.

One possibility likely to benefit all youth is a return to the vision of the Juvenile Delinquents Act, which regarded youth offending as an indication that supports and resources should be provided to the youth and/or the family (Muncie, 2006). This approach is consistent with the Article 3 provision of the UNCRC that the "best interests" of the child should be a primary consideration in all actions, courts, and law. Policy changes that move youth justice from punishment to diversion have resulted in substantial reductions in youth incarceration in many jurisdictions. The most drastic reductions have happened in Japan, Norway, and Sweden (Muncie & Goldson, 2013). Iceland, Norway, Sweden, Denmark, and Finland emphasize social and educational interventions and mediation, while Australia recently added restorative justice youth conferencing to its existing measures. While similar options exist in Canada, punishment and deterrence still dominate the Canadian approach.

# Child Protection

In Canada provinces and territories are responsible for child protection, with federal government responsibility limited to funding services for children on reserve. Every jurisdiction has legislation specific to the protection of children, as well as policies, standards, and protocols that specify categories of child maltreatment, define abuse and neglect, and outline criteria for intervention and the forms of intervention that might take place. Policies emphasize the assessment of child safety and maltreatment, and in some instances substitute care is required for children who have been or are likely to be harmed by parental action or inaction.

Despite variations across jurisdictions, the primary determinants of whether a family comes to the attention of authorities, whether authorities intervene, and how they intervene are race and class, with racialized, poor, or disabled families persistently over-represented and subject to more intrusive forms of state intervention (Bywaters, Brady, Sparks, & Bos, 2016). Indigenous people, who are among the poorest in Canada, are particularly over-represented on child protection caseloads (Lavergne, Dufour, Trocmé, & Larrivée, 2008). Although less than 4 per cent of Canadians identify as Indigenous, 22 per cent of investigations where child maltreatment was found to have occurred involved Indigenous children (Trocmé et al., 2010). The most recent available national study, the Canadian Incidence Study of Reported Child Abuse and Neglect (CIS-2008), determined child protection investigations almost doubled between 1998 and 2008, from 21.47 investigations per 1,000 children in 1998 to a rate of 39.16 per 1,000 children in 2008 (Trocmé et al., 2010). The out-of-home placement of children also continued to increase: between 1992 and 2007, the number of children placed increased from 42,000 (5.7 children per 1,000 children) to 67,000 (9.2 children per 1,000 children) (Mulcahy & Trocmé, 2010). These increases have been attributed in part to including emotional abuse and "exposure" to intimate partner violence as categories of child maltreatment; and in part to factors related to neglect, such as deepening poverty, the lack of accessible family supports and resources, and the absence of affordable, safe housing (Swift, 2011). The CIS was undertaken again in 2018. Findings will be made available on the Canadian Child Welfare Research Portal (http://cwrp.ca/overview).

All Canadian child welfare policies reflect the neo-liberal emphasis on individual rather than societal responsibility. Individual families are expected to care for, supervise, and protect their children even if their efforts are constrained by poverty or other factors. Although children have a right to this form of "protection" and legislation identifies the family as the best place for them, children do not have legislated rights to resources and supports that could maintain them within their families and communities. Additionally, while the state's role in protecting children from harm related to parental conduct is enshrined in law and policy, no corollary provisions exist to tackle those forms of harm (unsafe drinking water, inadequate housing, poverty) related to state conduct. This approach contrasts starkly with Nordic social welfare systems in which all families, not just those targeted under legislation, are entitled to a broad range of supports (Walmsley & Tessier, 2014–15). Canada's approach is also markedly different from the family welfare systems common to Western European countries, where supports are available to children and families. While children in any of these systems may sometimes be placed outside the home, in social and family welfare systems this usually comes about through voluntary agreements with parents, whereas in child protection systems like Canada's most placements are compelled through court orders (Gilbert, 2012).

The Truth and Reconciliation Commission (TRC) of Canada (2015) issued 94 Calls to Action in the form of present and future obligations of Canadians as *treaty people*; many of these are child protection obligations and recommendations for policy and practice changes. State removals of Indigenous children have been classified as a genocidal practice that continues in the present with ongoing removals and over-representation of Indigenous children in protection systems governed under non-Indigenous law. The TRC identified that Canada perpetrated not only cultural but also physical and biological genocide against Indigenous peoples, in part through residential schools and the "Sixties Scoop" when social workers arranged permanent adoptions for Indigenous children outside of their communities, primarily with white families. In 2008, the Auditor General of Canada identified that funding for Indigenous child welfare services living on reserve was 22 per cent less than funding for similar services for all other children residing in Canada. Subsequently, the First Nations Child and Family Caring Society initiated various legal actions in an attempt to compel equitable funding, which the federal Conservative government fought at every turn (Blackstock, 2015). A human rights tribunal initiated by Cindy Blackstock in 2007 declared in 2016 that the federal government was discriminating against the human rights of Indigenous children living on reserve, and ordered the government to provide equitable funding. After the tribunal initiated a number of non-compliance orders, the federal Liberal government announced in its 2018 budget, earmarked "reconciliation," a commitment to redress funding gaps for on-reserve child welfare services.

## Chapter Summary

As has been consistently demonstrated in our discussion of various social policy areas, the well-being and life chances of children and youth are intertwined with those of their parents or caregivers and communities. In the case examples at the start of the chapter, Nicole's parents can optimize her childhood through a heady mix of public and purchased resources and supports. Theresa's and Noah's parents have no discretionary funds to purchase either essential or enhanced services and constantly navigate trade-offs between, for example, minimally adequate housing and minimally adequate nutrition. Robert has access to resources the state provides for his care, but lacks a supportive family network and anything above the minimum needed to optimize his life chances.

Over the last few decades, widening inequalities in Canada are accompanied by greater disparities in child development, especially for Indigenous, immigrant, and refugee children and youth (CCRC, 2011). The situation of Indigenous children is particularly alarming. The Indian Act is the only raced-based legislation in the industrialized Western world (Blackstock, 2016). It has been used by government as a tool of genocide and facilitates discrimination against Indigenous children. Although there has been ample documentation of the situation of Indigenous children and a high level of consensus in the analysis and recommendations for action, the social policy response at all levels of government has been inadequate. The current federal government's 2018 budget implies it will implement a nation-to-nation relationships with Indigenous peoples and will make revisions to the Indian Act so that Indigenous people are in control of their own decision-making and futures. This budget also includes funding to redress inequities for Indigenous people across a number of key domains, including health, child welfare, education, and housing (see Government of Canada, 2018b).

At the time of this writing, it is too soon to know precisely how these commitments will be implemented or to determine their outcome. What is known, however, is that international comparisons provide compelling evidence that political choices different from those made in Canada over the last decades lead to social policies that effectively redress inequities. Unless Canada moves forward within nation-to nation relationships with Indigenous peoples and creates legislation and policy to increase and equitably distribute the quality of social goods, the inequalities that fundamentally frame life experiences and outcomes for Indigenous and other marginalized children will remain the same or deteriorate further.

## Discussion Questions

1. List the most significant policies that optimize the lives of Theresa, Noah, Nicole, and Robert, and those that buttress their existing inequalities.

2. What policy changes are needed to further optimize their lives and create equity?

3. What are the first three steps you recommend the federal government take to enhance the lives of Indigenous children and youth?

## References

Abreu, R. L., Black, W. W., Mosley, D. V., & Fedewa, A. L. (2016). LGBTQ youth bullying experiences in schools: The role of school counselors within a system of oppression. *Journal of Creativity in Mental Health, 11*(3–4), 325.

Allen, M. K., & Superle, T. (2016). Youth crime in Canada, 2014. *Juristat: Canadian Centre for Justice Statistics*, 1.

Auditor General of Canada (2011). *The 2011 status report of the Auditor General of Canada to the House of Commons*. Chapter 4: Programs for First Nations on reserves. Ottawa, 2011. Retrieved from http://www.oagbvg.gc.ca/internet/docs/parl_oag_201106_04_e.pdf

Baker, M. (2007). Managing the risk of childhood poverty: Changing interventions by the state. *Women's Health and Urban Life, 6*(2), 8–21.

Bateman, T. (2011). Youth justice news. *Youth Justice 11*(3), 282–91.

Battle, K., & Torjman, S. (2015, May). *Child benefit reform is back on track*. Ottawa: Caledon Institute of Social Policy. Retrieved from

http://www.caledoninst.org/Publications/
PDF/1065ENG%2Epdf

Blackstock, C. (2015). Should governments be above
the law? The Canadian Human Rights Tribunal and First Nations child welfare. *Children
Australia, 40*(2), 95–103.

———. (2016, 3 Apr.). Justice long overdue for First
Nations [Video file]. Retrieved from https://
www.youtube.com/watch?v=LfMUKllM224

Bogt, T. F. M., Looze, M. D., Molcho, M., Godeau,
E., Hublet, A., Kokkevi, A., & Pickett, W. (2014).
Do societal wealth, family affluence and gender
account for trends in adolescent cannabis use?
A 30 country cross-national study. *Addiction,
109*(2), 273–83.

Boucher, E. (2014). *Empire's children: Child emi-
gration, welfare, and the decline of the British
world, 1869–1967.* Cambridge: Cambridge
University Press.

Brenner, S. L., Southerland, D. G., Burns, B. J., Wagner,
H. R., & Farmer, E. M. Z. (2014). Use of psychotropic medications among youth in treatment
foster care. *Journal of Child and Family Studies,
23*(4), 666–74.

British Columbia. (2009). *Kids, crime and care—
Health and well-being of children in care: Youth
justice experiences and outcomes.* Victoria:
Representative for Children and Youth.

Bywaters, P., Brady, G., Sparks, T., & Bos, E. (2016).
Inequalities in child welfare intervention rates:
The intersection of deprivation and identity.
*Child & Family Social Work, 21*(4), 452–63.

Campaign 2000. (2015). *Let's do this; Let's end child
poverty for good: Campaign 2000 report card
on child & family poverty in Canada.* Retrieved
from http://campaign2000.ca/wp-content/
uploads/2016/03/2015-Campaign2000-Report-
Card-Final-English.pdf

Canadian Coalition for the Rights of Children
(CCRC). (2011). *Right in principle, right in
practice: Implementation of the Convention on
the Rights of the Children in Canada.* Toronto:
CCRC.

Canadian Council on Refugees. (n.d.). Unaccompanied minors. Retrieved from http://ccrweb.ca/en/
content/unaccompanied-minors

*CBC News.* (2016, 11 July). 5 things to know about
the new Canada Child Benefit. Retrieved
from http://www.cbc.ca/news/politics/
canada-child-benefit-july-rollout-1.3668698

———. (2017, 21 July). Many Indigenous families
not applying for Canadian child benefit: Documents. Retrieved from http://www.cbc.ca/news/
politics/canada-child-benefit-indigenous-
1.4211545

Central Intelligence Agency (CIA). (2014). *The world
factbook: Country comparison.* https://Www.Cia
.Gov/Library/Publications/The-World-Factbook/

Citizenship and Immigration Canada. (2012). *Facts
and figures 2012—Immigration overview:
Permanent and temporary residents.* Ottawa:
Citizenship and Immigration Canada.

Clark, N. (2012). *Perseverance, determination and
resistance: An Indigenous intersectional-based
policy analysis of violence in the lives of Indigenous girls.* Retrieved from http://learningcircle
.ubc.ca/files/2013/10/7_Indigenous-Girls_
Clark-2012.pdf

Corak, M. (2011). *Age at immigration and the educational outcomes of children.* Ottawa: Minister of
Industry, Statistics Canada.

Corrado, R. R., Freedman, L. F., & Blatier, C. (2011).
The over-representation of children in care in
the youth criminal justice system in British
Columbia: Theory and policy issues. *Inter-
national Journal of Child, Youth and Family
Studies, 2*(1–2), 99–118.

———, Kuehn, S., & Margaritescu, I. (2014). Policy
issues regarding the overrepresentation of
incarcerated aboriginal young offenders in a
Canadian context. *Youth Justice, 14*(1), 40–62.

Denov, M., & Bryan, C. (2010). Unaccompanied refugee children in Canada. *Settlement of Newcomers to Canada, 12,* 67–75.

——— & ———. (2012). Unaccompanied refugee children in Canada: Experiences of flight and resettlement. *Canadian Social Work, 12*(2), 67–75.

Dhillon, J. K. (2015). Indigenous girls and the violence
of settler colonial policing. *Decolonization: Indigeneity, Education & Society, 4*(2), 1–31.

Faucher, C. (2009). Fear and loathing in the news:
A qualitative analysis of Canadian print news
coverage of youthful offending in the twentieth
century. *Journal of Youth Studies, 12*(4), 439–56.

Ferrer, A., Picot, G., & Riddell, W. (2014). New directions in immigration policy: Canada's evolving
approach to the selection of economic immigrants.
*International Migration Review, 48*(3), 846–67.

Findlay, L. C., Langlois, K. A., & Kohen, D. E. (2013).
Hunger among Inuit children in Canada. *International Journal of Circumpolar Health, 72.*

Finkel, A. (2006). *Social policy and practice in Canada:
A history.* Waterloo, ON: Wilfrid Laurier University Press.

Fitzgerald, R.T., & Carrington, P.J. (2011). Disproportionate minority contact in Canada: Police
and visible minority youth. *Canadian Journal
of Criminology and Criminal Justice/La Revue
canadienne de criminologie et de justice pénale,
53*(4), 449–86.

Freeman, J. G., King, M. A., Pickett, W., Craig, W., Elgar, F., Janssen, I., & Klinger, D. (2011). *The health of Canada's young people: A mental health focus*. Ottawa: Public Health Agency of Canada.

Gabriel, C. (2017). Framing families: Neo-liberalism and the family class within Canadian immigration policy. *Atlantis: Critical Studies in Gender, Culture & Social Justice, 38*(1), 179–94.

Garnett, B. R., Masyn, K. E., Austin, S. B., Miller, M., Williams, D. R., & Viswanath, K. (2014). The intersectionality of discrimination attributes and bullying among youth: An applied latent class analysis. *Journal of Youth and Adolescence, 43*(8), 1225–39.

Gilbert, N. (2012). A comparative study of child welfare systems: Abstract orientations and concrete results. *Children and Youth Services Review, 34*(3), 532–6.

Goldring, L., & Landolt, P. (2013). The conditionality of legal status and rights: Conceptualizing precarious non-citizenship in Canada. In L. Goldring & P. Landolt (Eds), *Producing and negotiating non-citizenship: Precarious legal status in Canada* (pp. 3–27). Toronto: University of Toronto Press.

Gorski, P. C. (2012). Perceiving the problem of poverty and schooling: Deconstructing the class stereotypes that mis-shape education practice and policy. *Equity & Excellence in Education, 45*(2), 302–19.

Government of Canada. (2018a). Suicide prevention. Retrieved from https://www.canada.ca/en/indigenous-services-canada/services/first-nations-inuit-health/health-promotion/suicide-prevention.html

——. (2018b). Budget 2018. Reconciliation. Retrieved from https://www.budget.gc.ca/2018/docs/plan/chap-03-en.html

Heckman, J. J., & Masterov, D. V. (2007). The productivity argument for investing in young children. *Review of Agricultural Economics, 29*(3), 446–93.

Hou, F., & Bonikowska, A. (2016). *Educational and labour market outcomes of childhood immigrants by admission class*. Ottawa: Statistics Canada

Hudson, G., Atak, I., Manocchi, M., & Hannan, C.-A. (2017). *(No) access T.O.: A pilot study on sanctuary city policy in Toronto, Canada*. RCIS Working Paper No. 2017/1. Toronto: Ryerson Centre on Immigration and Settlement.

Kalaichandran, A. (2017, 16 Mar.). Advocates concerned about unaccompanied minors seeking asylum in Canada. The Canadian Press. Retrieved from http://www.citynews.ca/2017/03/16/advocates-concerned-about-unaccompanied-minors-seeking-asylum-in-canada/

Kalant, H. (2015). Cannabis control policy: No rational basis yet for legalization. *Clinical Pharmacology & Therapeutics, 97*(6), 538–40.

Ke, J., & Ford-Jones, E. L. (2015). Food insecurity and hunger: A review of the effects on children's health and behaviour. *Paediatrics & Child Health, 20*(2), 89–91.

Kutcher, S., & McLuckie, A. (2011). Evergreen: A child and youth mental health framework for Canada. *Paediatrics & Child Health, 16*(7), 388.

Lavergne, C., Dufour, S., Trocmé, N., & Larrivée, M. C. (2008). Visible minority, Aboriginal, and Caucasian children investigated by Canadian protective services. *Child Welfare, 87*(2), 59.

Lessa, I. (2012). Single motherhood in the Canadian landscape. In A. Westhues & B. Wharf (Eds), *Canadian social policy: Issues and perspectives* (5th edn, pp. 147–66). Waterloo, ON: Wilfrid Laurier University Press.

Levasseur, J., & Marcoux, J. (2015, 14 Oct.). Water advisories chronic reality in many First Nations communities. Retrieved from http://www.cbc.ca/news/canada/manitoba/bad-water-third-world-conditions-on-first-nations-in-canada-1.3269500

Minkes, J. (2007). Review essay: Change, continuity, and public opinion in youth justice. *International Criminal Justice Review, 17*(4), 340–9.

Mukhtar, M., Dean, J., Wilson, K., Ghassemi, E., & Wilson, D. H. (2016). "But many of these problems are about funds . . .": The challenges immigrant settlement agencies (ISAs) encounter in a suburban setting in Ontario, Canada. *Journal of International Migration and Integration, 17*(2), 389–408.

Mulcahy, M., & Trocmé, N. (2010). *CECW information sheet #78. Children and youth in out-of-home care in Canada*. Montreal: Centre for Research on Children and Families, McGill University.

Muncie, J. (2006). Governing young people: Coherence and contradiction in contemporary youth justice. *Critical Social Policy, 26*(4), 770–93.

——& Goldson, B. (2013). Youth justice: In a child's best interests? In J. Simon & R. Sparks (Eds), *The SAGE Handbook of Punishment and Society* (pp. 341–55). Thousand Oaks, CA: Sage.

National Alliance for Children and Youth (NACY). (2014). An action framework for children and youth in Canada. *The Philanthropist, 26*(2), 145–79.

National Crime Prevention Centre. (2012). *A statistical snapshot of youth at risk and youth offending in Canada.* Ottawa: National Crime Prevention Centre, Public Safety Canada.

Porath-Waller, A. J., Brown, J. E., Frigon, A. P., & Clark, H. (2013). *What Canadian youth think about cannabis: Technical report.* Ottawa: Canadian Centre on Substance Abuse.

Public Health Agency of Canada. (2008). *Bullying and fighting among Canadian youth.* Ottawa. Retrieved from http://publications.gc.ca/site/archiveearchived.html?url=http://publications.gc.ca/collections/collection_2009/aspc-phac/HP15-2-3-2008E.pdf

Rose-Jacobs, R., Black, M. M., Casey, P., Cook, J., Cutts, D. B., Chilton, M., et al. (2008). Household food insecurity: Association with at-risk infant and toddler development. *Pediatrics, 212,* 65–72.

Rossiter, M., Hatami, S., Ripley, D., & Rossiter, K. (2015). Immigrant and refugee youth settlement experiences: "A new kind of war." *International Journal of Child, Youth and Family Studies, 6,* 746–70.

Saint-Martin, D. (2007). From the welfare state to the social investment state. In M. Orsini & M. Smith (Eds), *Critical policy studies* (pp. 280–98). Vancouver: University of British Columbia Press.

Schissel, B. (2008). Justice undone: Public panic and the condemnation of children and youth. In *Moral panics over contemporary children and youth* (pp. 15–30). Farnham, UK and Burlington, VT: Ashgate.

Séguin, L., Nikiéma, B., Gauvin, L., Zunzunegui, M.-V. & Xu, Q. (2007). Duration of poverty and child health in the Quebec longitudinal study of child development: Longitudinal analysis of a birth cohort. *Pediatrics, 119*(5), e1063–e1070.

Sherlock, T. (2017, 31 July). Cindy Blackstock says Trudeau government's "making excuses" for neglecting Indigenous children. *National Observer.* Retrieved from http://www.nationalobserver.com/2017/07/31/news/cindy-blackstock-says-trudeau-governments-making-excuses-neglecting-indigenous

Silcox, J. (2016). *Representations of youth crime in Canada: A feminist criminological analysis of statistical trends, national Canadian newspapers, and moral panics* (Unpublished doctoral dissertation). University of Western Ontario, London, ON.

Strong-Boag, V. (2002). Getting to now: Children in distress in Canada's past. In B. Wharf (Ed.), *Community work approaches to child welfare* (pp. 29–46). Peterborough, ON: Broadview Press.

Swift, K. J. (2011). Canadian child welfare: Child protection and the status quo. *Child protection systems: International trends and orientations,* 36–59.

Trocmé, N. (2010). *Canadian incidence study of reported child abuse and neglect, 2008: Major findings.* Ottawa: Public Health Agency of Canada.

——, Fallon, B., MacLaurin, B., Sinha, V., Black, T., Fast, E., & Holroyd, J. (2010). *Canadian incidence study of reported child abuse and neglect—2008: Major findings.* Ottawa: Public Health Agency of Canada.

Truth and Reconciliation Commission of Canada. (2015). *Calls to action.* Winnipeg. Retrieved from http://www.trc.ca/websites/trcinstitution/File/2015/Findings/Calls_to_Action_English2.pdf

UNICEF. (2016). *Report Card 13: Fairness for children.* Retrieved from http://www.unicef.ca/en/unicef-report-card-13-fairness-for-children

UNICEF Canada. (2016). *Child well-being in rich countries: A comparative overview: Canadian companion.* Retrieved from http://www.unicef.ca/sites/default/files/legacy/imce_uploads/DISCOVER/OUR%20WORK/ADVOCACY/DOMESTIC/POLICY%20ADVOCACY/DOCS/unicef_rc_11_canadian_companion.pdf

United Nations (UN). (2010). *The rights and guarantees of internally displaced children in armed conflict.* New York: UN.

Walmsley, C., & Tessier, L. (2014–15). Children's welfare: A comparison of Nordic and Canadian approaches. *CCPA Monitor: Economic, Social and Environmental Perspectives, 21*(7), 30–4.

White, J. (2009). *Doing youth suicide prevention critically: Interrogating the knowledge practice relationship.* Victoria, BC: Federation of Child & Family Services of BC.

Wilkinson, L. (2008). Labor market transitions of immigrant-born, refugee-born, and Canadian-born youth. *Canadian Review of Sociology / Revue canadienne de sociologie, 45*(2), 151–76.

Wilkinson, R. G., & Pickett, K. (2009). *The spirit level: Why more equal societies almost always do better.* London: Allen Lane.

# III Social Policy for Social Issues

# 12 Post-Secondary Education Policy in Canada

## Merit, Right, or Social Investment?

*Christopher Walmsley, Robert Harding,*
*and Daphne Jeyapal*

---

### Chapter Objectives

*This chapter will help you to develop an understanding of:*
- Canada's major post-secondary education (PSE) policy options and the strengths and limitations of each;
- how social location informs the individual experience of PSE;
- PSE policy proposals of the major political parties in Canada;
- differences between Canada's PSE tuition policies and those of the United States and Nordic countries.

---

## Introduction

In this chapter, you will meet six students working towards a BSW degree in Canada.[1] They attend universities in different provinces, and have different life circumstances and different levels of access to economic resources. These stories are a starting point to better understand one Canadian social policy field—post-secondary education—and explore who has access, how it is funded, why the cost varies from one region to another, what the benefits are, and what discourses accompany spending on post-secondary education. Should post-secondary education be viewed as a universal social right, a commodity to be bought and sold, a charitable good, or a social investment?

## Meet Christa, Melissa, Nadege, Farzana, Gwen, and Mike

### 1. Christa

Christa's father is a chartered accountant with a major firm in downtown Toronto, and her mother is a registered nurse. Although the family home in northwest Toronto is only 45 minutes from York University by subway and bus, Christa has lived in her own apartment in Vaughan since the beginning of second year. It is a short 20-minute commute to campus by car. Christa chose to move to Vaughan to create greater physical and emotional distance from a friend of the family who sexually assaulted her on a family skiing weekend when she was in Grade 12, but she hasn't shared the full complexity of her reasoning with her parents.

Christa completed high school at a private girls' school in Toronto, earned an entrance scholarship for first-year university, and has been supported financially by her parents for most of her expenses. Her parents started saving for her education through a registered education savings plan (RESP) when she was born. They added the maximum of $2,500 to the plan annually, and the federal government, through the Canada Education Savings Grant (CESG), contributed another $500 each year. At the time of her high school graduation, the plan had accumulated a principal of $54,000 plus $34,617 interest (at a 5 per cent annual rate of return), which her father is using to support her education.

Since Christa lived at home during first year and had an entrance scholarship, her expenses were minimal—books, clothing, and recreation, which she covered through a summer job as a camp counsellor. She began to draw on the RESP funds in second year, and had a budget of $3,100 per month ($37,200 per year) to cover tuition, books, rent, food, transportation, clothes, and recreation. Christa also received a $50,000 inheritance from her grandmother, with which she purchased a new Toyota Prius and a top-of-the-line computer. She and her father anticipate that the inheritance will be needed to pay for part of her last year if she doesn't earn enough at her summer job. Her mother, who hasn't worked in many years due to chronic fatigue syndrome, edits all of Christa's papers for spelling and grammar. As she is financially dependent on her parents, her father deducts her tuition, living expenses, and books from his taxes. He passes on the $1,100 value of the deduction to her, which she uses to subsidize her winter vacation in the Caribbean. She will graduate debt-free.

## 2. Melissa

Melissa was first removed from her mother at the age of two due to her mother's ongoing drug addiction and placed with foster parents in Prince George. After five years in foster care she was returned to her mother for a six-month period, but due to the frequent violence of her mother's partner, she was removed again and a permanent custody order was put in place. Melissa turned 19 in foster care, having had three different sets of foster parents.

A good student all through elementary and secondary school, she enrolled at the University of Northern British Columbia (UNBC). Her last foster parents permitted her to live with them rent-free after she "aged out of care" but asked her to pay a board allowance of $250/month. She is responsible for all her own living and educational expenses. Her tuition and compulsory fees are about $6,200 a year, including a health and dental plan not available through her two part-time jobs. UNBC opted not to provide tuition waivers for former foster children in response to a 2013 challenge by BC's Representative for Children and Youth, the province's child advocate. However, on 1 September 2017, the NDP/Green coalition government eliminated tuition fees for all former children in care attending BC's 25 post-secondary institutions.

Melissa is now entering her fourth and final year. While the announcement from the coalition government will save her about $6,000, she anticipates her debt at graduation will still be about $24,000 as she uses her student loan only for tuition and books and covers her living expenses through her part-time work. Melissa works evenings for a car rental company, which works well with her class schedule. She also puts in overnight shifts every Saturday and Sunday at a local group home for slightly more than minimum wage. After two years of employment, she became eligible for a $1,000 bursary from the group home.

## 3. Nadege

Nadege's family moved from Rwanda to the Côte-des-Neiges neighbourhood of Montreal a few years after the 1994 genocide. In Rwanda, her father worked as an engineer, but he was unable to attain equivalency for his professional qualifications in his new country. He found work as a taxi driver until his death from a heart attack at the age of 48, when Nadege was seven. Following his death, Nadege's mother found work as a cashier at Chez Cora, a breakfast-lunch restaurant in downtown Montreal. She earns one dollar above the provincial minimum wage and holds the same job today. Her two older brothers, teenagers at the time of their father's death, found part-time work to help support the family until they left home in their late teens for work in the trucking industry. Today, each makes an annual income over $80,000 with a high school diploma, but they do not financially support their mother or sister. Nadege worked part-time through high school, initially during summer at the local Dairy Queen, then bussing tables at Chez Cora where her mother works year-round.

Nadege is an honours student and bilingual. She decided after two years of CEGEP to apply to the social work program at the Université de Montréal as her first language is French. She received an entrance scholarship of $3,000 for her first year, but since Nadege lives at home she gives her mother $500 per month room and board, which her mother needs to make ends meet. With her summer work and her 10 hours per week of work during the academic year, she defrays the cost of her books, clothing, transportation, and some of her tuition. However, she still needs a student loan to cover the cost of her living expenses and the rest of her tuition expenses. Due to her low income, she was eligible for a grant of $2,000/year as part of her student loan application. While tuition fees in Quebec are among the lowest in Canada, Nadege is nevertheless accumulating a debt of about $4,000 per year. She took two years off between her CEGEP studies and university to pay off her accumulated student loan, as she was anxious about the debt. She anticipates it will rise again to $13,000 by the time of her BSW graduation.

Her mother is proud of her daughter's achievements, is supportive of her studies, and looks forward to the day when Nadege will be a professional and financially independent. However, she worries about how she will support herself when her daughter leaves home.

## 4. Farzana

Farzana was born in Afghanistan and migrated to Canada at the age of seven with her mother, father, and younger sister, who was three at the time. Her father was a driver and translator for a *Globe and Mail* correspondent posted in Afghanistan. The reporter assisted the family in immigrating to Canada, with his parents, their friends, and his parents' church in Regina organizing their sponsorship.

Farzana's parents opened a convenience store in the community, but when she was 11 her father was the victim of an armed robbery at the store, which was a trigger for his pre-existing post-traumatic stress disorder (PTSD) due to the violence he experienced during the Afghan war. He had a series of PTSD-related episodes that left the family fearing for their safety. He was hospitalized for a few weeks at the psychiatric unit of the local hospital and released back into the community. However, he continued to struggle with his mental health, and a year later Farzana's mother separated from him. He is now unable to work, lives in a psychiatric boarding home, and sees his daughters once or twice a year. His wife has taken over the business with the help of her daughters.

Farzana lives at home, is employed about 30 hours a week at the store, and studies part-time towards her BSW at the University of Regina. She pays for her tuition as she goes, enrolling in only the number of courses each term that she can afford, and co-ordinates her class schedule around her work schedule. While she has maintained passing grades, she finds writing essays particularly challenging and relies on friends to review her assignments. She has been working towards her BSW for seven years and hopes to complete it in two more years.

## 5. Gwen

Gwen is the oldest of five children whose parents were residential school survivors. She attended elementary school on reserve in her small home community of about 1,000 residents in northern Ontario. Since there was no local high school, she had to attend high school in Thunder Bay, several hours away. There, she boarded with a local Indigenous family for 10 months of the year. She continued her studies after high school at the local college, enrolling in a two-year social service diploma program, with financial support from her local band. When she wanted to continue towards a BSW degree at Lakehead University, her band's education co-ordinator refused to support her plan, saying that others needed a chance, and that support for two years of post-secondary education was already more than most band members received. Gwen decided to continue on her own, taking out student loans, and working part-time.

While she enjoys her social work courses and is proud of how hard she worked to get into the program, she has found her time in university very challenging. She anticipates having a debt of over $30,000 upon graduation, and because she is not living on reserve or working for a First Nation, she pays the same taxes as other Canadians. In her job as a server at the local tavern, she frequently fends off accusations that she pays no taxes. At university, she encounters students who believe she pays no tuition or taxes and is only in the BSW program due to an affirmative action program.

Gwen's family and community are not enthusiastic about her decision to become a social worker. Her aunt remembers when social workers took Gwen's uncle and three of his cousins away to a foster home. Only one cousin is still alive.

## 6. Mike

Mike was a journeyman carpenter in Halifax, making about $60,000 a year until an industrial accident severely damaged his back, making a return to carpentry or any other trade that demanded physical work impossible. While on Employment Insurance (EI) and waiting for his claim to be processed at Workers' Compensation, he began to volunteer at the Boys and Girls Club. He received so much positive feedback from the staff that the director took him aside and suggested he explore a career in social work.

The Workers' Compensation Board (WCB) tried to find other work that Mike could do in his field, and offered to retrain him as an excavator operator or construction estimator. When he made clear his intention to study social work, the maximum they would provide was the equivalent of tuition fees for excavator operator training (about $15,000) and wage-loss benefits of six months, the length of the training period (about $20,000). However, he needed to establish to WCB's satisfaction that he could obtain the additional funds necessary to complete his choice of retraining plan—a BSW. This proved difficult as he knew he would need a student loan to support his BSW studies, and he couldn't apply for one until he was admitted to university.

Mike and his wife talked about the possibility of applying to Memorial University in St. John's, Newfoundland and Labrador, where the fees were considerably less—$11,500 versus about $34,000 for a four-year BSW at Dalhousie University in Halifax. However, she didn't see a way to open a daycare in St. John's to maintain her income. The cost for Mike to travel, pay additional living costs, and not be available to help at home contributed to their decision to stay in Halifax. As a person with a disability, Mike became eligible for a grant of $2,000 per year as part of his student loan application. He also applied for and

---

**Box 12.1**  Tuition and Other Fees at Canadian, American, and Nordic Universities, 2015–16

| | |
|---|---|
| **Canada** | |
| Average tuition and other fees at Canadian universities | Cdn$7,029 |
| **United States** | |
| Public four-year colleges (in-state fees) | US$9,420 |
| Public four-year colleges (out-of-state fees) | US$24,070 |
| Private non-profit four-year colleges | US$32,330 |
| **Nordic Countries** | |
| Finland | 0.0 |
| Sweden | 0.0 |
| Norway | 0.0 |
| Denmark | 0.0 |

Sources: Statistics Canada (2015); College Board (2016); Välimaa (2015).

received a scholarship from the National Educational Association of Disabled Students (NEADS) for $1,200. Between his WCB allowance, student loans, summer work at the Boys and Girls Club, his spouse's income from operating a small daycare out of their house, and a campus work-study position, the couple are just able to support themselves and their two small children. However, they estimate they will have a student loan debt of $17,000 when he graduates.

As Mike's injury left him unable to drive or take conventional public transportation, and because his spouse's early morning daycare responsibilities precluded her from giving him a ride in the morning, he could get to the university only if he qualified for Halifax's Access-A-Bus service. Fortunately, based on his doctor's recommendation, he qualified for this service, which provided door-to-door transit service for people unable to use the public transit system due to a disability.

Christa, Melissa, Nadege, Farzana, Gwen, and Mike have all been admitted to a BSW program at their respective universities. They have all met the standard qualifications for admission, successfully competed through the admissions process, and thereby obtained

**Table 12.1**  University Tuition Fees in Canada in 2016

| Province | Student | Tuition Fees* (2015–16) | Additional Compulsory Fees** | Tuition and Compulsory Fees (2015–16) | % Change from 2014–15 Tuition Fees | Estimated Tuition Fees and Compulsory Fees for Four-Year BSW (2016 dollars)*** |
|---|---|---|---|---|---|---|
| Newfoundland and Labrador | | 2,660 | 229 | 2,889 | 0.0 | 11,556 |
| Prince Edward Island | | 6,119 | 626 | 6,745 | 4.6 | 30,433 |
| Nova Scotia | Mike | 6,817 | 784 | 7,601 | 5.2 | 34,296 |
| New Brunswick | | 6,353 | 531 | 6,896 | 0.9 | 31,115 |
| Quebec | Nadege | 2,799 | 823 | 3,622 | 2.2 | 16,342 |
| Ontario | Christa Gwen | 7,868 | 903 | 8,771 | 4.0 | 39,575 |
| Manitoba | | 3,930 | 673 | 4,603 | 1.9 | 20,769 |
| Saskatchewan | Farzana | 6,885 | 407 | 7,292 | 2.9 | 32,902 |
| Alberta | | 5,738 | 1,142 | 6,810 | 0.0 | 27,240 |
| British Columbia | Melissa | 5,305 | 644 | 5,949 | 2.0 | 26,842 |
| Canada (average) | | 6,191 | 838 | 7,029 | 3.2 | 31,715 |

*Actual BSW tuition fees are assumed to resemble the weighted provincial average of undergraduate tuition fees provided by Statistics Canada. In Quebec and Nova Scotia, out-of-province students pay significantly higher fees. This is factored into the weighted average for those provinces.
**This amount does not include partially compulsory health and dental fees, as students with alternative coverage can opt out of these fees.
***The calculations in this column make several assumptions: (1) the Canadian average annual fee increase of 3.2 per cent continues for the next four years; (2) the tuition freeze implemented by the Newfoundland and Labrador government in 2003 continues for another four years; (3) the tuition fees in Quebec continue to rise at the same rate as the 2014–15 to 2015–16 Canadian average increase (3.2 per cent); and (4) the tuition freeze implemented by the Alberta government in 2015 continues for an additional four years.
Source: Statistics Canada (2015).

**Table 12.2**  Estimated Student Debt at Graduation

| Student | Years to Complete BSW | Debt at Graduation |
|---|---|---|
| Christa | 4 | 0.00 |
| Melissa | 5 | $24,000 |
| Nadege | 6 | $13,000 |
| Farzana | 9 | 0.00 |
| Gwen | 5–6 | $30,000+ |
| Mike | 4 | $17,000 |

access to a professional degree education program. However, their stories reveal remarkably different economic and social circumstances, varying levels of social supports, and potentially different levels of institutional inclusion once they are in the program. If they complete their programs, they will graduate with vastly different levels of debt, or none at all (see Table 12.2).

# The Cost of Post-Secondary Education

In 2016, the average annual cost of university education was reported to be $7,029 (Table 12.1), an increase of 3.2 per cent over the year before (Statistics Canada, 2015). However, this only considers tuition and ancillary fees charged by the university, and doesn't include living costs, books, transportation, health care, and recreation. An average cost is one way to summarize the expense of university education, but it hides important regional differences. As Table 12.1 shows, students pay vastly different amounts for the same degree in different parts of Canada. They also enter post-secondary education from different historical contexts, with differential levels of social inclusion, and with more or less economic and **social capital**, that is, "the power within society that the individual derives from attachment to social networks, such as work, church groups, community associations, clubs, and the like" (Brooks, 2012, p. 563). For example, Christa will graduate with no debt and can focus exclusively on her studies. Melissa and Gwen, on the other hand, largely rely on their own resources to put themselves through university. While Melissa obtained a $1,000 bursary from her employer towards her degree, she was only eligible once, and this was a minor portion of her overall annual fees of about $6,000.

Gwen is a status Indian, as recognized by the federal government, so she received financial support from her band for two years of post-secondary education through Indigenous and Northern Affairs[4] funding. However, because of limited resources and the expectation from her band that educational support would lead directly to employment after two years, she has had to cover the rest of her educational costs herself. Gwen and Melissa, unlike Christa, are the only ones in their families and social circles to pursue post-secondary education. While Melissa can count on a level of encouragement from her former foster parents, they are also unsure of her choice, as they only completed high school. Gwen's parents, aunts, uncles, and cousins have not completed high school. Her younger siblings, while proud of her accomplishments, find what she is doing completely foreign. Her family is also distrustful when she says she wants to become a social worker due to the problematic relationships social workers have had within Indigenous communities in the past.

Mike will have a lower debt level than Gwen and Melissa, as he is receiving a WCB training allowance, over $10,000 in Canada Student Grants, and a university scholarship. He is also studying with the interest and support of his partner and colleagues at the Boys and Girls Club. Some are recent BSW graduates who know the faculty and curriculum, and encourage him to discuss his school experience with them on an ongoing basis. While he will have a debt of $17,000, it would have been $37,000 without the financial support he received.

At the middle on the continuum of indebtedness are Farzana and Nadege. Farzana's parents were both professionals in Afghanistan, earned university degrees, and value a post-secondary education for their daughter. They also strongly believe in working hard, staying debt-free, and depending exclusively on family resources. Farzana will graduate without debt despite having had no external support—no bursaries, scholarships, or student loans. Nadege, like Farzana, had a father with a university education, but her mother only completed high school and saw herself primarily as a stay-at-home parent. Although she is an excellent student and received an entrance scholarship like Christa, since her father's untimely death, life has been an economic, social, and personal struggle. Although members of her church are excited that she is attending university, no other supports are available to her.

Financial struggles exacerbate the ways in which some students experience their sense of belonging within the post-secondary context. Those whose access to education is complicated by race, class, and gender exclusions ingrained in Canadian society may experience further marginalization in the classroom.

These discrepancies in access to and inclusion within post-secondary education raise several questions. Should Canada's social policies address the inequities these students face at the beginning of their post-secondary education? Should one's individual success be based on a notion of **meritocracy**, the idea that success derives solely from one's own ability, talent, and hard work? Is post-secondary education a commodity to be bought and sold, with the price determined by what the (student) buyer is willing to pay, or is it a right of citizenship that should be equally available to all? Furthermore, should those with less economic resources be given extra financial help? If so, should it be a charitable good made available through corporate and individual donations only to those deemed worthy or deserving? To understand how Canadians collectively view and value post-secondary education, an analysis of existing policy options follows.

# Canadian Post-Secondary Education Policy Options

Through public policy, charitable donations, and **intergenerational transfers** (assets or benefits transferred within the family from a member of an older generation to a member of a younger generation),[5] Canadians support universities and post-secondary students. The principal mechanisms are government grants to universities, tax deductions, student loans, Canada Education Savings Grants, and scholarships and bursaries.

## Federal and Provincial Grants to Universities

Historically, the most substantial source of revenue for Canadian universities has been government grants. At the national level, the Canada Social Transfer is the mechanism through which the federal government transfers funds to the provinces for post-secondary education and various social services. This now exceeds an estimated $3.7 billion[6]

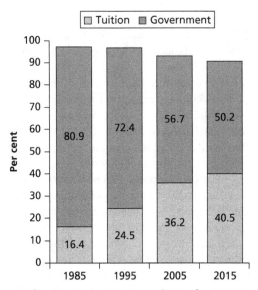

**Figure 12.1** Government funding and tuition as a share of university operating revenue
Source: CAUT (n.d.).

(Parliamentary Budget Officer [PBO], 2016). Provincial governments draw on these funds as well as their own to provide annual operating grants to universities. In 1985, government funding comprised 80.9 per cent of university operating revenue, while student tuition fees comprised an average of only 16.4 per cent. By 2015, however, this ratio had changed substantially. Government grants declined to 50.2 per cent of the total, and tuition fees rose to 40.5 per cent of operating revenue (Figure 12.1) (CAUT, n.d.).

At the same time, important regional differences exist. In 2015, the Newfoundland and Labrador government covered 79.8 per cent of university operating revenue, with student tuition fees comprising only 12.6 per cent of the total. By contrast, the Ontario government contributed only 39.3 per cent of university operating revenue with tuition fees making up 52.4 per cent of the total. In Quebec, the provincial government funded 66.4 per cent of university operating costs whereas tuition fees covered only 25.7 per cent. The pattern in most provinces, though, changed substantially in the past 30 years. Students, in 1982, covered under one-seventh of the operating costs of their university, but now they cover over one-third. This is more extreme in Ontario and British Columbia, where student tuition fees now comprise almost half the operating revenue of Ontario universities and over 40 per cent of those in British Columbia. This reality is closely tied to policy decisions made by successive neo-liberal governments, not just to the fact that the provinces are larger and wealthier. Differences in how provincial governments support universities have a marked impact on tuition fees at individual universities.

## Income Tax Deduction for Tuition Fees, Living Costs, and Textbooks

The Canada Revenue Agency permits students to deduct tuition fees as well as two additional amounts from their income taxes. The first, known as the "Education Amount," represents a student's living costs, and the second, the "Textbook Amount," covers books. In 2016, the education and textbook amounts had these values:

**Education amount**:  $400/month × months in full-time attendance
                       $120/month × months in part-time attendance
**Textbook amount**:   $65/month × months in full-time attendance
                       $20/month × months in part-time attendance
                                         (Canada Revenue Agency, 2016)

Students can also carry forward all or a portion of these deductions to a year in which their income is higher and thereby receive the full benefit of the deduction. At the same time, they can transfer unused amounts to partners, parents, or grandparents so that they can claim the deduction.[7] For the student taxpayer (or family member), this group of tax deductions is estimated to reduce taxes by $848 to $1,191 per year (PBO, 2016, p. 16). Formally these are known as **tax expenditures**, a policy mechanism that reflects a decision to leave certain amounts with the taxpayer to compensate for expenses in defined areas. In effect, it is a decision by government to *not* collect taxes. The total tax expenditure arising from the tuition, education, and textbook deductions is estimated to be $1.8 billion (PBO, 2016, p. 13).

The amount of money allocated to these tax expenditures is impressively large, but is it an effective way to support post-secondary students? The federal government announced the planned elimination of the tuition, education, and textbook deductions in the 2016 budget in favour of an increase in the Canada Student Grants program (PBO, 2016, p. 31). There are likely several reasons for this:

1.  Income tax deductions do not aid students in financial need when they most need it. Tuition fees are normally due in late summer, but students do not receive the benefit of the tax deduction until 8 to 10 months later after their income tax return for the previous year has been filed. If they don't have family members to whom they can transfer the unused portion of their deductions, it may be years before they receive the full benefit of the deduction—once their degree is finished and their income begins to increase.
2.  Between 150,000 and 200,000 students appear not to be claiming the tax credits to which they are entitled (PBO, 2016, p. 33). Students with low taxable income may not realize that the unclaimed amounts of their deductions in one taxation year can be brought forward in succeeding years. Also, they may not know that they can transfer their unused deductions to a family member.
3.  Tax deductions disproportionately benefit higher-income individuals and families. They are an ineffective policy option to increase the participation of marginalized students in post-secondary education. The PBO found that families in the top 20 per cent of after-tax income received 37.7 per cent of the total value of these tax expenditures whereas the families with the lowest 20 per cent of after-tax income received only 17.2 per cent of the expenditures (PBO, 2016, p. 19).

## Federal/Provincial Student Loans

Canada had over 2 million full- and part-time students enrolled in post-secondary education in 2013. Of these, 46 per cent graduate with a student loan and an average debt of $22,276 (PBO,

2016, p. 10). Clearly, a student loan is the policy option "of choice" for almost half of Canada's post-secondary students. In 2013–14 the value of new student loans was $2.7 billion. However, a growing number of students are holding a debt at graduation greater than $25,000:

> the data suggest a growing divide among the postsecondary student popula-tion. The overall percentage of recent graduates with student debt has actually declined slightly. Yet the percentage of recent graduates with large amounts of debt is growing, along with the average amount of debt owed at graduation. This is especially true of university graduates. The trend amounts to fewer students holding larger average debt at graduation. (PBO, 2016, p. 53)

The Canada Student Loans Program (CSLP) provides up to 60 per cent of a full-time student's assessed need to a maximum of $210 per week. However, this $210-a-week loan limit has been unchanged since the 2005–6 loan year, despite the consumer price index rising 19.6 per cent since then (Statistics Canada, 2016). This means that today's student can purchase 20 per cent less than a student in 2005–6. In addition, loans don't account for the vastly different tuition fees and cost of living across the country.

Students from low-income families can also receive Canada Student Grants, a non-repayable amount of $250 per month of study. If the student is from a middle-income family, she or he can receive $100 per month of study, and if students have dependants under the age of 12 or a dependant with a permanent disability they can receive grants of $200 per month of study per child. Part-time students from low-income families may also be eligible for financial support.

In 2016, the Liberal government announced a plan to focus its post-secondary policy on an increase to the Canada Student Grant. Specifically, this plan has several objectives:

- increase Canada Student Grant amounts by 50 per cent for both full- and part-time students from low- and middle-income families starting in 2016–17. Cost: $1.53 billion over five years and $329 million per year thereafter;
- expand Canada Student Grant eligibility by 2017–18. Cost $790 million over four years starting in 2017–18;
- simplify Canada Student Grant program requirements so that students will be re-quired to contribute a flat amount each year towards the costs of their education, and financial assets and student income will no longer be considered. Cost: $267.7 million over four years, starting in 2017–18;
- raise the income threshold for the Repayment Assistance Plan of the Canada Student Loan Program. The threshold will be increased so that no student will have to repay her/his Canada Student Loan until earning at least $25,000 per year. This will cost an additional $131.4 million over five years, beginning in 2016–17, and $31 million per year thereafter. (PBO, 2016, p. 28)

As noted above, these policy objectives will be accomplished by eliminating the federal tax deduction for tuition, living expenses, and textbooks. This suggests the monthly grant for full-time low-income students will rise to $500 per month, or $4,000 per academic year. Although the tax deduction had an average value of about $1,000 per year and the existing CSG had a value of $2,000 per year, in effect, the proposed changes represent a $1,000 per year overall increase in the CSG. However, the increased grant becomes available during the school year, rather than 18 months after. Increasing the CSG eligibility criteria, simplifying the program requirements, and raising the income threshold for loan repayment appear, on the surface, to be positive moves to enable a greater number of students to participate in the program. Will this ensure a greater number of students have access to post-secondary education, graduate with lower debt, and are better able to repay their loans? Without specific changes of policy and implementation to assess, it remains to be seen whether or not the Liberal government's plan will be successful.

## Canada Education Savings Grants (CESG)

Parents who open a registered education savings plan (RESP) to save for their child's university education can put aside up to $2,500 per year tax-free, but they are also entitled to a grant of $500 per year under the federal government's Canada Education Savings Grant (CESG).[8] As demonstrated above with Christa, parents who opened an RESP for their child at birth and contributed the maximum of $2,500 per year would have over $50,000 available for their child's university education. The Parliamentary Budget Office estimates federal spending on the CESG and related programs at $1.1 billion, with 49 per cent of the expenditures going to families with an annual income over $90,000 (PBO, 2016, p. 20).

## Scholarships and Bursaries

Each university has an increasing range of student awards available at entrance and after the first year, based on merit, need, or recognition of a specific ability, interest, or affiliation. Across Canada, this aspect of university funding has increased 152.9 per cent between 2000–1 and 2012–13, or 12.7 per cent per year. Overall, this has been the largest percentage increase of any area of university spending since 2000–1 (CAUT, 2015, p. 9). Tuition fees increased 111.8 per cent over the same period (9.3 per cent per year), whereas provincial government grants increased a total of 55.1 per cent (4.6 per cent per year) (CAUT, 2015, p. 4). This suggests universities are attempting to address the shortfall in government grants and student tuition by turning towards corporate and individual donors. It is not uncommon to see evidence of the gifts of major donors in the names given to buildings, research chairs, sports facilities, labs, and classrooms. Scholarships and bursaries are another site of donors' gifts, but are they an effective way to finance a university education? Are such gifts targeted to students with the greatest need, or do they meet an academic or interest criteria of donors and thereby indirectly reward students who are financially well off?

In our student stories, Christa and Nadege received entrance scholarships based on their grades, and Mike received a small scholarship based on his disability. But Melissa and Gwen, who live in provinces with some of the highest tuition fees and who have the least financial support from their families, received no university scholarships or bursaries—although Melissa did receive a small bursary from her employer. Farzana did not receive a scholarship or bursary from her university. Is this because she did not know that such funds exist? Did she believe she did not qualify as she had neither outstanding academic merit nor exceptional need? Did she assume the time involved in submitting an application was not worth the slim chance of receiving an award? Or was she ineligible because she was attending part-time?

Increased university fundraising appears to be one direction for the future, which suggests Canadian universities might increasingly resemble those in the United States, where 70 per cent of students receive financial aid to offset the high cost of fees (College Board, 2016). Is this direction inevitable? During a federal election, future directions for Canada become visible in the proposals political parties present to the electorate.

# Policy Proposals

Prior to a federal or provincial election in Canada, political parties announce a range of policies they hope will increase their support with different segments of the electorate and thus ensure their party's electoral success on voting day. Each of the major parties developed post-secondary education policy proposals during the 2015 federal election. These are summarized below.

*Green Party*

- Abolish tuition fees for post-secondary education by 2020.
- Eliminate any existing or future student federal debt above $10,000.
- Abolish interest on new student loans and increase available funding for bursaries (Green Party of Canada, 2015).

*Liberal Party*

- Increase the maximum Canada Student Grant (CSG) for low-income students to $3,000 per year for full-time students and to $1,800 per year for part-time students.
- Increase the income thresholds for eligibility to the CSG, giving more Canadian students access to larger grants.
- Ensure that no graduate with student loans will be required to make any repayment until that individual is earning an income of at least $25,000 per year (Liberal Party of Canada, 2015).

*New Democratic Party*

- Invest $250 million in additional federal student grants over four years, with an emphasis on helping students who need it most, creating as many as 50,000 new grants.
- Immediately begin phasing out interest on federal student loans, eliminating it completely by Year 7 and saving the average student $4,000 (New Democratic Party of Canada, 2015).

*Conservative Party*

- Support Canadian families saving for their child's education by enhancing the Canada Education Savings Grants—the matching contribution to registered education savings plans—for low- and middle-income families.
- Doubling the enhanced grant for middle-income families from 10 cents to 20 cents per dollar on the first $500 contributed each year.
- Doubling the enhanced grant for lower-income families from 20 cents to 40 cents per dollar on the first $500 contributed each year (Conservative Party of Canada, 2015).

# Post-Secondary Education as a Political Issue

The parties' proposals reflect differing views about responsibility to provide post-secondary education in Canada. The Green Party plan implies the greatest responsibility lies with the government, and their plan to eliminate tuition fees would accentuate this role. The Liberals and the New Democrats appear to place primary responsibility on students to finance their own education, with government's role being increased support to those with low income. The Conservatives' plan suggests that financing a university education is the family's responsibility, with government providing incentives so that parents can save towards that goal. Clearly, the parties' proposals express different social values and political philosophies. How do Canadians, and young adults specifically, view the responsibility to fund post-secondary education? In the past 30 years, students have become responsible for a greater share of the cost of operating their universities. They don't appear to object to this trend or demand a greater say in university governance in exchange for their increased role in funding the university. In English Canada, rising student fees appear generally accepted by students and the public, albeit with some resistance organized by the Canadian Federation of Students. In Quebec, however, student protest about university fees has been forceful and ongoing. Remarkably, it has been the province with the lowest tuition until recently. Notably, "unlike students in other Canadian provinces, Quebec students are used to strikes and to obtaining gains through strikes" (Bégin-Caouette & Jones, 2014, p. 416). Here is a brief chronology of Quebec students' activism over the past five decades:

> 1968: Strike for tuition fees
> 1974: Strike for increased funding and loans
> 1978: Strike for accessible loans and scholarships
> 1986: Strike for a tuition freeze
> 1988: Strike for increased aid to part-time students
> 1990: Strike against tuition increases
> 1994: Strike against tuition increases
> 2005: Strike to oppose the conversion of student funding grants into loans
> 2007: Strike against tuition increases
> 2012: Strike against tuition increases
>
> (Bégin-Caouette & Jones, 2014, p. 416)

The 2012 strike mobilized students from across the province. It was precipitated by the 2010–11 Quebec government's plan to increase tuition fees over five years from $2,200 per year to $3,800 per year, a total increase of $1,625 or $325 per year. There were marches of 150,000–200,000 protestors in Montreal, and it became the largest student protest in Quebec history (Bégin-Caouette & Jones, 2014). Ideologically, it was a debate about the role of higher education in society, "and the discourse used by the student movement [was] based on a set of social-democratic values that resonate with the collective imaginary of Quebec society" (Bégin-Caouette & Jones, 2014, p. 418). The relative absence of debate and protest about rising tuition fees in other provinces suggests that different values inform the public's thinking about post-secondary education or public protest in anglophone provinces. But if that is the case, how does one explain the much greater public investment in post-secondary education in Newfoundland and Labrador and the long-standing tuition freeze in that province?

# The Post-Secondary Education Policy Narrative in Canada

The discussion above suggests more than one policy narrative informs post-secondary education. Some appear to view post-secondary education as the family's responsibility to save for the education of their members, with the state's role limited to incentives to help the family save. By extension, universities should be free to charge students the fees they choose to provide a quality education without government intervention. Others frame the narrative in terms of "opportunity"—all citizens should have the opportunity to participate in post-secondary education so they can pursue their preferred careers, obtain a decent standard of living, have upward mobility in society, provide for their families, and have a secure retirement. Loans and grants increase opportunities for students to participate in education and its benefits, but the individual is responsible for shouldering the greater burden of its cost. Still others view post-secondary education as a right of citizenship, like the K–12 education system, and believe all citizens should have the right to a publicly funded university education without fees. The large Quebec protests over the modest tuition fee increase suggest many in that province view post-secondary education as a right.

## Busting the "Barista" Barrier

Recent media discourse about BA graduates working as baristas, servers, clerks, couriers, and stockers, as well as less safe and socially sanctioned employment, suggests that a post-secondary education may not be worth it today (Pettigrew, 2013). Unable to move into well-paying middle-class jobs and saddled with student loan debt, they are being described as the "new underclass" (Sorensen, 2013) or "generation jobless" (Bartlett & LeRose, 2015). Student fees in 8 out of 10 Canadian provinces are rising faster than inflation, and a greater number now graduate with debt over $25,000. In most English Canadian provinces, an absence of political pressure exists to change this reality. Yet, Canada has one of the most highly educated populations among the member nations of the Organisation for Economic Co-operation and Development (OECD). With 57.3 per cent between the ages of 25 and 34 having either a college diploma or university degree in 2012, this is the third highest among OECD countries, following South Korea at 65.7 per cent and Japan at 58.6 per cent. Is there a surplus of graduates in Canada that prompts prospective students as well as graduates to ask, "Is post-secondary education worth the investment?"

Research suggests that students with lower economic and social capital are more likely to question the value of post-secondary education, believing that mounting debt is a likely outcome of studies. Young adults with parents who have not attended university are more likely to see higher tuition fees as a barrier to their participation (Johnson, 2008), and "students from racialized communities and lower income backgrounds, as well as single parents are more likely to hold negative feelings about taking on student debt" (Canadian Federation of Students, 2013, p. 1), for various complex social, cultural, political, and economic reasons.

Students with more limited economic means would be more likely to select themselves out of the uncertain future of a BA and towards the greater certainty of a short-term diploma or certificate with its prospect of tangible employment. In 2006, youth aged 18–24 with parents earning more than $100,000 in pre-tax income were found to be almost twice as likely (49 per cent) to have enrolled in university as those whose parents earned less than $25,000 (28 per cent) (CAUT, 2014–15, p. 15). In 2016, the Parliamentary Budget Office estimated "that roughly 60 per cent of postsecondary students belonged to higher-income families (that is, the two highest after-tax or disposable income quintiles)" (PBO, 2016, p. 4). It also found that 54 per cent of graduates didn't have student loans, suggesting that their families provided considerable support to their education so that a loan was unnecessary (PBO, 2016, p. 7). Clearly, upper middle-class youth, raised with expectations of university attendance, do not face the issue of whether they can go to university. Instead, they face the issue of which university and what program to choose.

A possible exception to this trend is the university participation of first- and second-generation immigrants, as shown in a Statistics Canada study:

> In Canada, students of the first generation were 12 percentage points more likely to attend a postsecondary institution by age 23 than students of the third and higher generations (i.e., those with Canadian-born parents); students of the second generation—those born in Canada to immigrant parents—were about 18 percentage points more likely to do so. (Picot & Hua, 2012, p. 2)

The study found 49 per cent of first-generation youth had two parents with post-secondary credentials (Picot & Hua, 2012, p. 1), suggesting that almost half of these youth were raised with a family expectation of university attendance, but perhaps not the economic resources to match. The study doesn't distinguish the country of origin, social class, and ethnicity of immigrants, and doesn't consider differences in outcome based on these factors. Nevertheless, it is evident that clear policy initiatives are needed to encourage and support the participation of lower-income youth. Otherwise, universities are in danger of becoming the exclusive space of the economically advantaged.

Does a post-secondary education pay off irrespective of one's class background and debt load at graduation? Research by the Education Policy Research Initiative (EPRI) used administrative student data held by 14 post-secondary education institutions in four different regions of the country and linked these data with tax files from Statistics Canada. It tracked students' post-graduation earnings from 2005 through 2013. Overall, 2005 bachelor's degree graduates had average annual earnings of $45,200 (in 2014 dollars) in the first year after graduation, and this grew by 66 per cent to reach $74,900 eight years out. Engineering, mathematics, computer science, and business graduates had greater incomes and earnings growth than the other groups, but social sciences BA graduates also did well, with average earnings of $36,300 immediately after graduation, which grew to just under $62,000 eight years later (up 71 per cent). Humanities grads also experienced steady growth, with a 74 per cent increase starting at $32,800 and reaching $57,000 in eight years. The study estimates a hypothetical barista working full-time would likely earn about $22,000, and there would be little growth over time (Finnie, 2016; Finnie, Afshar, Bozkurt, Miyairi, & Pavlic, 2016). Those in more marginalized employment contexts earn even less.

# Chapter Summary

Canadian university education is moving strongly in the direction of a private commodity rather than a public good, in all provinces except Quebec and Newfoundland and Labrador. It is beginning to resemble post-secondary education in the United States more closely than that in Nordic countries. The 2016 Liberal government reforms appear intended to reduce the harsher aspects of student debt with increased student grants and an income threshold before debt repayment begins, but they are not significant moves to strengthen universities themselves as public goods. The Parliamentary Budget Officer summarizes the essential public discourse regarding post-secondary education in Canada:

> an important goal of postsecondary institutions is to train students and thus create a high-quality workforce. Much of the benefit of this training will be captured by the students themselves through higher earnings over their lifetime. Some of this benefit, however, will spill over to the larger society through improved long-term economic growth, lower unemployment and increased productivity, as well as greater equity and economic mobility. (PBO, 2016, p. 6)

Although some evidence supports the higher earnings assertion, and Canada has a greater percentage of post-secondary graduates than most OECD countries, there is no clear path to opportunity for those with low social and economic capital. Public discourse about the rising level of student indebtedness and diminished opportunities for graduates suggest that an increasing number of low-income young adults will not take the risk of post-secondary education. While some policies exist to support the participation of low-income, Indigenous, and disabled students, as this chapter indicates, these do not mitigate the overall commodification of Canadian post-secondary education.

# Discussion Questions

1. Place the students discussed in this chapter on a continuum from most likely to least likely to complete a BSW degree. Discuss the reasons for your ranking. What do you believe are factors that contribute to successful completion of post-secondary education?

2. What should the aim of government policy be with respect to post-secondary education?

   a. reduce tuition fees to zero;

   b. substantially increase bursaries for students in financial need;

   c. eliminate interest on student loans.

   Justify the rationale behind each option, and discuss the merits and limitations of each.

3. How do a student's gender, Indigeneity, race, and class inform participation and completion of post-secondary education?

4. If tuition waivers for specific groups were to be provided by the federal government, provincial government, or your university, which groups should be prioritized? Why?

5. What are the arguments for extensive public funding of post-secondary education? What are the arguments for individuals and families being the major funder of post-secondary education?

# Notes

1. Although the students described in this chapter are fictitious, their stories are intended to illustrate the lives of actual students studying social work in Canada today.

2. More than 70 per cent of full-time undergraduate students receive grants to reduce the actual price of college. Also, many political jurisdictions and institutions grant tuition waivers to groups such as veterans, teachers, or dependants of employees. It should be noted that significant variation in tuition fees within each type of institution exists. For example, prestigious public universities may have fees as high as those in the private sector. The University of Michigan (the highest-ranked public US university) estimated fees for new out-of-state students in 2014–15 at US$41,906 (College Board, 2016).

3. Students from European Union countries and European Economic Area countries (the EU member countries plus Norway, Iceland, and Liechtenstein) are entitled to pay no tuition fees as well (Välimaa, 2015).

4. The department's name at the time.

5. In this case, usually a parent or grandparent transfers a resource to a child/grandchild to support university education. It may be such items as a car, tuition payment, condo purchase, groceries, fitness membership, or clothing.

6. The CST is a block transfer payment from the federal government to the provinces to support child care, social services, income assistance, and post-secondary education: "Because the various social supports within the CST are all rolled up into one block payment, there is no way to definitively capture the portion of CST earmarked for postsecondary education." Moreover, there is no process to track the CST once it enters provincial accounts. The postsecondary portion of the CST is, therefore, notional and only can be estimated based on Department of Finance assumptions and data (PBO, 2016, p. 27).

7. A student with a physical or mental disability attending university part-time can receive the $400/month full-time education deduction with supporting documentation.

8. To a maximum of $7,200.

# References

Bartlett, S., & LeRose, M. (2015, 25 Apr.). *Generation jobless*. Toronto: Dreamfilm Productions/CBC-TV. Retrieved from http://www.cbc.ca/doczone/episodes/generation-jobless

Bégin-Caouette, O., & Jones, G. A. (2014). Student organizations in Canada and Quebec's "Maple Spring." *Studies in Higher Education, 39*(3), 412–42.

Brooks, S. (2012). *Canadian democracy* (7th edn). Toronto: Oxford University Press.

Canada Revenue Agency. (2016). Education deductions and credits. Retrieved from https://www.canada.ca/en/revenue-agency/services/tax/individuals/topics/about-your-tax-return/tax-return/completing-a-tax-return/deductions-credits-expenses/education-deductions.html

Canadian Association of University Teachers (CAUT). (n.d.). *CAUT almanac of post-secondary education in Canada*. Retrieved from https://www.caut.ca/resources/almanac/finance

———. (2014–15). *CAUT Almanac of Post-Secondary Education in Canada*. Ottawa: CAUT.

———. (Spring 2015). *CAUT education review*. Ottawa: CAUT.

Canadian Federation of Students. (2013, Fall). *Student debt in Canada: Education shouldn't be a debt sentence*. Retrieved from http://dev.cfswpnetwork.ca/wp-content/uploads/sites/71/2015/07/Factsheet-2013-11-Student-Debt-EN.pdf

College Board. (2016). Average published undergraduate charges by sector, 2016–17. Retrieved from https://trends.collegeboard.org/college-pricing/figures-tables/average-published-undergraduate-charges-sector-2016-17

Conservative Party of Canada. (2015, 8 Sept.). Prime Minister Harper announces further support for families saving for their children's education. Retrieved from www.conservative.ca/prime-minister-harper-announces-further-support-for-families-saving-for-their-children's-education

Green Party of Canada. (2015, 16 Sept.). Greens' pledge to abolish tuition fees, invest in youth. Retrieved from https://www.greenparty.ca/en/...09.../greens'-pledge-abolish-tuition-fees-invest-youth

Finnie, R. (2016, 8 Aug.). Busting the barista myth—higher education is linked to higher salaries. *Ottawa Citizen*. Retrieved from http://ottawacitizen.com/opinion/columnists/finnie-busting-the-barista-myth-higher-education-is-linked-to-higher-salaries

———, Afshar, K., Bozkurt, E., Miyairi, M., & Pavlic, D. (2016, 26 July). *Barista or better? New evidence on the earnings of post-secondary education graduates: A tax linkage approach.* Ottawa: Education Policy Research Initiative, University of Ottawa.

Johnson, D. (2008). *Inter-Provincial Variation in University Tuition and the Decision to Attend University Immediately after High School Graduation: Evidence from the Youth in Transition Survey in Canada.* MESA Project Research Paper 2008-4. Toronto: Canadian Education Project. Retrieved from www.mesa-project.org/research.php

Liberal Party of Canada. (2015). Postsecondary education. Retrieved from https://www.liberal.ca/realchange/post-secondary-education/

New Democratic Party of Canada. (2015, 1 Oct.). College, university to be more affordable under NDP. Retrieved from https://www.ndp.ca/news/college-university-to-be-more-affordable-under-ndp

Parliamentary Budget Officer, Office of the (PBO). (2016, 5 May). *Federal spending on postsecondary education.* Ottawa.

Pettigrew, T. (2013, 8 Feb.). In defence of the barista with the B.A. What's wrong with well-educated coffee servers? *Maclean's.* Retrieved from: http://www.macleans.ca/education/uniandcollege/in-defence-of-the-barista-with-the-b-a/

Picot, G., & Hua, F. (2012). *Immigrant postsecondary education: A comparison of Canada and Switzerland.* Ottawa: Statistics Canada.

Sorensen, C. (2013, 16 Jan.). Why a generation of well-educated, ambitious, smart young Canadians has no future. *Maclean's.* Retrieved from http://www.macleans.ca/society/life/the-new-underclass/

Statistics Canada. (2015, 9 Sept.). University tuition fees, 2015/2016. *The Daily.*

Statistics Canada. (2016). Consumer price index, historical summary 1996 to 2015.

Välimaa, J. (2015, 17 Feb.). Why Finland and Norway still shun university tuition fees—even for international students. *The Conversation.* Retrieved from https://theconversation.com/

# 13 Homelessness and Housing Insecurity

## Government Inaction in the Creation of a Major Crisis

*Terry Kading*

---

### Chapter Objectives

*This chapter will help you to develop an understanding of:*
- sources of homelessness and housing insecurity in Canada;
- the strengths and limitations of various responses by the government of Canada to date;
- challenges in addressing homelessness in Canada;
- the intersections of homelessness, housing insecurity, and poverty in Canada.

---

## Introduction

Media coverage corroborates what has been recognized by many local governments and homeless advocates for decades—Canada is in the midst of a crisis of affordable housing affecting broad segments of the population. In a global study of the least affordable places to live "on a housing-cost-to-income basis," Vancouver is the world's third least affordable city (after Hong Kong and Sydney) and Toronto is ninth, and "seven of Canada's largest 40 metro areas are severely unaffordable, 10 are seriously unaffordable, 13 are moderately unaffordable, and 10 are unaffordable" (Florida, 2017). High and rising prices to rent or purchase housing, with an insufficient supply of government-subsidized housing, have resulted in a severe crisis of housing affordability, in which evident homelessness has expanded beyond males in their forties and fifties to seniors, youth, women with children, and impoverished families (FCM, 2012; SPARC-BC, 2011; Grenier, Barken, Sussman, Rothwell, & Bourgeois-Guérin, 2016; Gaetz, 2014).

Understanding the dimensions of the "housing crisis" in this country is essential to appreciating the difficulties confronted by community organizations, local governments, front-line staff, and administrators in provincial agencies tasked with meeting one of the most basic needs of citizens. The extent of homelessness and the affordable housing crisis have forced social workers to confront the intersectionality of poverty, income insecurity, race, and gender that underlies inadequate responses to these crises. Since the late 1990s, increasing numbers of visibly homeless citizens testify not just to a homeless-ness crisis but to a more generalized crisis in affordable housing:

> More than 1.5 million Canadian households are paying more than 30 per cent of their income on rent—CMHC's (Canadian Mortgage and Housing Corpor-ation) standard for affordability. Over half of these households are in extreme core-housing need (living in poverty and spending more than 50 per cent of income on housing). Worse still, every night more than 35,000 Canadians will be homeless as part of the more than 235,000 who experience homelessness at some point every year. (Barata & Richter, 2017)

---

## Case Examples    Faces of a Housing Crisis

---

**John**, 22, is living on the streets of a mid-sized city. After a family crisis in his early teens, he was placed in foster care where a family of modest means provided food and shelter but little else. His government caseworker had little time for him due to her workload. With unaddressed abuse and trauma, he was unable to complete high school and turned to alcohol and recreational drugs to cope. By his late teens, he had connected with other street-engaged young adults as the only peer group that offered a reliable social connec-tion. Having aged out of the foster care system with inadequate education or basic life skills to pursue other opportunities, John found himself increasingly depressed and turned to harder street drugs. While he has connected with a local community organization for support, due to the extent of his mental health and life skill needs, he is on a long waiting list for housing that offers the services required to address over a decade of unmet needs.

**Kate** and **Matthew** are in their late twenties with two children, aged three and five, living in a large urban centre. Both are Indigenous and come from impoverished backgrounds. They have completed short professional programs through community colleges. They have an annual combined income of about $30,000. Due to the high cost of child care, Kate has been able to work only part-time, that is, when Matthew is at home. Though they started their life together with a spacious two-bedroom apartment, rapidly rising rents have compelled them to look for a smaller, less expensive place. Even though they met with landlords at over a dozen accom-modations, they never received a call back. Matthew is convinced that racism was behind these rebuffs. Eventually, they had to move into a one-bedroom basement suite in a part of town with a high crime rate. It is located a considerable distance from work, friends, and family. They are angry about the racism they have experienced. They also feel isolated and frustrated as oppor-tunities for more education are expensive, the costs of raising two children keep rising, and rents and child-care costs prohibit their exploring other opportunities. They are fearful, as they have no savings, even for emergencies. They are relying increasingly on the food bank and on other charities to meet basic needs. They are running out of housing options as rents and other costs for their children keep going up.

**Paula**, 66, lives in her own small home in a remote town in decline. Her marriage ended decades ago. She raised two children on her own through various low-paying jobs, social assistance, and community services. Her two daughters have moved to large urban centres looking for steady work. She has no savings or pension from an employer and relies on the Canadian Pension Plan, Old Age Security, and the Guaranteed Income Supplement, which total about $21,000 a year. While she owns her own home, it is in dire need of major repairs that she cannot afford. In the state of the local economy it would be impossible to sell. As her health declines, she finds travel to larger urban centres for health care and treatments a major expense. She does not have enough income to cover the increasing costs of property taxes, utilities, and a vehicle, while supporting some of the living expenses for her two daughters, who also are struggling. Paula would like to move to a larger town with assisted living, but she cannot afford this type of housing on her income. She is worried about the level of credit card debt she has accumulated, since she is no longer able to work. This high level of economic and housing insecurity was not the type of retirement she had imagined.

## News, Discourse, and Housing

Communications researchers have found that the media have done little to educate the public about the government policy-making that has generated poverty, housing insecurity, and homelessness (Best, 2010; Martin, 2011; Calder, Richter, Burns, & Mao, 2011; Schneider, 2011; Schwan, 2016). The affordable housing crisis has garnered significant media attention as the effects are felt by a large cross-section of Canadian society, particularly in our largest urban centres where the media presence is greatest. At the federal level, more onerous terms for borrowing have been adopted by the federal government in the hope that housing prices will come down to more reasonable levels for middle-income earners and that more housing will be developed to meet the needs of these young families and professional sectors. However, this emphasis on higher-income earners favours the needs of home *buyers* over the rental needs of the poor. People who can find financing for a home contribute to an important sector of the economy (Martin, 2011, p. 16). This inequity has sidelined the media focus on homelessness and related issues of poverty that was more evident, thanks to advocacy, in the late 1990s and briefly in 2007–8 when particular provinces raised the profile on homelessness (Schwan, 2016).

Reporting on homelessness tends to be related to "high-profile events," which lead to episodic coverage, for example, in response to a homeless death or to local crime involving homeless individuals or to a public order issue. These contexts individualize persons' failings that have resulted in their being homeless and perpetuate stereotypes of the homeless—such as homeless camps being associated with social deviance—*dirtiness, drugs*, and *danger* (Toft, 2014; Best, 2010; Calder et al., 2011; Martin, 2011). Testimonies by homeless individuals further "promote their continued marginalization and undermine their potential for social inclusion and citizenship" (Schneider, 2011, p. 74). Thus, sympathetic but individualized media portrayals compete with negative characterizations and concerns over "crime and public safety" arising from the increase in homeless citizens. As a result, Canadians may never read news stories that examine the "connections between homelessness and racism, patriarchy, colonialism, or other systems of oppression and inequality" (Schwan, 2016, p. 64).

The media have not held the federal or provincial governments responsible for these outcomes. Rather, reporting is complacent about official pronouncements that initiatives are in place and is accepting of a political strategy of "managing" instead of solving homelessness (Schwan, 2016). Advocates have noted that "people in positions of power have confused the public about what can be done," passing blame to other levels of government and obscuring the role of government in creating poverty (Schwan, 2016, p. 123). Rarely have anti-poverty and housing advocates been able to foster a sustained media focus on the policy context that creates poverty and homelessness, even though this has been recognized as the most effective way to bring attention to social problems (Best, 2010, p. 75). Despite government discourse that confuses the public as to who is responsible for homelessness, advocates believe a more positive shift in attitudes is the result of more people experiencing heightened economic insecurity (Schwan, 2016, p. 118). While citizens may rationalize their reluctance to be part of the solution to a problem that seems too large to solve, they have become more sympathetic towards the homeless and frustrated by government inaction (Schneider, 2014, pp. 243–4), believing that governments have the latitude to act. (For more about discourse and poverty, see Chapter 18.)

## Background to a Needless Crisis in Affordable Housing

In the face of an evident affordable housing crisis in many urban centres in Canada, the budget of the government of Canada in 2017 has been referred to as a "game-changer" as it makes a funding commitment of $11.2 billion over 11 years to affordable housing (FCM, 2017). This commitment is significant because it has been over three decades since the government of Canada made a long-term commitment to funding affordable housing. The budget also commits $2.1 billion over 11 years to continued funding to address homelessness. While far from the more than $43 billion needed to address this crisis (Gaetz, Dej, Richter, & Redman, 2016), this commitment represented the return of the federal government to the forefront of this issue. This shift was undeniably a result of two decades of research and advocacy by homelessness and housing advocates from across the country recognizing that inaction has caused needless suffering, insecurity, illness, and death (Schwan, 2016; Condon, 2016).

Federal and provincial governments are slowly returning to what was understood as a simple truth in the mid-twentieth century—affordable and appropriate housing becomes a reality only if governments fund the construction and maintenance of appropriate housing, services, and incomes for housing-insecure citizens. This crisis is not due to unforeseen circumstances. In the 1970s and 1980s, Canada was a model to other countries in financing and designing award-winning approaches to the diverse housing needs of citizens (Layton, 2008; Duffy, Royer, & Beresford, 2014). Irresponsible cuts and the downloading of responsibilities to provincial and local governments created the current housing crisis. Historically, all three levels of government have had a role in the provision of housing. What has varied over recent times is the level of government that has played the dominant role. Clearly, significant progress has been made in addressing the housing needs of citizens only when the federal government has taken a lead role—a position it is being forced to resume due to the extent of the current crisis.

## Governments and Housing

What constitutes the category of "housing" or "housing provision" is a complex field involving numerous stakeholders from the private for-profit sector, from the non-profit sector, and from all three levels of government. The dominant sector is the private for-profit sector, comprised of home builders (single-family dwellings, duplexes, row housing, condominiums, and apartments), property developers, property owners, realtors, architects, and construction companies, all of which combine to provide the majority of citizens with the opportunity to rent or to own shelter based on income level and lifestyle preferences. The non-profit sector tends to be geared towards providing more affordable or accessible forms of housing to rent or own, or providing relief from the elements or from abuse. These range from single-family dwellings for purchase, to apartments for rent, to transitional housing facilities and temporary/emergency shelter facilities—overseen by notable organizations such as Habitat for Humanity, the John Howard Society, and the Elizabeth Fry Society. In addition, all three levels of government to various degrees are engaged in the provision of "social housing" for low-income families and individuals. The provinces and largest urban centres, such as Toronto and Vancouver, have significant but inadequate stocks of social housing, and the government of Canada provides housing to military personnel and public servants employed in remote areas. It is also responsible for the housing needs of Indigenous people. The overlapping roles of each level of government are examined in Box 13.1.

---

### Box 13.1    Government Roles in Housing Provision

*Federal Government*
- Policies, budgets, and programs that transfer money each year to provincial and municipal governments that support housing construction, services, or incomes for citizens to access housing, or that direct forms of support to promote housing security, e.g., Employment Insurance, the Canada/Quebec Pension Plan, and Old Age Security.
- Bank of Canada—sets interest rates, which determine the cost of borrowing money and, therefore, access to the housing market for those interested in purchasing their own home or in investing in housing for rental or resale purposes.
- Canadian Mortgage and Housing Corporation—provides mortgage home insurance to increase accessibility to home ownership, financing for affordable housing, and housing for Indigenous peoples.

*Provincial Government*
- Regulations for the housing industry and related services, e.g., building codes, professional and trades certification.
- Regulation of for-profit and non-profit sectors providing housing.
- Financing for the building of affordable housing.
- Income supports to citizens to ensure housing security, e.g., seniors, individuals with disabilities, foster care.

*continued*

- Financial support to non-profit organizations for building, maintenance, and support services for affordable, transitional, and temporary/emergency housing.

*Local Government*
- Land-use planning and zoning laws for particular forms of housing to meet expected needs of residents.
- Development charges, allocations of property, and vetting of zoning applications for the building of housing.
- Financial incentives to redevelop areas or to encourage the building of certain types of housing.
- Property tax breaks and monetary awards to support non-profit community organizations providing emergency, transitional, or permanent housing, and services for low-income residents.

The housing sector involves a wide variety of rules, regulations, programs, and funding from all three levels of government. Under the 1867 British North America Act (now called the Constitution Act, 1867) there is no explicit reference to "housing." However, housing appears captured under the *property and civil rights* category, with social services to support families and individuals recognized as under provincial jurisdiction. This constitutional criterion, though, has never prevented the federal government from having authority in these provincial areas of responsibility as long as the federal government covered the majority of the costs, an advantage this level of government has through broader means of taxation (both direct and indirect). Thus, the National Housing Act (1944) "recognized shelter as a basic human need" and included a federal/provincial cost-sharing formula where 75 per cent was funded from the federal level and 25 per cent was funded provincially for the following expenses: the costs of land acquisition, public housing construction, operating costs, and rental subsidies. The creation of the Canadian Mortgage and Housing Corporation (CMHC) through this Act placed the federal government at the centre of housing policy, and from this institution would flow innovative approaches to housing.

## From Housing Success to Housing Crisis

With an aggressive urban renewal strategy through the 1950s and 1960s targeting Canada's largest urban centres, governments made significant gains in the construction of public housing. By the 1970s, small-scale projects that housed residents with a range of incomes received federal funding in the form of 100 per cent mortgage assistance. These mixed-income projects were provided by non-profit or co-operative housing corporations. The federal government subsidized the rents of low-income tenants, and directly funded more than a million new housing starts, with a particular concern for creating low-income housing (Murphy, 2000; Coutts, 2000). Federal and provincial cost-sharing arrangements made important progress in addressing multiple shortcomings in housing and social assistance. However, a stagnant national economy, high unemployment, and rising provincial and federal debts initiated the gradual elimination of these supports and incentives to create affordable housing (Murphy, 2000; Layton, 2008). By 1994, federal funding cuts to housing programs would amount to $1.8 billion, the CMHC role in affordable housing was diminished, and in 1996 the federal government announced plans to download existing federal housing programs to the provinces, phasing out all federal funding by the third decade of the twenty-first century (Layton, 2008). The same cuts by provincial governments through the 1990s resulted in only a very small number of affordable housing units being built across Canada, and the majority of subsidies were whittled away in a drive to restrain spending or to advance tax cuts at election time. By the late 1990s, the cost-sharing formula became 33 per cent federal, 33 per cent provincial, and 33 per cent local—a significant download of costs onto local governments, which many are unable to afford. As Barbara Murphy (2000) noted at this time, the failure to address the needs of those with mental health challenges, combined with a "growing number of poor and a growing number of expensive housing units" (p. 19), means we have more people on the streets.

Through federal and provincial government disengagement, housing availability and affordability have become far worse since the late 1990s. A "homelessness crisis" had become a generalized "affordable housing crisis." By 2015–17 waiting lists for social housing across Canada totalled: Fredericton—500; Montreal—24,000; Ottawa—10,900; Toronto—90,900; Vancouver—9,500; Winnipeg—2,855 (Aleman, 2016); Calgary—3,000+ (City of Calgary, 2017); and Edmonton—4,500 (Theobald, 2016). In the province of Ontario alone estimates were of 171,360 families, seniors, and single adults and couples waiting for rent-geared-to-income housing and of thousands of units in urgent need of repair (Aleman, 2016). The "downloading" of this responsibility to local governments and communities was not a co-ordinated plan, but a persistent unwillingness of higher levels of government to recognize housing as a priority. Federal–provincial and municipal–provincial jurisdictional disputes and evasion have stalled the implementation of an effective strategy for affordable housing to the point that **housing insecurity** (Ling, 2008; CMHC, 2017) now affects broad segments of our population. Seniors relying on fixed incomes confront ever-rising mortgage rates and house lines of credit rates, rising rents, and escalating living costs (Sheridan, 2016). Low-income working families and new immigrants often cannot find rental accommodations appropriate for the size of their families. Rising rents preclude the ability to save to purchase a home (McMahon, 2015). Indigenous people experience shortages and dilapidated housing conditions on reserves and face discrimination when seeking housing in urban centres (Adams & Gosnell-Myers, 2013; Patrick, 2014; Lambert, 2016). As university students and young professionals increasingly experience housing insecurity, the topic has become the focus of news coverage concerning their aspirations for home ownership (Dyck, 2016; Chiosa, 2016). These problematic features of the housing sector have been most evident in government responses to homelessness, as 15 years of federal–local collaboration to address this issue have resulted only in an increase in visible homelessness.

# From National Homelessness Initiative to Homelessness Partnering Strategy

In late 1999, the government of Canada made a three-year commitment of $753 million with the National Homelessness Initiative (NHI) in an effort to support communities in managing the significant rise in visible homelessness (Smith, 2004). Originally intended for Canada's 10 largest cities, by 2000 this initiative would include another 51 smaller urban centres and regional areas tasked with the responsibility of finding local solutions to meet the needs of their homeless residents. The National Homelessness Initiative aimed to "facilitate community capacity by coordinating Government of Canada efforts and enhancing the diversity of tools and resources" (HRSDC, 2011). Initiated with no guarantee of renewed funding and with the government of Canada only committed to funding a maximum of 50 per cent of the overall initiative, renewals of the NHI would not be introduced until 2007–8, at which time NHI was replaced with the Homelessness Partnering Strategy (HPS).

The NHI had three components: Supporting Communities Partnerships Initiative (SCPI), a Youth Homelessness Strategy, and an Urban Aboriginal Strategy (National Homelessness Initiative, n.d.). Of the three branches, the SCPI was the largest, establishing nine criteria for an acceptable planning process as the basis for accessing available funds. The clear identification of "assets and gaps" was the most important strategy to create a "seamless underpinning of support" leading to self-sufficiency. This local "leadership" role was comprised of quite significant demands in service assessments, matching funding, evaluations, reporting, and community engagement. Overall, the model was comprised of a comprehensive approach that ensured spending be targeted towards those measures most effective in addressing immediate local needs.

Feedback to the federal government from community partners on the usefulness of the NHI was generally positive (Standing Senate Committee, 2009), but the main problem was the lack of a long-term commitment by the federal government to these communities, which created a "lack of predictability and sustainability" in responding to the homelessness crisis (Kelowna Committee, 2009; Interviews, 2010–15). Despite the progress made in meeting the immediate needs of homeless residents, most communities identified the main gap in their supports as affordable housing, which was not in the "mandate of the NHI" (Human Resources and Skills Development Canada, 2008). In response to these shortcomings, the NHI was reintroduced in 2007–8 as the Homeless Partnering Strategy (HPS).

The HPS would commit to a longer overall funding horizon, with financial commitments until 2014. There was also a financial commitment of over $1.9 billion to affordable housing over five years via the distribution of funds to provincial governments. At the local level, the conditions for funding had compelled a number of positive outcomes, even though engagement in the process has varied considerably depending on local capacities. For the first time, numerous municipal governments engaged in social planning and developed social plans identifying the needs of a broad range of residents. Local research on homeless needs and numbers provided the grounds for advocacy based on accumulated data, and HPS support for multi-community studies has provided important data on the extent of hidden homelessness, the identification of at-risk populations, and levels of housing insecurity (SPARC-BC, 2011).

Where community engagement has been strong, action plans and homeless counts have raised the profile on homelessness. Insights from individuals with lived experience have identified systemic deficiencies at the local and provincial levels and have confirmed that the vast majority are on the street due to a lack of money—not a lifestyle preference. Many adults who are homeless first experienced homelessness in their youth, and homelessness has contributed to the severity of mental health and addictions issues (National Learning Community, n.d.; Waegemakers Schiff & Rook, 2012). At the local level, there is agreement with the federal government that all three levels of government need to contribute to a long-term solution (Interview, 2010–15). Despite these notable outcomes from a multi-level approach, serious reservations persist.

Community organizations, after more than 15 years of "partnering" with the federal government, have little trust in the federal commitment to address homelessness. This mistrust is rooted in the fact that the basis of the "homeless crisis" resides in the short-sighted and irresponsible federal and provincial budget cuts of the 1990s and the downloading of responsibility that was sold to the local level as "empowerment" (Interview, 2010–15). With no declines in homelessness, "to say that we are eradicating homelessness is a total fallacy" (Interview, 2010–15). Onerous applications, reporting, and oversight requirements for community organizations are burdensome at the expense of addressing local needs. Staffing and time costs are absorbed by local organizations that can ill afford them, further reinforcing the impression that community organizations are being used as a low-cost response to a responsibility that should be federal and provincial.

Perhaps the strongest criticism of the NHI/HPS is that the federal government does not *want* to understand what is necessary to generate successful responses to homelessness, as the federal government has not been interested in whether or not homelessness has actually declined in designated communities receiving funding. Instead, success has been measured by the extent to which matching funds exceeded 50 per cent (Graham, 2011). Even though the overall funding horizons have increased, approved initiatives still are funded for only short periods of time.

> The federal government's approach to addressing homelessness and working with local groups is totally disrespectful. It has no sense of the legitimacy of running programs and how long it takes to build an effective, solid program. If you've got to write a contract to say you are going to resolve the issues that you've encountered, such as homelessness, in a two- or three-year span . . . I don't know how you do that. (Interview, 2010–15)

Such evaluations by advocates for the homeless clearly contradict the dominant discourse by governments and the media, but they are seldom heard due to the lack of a sustained media focus on the structural inequities and government policies that generate poverty and housing insecurity in Canada.

This funding uncertainty and lack of federal and provincial resolve on homelessness and affordable housing were confirmed in mid-2011, when it was reported that a federal–provincial agreement on the issue of "affordable housing" would require two years of talks just to establish a "framework" in which specific terms would be negotiated separately with each individual province (Scoffield, 2011). Thus, it was only by the end of 2014 that separate provincial agreements were reached with all provinces for the use of matching funds for affordable housing—just as the HPS funding was set to expire (CMHC, 2015). As the announcement on renewal of the HPS after 2014 was continually postponed and restraints were imposed on funded projects, there was a strong sense that the federal government was about to terminate the HPS and retreat from any further commitments to affordable housing. This intention was later confirmed, but renewal of the HPS for another five years had been saved only after a significant level of lobbying by national organizations.

The initial results of a research project by the Mental Health Commission of Canada demonstrated the effectiveness and potential cost savings of a "Housing First" (HF) approach to homelessness (McNaughton, Nelson, Goering, & Piat, 2016). Thus, it was not the increased illness, suffering, or deaths due to homelessness that moved the federal government. Only the realization that there was a "cost-saving" to a new approach kept the federal government engaged, suggesting that with no proven monetary savings the HPS would have been ended.

## The "Housing First" Approach

The renewal of the Homelessness Partnering Strategy for 2015–19 came with new conditions on the use of matching funds, of which the most significant was that the majority of the money was to be dedicated to Housing First initiatives. Recognized as a highly effective model in addressing formerly homeless individuals with complex mental health issues and/or addictions, the model places high expectations on community organizations, provincial and local governments, and local property owners to achieve desired outcomes (Waegemakers Schiff & Rook, 2012; CHRA, 2013; MHCC, 2014). Targeting the most visibly "street-entrenched" individuals, the premise of HF is that nothing meaningful can be achieved unless homeless individuals first are provided with stable housing, with the means necessary to preclude them from having to return to the streets, e.g., medical care, sufficient incomes, food, life skills, and organizational representation. The most effective model is a sophisticated collaboration of congregate and scattered site housing options offering a broad range of services tailored to the individual. **Congregate housing** is a housing facility offering a range of housing units with full-service supports to meet all the needs of residents. **Scattered site housing** is offered as an option for more independent living, supporting placement in private apartments with varied levels of ongoing support by community organizations and provincial agencies.

Community organizations that have implemented a Housing First approach in various urban centres in Canada have all attested to the improved physical and mental health of participants, with reductions in interactions with police and emergency services (Kading & Norman, 2014). They have also identified the following challenges to implementing the Housing First approach. Individuals will likely suffer financial shortcomings. Community organizations with Housing First programs experience staff burnout and high turnover in fulfilling individualized support. "First-come, first-served" waiting lists for Housing First programs prevent community organizations from prioritizing clients with the greatest needs. Low vacancy rates limit workers from meeting the first requirement of Housing First: a viable home. A more general critique is that Housing First prioritizes the "street-entrenched/hardest to house," which favours older males under the age of 65, and does not address the needs of homeless youth, women (with or without children), and seniors, particularly of Indigenous heritage—whose numbers are increasing but who tend to be less visible on the streets. The main restrictions to an effective HF response arise within provincial jurisdictions, where large gaps exist between the HPS mandates and the level of financial support for community organizations, health care services, and the provision of adequate incomes. Thus, it is not apparent that the provinces are on board with HF requirements, even as an exercise in saving costs.

Despite limitations in adopting Housing First, in the time it took for the federal and provincial governments to resolve the modest 2009 federal pledge on affordable housing and endorse a Housing First approach, the "homelessness crisis" had become a more generalized "affordable housing" crisis affecting much broader segments of society, including youth, seniors, post-secondary students, Indigenous people, low-income working adults and families, recent immigrants, and young professionals (Conference Board of Canada, 2010; FCM, 2012; CHRA, 2013; Gaetz et al., 2016; Grenier et al., 2016; Chiosa, 2016). Competition for rental spaces has escalated in response to a diminishing supply of affordable housing spaces, advantaging those in the rental market who are employed and more financially secure and able to pay higher and rising rents on a long-term basis, specifically, young professionals and seniors. This skewing of power within available housing has further eroded the ability of workers to implement a Housing First approach to address street-entrenched and hidden forms of homelessness. Notably, only the expansion of the crisis into populations that enjoy more prestige pushed the federal government into action.

## Social Policy Change in Action

### A Way Home: Working Together to End Youth Homelessness in Kamloops, BC

*by Katherine McParland*

*The ongoing success of a collaborative program to address youth homelessness in the small city of Kamloops, BC, is a result of a social work graduate from Thompson Rivers University—Katherine McParland, the Youth Homelessness Manager for the A Way Home Committee.*

In 2012, I was working at an adult Housing First building and began to identify many more youth on the street. Upon further conversations, I discovered that many of these youth had aged out of foster care and did not have the support they needed to secure housing. This resonated with me, as I remembered my own experience of aging out of the system and subsequently ending up homeless. I knew it would take a community to create change and act like family to those kids who have none, so I created a community group, the "Former Youth in Care Supportive Housing Committee." At the same time, Kamloops had been named a pilot community in a national initiative aimed at ending youth homelessness. The result was A Way Home—a plan to end youth homelessness in Kamloops. The plan was released in 2014, and the Former Youth in Care Supportive Housing Committee adopted it as our own and became the A Way Home movement. Recognized for our momentum in implementing the plan and generating solutions to end youth homelessness that could be replicated in other communities, it became A Way Home Canada. It has also become an international phenomenon with A Way Home America and A Way Home Scotland.

A Way Home Kamloops has 120 members from all sectors, including non-profits, Indigenous organizations, businesses, landlords, youth, and community members. We are all brought together with the same vision of preventing, reducing, and ending youth homelessness in our community.

*continued*

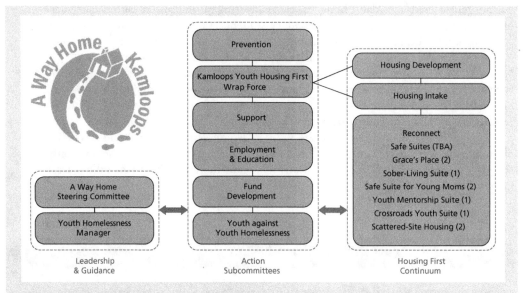

**Figure 13.1 A Way Home: Guiding Structure**
Source: A Way Home Kamloops. Courtesy of Katherine McParland.

Through co-ordinating services, we have developed the Kamloops Youth Housing First Wrap Force. This is a centralized housing and supports intake system for youth experiencing homelessness. Nineteen different organizations have identified one Youth Homelessness Champion, who would connect youth to the Wrap Force. The goal is that there will be no wrong door for youth to access housing. The impact of co-ordinating services was evident—without any new money, 14 new units of youth program housing were created within a year. This momentum led to a continuum of housing and wraparound supports for an inter-agency team for housing sustainability (Figure 13.2).

Gaps are identified and housing is created to meet those needs. We have also created scattered-site housing where agencies take out leases on apartments to reduce risks for landlords. The business sector has been engaged and sponsors youth by providing year-long rental subsidies. A Way Home's focus has also been prevention, where we have created a ConNext table—a space where the youth meets with the social worker and a team of community supports who will help to ensure the transition from the foster-care system is successful—to connect youth aging out of foster care with supports and housing. To further community education we conducted Canada's first Youth Homelessness Count. We identified over 129 youth who have experienced homelessness, with 56 of these youth being homeless during 13–24 October 2016. Our hope is other communities will conduct counts to educate government on the resources we need.

Our work is grounded in the lives of youth who have experienced homelessness. We are looking to the provincial and federal governments to support this municipal work. We have learned that we will never end youth homelessness without policy changes and the resources we need to ensure every youth has A Way Home.

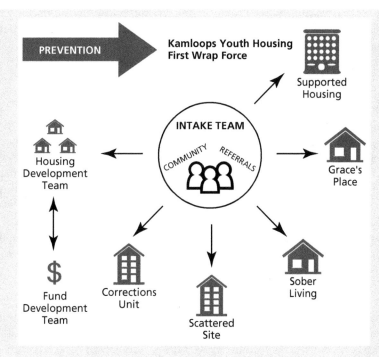

**Figure 13.2 Kamloops Youth Housing First Wrap Force**
Source: A Way Home Kamloops. Courtesy of Katherine McParland. Building icons:
© ronnarid somphong/123RF. People icon: © pensiri saekoung/123RF

# The Return to a National Housing Strategy

Only with the increased media exposure of a broadening crisis in affordable housing was the problem finally picked up as an issue in the 2015 federal election. The Liberal Party of Canada came into power on its promise of a national strategy on housing—this from the very governing party that had been committed in the 1990s to getting the federal government "out of housing" by early in the twenty-first century. The prompt response and the return of a federal role in affordable housing are an admission of this failure of leadership and responsibility at the federal and provincial levels. In addition, it is still evident that this is not caused by concern for the most vulnerable on the streets, but by the fact that a basic human need such as "appropriate housing" has become a challenge for millions of Canadians and has drawn the persistent criticism of big-city mayors, housing advocates, and national organizations representing seniors and health care professionals. It is also a context that will only get worse before the latest federal initiatives on housing effect any change.

The first Liberal government budget of 2016 allocated $2.3 billion to housing and homelessness over two years, of which $111 million went to bolster HPS funding, followed by a consultation process for the creation of a National Housing Strategy (CAEH, 2016). The 2017 federal budget then added another $11 billion and laid out a strategy for the next decade (Government of Canada, 2017), which "will provide a roadmap for governments and housing providers across the country" and includes a "renewed partnership between the Government and provinces and territories to better support key housing priorities." There will be a new $5 billion National Housing Fund to address critical housing issues and to better support vulnerable citizens. This will provide municipalities and other housing partners with sustained and improved access to low-cost loans for the repair and renewal of housing units, as well as for the construction of new affordable housing. There will also be temporary funding for income supports linked to rents, and targeted support for northern housing and Indigenous people not living on-reserve.

These funding initiatives acknowledge the broad extent of the housing crisis in Canada, including the disrepair of social housing that was transferred to the provinces at the beginning of the twenty-first century (Tory & Iveson, 2016; Gray, 2017). Of note, it is only with the 2017 budget that the CMHC and Statistics Canada have a mandate to discern the extent of homelessness and housing insecurity in Canada. While important gains have been achieved in acquiring a renewed federal focus on homelessness and housing insecurity, there are no decisive goals in place to "end homelessness" (Press, 2017a). Federal support does not match estimates on the monies needed to address these crises, and it remains unclear if "renewed partnership" with the provinces will ensure the necessary financial resources or, instead, generate conflict.

Anti-poverty and homeless advocates in Canada tend to be aware of several communities in Alberta that have had success in reducing homelessness, particularly the small city of Medicine Hat (Lawrynuik, 2017). Within three days of being recognized as homeless, an individual has a support worker, with the goal of a permanent "roof over their head" within 10 days. Less known is the fact that in 2008 the government of Alberta launched a comprehensive 10-year strategy to end homelessness in the province (Alberta Secretariat, 2008), in which the principles of "affordable housing for all" and a Housing First approach were primary. At the centre of the plan was a calculation of the costs of maintaining the status quo for the some 11,000 homeless (at the time) over 10 years—estimated at $6.65 billion (with minimal change in their condition), where an investment of $3.36 billion in affordable housing and a Housing First approach over these 10 years would result in a saving of $3.334 billion to the province (while providing secure housing and a better quality of life). Calculating the anticipated growth in the homeless population over these 10 years suggested that by spending $7.7 billion, the province would save $6.5 billion. Notable are the large upfront monetary sums committed to end homelessness in just this one province, financial commitments that are not commensurate at the federal level to address similar needs across the country. Still, the 2017 federal budget marked a turnaround in the federal government position that advocates for the homeless hope can be expanded in financial resolve and commitments.

## International Comparisons

### Housing Challenges and Government Responses in Other Countries

Challenges of homelessness and housing insecurity have become generalized across most European countries and the United States, exacerbated by the increased unemployment from the global financial crisis of 2008 and the rising costs of rents or home ownership (Foundation Abbé Pierre—FEANTSA, 2017; National Alliance, 2017). Most alarming was that in all EU countries "young people are more vulnerable to prohibitive housing costs, over-crowding and severe housing deprivation than the rest of the population" (Foster, 2017a). Only Finland has reported a steady decline in homelessness due to the aggressive application of a Housing First model since 2008 as a national strategy (Foster, 2017b).

Germany and Switzerland had been recognized for having the best policies for ensuring a range of housing options at the local level. In these countries local governments are allowed to determine local needs and to offer the types of financial incentives and subsidies required to encourage property developers to build innovative and appropriate rental housing to meet the varied housing needs of the population (Hugentobler, 2015; Phillips, 2014). Due to heavy regulations in Germany and Switzerland, renting has been far cheaper compared to the costs of home ownership, as the building of rental housing has been supported by the government as a priority over incentives to encourage home ownership. However, these policies have not prevented an increase in homelessness. The example of Finland demonstrates that a priority on homelessness over and above providing affordable housing options is required to meet the needs of homeless citizens.

# Chapter Summary

This chapter has provided an overview of the complex and changing dynamics surrounding housing insecurity and homelessness in Canada, beginning with the cutbacks to affordable housing in the 1980s, the homelessness crisis that had developed by the 1990s, followed by a more general crisis in affordable housing in the early 2000s, leading in 2017 to renewed funding commitments by the government of Canada. Revisiting the Case Examples at the start of the chapter, we see that John, Kate and Matthew, and Paula represent different demographics and urban contexts affected by the decisions of the federal and provincial governments. A combination of events beyond their control, including limited financial resources, has left them few options and has generated deep insecurities. While more federal and provincial commitments to various types of affordable housing have emerged, it will be many years before these individuals see the benefits of such changes.

During that time interval, John could quite easily develop greater mental health and addictions challenges leading to death, despite a renewed federal commitment and more money to youth homelessness and Housing First (Zimonjic, 2017). As funding and programming will not be rolled out until 2020, existing housing and services for youth are limited. Far more funding is required to address the level of need (see the Social Policy Change in Action box). Mounting financial stress could easily lead to Kate and Matthew's partnership breakdown, with Kate then likely to be reliant on social assistance to raise two children. However, if they can make it as a couple until 2020, they may be eligible for the "portable housing benefit" of $2,500 a year to help cover rent (Press, 2017b; Zimonjic, 2017). In addition, separate but ongoing negotiations with Indigenous housing organizations may lead to more housing options for off-reserve urban populations, increasingly supported by important national and provincial organizations (see National Association of Friendship Centres, 2017).

Paula's health could rapidly decline as it becomes more difficult to access health care. Her financial circumstances could worsen and her living conditions deteriorate. At this time, federal support is limited to tax rebates for renovations paid in advance, with only select provinces offering additional support (Government of Canada, Employment and Social Development Canada, 2017). Still, the Canadian Association of Retired Persons is supportive of federal government commitments under the proposed National Housing Strategy to build more affordable housing, repair existing affordable housing stock, and identify vulnerable seniors (CARP, 2017). At this time, all of these scenarios add considerable time and costs to the health care, social services, and justice systems, and these issues could have been prevented had there been services and affordable housing options in place to meet the needs of these individuals before the needs became critical.

As both levels of government begin to understand the needless costs generated by inaction, it is important to emphasize that increasing access to affordable housing is not just a cost-saving exercise. Rather, it is necessary to recognize that the insecurity, suffering, illness, and deaths caused by existing policies, practices, and relationships among our three levels of government are fundamentally unjust and must be changed.

## Discussion Questions

1.  How visible is homelessness in your community? How has this chapter changed your perceptions of the needs of homeless residents?

2.  What action plans does your community have in place to address homelessness, poverty, and/or affordable housing needs? Do they incorporate a Housing First approach?

3.  What is your opinion of federal and provincial responses to homelessness and affordable housing? Does the 2017 federal budget offer the potential to reverse these crises?

## References

Adams, M., & Gosnell-Myers, G. (2013, 22 Jan.). Don't forget Canada's urban aboriginals. They're not just passing through. *Globe and Mail*. Retrieved from https://www.theglobeandmail.com/opinion/dont-forget-canadas-urban-aboriginals-theyre-not-just-passing-through/article7599448/?arc404=true

Alberta Secretariat for Action on Homelessness. (2008). *A plan for Alberta: Ending homelessness in 10 years*. Edmonton: Government of Alberta.

Aleman, A. (2016, 21 Oct.). With long wait times for social housing, what can be done to meet the housing needs of homeless people and those at-risk? *The Homeless Hub*. Retrieved from http://homelesshub.ca/blog/long-wait-times-social-housing-what-can-be-done-meet-housing-needs-homeless-people-and-those

A Way Home Committee. (2018). A Way Home Kamloops. Retrieved from https://www.awayhomekamloops.com/

Barata, P., & Richter, T. (2017, 20 Mar.). A portable housing benefit could ease our homeless crisis. *Globe and Mail*, p. A11.

Best, R. (2010). Situation or social problem: The influence of events on media coverage of homelessness. *Social Problems, 57*(1), 74–91.

Calder, M., Richter, S., Burns, K., & Mao, Y. (2011). Framing homelessness for the Canadian public:

The news media and homelessness. *Canadian Journal of Urban Research, 20*(2), 1–19.

Canada Mortgage and Housing Corporation (CMHC). (2015). Investment in affordable housing bilateral agreements and public reporting. Retrieved from http://www.cmhc-schl.gc.ca/en/inpr/afhoce/fuafho/iah/iah_003.cfm

——. (2017). What is core housing need? Retrieved from https://www.cmhc-schl.gc.ca/en/hoficlincl/observer/observer_044.cfm

Canadian Alliance to End Homelessness (CAEH). (2016). Budget 2016 invests $2.3 billion over two years on housing & homelessness. Retrieved from http://www.caeh.ca

Canadian Association of Retired Persons (CARP). (2017). Canada's first ever national housing strategy. Retrieved from http://www.carp.ca/2017/11/23/canadas-first-ever-national-housing-strategy/

Canadian Housing and Renewal Association (CHRA). (2013, Apr.). Presentations from annual meeting. Edmonton, Alberta.

Chiosa, S. (2016, 24 May). Academic housing & universities struggle to find affordable housing. *Globe and Mail.* pp. A1, A6–A7.

City of Calgary. (2017). Applicant information. Retrieved from http://www.calgary.ca/CSPS/ch/Pages/Applicant-information/Waiting-list-for-housing.aspx

Condon, S. (2016, Mar.). *Still dying on the streets: Homeless deaths in British Columbia* (2nd edn). Vancouver: Street Corner Media Foundation.

Conference Board of Canada. (2010). *Building from the ground up: Enhancing affordable housing in Canada.* Toronto: Conference Board of Canada.

Coutts, J. (2000). Expansion, retrenchment and protecting the future: Social policy in the Trudeau years. In T. Axworthy & P. Trudeau (Eds), *Towards a just society: The Trudeau years* (pp. 221–45). Toronto: Penguin.

Duffy, R., Royer, G., & Beresford, C. (2014, Sept.). *Who's picking up the tab? Federal and provincial downloading onto local governments.* Vancouver: Columbia Institute—Centre for Civic Governance.

Dyck, D. (2016, 14 Mar.). Millennials fleeing Vancouver for cities with more affordable housing, threatening city's tech economy. *Financial Post.* Retrieved from http://business.financialpost.com/personal-finance/mortgages-real-estate/millennials-fleeing-vancouver-for-cities-with-more-affordable-housing-threatening-citys-tech-economy

Federation of Canadian Municipalities (FCM). (2012). *No vacancy: Trends in rental housing in Canada.* Ottawa: FCM.

——. (2017, 22 Mar.). Federal budget a game-changer for municipalities. Retrieved from https://fcm.ca/home/media/news-and-commentary/2017/federal-budget-a-game-changer-for-municipalities.htm

Florida, R. (2017, 24 Apr.). It's more than a housing crisis. *Globe and Mail,* p. A11.

Foster, D. (2017a, 21 Mar.). Homelessness and housing problems reach crisis point in all EU countries—except Finland. *The Guardian.* Retrieved from https://www.theguardian.com/housing-network/2017/mar/21/homelessness-housing-problems-crisis-point-all-eu-countries-except-finland

Foster, D. (2017b, 22 Mar.). What can the UK learn from how Finland solved homelessness? *The Guardian.* Retrieved from https://www.theguardian.com/housing-network/2017/mar/22/finland-solved-homelessness-eu-crisis-housing-first

Foundation Abbé Pierre—FEANTSA. (2017, 21 Mar.). *Second overview of housing exclusion in Europe.* Retrieved from http://www.feantsa.org/en/report/2017/03/21/the-second-overview-of-housing-exclusion-in-europe-2017

Gaetz, S. (2014). *Coming of age: Reimagining the response to youth homelessness in Canada.* Toronto: Canadian Homelessness Research Network Press.

——, Dej, E., Richter, T., & Redman, M. (2016). *The state of homelessness in Canada 2016.* Toronto: Canadian Observatory on Homelessness Press.

Government of Canada. (2008). *The Homelessness Partnering Strategy: Partnerships that work.* Ottawa: Government of Canada.

——. (2017). *Building a strong middle class.* Retrieved from http://www.budget.gc.ca/2017/docs/plan/budget-2017-en.pdf

——, Employment and Social Development Canada. (2017). Retrieved from https://www.canada.ca/en/employment-social-development/services/benefits/housing/buying-home.html

Graham, A. (2011). Vision, collaboration, persistence and hard work: The Canadian federal government's homeless partnering strategy. In J. Bourgon (Ed.), *A new synthesis of public administration: Serving in the 21st century* (pp. 167–81). Montreal & Kingston: McGill-Queen's University Press.

Gray, J. (2017, 27 Apr.). New funding for Toronto transit, social housing left out of Ontario budget. *Globe and Mail.* Retrieved from http://www.theglobeandmail.com/news/politics/new-funding-for-toronto-transit-social-housing-left-out-of-ontario-budget/article34840368/

Grenier, A., Barken, R., Sussman, T., Rothwell, D., & Bourgeois-Guérin, V. (2016). Homelessness among older people: Assessing strategies and frameworks across Canada. *Canadian Review of Social Policy / Revue Canadienne de Politique Sociale, 74*, 1–39.

Homeless Hub Newsletter. (2017). Canadian Observatory on Homelessness welcomes the 2017 federal budget. Retrieved from http://us1 .campaign-archive2.com/?u=61233be4a0bcc87 d8977b631e&id=e289d3c399&e=f966839972

Hugentobler, M. (2015, 27–9 Aug.). The provision of social housing as a key aspect for social inclusion in cities. RC21 International Conference, Urbino, Italy.

Human Resources and Skills Development Canada (HRSDC). (2011). *National Homelessness Initiative—background*. Ottawa: Government of Canada.

———, Strategic Policy and Research Branch. (2008). *Summative evaluation of the national homelessness initiative—Final report*. Ottawa: Government of Canada.

Interviews. (2010–15). Semi-structured interviews conducted with social planners, community organizations, and city councillors from Victoria, Vancouver, Kamloops, Kelowna, Prince George, and Nanaimo.

Kading, T., & Norman, T. (2014, 26 Mar.). *"Housing First"—Research findings*. Report presented to the Kamloops Working Group on Homelessness.

Kelowna Committee to End Homelessness. (2009). *Home for good: Kelowna's ten year plan to end homelessness*. Retrieved from www.castanet .net/content/1243913711AFT.pdf

Lambert, S. (2016, 2 Nov.). First Nations housing crisis will take a lifetime to solve: AFN regional chief. *CBC News*. Retrieved from http://www .cbc.ca/news/canada/manitoba/first-nations-housing-crisis-will-take-a-lifetime-to-solve-1.3833792

Lawrynuik, S. (2017, 26 Jan.). Medicine Hat maintaining homeless-free status 2 years on. *CBC News*. Retrieved from http:// www.cbc.ca/news/canada/calgary/ medicine-hat-homeless-free-update-1.3949030

Layton, J. (2008). *Homelessness: How to end the national crisis* (2nd edn). Toronto: Penguin.

Ling, T. (2008). *The reality of housing insecurity*. Ottawa: Citizens for Public Justice. Retrieved from https:// www.cpj.ca/files/docs/PJ-Backgrounder-on-Housing-and-Homelessness3.pdf

McMahon, T. (2015, 10 Sept.). Affordable housing crisis affects one in five renters in Canada: Study. *Globe and Mail*. Retrieved from https://beta.theglobeandmail.com/ report-on-business/economy/housing/the-real-estate-beat/affordable-housing-crisis-affects-one-in-five-renters-in-canada-study/ article26287843/

McNaughton, E., Nelson, G., Goering, P., & Piat, M. (2016, 27 Sept.). *The At Home / Chez Soi Project: Moving evidence into policy. The story of the At Home Chez Soi initiative's impact on federal homelessness policy in Canada*. Ottawa: Mental Health Commission of Canada. Retrieved from mentalhealthcommission.ca

Martin, L. (2011). Good deals for homebuyers, not for the poor: Erasing poverty from affordable housing discourse. *Journal of Poverty, 15*, 3–21.

Mental Health Commission of Canada (MHCC). (2014). *At Home / Chez Soi: National final report*. Retrieved from http://www .mentalhealthcommission.ca/English/ initiatives-and-projects/home

Murphy, B. (2000). *On the street: How we created the homeless*. Winnipeg: J. Gordon Shillingford Publishing.

National Alliance to End Homelessness. (2017). Homelessness in America. Retrieved from https://endhomelessness.org/ homelessness-in-america/

National Association of Friendship Centres (NAFC). (2017). About the NAFC. Retrieved from http:// nafc.ca/en/who-we-are/about-nafc/

National Homelessness Initiative. (n.d.). *A guide to the Supporting Communities Partnerships Initiative (SCPI)*. Ottawa: Government of Canada.

National Learning Community on Youth Homelessness. (n.d.). *National housing strategy recommendations*. Retrieved from http:// learningcommunity.ca/

Patrick, C. (2014). *Aboriginal homelessness in Canada: A literature review*. Toronto: Canadian Homelessness Research Network Press. Retrieved from http://www.homelesshub.ca/ sites/default/files/AboriginalLiteratureReview .pdf

Phillips, M. (2014, 23 Jan.). Most Germans don't buy their homes, they rent. Here's why. *Quartz*. Retrieved from https://qz.com/167887/ germany-has-one-of-the-worlds-lowest-homeownership-rates/

Press, J. (2017a, 22 Apr.). Liberals aim to cut number of "chronic" homeless in half. *Huffington Post*. Retrieved from http://www.huffingtonpost .ca/2017/04/22/liberals-set-homeless-reduction-targets-ahead-of-provincial-talks_n_16170918 .html

———. (2017b, 21 Nov.). New housing strategy could cut into child poverty rates, groups say. *CBC News*. http://www.cbc.ca/news/politics/campaign-2000-child-poverty-1.4411820

Schneider, B. (2011). Sourcing homelessness: How journalists use sources to frame homelessness. *Journalism, 13*(1), 71–86.

———. (2014). Homelessness: Emotion discourse and the reproduction of social inequality. *Canadian Journal of Communication, 39*, 235–48.

Schwan, K. (2016). *Why don't we do something? The societal problematization of "homelessness" and the relationship between discursive framing and social change* (Unpublished doctoral dissertation). University of Toronto, Toronto, Canada.

Scoffield, H. (2011). Ottawa and provinces reach $1.4 billion deal on affordable housing. Retrieved from http://homelesshub.ca/resource/ottawa-and-provinces-reach-14-billion-deal-affordable-housing?_ga=2.37303328.1695655720.1509806208-886663890.1509806208

Sheridan, S. (2016, 22 Nov.). Low-income seniors also victim to affordable housing crisis. *Policynote*. Retrieved from http://www.policynote.ca/low-income-seniors-also-victim-to-affordable-housing-crisis/

Smith, R. (2004). Lessons from the National Homelessness Initiative. In *Special Studies: Policy Development and Implementation in Complex Files*. Government of Canada/Canada School of Public Policy.

SPARC-BC. (2011). *Knowledge for action: Hidden homelessness in Prince George, Kamloops, Kelowna, Nelson and Nanaimo*. Retrieved from www.sparc.bc.ca

Standing Senate Committee on Social Affairs, Science and Technology. (2009). *In from the margins: A call to action on poverty, housing and homelessness*. Ottawa: Senate of Canada, Report of the Subcommittee on Cities. Retrieved from www.parl.gc.ca/Content/SEN/Committee/402/citi/rep/rep02dec09

Theobald, C. (2016, 30 May). Waiting list for affordable housing in Edmonton tripled to about 4,500 families in 2015. *Edmonton Journal*. Retrieved from http://edmontonjournal.com/news/local-news/wait-list-for-affordable-housing-in-edmonton-tripled-to-about-4500-families-in-2015

Toft, A. (2014). Contesting the deviant other: Discursive strategies for the production of homeless subjectivities. *Discourse & Society, 25*(6), 783–809.

Tory, J., & D. Iveson. (2016, 30 Sept.). How to tackle the housing crisis in Canada's cities. *Globe and Mail*. Retrieved from http://www.theglobeandmail.com/opinion/how-to-tackle-the-housing-crisis-in-canadas-cities/article32151195/

Waegemakers Schiff, J., & Rook, J. (2012). *Housing first: Where is the evidence?* Toronto: Homeless Hub.

Zimonjic, P. (2017, 22 Nov.). Liberals detail $40B for 10-year national housing strategy, introduce Canada Housing Benefit. *CBC News*. Retrieved from http://www.cbc.ca/news/politics/housing-national-benefit-1.4413615

# 14 Reaching beyond Hunger

## The Right to Food and Food Sovereignty

*Nettie Wiebe*

---

### Chapter Objectives

*This chapter will help you to develop an understanding of:*
- the importance of social policy on food security for physical, social, cultural, and environmental health and well-being;
- the difference between food security and food sovereignty;
- some consequences of the corporate food system that undermine food security;
- some key social policy changes that are necessary for realizing the right to food and achieving food sovereignty.

---

## Introduction

Food is a basic necessity for life, health, and social well-being. Whether, what, and how well people eat depends on income, economic and social status, food cultures, food systems, political structures, and ecological contexts. Although these factors are inextricably interrelated, in Canada, the primary social policy response to **food insecurity** and hunger has been an economic one channelled through welfare payments, supplemented in some jurisdictions with school lunch programs and backstopped by food banks. These strategies are embedded in an economic and societal context where food is treated as a marketable commodity, and its production, distribution, and consumption are dictated by affordability and efficiency.

In this chapter, I argue for a more complex discourse on food that takes into account the ecological and social dimensions of **food systems** and acknowledges the impact of increasing corporate control over food resources and choices. Social policy aimed at achieving food security must not only deal with the immediate access to and affordability of food but also the longer-term ecological, economic, cultural, and political impacts of food systems on citizens and communities. It must also respond to the urgent call of **food sovereignty** movements that demand the right to sustainable and culturally appropriate food, alongside people's right to define their own agricultural practices and food systems. I develop a critical conceptual framework of food sovereignty to explore social policy measures that promote social equality, ensure ecological care as a means to obtaining food security, and honour Indigenous food systems and sacred relationships within the environment.

# Canada's Current Food Policy Menu

Much of the public discourse on food deals with immediate experiences of food—the taste, cost, enjoyment, ease of preparation, calories, and nutritional benefit of various foods. The most frequent and high-impact exposure to food news and views is driven by those who market food, particularly processed and fast foods. The billions of dollars that food corporations spend on advertising their products effectively penetrate public consciousness and affect menus. McDonald's and Coca Cola are among the most recognized brands in the world (Statista, n.d.). Highly processed foods make up more than 60 per cent of the average Canadian family's food purchases (Picard, 2017).

However, the power of corporate food messaging is being challenged on several fronts. For example, the preponderance and deleterious impact of fast-food advertising campaigns that specifically target children has recently provoked Health Canada to hold consultations on regulating and restricting such advertising (Health Canada, 2017; Picard, 2017). Furthermore, a growing skepticism about food advertisers' health and content claims are erupting into more battles over labelling (Knezevic, 2017). Although researchers in university and government agriculture departments continue to focus almost exclusively on industrial production and processing, academics and writers in other disciplines are publishing critical assessments of this system (Koc et al., 2017). The industrial food system is subjected to widespread and deep critiques focused on its effects on human health, environments, and food production, as well as on its economic and social impacts (Kneen, 1989; Schlosser 2001; Pollan, 2006; Patel, 2007; Winson, 2013). Small-scale farmers, fishers, dieticians, health care advocates, environmentalists, political economists, Indigenous scholars, and many other groups are engaging in critical discourse and action to challenge the current food and social policy framework. So while food advertisers are urging Canadians to buy and eat more, and media stories of food shortages are mostly located in faraway, war-torn, or famine-stricken places, food discourse in Canada now includes, but also extends beyond, economic and production issues. Food is an important and complex human rights and social justice issue (Wiebe & Wipf, 2011).

---

**Case Examples**   Contexts of Food Shortage

---

A single mother in Toronto is concerned about being able to afford food as the rent for her housing is rising while her wages are stagnant. Her full-time job barely covers current living costs. Buying school supplies and clothes for her two children cannot be avoided, so cutting back on grocery bills remains one of the few cost-saving strategies open to her.

A family in Rosetown, Saskatchewan, is subject to a variable job market and low welfare rates, which make an occasional visit to the local food bank necessary (see Box 14.1). Having moved to a smaller town because housing is more affordable there, their employment

*continued*

options are seasonal, and the transportation costs to jobs in Saskatoon are too high to make that option financially viable.

The Inuit children in a Cape Dorset family don't always get enough to eat and rarely get fresh fruits and vegetables because food is expensive, fresh foods are usually not available, and the household income is too low to afford nutritious, fulsome diets for everyone. The stories their grandparents and Elders tell of "living off the land" seem remote and don't change their reality of heading to school on empty stomachs some mornings.

Each of the three households in the case examples suffers from food shortages that appear to be primarily economic in nature. However, a closer analysis of the context and genesis of these situations raises critical questions about the ecological, cultural, and political characteristics of our current food system. These questions, which will be revisited elsewhere in this chapter, are:

1. What is the real remedy to food insecurity if employment does not provide relief from the kind of poverty that causes food insecurity?
2. What is the structure of, and what are the values underpinning, a food system that produces large volumes of grain and livestock but leaves families food insecure in the midst of this abundance of food?
3. What has driven the transition from communities of traditionally self-sufficient ancestors who lived off the land to children who have tenuous access to imported foods?

While the three case examples are located in different geographic, social, and cultural spaces, they share the common experience of having more limited food choices than middle- or high-income Canadians. For example, their economic circumstances likely preclude culturally preferred organic foods or even health-related diet requirements where these are higher-cost food options. Menus may not be determined by class location but they certainly are influenced and constrained by it.

Canada's status as a wealthy country with economic opportunity and a good quality of life continues to be confirmed both here and abroad.[1] However, this is tempered by other data indicating that this good quality of life does not accrue to everyone. Despite being a major producer and exporter of food, and having a suite of social policies that are supposed to provide a strong safety net for all, many people in Canada are not assured of that basic necessity for life—food.

## Food Insecurity in Canada

The annual report *Hunger Count* released by Food Banks Canada illustrates that hunger and uncertain access to food haunts many Canadians in all parts of the country (Food Banks Canada, 2016). The data of food bank use in March 2016 show that 863,492 people received food from food banks in Canada, a 1.3 per cent rise from the 2015 survey. The trend on food bank use has been rising in most parts of Canada with a sharp increase of more than 17 per cent in Alberta, Saskatchewan, and Nova Scotia. There has been an overall rise of 28 per cent since 2008. More than a third of those receiving sustenance from food banks are under the age of 18. The profile of those who use the food bank includes some who are, or have recently been, employed (almost 20 per cent), many who receive social assistance (45 per cent), and a smaller percentage (8 per cent) who rely on pensions.

The *Hunger Count* presents a grim and disturbing picture of the number of people who are unable to secure food by buying groceries or by growing enough food for themselves, and who are able and willing to supplement their meals with food bank hampers. This leaves uncounted those who are hungry but are not near enough or mobile enough to get to a food bank. It also leaves out those who are not aware of the food bank option or who find it too humiliating to use that option.

In an effort to achieve a more accurate picture of the real and experienced level of food insecurity in Canada, a team of researchers at PROOF Food Insecurity Policy Research, supported by the Canadian Institutes of Health Research, has developed more robust data-gathering along with more nuanced definitions to describe the conditions that constitute household food insecurity (Tarasuk, 2016). Whereas getting food from a food bank definitely signals that the recipient does not have adequate food, there are various levels of food insecurity. A household where members "miss meals, reduce food intake, and at the most extreme go day(s) without food" is listed as suffering **severe food insecurity**. **Moderate food insecurity** occurs where households "compromise in quality and/or quantity of food due to a lack of money for food." But any household that must "worry about running out of food and/or limit food selection because of lack of money for food" is deemed to be in the **marginal food insecurity** category. While the latter two kinds of households may never access a food bank, they are **food vulnerable** in ways that compromise their health and well-being (Vozoris & Tarasuk, 2003; Dachner & Tarasuk, 2017). Using data collected by the Canadian Community Health Survey (CCHS), the annual reports published by the PROOF team show ongoing and increasingly severe problems of food insecurity in certain segments of the population and areas of the country. For example, lone-parent families headed by women were the most vulnerable demographic in 2014, with 33.5 per cent of these families rating as food insecure. Food insecurity registered the highest in northern Canada, where 60 per cent of children in Nunavut live in food-insecure households.

Food insecurity has well-known harmful effects on the health and well-being of individuals, families, and their communities and is especially damaging to the development and health of children (Dachner & Tarasuk, 2017; Kirkpatrick et al., 2010). It should provoke an urgent and effective policy and action response.

---

## Box 14.1   Rosetown Food Bank

The Rosetown & District Food Bank was formed in 2003. The catchment area extends beyond Rosetown (population: 2,451) to include farms and villages within a 50 km radius of Rosetown, Saskatchewan. The area is known for its rich, productive farmland and also has oil wells on the western edge.

*continued*

Food is packed once per month but a hamper can be requested at any time for emergencies. The regular food hamper contains dry and canned foods, coupons for a litre of milk per person that can be redeemed at the local Co-op grocery store, and other items as available. Service users are given enough food to last five to eight days.

All food is donated or purchased in the community. Collection bins are located in grocery stores and the United Church. Fundraisers are held periodically in Rosetown and other communities to support the food bank. The food bank is operated by adult and student volunteers and has a volunteer board.

The food bank is experiencing a sharp increase in the need for its services. Usage has tripled over the past six years. Their June 2017 report[2] indicates a hundred people (60 adults and 40 children, 15 of whom were under the age of five) received food that month. The recipients include young families where one or both parents have jobs, seniors, welfare recipients, unemployed persons, and persons with addictions.

## Charity Instead of Policy Responses

The Canadian public policy response, with few exceptions, has been neither urgent nor effective. The food insecurity data discussed above clearly demonstrate that many Canadians are living in poverty. Economic policy and social policy have failed to ensure that citizens' basic human needs can be met. Government programs, such as Employment Insurance, disability pensions and social assistance (welfare), social housing, and seniors' pensions were designed to support citizens during times of economic hardship, vulnerability, and joblessness. But **neo-liberal** economic policies (deregulation, privatization, and globalization) coupled with a paring down of government supports have left a growing number of citizens unable to meet their basic needs.

Citizens have attempted to step into the breach. The first food bank in Canada opened in Edmonton in 1981 in the context of a downturn in the oil industry (Riches, 1986, 2002). It offered a more centralized response than the variety of charitable initiatives that labour, social, and religious organizations had organized in previous times of need, such as during the Great Depression of the 1930s. As in the United States, where the world's first food bank was established in Arizona in 1967, the food bank was seen as an effective emergency measure to stem hunger in the short term until economic conditions improved. But this institutional model has persisted and proliferated (Riches, 2002; Poppendieck, 1998). Almost four decades later, there are 550 food banks in Canada operating more than 3,000 food programs. The trend is not abating.

In light of this history, it is clear that food banks are no longer a short-term emergency measure but have become an entrenched component of the Canadian food and social policy landscape. Far from acknowledging that food banks represent a policy failure, as "concrete evidence of the breakdown of Canada's social safety net, particularly the federal unemployment insurance program and provincial social assistance," governments have welcomed these cost savings (Riches, 1986).

The charity response to food insecurity has several practical shortcomings. Relying on food donations and/or thrifty food purchases means that the food supply is limited, variable, and uncontrollable (Tarasuk & Eaken, 2003). Nutritional balance is hard to achieve. The kinds of foods distributed are predominantly processed, non-perishable, highly packaged groceries, despite efforts to source fresh foods. Furthermore, what is on offer cannot be tailored to clients' needs and choices, which renders unmet needs invisible (Tarasuk & Eaken, 2003). Even with a growing network of outlets, food banks can only meet a fraction of basic food needs, and only for those who are able to access them.

The offloading of government responsibility to vulnerable citizens has created a void too large for charitable individuals and community organizations to fill, so the corporate sector has become a major player in supporting Food Banks Canada through avenues like the Retail Food Program. Corporate retail giants, such as Loblaws and Walmart (the latter featured prominently on the Food Banks Canada home webpage (https://www.foodbankscanada.ca), make donations and channel their customers' donations to food banks. These highly visible corporate interventions not only help to burnish their images as socially responsible corporations (Riches, 2002), but are also used to move along large volumes of goods that are no longer suitable for retail sales. Diverting surplus food from landfills to food banks is an efficient, cost-saving measure and, along with the charitable tax credits available for donations, turns the privatization of the hunger response into a useful corporate instrument. But, as Riches points out, "the structural causes of food poverty are not addressed by surplus food redistribution" (Riches, 2002, p. 651).

The benevolence, compassion, and commitment of the thousands of volunteers working in and donating to food banks are unquestionable and laudable. Close to 40 per cent of food banks are run solely by volunteers, and the remainder rely heavily on volunteer assistance (Food Banks Canada, 2014). However, food banks are neither an adequate nor an appropriate vehicle to deal with food insecurity, as charity cannot be a substitute for coherent, adequately funded, reliable public policy that is necessary for the realization of the human right to food (Riches, 2002).

## Improving the Policy Responses

Decades of neo-liberal policies have changed the public discourse and expectations in such a way as to place a greater focus on individual efforts and failures rather than on social commitments owed to citizens by their elected governments. Citing unmanageable public debt and global competition, neo-liberal governments of the 1980s curtailed public spending by cutting existing programs and refusing to institute new ones. Their narrative that social programs were unaffordable and would render the Canadian economy uncompetitive was regularly reinforced by corporate-owned media and right-wing think-tanks. Cutting taxes and deficits eclipsed social expenditures as public/political priorities. (For more about public policy priorities and decision-making processes, see Chapter 4.)

This influence is particularly evident in the discourse on hunger. The shift from food security being a public responsibility to being a voluntary action to feed hungry people locates both the action and the focus away from government into the domain of non-governmental organizations, private-sector business, and individuals. In effect, it excuses government inaction. By privatizing both the problem and the responses, it depoliticizes the issue of food insecurity (Riches, 2011a). Government budgets have redirected public investment from social programs into physical infrastructure, business incentives, and job training. The well-being of citizens is now mediated through the job market.

This shift represents a further commodification of social relations where the right to food and the public responsibility for food policy drop out of public discourse. However, according to CCHS data, the majority of food-insecure households in Canada (62.2 per cent) were reliant on wages or salaries from employment (Tarasuk et al., 2016). The relentless corporate drive to achieve higher profits and greater market share through lowering wages and demanding a flexible workforce, aided by neo-liberal trade agreements and deregulation, is effectively undermining workplace security. Low-wage, part-time, and precarious employment leaves many workers without adequate incomes to pay for basic needs.

Responding to the question raised in the Case Examples box of the working single mom in Toronto requires challenging economic and social policies. While economic growth and low unemployment rates are positive indicators for food security, they are not efficacious unless the benefits of that economic strength are fairly distributed (Yalnizyan, 2013). This has not been the case in Canada. More than half of the growth in Canadian incomes since 2009 has accrued to the top 10 per cent of earners, with the top 1 per cent taking the majority of that increase. Furthermore, while the income gap in Canada is growing, the wealth gap is even greater (Macdonald, 2014). This gap means that property, including housing, is owned by fewer people and is increasingly out of range for lower-income earners. Without a radical restructuring of the economy to raise minimum wages, regulate job security, enforce corporate responsibility to employees, and ensure more equitable distribution of created wealth, the jobs strategy is not enough.

Those who are unable to find jobs or who are unable to work are vulnerable—60.9 per cent of households whose major source of income was social assistance lack food security. This situation attests to the inadequacy of these supports. Many advocacy groups and experts call for an increase in welfare payments and other social supports (Food Banks Canada, 2014; Dachner & Tarasuk, 2017; Food Secure Canada, 2016). Some argue that an even more comprehensive and reliable strategy to eliminate food insecurity and fight poverty would be to guarantee households a **basic income** (Kimmet, 2017; Cooper, 2017).

Another, more limited, policy is the school lunch program. While lunch programs target hungry children with the attendant risk of stigmatizing them, a variety of school lunch programs are now funded by school boards, as well as by provincial and municipal levels of government. The funding structures and sources for these vary a lot and no program is designed to do more than supplement students' daily food intakes by offering either breakfasts or lunches at school. However, if such programs became "universal, healthy-food school lunches," that strategy would de-stigmatize current programs, protect vulnerable children, enhance their development, and weave a needed thread into Canada's social safety net. There are international precedents for effective, universal school lunch programs, for example, in Japan and Finland (Weller, 2017).

---

## Box 14.2 School Lunches in Finland

Since 1948 Finland has had a universal school lunch program, with free school meals seen as an entitlement and not connected in any way to charity or food aid. The scope of this school lunch program includes focus on healthy meals and developing students' interest in and taste for nutritious food (http://www.oph.fi/download/47657_school_meals_in_finland.pdf).

As a Nordic welfare state, Finland has a strong tradition of meeting the basic welfare needs of all its citizens, and school lunches are part of that history and tradition. Nonetheless, current economic and social challenges in Finland have provoked the need for some charitable food distribution (Silvasti & Karjlainen, 2014). Given the experience and success of this non-stigmatizing program, an important policy option today is for Canada to develop a national school lunch program—some 70 years after such a program was established in Finland.

All of the above suggested policy changes, if implemented, would help to decrease the levels of food insecurity and extreme poverty in the short term. However, in order to secure long-term food security here and elsewhere, the food system itself will have to remain viable. In what follows, I examine the political, ecological, and structural impediments to securing the long-term right to food and I argue that major structural and political changes are required.

# Contextualizing the Right to Food

Canada has signed important international agreements to respect, protect, and fulfill the human right to food. The International Covenant on Economic, Social, and Cultural Rights (1976), the International Convention on the Rights of the Child (1992), the World Declaration on Nutrition (1992), and the Declaration on World Food Security (FAO, 1996) all include commitments to implement the right to food.

The first step to fulfilling the "right to food" commitment is to ensure food security. As discussed above, this requires fundamental changes in the content and direction of current social policy. Governments would have to fund programs that delivered adequate household incomes as well as ensure the availability and access to affordable food for all Canadians.

The United Nations **Food and Agriculture Organization (FAO)** defines *food security* as "a situation that exists when all people, at all times, have physical, social and economic access to sufficient, safe and nutritious food that meets their dietary needs and food preferences for an active and healthy life" (FAO, n.d., p. 28). This definition leaves open the questions of where the food comes from, under what conditions it was grown, and who controls the food markets and resources. It delineates food as a commodity without capturing the complex ways in which food interacts with, and defines, social and psychological well-being.

Food should not be viewed merely as a marketable commodity necessary for physical health. It shapes social well-being and plays a significant role in cultural and community identities, relationships, and meaning. So, while ensuring that everyone gets enough to eat is a necessary part of food security, it is not sufficient.

The full and secure enjoyment of the right to food is only possible in a context where other rights are respected, persons are accorded the agency to determine their diets, and communities can participate in shaping food cultures. Furthermore, the possibility of fulfilling the right to food depends on the natural environments necessary for agricultural production, fishing, gathering, and hunting. Abundant and healthy food relies on healthy

## Social Policy Change in Action

### Social Work and Social Policy: Vancouver's Downtown Eastside

*by Anna Cavouras*
*Anna Cavouras is a policy advocate and community researcher now based in Toronto.*

The complex issues and daily challenges of navigating a charitable food system—lineups, ID requirements, dietary restrictions, specific meal times, memberships—demand that social workers use policy as a powerful advocacy tool. The larger context of poverty and unemployment, combined with racism, classism, and social isolation, only emphasize this necessity.

Potluck Café Society is a financially sustainable social enterprise in Vancouver's Downtown Eastside (DTES) with a focus on ending the cycle of poverty and addressing the needs of the most nutritionally vulnerable residents. With this dual mandate, they seek to connect a "right-to-food" philosophy with community-minded solutions for the neighbourhood. One of the programs, DTES Kitchen Tables, employs a comprehensive systems change approach to working with residents, community food providers, and other stakeholders in the local food system.

DTES Kitchen Tables launched a series of initiatives to connect residents' voices to policy-makers and to educate the community about the relevance of food policy, specifically as it relates to the charitable food system. One such initiative, From Plate to Policy: A Photo-Journey of the Plates in the DTES (FPTP), was centred on residents' voices and their stories about the charitable food system in the DTES. It comprised a collection of photographs and quotes from community residents, each speaking about personal experiences of food (in)security. Participants were asked questions that centred their experiences as "eaters," not merely as recipients of charitable food. The first question was, "What does a meal mean to you?" followed by, "What is your favourite food memory?" These questions were meant to highlight the individuality of each person and to show food as a source of joy and nourishment, not just sustenance. Participants were also asked how they would improve food in the DTES.

The intention of FPTP was to share lived experiences from people directly impacted by the charitable food system in the DTES. Invited guests to the showcasing event, where participants presented their "photo journeys" to policy-makers as part of the project, included city of Vancouver staff, organizations that serve food in the DTES, funders from granting organizations, and the food bank.

It became apparent while working on this project that there is a place for policy in the smallest of details. Participants mentioned things such as being able to sit for a meal, or having the opportunity to choose what might go on their plate. The day-to-day actions of service providers matter in a right-to-food context, where this right can still be exercised through food served with dignity and choice, with the opportunity for meaningful dialogue and input by those who access the services. Social work plays a pivotal role in linking larger policies with organizational procedures. This project helped bring that reality to the forefront. Additionally, becoming vocal in provincial and federal policies around income and health can be done by organizations through the smallest of actions, such as providing meeting space for groups, up to larger actions, such as supporting political candidates or using social media to raise awareness.

The environment created by FPTP gave service providers the opportunity to listen to the voices of community residents. Attendees reflected on how this photo display gave true insight into how policies directly affect the people they work for. Building these connections through powerful personal narratives is an essential part of the role of social workers in a policy context.

ecological contexts. The right to food cannot be exercised in a context of degraded environments and unpredictable climates because these inhibit the production of needed food as well as the possibility of living healthy and active lives. Achieving the right to food is wholly dependent on protecting the environment.

## Current Food System: Environmental Impact

The story of agriculture in Canada is one of change and movement. From the immigrant farmers who largely displaced Indigenous hunter-gatherer food systems (Hurt, 1987) to the current high-tech, high-input, corporate-controlled agriculture displacing family farming, our food system continues to undergo rapid and radical changes. These changes have been driven largely by technology, trade, urbanization, and the politics of agriculture (Wiebe, 2017). Most of our agriculture system is highly industrialized, relying on fossil fuels, on chemicals and chemical fertilizers, and on genetic and information technologies. Canadian agricultural policy is dedicated to ramping up production and increasing exports. Under the neo-liberal policy agenda, these goals overshadow domestic concerns such as ensuring that Canadians enjoy food security or that food-producing resources are protected and enhanced. Agriculture policy is subsumed under economic goals shaped by trade policy.

Over the past two decades, Canadian governments and transnational agribusiness corporations have set aggressive food export targets and achieved them—tripling our agri-food exports between 1989 and 2014 (AAFC, 2010, 2015). Total Canadian agri-food exports had grown to over $55 billion per year by 2015, and the sights are set even higher. The government is targeting a rise in exports in the agricultural and food category to $75 billion a year by 2025 (Qualman, 2017). Meanwhile, Canadian food imports have more than tripled during the 1989–2014 period to $45 billion. If these trends continue, reaching the 2025 export target will mean that we will also be importing $65 billion of food by then— about $8,000 annually for an average family of four. In addition to the environmental impact of transporting massive amounts of food around the world, the increasing reliance on imported foods undermines local food production and markets. It binds citizens into the global food trade, ceding control over production, processing, pricing, and marketing to global agribusiness.

Industrial agriculture, with its reliance on fossil fuels and nitrogen fertilizers, is a key reason for Canadians having among the highest per capita rates of greenhouse gas (GHG) emissions (Weis, 2017). The attendant climate change is linked to an increase in catastrophic climate events such as droughts and floods that destroy crops. As Tony Weis notes, "Industrial agriculture is at once deeply implicated in and threatened by climate change, as well as in soil degradation and the over-consumption and pollution of water" (Weis, 2017, p. 132).

An estimated 70 per cent of the freshwater supplies globally are consumed by agriculture. This level of water use is unsustainable. Although Canada boasts a plentiful supply of fresh water, the high use of agricultural chemicals, fertilizers, and pesticides and the wastes from intensive livestock operations are causing serious water pollution in parts of the country. For example, Lake Winnipeg, the third largest freshwater lake in Canada (excluding the Great Lakes), was deemed "the most threatened lake" in 2013 largely due to agricultural runoff (Environment Canada, 2011; *CTV News*, 2013). The trend is towards more input usage, not less (Qualman, 2011) because the mining of soils for more production requires ever-more fertilizer as these soils become more degraded.

Current farming systems also are responsible for a sharp decline in biodiversity, which is among the biggest threats to future food security. The key benefit of high-input, intensive agriculture systems is its ability to produce large volumes of uniform, standardized product. Modern food processing, packing, and marketing industries require that, and consumers have come to expect it.

This situation raises two issues. First, because food comes from living organisms, the drive to achieve massive quantities of uniform "products," whether pigs or tomatoes, can only be successful if genetic diversity is suppressed, growing environments are artificially controlled, and all inputs such as feed or fertilizer are standardized and uniform. In short, the natural diversity of living, interacting organisms must be ruthlessly thwarted to achieve the industrial uniformity desired for the shelves of the supermarket (De Schutter, 2017). Second, while the standardization strategy is efficient for large-scale operations and global trade, it also results in a great deal of waste. The surplus that food corporations channel towards food banks is only part of the huge amount of unusable production or unmarketable food created by this system (*CBC News*, 2016). Valiant efforts to reduce food waste with manipulations to increase shelf life or to survive long-distance transport are only partially successful in reducing food waste—and come at an additional environmental cost.

But the future of food production depends on biological diversity, especially in the face of the changing climate. Resilience and adaptability, the hallmarks of diversity, are key to long-term food security. As a recent United Nations report to the Human Rights Council concluded:

> Today's dominant agricultural model is highly problematic, not only because of damage inflicted by pesticides, but also their effects on climate change, loss of biodiversity and inability to ensure food sovereignty. These issues are intimately interlinked and must be addressed together to ensure that the right to food is achieved to its full potential. (Human Rights Council, 2017)

Halting the ecological damage of the current food production system in Canada will require some fundamental changes to food and agriculture policy and practice. Food, farming, and the environment will have to be re-evaluated and revalued with a focus on sufficiency, ecological care, and biodiversity. Massive, concentrated production for export will have to give way to smaller-scale, environmentally sustainable, diverse farming along with more equitable and localized distribution, consumption, and marketing practices.

## Current Food System: The Corporate Role

Global trade and technological changes have moved food production from small-scale family-owned farms to corporate enterprises. As farm numbers continue to decline, rural communities are losing ground (Wiebe, 2017). The key beneficiaries of this trend have been agribusiness corporations and financiers, who have succeeded in gaining ownership of many food-producing resources and control much of the global and domestic food market (Qualman, 2001). The corporate drive for profits, production, and market power frequently overrides ecological care, culture, and democracy (Patel, 2007). A pattern of landownership concentration is occurring in parts of Canada as corporate investors seek to gain a firmer hold on the food system (Desmarais et al., 2016). Rural people, farmers, and Indigenous peoples are expendable where they interrupt the exploitation ("development") of natural resources. Exploitable farm labour, available through the Temporary Foreign Worker Programs, is used extensively.[3] Approximately 30,000 migrant farm workers come to Canada annually (De Schutter, 2012) (see Chapter 17).

The corporate control over all parts of the food system is global and consolidating. Governments have aided and abetted this concentration of corporate power through trade agreements and the deregulation of financial and agricultural markets. Mergers of major global agribusiness corporations are proceeding rapidly. The most recent round, when completed, could leave just three corporations controlling more than 60 per cent of the agrichemical and seed markets (ETC Group, 2016; Clapp, 2016).

Having so much control concentrated in a few corporate boardrooms makes the entire food system vulnerable. Food prices can rise rapidly, creating a crisis especially for those who rely on imported foods, as happened in 2008 (Bello & Baviera, 2010). While large quantities of agricultural products (primarily corn) were being diverted into the production of agro-fuels, human hunger abounded (Holt-Gimenez & Shattuck, 2010; La Via Campesina, 2008). Low-income countries and regions that had converted from self-sufficiency in basic staples to cash crops for export were the most vulnerable to shortages, being unable to soften the price hike.

The vexing question raised by the Rosetown family living in a productive, food surplus area (see Case Examples box) illustrates that the availability and proximity of food do not overcome the economic and power distances embedded in the current food system. The commodification and globalization of food markets create great distances between food and eaters (Kneen, 1989). Market mechanisms and values controlled by agribusiness corporations remove key food policy decisions affecting citizens' food security, food quality, and environments from public and democratic control, leaving hungry families in the midst of food abundance (Haynes, 2011). For example, the dismantling of the Canadian Wheat Board and changes to the Seeds Act have undermined farmers' seed saving and grain marketing power, handing these key components of agriculture over to transnational entities while concentration of landownership (noted above) gives investors control over essential food-producing resources (NFU, 2015a, 2015b). Meanwhile, citizens are denied knowledge about many of the supermarket foods they are buying (Knezevic, 2017).

How can the fundamental right to food be defended and exercised in this context?

# Food Sovereignty: The Right to Food

Neo-liberal changes to agriculture and food policy were catapulted into the international arena when negotiations on agriculture became a key component of the General Agreement on Tariffs and Trade (now the **World Trade Organization** [WTO]). This represented a green light for the revamping of food production and the consolidation of power for global food traders, undermining local food production and markets and threatening the survival of peasant and small-scale farmers.

Progressive peasant and farmer organizations responded to this danger by building a solidarity movement, **La Via Campesina**, to resist this agenda and envision a different framework—that of food sovereignty (see International Comparisons box). Food sovereignty "puts people at the centre of food, agriculture, livestock and fisheries policies, ensuring sufficient, healthy and culturally appropriate food for all individuals, peoples and communities; and rejects the proposition that food is just another commodity or component for international agri-business" (Nyeleni, 2007). It was understood from the outset that defence of peoples' rights to food and the protection of rural environments and cultures could only be done by retaking control of the food system from corporate agribusiness and financiers and placing it back in the hands of citizens, peasants, small-scale farmers, and local communities (La Via Campesina, 1996). The language of food sovereignty recognizes and articulates that food is political and that control over food systems is fundamental to democracy, justice, and social equity.

What began as a movement of peasant, Indigenous, rural workers', women's, and small-scale farmers' organizations in 1993 has grown into a global peoples' movement struggling for the fundamental reorientation of food production and an inclusive vision of ecological and social justice that cherishes cultural and biological diversity. The National Farmers Union, a founding member, was the only Canadian participant initially but the Quebec-based Union Paysanne is now also a member. As the former UN Special Rapporteur on the Right to Food, Olivier De Schutter, observed:

> The early food-sovereignty activists of La Via Campesina were quite prescient when it came to understanding how international trade could—and would shape food systems: standardizing farmers as well as the commodities they produce, encouraging the unsustainable growth of long-distance trade controlled by the agrifood behemoths, and neglecting local and regional markets. Resilience requires diversity, these activists campaigned, including a diversity of markets. (De Schutter, 2015)

The conceptual framework of food sovereignty has become a powerful instrument of advocacy and solidarity for environmental, social justice, and food movements and agencies around the world. Reframing the discourse has helped clarify and articulate values and relationships that challenge corporate, neo-liberal ideologies. For example, by refusing to adopt the individualizing discourse that constructs "household food security" by channelling the conversation into issues of quantity, quality, and accessibility of food, the food sovereignty perspective enables a different way of defining food problems and solutions. The breadth and vision of the framework concept of food sovereignty invite citizens, organizations, agencies, and movements into a discourse that is not limited to, or by, economic or market parameters. As the Havana Declaration states: "We affirm that food is not just another merchandise and that the food system cannot be viewed solely according to market logic" (WFFS, 2001).

The struggle for food sovereignty is a practical one. How can enough food be produced in ecologically sustainable ways to ensure that everyone's right to food can be fulfilled? Peoples who have lived within complex, diverse ecosystems have garnered extensive knowledge about living sustainably in those places. Peasants, Indigenous peoples, and some agronomists (Altieri, 2010) are developing, practising, and researching agro-ecology—integrated, small-scale production systems that reduce external inputs, recycle wastes, and combine elements of nature to maximize synergies. Agro-ecological food systems are not only highly productive but, by reducing inputs and working in harmony with nature, are enhancing biodiversity and "helping to cool the planet" (La Via Campesina, 2015). These food systems are focused on localizing food production and eliminating GHG emissions and the pollution of industrial agriculture.

## Indigenous Food Sovereignty

The damaging outcomes and dangers of Canada's current food system are clearly evident in many Indigenous communities. However, Indigenous peoples also offer examples of resilience and wisdom as a way forward for everyone (Dahlberg, 1994; LaDuke, 2008a).

As the data discussed earlier in this chapter show, there is an ongoing crisis of food insecurity in northern Indigenous communities that is especially acute for children (Food Secure Canada, 2017). Northern Canada is also experiencing the most radical

## International Comparisons

### La Via Campesina

La Via Campesina (LVC) is an international movement comprised of 164 local and national organizations in 73 countries from Africa, Asia, Europe, the Middle East, and the Americas. Altogether it represents about 200 million people of the land—peasants, small- and medium-scale farmers, landless people, pastoralists, rural women and youth, Indigenous peoples, migrants, and agricultural workers. The movement was founded in 1993 to resist the liberalization of agricultural trade and to defend small-scale food production, local markets, diverse cultures, and environments against corporate globalization and exploitation.

LVC first presented the basic principles of food sovereignty at the World Food Summit in Rome in 1996. Since then, food sovereignty has become a defining conceptual framework for food system analysts and activists. It has been incorporated into legislation and/or constitutions in Venezuela, Ecuador, Bolivia, Nicaragua, Mali, Brazil, Nepal, and Senegal.

LVC organizations have engaged in a wide range of struggles to retain or regain local control over land, territories, markets, and seeds. The movement has also integrated into its solidarity work gender equality, campaigns to stop violence against women, solidarity with migrant workers, and other social justice issues.

For more information on La Via Campesina, see https://viacampesina.org/en/.

effects of climate change. Melting pack ice, thawing permafrost, and the intrusion of new insects have become harbingers of what is to come.

The relationship between these two stark realities—food insecurity and severe climate change—is obviously complex. But the overarching issues are ones of colonial economic expansion supplanting traditional food systems. Resource extraction and other industrial intrusions have changed the physical landscape, and climate change is altering the ecology. Colonial policies such as forced relocation, settler education, residential schools, and a history of marginalization have undermined cultural practices and community structures. Meanwhile, the importation of southern foods and commercial food retailing is an inadequate substitute for what has been disrupted and destroyed.

In describing the dire situation of hunger in the North, Food Banks Canada notes that there is a food crisis among:

> First Nations, Métis and Inuit populations, who are experiencing a destabilizing transition from a subsistence to a market/mixed economy. Decreased access to traditional foods and increased reliance on store-bought foods are central aspects of this transition. In the North, the cost of store-bought food can be astronomical. The high cost of food, a lack of job opportunities, high levels of poverty, and decreasing consumption of traditional foods have combined to create a serious and pressing public health emergency.... (https://www.foodbankscanada.ca/Home.aspx)

In a critical analysis of how northern food issues are covered in the media, Hiebert and Power note that much of the public discourse is framed assuming the inevitability of the shift from "traditional to market-based diets, as food became tied to Western market participation and the involvement with settler endeavours" (Hiebert & Power, 2016, p. 107). This discourse focuses on the costs and availability of food items. Stories of the shockingly high costs of particular items, along with high shipping costs and the impossibility of getting some items, captivate the debate. In this context, government efforts to lower costs with subsidies and charitable donations seem like a reasonable, even heroic, response. But as Hiebert and Power point out, this scenario replicates the narrative of Inuit as passive, inferior, troubled recipients, reinforcing a colonial discourse and framing food insecurity as primarily a market issue.

The United Nations Special Rapporteur on the Right to Food visited some northern communities and reserved a section in his report for this issue. He reminded the government of its "duty to respect, protect and fulfill the right to food" (De Schutter, 2012, p. 5). He also noted that studies involving Inuit adults found that they had higher levels of several key vitamins and minerals on days when they ate "country food." This research uncovers the critical relationship between access to country foods and health (De Schutter, 2012).

Juxtaposing these findings with the ongoing destruction of northern environments raises the question of whether the "transition from a subsistence to a market/mixed economy" noted in the Food Banks Canada description is a solution to northern food insecurity or an extension of the problem. Strategies based on market ideology and economic individualism undermine traditional cultures that were based on subsistence provisioning and intra-community support, threatening the collapse of Indigenous cultures (Hiebert & Power, 2016). The hunger and high rates of diet-related diseases, such as diabetes, suffered by the children of the Cape Dorset family in the Case Examples box are an outcome of a complex array of factors that require a fundamental reorientation of perspectives and policies.

Health researcher Debbie Martin, having studied the relationship between Indigenous peoples' health and food, argues that approaching the problem as one of how to deliver more food from elsewhere "distances individuals from the contexts in which their foods are eaten and reinforces a growing ignorance about the interconnectedness of the health of people and the health of the planet" (Martin & Amos, 2017, p. 206). The current market-driven, industrial food system leaves many Indigenous people food insecure and ill. Winona LaDuke, Anishinaabekwe activist, environmentalist, economist, and writer, puts it succinctly when she claims that "the recovery of the people is tied to the recovery of food, since food itself is medicine not only for the body, but for the soul, for the spiritual connection to history, ancestors, and the land" (LaDuke, 2008b, p. 209).

**Indigenous food sovereignty** presents a complex set of challenges (Daigle, 2017). Although treaty rights relating to traditional forms of food provisioning such as hunting, fishing, and trapping are recognized and affirmed in the Constitution Act, 1982 (section 35), ongoing legal and economic barriers to exercising these rights persist at the provincial level.[4] Cultural disruption and displacement leave many outside of their traditional territories. Furthermore, the ecological damage inflicted on these territories is irreversible.

But Indigenous food sovereignty advocate Dawn Morrison, working within the Indigenous Food Systems Network, describes what this vision means and how it fits into the traditional values of her people. The first of the four principles that guide Indigenous communities striving for food sovereignty is:

> Food is a gift from the Creator. In this respect, the right to food is sacred and cannot be constrained or recalled by colonial laws, policies or institutions. Indigenous food sovereignty is ultimately achieved by upholding our long-standing sacred responsibilities to nurture healthy, interdependent relationships with the land, plants and animals that provide us with our food. (Morrison, 2011, p. 100)

## Expanding Social Work Praxis

The ecological damage of industrial, globalized agriculture is coupled with a failure to meet the basic human need for, and right to, food.

Arguing for "the inclusion of environmental justice in contemporary social work practice as one way of promoting inclusionary social work that meets some of the challenges of the 21st century" (Dominelli, 2014, p. 338), Lena Dominelli holds that current development models exacerbate inequalities and social injustice (Dominelli, 2012, 2013, 2014). This is made more evident in times of crisis when marginalized people often suffer the brunt of the disasters and when the inequalities of the underlying socio-economic, political, and cultural structures are exposed (Dominelli, 2014). She urges social work practitioners to broaden the scope of their analysis and work to take "environmental injustice" into account:

> I define environmental injustice as society's failure to ensure the equitable distribution of the Earth's resources in meeting human needs, simultaneously providing for the well-being of people and planet Earth today and in the future. Through this definition, I suggest that the current model of industrial development is "not fit for purpose" and that social workers have a role to play in formulating alternative models of socio-economic development by promoting environmental justice and organizing and mobilizing communities in meeting human need "without costing the earth" (Dominelli, 2014, p. 339).

Social work that embraces environmental justice includes advocating for, and helping to create, sustainable food systems that erase food insecurity.

## Chapter Summary

The arguments presented in this chapter reveal the deep interconnections among poverty, food security, rights, cultures, relationships, and the environment. Food issues are not just economic issues but have important political, social, and ecological dimensions.

Food security is necessary for physical, social, and psychological well-being. But the data and critique presented above clarify that neither charitable efforts nor corporate interests are adequate to ensure food security for all Canadians. The corporate sector, while highly influential in shaping menus, food consciousness, and markets—and increasingly controlling food-producing resources—does not have either the mandates or incentives to ensure food security.

In order to realize the right to food, governments must shed the neo-liberal agenda and refocus economic and social priorities. Implementing the right to food means that social policy respects the culture, dignity, and decision-making of individuals and communities, as well as allocating resources more equitably to combat inequality and vulnerability. This agenda is especially challenging in Indigenous communities where injustices and environmental destruction undermine traditional, sustainable food systems.

Ecological degradation and climate change pose a growing problem for food production and, hence, food security. In light of increasing evidence that industrial agriculture and the global, corporate-controlled food system are ecologically unsustainable, I argue that food and agriculture policy and practice must be radically restructured.

The above analysis opens the way to reformulate social policy on food. Using a critical food sovereignty framework moves food policy and activism beyond the immediate necessity of enough food for everyone to also engage with the deeper, longer-term viability of food systems. Long-term food security requires care for our ecological home (Mother Earth) along with social inclusion, equity, respect, and local democratic control over food resources and markets, that is, food sovereignty. Realizing the right to food entails all of these elements, which, when woven together in practical, effective ways, will enrich, inform, and enhance social work practices.

# Discussion Questions

1. What social policy changes would effectively resolve the food insecurity problems confronting vulnerable Canadians in the short term?

2. What are some of the current policies and practices that threaten long-term food security?

3. How does the industrialized global food system help to achieve food security in Canada? How does it hinder food security?

4. What are some of the necessary conditions for realizing the right to food? What role does food sovereignty have in achieving this?

# Notes

1. This reputation is confirmed by United Nations Human Development reports as well as by the popular media (see, e.g., Frisk, 2017).

2. Information given by a Rosetown Food Bank volunteer in a telephone interview, 10 August 2017.

3. For a cogent analysis of how a growing pool of surplus labour is affecting the dynamics of development, political economies, and food systems globally, see Wise and Veltmeyer (2016).

4. Criminal charges against Indigenous people for violating provincial hunting and fishing regulations are so prevalent that a pamphlet on how to deal with these offers guidance to Indigenous and Métis peoples in British Columbia: https://www.firstpeopleslaw.com/database/files/library/A_Guide_to_Aboriginal_Harvesting_Rights.pdf. For recent cases, see Poitras (2016).

# References

Agriculture and Agri-Food Canada (AAFC). *Canada's trade in agricultural products*. Various years. Ottawa: Supply and Services Canada.

———. (2010). Canadian trade highlights. Retrieved from www.agr.gc.ca

———. (2015). Import and export data: Canada at a glance. Retrieved from http://www5.agr.gc.ca/resources/prod/Internet-Internet/MISB-DGSIM/ATS-SEA/PDF/4679.pdf

Altieri, M.A. 2010. Scaling Up Agroecological Approaches for Food Sovereignty in Latin America. In *Food Sovereignty: Reconnecting Nature and Community*. ed. Wittman, H., Desmarais, A.A., and Wiebe, N. Halifax: Fernwood (pp. 120–32).

Bello, W., & Baviera, M. (2010). Capitalist agriculture, the food price crisis and peasant resistance. In H. Wittman, A.A. Desmarais, & N. Wiebe (Eds), *Food sovereignty: Reconnecting nature and community* (pp. 62–74). Halifax: Fernwood.

CBC News. (2016, 26 Oct.). A $31B problem: How Canada sucks at reducing food waste. Retrieved from http://www.cbc.ca/news/business/canada-food-waste-1.3813965

Clapp, J. (2016). Bigger isn't always better: What the proposed agribusiness mega mergers could mean for Canada. Retrieved from https://foodsecurecanada.org/resources-news/news-media/big-6-agribusiness-mega-mergers-canada

Cooper Institute. (2017). Liveable incomes. http://www.cooperinstitute.ca/content/page/programs_income/livable-income.html

CTV News. (2013, 5 Feb.). Lake Winnipeg named world's most threatened lake in 2013. Retrieved from http://www.ctvnews.ca/canada/lake-winnipeg-named-world-s-most-threatened-lake-in-2013-1.1143414

Dachner, N., & Tarasuk, V. (2017). Origins and consequences of and responses to food insecurity in Canada. In M. Koc, J. Sumner, & A. Winson (Eds), *Critical perspectives in food studies* (pp. 221–36). Toronto: Oxford University Press.

Dahlberg, K. A. (1994). A transition from agriculture to regenerative food systems. *Futures, 26*(2), 170–9.

Daigle, M. (2017). Tracing the terrain of Indigenous food sovereignties. *Journal of Peasant Studies*, 1–19. doi:10.1080/03066150.2017.1324423. Retrieved from http://dx.doi.org/10.1080/03066150.2017.1324423

Desmarais, A.A., Qualman, D., Magnan, A., & Wiebe, N. (2016). Investor ownership or social investment? Changing farmland ownership in

Saskatchewan, Canada. *Agriculture and Human Values*. Published online 11 Apr.

De Schutter, O. (2012). *Report of the Special Rapporteur on the Right to Food*. Retrieved from http://www.srfood.org/images/stories/pdf/officialreports/20121224_canadafinal_en.pdf

———. (2015). Don't let food be the problem: Producing too much food is what starves the planet. *Foreign Policy*. Retrieved from http://foreignpolicy.com/2015/07/20/starving-for-answers-food-water-united-nations/

———. (2017, 9 Jan.). Modern agriculture cultivates climate change—we must nurture biodiversity. *The Guardian*.

Dominelli, L. (2012). *Green social work*. Cambridge: Polity Press.

———. (2013). Environmental justice at the heart of social work practice: Greening the profession. *International Journal of Social Welfare*. *22*(4), 431–9. doi:10.1111/ijsw.12024

———. (2014). Promoting environmental justice through green social work practice: A key challenge for practitioners and educators. *International Social Work*, *57*(4), 338–45.

Environment Canada Manitoba Water Stewardship. (2011, June). *State of Lake Winnipeg: 1999 to 2007*. Retrieved from http://www.gov.mb.ca/waterstewardship/water_quality/state_lk_winnipeg_report/pdf/state_of_lake_winnipeg_rpt_technical_low_resolution.pdf

ETC Group. (2009). Who will feed us? Questions for the food and climate crises. Retrieved from http://www.etcgroup.org/en/node/4921

———. (2016). Merge-santo: New threat to food sovereignty. Retrieved from http://www.etcgroup.org/content/merge-santo-new-threat-food-sovereignty

Fairbairn, M. (2010). Framing resistance: International food regimes and the roots of food sovereignty. In H. Wittman, A.A. Desmarais, & N. Wiebe (Eds), *Food sovereignty: Reconnecting nature and community* (pp. 15–32). Halifax: Fernwood.

Food and Agriculture Organization 1996 Rome Declaration on World Food Security. http://www.fao.org/docrep/003/w3613e/w3613e00.htm

Food Banks Canada. (2014). *Hunger Count 2014*. Retrieved from https://www.foodbankscanada.ca/Hunger-in-Canada/Food-Banking-in-Canada.aspx

Food Secure Canada. (2016). *Zero hunger*. Retrieved from https://foodsecurecanada.org/resources-news/news-media/we-want-canada-zero-hunger

———. (2017). *Discussion Paper 1—Indigenous Food Sovereignty*. Retrieved from https://foodsecurecanada.org/sites/foodsecurecanada.org/files/DP1_Indigenous_Food_Sovereignty.pdf

Frisk, A. (2017, 7 Mar.). Canada named 2nd best country in the world . . . again, report finds. *Global News*. Retrieved from http://globalnews.ca/news/3293192/canada-2nd-best-country-2017-world-rankings-survey

Haynes, M. (2011). Hunger in the midst of plenty. *Socialist Review* (July/Aug.). Retrieved from http://climateandcapitalism.com/2011/07/16/hunger-in-the-midst-of-plenty/

Health Canada. (2017). Restricting unhealthy food and beverage marketing to children. Retrieved from https://www.canada.ca/en/health-canada/programs/consultation-restricting-unhealthy-food-and-beverage-marketing-to-children.html

Hiebert, B., & Power, E. (2016). Heroes for the helpless: A critical discourse analysis of Canadian national print media's coverage of the food insecurity crisis in Nunavut. *Canadian Food Studies*, *3*(2), 104–26. doi:http://dx.doi.org/10.15353/cfs-rcea.v3i2.149. Retrieved from http://canadianfoodstudies.uwaterloo.ca/index.php/cfs/article/view/149/164.

Holt-Gimeniz, E., & Shattuck, A. (2010). Agrofuels and food sovereignty: Another agrarian transition. In H. Wittman, A.A. Desmarais, & N. Wiebe (Eds), *Food sovereignty: Reconnecting food, nature and community* (pp. 76–90). Halifax: Fernwood.

Human Rights Council, United Nations. (2017). Report of the Special Rapporteur on the Right to Food on Pesticides. A/HRC/34/48.

Hurt, R. D. (1987). *Indian agriculture in America: Prehistoric to the present*. Lawrence: University Press of Kansas.

Kimmet, C. (2017). The poor need a guaranteed income, not our charity. *The Walrus*. Retrieved from https://thewalrus.ca/the-poor-need-a-guaranteed-income-not-our-charity/

Kirkpatrick, S., McIntyre, L., & Potestio, M. (2010). Child hunger and long-term adverse consequences for health. *Archives of Pediatrics and Adolescent Medicine*, *164*(8), 754–62.

Kneen, B. (1989). *From land to mouth: Understanding the food system*. Toronto: NC Press.

Knezevic, I. (2017). Making wise food choices: Food labelling, advertising, and the challenge of informed eating. In M. Koc, J. Sumner, & A. Winson (Eds), *Critical perspectives in food studies* (2nd edn, pp. 239–52). Toronto: Oxford University Press.

Koc, M., Bancerz, M., & Speakman, K. (2017). The interdisciplinary field of food studies. In M. Koc,

J. Sumner, & A. Winson (Eds), *Critical perspectives in food studies* (2nd edn, pp. 3–18). Toronto: Oxford University Press.

LaDuke, W. (2008a). Anishinaabe prophecy: Communities must choose the green path for food, energy. *Tribal College: Journal of American Indian Higher Education, 20*(2), 60–1. Retrieved from http://www.tribalcollegejournal.org/anishinaabe-prophecy-communities-choose-green-path-food-energy/

———. (2008b). Protecting the culture and genetics of wild rice. In M. K. Nelson (Ed.), *Original instructions, Indigenous teachings for a sustainable future* (pp. 206–14). Rochester, VT: Bear & Company.

La Via Campesina. (1996). The right to food and access to land. Position of La Via Campesina presented at the World Food Summit, Rome, 13–17 Nov. Retrieved from https://viacampesina.org/en/

———. (2008). Small farmers feed the world, industrial agro-fuels fuel hunger and poverty. Position Paper.

———. (2013, 23 Apr.). To reclaim our future, we must change the present: Our proposal for changing the system and not the climate. Press release. Retrieved from https://viacampesina.org/en/index.php/actions-and-events-mainmenu-26/world-social-forum-mainmenu-34/1405-to-reclaim-our-future-we-must-change-the-present-our-proposal-for-changing-the-system-and-not-the-climate

———. (2015). Food sovereignty: 5 steps to cool the planet and feed its people. Retrieved from https://www.viacampesina.org/en/index.php/actions-and-events-mainmenu-26/-climate-change-and-agrofuels-mainmenu-75/1717-food-sovereignty-5-steps-to-cool-the-planet-and-feed-its-people

Macdonald, D. (2014, Apr.). Outrageous fortune: Documenting Canada's wealth gap. Canadian Centre for Policy Alternatives. Retrieved from https://www.policyalternatives.ca/sites/default/files/uploads/publications/National%20Office/2014/04/Outrageous_Fortune.pdf

Martin, D., & Amos, M. (2017). What constitutes good food? Toward a critical Indigenous perspective on food and health. In M. Koc, J. Sumner, & A. Winson (Eds), in *Critical Perspectives in Food Studies* (pp. 205–20). Toronto: Oxford University Press.

Morrison, D. (2011). Indigenous food sovereignty: A model for social learning. In H. Wittman, A.A. Desmarais, & N. Wiebe (Eds), *Food sovereignty in Canada: Creating just and sustainable food systems* (pp. 97–113). Halifax: Fernwood.

National Farmers Union (NFU). (2015a). Losing our grip. Retrieved from http://www.nfu.ca/issues/losing-our-grip-2015-update

———. (2015b, Feb.). Save our seed. Retrieved from http://www.nfu.ca/issues/save-our-seed

Nyeleni. (2007). *Proceedings of the Forum for Food Sovereignty*, Selingue, Mali, 23–7 Feb. Retrieved from www.nyeleni.org.

Patel, R. (2007). *Stuffed and starved: Markets, power and the hidden battle for the world's food system.* Toronto: HarperCollins.

Picard, A. (2017, 7 Mar.). Children don't need a daily diet of junk-food ads. *Globe and Mail.* Retrieved from https://beta.theglobeandmail.com/opinion/children-dont-need-a-daily-diet-of-junk-food-ads/article34221537/?ref=http://www.theglobeandmail.com&

Poitras, J. (2016, 8 Mar.). Province should resolve grey area in aboriginal hunting rights, 2 judges say. *CBC News.* Retrieved from http://www.cbc.ca/news/canada/new-brunswick/judges-aboriginal-treaty-rights-hunting-1.3480886

Pollan, M. (2006). *The omnivore's dilemma: A natural history of four meals.* New York: Penguin.

Poppendieck, J. (1998). *Sweet charity: Emergency food and the end of entitlement.* New York: Penguin.

Qualman, D. (2001). *The farm crisis and corporate power.* Ottawa: Canadian Centre for Policy Alternatives.

———. (2011). Advancing agriculture by destroying farms? The state of agriculture in Canada. In H. Wittman, A.A. Desmarais, & N. Wiebe (Eds), *Food sovereignty in Canada: Creating just and sustainable food systems* (pp. 20–42). Halifax: Fernwood.

———. (2017, 25 Apr.). Far-flung food: Local food falls victim to a fixation on food exports. *Graphic Descriptions Blog.* Retrieved from www.darrinqualman.com

Riches, G. (1986). *Food banks and the welfare crisis.* Ottawa: Canadian Council on Social Development.

———. (2002). Food banks and food security: Welfare reform, human rights and social policy. Lessons from Canada? *Social Policy & Administration 36*(6), 648–63.

———. (2009). Right to food within Canada: International obligations, domestic compliance. In G. G. James, R. Ramsay, & G. Drover (Eds), *International social work: Canadian perspectives.* Toronto: Thompson Educational Publishing.

———. (2011a). Why governments can safely ignore hunger: Corporate food charity keeps hunger off political agenda. Ottawa: Canadian Centre for Policy Alternatives. Retrieved from https://www.policyalternatives.ca/publications/monitor/why-governments-can-safely-ignore-hunger

———. (2011b). Thinking and acting outside the charitable food box: Hunger and the right to food in rich societies. *Development in Practice, 21*(4–5). Retrieved from http://www.tandfonline.com/doi/abs/10.1080/09614524.2011.561295

Schlosser, E. (2001). *Fast food nation: The dark side of the all-American dream.* New York: Houghton Mifflin.

Silvasti, T., & Karjlainen, J. (2014). Hunger in a Nordic welfare state. In G. Riches & T. Silvasti (Eds), *First world hunger revisited: Food charity or the right to food?* (pp. 72–86). London: Palgrave Macmillan.

Statista. (n.d.) Food advertising—statistics & facts. Retrieved from https://www.statista.com/topics/2223/food-advertising/

Tarasuk, V., & Eaken, J. (2003). Charitable food assistance as symbolic gesture. *Social Science & Medicine, 56*, 1505–15.

———, Mitchell, A., & Dachner, N. (2016). *Household food insecurity in Canada, 2014.* Toronto: PROOF. Retrieved from http://proof.utoronto.cahttp://proof.utoronto.ca/wp-content/uploads/2016/04/Household-Food-Insecurity-in-Canada-2014.pdf

United Nations Human Development Report. (2016). Retrieved from http://hdr.undp.org

Vozoris, N., & Tarasuk, V. (2003). Household food insufficiency is associated with poorer health. *Journal of Nutrition, 133*(1), 120–6.

Weis, T. (2017). The political ecology approach to industrial food production. In M. Koc,

J. Sumner, & A. Winson (Eds), *Critical perspectives in food studies* (pp. 118–34). Toronto: Oxford University Press.

Weller, C. (2017, 2 Aug.). Japan's mouth-watering school lunch program is a model for the rest of the world. *Tech Insider.* Retrieved from http://www.businessinsider.com/japans-amazing-school-lunch-program-2017-7

Wiebe, N. (2017). Crisis in the food system: The farm crisis. In M. Koc, J. Sumner, & A. Winson (Eds), *Critical perspectives in food studies* (pp. 138–53). Toronto: Oxford University Press.

——— & Wipf, K. (2011). Nurturing food sovereignty in Canada. In H. Wittman, A. Desmarais, & N. Wiebe (Eds), *Food sovereignty in Canada: Creating just and sustainable food systems* (pp. 1–19). Halifax: Fernwood.

Winson, A. (2013). *The industrial diet: The degradation of food and the struggle for healthy eating.* Vancouver: University of British Columbia Press.

Wise, R. D., & Veltmeyer, H. (2016). *Agrarian change, migration and development.* Halifax: Fernwood.

World Forum on Food Sovereignty (WFFS). (2001). *Final Declaration of the World Forum on Food Sovereignty.* Havana, Cuba. Retrieved from fao.org/righttofood/kc/down-loads/vl/docs/AH290.pdf

Yalnizyan, A. (2013, 19 Sept.). Five years of economic recovery have been far from equal. *Globe and Mail.* Retrieved from https://beta.theglobeandmail.com/report-on-business/economy/economy-lab/five-years-of-economic-recovery-have-been-far-from-equal/article14403689/?ref=http://www.theglobeandmail.com

# 15 Canadian Health Care Policy

## Gaps, Inequalities, and Solutions

*Daniyal Zuberi and Melita Ptashnick*

---

### Chapter Objectives

*This chapter will help you to develop an understanding of:*

- the structure of Canada's health care system and contemporary debates on cost, equity, access, and outcomes;
- the strengths and weaknesses of Canada's health care system;
- how different people experience the health care system based on their social location;
- proposals for improving the quality of Canada's health care system.

---

## Introduction

This chapter will evaluate the effectiveness of health care policy in Canada by examining contemporary debates about cost, comprehensiveness, access, and equity. Canadians value the country's universal health care system, but the system is under pressure due to the growing needs of patients. National health care expenditure as a percentage of gross domestic product (GDP) is inadequate to meet current needs, especially in light of population growth and inflation. Perceived costs have slowed progress towards universal public insurance coverage for prescription medications in Canada (Morgan, Law, Daw, Abraham, & Martin, 2015). The comprehensiveness of public health insurance coverage remains too narrow, as it is focused primarily on physician and hospital services.

While Canada's health care system is performing better than those of many other countries in terms of access, more work needs to be done to address access and equity challenges. Canada ranked 17th out of 195 countries in health care access and quality in 2015 (GBD 2015 Healthcare Access and Quality Collaborators, 2017). Yet, a shortage of family physicians exists, particularly in rural areas, and long wait times persist for priority treatments, such as cataract and joint replacement surgeries (McGurran, 2013). In addition, despite policies to provide universal access, the health care system struggles to address systemic inequities between different individuals and regions. Individual Canadians experience health care differently, depending on their access to resources, health needs, social and cultural capital, and geographic location. Indigenous people, rural and remote residents, and low-income Canadians are most disadvantaged by these inequities.

---

### Case Examples    Health and Socio-economic Context

**George**, 73, has lung cancer and heart disease. He is Métis, speaks Dene K'e, and lives with his daughter's family in a rural town in northeastern British Columbia.

**Amy**, 41, completed an undergraduate degree in computer science at Carleton University in Ottawa. She works as a software engineer at a major technology company downtown. The combined annual income for Amy and her husband is over $100,000. Amy's 15 year-old daughter competes in Scottish Highland dance competitions on weekends to connect with her grandparents' heritage.

**Hanan**, 34, is an immigrant from Lebanon, who lives with her husband and two young children in a low-rent apartment in rural New Brunswick. Hanan's husband works part-time as a general labourer. Due to depression, child-care responsibilities, and lack of a social network, Hanan has struggled for more than a year after arrival trying to find a job.

---

In this chapter, we start with a brief review of the socio-historical context of the Canadian health care system. Next, we address physician shortages and surgical wait times before delving into service inequalities experienced by segments of the Canadian population. The chapter concludes with a section on mental health care issues and a summary.

# The Socio-Historical Context of Health Care Policy in Canada

According to the Canada Health Act, the goals of Canadian health care policy are to preserve the physical and mental well-being of Canadians and support access to health services without barriers (Government of Canada, 2012b). The Canada Health Act defines the criteria related to the principles of comprehensiveness, universality, accessibility, portability, and public administration for insured health services and extended health care services that provinces must meet to receive Canada Health Transfer funds from the federal government. Provincial health insurance plans must cover health services from medical practitioners and hospitals without impeding access for all insured provincial residents.

In practice, the comprehensiveness of public health insurance in Canada is narrow, focusing mainly on physician and hospital services (Adams, 2016). There are some provincial government subsidies for long-term care and prescription medications, but they often target populations based on income or age and may involve user fees (Marchildon, 2013). While extended care services, such as home care and nursing home services, are not insured under the Canada Health Act, they can be provided if a province so chooses (Lanoix, 2017). However, the availability of home care varies across the nation because the five principles of the Canada Health Act do not regulate these services. Unmet long-term care needs are burdening the acute care system, where 15 per cent of the beds are occupied by seniors waiting for long-term care, such as nursing home services (Adams & Vanin,

2016). An increased focus on disease prevention programs is needed to reduce the long-term care requirements of Canada's aging population.

The Romanow Report (2002) recommended that insured health services in the Canada Health Act be expanded to include prescription medications. Canada is the only nation with a universal health insurance program that does not include universal coverage for prescription medications (Morgan, Law, Daw, Abraham, & Martin, 2015). Canadians without medication insurance coverage, those from low-income house-holds or those in poor health are the most likely not to fill their prescriptions for cost reasons(Law, Cheng, Dhalla, Heard, & Morgan, 2012). A study estimated that publicly funded universal prescription medication coverage in Canada would increase government expenditures by $1 billion and reduce private-sector costs by $8.2 billion (Morgan et al., 2015). However, this estimate of government expenditures is likely too high because a universal public medication insurance plan would also eliminate the need for tax sub-sidies for employer-sponsored private medication insurance plans (Morgan, Daw, & Law, 2013). In the 2018 Budget Plan, the federal government reported that an Advisory Council will study options about the implementation of a national pharmacare program (Department of Finance Canada, 2018).

## International Comparisons

### Long-Term Care Reform in the Netherlands: Universalism versus Expenditure

In 1968, the Dutch Exceptional Medical Expenses Act created a national compulsory social insurance scheme to cover excessive long-term residential care costs in facilities, such as care homes and nursing homes; later, home-care coverage was added for long-term care services at home (Da Roit, 2012; Kroneman et al., 2016). Taxes and income-based contributions, later supplemented by co-payments, finance the system (Da Roit, 2012). Public regulations control private care delivery mainly through non-profit provider organizations, and there is no discrimination in long-term care insurance coverage based on income, age, residence location, or disability type (Da Roit, 2012; Maarse & Jeurissen, 2016).

Differences in public expenditure for long-term care among Organisation for Economic Co-operation and Development (OECD) countries mainly reflect variation in formal long-term care arrangements as compared to informal care provision by family members (OECD, 2015). Canada under-invests in long-term care as compared to other OECD countries (Table 15.1).

Even in the Netherlands, which features high levels of long-term care expenditures, potential increases in demand from an aging population and an expanding deficit from the economic crisis have challenged the universal nature of the Dutch long-term care insurance plan and its financial sustainability, which resulted in comprehensive reform from 2006 to 2015 (Da Roit, 2012; Kroneman et al., 2016; Maarse & Jeurissen, 2016). Only those requiring 24-hour care can now access residential long-term care, as the reform aims to shift to an aging-at-home paradigm (Maarse & Jeurissen, 2016). Home nursing and personal care

*continued*

**Table 15.1**  Long-Term Care Public Expenditure for OECD Countries, 2013 (% of GDP)

| | |
|---|---|
| Netherlands | 4.3 |
| Sweden | 3.2 |
| Norway | 2.4 |
| Denmark | 2.3 |
| Finland | 2.2 |
| Japan | 2.1 |
| France | 1.9 |
| Belgium | 1.9 |
| Switzerland | 1.8 |
| Iceland | 1.8 |
| OECD average | 1.7 |
| Luxembourg | 1.3 |
| Austria | 1.2 |
| Canada | 1.2 |

Source: Data from OECD (2015).

funding are now decentralized to health insurers, who are responsible for contracting these services. The responsibility for supports for people at home, such as housekeeping and meals, is now decentralized to municipalities, and the budget for these activities has been reduced (Kroneman et al., 2016).

The underlying policy assumptions that social care services can be provided more efficiently by family members and community networks are contested (Maarse & Jeurissen, 2016). Critics point out that a considerable amount of informal care was already being provided by family members and estimates of capacity to increase informal care were inflated. In the past, eligible clients had the right to professional domestic care and social support, but now municipalities can substitute professional care with care from volunteers or neighbours. Furthermore, some municipalities discontinued domestic care or severely decreased the care hours, while lawsuits revealed that municipalities did not accurately assess clients' needs before reducing care.

## Funding Trends

Economic and political contexts affect health care system outcomes. After decades of deficit financing, a recession in the 1990s caused provincial governments in Canada to implement regionalized health care systems in an attempt to control costs (Marchildon, 2016). However, by the end of the decade, some provinces consolidated regional health authorities to gain economies of scale. A major obstacle to the success of regionalization was that the regional health authorities lacked the mechanisms to co-ordinate primary health care (Marchildon, 2015). While statutes indicated that regional health authorities would be expected to co-ordinate primary health care, the provincial ministries of health retained centralized control of physician payments because medical organizations would not support contract arrangements that made physicians accountable to the regional health authorities. This legacy of medical organizations' power dates back to the beginnings of public health insurance in Canada, when each province adopted the fee-for-service schedule for physician services from the existing insurance company that was approved by the medical association in the province (Lazar, 2013). Thus, historically, provincial governments recognized the medical associations as the bargaining agents for physicians, which solidified the associations' insider status.

From 2004 to 2011, right-of-centre provincial political environments tended to curtail progressive change in the health care system, despite increased federal spending. The Romanow Report recommended that the Canada Health Transfer include an increased share of federal funding to rebalance funding between federal and provincial governments, plus an escalator provision proportionate to the country's economic growth and payment capacity. However, additional federal funding in 2003–4 resulted in smaller changes in medicare compared to the 1990–2003 period. As a result of the political shift to the right, most newly elected governments lacked strong election commitments to health care policy change (Lazar, 2013). One change of note that did occur during the 2004–11 period was a shift in public opinion, which allowed private for-profit hospitals and clinics to play a larger role within the publicly funded system.

By 2010, total health expenditure was 11.4 per cent of GDP in Canada, compared to an OECD average of 9.5 per cent (McGurran, 2013). In Canada, 71.1 per cent of health care expenditure was public. However, in 2011 the federal government announced its plan to implement **per capita funding** for health care in 2014–15 and reduce annual funding increases from 6 per cent to a GDP-linked amount that could be as low as 3 per cent in 2017–18, creating potential fiscal stress for the provinces (Gardner, Fierlbeck, & Levy, 2014; Marchildon & Mou, 2014). The per capita funding model will potentially affect most adversely British Columbia, Quebec, and Atlantic Canada due to their high proportion of seniors or small total population size with a high percentage of rural residents (Marchildon & Mou, 2014). Mainly due to government fiscal restraints and modest economic growth over the 2011–16 period, Canadian health care expenditure as a proportion of GDP trended down from its 2010 peak, and spending per capita barely met inflation and population growth rates (CIHI, 2016a). Fiscal restraint in the face of growing needs has translated into a failure to address systemic challenges within Canada's health care system in several equity and access domains.

## Towards Self-Management of Health Care for Indigenous Peoples

The legacy of colonial policies in Canada created the marginalization of Indigenous peoples and inequitable health outcomes (Fridkin, 2012). Direct involvement of Indigenous peoples in health policy decisions can address power imbalances in the policy creation process and the resulting health inequities. The self-government agreements achieved by such groups as the James Bay Cree, the Nisga'a, and the Inuit of Nunavut and northern Quebec provide opportunities for Indigenous engagement in health policy, planning, and delivery (National Collaborating Centre for Aboriginal Health, 2011). (See Chapter 6 for more on Indigenous engagement in health care planning.) Until recently at the provincial level, only the Ontario and BC health systems had formal avenues for Indigenous input into regionalized health structures and these avenues were only advisory in nature (Lavoie, Kornelsen, Boyer, & Wylie, 2016). However, the new First Nations Health Authority in BC is anticipated to play a more direct role in determining health care services for Indigenous people in the province.

Consensus among First Nations and federal and provincial governments resulted in a new First Nations health governance structure in BC with the goal of returning decision-making to First Nations communities (Gallagher, Mendez, & Kehoe, 2015). The tripartite agreement focuses on the transfer of federal health programs to the First Nations Health Authority, the service delivery section of the new First Nations health governance structure (Gallagher et al., 2015; Her Majesty the Queen in Right of Canada, Her Majesty the Queen in Right of the Province of British Columbia, & First Nations Health Society, 2011). The programs are for status First Nations residents on reserve or, in the case of the Non-Insured Health Benefits Program, for status First Nations residents in the province (Her Majesty the Queen in Right of Canada et al., 2011). The First Nations Health Authority focuses on community-based prevention and primary care services using traditional and Western practices to provide culturally safe and effective services (Gallagher et al., 2015). The First Nations Health Authority does not duplicate health services already provided by the provincial Ministry of Health or regional health authorities.

## Shortage of Family Physicians

All too many Canadians continue to struggle to secure a regular family physician. Instead, these individuals must resort to drop-in health clinics or emergency rooms for care when ill. This lack of access disproportionately impacts those who are most vulnerable and who would benefit from the consistency of care provided by a family physician. For example, in addition to providing direct patient care, primary care physicians also act as gatekeepers to specialists and advanced medical care in cutting-edge facilities through the referral process in the Canadian health care system (Bissonnette, Wilson, Bell, & Shah, 2012).

Shortages of general practitioners are particularly acute in rural areas and thus are often a subject of focus for redistribution and retention policies. In New Brunswick, for example, provincial government policy initiatives sought to increase health care services to the province's under-served rural francophone minority by offering opportunities for members of this population to complete their medical training in their home communities (Beauchamp et al., 2013). However, while follow-up research showed that New Brunswick francophone family physicians with a rural background were more likely than their urban counterparts to open their initial practice in a rural community, a rural background did not confer a higher likelihood than an urban background of continuing to practise in a rural community. Research on physician retention in rural Alberta showed a combination of professional, personal, and community factors, such as workload, connections to community members, and fundraisers for health facilities, encouraged physician retention (Cameron, Este, & Worthington, 2012).

Turnover and retirement of family physicians exacerbate endemic shortages, particularly in rural regions (Randall, Crooks, & Goldsmith, 2012). In rural Ontario, a study of chronically ill patients needing to transition to new family doctors due to practice closures found that a relative absence of referrals often led to months or years without a regular family physician for study participants. In the absence of a regular family doctor, patients can experience barriers in accessing preventative care, such as regular monitoring of laboratory tests, and often lack access to assistance programs that require a family physician's forms or referrals, such as for disability benefits and specialist care (Crooks, Agarwal, & Harrison, 2012).

Some policy approaches seek to alter Canadians' access to primary health care by increasing the number of patient attachments to general practitioners. From 2014 to 2016, the General Practice Services Committee, a collaboration of the BC government and physicians, created and financially supported the "A GP for Me" initiative (General Practice Services Committee, 2015). The program brought 416 new physicians to the province, attached 178,000 residents without a family doctor to a general practitioner, and transferred 130,000 patients from closing practices to new family doctors.

Yet, access to care is not just about the number of family physicians but also about the comprehensiveness of care. In the period 2011–14, the number of family physicians per 100,000 Canadians rose from 106 to 114, ranking Canada eighth out of 34 OECD countries in family doctor to population ratio. However, nearly 15 per cent of Canadians over the age of 11 still could not access a regular general practitioner (CIHI, 2016b; OECD, n.d.; Statistics Canada, 2015). Per capita measures do not capture the comprehensiveness of care provided.

Fewer family physicians now undertake the responsibility of providing comprehensive care for patients (Ladouceur, 2012). In one 2007–12 study in BC, 24 per cent of the province's family physicians were deemed to have **high-responsibility practice styles** and 36 per cent to have **low-responsibility practice styles** (McGrail et al., 2015). High-responsibility physicians had seen 87 per cent of their patients repeated times during the period. Increased continuity of care through a regular family doctor reduces avoidable emergency department visits and hospitalizations (CIHI, 2015). In contrast, low-responsibility physicians had seen only 33 per cent of their patients more than once in the five years, suggesting the growing influence of walk-in clinics in provision of care (McGrail et al., 2015). High-responsibility family physicians scored 8 to 12 times higher than low-responsibility doctors for referrals to specialists and prevention activities—patterns of practice consistent with comprehensive care.

Policy reforms aim to build multidisciplinary teams of health care professionals. From 2000 to 2006, the federal Primary Health Care Transition Fund provided funding to provinces and territories to support reforms, such as creating primary health care multidisciplinary teams to provide comprehensive care, including co-ordination with other care levels (Government of Canada, 2012a). In rural British Columbia, inclusion of nurse practitioners in practices with family doctors increased access to primary care, reduced hospital admissions, and encouraged retention of physician colleagues (Roots & MacDonald, 2014). The salaried fee schedules for nurse practitioners supported longer patient appointments, which boosted preventative care and treatment for multiple health concerns. This resulted in a decreased need for future appointments. Wait times for appointments decreased, resulting in significantly fewer emergency room visits and hospital admissions.

# Priority Treatment Wait Times

In Canada, policy innovation to reduce wait times has been a key priority for many years. Excessive wait times for health care services, such as surgery, fail to meet the accessibility principle of the Canada Health Act (McGurran, 2013). To decrease wait times and increase access, Canadian national and regional governments initiated the 10-Year Plan to Strengthen Health Care in 2004, which focused on priority areas, such as joint replacement and sight restoration.

Wait times for surgeries for eye cataracts or joint replacement require improvement. From 2012 to 2016, the proportion of patients receiving cataract surgery within the benchmark of 112 days decreased from 83 per cent to 73 per cent in Canada. In particular, patients in Manitoba, Nova Scotia, and BC often had to wait beyond the benchmark time for their cataract or joint replacement surgery. In Manitoba, 66 per cent had their cataract surgeries after the benchmark of 16 weeks. In Nova Scotia, 62 per cent waited beyond the six-month benchmark for knee surgery.

Nationally, it has been difficult to sustain an initial surge in joint replacement surgeries. From 2000 to 2009 knee replacement surgeries increased by 96.8 per cent and hip replacements rose by 56.1 per cent in Canada (McGurran, 2013). However, a study found that a hospital factory model, which allowed a motivated team to focus exclusively on simple hip and knee surgeries without complications, and no issues of staffing, operating theatre, or bed capacity, was required to comply with orthopedic surgery wait time goals (Amar, Pomey, SanMartin, De Coster, & Noseworthy, 2015). National wait times for joint replacement plateaued from 2012 to 2016: 79 per cent of hip replacement patients and 73 per cent of knee replacement patients received their surgery within the benchmark of 182 days in 2016 (CIHI, 2017).

Long waits reduce the quality of life for patients. In Quebec, a follow-up study six months after total knee replacement surgery found that patients who had waited more than nine months for the surgery experienced the worst pain in the other knee and the most difficulties with work or daily activities compared to patients who had received more timely surgery (Desmeules, Dionne, Belzile, Bourbonnais, & Frémont, 2012).

# Inequitable Distribution of the Social Determinants of Health

While many government documents in Canada contain concepts about the social determinants of health—how social and economic circumstances influence the health of individuals and communities—limited attention is paid to these concepts in general public health practice and mainstream media discourse (Hayes et al., 2007; Raphael, 2000, 2011). The **social determinants of health** depict the resources a society distributes to its members (Raphael, 2011). Raphael (2011) argues that the unequal distribution of the social determinants of health to a society's members is due to the power of those who devise and profit from health and social inequities. Raising public awareness about the class-related influences that shape policy is one avenue to counter power groups.

# Inequality in Health Care Provision

## Geographic Inequalities

Residents of rural and remote communities face challenges accessing emergency, surgical, and maternity care close to home. Policies supporting enhanced physician training strategies, the re-emergence of midwifery, and inter-professional collaboration provide avenues to address care barriers in rural and remote communities. In the Northwest Territories, emergency care was particularly challenging for communities without hospitals due to the lack of qualified staff and the reliance on medical air transport (Oosterveer & Young, 2015). Canadians in the northern territories most frequently report not having a regular family doctor: Nunavut 82.5 per cent, Northwest Territories 57.7 per cent, and Yukon 26.1 per cent (Statistics Canada, 2015). Except for ice roads for a period during the winter, some communities in the Northwest Territories can only be reached by air, and weather conditions can delay emergency air transport up to six days (Oosterveer & Young, 2015).

In light of weather, local geography, and expense affecting transportation, some researchers, in a "Joint Position Paper on Rural Surgery and Operative Delivery," have recommended that rural patients receive surgical care as close to home as possible from services that are best able to meet their predicted requirements (Iglesias et al., 2015). Health care restructuring and difficulties in recruiting and retaining practitioners had led to a decline in small surgical services in Canadian rural communities, often forcing women to travel to regional centres for maternity care (Grzybowski, Stoll, & Kornelsen, 2013). To reverse this trend, general practitioners with enhanced surgical skills, who can perform certain surgeries such as Caesarean deliveries, can provide operative care in rural communities that are too small to support obstetricians. In BC rural communities that are supported by general practitioners with enhanced surgical skills, nearly 80 per cent of women deliver locally, whereas only one-quarter of women deliver in their local hospital when no local surgical services are present. Furthermore, surgical outcomes for general practitioners with enhanced surgical skills and obstetricians are comparable. In addition to increasing access equity, local surgical services aid community recruitment and retention of family physicians, which supports broader health care services, including emergency care (Iglesias et al., 2015).

Policy statements supported by the Society of Rural Physicians of Canada outline training strategies to enhance the skills of general practitioners and specialists in rural medical practices. Iglesias et al. (2015) recommend that core competency curricula for operative delivery (e.g., C-sections) and enhanced surgical skills be developed and delivered in recognized programs to train and certify general practitioners. The Society of Rural Physicians of Canada also recommends identifying which specialties are required as core services for community health centres and supporting these core specialties through curricula and non-urban training rotations (Hillyard et al., 2012).

Midwifery may be a potential solution to the shortage of maternity care providers in rural and remote regions (Stoll & Kornelsen, 2014). After the medicalization of childbirth starting in the mid-nineteenth century eventually led to the sidelining of midwifery practice in the mid-twentieth century in Canada, midwifery began to reappear in the formal health care system of some provinces in the 1990s (Olson & Couchie, 2013). A study of midwife-involved births in rural BC for the period 2003–8 found that the incidence of poor outcomes for newborns was very low, although the perinatal death rate (stillbirth or death within seven days of birth) was higher for women who lived in communities more than two hours away from a hospital with maternity services (Stoll & Kornelsen, 2014). The rate of transferring care from a midwife to a doctor was highest for women who resided in communities more than one hour away from access to C-sections.

Primary maternity care collaboration among physicians, nurses, and midwives may be another potential solution to shortages of family physicians and obstetric nurses in rural Canada, but macro-level barriers to collaboration need to be resolved (Munro, Kornelsen, & Grzybowski, 2013). A study in rural BC found that inequities in payment models between physicians and midwives caused physicians to display territorialism about their patient group. Physician-controlled medical advisory committees also rejected midwives' applications for hospital admitting privileges. An integrated, inter-professional mode of contract negotiations between the professional organizations and the government is needed to assist policy creation of an inter-professional funding model and hospital privileging process.

## Indigenous Peoples

Discrimination embedded in health care education institutes and practised in health care facilities reinforces stereotypes of Indigenous peoples and contributes to their suboptimal health care experiences. At the University of Calgary, medical students described discriminatory attitudes of instructors towards Indigenous people (Ly & Crowshoe, 2015). While medical students tended to understand that stereotyping was associated with discrimination, they also postulated that such stereotypes were grounded in reality. At the health care facility level, a study of health care access of Indigenous and non-Indigenous patients to the non-urgent section of an emergency department in a western Canadian city hospital found that providers exercised social control over racialized and poor patients, resulting in inferior care (Tang, Browne, Mussell, Smye, & Rodney, 2015). The care of racialized and poor patients was constrained by "disciplinary" actions, such as longer waits or the discounting of their health concerns. Previous discriminatory health care experiences caused many study participants to delay coming to the hospital. Thus, health care as a social institution of the state reproduced race and class inequalities by restricting opportunities to gain better health.

To address issues of discrimination researchers recommend that health care curricula and practice be aligned with cultural safety. The concept of **cultural safety** acknowledges the impact of colonialism and socio-economic position on health services for Indigenous people (Gerlach, 2012). Ly and Crowshoe (2015) argue that core courses and field training throughout the medical curricula should facilitate critical thinking to deconstruct racism, harmful representations of Indigenous people, and their negative outcomes on health care interactions. Research studying the access of Cree- and English-speaking Indigenous patients to hospital emergency departments in a large western Canadian city found that the presence of Cree-speaking Indigenous community health representatives increased respect for Indigenous patients, removed the language barrier, and supported patient participation in their own care (Cameron, Camargo Plazas, Salas, Bearskin, & Hungler, 2014).

Returning to the brief sketches in the Case Examples box, neither George's family doctor nor the nurse from the cancer counselling group in his rural BC town had the expertise to advise George about whether or not to have cancer surgery or where to have the surgery as he also had heart disease. George had to make these decisions on his own. At the regional hospital, George could use only a few English words to try to tell the doctor about his lung problem, but many technical terms inhibited communication. No interpreter was available and the bad-tempered white doctor showed discrimination against non–English-speaking people, so George decided to have his cancer surgery at the Vancouver hospital that had an interpreter.

Splintered health insurance coverage, jurisdictional disputes, and residential remoteness cause disparities in health care among different Indigenous communities. Exclusion from some government-funded health care insurance benefits is an obstacle to access for some Indigenous people. While status or registered First Nations individuals and Inuit are eligible for non-insured health benefits from the First Nation and Inuit Health Branch, such as dental, vision, and prescription medication coverage, Métis and non-status First Nations individuals are not eligible to receive these benefits (Ghosh & Spitzer, 2014). Research in an eastern Ontario urban community found that the cost of medications and supplies for Métis and non-status First Nations participants made it difficult for them to prevent or slow the progress of diabetes.

While the federal government usually funds government services, including for health care, for status First Nations people residing on reserves, the services are regulated under provincial or territorial legislation and delivered by First Nations or provincial or territorial providers. **Jordan's Principle** is a child-first principle intended to prevent delay, denial, or disruption of government services to First Nations children due to jurisdictional disputes (Blumenthal, 2015). The principle directs "the government (federal or provincial/territorial) that first receives a request to pay for services for a Status Indian child, where that service is available to other children, [to] pay for the service without delay or disruption" (MacDonald & Walman, 2005, p. 107).

Although Jordan's Principle passed in the House of Commons in 2007, implementation is limited in scope and jurisdictional consistency (UNICEF Canada, 2012). Currently, the principle is applied only to children diagnosed with multiple disabilities requiring service from multiple providers, excludes intra-governmental jurisdictional disputes, and proceeds through multiple administrative steps and delays before service provision and payment (Blumenthal, 2015; Jordan's Principle Working Group, 2015). In 2016, the Canadian Human Rights Tribunal ordered the federal government to immediately implement the complete scope and meaning of Jordan's Principle (*First Nations Child and Family Caring Society of Canada and Assembly of First Nations v. Attorney General of Canada*, 2016). (See Chapter 6 for more on Jordan's Principle.)

## Low-Income Populations

The Canadian health care system exhibits three strata of state stewardship and financing, each stratum with its own avenues to access inequities based on income (Marchildon & Allin, 2016). Federal and provincial governments regulate and finance physician and hospital services. In the second level, prescription medications and long-term care are accountable to some provincial regulations via targeted subsidy policies that cover gaps not addressed by the private sector. Dental care exemplifies the private delivery and financing layer, the third stratum.

In the Case Examples box, Amy is fortunate because she works in a job with a living wage and good employee benefits. Her employer, Big Tech, covers 50 per cent of the provincial health care premium for the family and her husband's employer covers the other half of the premium. Amy also has private health insurance coverage through her employer, which annually covers up to $2,300 in dental and medical costs, including prescription medications, for her and her family.

However, while the intention of universal health care is that all Canadians are to receive physician services based on medical need rather than income level, income inequalities affect use of physician care (Marchildon & Allin, 2016). Lower rates of visits to family doctors for low-income Canadians are coupled with an inability to afford prescription medications. Less-educated, low-income individuals are also less likely to advocate for specialist referrals from their general practitioners.

While Canadians employed in good jobs have sufficient outpatient prescription medication coverage through private health insurance, the working poor and seniors face deductibles and user fees associated with provincial drug plans to access outpatient prescription medications. A study of patients in Ontario with diabetes, asthma, or high blood pressure found that those with private medication insurance coverage were more likely to use essential prescription medications than those without private insurance (Kratzer, Cheng, Allin, & Law, 2015). Thus, these policies lead to medication non-compliance and associated worse health outcomes for lower-income Canadians (Marchildon & Allin, 2016). Policy to lower deductibles and co-payments in public medication insurance could address this access inequality for prescription medications (Kratzer et al., 2015).

The exclusion of long-term care from universal health coverage also creates a two-tier system for elderly Canadians (Marchildon & Allin, 2016). Seniors who can afford private care facilities quickly access 24-hour care, while low-income individuals wait for a spot in publicly financed facilities plagued by supply constraints. A report from the Wellesley Institute found that seniors in Toronto who could afford to pay for private or semi-private rooms in a long-term care facility were placed almost three months faster than those who sought basic accommodation (Um, 2016). Low-income residents could only apply for government financial support for the basic rooms. Similarly, low-income seniors face financial obstacles for home care beyond the limited publicly funded services (Marchildon & Allin, 2016).

The working poor also face financial barriers to accessing preventative and therapeutic dental care. Most dental care coverage is provided through employment-based private insurance plans in occupation groups with high salaries. Government policy extends publicly funded dental coverage only to social assistance recipients provincially and to eligible First Nations individuals and Inuit under the Non-Insured Health Benefits program federally. As the working poor are excluded from private and public dental coverage, the result is poorer oral health for them when they cannot afford dental care.

# Mental Health Services

Nearly one-third of Canadians requiring mental health care have unmet mental health care needs (Baiden, den Dunnen, & Fallon, 2017). In 2007 the federal government tasked the newly established Mental Health Commission of Canada with creating a national mental health strategy (Goldbloom & Bradley, 2012). The 2012 Mental Health Strategy for Canada included a focus on reducing disparities in access to mental health care.

Factors associated with unmet mental health care needs include younger age, low income, and immigration status (Baiden, den Dunnen, & Fallon, 2017; Slaunwhite, 2015; Thomson, Chaze, George, & Guruge, 2015). A study in Ontario found that 53.5 per cent of youth during the period 2010–14 who came to the emergency department with a new mental health disorder had not previously sought mental health care from a physician in a community setting (Gill et al., 2017). Youth without a regular primary care provider had the highest risk of using the emergency department as the first contact for a new mental health condition. Timely access to primary care physicians with better mental health awareness could likely prevent some of these emergency department visits. Youth whose primary care physicians participated in a capitation-based model with after-hours access or who had a high focus on mental health were more likely to have used primary care for mental health issues before resorting to the emergency department.

Low-income Canadians are three times more likely than their high-income counterparts to report accessibility and availability barriers to mental health care (Slaunwhite, 2015). Accessibility barriers include inability to pay for care, lack of transportation, or lack of child care. Long wait times or unavailability of an appropriate mental health care professional at the time or in the area exemplify availability obstacles. Canadians with lower socio-economic status face further difficulties after accessing the mental health system. A study of adults in Ontario community mental health programs examined the likelihood of receiving the correct level of care based on type of income source (Durbin, Bondy, & Durbin, 2012). Those living on a public assistance income had a higher risk of being severely under-served than those with other types of income sources.

Referring back to the Case Examples box, several months after immigrating to join her extended family, Hanan's sister offered to look after her five-year-old twin nieces so that Hanan could seek medical assistance for her depression. The family did not have a general practitioner, so Hanan went to a walk-in clinic. After an initial assessment, the clinic staff provided Hanan with a list of family doctors and some pamphlets about mental health options. However, when Hanan called some of the listed doctors, she was informed that they were no longer accepting new patients. She tried contacting several mental health services noted in the pamphlets, but was notified that she needed a referral from a family doctor. Her depression inhibited her ability to seek further assistance.

Barriers to mental health services for immigrants to Canada include a limited number of linguistically and culturally appropriate services, difficulty navigating the mental health system, and long wait times (Thomson et al., 2015). In Montreal, a study of primary care mental health practitioners found that 37.6 per cent frequently reported difficulty working with patients whose first language was neither French nor English (Brisset et al., 2014). Only 35.4 per cent of the practitioners in the study could access linguistic resources through their institutions. To improve access to and quality of mental health care, policies need to address training for practitioners about available linguistic resources, the different types and roles of interpreters, and factors that produce successful interpreted encounters in a mental health care setting.

One study in Toronto found that racialized immigrants and refugees living with HIV/AIDS encountered difficulties navigating the system and long wait times when seeking mental health services (Chen, Li, Fung, & Wong, 2015). Newcomers found it difficult to distinguish and choose among the different types of services in the mental health system. Study participants suggested a more **holistic care model,** in which navigation assistance and health, social, and legal services could be accessed at the same location.

A holistic care model is encouraged since people with mental health issues may have associated unmet needs in other aspects of daily life. To promote integration of individuals with severe mental health issues into the community the 2005 Quebec health ministry's Mental Health Action Plan transferred many mental health professionals from hospitals to primary care organizations in the communities and improved access to psychiatric consultations (Fleury et al., 2016). A study found that the perceived adequacy of help received remained stable for individuals with severe mental disorders two years after their transfer to the community but decreased at the five-year point. At the two-year follow-up, an increase of the perceived adequacy of help received for health care needs indicated that health services had responded appropriately to needs. However, at the five-year point, food, housing, education, and transportation needs rose in prominence and best-practice services (such as supervised housing and supported education) to adequately meet those needs had yet to be fully implemented under the Mental Health Action Plan (see Chapter 16 for more about issues of access to mental health services for marginalized populations).

## Social Policy Change in Action

### Social Workers Resist Policies to Standardize Care

The 2005 mental health reform in Quebec created a contradiction for social workers between process-oriented recovery services and outcome-based management practices (Khoury & Rodriguez del Barrio, 2015). The structural focus on standardized care and performance outcome measures, which aimed for cost reduction and efficiency, created systemic constraints to the flexibility of approaches, which social workers needed to practise within a mental health recovery philosophy. This philosophy frames mental health recovery as an individualized journey towards well-being in the community. A study found that some mental health social workers, who held a management position, seniority, or experience, could influence policy implementation and create room for flexible approaches during individual care interventions.

In the same year, the Ontario provincial government mandated the use of a computerized psychosocial assessment tool to mediate funding for mental health care in hospitals (O'Neill, 2015). The information technology instrument exemplifies how neo-liberalism and private-sector strategies infiltrate public health care through management tactics of standardization, surveillance, and work intensification, which shift care from a patient-centred approach to management-centred control in an effort to increase efficiency and cut costs. Social workers experienced a competition between maintaining patient care and completing the mandated documentation.

The computer-based assessment tools contributed to work intensification, decreased efficiency, and deskilling, all of which impeded social workers' ability to provide patient care. Patient care time was usurped by time needed for double documentation, since the computerized documentation met neither the requirements of the professional college nor the complex combination of health problems experienced by patients. The inflexible, standardized computerized assessment tools constrained the professional scope of practice, skills, and training that social workers employed to care for complex mental health patients.

While the high level of work intensification made it difficult for social workers to have sufficient critical thinking time to overtly challenge policies associated with standardization procedures, some engaged in covert tactics. Resistance strategies included delaying training on the computerized system, refusing to complete the standardized assessments for patients they had never met, and over-reporting the services required or the severity of symptoms for some patients. Despite potential disciplinary action for failure to complete the assessments in a timely manner, many social workers resisted because they saw providing direct patient care as their primary role and completing the assessments as an administrative task.

## Chapter Summary

To address gaps and inequities in the Canadian health care system, policies should promote holistic care and greater assistance to patients to navigate the system. Holistic care models would expand the number and professional scope of primary health care teams in rural and remote regions (ideally with co-located mental health and social services) (Fleury et al., 2016; Grzybowski, Stoll, & Kornelsen, 2013; Hillyard et al., 2012; Munro et al., 2013). Fundamentally enhancing universal access requires an emphasis on targeting resources towards the vulnerable and marginalized because successfully navigating the health care system is a challenge for many. Providing culturally appropriate health representatives in health care settings improves the care interactions and experiences (Cameron et al., 2014). Enhanced anti-discrimination curricula for health care providers would also support more positive health care interactions and outcomes (Ly & Crowshoe, 2015).

Overall, policy-makers need to increase investment in health care. The Canada Health Act should be broadened to include outpatient prescription medications (Romanow, 2002) and midwifery services, for example. There is a need for greater investment in support services, such as home care, to allow individuals to age in place. Through investment, research, and monitoring, Canadian policy-makers should target additional resources towards prevention and enhancing access to health care for vulnerable populations with the goal of improving health outcomes for all Canadians.

## Discussion Questions

1. As a voter, would you support a political platform policy that pledges to increase the number of medical graduates in the province or a platform policy to create multi-disciplinary primary care team centres across the province? Why?

2. What public and private health care insurance coverage do you have? Prioritize the three gaps in your coverage of most concern to you and create policies to close these gaps. Discuss whether your policies should cover specific groups or everybody.

3. Discuss how race, gender, and socio-economic position may affect decisions to seek health care.

4. Think about factors within the health care system that caused a delay in surgery for someone you know. Propose a policy reform to address the main factor that you identified as causing this delay.

# References

Adams, O. (2016). Policy capacity for health reform: Necessary but insufficient: Comment on "Health Reform Requires Policy Capacity." *International Journal of Health Policy and Management, 5*(1), 51–4.

——— & Vanin, S. (2016). Funding long-term care in Canada: Issues and options. *Healthcare Papers, 15*(4), 7–19.

Amar, C., Pomey, M.-P., SanMartin, C., De Coster, C., & Noseworthy, T. (2015). Sustainability: Orthopaedic surgery wait time management strategies. *International Journal of Health Care Quality Assurance, 28*(4), 320–31.

Baiden, P., den Dunnen, W., & Fallon, B. (2017). Examining the independent effect of social support on unmet mental healthcare needs among Canadians: Findings from a population-based study. *Social Indicators Research, 130*(3), 1229–46.

Beauchamp, J., Bélanger, M., Schofield, A., Bordage, R., Donovan, D., & Landry, M. (2013). Recruiting doctors from and for underserved groups: Does New Brunswick's initiative to recruit doctors for its linguistic minority help rural communities? *Canadian Journal of Public Health, 104*(6, Suppl. 1), S44–S48.

Bissonnette, L., Wilson, K., Bell, S., & Shah, T. I. (2012). Neighbourhoods and potential access to health care: The role of spatial and aspatial factors. *Health & Place, 18*, 841–53.

Blumenthal, A. (2015). No Jordan's Principle cases in Canada? A review of the administrative response to Jordan's Principle. *International Indigenous Policy Journal, 6*(1), Article 6.

Brisset, C., Leanza, Y., Rosenberg, E., Vissandjee, B., Kirmayer, L. J., Muckle, G., et al. (2014). Language barriers in mental health care: A survey of primary care practitioners. *Journal of Immigrant and Minority Health, 16*(6), 1238–46.

Cameron, B. L., Camargo Plazas, M. d. P., Salas, A. S., Bearskin, R. L., & Hungler, K. (2014). Understanding inequalities in access to health care services for Aboriginal people: A call for nursing action. *Advances in Nursing Science, 37*(3), E1–E16.

Cameron, P. J., Este, D. C., & Worthington, C. A. (2012). Professional, personal and community: 3 domains of physician retention in rural communities. *Canadian Journal of Rural Medicine, 17*(2), 47–55.

Canadian Institute for Health Information (CIHI). (2015). *Continuity of care with family medicine physicians: Why it matters.* Ottawa: CIHI.

———. (2016a). *National health expenditure trends, 1975 to 2016.* Ottawa: CIHI.

———. (2016b). *Supply, distribution and migration of physicians in Canada, 2015: Data tables.* Ottawa: Canadian Institute for Health Information.

———. (2017). *Wait times for priority procedures in Canada, 2017.* Ottawa: Canadian Institute for Health Information.

Chen, Y. B., Li, A. T.-W., Fung, K. P.-L., & Wong, J. P.-H. (2015). Improving access to mental health services for racialized immigrants, refugees, and non-status people living with HIV/AIDS. *Journal of Health Care for the Poor and Underserved, 26*(2), 505–18.

Crooks, V. A., Agarwal, G., & Harrison, A. (2012). Chronically ill Canadians' experiences of being unattached to a family doctor: A qualitative study of marginalized patients in British Columbia. *BMC Family Practice, 13*(69), 1–9.

Da Roit, B. (2012). The Netherlands: The struggle between universalism and cost containment. *Health and Social Care in the Community, 20*(3), 228–37.

Department of Finance Canada. (2018). *Equality and growth: A strong middle class.* Retrieved from https://www.budget.gc.ca/2018/docs/plan/toc-tdm-en.html

Desmeules, F., Dionne, C. E., Belzile, É. L., Bourbonnais, R., & Frémont, P. (2012). The impacts of pre-surgery wait for total knee replacement on pain, function and health-related quality of life six months after surgery. *Journal of Evaluation in Clinical Practice, 18*(1), 111–20.

Durbin, A., Bondy, S. J., & Durbin, J. (2012). The association between income source and met need among community mental health service users in Ontario, Canada. *Community Mental Health Journal, 48*(5), 662–72.

*First Nations Child and Family Caring Society of Canada and Assembly of First Nations v. Attorney General of Canada.* (2016). 2016 CHRT 2, T1340/7008 (Canadian Human Rights Tribunal, 26 Jan. 2016).

Fleury, M.-J., Bamvita, J.-M., Grenier, G., Schmitz, N., Piat, M., & Tremblay, J. (2016). Adequacy of help received by individuals with severe mental disorders after a major healthcare reform in Quebec: Predictors and changes at 5-year follow-up. *Administration and Policy in Mental Health and Mental Health Services Research, 43*(5), 799–812.

Fridkin, A. J. (2012). Addressing health inequities through Indigenous involvement in health-policy discourses. *Canadian Journal of Nursing Research, 44*(2), 108–22.

Gallagher, J., Mendez, J. K., & Kehoe, T. (2015). The First Nations Health Authority: A transformation in healthcare for BC First Nations. *Healthcare Management Forum, 28*(6), 255–61.

Gardner, W., Fierlbeck, K., & Levy, A. (2014). Breaking the deadlock: Towards a new intergovernmental relationship in Canadian healthcare. *Healthcare Papers, 14*(3), 7–15.

GBD 2015 Healthcare Access and Quality Collaborators. (2017). Healthcare access and quality index based on mortality from causes amenable to personal health care in 195 countries and territories, 1990–2015: A novel analysis from the Global Burden of Disease Study 2015. *Lancet, 390*(10091), 231–66.

General Practice Services Committee. (2015). A GP for me. Retrieved from http://www.gpscbc.ca/what-we-do/innovations/a-gp-for-me

Gerlach, A. J. (2012). A critical reflection on the concept of cultural safety. *Canadian Journal of Occupational Therapy, 79*(3), 151–8.

Ghosh, H., & Spitzer, D. (2014). Inequities in diabetes outcomes among urban First Nation and Métis communities: Can addressing diversities in preventive services make a difference? *International Indigenous Policy Journal, 5*(1), Article 2, 1–24.

Gill, P. J., Saunders, N., Gandhi, S., Gonzalez, A., Kurdyak, P., Vigod, S., et al. (2017). Emergency department as a first contact for mental health problems in children and youth. *Journal of the American Academy of Child and Adolescent Psychiatry, 56*(6), 475–82.

Goldbloom, D., & Bradley, L. (2012). The Mental Health Commission of Canada: The first five years. *Mental Health Review Journal, 17*(4), 221–8.

Government of Canada. (2012a). About primary health care. Retrieved from https://www.canada.ca/en/health-canada/services/primary-health-care/about-primary-health-care.html

———. (2012b). Canada Health Act. Retrieved from http://laws-lois.justice.gc.ca/eng/acts/c-6/page-1.html#docCont

Grzybowski, S., Stoll, K., & Kornelsen, J. (2013). The outcomes of perinatal surgical services in rural British Columbia: A population-based study. *Canadian Journal of Rural Medicine, 18*(4), 123–9.

Hayes, M., Ross, I. E., Gasher, M., Gutstein, D., Dunn, J. R., & Hackett, R. A. (2007). Telling stories: News media, health literacy and public policy in Canada. *Social Science & Medicine, 64*(9), 1842–52.

Her Majesty the Queen in Right of Canada, Her Majesty the Queen in Right of the Province of British Columbia, & First Nations Health Society. (2011). *British Columbia Tripartite Framework Agreement on First Nation Health Governance*. Retrieved from http://www.fnha.ca/Documents/framework-accord-cadre.pdf

Hillyard, J., Reilly, D., Rogers, J., Amit, M., Wilson, R., Fitzgerald, W., et al. (2012). Specialist physicians for rural and remote populations in Canada. *Canadian Journal of Rural Medicine, 17*(1), 26–7.

Iglesias, S., Kornelsen, J., Woolard, R., Caron, N., Warnock, G., Friesen, R., et al. (2015). Joint position paper on rural surgery and operative delivery. *Canadian Journal of Rural Medicine, 20*(4), 129–38.

Jordan's Principle Working Group. (2015). *Without denial, delay, or disruption: Ensuring First Nations children's access to equitable services through Jordan's Principle*. Ottawa: Assembly of First Nations.

Khoury, E., & Rodriguez del Barrio, L. (2015). Recovery-oriented mental health practice: A social work perspective. *British Journal of Social Work, 45*(Suppl. 1), i27–i44.

Kratzer, J., Cheng, L., Allin, S., & Law, M. R. (2015). The impact of private insurance coverage on prescription drug use in Ontario, Canada. *Health Care Policy, 10*(4), 62–74.

Kroneman, M., Boerma, W., van den Berg, M., Groenewegen, P., de Jong, J., & van Ginneken, E. (2016). The Netherlands: Health system review. *Health Systems in Transition, 18*(2), 1–239.

Ladouceur, R. (2012). What has become of family physicians? *Canadian Family Physician, 58*(12), 1322.

Lanoix, M. (2017). No longer home alone? Home care and the Canada Health Act. *Health Care Analysis, 25*(2), 168–89.

Lavoie, J. G., Kornelsen, D., Boyer, Y., & Wylie, L. (2016). Lost in maps: Regionalization and Indigenous health services. *Healthcare Papers, 16*(1), 63–73.

Law, M. R., Cheng, L., Dhalla, I. A., Heard, D., & Morgan, S. G. (2012).The effect of cost on adherence to prescription medications in Canada. *Canadian Medical Association Journal, 184*(3), 297–302.

Lazar, H. (2013). Why is it so hard to reform healthcare policy in Canada? In H. Lazar, J. N. Lavis, P.-G. Forest, & J. Church (Eds), *Paradigm freeze: Why it is so hard to reform health care in Canada* (pp. 1–20). Montreal & Kingston: Queen's University Press.

Ly, A., & Crowshoe, L. (2015). "Stereotypes are reality": Addressing stereotyping in Canadian Aboriginal medical education. *Medical Education, 49*(6), 612–22.

Maarse, J., & Jeurissen, P. (2016). The policy and politics of the 2015 long-term care reform in the Netherlands. *Health Policy, 120*(3), 241–5.

MacDonald, K. A., & Walman, K. (2005). Jordan's Principle: A child first approach to jurisdictional issues. In C. Blackstock, T. Prakash, J. Loxley, & F. Wien (Eds), *Wen:de: We are coming to the light of day* (pp. 87-112). Ottawa: First Nations Child and Family Caring Society of Canada.

McGrail, K., Lavergne, R., Lewis, S. J., Peterson, S. L., Barer, M., & Garrison, S. R. (2015). Classifying physician practice style: A new approach using administrative data in British Columbia. *Medical Care, 53*(3), 276–82.

McGurran, J. J. (2013). Canada. In L. Siciliani, M. Borowitz, & V. Moran (Eds), *Waiting time policies in the health sector: What works?* (pp. 99–113). Paris: OECD Health Policy Studies, OECD Publishing.

Marchildon, G. P. (2013). Canada: Health system review. *Health Systems in Transition, 15*(1), 1–179.

———. (2015). The crisis of regionalization. *Healthcare Management Forum, 28*(6), 236–8.

———. (2016). Regionalization: What have we learned? *Healthcare Papers, 16*(1), 8–14.

——— & Allin, S. (2016). The public–private mix in the delivery of health-care services: Its relevance for lower-income Canadians. *Global Social Welfare, 3*(3), 161–70.

——— & Mou, H. (2014). A needs-based allocation formula for Canada Health Transfer. *Canadian Public Policy, 40*(3), 209–23.

Morgan, S. G., Daw, J. R., & Law, M. R. (2013). *Rethinking pharmacare in Canada.* Toronto: CD Howe Institute.

———, Law, M., Daw, J. R., Abraham, L., & Martin, D. (2015). Estimated cost of universal public coverage of prescription drugs in Canada. *Canadian Medical Association Journal, 187*(7), 491–7.

Munro, S., Kornelsen, J., & Grzybowski, S. (2013). Models of maternity care in rural environments: Barriers and attributes of interprofessional collaboration with midwives. *Midwifery, 29*(6), 646–52.

National Collaborating Centre for Aboriginal Health. (2011). *Looking for Aboriginal health in legislation and policies, 1970 to 2008: The policy*

*synthesis project.* Prince George, BC: National Collaborating Centre for Aboriginal Health.

O'Neill, L. (2015). Regulating hospital social workers and nurses: Propping up an "efficient" lean health care system. *Studies in Political Economy, 95*(1), 115–36.

Olson, R., & Couchie, C. (2013). Returning birth: The politics of midwifery implementation on First Nations reserves in Canada. *Midwifery, 29*(8), 981–7.

Oosterveer, T. M., & Young, T. K. (2015). Primary health care accessibility challenges in remote Indigenous communities in Canada's North. *International Journal of Circumpolar Health, 74*(1), 1–7.

Organization for Economic Co-operation and Development (OECD). (n.d.). OECD Stat: Health care resources. Retrieved from http://www.oecd-ilibrary.org/economics/data/oecd-stat_data-00285-en

———. (2015). *Health at a glance 2015: OECD indicators.* Paris: OECD Publishing.

Randall, E., Crooks, V. A., & Goldsmith, L. J. (2012). In search of attachment: A qualitative study of chronically ill women transitioning between family physicians in rural Ontario, Canada. *BMC Family Practice, 13*(125), 1–12.

Raphael, D. (2000). Health inequalities in Canada: Current discourses and implications for public health action. *Critical Public Health, 10*(2), 193–216.

———. (2011). A discourse analysis of the social determinants of health. *Critical Public Health, 21*(2), 221–36.

Romanow, R. J. (2002). *Building on values: The future of health care in Canada—Final report.* Ottawa: Government of Canada.

Roots, A., & MacDonald, M. (2014). Outcomes associated with nurse practitioners in collaborative practice with general practitioners in rural settings in Canada: A mixed methods study. *Human Resources for Health, 12*(69), 1–11.

Slaunwhite, A. K. (2015). The role of gender and income in predicting barriers to mental health care in Canada. *Community Mental Health Journal, 51*(5), 621–7.

Statistics Canada. (2015). Access to a regular medical doctor, 2014. Retrieved from http://www.statcan.gc.ca/pub/82-625-x/2015001/article/14177-eng.htm

Stoll, K., & Kornelsen, J. (2014). Midwifery care in rural and remote British Columbia: A retrospective cohort study of perinatal outcomes of rural parturient women with a midwife involved in their care, 2003 to 2008. *Journal of Midwifery & Women's Health, 59*(1), 60–6.

Tang, S. Y., Browne, A. J., Mussell, B., Smye, V. L., & Rodney, P. (2015). "Underclassism" and access to healthcare in urban centres. *Sociology of Health & Illness, 37*(5), 698–714.

Thomson, M. S., Chaze, F., George, U., & Guruge, S. (2015). Improving immigrant populations' access to mental health services in Canada: A review of barriers and recommendations. *Journal of Immigrant and Minority Health, 17*(6), 1895–1905.

Um, S.-g. (2016). *The cost of waiting for care: Delivering equitable long-term care for Toronto's diverse population.* Toronto: Wellesley Institute.

UNICEF Canada. (2012). *Invited response to concluding observations for the United Nations Committee on the Elimination of Racial Discrimination: Canada's 19th and 20th reports on the International Convention on the Elimination of All Forms of Racial Discrimination (CERD).* Toronto: UNICEF Canada.

# 16 Justice for Whom? The Effect of Criminalization for Marginalized Peoples

*Juliana West and Jennifer Murphy*

---

## Chapter Objectives

*This chapter will help you to develop an understanding of:*
- criminalization as contemporary colonialism and as structural violence under neo-liberalism;
- criminal justice policies and processes including profiling, sentencing, confinement, release, and risk assessment;
- who is under correctional supervision in Canada;
- how criminalization affects Indigenous and racialized peoples;
- why understanding criminalization is key for social work and how social workers can take action.

---

## Introduction

How do we understand the specific criminal justice experiences of David, Lorrie, and Grant in the case examples below? In thinking about David's experience, we might argue he either was very unlucky or should have known better than to help someone he knew only as a neighbour. Or, comparing Lorrie's number of charges and the amount of time she has spent incarcerated to Grant's lack of convictions, we could be inclined to assume that Lorrie, rather than Grant, was a more dangerous and criminally inclined individual. We might further believe that Lorrie's convictions are a testimony to her guilt and Grant's lack of convictions to his innocence. And although curious, we might consider that David, Lorrie, and Grant's experiences are more relevant to criminology rather than to social work students, and we may assume that if people have been drawn into the criminal justice system they must have done something worse than people who have not.

This chapter will challenge those beliefs and help you to understand how criminalization is a function of marginalization and upholds the colonial, structurally violent, and neo-liberal processes creating the over-representation of Indigenous and racialized peoples as defendants in criminal courts and as inmates in prisons and jails. We will explain how the social work commitment to working with the most marginalized must include a critical analysis of key Canadian criminal justice policies and processes, including profiling, sentencing, confinement, release, and risk assessment. We will also encourage

---

**Case Examples**  Social Position and Criminalization

---

**David** is a 58-year-old Black man. He was a nurse practitioner in Toronto for 23 years, and most recently he worked as a foster care provider. When David's neighbour asked for help with moving across the city, David was racially profiled and pulled over by police for allegedly failing to signal. After the police officer asked to look in the duffle bags in the back seat of David's car, David consented and nine boxes of cold medication containing pseudoephedrine (an ingredient commonly stolen and used to cook crystal meth) were found among his neighbour's belongings. Despite David not having knowledge of the contents of the belongings, he was charged with the possession of stolen property. David took the advice of his appointed Legal Aid lawyer and pled guilty in exchange for a conditional discharge. David was not informed that the conditional discharge would remain on his record for three years and because he told his employer what occurred, David could no longer provide a satisfactory criminal record check. His conviction resulted in the revocation of his foster home licence and his inability to work in a nursing or home-care capacity.

**Lorrie** is a 27-year-old Anishinaabe woman and mother of four children, all of whom have been taken from her by the child welfare system. Lorrie was removed from her own family when she was nine, was a ward of the child welfare system until she turned 18, and had to quit her last year of high school in order to support herself. Lorrie has lived with homelessness, shelter insecurity, and poverty for most of her adult life. Lorrie has been convicted of nine poverty-related offences over the last eight years: theft under $5,000 (shoplifting $50 worth of food items), trespassing at night, failure to appear, public disturbance, and solicitation. She has been incarcerated five times for a total of 25 months and is currently completing probation.

**Grant** is a 44-year-old white father of two teenage children who live with their mother and visit Grant and his wife on school holidays. Grant grew up on his parent's farm until he finished high school, when he married and started a commercial equipment leasing and transporting business where he employs nine staff. Grant was charged with tax evasion (not declaring $47,000 of income) and dangerous driving, but after both charges were withdrawn, he was not convicted.

---

you to cultivate a curiosity and competency in locating criminalization within broader processes of cultural discourse, privilege, colonialism, racialization, and oppression.

# Criminalization

**Criminalization** is the process where some actions and some people are labelled as criminal whereas other people involved in the same behaviours are not. Probation and parole officers have considerable latitude in interpreting a person's compliance or lack of compliance with their release conditions. Prison staff have discretion regarding who is labelled a difficult or a compliant prisoner and how they punish or reward prisoner behaviour. And police too often arbitrarily question marginalized individuals for occupying public space.

Criminalization refers to the process of creating the social reality of crime involving labelling procedures and "discovering" criminals. In particular, it is how "state authorities, media and citizen discourse define particular groups and practices as criminal, with prejudicial consequences" (Schneider & Schneider, 2008, p. 351). In other words, criminalization involves processes of oppression and privilege apparent at the personal, cultural, and structural levels (Mullaly & West, 2018).

## Criminalization at the Personal Level

Racialization,[1] or the processes by which meanings are attached to an individual's behaviour based on his or her perceived race, is a key component of criminalization (Chan & Chunn, 2014). In Case Examples box, David was profiled as "driving while Black" (being stopped by the police because of racial discrimination). And because he was racialized by his lawyer (the lawyer made assumptions about David having a criminal history based on his skin colour), the lawyer withheld the consequences a conditional discharge would have for David's criminal record and, consequently, for his employment. Similarly, Lorrie was charged with public disturbance for swearing and shouting in a public park when she was there with three of her extended family members. Because she was racialized and deemed dangerous, her behaviour was labelled as criminal. When Grant, however, was "hollering and cussing" in the same public park while throwing a football with his white middle-aged buddies, his behaviour was perceived as acceptable and entertaining.

## Profiling

Profiling has involved police and politicians working in tandem to develop policies and strategies that would both deter "criminals" from committing "crimes" and support "law-abiding citizens" to feel safe in their communities. The broken windows approach[2] argues that addressing the visible signs of public disorder in a neighbourhood, such as broken windows in vacant houses and abandoned warehouses, would have the concomitant effect of reducing more serious criminal behaviour through a visible police presence in these poorer communities.[3] Despite this "common-sense" approach not being based in empirical research, it became one of the dominant doctrines of law enforcement in the 1990s in the United States and later in Canada, and influences public attitudes towards intolerance and exclusion. It has led to what Garland (2001) describes as the return to the punitive rather than rehabilitative model, placing victim narratives at the centre of penal policy and focusing on identifying "outsiders" as dangerous.

The broken windows approach has been applied disproportionately to impoverished neighbourhoods with large percentages of racialized peoples (Oberman & Johnson, 2016). As understood through an intersectional analysis, this flawed approach to policing and the emphasis on the law-and-order mantra obscure discussion of racism and classism. A form of this approach is used in the Downtown Eastside of Vancouver (DTES), where policing is concentrated on minor bylaw infractions leading to tickets and fines that most people are unable to pay. In 2013, a complaint was made about the number of jaywalking tickets issued to DTES residents—2,050 tickets between 2008 and 2012 compared to zero jaywalking tickets issued in two nearby wealthy neighbourhoods in the same time period. The net effect of this policing policy is to criminalize the poor and disadvantaged, confirming concerns "that city bylaws are not being enforced for reasons of public safety, but to circumvent the constitutional protections in this country against profiling and arbitrary detention" (Crawford, 2013, p. 3).

## Criminalization at Cultural and Structural Levels

Criminalization is not just about individual police officers profiling marginalized individuals; it is also reproduced at the cultural level: in the media, by politicians, and by the language we use. Mullaly and West (2018) offer a detailed discussion of how the discourses constructing marginalized groups as "Other," criminal, or dangerous are part of neo-liberal culture. For example, television shows such as *Cops* reproduce beliefs that the only people who commit crimes are people of colour and that police protect the community (Chan & Chunn, 2014; Mullaly & West, 2018). Politicians win campaigns on tough-on-crime platforms despite the fact that crime rates[4] have consistently fallen for decades (Webster & Doob, 2007). And social workers adopt oppressive language such as "offender" when referring to criminalized individuals when, in fact, we all have broken the law whether by jaywalking or driving over the speed limit (West, 2014).

Criminalization is also maintained and reproduced at the structural level in the space between how criminal justice policy and practices are perceived by privileged populations (fair and just) and the discrepancies and discretion operating at each level (arbitrary and biased). For example, the far-too-regular occurrence of murders of Black men by police in the United States is viewed with horror here in Canada. Yet, seemingly forgotten are the documented cases of the murder of Black and Indigenous men across the country by our own police departments, including the "starlight tours" (Comack, 2012) whereby the police drive Indigenous men and women (who *might* have been charged with public drunkenness) beyond the city limits and leave them to walk back in well-below-freezing temperatures, often without their shoes or coats.[5] In other words, criminalization refers to the processes whereby marginalized individuals and groups are controlled and supervised by the police, the courts, and the corrections industry, leaving privileged people far less scrutinized:

> Acts that result in structural violence such as large-scale pension/investment theft, environmental/occupational illness or death, unsafe drinking water, or the murder and rape committed by state sanctioned residential school contractors, fly under the radar of reported crime rates even though they cause greater harm to more people than the acts committed by those who are poor and marginalized. (West, 2014, p. 75)

As Chan and Chunn (2014) describe, people at all levels have considerable discretion in how they carry out their roles in deciding who and what is criminal. Police have the power to decide which calls they respond to, whom they charge, and whom they ignore or let off with a warning. Lawyers have the power to offer competent and considered advice to those clients they deem worthy (or are able to pay), and the power to give marginal representation to the rest. And judges have discretion in how they interpret the law, what they perceive will be a deterrent, whom they go hard on and with whom they display mercy, and the sentences they hand down.

## Sentencing

Canadian sentencing is presumed to occur within a neutral, unbiased system, what Naffine (1990) calls "the Official Version of Law" (cited in Comack, 2012, p. 11). Naffine argues, however, that the attributes of judges, who are overwhelmingly male, white, and middle class, contribute to systemic bias against those individuals deemed to be "Other." Sentencing is generally left to the discretion of the judge, who determines an appropriate sentence following precedents from previous similar cases and the guidelines laid down in section 718 of the Criminal Code (1985). Mandatory minimum sentences, however, which remove sentencing discretion for judges, were increased for a number of offences by the Harper government between 2006 and 2015. Under the current Trudeau government, all mandatory minimum sentencing provisions will be subsequently reviewed[6] but some will be kept for the most serious offences (Crawford, 2017). Furthermore, under the 1999 *Gladue*[7] principles (section 718.2[e] of the Criminal Code), all options other than incarceration are to be considered first for Indigenous individuals (see Chapter 6 for more about the *Gladue* principles). Unfortunately, the disproportionate over-incarceration of Indigenous people has continued unabated post-*Gladue*[8] (Milward & Parkes, 2014).

# Criminalization as Contemporary Colonialism

While countries across the European Union (EU) imprison new immigrants at six times the rate of EU citizens (De Giorgi, 2010), Bracken, Deane, and Morrissette (2009) caution that the processes and effects of colonialism, in addition to racialization, make over-representation even more substantial for Indigenous peoples. Colonialism[9] is not only a historical reality in Canada, its contemporary processes, policies, and structures are active today (Adams, 1999; Frideres & Gadacz, 2012; Hart, 2009; Monchalin, 2016; Razack, 2015; Smith, 2000; Wilson & Yellow Bird, 2005). Contemporary examples of colonialism include the criminalization of Indigenous people and enforcement of child welfare policies to maintain a system of domination (West, 2014). The criminal justice system, the latest incarnation of the 1876 Indian Act, now moves Indigenous people from reserves to prisons (Monture-Angus, 2000):

> There are perhaps no better indicators of continuing colonization and its accompanying spatial strategies of containment than the policing and incarceration of Aboriginal people.... Over-policed and incarcerated at one of the highest rates in the world, their encounters with white settlers have principally remained encounters in prostitution, policing, and the criminal justice system. (Razack, 2002, pp. 133, 127)

The Truth and Reconciliation Commission (2015a) reiterated what the Aboriginal Justice Inquiry (Hamilton & Sinclair, 1991) identified 25 years prior—the roots of over-representation are enmeshed in colonial processes. The criminal justice system, the courts, and the police discriminate against and criminalize Indigenous people, and Indigenous people have greater involvement with the criminal justice system, both as perpetrators and as victims, as a result of racism, poverty, marginalization, exclusion, and residential school and child welfare involvement. Indigenous people are more likely to be arrested, to face multiple charges, to spend more time in remand awaiting trial, to be denied bail, to have less time with a lawyer, to be found guilty, to be sentenced to incarceration rather than community supervision or a fine, to have longer sentences, to have an assessed higher risk, and to be less likely to obtain early release than their non-Indigenous counterparts (Hamilton & Sinclair, 1991; Monchalin, 2016; TRC, 2015a). Turnbull (2016) highlights that despite the Parole Board of Canada claiming it has made accommodations for the realities that Indigenous prisoners face, the official rhetoric glosses over the ongoing discrimination entrenched in the criminal justice system and institutions of confinement.

## Confinement

While the effects of poverty, residential schools, and child welfare systems are mitigating factors to be considered in sentencing Indigenous individuals following the *Gladue* decision, Correctional Service of Canada (CSC) policy states it also incorporates this analysis with confinement within the penitentiary system when determining security classification, with transfers between institutions, and with solitary confinement (Sapers, 2016, p. 45). There is, however, little transparency about how the CSC applies this policy in practice with the result that Indigenous prisoners are disproportionately classified as high risk and placed in maximum security penitentiaries, are less likely to gain access to community supervision programs, and are more likely to be placed in solitary confinement and be involved in incidents of self-harm (Sapers, 2012).

The Corrections and Conditional Release Act (CCRA) (1992) included provisions under section 81 for healing lodges, in partnership with Indigenous communities, to hold federal prisoners who otherwise would be housed in institutions. Under section 81, only 68 beds were available nationwide as of 2012 (Sapers, 2012) and it was not until 2011, or 20 years post-Act, that any beds were available for Indigenous women. There is also considerable controversy about the efficacy of healing lodges. A penitentiary setting, however ostensibly progressive, cannot provide a setting to empower and heal women. CSC has ignored issues of race and class in promoting the Okimaw Ochi Healing Lodge in Saskatchewan by assuming a homogeneity of Indigenous women's experiences that enforces systemic racism. In other words, a prison is still a prison (Hannah-Moffat, 2001).

Federal prisoners are more likely to live with mental health issues (Sapers, 2015). For example, at admission to federal institutions, 30 per cent of incarcerated women had previous hospitalization in psychiatric wards, 60 per cent were prescribed psychotropic medication once in prison, and almost 40 per cent of incarcerated men required further assessment of their mental health (Sapers, 2015). Federal prisons are in effect "housing the largest psychiatric populations in the country" (Sapers, 2009, p. 4).

In addition, almost 70 per cent of incarcerated women have been sexually assaulted, 86 per cent of women report previous physical abuse, and 80 per cent of incarcerated men have substance abuse issues (Sapers, 2015). Coupled with low educational levels and limited employment experience, federally sentenced prisoners, both men and women, are already among the most at-risk population for homelessness, unemployment, exploitation, and victimization once released. While one could argue that more programs are needed for prisoners, Pate (2003) and Hannah-Moffat (2001) suggest people should have access to needed community resources and not be sent to prison to get the treatment they need.

The conditions of confinement are also an exacerbating factor in contributing to mental health issues for federal prisoners. "Administrative segregation" or solitary confinement, the removal of a prisoner from the general population to maintain the safety and security of the penitentiary and to prevent harm to the individual or others, is supposed to be used sparingly, as a last resort, and for the shortest possible length of time (Sapers, 2015). However, as Howard Sapers, the Correctional Investigator of Canada from 2004 to 2016, laments, no limitations are placed on the amount of time that prisoners spend in segregation, with some spending years in indefinite segregation, nor has there been a reduction in the over-reliance of its use with women, Indigenous and Black prisoners, and those with mental health issues.

## Release from Prison

Marginalized prisoners are also disadvantaged when applying for parole.[10] Indigenous individuals have higher program completion rates while in prison but are released later on parole and their parole is revoked more frequently (Sapers, 2016). The trend towards keeping prisoners incarcerated longer until their statutory release (after having served two-thirds of their sentence) rather than on parole (having served one-third of their sentence) is exacerbated for Indigenous inmates. A large majority (84 per cent) are incarcerated until their statutory release date compared to 66 per cent of non-Indigenous persons. Additionally, only 15 per cent of Indigenous persons were released on day parole compared to 31 per cent of non-Indigenous inmates (Corrections and Conditional Release Statistic Overview, 2015). Being released later means less connection to family and community resources and fewer programs that can be accessed through probation or parole.

In addition to and because of being criminalized, Indigenous people in the community and particularly after release from prison (due to increased risk for exclusion, homelessness, and poverty) are also at a much higher risk of being victimized by crime and not deemed worthy of police protection. Indigenous people are victims of violent assaults, murders, and multiple victimizations (Monchalin, 2016), they are the target of police brutality and racialized policing (Comack, 2012; Razack, 2015), and, as in the cases of over 1,200 missing and murdered Indigenous women and girls, Indigenous people are rarely afforded the investigative attention and service of the police after having been victimized (Chan & Chunn, 2014; Palmater, 2016).

## Criminalization as Structural Violence under Neo-Liberalism

Sociologist Johan Galtung (1969) originally framed the concept of structural violence to mean the number of avoidable deaths or constraints to human potential caused by economic, social, and political systems. West (2014) argued that the criminalization of Indigenous people results in structural violence—it may not be as immediate as being assaulted in the street, but its long-term effects on Indigenous people's health and well-being are no less traumatic. Having a criminal record can impair a person's ability to obtain employment, to access subsidized housing, to become a social worker. Being imprisoned is a risk to one's health resulting in malnutrition from substandard nutrition, delayed access to health care, or increased exposure to HIV, hepatitis C, and tuberculosis. Moreover, as Razack (2015) has emphasized after reviewing the innumerable deaths of Indigenous people detained, being taken into custody involves the real risk of not coming out alive. A prison sentence can also mean the loss of one's housing (and ensuing homelessness once released) and, for women, the loss of one's children to child welfare, thereby fuelling the child welfare/criminal justice pipeline once again. Monture (1989–90, p. 5) stated:

> I am deliberately connecting child "welfare" law with the criminal "justice" system. From the perspective of a traditional First Nations woman, I see the child welfare systems as being on a continuum with the criminal justice system. Both institutions remove citizens from their communities . . . both the child welfare system and the criminal justice system are exercised through the use of punishment, force, and coercion.

Criminalization is much more than persons in power making arbitrary and biased assessments about marginalized people's behaviours; criminalization is also inherent to neo-liberalism. As the neo-liberal shift away from the welfare state saw an increased emphasis on individual responsibility, risk-thinking ideology and risk assessments, and security through surveillance (Parton, 1996), it meant a deregulation of both the economy and privileged people and the increased regulation and surveillance of people living with marginalization (Peck, 2003). Neo-liberal governance and crime control policies are intrinsically connected (Wacquant, 2009)—the criminal justice, policing, and legal systems protect the dominant class by regulating and punishing the poor (De Giorgi, 2010; Monture-Angus, 2000; Pollack, 2004; Reiman & Leighton, 2017; Wacquant, 2009). Crime control has resulted in the criminalization of social policy where "social welfare issues become redefined as crime problems" and crime control policies take precedence over health care, housing, and employment (Knepper, 2007, p. 139). In addition, there is an increasing production of moral indifference (Bauman, 1989; Christie, 1994) where criminalized people are constructed to be deserving of being treated inhumanely by the state. The United States has become the chief global exporter of penal policy since the early 1990s, replacing welfare with prisons and placing crime control as a rallying point for neo-liberal agendas (Wacquant, 1999).

## Risk Assessments

Risk assessments are inherent to neo-liberalism, placing responsibility on individuals while simultaneously eroding and undermining the welfare state (Culpitt, 1999). Risk assessments are used by criminal justice (and child welfare systems) and promise community safety by pledging to identify who is a high risk to engage in an unwanted behaviour (Silver & Miller, 2002). They are concerned with managing risk by profiling categories of people (Webb, 2006) and are based on normative assumptions of white, cis-male, heterosexual, monogamous, middle-class lifestyles (Hannah-Moffat, 2005). Risk assessments identify marginalization as risk and result in further oppression and punishment (Canadian Human Rights Commission, 2003). The Canadian Human Rights Commission further asserts that criminogenic risk assessment tools are a violation of the Canadian Human Rights Act in that they identify social locations such as race, gender, disability, and religion as risk factors, and thusly discriminate against and overclassify, and should not be used on women,[11] racialized, or Indigenous people.

As long as risk assessments continue to be used, Hannah-Moffat (2016) argues[12] that socio-structural issues (for example, poverty, homelessness, unemployment, victimization, racism, classism, sexism) should be included so that the specific marginalization faced by groups of criminalized individuals could be addressed differentially according to need. This approach would supersede risk factors and look instead at a more complete picture of life on the "outside" for women and Indigenous and racialized individuals.

## Who Are We Talking About?

According to Statistics Canada (2017) (see Figure 16.1), on any given day in 2015–16 over 143,000 adults were under correctional supervision[13] in Canada: 27 per cent were incarcerated while 73 per cent were supervised in the community. While over half of all adult prisoners are under 35 years of age, the number of older prisoners (50 years and older) in federal institutions has increased 22 per cent since 2010. The minority of people incarcerated are serving federal sentences of two years or more (16 per cent) compared to most prisoners (84 per cent) who are under provincial jurisdiction (their sentences are less than two years). Furthermore, 60 per cent of people in provincial jails are incarcerated despite

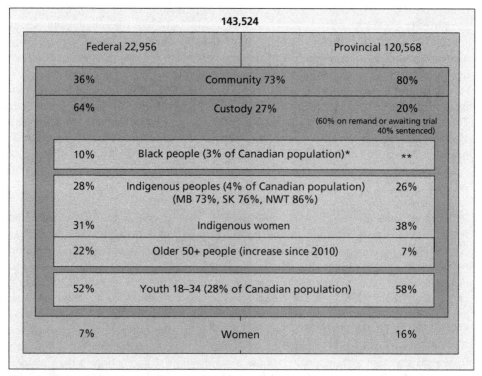

**Figure 16.1** Average 2015–16 daily count of adults under Canadian correctional supervision

not having yet been sentenced; they are on remand status—either awaiting trial and not yet proven guilty or awaiting sentencing.

Indigenous people are over-represented in both federal and provincial prisons and jails, making up over 25 per cent of inmate populations while only representing 4 per cent of the total Canadian population. This over-representation is greater for Indigenous women, and in the Prairie provinces Indigenous people make up over 75 per cent of those incarcerated in provincial jails (Statistics Canada, 2017).

Despite women representing only 15 per cent of all people under correctional supervision (Statistics Canada, 2017), young, poor, Indigenous, and racialized women are convicted predominantly for poverty-related offences[14] and are one of the fastest-growing prison populations in Canada and the world (Pate, 2006). For example, Indigenous women comprise 33 per cent of women within federal prisons (Correctional Service Canada, 2014), yet their numbers increased 58 per cent from 159 in 2006–7 to 251 in 2015–16 (Public Safety Canada, 2016).

Black[15] prisoners are another growing prison population. While Blacks represent only 3 per cent of the Canadian population, they comprise 14 per cent of federal prisoners with their numbers increasing 75 per cent in the decade preceding 2012 (Sapers, 2013).

Canada has 216 adult institutions—43 federal and 173 provincial/territorial (World Prison Brief, 2013). Conditions for prisoners within these institutions are exacerbated for Indigenous and racialized prisoners due to racism and discriminatory assessments and include: overcrowding; a lack of vocational and educational programs; ineffective mental health and substance dependence treatment; an increasing number of preventable deaths; inadequate nutrition; poor access to medical and dental care; overuse of punishment, solitary confinement, force, and inflammatory agents such as pepper spray; and poor quality of case management (Sapers, 2016).

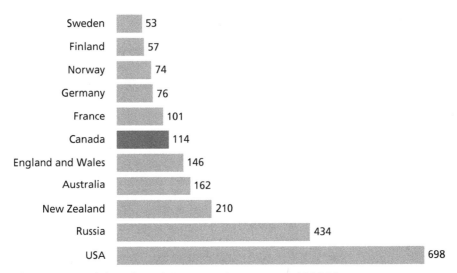

**Figure 16.2** Adult and youth incarceration rates per 100,000
Source: Data from World Prison Brief (2017).

While Canada has an overall incarceration rate of 114 people per 100,000 (see Figure 16.2), higher than that of most European countries but less than one-sixth of the rate of the United States (World Prison Brief, 2017), Canada's record in criminalizing Indigenous and racialized people is noteworthy. The Office of the Correctional Investigator (Sapers, 2006b) noted the incarceration rate for Indigenous people was nearly nine times greater than for the total population—1,024 per 100,000.

Despite the over-representation rates of Indigenous people in Canadian prisons, these are still lower than the actual numbers. According to the Canadian Centre for Justice Statistics (2005), nearly half of all people charged by Canadian police did not have their ethnic origin recorded, and for those who did it was often determined by police guesswork. Similarly, while prisons do record ethnic status, they rely on people self-identifying as Indigenous within a system where racism is systemic.

Also, while the overall crime rate in Canada has fallen 35 per cent—property crime has decreased 45 per cent since 1998 and violent crime has dropped 30 per cent since 2000 (Public Safety Canada, 2016)—and rates of incarceration for non-Indigenous prisoners have decreased (Sapers, 2006a), incarceration rates for Indigenous people have increased dramatically. In the 10 years from 2005 to 2015, numbers of Indigenous federal prisoners have increased 45 per cent and Indigenous federal women prisoners 58 per cent (Public Safety Canada, 2016). This is a relatively new phenomenon. In Manitoba in 2015, for example, Indigenous inmates were 73 per cent of the prison population (Statistics Canada, 2017); in 1949, they comprised 3 per cent (Singleton, 2001).

Whereas Indigenous people's interactions with criminal justice systems in Canada have been well documented, the experiences of racialized people with over-representation and systemic racism at all levels of the justice system (with police, in the court systems, in prisons, on probation/parole) have been frequently ignored (Chan & Chunn, 2014). Sapers (2013) reminds us that Black federal prisoners in Canada represent a diversity of ethnic, religious, and social backgrounds: half were born outside of Canada, half are under 30 years old, 23 per cent are Muslim, and only 4 per cent are women. Sapers noted that half of Black women serving federal sentences were convicted of drug trafficking charges and "many indicated that they willingly chose to carry drugs across international borders, primarily as an attempt to rise above poverty. There were some who reported having been forced into these activities with threats of violence to their children and/or families" (Sapers, 2013, p. 10). Common for all Black and racialized prisoners and despite having a lower risk to reoffend is that they were more likely to be placed in maximum security and isolation, to be labelled as gang members, and to be released from prison later in their sentences.

While the experiences of racialized prisoners in the US have been frequently profiled, Chan and Chunn (2014) argue that racism and racialization are fundamental yet rarely acknowledged realities when looking at the Canadian criminal justice context. This is evidenced by the media's racist portrayal of racialized peoples as "dangerous," as "illegal" or "aliens," or as victims who were somehow complicit in their fate. It is apparent in the essentializing of all people with brown skin as potential terrorists or gang members. It is obvious in the realities faced by racialized peoples in Canada. They are more likely to be targeted for arbitrary traffic stops and searches,

**Total inmate population: 14,615 (Average Daily Count)**

Inmate Population Diversity

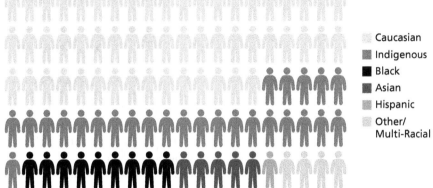

Caucasian
Indigenous
Black
Asian
Hispanic
Other/
Multi-Racial

**$111,202**

**Average Annual
Cost (2013-14) of
Incarcerating a Male
Inmate**

(Women Inmates cost
twice as much)

**1 in 4**
**inmates are Indigenous**
(36% of women inmates are Indigenous)

**1 in 4**
**inmates are over the age of 50**

**Almost 60%**
**of inmates are classified as
medium security**

**1 in 5**
**inmates are serving a life sentence**

**More than
Half**
**of all women inmates
have an identified
mental health need**
(compared to 26% of
male inmates)

**4 in 10**
**inmates are serving
a sentence of
2 to 4 years**

**Figure 16.3** Canadian prisoner demographics
Source: Sapers (2016, p. 8).

to have their 911 calls given a lower priority, to be the victims of police and corrections officers' violence, to experience a lower standard of legal representation, and to cope with more punitive sentencing. It is observable in racialized people's experiences being portrayed as isolated incidents carried out by a troubled police officer or a rogue judge. This is seen, in the Case Examples box, in David's experience in being stopped and searched, and being counselled by his lawyer to plead guilty despite his innocence. In contrast to Canada tending towards adopting American crime control penology, Finland offers an example of the transformation so desperately needed (see International Comparisons box).

## International Comparisons

### Finland

Pratt and Eriksson (2011) present Finland as an example of progressive policy development. As a result of a number of social movements in the early 1970s in Finland, discussions between prisoners, their advocates, and prison officials resulted in a fundamental shift in Finland's penal policy and in moving from a high incarceration rate to one of the lowest in the world. This shift toward a policy of normalization, where prisons reproduce the living conditions of Finnish society, meant prison reform was linked to a "broader Social Democratic programme of equality and social cohesion" (Pratt and Eriksson, 2011, p. 17). Finland's prisons are smaller, are located near or in urban centres, and are frequently open (without gates or fencing). Prisoners enjoy a quality of life that is significantly better than in Canadian and American prisons—Finnish prisoners are connected to their communities and are engaged in flexible case planning that promotes community employment and education.

# What Can Social Workers (and the Social Work Profession) Do?

A critical understanding of the effect of criminalization for marginalized people has been lacking in social work literature (Hannah-Moffat & Shaw, 2000; Monture-Angus, 2000; Reamer, 2004).[16] And while only a small percentage of social workers are employed as probation or parole officers, most social workers will work predominantly with marginalized people. Criminalization affects people who are the most marginalized (Pollack, 2004; Reamer, 2004), and social work has a dual mandate to work with the most marginalized and to work for social justice (CASW, 2005).

## Social Policy Change in Action

### British Columbia's Fondly Remembered Premier Was a Social Worker

David Barrett (1930–2018) was a retired social worker and politician. He was the Premier of British Columbia from 1972 to 1975 and received the Order of British Columbia in 2012. When interviewed about his career and what his greatest achievements were, Barrett replied it was the closing of two youth jails, the Willingdon Industrial School for Girls in Burnaby and the Brannan Lake Industrial School for Boys in Nanaimo. "We had kids going into adult prisons. . . . There were boys in Brannan Lake as young as nine years old" (*Times Colonist*, 2010). Although these centres were run by child welfare, youth were sent there from juvenile courts for offences including "incorrigibility and sexual immorality" (British Columbia, n.d.).

Before being elected to the BC legislature in 1960, Barrett worked in prisons, at the Oakalla Prison Farm in Burnaby and later at the Haney Correctional Institute in Maple Ridge.

In a lecture given in 2008, Barrett (2008) shared, "Who was it that I was responsible for in that prison? All children of poor families. Rich kids were not in jail: they could hire a lawyer and make an appeal to the judge, so they didn't go to jail."

After training as a social worker and working as a public official, Barrett used his position to educate social workers:

> I ordered all the social workers brought down to Victoria for a three-day conference and I stood up in front of them, and I said, "My fellow professionals, it is the edict of this government that we are closing the Willingdon School for Girls. If you have a troubled youngster in your community . . . we will provide facilities and services for a child who needs some time away from parents, or the setting that she is in. . . ." There was dead silence in the room. But then . . . they said, "We can't do all of that!" I asked, "Why?" "We don't have the money for all that." I said, "the money will be there, are you still in favour of it?" "Well, no." I said, "Fine. All you have to do is quit. I will not have a social worker working for the provincial government continuing the potential wasting of a young girl's life by sending her down to the Willingdon School for Girls as an excuse" . . . we have a responsibility to each other as human beings. (Barrett, 2008)

Social workers are in a primary position to understand how marginalization and oppression affect people's experiences and behaviour, and how the social labelling of those behaviours leads to criminalization (Pollack, 2004). Social workers have a particular responsibility to be informed, to be engaged with understanding how processes of criminalization occur, *and* to work for the eradication of those processes and their effects for marginalized people:

> Many of our social work interventions shift our focus from the sources of social problems to their symptoms; we too often concentrate only on improving life skills and providing tangible and referred resources. Nevertheless, sources and processes of overrepresentation, colonization, and social injustice should be of central importance to social work. Our areas of practice and work with marginalized populations automatically require social work to reconsider its role not only in the processes leading to the child welfarization and criminalization processes but also in the prevention of those processes for Aboriginal peoples. (West, 2014, p. 27)

## Chapter Summary

This chapter introduced criminalization as a framework to understand marginalized people's experiences with the criminal justice system and the harm this system poses specifically to racialized and Indigenous people. By linking criminalization with colonialism, structural violence, and neo-liberalism, we can understand how policies and processes of profiling, sentencing, confinement, release, and risk assessment pose tangible risk for the very people social work is mandated to serve.

Going back to the case examples at the start of this chapter, this framework helps us in understanding how Grant's privilege as a white middle-class man increased his ability to have his charges dropped and how Lorrie's and David's marginalization increased their criminalization. It assists us in reframing people's behaviours as resistance to oppression rather than assuming a pathology in their intent. It provides evidence for us when we challenge notions that the criminal justice is fair, that the police always protect, or that the assessment tools we use are above reproach. It holds us accountable to use language that promotes the inherent dignity of people who have been criminalized and to challenge mainstream theories that further marginalize the people we are mandated to serve. It can also inspire us to vote for and support politicians who resist crime control platforms, who support human rights for all, who work to decriminalize social problems, and who are committed to social justice.

## Discussion Questions

1.  How can the criminal justice system be perceived as fair and just by Canadians belonging to privileged groups?

2.  Why should social workers be concerned with who is criminalized?

3.  How is the criminal justice system a form of contemporary colonialism for Indigenous people?

4.  Given that Finland has for nearly 50 years successfully used a very different criminal justice approach than that of Canada, how can social workers ethically support Canadian criminal justice policy and the risk it poses to marginalized people?

## Notes

1.  Chan and Chunn (2014) remind us that racialization is produced and maintained through the intersectionality of racism, sexism, ableism, heterosexism, xenophobia, and so on.

2.  The broken windows approach, based on earlier research by Philip Zimbardo, was first widely discussed in an *Atlantic Monthly* article by Kelling and Wilson (1982).

3.  Visible police presence in communities was often described as the return to beat patrol where police officers would leave their patrol cars and walk through neighbourhoods.

4.  While profiling members of impoverished communities and racialized minorities in a "get tough on crime" approach has been documented in a number of major cities in Canada, statistics on charge rates delineating race/ethnicity generally are not collected by Canadian police forces. Instead, statistics are collected using police reports, and these are divided into categories of crimes and their severity (Crime Severity Index and Violent Crime Severity Index), along with geographical locations of criminal activity (Allen, 2015). Overall, crime statistics from 1998 to 2015 show that serious crime has been in decline across Canada, with small pockets of fluctuating crime in 2003 and 2015 (Allen, 2015). In 2015, Alberta was a crime hot spot, with the largest increase in provincial crime statistics, up 18 per cent over 2014. Other provinces with increased crime rates include Newfoundland and Labrador, Manitoba, and Saskatchewan, all provinces also struggling with economic downturns and increasing poverty. Only the Northwest Territories had an

increase in violent crime: a 10 per cent increase in homicide and serious assault.

5. "Starlight tours" reportedly originated with the Saskatoon police practice of arresting Indigenous men and women for misdemeanours and then dumping them at the edge of the city. This practice has been occurring across the Prairies.

6. Justice Minister Jody Wilson-Raybould's rationale for the review on mandatory minimum sentences was based on two principles: first, that it is part of a judge's role to determine sentencing, and second, that mandatory minimum sentencing contributes to the significant backlog of criminal cases in the Canadian court system, as accused people tend to choose a trial (and possible not guilty verdict) over a plea bargain when faced with a minimum sentence.

7. This principle was established following the Supreme Court of Canada ruling in the *Gladue* case in 1999, in an effort to reduce the over-incarceration of Indigenous prisoners in the criminal justice system. The Truth and Reconciliation Committee's Calls for Action echo this sentiment: "30. We call upon federal, provincial, and territorial governments to commit to eliminating the overrepresentation of Aboriginal people in custody over the next decade, and to issue detailed annual reports that monitor and evaluate progress in doing so." (TRC, 2015b, p. 3)

8. While the intention of the *Gladue* ruling was to decrease the numbers of Indigenous people incarcerated in Canadian prisons, the effects have been negligible in reducing incarceration and have been undermined by "the focus on individualized justice and the presence . . . of retributive sentencing objectives" (Milward & Parkes, 2014, p. 117).

9. While colonialism and colonization are often interchanged in the literature, Osterhammel (2005, p. 4) differentiates colonization from colonialism: "'colonization' designates a process of territorial acquisition . . . and 'colonialism' a system of domination." As Hart (2002, pp. 26–7) explains, colonialism "is driven by a world-view and processes that embrace domination, self-righteousness, and greed and affects all levels of Indigenous peoples' lives."

10. The parole board is independent from the federal government and operates under the mandate of the CCRA. Federal prisoners can apply for parole after completing one-third of their sentence (CCRA, section 120.1) and are eligible for statutory release after completing two-thirds of their sentence (CCRA, section 127.3).

11. For example, women prisoners face specific barriers to release, particularly within the actuarial system of risk considered by parole boards (Hannah-Moffat & Yule, 2011). Parole eligibility is determined by reviewing the prisoner's case file and holding a parole hearing. The case file includes extensive information about her criminal record, social history, and conduct while incarcerated, but is not an objective documentation of risk. Rather, "early characterizations of an offender's criminogenic risk/need, offence cycle and social history were often repeated verbatim in subsequent reports in her file and, ultimately, in the decision narrative" (p. 153). Parole boards then have to balance whether the past determines the future risk to reoffend.

12. Hannah-Moffat's (2016) discussion of "dynamic structural risk" is informed by Maruna's (2001) work on desistance theory, which argues that mainstream criminological theories positing that pathways to crime start in adolescence and continue inexorably throughout adulthood in a form of criminal essentialism is not substantiated by empirical evidence. Rather, most individuals involved in the juvenile justice system do not progress inevitably to the adult system, and illegal behaviour for adults tends to end before the age of 30 in the "aging-out phenomenon" (Maruna, 2001). The difficulty he addresses in some detail is how to define desistance from crime; if criminal behaviour is not a stable or permanent trait, but rather a more sporadic event, then defining desistance from crime can be problematic and should be determined more along a continuum that views refraining from crime as a process rather than an abrupt change from criminal to non-criminal. Societal pressures are also then considered as important factors in criminal risk and recidivism.

13. We use the term "correctional supervision" to refer to all people who, once charged, either are in prison serving their sentence or awaiting trial, or are being monitored in the community through either provincial probation or federal parole. The direct implications of being under correctional supervision include being regularly monitored by criminal justice systems (police, prison, probation, parole), having restrictions placed on one's liberty (for example, where one lives; where or what one does for employment; where and when one can physically move, eat, or sleep; the kinds of substances one can legally use, such as nicotine or alcohol); having one's privileges revoked (having a curfew imposed if in the community, being revoked from the community and returned to prison, or being held in solitary confinement); and having a record,

14. MacFarlane and Milaney (2008, p. 2) define poverty-related offences as "attempts to cope with the restrictions of poverty using a social inappropriate but readily available means." This would include shoplifting, welfare fraud, prostitution, transporting or carrying drugs across international borders, failure to pay a fine for owning a dog without a licence, riding the subway without a ticket, or urinating in a park. We would temper that definition by adding that the means available to people coping with poverty are often criminalized. For example, welfare rates are so low that it is nearly impossible to survive without finding other ways of fulfilling basic needs, such as by stealing food (shoplifting), not declaring additional sources of revenue (welfare fraud), agreeing to exchange sexual services for remuneration (prostitution), or being promised $1,000 to be a drug mule (trafficking).

15. Correctional Service Canada (CSC), the body that oversees all federally sentenced persons, uses 28 categories for racial identities in its intake process, including Black, Caribbean, or sub-Sahara African. While racialized individuals may have self-identified at intake using any of the 28 categories, Sapers (2013) used the term "Black" to be consistent with how CSC compiled and reported the data.

16. Bracken, McNeill, and Clarke (2010) noted that while nearly 20 per cent of probation officers in Canada were social workers, the only Canadian social work academic journal published just two articles on social work criminal justice within a recent 20-year period.

# References

Adams, H. (1999). *Tortured people: The politics of colonization*. Penticton, BC: Theytus Books.

Aglias, K. (2004). Women in corrections: A call to social work. *Australian Social Work*, *57*(4), 331–42. doi:10.1111/j.0312-407X.2004.00163.x

Allen, M. (2015). Police-reported crime statistics in Canada, 2015. Retrieved from http://www.statcan.gc.ca/pub/85-002-x/2016001/article/14642-eng.htm

Barrett, D. (2008). A lecture by David Barrett, 27 Oct., Thompson Rivers University, Kamloops, BC.

Bauman, Z. (1989). *Modernity and the Holocaust*. Ithaca, NY: Cornell University Press.

Bracken, D., Deane, L., & Morrissette, L. (2009). Desistance and social marginalization: The case of Canadian Aboriginal offenders. *Theoretical Criminology*, *13*(1), 61–78. doi:10.1177/1362480608100173

——, McNeill, F., & Clarke, A. (2010). Social work, criminal justice and their reconfiguring relationships. Revista de *Asistenţă Socială*, (1), 114–24. Retrieved from www.ceeol.com

British Columbia. (n.d.). 1950s: The Brannan Lake Industrial School and Willingdon Industrial School. https://www2.gov.bc.ca/gov/content/justice/criminal-justice/corrections/about-us/history/youth/1950

Canadian Association of Social Workers (CASW). (2005). *Code of ethics*. Ottawa: CASW. Retrieved from https://www.casw-acts.ca/sites/default/files/attachements/casw_code_of_ethics_0.pdf

Canadian Centre for Justice Statistics. (2005). *Collecting data on Aboriginal people in the criminal justice system: Methods and challenges*. Retrieved from http://www.statcan.ca/cgi-bin/downpub/listpub.cgi?catno=85-564-XIE2005001

Canadian Human Rights Commission. (2003). *Protecting their rights: A systemic review of human rights in correctional services for federally sentenced women*. Ottawa.

*CBC News*. (2013). Aboriginals, black people over-represented at Hamilton jail. Retrieved from http://www.cbc.ca/news/canada/hamilton/news/aboriginals-black-people-over-represented-at-hamilton-jail-1.2451143

Chan, W., & Chunn, D. (2014). *Racialization, crime, and criminal justice in Canada*. Toronto: University of Toronto Press.

Christie, N. (1994). *Crime control as industry: Towards gulags, western style*. London: Routledge.

Comack, E. (2012). *Racialized policing: Aboriginal people's encounters with the police*. Winnipeg: Fernwood.

Corrections and Conditional Release Act, SC, 1992, c. 20.

Corrections and Conditional Release Statistics Overview. (2015). Retrieved from https://www.publicsafety.gc.ca/cnt/rsrcs/pblctns/ccrso-2015/index-en.aspx

Correctional Service Canada. (2013). Institutional profiles. Retrieved from http://www.csc-scc.gc.ca/institutions/001002-4003-eng.shtml

———. (2014). Research results women offenders: Quick facts. Retrieved from http://www.csc-scc.gc.ca/publications/005007-3014-eng.shtml#_ftnref3

Crawford, A. (2017, 11 Feb.). Liberals looking to eliminate many minimum mandatory sentences, justice minister says. *CBC News*. Retrieved from http://www.cbc.ca/news/politics/mandatory-minimum-sentences-justice-1.3976205

Crawford, T. (2013, 6 July). Vancouver police asked to explain huge disparity in ticketing between wealthy, impoverished neighbourhoods. *Vancouver Sun*. Retrieved from http://www.vancouversun.com/vancouver+police+asked+explain+huge+disparity+ticketing+being poor/

Criminal Code, RSC, 1985, c C-46.

Culpitt, I. (1999). *Social policy and risk*. London: Sage.

De Giorgi, A. (2010). Immigration control, post-Fordism, and less eligibility: A materialist critique of the criminalization of immigration across Europe. *Punishment & Society, 12*(2), 147–67. doi:10.1177/1462474509357378

DeKeseredy, W. S., & Perry, B. (Eds.). (2006). *Advancing critical criminology: Theory and application*. Oxford, UK: Lexington Books.

Doyle, A., & Moore, D. (Eds.). (2011). *Critical criminology in Canada: New voices, new directions*. Vancouver: University of British Columbia Press.

Frideres, J., & Gadacz, R. (2012). *Aboriginal peoples in Canada*. Toronto: Pearson.

Galtung, J. (1969). Violence, peace, and peace research. *Journal of Peace Research, 6*(3), 167–91. doi:10.1177/002234336900600301

Garland, D. (2001). *The culture of control: Crime and social order in contemporary society*. Chicago: University of Chicago Press.

Hamilton, A., & Sinclair, C. (1991). *Report of the Aboriginal justice inquiry of Manitoba: The justice system and Aboriginal peoples* (Vol. 1). Winnipeg: Queen's Printer. Retrieved from http://www.ajic.mb.ca/volumel/toc.html

Hannah-Moffat, K. (2001). *Punishment in disguise: Penal governance and federal imprisonment of women in Canada*. Toronto: University of Toronto Press.

———. (2005). Criminogenic needs and the transformative risk subject. *Punishment & Society, 7*(1), 29–51. doi:10.1177/1462474505048132

———. (2016). A conceptual kaleidoscope: Contemplating "dynamic structural risk" and an uncoupling of risk from need. *Psychology, Crime and Law, 22*(1–2), 33–46.

———. & Shaw, M. (Eds). (2000). *An ideal prison? Critical essays on women's imprisonment in Canada*. Halifax: Fernwood.

———. & Yule, C. (2011). Gaining insight, changing attitudes and managing "risk": Parole release decisions for women convicted of violent crimes. *Punishment & Society, 13*(2), 149–75.

Hart, M. (2002). *Seeking Mino-Pimatisiwin: An Aboriginal approach to helping*. Halifax: Fernwood.

———. (2009). Anti-colonial Indigenous social work: Reflections on an Aboriginal approach. In R. Sinclair, M. Hart, & G. Bruyere (Eds.), *Wicihitowin: Aboriginal social work in Canada* (pp. 25–42). Toronto: Brunswick Books.

Kelling, G. L., & Wilson, J. Q. (1982, Mar.). Broken windows: The police and neighborhood safety. *Atlantic Monthly, 249*(3), 29–38. Retrieved from https://www.theatlantic.com/magazine/archive/1982/03/broken-windows/304465/

Knepper, P. (2007). *Criminology and social policy*. London: Sage.

Lappi-Seppälä, T. (2009). Imprisonment and penal policy in Finland. *Scandinavian Studies in Law, 54*, 333–80.

Luck, S. (2016, 20 May). Black, Indigenous prisoners over-represented in Nova Scotia jails. *CBC News*. Retrieved from http://www.cbc.ca/news/canada/nova-scotia/black-indigenous-prisoners-nova-scotia-jails-1.3591535

MacFarlane, C., & Milaney, K. (2008). *Crimes of desperation: The truth about poverty-related crime*. Calgary: United Way of Calgary. Retrieved from http://www.calgaryunitedway.org/images/uwca/our-work/communities/public-policy-research/Crimes%20of%20%20Desperation%20Final%20mar08.pdf

Maruna, S. (2001). *Making good: How ex-convicts reform and rebuild their lives*. Washington, DC: American Psychological Association.

Milward, D., & Parkes, D. (2014). Colonialism, systemic discrimination, and the crisis of Indigenous over-representation: Challenges of reforming the sentencing process. In E. Comack (Ed.), *Locating law: Race, class, gender, sexuality, connections* (3rd edn, pp. 116–42). Halifax: Fernwood.

Monchalin, L. (2016). *The colonial problem: An Indigenous perspective on crime and injustice in Canada*. Toronto: University of Toronto Press.

Monture, P. (1989–90). A vicious circle: Child welfare and First Nations. *Canadian Journal of Women and the Law, 3*(1), 1–17.

Monture-Angus, P. (2000). Lessons in decolonization: Aboriginal overrepresentation in Canadian criminal justice. In D. Long & O. Dickason (Eds), *Visions of the heart: Canadian Aboriginal issues* (2nd edn, pp. 361–86). Scarborough, ON: Nelson.

Mullaly, B., & West, J. (2018). *Challenging oppression and confronting privilege: A critical approach to anti-oppressive and anti-privilege theory and practice* (3rd edn). Toronto: Oxford University Press.

Oberman, J., & Johnson, K. (2016). Broken windows: Restoring social order or damaging and depleting New York's poor communities of color? *Cardozo Law Review, 37*(3), 931–54.

Osterhammel, J. (2005). *Colonialism: A theoretical overview* (2nd edn, S. Frisch, Trans.). Princeton, NJ: Markus Wiener.

Palmater, P. (2016). Shining light on the dark places: Addressing police racism and sexualized violence against Indigenous women and girls in the National Inquiry. *Canadian Journal of Women and the Law, 28*(2), 253–84.

Parton, N. (1996). Social work, risk, and the "blaming system." In N. Parton (Ed.), *Social theory, social change and social work* (pp. 98–114). New York: Routledge.

Pate, K. (2003). Prisons: The latest solution to homelessness, poverty and mental illness. Presented at the WomenSpeak Series, Calgary. Retrieved from http://www.caefs.ca/wp-content/uploads/2013/04/prison.pdf

———. (2006). Advocacy, activism and social change for women in prison. *Canadian Woman Studies, 25*(3–4), 81–99.

Peck, J. (2003). Geography and public policy: Mapping the penal state. *Progress in Human Geography, 27*(2), 222–32. doi:10.1191/0309132503ph424pr

Pollack, S. (2004). Anti-oppressive social work practice with women in prison: Discursive reconstructions and alternative practices. *British Journal of Social Work, 34*(5), 693–707. doi:10.1093/bjsw/bch085

Pratt, J., & Eriksson, A. (2011). "Mr. Larsson is walking out again": The origins and development of Scandinavian prison systems. *Australian & New Zealand Journal of Criminology, 44*(1), 7–23.

Public Safety Canada. (2016). Corrections and conditional release: Statistical overview 2015. Retrieved from http://www.publicsafety.gc.ca

Razack, S. (2002). Gendered racialized violence and spatialized justice: The murder of Pamela George. In S. Razack (Ed.), *Race, space and the law: Unmapping a white settler society* (pp. 121–56). Toronto: Between the Lines.

———. (2015). *Dying from improvement: Inquests and inquiries into Indigenous deaths in custody.* Toronto: University of Toronto Press.

Reamer, F. (2004). Social work and criminal justice: The uneasy alliance. *Journal of Religion & Spirituality in Social Work, 23*(1–2), 213–31.

Reiman, J. & Leighton, P. (2017). *The rich get richer and the poor get prison: Ideology, class, and criminal justice* (11th ed.). New York: Routledge.

Sapers, H. (2006a). Backgrounder: Aboriginal inmates. Retrieved from http://www.oci-bec.gc.ca/newsroom/bk-AR0506_e.asp

———. (2006b). *Annual Report of the Office of the Correctional Investigator 2006–2007.* Retrieved from http://www.oci-bec.gc.ca/cnt/rpt/annrpt/annrpt20062007-eng.aspx

———. (2009). *Annual Report of the Office of the Correctional Investigator (2008–2009).* Catalogue no. PS100E-PDF. Ottawa: Minister of Public Works and Government Services Canada.

———. (2012). *Spirit matters: Aboriginal people and the Corrections and Conditional Release Act.* Catalogue no. PS104-6/2013E-PDF. Ottawa: Minister of Public Works and Government Services Canada.

———. (2013). *A case study of diversity in corrections: The Black inmate experience in federal penitentiaries: Final Report.* Catalogue No. PS104-8/2013E-PDF. Ottawa: Correctional Investigator of Canada.

———. (2015). *Annual Report of the Office of the Correctional Investigator (2014–2015).* Catalogue no. PS100E-PDF. Ottawa: Minister of Public Works and Government Services Canada.

———. (2016). *Annual Report of the Office of the Correctional Investigator (2015–2016).* Catalogue no. PS100E-PDF. Ottawa: Minister of Public Works and Government Services Canada.

Schissel, B., & Brooks, C. (Eds). (2002). *Marginality and condemnation: An introduction to critical criminology.* Halifax: Fernwood.

Schneider, J., & Schneider, P. (2008). The anthropology of crime and criminalization. *Annual Review of Anthropology, 37*(1), 351–73. doi:10.1146/annurev.anthro.36.081406.094316

Silver, E., & Miller, L. (2002). A cautionary note on the use of actuarial risk assessment tools for social control. *Crime & Delinquency, 48*(1), 138–61. doi:10.1177/0011128702048001006

Singleton, W. (2001). *Beyond the attic door: A feminist social history of imprisonment at the Portage*

*Gaol from 1945 to 1970* (Unpublished master's thesis). University of Manitoba, Winnipeg.

Smith, G. (2000). Protecting and respecting Indigenous knowledge. In M. Battiste (Ed.), *Reclaiming Indigenous voice and vision*. Vancouver: University of British Columbia Press.

Statistics Canada. (2017). Adult correctional statistics in Canada, 2015/2016. Ottawa: Statistics Canada. Retrieved from http://www.statcan.gc.ca/pub/85-002-x/2017001/article/14700-eng.htm

*Times Colonist*. (2010, 1 Oct.). Barrett: Still cheeky as he turns 80. Retrieved from https://web.archive.org/web/20160208124233/http://www.canada.com/story_print.html?id=2c5ec4e1-ab01-4e9b-a501-e1c64ac8d5ad&sponsor=

Truth and Reconciliation Commission of Canada (TRC). (2015a). *Final Report of the Truth and Reconciliation Commission of Canada. Volume One: Summary*. Winnipeg.

———. (2015b). *Calls to action*. Winnipeg.

Turnbull, S. (2016). *Parole in Canada: Gender and diversity in the federal system*. Vancouver: University of British Columbia Press.

Wacquant, L. (1999). How penal common sense comes to Europeans: Notes on the transatlantic diffusion of the neoliberal doxa. *European Societies, 1*, 319–52.

———. (2009). *Punishing the poor: The neoliberal government of social insecurity*. Durham, NC: Duke University Press.

Webb, S. (2006). *Social work in a risk society: Social and political perspectives*. New York: Palgrave Macmillan.

Webster, C., & Doob, A. (2007). Punitive trends and stable imprisonment rates in Canada. *Crime and Justice, 36*(1), 297–369.

West, J. (2014). *The role of social work in contemporary colonial and structurally violent processes: Speaking to Aboriginal social workers who had child welfare and/or criminal justice involvement as youth* (Unpublished PhD thesis). University of Manitoba, Winnipeg. Retrieved from http://mspace.lib.umanitoba.ca/handle/1993/23854

Wilson, W., & Yellow Bird, M. (2005). Beginning decolonization. In W. Wilson & M. Yellow Bird (Eds), *For Indigenous eyes only: A decolonization handbook* (pp. 1–7). Santa Fe, NM: School of American Research.

World Prison Brief. (2013). Canada. Retrieved from http://www.prisonstudies.org/country/canada

———. (2017). Highest to lowest prison population total. Retrieved from http://www.prisonstudies.org/highest-to-lowest/prison-population-total

# 17 Nationalism, Neo-liberalism, and the Securitization of Canadian Immigration Policy

*Daphne Jeyapal*

## Chapter Objectives

*This chapter will help you to develop an understanding of:*

- migration policy as a regulatory mechanism that determines who can enter Canada, when, and on what terms;
- public and policy discourses of nationalism, neo-liberalism, and securitization and their influence on immigration policy;
- the role of the field of migration in shaping Canadian race relations and the politics of citizenship in the age of terror.

## Introduction

On 28 January 2017, following US President Donald Trump's infamous ban on refugees and travellers from seven predominantly Muslim countries, Prime Minister Justin Trudeau tweeted:

**Justin Trudeau** ✔
@JustinTrudeau

✈ Follow

To those fleeing persecution, terror & war, Canadians will welcome you, regardless of your faith. Diversity is our strength #WelcomeToCanada

12:20 PM - 28 Jan 2017

↩  ↻ 425,556   ♥ 778,116                          ⓘ

**Figure 17.1** Prime Minister Trudeau tweets that all are welcome in Canada
Source: Twitter @Justin Trudeau, 28 Jan. 2017.

Minutes later, he shared the 2015 photograph of himself welcoming Syrian refugees at an airport in Toronto, trending #WelcomeToCanada (see Figure 17.2). When this photo was first published, it exemplified the fanfare around the Prime Minister's compassion and inclusivity because his newly elected party had just pledged to resettle 25,000 Syrian refugees within months. Personally handing them winter coats, he was reported telling the first refugee to disembark from government planes, "You're safe at home now."

The image of Canada as a welcoming nation to people from all over the world is an enduring one. Canadian national identity relies on it (see Chapter 7). Trudeau's political platform for the 2015 federal election included promises to welcome Syrian refugees escaping persecution. During his inaugural speech, he proudly reiterated, "A Canadian is a Canadian is a Canadian." Following nine years of former PM Stephen Harper's conservative immigration statements and policies, most people perceived Trudeau as a welcome change. For many, he symbolized a return to Canada's high-profile liberal rhetoric of multiculturalism, inclusivity, and international peacekeeping. Furthermore, in stark contrast to the current repressive US administration, this characterization may seem apt. But are these feel-good politics and inclusive imagery an accurate depiction of immigration policy in Canada?

In 2016 the Angus Reid Institute, in partnership with the Canadian Broadcasting Corporation, conducted a national poll. Contrary to popular belief, it indicated that the Canadian public views immigration less favourably than our southern neighbours. Compared to an almost 50/50 split among the US public, two out of three Canadians, rather

**Figure 17.2** Prime Minister Justin Trudeau greets a Syrian girl at Toronto's Pearson Airport in 2015

Source: Prime Minister Justin Trudeau on Twitter.

---

## Case Examples   Coming to Canada

---

**Marcos**, 35, has spent the last 14 years going back and forth between Jamaica and Canada through the Seasonal Agricultural Worker program. On average, he works 70 to 80 hours a week for less than minimum wage. Most of the money he earns—significantly less than his Canadian counterparts—supports his wife and children. Because Ontario has no laws to protect farm workers who work in extreme heat, Marcos labours in unbearable conditions during the summer months. Despite being injured numerous times, he has learned not to complain because he has seen that those who protest tend to be deported and do not return.

**Elaina**, 46, is an asylum seeker from Mexico. After numerous attempts to leave her abusive partner, Elaina got help from her parents, who collected the money necessary to purchase airfare for their daughter and two grandchildren to leave the country. Arriving in Manitoba, Elaina is informed that because she is from a **designated country of origin**, she is assumed to be "safe" by the Canadian government. Despite physical and emotional injuries, Elaina now has only 15 days to complete her application. She learns that her application would be strengthened with proof of abuse that she was unable to secure before her escape.

**Michael**, 55, the descendant of Irish immigrants, was born and raised in Chicago, where he currently works as an architect. As a result of protections offered by NAFTA, Michael has spent periods of time working in Canada. After the recent US presidential election, Michael, a card-carrying Democrat, does not want to live in the US. He was one of the 200,000 people accessing Canada's immigration website causing it to crash on election night. He has bought a three-bedroom home in Toronto and found a job that pays him more than what he previously earned. At his job interview, he was not asked if he has "Canadian experience."

than encouraging cultural diversity, would prefer that minorities "do more to fit in" with mainstream Canada. In answer to another survey question, one-third expressed dissatisfaction with how new immigrants are integrating into their communities. On immigration and refugee policies, the majority believe that Canada should put its economic needs before humanitarian considerations: 79 per cent believe it should prioritize its own economic and workforce needs above people in crisis abroad.

Migration is a highly contested area of social policy that speaks to the core question of who is Canadian. It is a realm that requires a close consideration of how ideologies, cultural beliefs, and economic forces provide coherence and contradiction. This chapter examines the historical context of immigration policy to make sense of immigration in post-9/11 Canada, through the era of the Harper government's conservative politics, into the Trudeau government's liberal revisioning. I highlight three trends to unpack the construction and effect of immigration policy: **nationalism** (an ideology that places the needs and formation of the nation-state above all else), neo-liberalism (the social and economic policy trend towards privatization, competition, efficiency, and personal responsibility), and **securitization** (constructing a policy area as one with security implications). Applying these concepts to immigration policy helps us to uncover how government and public discourse on the current Immigration and Refugee Protection Act (IRPA), immigration reform through Bill C-24 and Bill C-31, and tightening anti-terror and security legislation influence race relations and the politics of citizenship in Canada.

# Contextualizing Immigration Policy

Immigration policy has always been central to colonialism and the dispossession of Indigenous peoples. Through the migration of white settlers, land was stolen and repopulated while Indigenous peoples were marginalized and murdered. The first government body overseeing immigration was called the Department of Immigration and Colonialism. The present-day migration of people, often themselves escaping the violence of post-colonialism, war, and deprivation in their own nations, further complicates the politics and conditions of Canada as a white settler society.

Immigration policy is a racialized, gendered, and class-based regulatory mechanism that continues to determine who can enter Canada, when, and on what terms. Some immigration streams have historically excluded people based on country of origin; others specify or favour gendered criteria (such as the Caregiver program or the Seasonal Agricultural Program), while interweaving economic and political ideologies that support the demand for cheap and often deportable labour. This policy field is filled with contradiction. It is also deceptive: political discourses of immigration policy are often inconsistent with the actual operation of immigration. The dominant (i.e., mainstream white) public, politicians, policy actors, and immigration officers make contradictory and sometimes arbitrary decisions about who deserves inclusion within Canada's borders. It marks "us" through the binary that allows judgement of "them." These exclusionary power relationships foster hierarchies of superiority and inferiority between dominant "Canadians" and "migrants": those who are accepted on Canadian soil in contrast to those who are not and those who are yet to be.

A **critical intersectional framework** allows us to examine immigration with respect to immigrants' demographic trends and the political, economic, and social processes linked to policy development and implementation, along with the discourses and rationales that support these legislative manoeuvres. As social workers, we emphasize respect for the inherent dignity and worth of all people, while examining conditions of social justice that connect the past to the present.

## Overview of Historical Immigration Trends

Each phase of Canada's immigration policy is framed through political rhetoric underlying economic need and social practices. The first Immigration Act (1869) pursued immigration through what is often referred to as an "open door policy," where Canadian leaders imagined the future nation as a European farming country. Not all were welcome, however, as barriers were in place against persons with disabilities, those convicted of a crime, the poor, and the ill. While racialized people were allowed entry or detained under specific economic and political categories, such as labourers, railroad builders, domestic workers, or other indentured workers, they remained at the margins of Canada's national narrative. Europeans were viewed as desirable, and Northern Europeans were preferred and privileged. Between 1900 and 1964, these countries, in particular Britain, were the primary source of migrants to Canada.

Overt exclusion laws kept out "undesirable" immigrants. The Chinese Head Tax and Exclusion Act (1885) imposed large taxes on immigrants and denied them citizenship. The Continuous Journey Regulation (1908) prohibited people who did not "come from the country of their birth or citizenship by a continuous journey"—applying specifically to those from India, from which there were no direct passenger shipping lines to Canada. The second Immigration Act (1919) officially excluded specific groups through section 38, which limited or prohibited the entry of "undesirable races or nationalities." The "none is too many" view of immigration officials turned away Jewish refugees prior to and during World War II.

In the 1960s, Canada's immigration policy shifted from explicitly race-based exclusion criteria to a "points system" (1967). Prospective immigrants were required to pass a points-based evaluation determined according to their skills and experience—a process still in effect today. This shift prioritized skilled immigrants who were necessary to shift Canada's agricultural-based economy to produce industrial goods for national consumption. The approach aligned with a growing national discourse of Canada as a welcoming nation. But points allocated for each category indicate implicit biases within the policy framework. For example, increased language points for fluency in English and French indicate a preference for those from Europe or previously colonized nations. Increased points for previously working in Canada indicate a preference for Canadian over foreign work experience. While Canada had previously admitted refugees on a case-by-case basis prior to 1969, by signing on to the UN Convention Relating to the Status of Refugees, the government formally recognized refugees as a class of immigrants. In keeping with Canada's growing embrace of multiculturalism, the 1975 Green Paper on immigration framed immigration as a source of welcome ethnic diversity. A new Immigration Act (1976) introduced the basic framework for Canada's contemporary immigration policy with new migrant categories such as family, assisted relatives, humanitarian, independent, and, a few years later, business classes. In 1977, Canada removed "homosexuality" from the list of inadmissible classes.

Three decades later, as Western nations continued to lead the way towards economic globalization, Canadian leaders framed the nation as post-industrial and in need of migrants to generate knowledge and efficiencies to ensure Canada's competitiveness internationally. In 2001, the federal government introduced the Immigration and Refugee Protection Act, which retained much of the previous legislation's framework while tightening eligibility criteria in some categories, such as refugees, skilled immigrants, and business immigrants, and expanding some entitlements, such as recognizing same-sex and common-law relationships. It also extended the government's reach in response to the terrorist attacks on the United States of 11 September 2001. Bill C-31, Protecting Canada's Immigration System Act, officially amended the IRPA in 2012, implementing a range of ideological and ad hoc changes, and altering much of the immigration terrain. Each shift of immigration policy leads to a unique emphasis on who gets in. These policy changes and discursive changes alter our social contexts.

## Current Context of Immigration Policy

Canada is a geographically vast nation with about 35.2 million inhabitants (2016), nearly one-fifth of whom were born in another country. With the exception of Indigenous peoples (approximately 5 per cent), the rest are migrants or descendants of migrants. Contextualizing migration this way acknowledges that immigration is not a new phenomenon: it is the story of colonialization, and new and not-so-new immigrants are part of Canada's national colonial story. Under Canada's Constitution, immigration is now a "concurrent power" where jurisdiction is formally shared between federal and provincial governments. Three departments oversee immigration administration and management. Immigration, Refugees and Citizenship Canada (IRCC) is responsible for the admission and integration of temporary and permanent immigrants; the Immigration and Refugee Board is an administrative tribunal overseeing humanitarian claims; and the Canada Border Services Agency (CBSA) oversees matters relating to border services and is thereby responsible for detaining or deporting those who are "illegalized," or deemed a threat to national security.

Today, immigration categories for permanent residents are established through economic, family, or humanitarian classes. Table 17.1 provides an overview of categories and admittance rates for 2016. While family-class immigrants and refugees lag behind in acceptance numbers, economic-class immigrants are the largest group of permanent migrants.

**Table 17.1**  New Permanent Residents Admitted in 2016

| Immigrant Category | Number Admitted in 2016 |
|---|---|
| Federal economic, skilled | 59,999 |
| Federal economic, caregivers | 18,467 |
| Federal economic, business | 867 |
| Provincial nominees | 46,170 |
| Quebec skilled workers | 25,857 |
| Quebec business immigrants | 4,634 |
| Total economic | 155,994 |
| Spouses, partners, and children | 60,588 |
| Parents and grandparents | 17,041 |
| Family, other | 375 |
| Total family | 78,004 |
| Protected persons in Canada and dependants abroad | 12,116 |
| Government-assisted refugees | 23,523 |
| Blended visa office-referred refugees | 4,434 |
| Privately sponsored refugees | 18,362 |
| Total protected persons and refugees | 58,435 |
| Humanitarian and other | 3,913 |
| **Total** | **296,346** |

Source: IRCC, Permanent Resident Data as of May 2017. Retrieved from https://www.canada.ca/en/immigration-refugees-citizenship/corporate/publications-manuals/annual-report-parliament-immigration-2017.html

**Table 17.2**   Top 10 Source Countries for Permanent Residents Admitted in 2016

| Rank | Country | Number |
|---|---|---|
| 1 | Philippines | 41,791 |
| 2 | India | 39,789 |
| 3 | Syria | 34,925 |
| 4 | China, People's Republic of | 26,852 |
| 5 | Pakistan | 11,337 |
| 6 | United States of America | 8,409 |
| 7 | Iran | 6,483 |
| 8 | France | 6,348 |
| 9 | United Kingdom and UK Overseas Territories* | 5,812 |
| 10 | Eritrea | 4,629 |
| Total top 10 | | 186,375 |
| All other source countries | | 109,971 |
| **Total** | | **296,346** |

*The United Kingdom currently maintains 14 Overseas Territories across the globe. These are the remnants of the once vast British Empire, and include Bermuda, the Turks and Caicos Islands, the British Virgin Islands, the Cayman Islands, Gibraltar, Montserrat, and the Falkland Islands.
Source: IRCC, Permanent Resident Data as of May 2017. Retrieved from https://www.canada.ca/en/immigration-refugees-citizenship/corporate/publications-manuals/annual-report-parliament-immigration-2017.html

Table 17.2 demonstrates the shifting face of immigration.

In addition to permanent immigrants, in 2015 IRCC also admitted 73,111 individuals to Canada under the Temporary Foreign Worker (TFW) Program and 176,772 under the International Mobility Program (IMP). This means that temporary migrants outnumber economic migrants. These statistics provide a glimpse into demographic trends that allow us to uncover a continuing hierarchy of migrants through explicit and implicit preferences, discourses, and rationales. Furthermore, a review of immigration trends provides insight into those who are "desirable" over others who are "undesirable" or altogether inadmissible.

## Social Policy Change in Action

### Social Work Advocacy to Challenge Discriminatory Immigration Policy

*by Ilaneet Goren*

*Ilaneet Goren, MSW, is the Director of Workplace Learning and Development at Harmony Movement.*

While Canada's immigration policy has evolved to redress exclusion of specific groups throughout history, people with physical, cognitive, and intellectual disabilities continue to be excluded on the basis of their disability. Section 38.1(c) of the Refugee and Immigration Protection Act deems foreign nationals inadmissible if their health condition "might reasonably be expected to cause excessive demand on health or social services." This means eligible applicants are being denied entry because they or someone in their family has a disability, while many families also lack the financial resources to participate in the lengthy appeal process. According to disability rights advocates, the inadmissibility criteria reproduce the bias and stereotype that disability is a "burden," a deficit within the individual, and an economic risk to Canadian health and social services. But this perception isn't grounded in reality because it fails to recognize that many people with disabilities can and do contribute to Canada's social and economic life.

This policy has led to immense stress and separation of families, exemplified in the 2016 case of Felipe Montoya's family. A professor at a major Canadian university who arrived on a work visa, Montoya was seeking permanent status for himself and his family. Their application was denied because Montoya's son, Nico, has Down syndrome, despite his good health status and no evidence of "burden" on the system. While the Montoya case garnered media attention that undoubtedly helped the cause, it was hardly unique. Several other cases of children with physical and intellectual disabilities being denied permanent status are emerging across Canada, including the case of a Filipina caregiver, Karen Talosig, who was told she couldn't bring her deaf teenage daughter to Canada because of the inadmissibility policy.

As a social worker and diversity manager at an agency supporting people with intellectual disabilities, I was part of a large community response to put pressure on the Minister of Immigration to make changes to this discriminatory policy. This included signing and circulating petitions and co-writing an article for a non-profit alternative online magazine to bring greater attention to the barriers and challenges some of the most marginalized people in Ontario experience because of race, disability, and immigration status. In facilitating equity and diversity workshops for developmental sector agencies, I engaged service providers and managers in conversations about the impact of the immigration policy on immigrants and refugees with disabilities, and what it means in terms of access to government services for people without legal status.

I also participated in organizing and facilitating a series of round tables in three communities across Ontario hosted by the Ontario Coalition of Agencies Serving Immigrants. The round tables brought disability and immigration workers together around a common goal of addressing barriers to access for immigrants with disabilities. These actions were pieces of the large community response and advocacy efforts led by Montoya's family and their allies and supporters. Although the initial decision was eventually overturned on compassionate grounds after several months of lobbying, allowing Montoya's family to stay in Canada, advocates continue to lobby for changes to Canada's inadmissibility policy.

# Theorizing Discourses of Immigration

Three theoretical frameworks can help us unpack evolving immigration trends. For each, I introduce the theory, followed by examples that suggest how it is constructed through immigration policy.

## Nationalism

> This is the voice of the West
> And it speaks to the world
> We hold by right
> And maintain by might
> Until the foe is backward driven
> White Canada forever
> White Canada forever
> White Canada forever
> Our watch word be
> God save the King.
> — early 1900s beer ballad

Nationalism prioritizes the nation's needs over all other considerations. Nationalism is core to immigration because the process of nation-building is integral to settler colonies such as Canada, Australia, and New Zealand that were historically planned from the outside and organized through the violence of conquest. They created their own self-colonizing practices and processes to mark their unique nationality. As the lyrics of a popular beer ballad of the early 1900s clearly express (Kazimi, 2004), Canada's legacy is deeply entrenched in the political, social, and racial construction of a white nation. Alongside the dispossession of Indigenous peoples, Canada actively pursued the formation of a white, predominantly British colony. Prime Minister John A. Macdonald referred to Canada as a "white man's country" in Parliament (Dua, 2000), and subsequent leaders, such as Mackenzie King, continued to foster this rhetoric of the "white" race as superior and thereby preferred. In a post–World War II speech, he emphatically defended this racial preference when he stated, "I wish to make quite clear that Canada is perfectly within her rights in selecting the persons whom we regard as desirable future citizens. It is not a 'fundamental human right' of any alien to enter Canada. It is a privilege. It is a matter of domestic policy" (quoted in Triadafilos, 2012, p. 15).

Dominant discourses distinguish between the plights of white colonials or nationals and immigrants (Thobani, 2007). Colonials and nationals are viewed as "overcoming adversity when founding the nation," and having "intrinsic worthiness." Because they are considered "compassionate" and "law-abiding," their failings are "individual and isolated." By contrast, racialized migrants are viewed as "responsible for importing their backward cultural practices and diseases," being "susceptible to lawlessness," and "tending to resort to deceit—placing loyalty to kin above all else." Their failings are thought to "reflect the inadequacies of their race." Thobani (2007, p. 18) argues that "racial domination lies at the very heart of Canadian nationhood, at the core of its identity and its social, judicial, and moral order."

Policy and legal processes legitimize the violence of conquest and the creation of a white settler society. While white citizens benefit from this construction, racialized migrants are transformed into objects of exploitation. Canada's treatment of early Chinese migrants clearly highlights this racial preference and pattern of keeping the "inferior" on the margins. After the Canadian Pacific Railway sought cheap, expendable labour to lay tracks, Parliament passed the Chinese Immigration Act of 1885, establishing a Chinese head tax on each Chinese person entering Canada. This policy was meant to dissuade and limit the immigration of Chinese people. Starting at $50, the tax went up to $500 in 1903 (the equivalent of two years' salary or a purchase of two homes at the time!), and stayed in place for 38 years. Explicitly, Asians were considered "undesirable" whereas the British were "desirable."

The *Komogata Maru* case challenged the "continuous journey" regulation to highlight how British citizenship alone did not make the ideal Canadian. When 376 citizens from British India arrived in Vancouver in 1914 fleeing the tumult of colonial India, only 24 were admitted. The rest were not allowed to disembark for two months, and then were forced to return to India and face imprisonment and, in some cases, death. The discourse surrounding this decision was entrenched in the passengers' "criminality" and attacked the authenticity of their legal claim to enter Canada, couched in racist views of morality, suitability, and civilization. Canada discriminated against British subjects at a time when the country was accepting huge numbers of European migrants (more than 400,000 arrived in 1913 alone). This case highlights Canada's preference for white immigrants. Policies like this placed those of European origin at the centre, with racialized subjects at the margins. Racialized people's claims to enter Canada could be denied based on moral, social, and political grounds, and their construction as inferior, criminal, violent, dangerous, disease-ridden, and deceptive were often evoked to justify their exclusion, if not their physical expulsion.

The discourse of "White Canada" may seem unfamiliar today. Unlike other nations like Germany, France, and Britain, which have disavowed multiculturalism, Canada continues to espouse it as state policy. We colloquially refer to ourselves as a "mosaic" in contrast to the "melting pot" of the United States. Since the inception of the "points system" in 1967, Canada has formally removed race-based preferences in its selection process. But Canadian society has consistently exalted white citizens through specific moral and social characteristics—they are "insiders" who determine the inclusion or exclusion of others. These preferences are often reflected in how points are quantified and distributed. Over time, commonsensical white preferences have erased the negative explicit connotations attached to "White Canada." As such, assumptions of race neutrality and discourses of inclusivity and merit incite many important questions: Has our national commitment to a "White Canada" truly been replaced by a desire for diversity? How does immigration policy continue to embed a racial hierarchy by constructing some migrants as "deserving" at the expense of others? Who is "Canadian"?

## The "Canadian" Experience

Despite a majority of migrants being racialized, nationalism endures through immigration policy biased towards markers of whiteness. Immigrants' foreign credentials and work experience are not consistently recognized by prospective employers. Immigrants are often overqualified for the jobs that they are hired for. Employers' demand for "Canadian experience" marginalizes immigrants within the labour market, and results in a "waste of valuable human capital" (Guo, 2009). Bauder (2003, p. 699) argues that "professional associations and the state actively exclude immigrant labour from the most highly desired occupations in order to reserve these occupations for Canadian-born and Canadian-educated workers." In light of the tremendous shortage of doctors across the country, foreign medical professionals denied recognition is one example. Many immigrants feel "tricked into this situation by Canadian immigration policies and labour market regulations that do not disclose to immigrants prior to their arrival in Canada that their human capital will be devalued" (Bauder, 2003, p. 713).

Despite decades of critique from immigration activists and social workers serving migrants, the Canadian government further legitimized "Canadian experience" by formalizing this problematic and controversial criterion as a source of exclusion in a new immigration category. Launching the Canadian Experience Class in 2008, the government claimed they would be encouraging the "best and the brightest" to migrate and succeed in Canada. Essentially, this program credits years of experience already earned within Canada, encouraging those who already work as temporary residents to seek permanent status. It is justified through the same rhetoric that justifies this preference within the labour market: "Canadian experience" is superior to "foreign experience." Whose credentials and experience are valued in the job market? Who gets to determine these criteria? Who do these systems and structures benefit? Unconscious Eurocentric preferences and racist discourses are woven through policy and legislation. These biases sustain and maintain a dominant white culture and systemic racism through immigration.

## Conditions on Being "Canadian"

Not all Canadians are treated equally through immigration policy. In fact, citizenship may not even be a permanent status. Through Bill C-24, the Strengthening the Canadian Citizenship Act passed by the Harper Conservative government in 2014, the Canadian government has the right of revoking "citizenship of dual citizens, who while they were Canadian citizens, engaged in certain actions contrary to the national interests of Canada, and permanently barring these individuals from reacquiring citizenship." Such a policy is reminiscent of the 22,000 Japanese Canadians who were placed in internment campus and the 4,000 who were stripped of their Canadian citizenship before being deported back to Japan during World War II (Japanese Canadian Centennial Project, 1978). Immigration authorities now have the power to arbitrarily revoke citizenship on the grounds of "false representation," "fraud," "knowingly concealing material circumstances," "treason," "terrorism," "espionage against Canada," or taking up arms against Canada. There is also a new resident provision that requires an applicant to be physically present in Canada for four out of six years. This requirement distinguishes between naturalized and other Canadian citizens to violate mobility rights (Canadian Bar Association, 2014)—a criterion that natural-born Canadian citizens do not face. The policy has been criticized for targeting people from the Middle East, Africa, Asia, and South America; for targeting people with dual citizenship; for making it more difficult to appeal court decisions; and for granting unprecedented power to the Minister of Citizenship and Immigration (Amin-Khan, 2015, p. 132; Canadian Civil Liberties Association, 2015). Problematically, the majority of revocation cases will be decided by the minister (or a delegate), not a federal court judge who will be involved for only "certain complex cases." This denies people the right to due process and gives immigration officials disproportionate discretion in determining whose citizenship is revoked.

The bill emphasizes "protecting and strengthening the great value of Canadian citizenship, and reminds individuals that citizenship is not a right, it's a privilege" (Black, 2014). It alters the construction of citizenship by echoing Mackenzie King's rhetoric of conditional citizenship for only the privileged. Critics argue that this creates a "two-tiered" immigration system for dual citizens; it illegalizes migrants without definitive evidence. As Amnesty International (2014, p. 3) states:

> These provisions risk fueling stereotypes that view Canadians of certain national origins who maintain (voluntarily or not) citizenship of those countries, as being less loyal to Canada; stereotypes that equate their particular foreignness with terrorism. Individuals who do not carry additional nationalities are seen as the "true" or "pure" Canadians; while individuals who carry other nationalities in addition to their Canadian citizenship are perceived to have suspect or divided loyalties.

Despite Liberal critiques of this bill while in opposition, and Trudeau drawing attention to the sanctity of citizenship during his election campaign, the Liberal government has used this bill to revoke citizenship at a far more aggressive rate than Harper's government did. As of February 2017, at least 236 people had received notice of their Canadian citizenship revocation since the Liberals came to power (Smith, 2017).

These examples demonstrate how the immigration system is intertwined with the criminal justice system. Where criminalized acts could be addressed through law, the immigration system has introduced increasingly interdependent criteria to create a two-tiered system of who is deserving. Where non-migrants are penalized through the law, migrants are additionally penalized through immigration policy. They are criminalized and constructed as "undeserving" of citizenship, figuratively and literally. This conditional citizenship is endorsed by the majority of the Canadian public. The Angus Reid Institute reports that compared to 21 per cent who want to abolish Bill C-24, 53 per cent urge that the legislation remain in place (Maloney, 2016). Eighty-four per cent of Conservative supporters and 38 per cent of Liberal supporters are in support of Bill C-24, while 40 per cent of those who support the NDP believe the bill should be left as is (Maloney, 2016).

## Neo-Liberalism

The country relies on immigration to maintain our economic and social systems. When the Canadian Pacific Railroad was under construction, workers from China were welcomed and encouraged to fulfill labour needs at great risk. Unlike white workers, who were paid between $1.50 and $2.50 per day and had their supplies included, Chinese workers were paid $1 a day and still had to pay for their food and camping and cooking gear. One worker died for every mile of track laid down through the Rocky Mountains between Calgary and Vancouver. Yet the 1902 Royal Commission on Chinese and Japanese Immigration clearly stated that the Chinese were "unfit for full citizenship . . . they are so nearly allied to a servile class that they are obnoxious to a free community and dangerous to the state."

Anti-Asian racism fuelled these oppressive immigration restrictions. In September 1907, over half of Vancouver's population of 30,000 attended a rally by the Asiatic Exclusion League wearing ribbons that said "For a White Canada." Homes and businesses in Chinatown were vandalized by approximately 7,000 men. The *Vancouver Province* reported that "the mob soon left the Chinese quarter and headed in the direction of Japtown. . . . The crash of glass was continual. Window after window was shattered in stores and boarding houses as the riotous gang pushed farther into the thoroughfare lined with nests of Japanese" (*CBC*, 2001). On 1 July 1923, colloquially referred to as "Humiliation Day," Chinese immigration was definitively banned; this legislation was not repealed for another 25 years. Immigration maintains the nation's labour force efficiently, at minimal cost to the state. The migrant worker bears the cost, risk, and loss. Then and now, migrants are continually constructed as "second-class citizens" who are a drain on our welfare systems, often scapegoated as being responsible for economic recessions (Li, 2003).

## The Neo-Liberalization of Migrants and the Settlement Sector

Today, preferred immigrants must be good neo-liberal subjects. Their success comes from personal responsibility, individual labour, and monetary security that they have earned themselves. Canada's immigration-settlement sector has been a victim of the Canadian government's neo-liberalization. Over the past decade, 19 citizenship and immigration offices have closed, limiting front-line positions and centralizing services. Social welfare has been downgraded to an individual responsibility. When migrants do not effectively or adequately integrate, they are blamed instead of the fault being found in the lack of needed supports and services.

Systematic and widespread cuts across the settlement sector reached their nadir between 2010 and 2013, when Harper's Conservative government enacted a 10 per cent cutback of $53 million. Community agencies, English as a second language (ESL) programs, advocates, and social service workers once available to support people through complex migration procedures were no longer available or had their services greatly reduced (Chua, 2014). The Interim Federal Health Program drastically limited services for refugee claimants (Eggertson, 2013). These cuts affect those most marginalized within the nation-state: those with few rights to rely on and those most in need of health, social, economic, and political supports. The government also effectively eliminated controversy by cutting funds to the advocacy groups that might critique these decisions.

At the same time, the government spent time and money introducing a series of bills designed to limit access to services and resources for asylum seekers and refugees, such as Bill C-43, which denies refugee claimants access to social assistance, and Bill C-51, which supports mandatory detention (Canadian Council for Refugees, 2014). These cutbacks imply that migrants who require supports are not the migrants Canada desires. Instead, Canada prefers migrants who can support the financial burden of their migration, settlement, and integration into society. Thus, in some instances refugees and asylum claimants are denied reasonable access to health care, and despite proficiency in one of Canada's two main languages being identified as the most important key to integration that supports immigrant "success," cutbacks to these programs have directly disadvantaged those not from Europe or from previously colonized countries.

## The Neo-Liberalization of Immigration Policy

The efficiency of processing immigration applications has dominated discourses on Canada's immigration system. Often this challenge is evoked in comparison to other Western nations whose immigration systems are "more efficient." In an effort to "manage" the system more efficiently, the government decided to eliminate 300,000 skilled-worker applications in 2012. Announcing this decision shortly after the Economic Action Plan 2012 was announced, Citizenship and Immigration Minister Jason Kenney informed the media: "All the applications in the skilled worker category that we received prior to February 28, 2008 will be returned. That will reduce the backlog from 420,000 to 160,000." According to Kenney, this decision supported "making our immigration system truly fast and flexible in a way that will sustain Canada's economic growth" and "make the Canadian economy better and wealthier." Thirty thousand visa applications were returned without acknowledgement of consequences to the applicants who had applied. The minister avoided responding to the question of his government being unfair to those applicants, some of whom had waited 11 years in queue (*Canadian Immigrant*, 2012).

### The Canadian Experience Class

Immigration categories themselves are now entrenched in neo-liberal rhetoric. The Canadian experience class (CEC) clearly signifies this neo-liberal preference. Finance Minister Flaherty drew on neo-liberal logics when he framed the CEC as a "key tool" that would modernize the immigration system (*Toronto Star*, 2008). The CEC requires prior work history in Canada in a "skilled" occupation and moderate proficiency in one of Canada's official languages to ensure that new immigrants can "hit the ground running." According to the government of Canada, "Through the Canadian Experience Class, newcomers will be more likely to make the most of their abilities while undergoing a more seamless social and economic transition to Canada. And, in turn, their cultural and economic contributions will enrich Canada" (Government of Canada, 2008). This emphasis masks how this immigration category makes temporary residency precarious (Bhuyan, Jeyapal, Ku, Sakamoto, & Chou, 2015). It glorifies temporary immigration streams as an opportunity for potential permanency. As Bhuyan and colleagues state, "the 'efficiency' of this modern approach is predicated on the potential exploitation of temporary migrants who must demonstrate their capacity to settle in Canada, without the use of public support that was historically provided to newcomers" (Bhuyan et al., 2015, p. 11). Canada prefers "desirable" subjects who have already demonstrated their ability to settle and integrate by finding employment to earn the elusive "Canadian experience," thereby proving themselves worthy candidates for citizenship. This rhetoric appears deracialized, despite being deeply embedded within nationalistic race-based constructions on criteria and conditions that make experience "Canadian" (Bhuyan et al., 2015). The requirement of Canadian experience itself has faced decades of resistance and critique, most recently by the decision of the Ontario Human Rights Commission (2013) to denounce it as "prima facie discrimination" (see Chapter 7).

### Temporary Foreign Worker Program

No immigration policy is as overtly discriminatory as the Temporary Foreign Worker Program. The program allows Canadian employers to hire foreign nationals to fill labour shortages when qualified Canadian citizens and permanent residents cannot be found. This translates to contexts where work conditions are so unfavourable, and pay is so unfair, that only the most marginalized, precarious, and desperate would consider this source of employment. Where workers in Canada refuse the inhumane conditions of this labour, those from elsewhere are brought in to work instead. It is easy to unpack the problematic logic underlying this program from the title of the category itself. This is an immigration category that constructs a worker as "temporary." However, these temporary labourers are often long-time residents of Canada, yet with none of the rights, social supports, or funding warranted for residents who are made permanent. These people, like Marcos in the Case Examples, are disposable, deportable, and transient by law. More people gain entry through the TFWP than as economic migrants. They inhabit a "liminal space" in Canadian public consciousness—their labour is fundamental to the nation, but their identities are made invisible from racism (Lee, 2003).

The TFWP is clearly designed to benefit employers' capitalist interests and supersede employee rights. For example, the Seasonal Agricultural Worker program has allowed Canadian farmers to rely on foreign workers—predominantly from Mexico and the Caribbean—for over five decades. The immigration category itself was introduced after Canadian farmers argued that local workers could no longer be persuaded to perform this low-paid, dangerous work. The program is constructed as a neo-liberal win-win: Canadian farmers have their labour needs met through a virtually unlimited pool of workers, while foreign workers are gifted the opportunity to work and earn in Canada. However, this "gift" requires that migrant workers are employed in unfree relationships as a condition of entering, inhabiting, and working in Canada. They enter through a "revolving door of exploitation" (Sharma, 2008). This includes an expectation to work unregulated hours (often 12-hour days, 7 days a week) for less than minimum wage with no possibility of overtime pay. They are continually exposed to dangerous working conditions, denied the protective equipment routinely provided to local workers, given little to no safety training, and discouraged from seeking treatment if they are injured on the job (Fudge, 2016; Faraday, 2014). Most are tied to a specific employer, making them more vulnerable and afraid to report their work conditions for fear of losing their jobs or being blacklisted or deported (Lee, 2003).

It is easy to see why critics argue that this program is a system of modern-day slavery that consistently allows employers to exploit workers who are denied the rights promised Canadians, including any possibility of applying for permanent residency (Liew, 2016). Through this program, workers will never gain Canadian citizenship. As Sharma (2008, p. 418) asserts, "the notion of citizenship is not a philosophical absolute but the mark of a particular kind of relationship that people have with one another." Citizenship is as much about formal status as it is about one's belonging, power, and inclusion within the nation-state. In this case, citizenship or its lack operates as a strategy of exploitation that reinforces the continuity of migrant workers as non-citizen subjects.

## Securitization

Securitization is the process of transforming a policy area, such as immigration, into the realm of security. But security for whom? To protect against whom? From what? Objective 1 of the Immigration and Refugee Protection Act (IRPA) (2001) is "to promote international justice and security by fostering respect for human rights and by denying access to Canadian territory to persons who are criminals or security risks." With these criteria undefined, much room for interpretation and bias exists. With an assumption that all immigrants have the potential to threaten national security, the realm of immigration categorically criminalizes, if not rejects, individuals deemed a threat. Securitization emphasizes national security where "all spaces are vulnerable" and "open to exploitation by terrorists and organized criminals" (Kruger, Mulder, & Korenic, 2004, p. 82), requiring government control and supervision. Consequently, migrants become an object of security threat. They are tracked, assessed, and monitored as part of the regulatory process.

As Amin-Khan (2015, p. 119) illustrates, the construction of securitization is closely woven through constructions of racialization:

> Securitization is a process whereby those who fit a certain identity-based profile— of the "terrorist" other or of someone viewed as liable to indulge in criminal activity to harm state and society—are targeted, treated suspiciously, and/or subjected to racism and harm from ordinary members of mainstream Western society, media, and security forces.

In immigration policy, securitization operates through racist assumptions and discourse. It creates and condones a sense of urgency that justifies measures of "survival" that often contradict, if not suspend, rights, laws, and political processes protecting citizens. Following the 9/11 attacks in the US, that country ushered in an explicit "war on terrorism"—i.e., war on terrorists or those with the potential to be terrorists—and called on many of its allies to join the cause.

## "Protecting" Canada's Immigration System

The threat of terrorism was again evoked when Tamil refugees arrived in 2009. Fleeing a 30-month-long military campaign by the Sri Lankan government against the Liberation Tigers of Tamil Eelam (LTTE), which resulted in the death of between 40,000 and 80,000 Tamil civilians and displaced over 130,000 people in 2009 alone (Amnesty International, 2009), 76 Tamils on board the *Ocean Lady* and 492 Tamils aboard the *Sun Sea* arrived on the shores of British Columbia. They were met with moral panic and racist discourse resembling the *Komagata Maru* incident of almost a century earlier. This time, three different tropes were employed: the "queue-jumper," the "terrorist," and the "breeder" (Krishnamurthi, 2013). Through her study of popular media reports on the 2010 arrival of the *Sun Sea*, Krishnamurthi uncovered how dominant discourses framed the asylum seekers as undeservingly entering through a back door and embodying the LTTE's criminality and terrorist threat. Their imagined offspring would also take away from more deserving Canadians. This incident demonized refugees during the 2011 federal election, when the Conservative Party branded itself as the only party that was "tough on human smuggling" by making direct reference to Tamil refugees. Immigration Minister Kenney commented:

> We proposed the measures in Bill C-31 to demonstrate to Canadians and the vast majority of immigrants who are law-abiding that we will not tolerate those who seek to abuse our generosity, including bogus asylum claimants, human smugglers and those who might represent a risk to Canadian security. (Government of Canada, 2012)

Bill C-31 criminalizes asylum seekers by defining "irregular arrival," which refers to a person who is unable to provide identifying documentation upon arrival, or who was suspected of being a victim of trafficking or of having an affiliation with a terrorist organization. Irregular arrivals can be detained without charge for up to 12 months in a detention centre or jail without any review of their file. If their claim is accepted, they will be released without the possibility of applying for permanent residency for five years. They cannot apply to travel outside the country or see or sponsor family members. If the claim is rejected, they have no chance of appeal but are instead deported back to the country they were originally fleeing. By contrast, human traffickers are not criminalized through this legislation.

Through this bill the Immigration Minister has the authority to determine "safe" and "unsafe" countries; only people fleeing "unsafe" countries are deemed deserving of asylum. Cases of asylum seekers from a "safe" or "Designated Country of Origin" are handled differently from those whose countries are not on the list (see Table 17.3). They are granted 15 days instead of 60 to file a claim and are given a hearing within 30 to 45 days. The hearing's outcome cannot be appealed (Bragg, 2013). This list results in a two-tier process based on ideology and statistics of violence rates, despite the fact that violence can take place anywhere. In the Case Examples box, Elaina's profile highlights this reality: all women across class, race, and country are vulnerable to gender-based persecution despite being from a "safe" country like Mexico. The focus remains on criminalizing migrants: "The Designated Countries of Origin policy is meant to deter abuse of the refugee system by people who come from countries generally considered safe. Refugee claimants from Designated Countries of Origin will have their claims processed faster" (Government of Canada, 2017b).

By criminalizing migrants, the bill effectively constructs them as deserving or undeserving, based on their country of origin. The mandatory detention of asylum seekers, including minors, is highly problematic. Between 2006 and 2014, over 87,317 migrants were jailed without charge (Never Home, n.d., para. 1), including 807 children annually. In Canada, migrants are the only people who can be jailed without being charged with any criminal offence. Discourses of criminalization have had differential impacts on racialized migrants because "racialized stereotypes have been mobilized to construct

**Table 17.3    Designated Countries of Origin**

| | | |
|---|---|---|
| Andorra | Iceland | Norway |
| Australia | Ireland | Poland |
| Austria | Israel (excludes Gaza and | Portugal |
| Belgium | the West Bank) | Romania |
| Chile | Italy | San Marino |
| Croatia | Japan | Slovak Republic |
| Cyprus | Latvia | Slovenia |
| Czech Republic | Liechtenstein | South Korea |
| Denmark | Lithuania | Spain |
| Estonia | Luxembourg | Sweden |
| Finland | Malta | Switzerland |
| France | Mexico | United Kingdom |
| Germany | Monaco | United States of America |
| Greece | Netherlands | |
| Hungary | New Zealand | |

Source: Government of Canada (2017b).

Muslims, Arabs, and South Asians (and all those who fit these stereotypes) as suspects through a security discourse that serves to criminalize their communities" (Tomasso, 2012, p. 334).

## "Securing" the Canada–United States Border

The Safe Third Country Act or STCA (2002) was implemented following the initial panic of 9/11, and it has bound Canada and the US through migration politics, policy, and administration in uniquely problematic ways. According to the Act, refugees can claim asylum only in the first country they landed in that was safe. It was one "part of the US–Canada Smart Border Action Plan in the wake of the September 11 attacks. That plan aimed to strengthen North American security while keeping a free flow for trade and commerce across the border." (Harris, 2017). The Act protects neo-liberal interests of desired trade, but criminalizes those seeking protection. It asserts that asylum seekers are equally safe in both countries. However, the Act applies only at designated crossings, therefore creating a loophole for migrants who cross the border irregularly to apply for refugee status.

This has had unprecedented implications under US President Donald Trump's administration. One of his first moves as President was to implement a ban on refugees from predominantly Muslim countries. However, Trump's executive order was overturned by the courts based on grounds that it "did not advance national security, said the administration had shown 'no evidence' that anyone from the seven nations—Iran, Iraq, Libya, Somalia, Sudan, Syria, and Yemen—had committed terrorist acts in the United States" (Liptak, 2017). The fear of continuing securitization and potential deportation by those seeking asylum in the US has resulted in people fleeing to Canada, and a third, somewhat watered-down iteration of Trump's Muslim ban was upheld by the US Supreme Court in June 2018. Despite people facing racially motivated hate and surveillance in the United States, the STCA prevents them from crossing into Canada if they first landed in the US and Canada is compelled to refuse their application for refugee status. Growing numbers of people are risking their lives as they attempt to irregularly cross the border into Canada.

Because asylum seekers are ineligible for federal settlement funding and caseloads are exponentially growing because of increasing numbers of refugees from the US, organizations serving asylum seekers such as the Inland Refugee Society in Vancouver face a predicament. On average, the Society serves 800 people annually, but within the first five months of 2017 it served 700 refugees. Executive Director Mario Alaya reported that "refugees tell him they've fled the US because they're 'afraid of the new government' and they decided to come to Canada after hearing Prime Minister Justin Trudeau's message of welcome to refugees" (Nuttal, 2017). Yet, organizations like this, with limited funding and no federal supports for asylum seekers, face closing and asylum seekers are often forced to go underground.

While asylum seekers confront an increasingly punitive experience moving from the US to Canada, potential permanent migrants from the US are increasingly welcomed. Migration from the US to Canada has always spiked following watershed political events. American immigration dramatically increased during the Vietnam War (falling in 1973 after the military draft ended) and doubled in the years of the US invasion of Iraq and in the years after 9/11. Preliminary signs—such as the overwhelming traffic to the Canadian immigration website during the US election that caused it to crash—indicate a similar spike following Trump's victory. In the days following the US election, new changes to the points system were launched. Potential migrants from the US already benefit from language criteria (they are likely to speak English or French) and education criteria (their degrees are more likely to be recognized) compared to migrants from other nations. Now, applicants can earn 50 additional points by working in Canada, which has been made possible and easier through NAFTA. Already having a job offer (which is the case for many applicants outside the US) was reduced from 600 to 50 points, significantly altering non-US applicants' competitiveness. These changes make it easier for Americans to work in Canada and become citizens once they are here (Cain, 2016). The biases implicit in the quantification of points indicate Canada's "desired" group of immigrants—a construction Michael in the Case Examples box benefits from when he decides it's time for a change. The nationalist and neo-liberal privileges implicit in the system make him a more "deserving" candidate for Canadian citizenship.

This construction of safety is evidently problematic: safe for whom? Safety from what/whom? The complex bureaucratic and legal structures that constitute these systems mask the subjective nature of how some regions are racialized as safe or unsafe, and how migrants from these areas are constructed as threatening the social and moral order of the nation while others are made invisible.

## Securitization amid Humanitarian Crises

The lifeless body of three-year-old Alan Kurdi, washed ashore on a Greek island, appeared on the front pages of international media and ushered in public global consciousness of the Syrian refugee crisis in September 2015. His family were Syrian refugees trying to reach Europe. They were crossing the Aegean Sea between Turkey and Greece when he, his brother, and mother died. Because the family was hoping to join their relatives in Vancouver after unsuccessful attempts of sponsorship, his death and the Syrian refugee crisis became a major issue during the 2015 Canadian federal election.

The Syrian crisis since 2011 has led to the death of 470,000 Syrians in their homeland, the displacement of 6.1 million from their homes, and 4.8 million seeking refuge in other countries (Human Rights Watch, 2016). Since Canada's commitment to resettle Syrian refugees was announced, 40,081 had arrived from 4 November 2015 to the end of January 2017. While the Syrian refugee policy explicitly aims to protect those most vulnerable (Government of Canada, 2017a, p. 1), markers of difference continue to operate through this regulatory mechanism. The government decided to marginalize single men through the program. By prioritizing families, women, children, and sexual minorities, the government argues that its primary aim is to help complete families move, despite the reality that Syrian men in their twenties form one of the groups most at risk in Syria. By excluding unaccompanied men as potential refugees, Canada walks an uncomfortable line between "a family first" ideology (which it does not necessarily enact towards Canadian families) and reinforcing a view of Syrian men as potentially more deviant and criminal. Through this logic, Alan Kurdi's father, who lost his entire family, would not be eligible without existing family ties in Canada.

Canada implements a comprehensive five-step process to screen Syrian refugees—initial registration, security screening, and selection process; a medical examination to screen for infectious diseases and identify health care needs; depending on clearance to

## International Comparisons

### Global Responses to the Syrian Refugee Crisis

Countries neighbouring Syria such as Turkey, Iraq, Egypt, Jordan, and Lebanon have provided immense protection to fleeing Syrians. Turkey is the largest host country with over 2.9 million registered Syrian refugees. Over 2.2 million refugees are estimated to be within Lebanon, and 1.2 million in Jordan. Despite significant adverse economic and social costs to these host countries, they have provided access to their territories and dedicated financial resources and social services to provide aid (Ostrand, 2015). More than 80 per cent of registered Syrian refugees in these countries live in cities and communities rather than in designated refugee camps.

The UN High Commissioner for Refugees has urged European nations to do more to support the countries bordering Syria, and expressed hope that "humanity will not be put on a ballot" in their upcoming elections (Weaver, 2017). He compared this unfolding crisis to World War II, and noted that during that time countries around the world supported Europe.

fly, a transportation period; security checks and medical screening upon arrival; and being placed in various communities depending on whether refugees are government-sponsored or privately assisted (Hansen & Huston, 2016). This process requires complex co-ordination and facilitation among the Canadian Border Services Agency; Department of National Defence/Canadian Armed Forces; Global Affairs Canada; Immigration, Refugee and Citizenship Canada; Public Health Agency of Canada; Public Services and Procurement Canada; and the Royal Canadian Mounted Police (Government of Canada, 2016).

Dominant discourses in news media suggest that while some support helping refugees, others argue that the state should prioritize the needs of vulnerable Canadians before supporting those from abroad, or, alternatively, that Canada should use its discretionary resources to guard against potential future terrorist attacks rather than welcome potential future terrorists. Overt violence, such as the pepper-spraying of Syrian refugees at a Muslim welcoming event in Vancouver, highlights the dissonance and violence underlying these tensions. Syrian refugees already face significant challenges in their settlement. Families have struggled to find apartments, have been forced to live in hotels, and have not been able to access language classes (Friesen, 2017).

## Chapter Summary

This chapter has examined how citizenship functions as a tool of political stratification that allows Canadian immigration policy, politics, and the public to segregate the "deserving" from the "undeserving," based on traits of racialization, economic worth, and risk in the age of terror. These are important considerations. Permanent residency and citizenship are critical factors that provide labour standards and wage structures, conditions of employment and social engagement, and access to rights, freedoms, and social services.

Citizenship determines the conditions of who belongs, whose safety takes precedence, and whose humanity is valued. Various current policies and processes, and the politics behind them, fundamentally erode democracy and the myth of Canada as a welcoming and inclusive nation.

Applying the concepts of nationalism, neo-liberalism, and securitization to immigration policy uncovers how government and public discourse on the current policies influence race relations and the politics of citizenship in Canada. It is difficult to separate immigration moves that are nationalist, neo-liberal, or based in securitized logic. Discourses of "us" and "them" operate alongside an emphasis on the primacy of the economy and a moral panic over perceived threats to national security. Processes of nationalism, neo-liberalism, and securitization are deeply intertwined through the terrain of Canada's immigration policy.

## Discussion Questions

1.  How and why does Canada continue to reinforce its image as an inclusive nation?

2.  Should Canada prioritize humanitarian need over economic need? What are the strengths and challenges of such an approach?

3.  What are the social, economic, and political implications of creating two-tiered immigration categories through immigration policy?

4.  How can social workers problematize the criminalization of migrants?

## References

Amin-Khan, T. (2015). Security and its impact on migrants and refugees. In H. Bauder & J. Shields (Eds), *Immigrant experiences in North America: Understanding settlement and integration*. Toronto: Canadian Scholars' Press.

Amnesty International. (2009). Sri Lanka's promise to free displaced must be followed by concrete action. Retrieved from https://www.amnesty.org/en/latest/news/2009/11/sri-lanka-promise-reedisplaced-must-followed-concrete-action-20091124

———. (2014). Amnesty International concerns regarding proposed changes to the Canadian Citizenship Act. Reviewed from https://www.amnesty.ca/sites/amnesty/files/c24_brief_amnesty_international_canada.pdf

Bauder, H. (2003). "Brain abuse," or the devaluation of immigrant labour in Canada. *Antipode*, 35(4), 699–717.

Bhuyan, R., Jeyapal, D., Ku, J., Sakamoto, I., & Chou, E. (2015). Branding "Canadian experience"

in immigration policy: Nation building in a neoliberal era. *Journal of International Migration and Integration*. Advanced online publication. doi:10.1007/s12134-015-0467-4

Black, D. (2014, 27 June). Immigration experts say Bill C-24 discriminatory and weakens citizenship. *Toronto Star*. Retrieved from https://www.thestar.com/news/immigration/2014/06/27/immigration_experts_say_bill_c24_discriminatory_and_weakens_citizenship.html

Bragg, B. (2013). Immigration policy guide: A guide to Canada's changing immigration policy. Ethno-cultural council of Calgary. Retrieved from http://www.ecccalgary.com/wp-content/uploads/Immigration_Policy_Guide_06-13.pdf

Cain, R. (2016, 18 Nov.). New immigration rules make it easier for Americans to work and stay in Canada. *Global News*. Retrieved from http://globalnews.ca/news/3075089/new-immigration-rules-make-it-easier-for-americans-to-work-and-stay-in-canada/

Carlier, M. (2016). Explaining differences in the Canadian and American response to the Syrian refugee crisis. *Virginia Policy Review, 9*, 56–106.

Canadian Bar Association. (2014). Bill C-24 Strengthening Canadian Citizenship Act. National Immigration Law Section. Retrieved from https://www.cba.org/CMSPages/GetFile.aspx?guid=97a417ea-9a17-446d-be2b-5a8ec6769aaf

Canadian Civil Liberties Association. (2015). Understanding Bill C-24 and recent changes to the Canadian Citizenship Act. Retrieved from https://ccla.org/understanding-bill-c-24/

Canadian Council for Refugees. (2014). *Canadian Council for Refugees Annual Report 2013–2014*. Ottawa, Canada. Retrieved from: http://ccrweb.ca/en/annual-report-2013-2014.

*Canadian Immigrant*. (2012, 29 Mar.). 300,000 skilled worker applications are being eliminated. Retrieved from http://canadianimmigrant.ca/slider/300000-skilled-worker-applications-are-being-eliminated

*CBC*. (2001). Legacy of hate: Chinese immigrants encounter prejudice and violence as they settled in Canada. Retrieved from http://www.cbc.ca/history/EPISCONTENTSE1EP11CH3PA3LE.html

Chua, S. (2014, 20 Apr.). Traumatized refugees lose most federal mental health funding in B.C. *Globe and Mail*. Retrieved from https://www.theglobeandmail.com/news/british-columbia/traumatized-refugees-lose-most-of-their-federal-mental-health-funding-in-bc/article18072522/

Dua, E. (2000). The Hindu woman's question. *Canadian Woman Studies, 20*(2), 108–16.

Eggertson, L. (2013). Health care organizations wait to talk to citizenship minister about cuts to refugee benefits. *Canadian Medical Association Journal, 185*(7), E279–80.

Faraday, F. (2014). Profiling the precarious: How recruitment practices exploit migrant workers. Metcalf Foundation. Retrieved from http://metcalffoundation.com/stories/publications/profiting-from-the-precarious-how-recruitment-practices-exploit-migrant-workers/

Friesen, K. (2017, 5 Jan.). Syrian exodus to Canada: One year later, a look at who the refugees are and where they went. *Globe and Mail*. Retrieved from https://www.theglobeandmail.com/news/national/syrian-refugees-in-canada-by-the-numbers/article33120934/

Fudge, J. (2016). Migrant domestic workers in British Columbia, Canada: Unfreedom, trafficking, domestic servitude. In J. H. Owens (Ed.), *Temporary labour migration in the global era* (pp. 151–71). Portland, OR: Hart Publishing.

Government of Canada. (2008). News release: Canada's government to help temporary foreign workers and foreign student graduates become permanent residents.

Government of Canada. (2012). Speeches for 2012—ARCHIVED—Speaking notes for The Honourable Jason Kenny. Retrieved from https://www.canada.ca/en/immigration-refugees-citizenship/news/archives/speeches-2012/jason-kenney-minister-2012-06-29.html-

———. (2016). #WelcomeRefugees: The road ahead. Retrieved from https://www.canada.ca/en/immigration-refugees-citizenship/services/refugees/welcome-syrian-refugees/looking-future.html

———. (2017a). #WelcomeRefugees: Canada resettled Syrian refugees. Retrieved from https://www.canada.ca/en/immigration-refugees-citizenship/services/refugees/welcome-syrian-refugees.html

———. (2017b). Designated countries of origin policy. Retrieved from http://www.cic.gc.ca/english/refugees/reform-safe.asp

Guo, S. (2009). Difference, deficiency, and devaluation: Tracing the roots of non-recognition of foreign credentials for immigrant professionals in Canada. *Canadian Journal for the Study of Adult Education, 22*(1), 37–52.

Hansen, L., & Huston, P. (2016). Health considerations in the Syrian refugee resettlement process in Canada. *Canadian Communicable Disease Report, 42*(2), S3–S7.

Harris, K. (2017, 26 February) Refugee influx: 5 things to know about illegal border crossings into Canada. *CBC*. Retrieved from: https://www.cbc.ca/news/politics/canada-us-border-illegal-border-crossings-1.3995768

Human Rights Watch. (2016). Syria: Events of 2016. Retrieved from https://www.hrw.org/world-report/2017/country-chapters/syria

IRPA. (2001). Government of Canada—Justice Laws Website. Retrieved from https://laws-lois.justice.gc.ca/eng/acts/I-2.5/section-3-20030101.html

Japanese Canadian Centennial Project. (1978). *1877–1977: The Japanese Canadians dream of riches*. Vancouver: Vancouver Publishing.

Kazimi, A. (2004). *Continuous Journey* [Documentary]. Canada: TV Ontario.

Krishnamurthi, S.(2013). Queue-jumpers, terrorists, breeders: Representations of Tamil migrants in Canadian popular media. *South Asian Diaspora, 5*(1), 139–57.

Kruger, E., Mulder, M., & Korenic, B. (2004). Canada after 11 September: Security measures and "preferred" immigrants. *Mediterranean Quarterly, 15*(4), 72–87.

Lee, M. S. (2003). *El contrato.* National Film Board of Canada.

Li, P. (2003). *Destination Canada. Immigration debates and issues.* Toronto: Oxford University Press Canada.

Liew, J. (2016, September 26). Let's make real reforms to the Temporary Foreign Worker program. *Ottawa Citizen.* Retrieved from: https://ottawacitizen.com/news/politics/liew-lets-make-real-reforms-to-the-temporary-foreign-worker-program

Liptak, A. (2017, 9 Feb.). Court refuses to reinstate travel ban. *New York Times.* Retrieved from https://www.nytimes.com/2017/02/09/us/politics/appeals-court-trump-travel-ban.html

Maloney, R. (2016, 18 Mar.). Bill C-24: Slim majority want Trudeau's Liberals not to repeal changes, poll suggests. *Huffington Post.* Retrieved from http://www.huffingtonpost.ca/2016/03/18/bill-c-24-justin-trudeau-liberals-harper-poll_n_9499608.html

Never Home. (n.d.). Legislating discrimination of Canadian immigrants. Retrieved from http://www.neverhome.ca/

Nuttal, J. J. (2017, 8 June). Refugees at risk after BC support group denied federal funds, critics say. *The Tyee.* Retrieved from https://thetyee.ca/News/2017/06/08/Inland-Refugee-Society-Denied-Funds/

Ontario Human Rights Commission. (2013). *Policy on removing the Canadian experience barrier.* Toronto: Ontario Human Rights Commission.

Ostrand, N. (2015). The Syrian refugee crisis: A comparison of responses by Germany, Sweden, the United Kingdom, and the United States. *Journal on Migration and Human Security, 3*(3), 255–79.

Sharma, N. (2008). On being not Canadian: The social construction of "migrant workers" in Canada. *Canadian Review of Sociology, 38*(4), 415–39.

Smith, M. (2017, 10 Feb.). Dramatic increase in people having Canadian citizenship revoked since Trudeau elected. *National Post.* Retrieved from http://news.nationalpost.com/news/canada/politics/dramatic-increase-in-people-having-canadian-citizenship-revoked-since-trudeau-elected

Thobani, S. (2007). *Exalted subjects: Studies in the making of race and nation in Canada.* Toronto: University of Toronto Press.

Tomasso, L. (2012). More equal than others: The discourse construction of migrant children and families in Canada. *International Journal of Child, Youth and Family Studies, 3*(2), 331–48.

*Toronto Star.* (2008, 19 May). PM unconvincing on immigration. Retrieved from http://www.pressreader.com/canada/toronto-star/20080519/282479999533957

Triadafilos, T. (2012). *Becoming multicultural: Immigration and the politics of membership in Canada and Germany.* Vancouver: University of British Columbia Press.

Weaver, M. (2017, 30 Mar.). Syrian refugees: More than 5M in neighbouring countries now, says UN. *The Guardian.* Retrieved from https://www.theguardian.com/world/2017/mar/30/syrian-refugee-number-passes-5m-mark-un-reveals

# 18 The Role of Policy in Sustaining or Eliminating Poverty

*Robert Harding*

---

## Chapter Objectives

*This chapter will help you to develop an understanding of:*
1. the role discourse plays in how we understand and find solutions to poverty;
2. how poverty is defined, who is poor, and who is most at risk of poverty;
3. what policies and programs are available to support the poor, what their deficiencies are, and how policy can lift people out of, or keep them in, poverty;
4. what policies and programs are needed to effectively address poverty and what policies have worked well in other countries.

---

## Introduction

*"Hey poor, you don't have to be poor anymore"*

> — from the song "Welcome to Paradise" by Front 242. By permission of Front 242.

This tongue-in-cheek lyric captures the neo-liberal attitude to people living in poverty, which is characterized by the "pull yourself up by the bootstrap" approach promoted in news discourse. This view reflects the myth of Canada as a meritocracy and a land of boundless opportunities, where some people "choose" to be poor because they are lazy or morally weak. If we conclude that poverty is a "choice" made by a few "bad" apples, then it is easy to blame the poor for their predicament and justify neo-liberal policies that either harm the poor or do little to help them. Yet poverty is related to conditions and systems over which individuals have little control, and thus is not related to individual choice, at least not on the part of the poor. While people do not choose to be poor, governments' conscious policy choices sometimes have the effect of creating or maintaining poverty.

High levels of poverty are easily explained: society is structured in ways that benefit wealthy people and corporations, while ensuring that a significant proportion of the population remains poor, marginalized, and desperate to take on low-paying work. Yet governments have tremendous potential to dramatically reduce poverty by prioritizing it through their policy decisions. Other countries have implemented pragmatic and effective anti-poverty policies that have helped them achieve far lower poverty rates than Canada—and greater social inclusion.

**Case Examples**   Being Poor in Canada

Meet Raphael, Andie, and Norma, three Canadians in distinct social locations, living in poverty.

**Raphael**, 77, is a widowed refugee from Guatemala. He came to Canada after his retirement and has no access to the Canada Pension Plan (CPP) or a private pension plan. He receives the maximum Old Age Security (OAS) benefit and Guaranteed Income Supplement (GIS), which provide him with $871.86 per month to live on, most of which is eaten up by the $600 rent and utilities bill for his studio apartment in Hamilton. Due to his disability, he finds it increasingly difficult to cook, clean, and get around, yet he receives very limited home care from the provincially funded program. Because the local food bank is a long bus ride away, he only accesses it once a month when a friend is available to drive him.

**Andie**, 49, is an HIV-positive trans woman. She receives $710 per month in social assistance. She considers herself fortunate to have found a **single-room occupancy (SRO) unit** in Vancouver's Downtown Eastside for the BC Shelter rate of $375, as most SROs in the neighbourhood are much more expensive. She has been undergoing periods of severe depression while awaiting gender confirmation surgery. Recent federal government cuts to the local Positive Living organization have reduced her access to diet supplementation, essential medical supplies, counselling services, and other needed services.

**Norma**, 27, is a lone mother of two children under the age of four. She moved to Winnipeg from a northern reserve to take a job as a teaching assistant, which pays $1,400/month after taxes and deductions. She struggles to pay the $900 rent on her basement suite, and has been forced to rely on unlicensed, and unsafe, daycare for her children, for which she pays approximately $400/month. To make ends meet, she often skips meals and relies on short-term high-interest loans from "payday" financial loan companies.

This chapter begins by addressing the question, *Who are the poor?* Then, we discuss poverty's ideological context, explore the influence of ideology on how we measure and define it, and assess the ways in which dominant discourse influences how we think and talk about it. Next, we assess how effective our income supplementation policies are in addressing the needs of the poor, and identify policies that serve to perpetuate or, in some cases, exacerbate poverty. Subsequent sections address promising new approaches and effective international poverty reduction policies, and propose concrete steps governments can take to make a real difference in the lives of the poor. In the final section, we contemplate the possibility of a brighter future, one where progressive policies transform the lives of the poor.

## Poverty and Social Location: Who Are the Poor?

Poverty can affect all of us despite how hard we work, how many skills we have, our level of educational attainment, or our social status. We've all heard stories about successful business people or professionals who suffer a sudden reversal, such as a debilitating accident, mental health episode, domestic violence, or change in family status, and are subsequently "plunged" into poverty and forced to go on welfare. After failing to make mortgage or rental payments, they end up destitute or even homeless. For many of us, there is truth in the adage that we are but one paycheque away from losing our home and living on the street. In fact, an IPSOS (2017) survey found that 52 per cent of Canadians are a mere $200 away from not being able to cover their monthly bills and expenses. Some Canadians end up living on the street simply because they don't have enough savings to cope with even a relatively minor unexpected expense. More than one out five people report that they would be unable to "come up with just $2,000 within a month for an emergency expense" (Canadian Payroll Association, 2017).

However, some people are more at risk of living in poverty than others. Vulnerable groups include children, students, women, female single parents, those on fixed incomes, recent immigrants, people of colour, Indigenous people, people living with disabilities or mental health issues, and people living alone. In the case of women, not only do they earn only 87 per cent of what men earn (Statistics Canada, 2017a), but also they are far more likely to be tasked with caring for children, elderly parents, and other relatives. Indeed, for many women, having children means living in poverty, especially for lone mothers or those who separate from their partners. The poverty rate for female lone-parent families is a staggering 34.5 per cent, meaning that more than one out of three such families are living in poverty (Statistics Canada, 2017b). Furthermore, due to gender discrimination and various policies that disadvantage women, they are far more likely than men to work part-time, work in low-wage jobs with no or low benefits and pensions, and take time out from working to care for children.

Given the economically disadvantaged position of many mothers, it is not surprising that children have the highest rate of poverty of any age group in Canada. (See Chapter 11 for more about economic issues affecting children.) In 2016, 1.3 million children, or one out of five Canadian children, live in poverty (Campaign 2000, n.d.). This risk is not spread evenly among all children: Indigenous children (40 per cent) and visible minority children (22 per cent) have far higher rates of poverty than non-immigrant and non-racialized children (13 per cent) (Children First Canada, 2016). Yet many countries have far lower rates of child poverty than Canada. Indeed, our child poverty rate is more than twice as high as those of Denmark, Iceland, Norway, and Finland, and an assessment of 37 countries' effectiveness at reducing child poverty ranked Canada fourth last (UNICEF Office of Research, 2017).

# Ideological Context of Poverty Policy

## Economic Globalization and Neo-liberal Economics: Laying the Structural Foundations of Poverty

It is impossible to talk about poverty policy without discussing the broader context of globalization and neo-liberal economics. Neo-liberal governments promote policies emphasizing individualism, privatization of government services, programmatic retrenchment of the welfare state, and reducing or eliminating government regulation of the corporate sector so that the economy is determined solely by market forces.

Today, while some may regard economic globalization as a relatively new phenomenon associated with free trade agreements in North America and Europe in the 1980s and 1990s, globalization of investment and trade has a long history, in that people from countries and continents far away from one other have been trading for thousands of years. What has changed more recently is the scale of investment and trade, and the state and international structures and trade agreements that facilitate it.

Neo-liberalism and economic globalization work hand in hand to ensure the free movement of goods, services, and capital across international borders, while pressuring governments to deregulate markets, lower taxation, cut services, and put downward pressure on wages. While these policies serve the interests of wealthy people and corporations well, vulnerable populations pay a hefty price. The rise of neo-liberalism has coincided with rising rates of income inequality, poverty, and massive growth in food banks and homelessness.

## Retrenchment of Government Programs, Services, and Infrastructure

Programmatic retrenchment is a neo-liberal trend in government to slash government spending by reducing or eliminating benefits, cutting social welfare programs, services, and infrastructure, and generally making social policy less generous. One form of retrenchment occurs when one level of government chooses to "claw back" benefits received by poor people in one program from another program, sometimes offered by a different level of government. Governments often target social assistance programs for cutbacks. For example, in 1997, after the federal government implemented the National Child Benefit, which provided about $120 per month to families living on income security, all but two provinces, New Brunswick and Newfoundland and Labrador, chose to take back this money from families' income security cheques (Raphael, 2011). Thus, the poorest and most vulnerable members of society bear the brunt of programmatic retrenchment. For example, in 2012, the Conservative federal government made changes to the Interim Federal Health Program that reduced the ability of refugees to access basic health care.

Yet programmatic retrenchment is not restricted to Conservative governments. In 2015, the Liberal Party was elected on a platform that included increased spending on social programs. However, shortly after taking power, this government cut programs for people living with HIV/AIDS and hepatitis C by changing the application process through the Public Health Agency of Canada. Some of the organizations providing these services are facing dramatic service cuts or even closure (Positive Living Fraser Valley, 2017). Positive Women's Network, the only such agency serving HIV women in British Columbia, was forced to close (Kane, 2017), leaving Andie (see Case Examples box) without much-needed social support and access to health and wellness programs. Stigmatized services and programs for poor and marginalized populations, whose voter turnout for elections is traditionally low and who have little political clout or leverage, present easy targets for cuts since they are often maligned or ignored in the media, and members of the public may be oblivious or unsympathetic to their plight. Program retrenchment pushes low-income people into poverty and exacerbates the lives of the poor.

# How Do We Talk about Poverty in Canada?

What kinds of conversations do Canadians have about poverty? Clearly, how we think and talk about it is influenced by a wide variety of factors, including our personal experiences and values, what we learn in school, what we see, hear, and read in the media, as well as by our conversations with friends, family, and colleagues. These discursive experiences, ideas, images, texts, and talk weave and build public discourses about poverty. Given the ideological context described at the beginning of this chapter, it is not surprising that neo-liberal discourses have dominated the conversation. These discourses about the poor may play a significant role in their exclusion from society. In Britain, sociologist Ruth Levitas (2005) found that the dominant discourses on poverty and "social exclusion" were the Moral Underclass (MUD), and the Social Integrationist (SID) discourses. An underlying assumption of MUD is that since the underclass is "culturally" inferior to mainstream society, poverty is legitimate and the poor deserve to be marginalized and excluded. According to SID, poverty results from unemployment, and therefore the solution is getting people into the workforce, which will result in their integration into society. Yet this discourse ignores other forms of structural inequality such as race, gender, and sexual orientation. In Canada, MUD is the main discourse for making sense of social policy on poverty-related issues, including income security, minimum wages, and measures related to Employment Insurance (Raphael, 2011). This discourse is part of a common-sense cognitive framework by which certain policies and approaches are justified and privileged over others. (See Chapter 2 for more about the influence of discourse on policy-making.)

Research indicates that discourses emerging from poverty policy include binaries that effectively separate the poor from other citizens. For example, in British Columbia, the classic binary of *deserving versus undeserving poor* is enacted in the law through the designation of two groups, those undeserving recipients on *temporary assistance* and the deserving poor on *continuous assistance*, which includes people with disabilities, people with multiple barriers to employment, and children (Jeppesen, 2009). Indeed, the phenomenon of programmatic retrenchment is based on the assumption that the poor do not deserve or need our help. If social programs are seen as "expendable," governments may justify policies and programs that *pathologize* poverty, such as the Ontario Works program, which aims to address individual deficiencies such as "lack of motivation and poor hygiene" (Fernando & Earle, 2011).

## The Role of Think-Tanks in Defining Poverty and Shaping Policy

Think-tanks are privately funded organizations that conduct research into a variety of public policy issues and advocate for specific policy changes, usually based on a specific set of political values and principles. In some ways, think-tanks do the heavy ideological lifting for political parties, corporations, and organizations with a political interest in defining, and measuring, poverty in public discourse and shaping policy designed to address it. Many think-tanks have registered charity status, and most of the larger ones are conservative, such as the Fraser Institute, the Frontier Centre for Public Policy, and the CD Howe Institute. These think-tanks have a corporate agenda that promotes increased oil and resource development, less government regulation, lower taxes, and less spending on social services. (See Chapter 4 for more about think-tanks and their role in policy-making.)

One way that conservative think-tanks promote neo-liberal discourses is by providing "media-friendly" reports to major news organizations. Conclusions from these reports are often uncritically accepted as fact by opinion and editorial writers in support of residual positions on poverty. As well, social policy "experts" appointed by conservative think-tanks are frequently afforded the opportunity to write opinion pieces about poverty. In one study of poverty discourse in 13 major daily Canadian newspapers, writers from conservative think-tanks authored two-thirds of the guest-written columns, while representatives of progressive or liberal think-tanks, such as the Caledon Institute and the Canadian Centre for Policy Alternatives (CCPA), did not write and were not mentioned in a single opinion piece (Harding, 2016). Furthermore, the ranks of senior journalists for some news organizations have been stacked with former employees of conservative think-tanks (Gutstein, 2014).

The way poverty is measured and defined is, in itself, highly ideological and political. Conservative commentators and think-tanks, such as the Fraser Institute through the work of Sarlo (2013) and others, promote **absolute measures of poverty** that downplay the magnitude and severity of the problem. Understating the scale of poverty is in line with the Fraser Institute's mandate, which promotes "individual responsibility" and scaling back or eliminating social programs and entitlements. If poverty can be defined as a benign problem affecting a relatively small number of Canadians, the argument follows by asking: Why do we need to change what we're doing? According to this script, Canada is a wealthy country that doesn't have "real" poverty, such as that experienced in the developing world. Here, people are spoiled and want to be looked after by the "nanny state."

## News Discourse

The news media have a profound influence on how people think and talk about poverty, and often the media portray poverty as difficult to define, and even more difficult to address. However, more than anything else, news discourse about poverty is defined by the absence of the voices of the poor themselves. Excluding poor people from the conversation about poverty leads to them being stereotyped and "othered," which limits the public's ability to understand their lived experiences. This allows major influencers of news discourse about poverty policy—pro-business economists, news pundits, politicians, and think-tanks—to reproduce dominant definitions of issues and promote solutions that reduce services and encourage individual "responsibility." (See Chapter 2 for more on how media discourse influences the making of social policy.)

*How do the news media frame policy solutions to poverty?* This question assumes that poverty is seen as problematic to begin with. Indeed, some news commentators frame poverty as a social condition essential to the maintenance of a healthy society and strong economy, and offer a simple prescription: *reduce government programming designed to alleviate poverty since it only serves to "enable" the poor and create dependency on the state* (Harding, 2016). Thus, income support, social housing, and other government-funded services and programs are viewed as not only unnecessary but counterproductive. The more the state gives to the poor, the lazier people become and the more likely they are to "choose" to go on welfare rather than work. According to this logic, the availability and quality of programs and services have an *inverse* relationship to the poverty rate.

A related discourse that emerges in poverty news is that *since we have no control over it, all we can do is deal with the consequences.* Opinion writers ascribe human attributes to poverty, describing it as "stubborn," "relentless," or "unforgiving." Personifying poverty signals to audiences that poverty represents a force of nature, one we have very little control over. Therefore, it is inevitable that we will not be able to contain it completely (Harding, 2016). Perhaps the most destructive consequence of this type of news discourse is that it may create uncertainty about the state's ability to ameliorate poverty or even give Canadians pause to consider whether governments ought to be involved in poverty reduction in the first place.

# How Do We Supplement the Income of Low-Income Canadians?

While many people associate income support exclusively with social assistance, or "welfare," in fact, the term includes a wide variety of other provincial and federal programs, including transfers or tax credits for low-income Canadians administered through the income tax system, age-related income support (for older Canadians and children), and unemployment benefits. Some of these programs are universal, while others are selective and means-tested. One thing clear about this fragmented patchwork quilt of programs—many of which were created over half a century ago during very different economic times—is that they have *not* been effective at eliminating poverty.

## Social Assistance

Social assistance policies have effectively legislated poverty since benefits leave beneficiaries significantly below the poverty line. The Caledon Institute found that, with one exception, all provincial social assistance rates for the four beneficiary categories—single employable; person with a disability; single parent, one child; couple with two children—left recipients well under the poverty line as measured by after-tax low-income cut-offs (LICOs) (Tweddle, Battle, & Torjman, 2017). The sole exception is Newfoundland and Labrador, where a single parent with one child receives an annual welfare income $1,627 over the poverty line. Couples with two children in British Columbia were the furthest under the poverty line with a poverty gap of $14,490. In Andie's case (see Case Examples box), the BC government raised the social assistance rate by $100 to $710 soon after coming into power in 2017—the first increase in a decade. Even with the increase, Andie is living well under the poverty line.

While European countries such as Switzerland set social assistance rates high enough for recipients to retain a sense of self-worth, thus enabling them to be socially engaged, Canada's programs seem designed to do the opposite—to ensure that recipients do *not* enjoy a "reasonable standard of living" (Raphael, 2011). Indeed, our **means and income-tested benefits** are perhaps our most heavily stigmatized form of social welfare, and recipients may be subjected to shame and embarrassment by social assistance workers. Depending on their province or territory of residence, people may be required to sell assets such as houses and vehicles, spend savings, and cash in pension plans in order to qualify for welfare. Some provinces force people to work in low-paying jobs, and many people may not be eligible for benefits at all, including students and immigrants.

## Income Support for Unemployed People

Canada's woefully inadequate **social insurance** program for unemployed workers represents a neo-liberal program retrenchment exercise that began in the mid-1990s, when the Unemployment Insurance scheme was stripped down and rebranded as the Employment Insurance (EI) program. In the years leading up to the passage of the Employment Insurance Act in 1996, Canada signed two major trade accords with our neighbours to the south: the Canada–US Free Trade Agreement in 1989, followed by the North American Free Trade Agreement (NAFTA) in 1994, which added Mexico as a free trade partner.

When these agreements were negotiated, Canadians were concerned about US demands that Canadian negotiators "harmonize" our unemployment insurance qualification rate of 83 per cent (in 1989) with the US federal unemployment program's 33 per cent qualification level (Tester & Case, 1999). The federal government offered assurances that our social programs were "sacrosanct" and would never be bargained away. Yet two years after NAFTA was signed, Canada passed the Employment Insurance Act, which resulted in the worker qualification rate declining until it was at roughly the same level as it was for US workers. This is an example of *social policy by stealth* (Battle, 1995) in which governments surreptitiously cut back programs and reduce social entitlements, effectively saying one thing but doing another.

Today only about one in three unemployed workers qualifies for EI in the first place. This is partly because benefit eligibility is now calculated based on the number of hours worked, as opposed to the previous regime that based eligibility on weeks of employment. This disadvantages people working part-time or in seasonal industries, often women, students, and younger workers. Furthermore, the EI benefit level is based on only 55 per cent of the claimant's maximum weekly insurable income ($543 in 2017), thus yielding a maximum weekly benefit of under $300. Recipients must begin repaying Employment Insurance benefits through the income tax system when their net annual incomes exceed $64,125 (2017). As well, there are eligibility disparities based on where you live: to be eligible for benefits, people living in regions with lower unemployment rates must work up to seven more weeks than those living in regions with higher unemployment. Many people receiving EI benefits are living at or under the poverty line, and when their benefits expire, they move even deeper into poverty as they often have little choice but to apply for social assistance.

## Income Support for Families with Children

In 2016, the Liberal government amalgamated the Canada Child Tax Benefit/National Child Benefit Supplement (CCTB/NCBS) and the Universal Child Care Benefit into the Canada Child Benefit (CCB), which provides eligible families with children under the age of 18 with a single non-taxable payment every month. When family income reaches $30,000 annually, the benefit is gradually clawed back by the government. As of July 2018, when the CCB was indexed to inflation, children under the age of 6 were eligible for $6,496 annually, while children between the ages of 6 and 17 received $5,481. Torjman, Mendelson, and Battle (2017) describe the CCB as the "most important poverty fighting measure in a generation," one that lifted 300,000 children out of poverty in its first year. (See Chapter 11 for more about income support for children and families.)

## Income Support for Older Canadians

While some older Canadians have private pension plans, savings, and investments to draw upon, many low-income people rely primarily on the Quebec/Canada Pension Plan (Q/CPP), which is, technically, a social insurance program, as well as federal income support programs, namely Old Age Security (OAS), the Guaranteed Income Supplement (GIS), and the Allowance. Q/CPP is based on employee and employer contributions—thus, the more months people make maximum contributions, the larger the pension they will receive at age 65 up to a ceiling of $1,134.17 monthly in 2018. While workers are able to drop 17 per cent of their lowest contribution months from the calculation of their pension benefit, older women are at a disadvantage as they are more likely than men to have worked in lower-paid sectors, to have worked part-time, and taken time off to care for children and other family members. Measured as a percentage of GDP, Canada's spending on public pension plans is lower than that of most European countries and even less than that of the US (Townsend, 2012).

The OAS is a flat-rate benefit paid to all Canadians 65 or older that is gradually clawed back when individuals reach a certain income threshold. The GIS is an income-tested supplement issued to low-income people aged 65 and older. Both benefits are adjusted for cost-of-living increases four times annually. The Allowance is another income-tested benefit available to spouses of OAS/GIS claimants between 60 and 64, and also for spouses of deceased claimants. In our Case Examples, Raphael and the many other Canadians who rely exclusively on the OAS and GIS maximum benefit of $871.86/month face poverty and hardship as they age.

The poverty rate for elderly people has been increasing for the last two decades. Between 2010 and 2015, the rate of poverty for people 65 years and older increased from 12 per cent to 14.5 per cent (Statistics Canada, 2017c). Even for middle-class Canadians, staying above the poverty line is a challenge as up to half of them face a "significant reduction in their living standards in retirement" (Wolfson, 2015, p. 5).

Groups most susceptible to poverty in old age include women, low-income people, Indigenous people, people with disabilities or mental health issues, and the chronically unemployed. Even more disturbing is older Canadians' increasing proportion of the homeless population. One-quarter of people accessing homeless shelters are over 50, and the number of homeless Canadians between 50 and 64, as well as Canadians 65 or older, is increasing (Gaetz, Dej, Richter, & Redman, 2016).

# What Policies Are Implicated in Perpetuating Poverty?

Poverty is a multi-faceted problem influenced by diverse factors and policies. Poor people and their families experience numerous obstacles and challenges, including in basic areas that most Canadians take for granted, such as having an adequate wage, food to eat, a roof over their heads, clothing to wear, reliable transportation, and access to legal counsel, to name but a few. Which government policies and programs hinder poor people's ability to address their essential needs?

## Housing

Having a roof over your head is a basic human need, so one would expect that governments would have a strong policy presence in housing. Yet, over 20 years ago the federal government cut all funds for new affordable housing (Irwin, 2004), and since then it has done little to ensure that Canadians have access to housing. Today, many low-income Canadians live in inadequate, low-quality housing, which may negatively impact their physical and mental health as well as their children's success at school (Silver, 2014, p. 81). While some people meet their housing needs through government-subsidized housing, housing co-operatives, or single-room occupancy units, most must rely on market housing in a situation where declining housing stock has resulted in increased demand and dramatic cost increases.

Four out of 10 renters are spending more than 30 per cent of their income on rent, a proportion that is generally considered to place people at risk of poverty. Nineteen per cent of Canadian renters are in an even more precarious situation, spending more than 50 per cent of their income on rent (Canadian Rental Housing Index, 2017). In the Case Examples at the start of the chapter, Andie and Raphael spend 53 per cent and 69 per cent of their income on rent, proportions that ensure poverty is a fact of life for them. Norma is the least at risk of our three Canadians, although even she spends 36 per cent of her total income (employment income plus CCB) on housing. (See Chapter 13 for more about housing policy.)

## Homelessness

The dramatic increase in homelessness in recent years is directly attributable to the federal government's "massive disinvestment in housing over the past quarter century" (Gaetz, Dej, Richter, & Redman, 2016). While poor people generally face a high risk of homelessness, certain factors in people's households render them even more susceptible. For example, youth aging out of the child welfare system face a far higher risk of homelessness, unemployment, and poverty than other youth. Indeed, there is a strong connection between involvement in child welfare systems and youth homelessness. Homeless youth are "193 times more likely than youth in the general population to report involvement with the child welfare system" (Nichols et al., 2017, p. 4). Furthermore, "Indigenous youth, LGBTQ2S youth, and racialized youth are overrepresented among youth experiencing homelessness" (p. 3). Indeed, due to racism, systemic oppression, and colonialism, Indigenous people of all ages are at far greater risk of homelessness than non-Indigenous people, representing more than a third of the total homeless population in many cities. While only 4.3 per cent of Canadians identify as Indigenous, 28–34 per cent of homeless shelter clients are Indigenous (Gaetz, Dej, Richter, & Redman, 2016). (See Chapter 13 for more about homelessness.)

## Minimum Wage

As with social assistance rates, minimum wages have been allowed to stagnate for many years. Indeed, due to the impact of inflation on buying power, minimum-wage workers in all provinces and territories are further behind today than they were 10 or 20 years ago.

As one labour leader put it, "minimum wage is a poverty wage" (*CBC News*, 2017b). Even in Alberta, where the NDP government implemented a $15 minimum wage in 2018, many people earning that wage, including most lone parents and their children, are still living well below the poverty line.

## Child Care

The cost of child care is a significant factor in poverty for women and children (Piano, 2014; Milne, 2016). Canadian families spend nearly a quarter of their total income on paying for child care, a much higher ratio than in most other OECD countries (Torjman, Mendelson, & Battle, 2017). Many parents face a difficult choice between paying for expensive child care and other work-related costs, or staying home and raising children while relying on social assistance or a partner's income. Both scenarios can result in families living below the poverty line.

Unlike many European countries, Canada's federal government does not have a free universal child-care plan and plays a very limited role in generating affordable quality child care. The lack of federal intervention in the supply of affordable, quality daycare spaces has led to a severe shortage of space, with more than 70 per cent of daycare centres maintaining wait lists and some charging wait list fees (Macdonald & Friendly, 2016).

Quebec stands out from other provinces and territories in its efforts to limit the costs of daycare for families as it sets a base daily fee for child care ($8.05/day as of 1 January 2018) for low- and modest-income families. This system actually generates a surplus for the province due to the additional taxes resulting from mothers' increased labour force participation, which more than offsets the government's investment in child care (Fortin, 2016).

## Food Security Policy

Access to adequate nutrition is a basic human need, so one would expect governments to elaborate policy that ensures this need is met. Yet, as with poverty reduction, the federal government does not have a national policy. One indicator of the scale of the food insecurity problem is food bank use. In March 2016, 863,492 Canadians accessed a food bank, an increase of 28 per cent over the previous eight years (Food Banks Canada, 2016). Given that social assistance rates are set below the poverty line, it is unsurprising that people relying on it represent nearly half of all food bank users. More than one in eight users are Indigenous people, which means that they are significantly over-represented in comparison to their share of Canada's population.

For homeless people, food insecurity is a daily reality. Approximately 35,000 people are homeless on any given night, and 235,000 Canadians experience homelessness annually (Gaetz, Dej, Richter, & Redman, 2016). Yet, food banks mostly serve people who have housing of one kind or another, with under 1 per cent of their clientele defined as "living in the street" (Food Banks Canada, 2016). Food banks may be located in areas that are not easily accessible to homeless people, and many of their foodstuffs require access to cooking facilities, something homeless people lack. (See Chapter 14 for more about food security.)

## Legal Aid

The right to justice ought to be universal. Nonetheless, many people are denied access to legal counsel simply because they lack the means to pay. Lawyers are very expensive, completely unaffordable for low-income people and beyond the means of many middle-class people. The average five-day civil trial costs $56,439—roughly $16,000 more than what a median single-parent family takes home in a year (Fraser, 2016). Provincial legal aid programs have been scaled back or allowed to erode over time. In Ontario, more than a million people slipped through the gap of eligibility and affordability from the mid-1990s to 2015, when eligibility for legal aid was frozen. During these years, a single person's income had to be $10,800 or under to qualify for full legal aid and $12,500 or under for partial coverage (Fraser, 2016).

Low-income people needing legal services may be faced with the prospect of having to liquidate all their assets, including savings and RRSPs, before they can qualify. Requiring people to sell limited assets and dip into meagre savings and RRSPs forces them to make a grim choice between going into poverty or going to court without a lawyer. Indeed, in Ontario, 57 per cent of Family Court litigants had no legal representation in 2014–15 (Fraser, 2016). Legal aid policy places vulnerable populations at risk of poverty, including women and children attempting to leave domestic violence. Since going to court without legal representation places people at an enormous disadvantage, inadequate legal aid policies actually *produce* poverty.

## Social Policy Change in Action

### Services for People Living with HIV/AIDS and Hepatitis C
*by Mike Zonta, on behalf of the Bachelor of Social Work Advocacy Task Group, University of the Fraser Valley*

### What Happened?

Until 2016, Positive Living Fraser Valley (PLFV) and other agencies providing services to people living with HIV/AIDS, hepatitis C, and other sexually transmitted and blood-borne diseases had been receiving most of their funding from the Public Health Authority of Canada (PHAC). That year, by reprioritizing where the money would go, PHAC defunded 42 agencies across Canada. The loss of PLFV would have created a gap in services affecting a population of 1.6 million people in BC's Lower Mainland. PLFV ensures that service users are supported in the areas of diagnosis, treatment, and follow-up care.

### Actions Taken
In fall 2016 we began raising public awareness about how losing these services would impact local communities. Together with PLFV members, 30 students and faculty from the School of Social Work and Human Services at the University of the Fraser Valley (UFV) boarded a bus to

deliver impact statements to Members of Parliament and BC's Legislative Assembly across the Fraser Valley. Stop after stop, we handed letters to MPs and MLAs—many of whom were unaware of the situation—and engaged them in candid discussions about this policy change. We also met with local supporters, one of whom was able to convey our concerns directly to the federal Health Minister.

We organized a community action round table that included MPs, MLAs, municipal representatives, service users and providers, UFV professors, and community members. The keynote speaker described what the community looked like before PLFV existed, what was accomplished through service provision, and what the impact would be of the loss of service. Students facilitated discussions at individual tables about how to support PLFV and its many members. At one table sat an MP, a mayor, a member of the local health authority, and two PLFV members living with HIV. Attendees shared a variety of promising ideas for action and support for PLFV.

### What Was Accomplished

Through our actions and the resulting pressure on decision-makers, we were successful in helping the PLFV access one more year of transitional funding. Although not a long-term solution, this allowed the agency to rally support for its services rather than cease operations. As an indirect result of our activism, PLFV initiated discussions with other funding agencies about accessing additional support that would enable their core services to continue. Most importantly, our actions as student social workers have fostered hope among marginalized and oppressed people who struggle with poverty.

# New and Proposed Policies That May Reduce Poverty

## Housing First

Communities across Canada have begun adapting a Housing First (HF) policy (see Chapter 13), an approach to homelessness that emerged in California in the late 1980s. HF emphasizes finding homeless people an apartment or similar long-term living facility immediately as opposed to the traditional approach of placing a person in a temporary shelter and assessing their "housing readiness" before gradually moving them through other forms of transitional housing and ultimately placing them in permanent, independent homes. HF is premised on the notion that housing is a basic need and human right, and that having safe, secure housing will enable people to deal with other challenges relating to employment, relationships, and substance abuse. However, full implementation of this policy requires governments to commit considerably more money to affordable housing. While its proponents stress the importance of building local partnerships with municipalities, police, the health sectors, and community organizations, ultimately the federal government must set aside substantial resources in order for HF to achieve its full potential.

## Living Wage

While non-indexed minimum wages do little to address poverty, living wage policies represent a proactive approach to poverty reduction. Instead of attempting to lift poorly paid workers out of poverty after the fact or limit the negative impacts of poverty, the living wage sets a minimum hourly wage—considerably higher than provincial or territorial minimum wages—calculated to maintain people *above* the poverty line. It is based on actual living costs for specific communities and is adjusted annually to reflect changes in the cost of living.

While living wages have been in place in some US jurisdictions for a number of years, New Westminster, BC, was the first Canadian jurisdiction to implement it in 2011. New Westminster (2011) defined the living wage as "the minimum hourly wage necessary for two working parents to pay for food, shelter, support the healthy development of their children, escape financial stress and participate in their community." In 2017, the city's living wage was $20.62/hour (Living Wage for Families, n.d.), almost $10/hour more than the provincial minimum wage of $10.85.

Municipal living wage policies are typically limited in their application in that only city employees or contractors working for the city are covered. Someone working at a local fast-food outlet or daycare centre in the city would not be covered, and probably would be earning the provincial minimum wage, or close to it. The greatest strength of this policy is that it sets a good example for other governments and employers. Soon after New Westminster enacted its policy, Vancity Credit Union implemented its own living wage policy, and since then other companies, as well as several municipalities, have followed suit. However, the commitment to pay workers a living wage is voluntary, and municipal governments and private employers that have implemented them had already been paying most employees at or above the living wage. For some low-wage employers such as daycare centres, implementing a living wage may be financially unsustainable unless the employer receives assistance from the government.

## Guaranteed Annual Income (GAI)

Ever since a successful experiment with a **guaranteed annual income** (GAI) program in Manitoba from 1974 to 1978, anti-poverty advocates have been promoting this as an alternative to social assistance. Under this approach, every citizen receives a guaranteed annual income that can paid be out in weekly, bimonthly, or monthly instalments. What distinguishes this from conventional "welfare" is that it does not carry a crippling stigma since it is not means-tested and does not require recipients to work. One of its main advantages over traditional cash benefits is its efficiency, since all income supplementation programs and tax measures, including social assistance, could potentially be rolled into the GAI and the costly administrative regimes associated these programs eliminated. For middle-class and well-off people, some or all of the GAI benefit could be recouped through the income tax system.

Finland began a GAI trial in 2017, which pays 2,000 unemployed citizens 560 euros a month (KELA, 2017), and basic income pilot programs are in progress in India, Kenya, Uganda, and Holland. In 2017, Ontario began piloting a GAI program in which 4,000 residents of three cities receive up to $17,000 annually, and other provinces have expressed an interest in GAI. Canada's national association of social workers recommended a "universal income" that would pay every citizen $20,000 per year tax-free (Kennelly, 2017).

Nonetheless, GAI is a controversial issue. Olli Kangas of KELA, the Finnish social insurance institution, observed that "some people think basic income will solve every problem under the sun, and some people think it's from the hand of Satan and will destroy our work ethic" (Cook, 2015). Not only is the GAI a divisive issue, it is also uniquely situated among poverty reduction proposals in that it has both conservative and progressive proponents and detractors. While Conservative Senator Hugh Segal (quoted in Martin, 2011, p. 50) described it as a policy that can "solve poverty: not dilute it, mitigate it, improve upon it, but actually solve it," the Fraser Institute declared that while the GAI may be appealing "in theory, in practice it's not likely to deliver" (Lammam & MacIntyre, 2015). Other conservative critics cite the program's potential to "sap" people's incentive to work. Yet previous GAI experiments in Manitoba and internationally have demonstrated that the program's predicted "excessive" disincentive on people's work ethic was actually "much smaller than predicted" (Martin, 2011).

Progressive critics, such as anti-poverty activist Jean Swanson, are skeptical about the GAI's effectiveness for completely different reasons. She argues that while powerful interests find it appealing due to is lower administrative costs, she fears that its implementation would result in the loss of other beneficial programs such as the GIS and important initiatives in areas such as social housing (*CBC News*, 2017a). Others fear it will subsidize irresponsible employers and let governments off the hook for providing quality training and education for workers and ensuring that employers meet high standards for working conditions, training, and benefits. Still, provided it is fully indexed and does not come at the expense of other valuable programs, a national GAI policy could transform the lives of the poor.

# International Policies We Can Learn From

## Gender Income Equality

An important factor in women's poverty is that women often receive less remuneration for the same or similar work done by men. Indeed, women's organizations and anti-poverty advocates have long criticized governments for failing to eliminate gender inequality when it comes to employment pay. In spite of the federal government's commitment to introduce pay equity legislation in 2018, and pay equity legislation in all 13 provinces and territories, women still earn significantly less than men, often have **precarious employment**, and are more likely to work in low-wage sectors, frequently in part-time positions with few if any benefits.

Perhaps Canada should look at the example set by Iceland. Already regarded as the best country in the world in terms of gender equality, Iceland legislated gender pay equity in 2017. This policy requires employers with more than 25 workers to "prove they give equal pay for work of equal value" (Lawless, 2017). Our government's adoption of similar policy would demonstrate that it is serious about eliminating gender inequities in pay and would make a material difference in many women's lives. (See Chapter 8 for more about policy affecting women.)

### Universal Free Post-Secondary Education

In many Northern European countries, post-secondary education is provided free, as a right of citizenship, and in some cases is even available to non-residents. In Canada, students face very different prospects. Over the last three decades, university tuition fees have been climbing at a far faster pace than inflation, increasing by 300 per cent between 1993–4 and 2015–16 (Shaker & Macdonald, 2015). While the federal and provincial governments provide students with a variety of loans, bursaries, and tax credits, earning a university degree often means living under the poverty line while in school—and for many years afterwards as students struggle to pay down heavy debt loads incurred during their studies. In addition to reducing student poverty rates and post-graduation debt loads, eliminating tuition would be a social investment that would enable people to pursue their educational aspirations, as well as an economic investment in a more skilled, better-educated workforce. (See Chapter 12 for more about post-secondary education policy.)

### Free Universal Child Care

The 2018 federal budget promised to invest $7.5 billion (over 11 years) in "high quality, affordable child care spaces," which will fund an additional 40,000 spaces over the first three years (Government of Canada, 2018, pp. 14–15). However, even with this investment, Canadians will still lack a free universal child-care program, such as is available in many European countries. Such a program would remove a significant obstacle from the path of caregivers, mostly women, who wish to join the workforce, pursue further education, or develop new skills. Free universal child care has the potential to reduce poverty rates for many parents and their children. Such a program would provide peace of mind and significant financial relief for Norma (see Case Examples box) as it would free up $400 for food, clothing, and other essential needs.

# The Way Forward: Can Policy Transform or Even Conquer Poverty?

A theme of news discourse about poverty is that it is inevitable and solutions to it are not entirely within our control but are determined by external factors, such as high unemployment or trends in the "global economy." At the same time, people living in poverty are constructed as architects of their own fate due to inherent flaws such as lack of ability or a strong work ethic. Yet when we look at successes achieved at home and abroad, we can see that policy decisions taken by government make tangible differences in poverty rates and in the lives of many people. Poverty is not the inevitable by-product of global or local "economic trends"—it results from conscious choices made by government, decisions that can be reversed or revised. Policy can transform poverty. Table 18.1 lists six transformative policy changes.

Before we can effectively tackle poverty, we need to reconceptualize how we think about it. When it comes to initiatives such as increasing social assistance rates or creating more subsidized housing, one of the first questions asked may be, *How much are these programs going to cost us? Or can we afford them?* But perhaps we should ask, *How can*

## Table 18.1 Policy Changes That Would Reduce Poverty

| Policy Change | Description | Benefit |
| --- | --- | --- |
| National poverty reduction plan | Comprehensive, co-ordinated, and rational planning involving multiple players, levels of government, and stakeholders, including poor people themselves | Effective planning and spending on poverty reduction |
| Indexation of benefits | All federal and provincial benefits and pro-grams, including social assistance and minimum wages are indexed to inflation along with all existing benefits | Benefit value would not decline over time due to inflation |
| National food security policy | Comprehensive planning and policy-making involving all levels of government to improve food production, distribution, and sustainability | Canadians have their nutritional needs met |
| National school lunch program | Co-ordinate and fund the provision of school lunches for all children who need them at Canadian schools | 1.2 million children living in poverty would have a nutritious lunch |
| Increase tax progres-sivity and eliminate tax shelters | Restore progressive tax rates for wealthy people and corporations, and eliminate tax loopholes and shelters | More revenue for ser-vices and programs; improved tax fairness |
| Invest more resources | Federal government increases transfer pay-ments to provinces and implements and enforces program standards, including univer-sality and benefit adequacy | New programs are created; existing ones are adequately funded |

*we not afford them?* We usually don't regard such programs as *investments* in our most valuable resource—the people—as many Northern European countries do. Perhaps we should focus on the *benefits* of poverty reduction and enhanced social inclusion, which include significant economic benefits such as higher productivity, a stronger economy, and lower costs associated with health care, substance abuse, and crime, to name but a few. In 2011, the Canadian Centre for Policy Alternatives quantified the economic costs of poverty in BC and determined that the province was paying between $8.1 billion and $9.2 billion every year for poverty-related costs in health care, crime, and foregone earn-ings and economic activity (Ivanova, 2011). But most importantly, lower poverty rates and higher social inclusion can result in better health outcomes, greater social harmony, and a higher quality of life for everyone.

## International Comparisons

### Reducing Poverty in Ecuador

While wealthy Northern European countries offer many examples of innovative and effective poverty reduction policies, even a small "developing" country such as Ecua-dor has demonstrated the difference a national commitment to poverty reduction can

*continued*

**Figure 18.1** Ministry of Social and Economic Inclusion Building in Cuenca, Ecuador
Source: Robert Harding.

make. In 2007, newly elected Indigenous President Raphael Correa implemented an aggressively redistributive social policy framework, which included dramatically improved health care services, free university education, and a ministry devoted to economic and social inclusion.

Today, Ecuador is seen as a leader in poverty reduction in Latin America (*Ecuador News*, 2016). In the decade Correa was in power, inequality dramatically decreased, the income poverty rate fell by 38 per cent, and the extreme poverty rate dropped by 47 per cent (Weisbrot, Johnston, & Merling, 2017), and the country has demonstrated "remarkable improvements" in human development, especially for its poorest citizens (Ordóñez, Samman, Mariotti, & Borja, 2015). In 2017, President Lenin Moreno, a wheelchair-bound Noble Prize winner, vowed to carry on the poverty reduction work of his predecessor, promising to "build a house for everyone and a free house for the poorest 191,000 people" (Nicolau, 2017). If Ecuador, a country with less than one-seventh of Canada's GDP,[1] can do this, why can't we?

## Chapter Summary

In this chapter, we have learned about who the poor are and how some groups, such as women, Indigenous peoples, recent immigrants, and people with disabilities or mental health issues, are disproportionately impacted by poverty as a consequence of their social location. These differential policy outcomes result from choices governments make, based on specific values and ideological beliefs. Indeed, the ways we talk and think about poverty, and how we define and respond to it with policy, are influenced by ideological discourses promoted in corporate media.

While some of our policies and programs make positive differences in the lives of the poor, many actually serve to exacerbate the problem. Some, such as legal aid and minimum wages, are simply inadequate, while in other policy areas the problem is a lack of government involvement, as in the case of housing and child care. Yet, a number of emerging approaches are on the horizon, such as the living wage and GAI, which offer opportunities to tackle poverty at its structural roots. These policies have the potential to ensure that people's incomes are sufficient to meet their basic needs, support their inclusion in society, and help them achieve their aspirations. Furthermore, we can learn from the experiences of other countries that have invested in innovative policies and programs that have proven highly effective in reducing poverty and increasing social inclusion, while strengthening the economy.

Sadly, many of our policies are mired in old ways of thinking, reproduce stereotypes about the poor, and reflect neo-liberal ideas such as meritocracy and the supposed disincentive created by social programs. We know that good policy can make a big difference in the lives of the poor—effective policies implemented in other countries and our own policy successes provide clear evidence of this. So we have the means to solve poverty—if we can only change the way we think about it.

## Discussion Questions

1. Put yourself in the shoes of Raphael, Andie, or Norma, all of whom live well below the poverty line (see the Case Examples box at the start of the chapter). It is the middle of the month and you've run out of money and have no food left. How would you survive? What options do you have? What steps would you take to ensure your basic needs and those of your family are met?

2. Many post-secondary students live under the poverty line, and even after graduation continue to live in poverty or low income while paying off heavy student loan debts. Describe three policy changes that would improve the situation.

3. In what ways do the social locations of Raphael, Andie, and Norma affect their experiences with poverty? How do dominant news discourses about the poor affect them?

## Note

1. In 2016, Ecuador's GDP per capita was US$5,968, while Canada's was US$42,157.

# References

Battle, K. (1995, May). Constitutional reform by stealth! *Caledon Commentary*. Ottawa: Caledon Institute of Social Policy. Retrieved from http://www.caledoninst.org/Publications/PDF/444ENG.pdf

——, Torjman, S., & Mendelson, M. (2016, 14 Apr.). The Canada Child Benefit needs to be fully indexed to inflation. *Globe and Mail*. Retrieved from http://www.theglobeandmail.com/report-on-business/rob-commentary/the-canada-child-benefit-needs-to-be-fully-indexed-in-inflation/article29619579/

Campaign 2000. (n.d.). 2016 Report Card. Retrieved from http://campaign2000.ca/wp-content/uploads/2016/11/NationalC2000Infographic2016.pdf

Canadian Payroll Association. (2017, 6 Sept.). National news release—9th annual survey. Retrieved from http://www.payroll.ca/cpadocs/npw/2017/CPA_NPW_Survey_-_national_news_release_-_2017_FINAL_EN.pdf

Canadian Rental Housing Index. (2017, 17 Apr.). Retrieved from http://www.rentalhousingindex.ca/#

*CBC News*. (2017a, 25 Feb.). Basic income in B.C.? Green Party wants it, but some welfare advocates don't. Retrieved from http://www.cbc.ca/news/canada/british-columbia/basic-income-in-b-c-green-party-wants-it-but-some-welfare-advocates-don-t-1.3999759

——. (2017b, 19 Sept.). "Minimum wage is a poverty wage": Rally calls for hike to $15/hour in Manitoba. Retrieved from http://www.cbc.ca/news/canada/manitoba/manitoba-minimum-wage-rally-1.4297636

Children First Canada. (2016). *The kids are not alright: It's time for Canada to measure up! A landmark report on the state of 2016 Canada's children*. Retrieved from https://static1.squarespace.com/static/5669d2da9cadb69fb2f8d32e/t/582e2fc13e00beacb43bde3e/1479421899329/The+kids+are+not+alright%21+Children+First+Canada+%E2%80%93+November+2016-3.pdf

City of New Westminster. (2011). What's new. Retrieved from http://www.newwestcity.ca/2010/05/13/living_wage_policy.php

Cook, L. (2015, 3 Mar.). Finland is giving 2,000 citizens a free basic income of 560 Euros a month. Retrieved from http://inhabitat.com/finland-prepares-universal-basic-income-experiment/

*Ecuador News*. (2016, 14 Mar.). Ecuador leads Latin America in poverty reduction but trend stalls in most of the region. Retrieved from https://www.cuencahighlife.com/poverty-rate-in-latin-america-stalls-after-years-of-decline-ecuador-leads-region-in-poverty-reduction-as-rates-continue-to-decline/

Fernando, S., & Earle, B. (2011). Linking poverty reduction and economic recovery: Supporting community responses to austerity in Ontario. *Canadian Review of Social Policy*, 65(6), 31–44.

Food Banks Canada. (2016). *HungerCount 2016*. Retrieved from https://www.foodbankscanada.ca/HungerCount.aspx

Fortin, P. (2016, 16 Dec.). Now is the right time for a national childcare policy. *Vancouver Sun*. Retrieved from http://www.ottawacitizen.com/Pierre+Fortin+right+time+national+childcare+policy/12539590/story.html

Fraser, L. (2016, 7 Mar.). Middle-class injustice: Too wealthy for legal aid, too pinched for "average" lawyers' fees. *CBC News*. Retrieved from http://www.cbc.ca/news/canada/legal-aid-middle-class-1.3476870

Gaetz, S., Dej, E., Richter, T., & Redman, M. (2016). *The state of homelessness in Canada 2016*. Toronto: Canadian Observatory on Homelessness Press.

Government of Canada. (2018, 17 Feb.). *Budget 2018. Equality + growth: A strong middle class*. Retrieved from https://www.budget.gc.ca/2018/home-accueil-en.html

Gutstein, D. (2014). *Harperism: How Stephen Harper and his think tank colleagues have transformed Canada*. Toronto: James Lorimer.

Harding, R. (2016). Limited and limiting conversations about the poor: Elizabethan prescriptions to poverty in the Canadian press. *Canadian Review of Social Policy / Revue Canadienne de Politique Sociale, 76*, 25–51.

Hugh, S. (2009, 24 Apr.). The last public policy frontier, eliminating poverty. Proceedings from the Annual Gow Lecture, Queen's University, Kingston, ON.

IPSOS. (2017, 8 May). Half of Canadians (52%) are $200 or less away from financial insolvency at the end of the month. Retrieved from http://www.ipsos-na.com/news-polls/pressrelease.aspx?id=7637

Irwin, J. (2004, 14 June). Commentary and fact sheets: Who's to blame for rising homelessness? Canadian Centre for Policy Alternatives

(CCPA). Retrieved from http://www.policy alternatives.ca/publications/commentary/ whos-blame-rising-homelessness

Ivanova, I. (2011, July). *The cost of poverty in BC.* CCPA. Retrieved from https://www.policy alternatives.ca/sites/default/files/uploads/ publications/BC%20Office/2011/07/CCPA_ BC_cost_of_poverty_full_report.pdf

Jeppesen, S. (2009). From the "war on poverty" to the "war on the poor": Knowledge, power, and subject positions in anti-poverty discourses. *Canadian Journal of Communication, 34*(3), 487–598.

Kane, L. (2017, 17 Sept.). B.C.'s only support group for HIV-positive women closes after funding cuts. *CBC News.* Retrieved from http://www.cbc.ca/ news/canada/british-columbia/b-c-s-only- support-group-for-hiv-positive-women- closes-after-funding-cuts-1.4294082

KELA. (2017). Basic income experiment 2017-18. Retrieved from http://www.kela.fi/web/en/ basic-income-experiment-2017-2018

Kennelly, C. (2017, Oct.*). Universal basic income guarantee: The next "big" thing in Canadian social policy.* Canadian Association of Social Workers. Retrieved from https://casw-acts.ca/ sites/casw-acts.ca/files/attachements/universal_ basic_income_guarantee_-the_next_big_ thing_in_canadian_social_policy_0.pdf

Lammam, C., & MacIntyre, H. (2015, 9 Jan.). Feds and provinces unlikely to ever agree on guaran-teed annual income. *Battlefords News-Optimist.* Retrieved from http://www.newsoptimist.ca/ opinion/columnists/feds-and-provinces- unlikely-to-ever-agree-on-guaranteed-annual- income-1.1725792

Lawless, J. (2017, 8 Mar.). Iceland will be first country to require firms to prove equal pay. *Globe and Mail.* Retrieved from https://beta.theglobe andmail.com/report-on-business/international- business/european-business/iceland-will-be- first-country-to-require-firms-to-prove-equal- pay/article34237414/?ref=http://www.theglobe andmail.com&service=mobile

Levitas, R. (2005). *The inclusive society: Social exclu-sion and new labour* (2nd edn). Basingstoke, UK: Palgrave.

Living Wage for Families. (n.d.). Living Wage Metro Vancouver. Retrieved from http://www.living wageforfamilies.ca/living_wages_in_bc_ and_canada

Macdonald, D., & Friendly, M. (2016, Dec.). A grow-ing concern: 2016 child care fees in Canada's big cities. CCPA. Retrieved from https://www .policyalternatives.ca/sites/default/files/uploads/

publications/National%20Office/2016/12/A_ Growing_Concern.pdf

Martin, M. (2011). International perspectives on guaranteed annual income programs. *Queen's Policy Review, 2*(1), 49–61.

Milne, K (2016, July). High stakes: The impacts of child care on the human rights of women and children. Vancouver: West Coast Women's Legal Education and Action Fund. Retrieved from http://www.westcoastleaf.org/wp-content/ uploads/2016/07/High-Stakes-low-resfor-web.pdf

Nichols, N., Schwan, K., Gaetz, S., Redman, M., French, D., Kidd, S., & O'Grady, B. (2017). *Child welfare and youth homelessness in Canada: A proposal for action.* Toronto: Canadian Observ-atory on Homelessness Press.

Nicolau, L. (2017, 20 Feb.). Ecuador: Approach to poverty could change under new government. *Humanosphere.* Retrieved from http://www .humanosphere.org/world-politics/2017/02/ ecuador-approach-to-poverty-could-change- under-new-government/

Ordóñez, A., Samman, E., Mariotti, C., & Borja, I. M. (2015, Oct.). Sharing the fruits of progress: Poverty reduction in Ecuador: Research reports and studies. Overseas Development Institute. Retrieved from https:// www.odi.org/publications/9958-ecuador- extreme-poverty-progress-reduction-inequality

Piano, M. (2014, January). Canada 2020 Analytical Commentary No. 6: Are we ready for universal childcare in Canada? Recommendations for equality of opportunity through childcare in Canada. Retrieved from http://canada2020 .ca/wpcontent/uploads/2014/01/Canada- 2020-Analytical-Commentary-No.-6- Universalchildcare-Jan-29-2014.pdf

Positive Living Fraser Valley. (2017). Current and coming events. Retrieved from http://www.plfv .org/events.html

Raphael, D. (2011). *Poverty in Canada: Implications for health and quality of life* (2nd edn). Toronto: Canadian Scholars' Press.

Sarlo, C. (2013). *Poverty: Where do we draw the line?* Vancouver: Fraser Institute. Retrieved from http://www.fraserinstitute.org

Shaker, E., & Macdonald, D. (2015, Sept.). *What's the difference? Taking stock of provincial tuition fee policies.* CCPA. https://www.policyalternatives .ca/sites/default/files/uploads/publications/ National%20Office/2015/09/Whats_the_ Difference.pdf

Silver, J. (2014). *About Canada: Poverty.* Halifax: Fernwood.

Stanford, J. (2015). *Economics for everyone: A short guide to the economics of capitalism* (2nd edn). London: Pluto Press.

Statistics Canada. (2017a, 8 Mar.). Women in Canada: Women and paid work. *The Daily*. Retrieved from https://www150.statcan.gc.ca/n1/daily-quotidien/170308/dq170308b-eng.htm

———. (2017b, 26 May). Table 206-0042—Low income statistics by economic family type, Canada, provinces and selected census metropolitan areas (CMAs), annual. *CANSIM database*. Retrieved from http://www5.statcan.gc.ca/cansim/a26?lang=eng&retrLang=eng&id=2060042&&pattern=&stByVal=1&p1=1&p2=31&tabMode=dataTable&csid=

———. (2017c, 9 Sept.). Household income in Canada: Key results from the 2016 Census. *The Daily*. Retrieved from http://www.statcan.gc.ca/daily-quotidien/170913/dq170913a-eng.htm

Tester, F. J., & Case, R. (1999). *Critical choices, turbulent times. Vol. II: Retreat and resistance in the reform of Canadian social policy*. Vancouver: School of Social Work, University of British Columbia.

Torjman, S., Mendelson, M., & Battle, K. (2017, Mar.). *The 2017 farewell budget*. Ottawa: Caledon Institute of Social Policy. Retrieved from http://www.caledoninst.org/Publications/PDF/1111ENG.pdf

Townsend, M. (2012, 1 Mar.). Undermining Canada's retirement income system: It's simply untrue Old Age Security is unsustainable. CCPA.

Tweddle, A., Battle, K., & Torjman, S. (2017, Nov.). *Welfare in Canada, 2016*. Ottawa: Caledon Institute of Social Policy. Retrieved from http://www.caledoninst.org/Publications/PDF/1119ENG.pdf

UNICEF Office of Research (2017). *Innocenti Report Card 14: Building the future: Children and the sustainable development goals in rich countries*. Florence, Italy: UNICEF Office of Research—Innocenti.

Weisbrot, M., Johnston, J., & Merling, L. (2017, Feb.). *Decade of reform: Ecuador's macroeconomic policies, institutional changes, and results*. Washington, DC: Center for Economic and Policy Research. Retrieved from http://cepr.net/images/stories/reports/ecuador-2017-02.pdf

Wolfson, M. (2015, June). *What me worry? Income risks for retiring Canadians*. CCPA Ontario. Retrieved from https://www.policyalternatives.ca/publications/reports/what-me-worry

# 19 Conclusion

## Social Policy and the Promise of Social Change

*Robert Harding and Daphne Jeyapal*

Social policy is deeply political. While laws and policies in Canada are usually written in neutral terms that may, at first blush, seem fair and egalitarian, they inevitably have unequal and inequitable impacts on people based on dimensions of their social location. We've seen that Indigenous people, racialized groups, women, LGBTQ people, people with disabilities, children and youth, the elderly, and those who are poor in Canada experience dramatically different outcomes based on policy. These differential impacts are based on assumptions of neutrality and funding formulas that are rationalized and supported by dominant discourses, which in turn are influenced and enforced by politicians, the corporate sector, news media, and other institutions, such as public education and the criminal justice system. Discourses delimit what is possible for social policy to achieve, and what is not, based on deeply held ideological assumptions, such as *Canada is a fair and just society for everyone* and *individuals are largely responsible for their own well-being.* This discourse assumes that everyone begins at the same starting point and requires the same intervention to arrive at the same destination. However, we know this is not the case.

As the chapters of this book highlight, communities and groups experience enduring historical, contemporary, and intersecting oppressions, exclusions, and discriminations that must first be addressed. While governments often perpetuate ineffective policy mired in outmoded assumptions, we have also seen new approaches to policy that attempt to produce equitable and anti-oppressive outcomes. In this chapter, we briefly highlight some of the lessons offered from around the world, from Canadian society, and from Indigenous communities who have been developing practices of social welfare to care for communities since time immemorial.

## Expanding Our Policy Universe beyond Canadian and American Borders

In Canada, our social policies are often compared to those in the US, with our much larger southern neighbour suffering badly in comparison. In the news media, Canada is portrayed as having a stronger social safety net and our citizens are seen as having far greater social entitlements, including something that many Americans covet—universal free health care. Dominant discourse constructs our citizens as fortunate to have such impressive benefits, which leads to the inevitable question, *How could our system be any more generous than it already is?* By presuming that our policy has gone as far as it can go in addressing people's needs, we delimit our future policy options.

Yet once we expand our policy analysis beyond the borders of Canada and the US, we find countless examples of highly effective policies that approach basic human needs in fundamentally different ways than we do: they provide profoundly different levels of entitlement and achieve far better outcomes in terms of equality, quality of life, and social inclusion. For example, while news media constantly reinforce the fact that our post-secondary tuition is lower than US fees, students in many other countries pay considerably less than ours or pay no tuition at all. In fact, Denmark, Finland, Norway, Sweden, and other European countries provide tuition-free post-secondary education to all their citizens. Even countries with far lower per capita GDPs than Canada, such as Ecuador and Brazil, offer free tuition for post-secondary education.

Cuba, another country with a low per capita GDP, demonstrates the difference policy can make when a government is committed to tackling issues of inequality. Despite Canada's persistent discourse that the fight for gender equality has already been won, women are still at a significant disadvantage to men. Cuba's commitment to gender equality begins with its constitution, which guarantees equal opportunities for all. Numerous practical policies ensure that this objective is achieved, including child-care centres, elderly residences, and paid maternity leave before and after childbirth. These policies have produced measurable positive results in employment, politics, and the criminal justice system that far exceed what we have accomplished in Canada.

It is also important not to underestimate the difference that recognizing a social policy issue as a national priority can make. It's hard to imagine a more fundamental need than food. Yet, we seem to be very far from having a national policy on food, an area that has been incorporated into policy and, in some cases, into the constitutions of countries such as Venezuela, Ecuador, Bolivia, Nicaragua, Mali, Brazil, Nepal, and Senegal. Canada has also yet to confront its rapid increases in homelessness as a national issue. Finland, on the other hand, has seen homelessness steadily decreasing ever since that country made reducing it a national priority. Even Ecuador, a so-called "poor, developing country," has dramatically reduced poverty and achieved major gains in human development. These improvements began in 2007 when its new government made poverty reduction and income redistribution a priority, implemented policies to achieve this in areas such as health care and education, and established a new ministry to oversee these changes. Today, Ecuador is seen as a poverty reduction leader in Latin America.

# Drawing Inspiration from Our Homegrown Policy Successes

While there are no shortages of effective international policies that Canada can look to, we can also take inspiration from our homegrown successes. One such policy is Quebec's universal government-subsidized daycare system, the only one of its kind in Canada.

While it is not free, at $7.75 a day, parents can access government-regulated daycare for far less than anywhere else in the country. Many parents face a difficult choice between paying for expensive child care or staying home and raising children while relying on social assistance, a sole (part-time and/or precarious) income, or a partner's income. All scenarios can result in families living below the poverty line. While far from perfect— there are limited daycare spaces and long waiting lists—Quebec's program represents an important step towards a universal daycare system, an approach that has the potential to help families out of poverty and enable single parents, especially women, to attain economic independence.

Also, for the first time in a long time, how we think and talk about core social policy issues in Canada is shifting. Conversations now include refreshing new ideas such as in-dexation of benefits, legalization or decriminalization of illegal drugs, living wages, and guaranteed annual income programs. In 2017, Ontario implemented a free undergraduate tuition policy for low-income students and introduced a basic income program on a trial basis in three communities; other provinces have now expressed an interest in piloting GAI programs. That same year, the federal government announced its intention to get back into the business of developing affordable housing, and has promised to launch a $40 billion National Housing Strategy.

# Learning from Indigenous Peoples about Effective Policies and Practices

Local social policy successes are not recent phenomena because Indigenous peoples relied on the principles of kinship, fellowship, and sociality to foster communal ties for millennia. Mutual support expressed in healing and helping traditions formed a coherent, autochthonous social welfare system that was sustained and supported by group members. Canada's approach to colonization left no room for these traditional ways of providing social welfare. Modern society saw no value in customary healing, which it disparaged as "heathenism" and regarded as an impediment to progress. As Canada grapples with the concept of reconciliation, Indigenous people are rediscovering the reality that healthy individuals enhance the well-being of their communities. Their experience might be the example that benefits the lives of all people in Canada.

One example offers a new way to think about "justice" itself. As Chapters 6 and 16 demonstrate, Indigenous people have been terribly harmed through the imposition of a racist criminal justice system, one that has resulted in extremely high rates of incarceration and caused inestimable destruction to individuals, families, and communities. Now, as Indigenous peoples reclaim responsibility for justice from settler authorities, they have been implementing traditional ways of dealing with these issues. For example, in British Columbia's Fraser Valley, the Stó:lō Nation's Qwí:qwelstóm program offers Indigenous offenders a peacemaking process, relying on Elders and consensus-based decision-making. Traditional restorative justice programs like this are helping Indigenous people across the country to resolve infractions and disputes in culturally appropriate ways and restore harmony, balance, and health to families and communities. Culturally restorative programs all over the country are confronting issues of social, political, economic, and legal justice relating to poverty, health care, housing, sexuality, gender rights, women's rights, and food sovereignty, among others. These avenues of Indigenous-led resistance and advocacy offer innovative ways through which our profession can learn, embody, and practise new ways of knowing and working towards social change.

# We Have the Power to Transform: Our Choices Make a Difference

When we reinvent policy conversations through lessons from home and abroad, we reposition ourselves as agents of change. While governments implement policy, our ideas and conversations about policy issues can justify a wide range of responses to them. As social workers, we need to be part of these conversations, challenge assumptions about neutrality, human nature, and the inequalities that inform them, and actively engage in policy-making processes. First and foremost, we must always challenge ourselves to think critically about social policy issues: How do we come to think about collective need in the ways that we do? How does a person's social location affect how policy impacts them? What values, ideologies, forces, and factors influence our support of one response over another? What sort of policy choices do dominant media and institutional discourses promote? How can we alter such discourses in the public, within communities, and within ourselves? These are some of the questions we must ask to promote policy that aligns with our professional values of pursuing social justice, combatting oppression, and promoting the equitable distribution of opportunities and resources. We must make our voices heard in policy debates, and counter dominant discourses that harm marginalized populations.

Our goal through this book has been to ground the realm of policy as one that, at its core, relates to choices made by people: choices made by people engaging in public discourse, choices made by policy-makers, choices made by the recipients of social policy, and choices made by social workers on whether, when, and how to implement policy when they work alongside those they serve. Each of the preceding chapters highlights narratives from social workers working within government organizations, the social service sector, and community-based settings who have chosen creative ways to challenge and change policy. Collectively, they showcase the potential and promise of social change by transforming policy contexts that restrain the lives and aspirations of those they serve. Their stories of advocacy and activism demonstrate how necessary and possible it is to resist and reform policy by viewing social policy as an investment in social justice. They challenge us to disrupt the ways in which social policy operates as a force of social injustice, and remind us that social policy can also be a site of critical, anti-oppressive social work practice. By confronting social work's convoluted past, we, as they do, believe our future legacies can embody new promises and potentials for social change and social justice in Canadian society.

# Glossary

**ableism:** The devaluing and oppression of (dis)Abled people while privileging, in comparison, able-bodied persons. Ableism is evident in personal attitudes, beliefs, and behaviours, as well as through social policies and organizational and societal infrastructures, that prevent (dis)Abled people from full participation in society.

**absolute and relative measures of poverty:** Absolute measures compare income with the costs for basic subsistence (food, clothing, shelter), so that those whose income does not meet basic needs are considered to be living in poverty; relative measures, in addition, also take into account the living standards of other people in the community.

**academic attendant:** A person who assists with activities of a (dis)Abled person beyond the duties of a regular attendant, such as, besides helping a worker dress for winter weather and assisting with getting the person to a meeting, but also helping with cognitive processing and the more academic-related aspects of a job, such as typing on a keyboard and conceptual presentation of thoughts. The person with the (dis)Ability has the expertise but conveying that knowledge is assisted by the academic attendant.

**agenda-setting:** The process by which news media focus on selected issues and topics, while marginalizing or ignoring others—in effect, determining what is on the agenda for public debate. In this way, the news media play a critical role in foregrounding what is important about social policy.

**all-in less cash transfers:** The combined central and sub-central government income tax plus employee social security contribution, less family benefits (in respect of dependent children) paid by government as universal cash transfers, as a percentage of gross wage earnings.

**anglosphere:** The white settler nations that grew out of British colonialism and still form the dominant culture of Canada, the United States, Australia, and New Zealand.

**backlash:** Adverse discursive, social, and political reactions, usually in response to social progress.

**basic income:** A policy intervention that guarantees a minimum income (also known as a *guaranteed annual income*), with the potential to reduce food insecurity in low-income households.

**binary opposition:** An argumentation strategy employed in news discourse, where two parties or ideas are constructed as being diametrically opposed to each other.

**bisexuals:** People who have desires towards and are sexually attracted to both men and women.

**cisgenderism:** A belief that remaining in the biological sex assignment at birth is normal and superior to transitioning from that assignment.

**citizens plus:** The concept that, in addition to the usual rights of Canadian citizenship, Indigenous peoples, many of whom signed peace agreements and treaties with the Canadian state or its colonial predecessors, possess additional rights as the original inhabitants of the land now called Canada.

**classical conservatism:** An ideology that accepts "human inequality—social, political, and economic—as part of the natural order of things" (Brooks, 2012, p. 38 [Chapter 3]) and stresses the importance of tradition, continuity with the past, the maintenance of law and order, support for the monarchy, and the belief that the well-off have an obligation to assist the poor.

**classical socialism:** An ideology, based on the principle of equality of condition, proposing that when individuals have roughly equivalent levels of wealth, power, and status, they will be better able achieve their full potential. Socialism, by definition, is critical of capitalism and the economic and social relations it creates.

**conflation:** When diverse groups and perspectives are subsumed into a single monolithic label. Conflation is a problematic feature of much racialized news coverage, especially when specific sets of behaviours or motivations are ascribed to all members of a particular racial group, such as Indigenous peoples or Muslims, and significant variations and differences are glossed over.

**congregate housing:** Housing facility offering a range of housing units with full-service supports to meet all the needs of residents, such as previously homeless people.

**contested space:** A place, such as the news media, where the meaning of texts can be and is challenged by alternative discourses. In contrast, corporate and political elites enjoy obvious advantages in getting their messages across.

**criminalization:** A process through which some actions and some people are labelled as criminal whereas other people involved in the same behaviours are not.

**critical discourse analysis (CDA):** A form of textual analysis that emphasizes how power operates through language.

It involves examining how word choice, argumentative strategies, ideology, and other textual features are used to frame social issues and create dominant discourses.

**critical intersectional framework:** A framework that forefronts critical theory and the concept of intersectionality to examine social issues and how they intersect with social identities and peoples' lives.

**critical race theory:** A field of study that examines the insidious nature of racialization, its entrenchment in social policy, and its different impacts.

**cultural safety:** Concept that acknowledges the impact of colonialism and socio-economic position on health care services for Indigenous peoples (Gerlach, 2012 [Chapter 15]).

**designated country of origin:** A term constructed through Bill C-31 that refers to a country assumed to be "safe" by the Canadian government. Cases of asylum seekers from "safe" or "designated countries," as listed by the Canadian government, are handled differently from and more quickly than those whose countries are not on the list.

**diasporas:** The dispersion of people and communities from their country of origin.

**(dis)Ability:** The term "disability" with emphasis on the multiple "Abilities" of people who live with impairment; "the results from the interaction between persons with impairments and attitudinal and environmental barriers that hinders their full and effective participation in society on an equal basis with others" (UN, 2008 [Chapter 10]).

**discourse:** Communication practices of all forms that are interconnected with the broader political, social, and cultural context.

**discrepancies:** The difference between the ratio of a particular group to the total population and the representation of that group in an identified circumstance. This difference suggests inequality.

**discursive formulation:** The social boundaries that define what can be said about a specific topic. They relate to the parameters of the language, social relations, and social identities that are considered true, relevant, and appropriate for a particular topic.

**dominant discourse:** The mainstream discourse on any issue, which is typically reinforced by those in positions of power.

**equality:** Defined by sociologists as equal status in measurements of population data in areas such as life expectancy, income, education, and employment opportunities.

**essentialism:** The idea that any individual can be identified by characteristics of the group.

**eugenics movement:** Social engineering movement that aimed to improve humanity through "measures to promote the survival of the fittest and to discourage the reproduction of undesirables in an attempt to purify society" (Mackelprang & Salsgiver, 2015, p. 7 [Chapter 10]).

**Fathers of Confederation:** The 36 white men who elaborated the founding document of Canada, the British North America Act of 1867.

**fiscal policy:** Economic policy related to public expenditures and taxation.

**flat tax:** A tax, such as property tax, applied at the same rate to all income levels, as opposed to progressive taxation, such as income tax, where those with more income pay proportionally more.

**Food and Agriculture Organization (FAO):** An agency of the United Nations that leads international efforts to defeat hunger. It serves developed and developing countries, and acts as a forum where states can negotiate agreements and debate policy.

**food insecurity:** A condition that exists when people do not have assured physical, social, or economic access to enough food to meet their dietary needs and food preferences. There are various levels of food insecurity: see *severe food insecurity, moderate food security, marginal food security,* and *food vulnerable.*

**food sovereignty:** A political framework developed by La Via Campesina that focuses on the right of peoples and government to determine their own agriculture systems, food markets, environments, and mode of production; a radical alternative to corporate-led, neo-liberal industrial agriculture.

**food system:** All of the activities and processes involved in the ways that people produce, obtain, consume, and dispose of their food, including the inputs and outputs required to run the system.

**food vulnerable:** Those who are uncertain of being able to secure the basic necessities for living and/or flourishing.

**framing:** How news media single out certain themes or storylines for attention while de-emphasizing or ignoring others.

**gays:** Men who have desires towards and are sexually attracted to other men. Historically and sometimes still used to include men and women with same-sex desires.

**gender:** The expression of what is socially and culturally constructed about the nature of femininity and masculinity, that is, the social norms and expectations around what it means to present as a man, woman, or other identity. Gender is different from the sex of a person, which is assigned at birth.

**guaranteed annual income (GAI):** An alternative to social assistance whereby every citizen receives a guaranteed income. This non-stigmatizing and non-means-tested policy approach does not require recipients to work, and is efficient since all income supplementation programs and tax measures can be rolled into the GAI and the costly administrative regimes eliminated. For middle-class and well-off people, some or all of the GAI benefit can be recouped through the income tax system.

**hashtag activism:** The strategic use of social media as means of social change, which has played a significant role in the rise, organization, and awareness of recent social justice movements such as Idle No More, Black Lives Matter, and Me Too.

**heteronormative:** Assumptions within society and its institutions that heterosexuality is the norm.

**heterosexism:** A belief that heterosexuality is normal and superior to any other sexual orientation.

**high-responsibility practice style:** A pattern of providing primary medical care with high-activity rates across the following categories: referrals to specialists, initial prescribing for long-term medications, repeat visits, patient oversight, and screening and risk management (McGrail, et al., 2015 [Chapter 15]).

**holistic care model:** An approach to health care in which transportation assistance and health, social, and legal services can be accessed at the same location.

**homo-bi-transphobia:** An irrational fear of those with same-sex or bisexual desires and/or transsexual, transgender people.

**homonormalizing:** What happens when lesbians, gays, and bisexuals ascribe to heterosexual norms in order to gain acceptance and respect, as is the case with same-sex marriage.

**housing insecurity:** A state of being determined by the physical condition of housing, its suitability for the number and the needs of the occupants (children, accommodate disabilities), and the affordability of the residence. Households are considered by the Canada Mortgage and Housing Corporation to be in "core housing need" (or "housing

insecure") when they live in housing that requires major repairs, does not have enough bedrooms for household size, and/or costs more than 30 per cent of before-tax household income.

**hypervisibility:** The news media's ability to draw intense attention to certain groups and populations, or to highlight some features of the news over others. See *agenda-setting*.

**imagined community:** Based on the work of Benedict Anderson (1983 [Chapter 2]), how nationhood and national identity are socially constructed through the imaginings of some citizens who perceive themselves as representative of a particular vision of their nation. News coverage of Indigenous peoples and racialized migrants sometimes constructs them as existing outside the symbolic borders of the imagined community of Canada.

**income-tested benefit:** Benefits for which eligibility is determined by the applicant's income.

**Indigenous food sovereignty:** A restorative framework for nurturing our relationship with one another and the culturally relevant plants, animals, and waterways that provide us with food.

**Indigenous peoples**: As defined by the section 35(2) of the Constitution Act, 1982, "the Indian, Inuit and Métis peoples of Canada."

**intergenerational transfer:** An asset or benefit transferred from one family member to another family member of a younger generation.

**intersectionality:** A conceptual tool that allows us to consider how social identities can be connected and interlocked in complex ways.

**intersex:** People born either with both male and female genitalia or with ambiguous genitalia.

**intertextuality:** How discursive texts shape each other, based on the reader's prior knowledge and frameworks.

**Inuit:** One of Canada's three constitutionally defined "aboriginal peoples." Inuit historically have lived above the treeline in the Arctic, in the areas of Canada now known as Nunavut, northern Quebec, Labrador, and the Northwest Territories.

**Jordan's Principle:** A principle established by the federal government in 2007 that obliges governments to act immediately in the best interests of Indigenous children before resolving jurisdiction disputes; after Jordan River Anderson, a Cree boy who died in hospital in 2005 at the age of five while federal and Manitoba officials argued over which jurisdiction was financially responsible for his in-home care.

**La Via Campesina:** An international movement that co-ordinates peasant organizations of small- and middle-scale producers, agricultural workers, rural women, and Indigenous communities in Asia, Africa, the Americas, the Middle East, and Europe. It is an important transnational social movement fighting for food sovereignty and against globalization.

**lesbians:** Women who have desires for and are sexually attracted to other women.

**lexical choices:** Conscious decisions made by editors or reporters to use particular words, often to convey specific meanings and definitions of events. Word choice can influence the way readers understand an issue, define solutions to a problem, or view an entire population or group of people.

**liberalism:** An ideology "associated with freedom of religious choice and practice, free enterprise and free trade in the realm of economics, and freedom of expression and association in politics"(Brooks, 2012, p. 37 [Chapter 3]).

**low-responsibility practice style:** A pattern of providing primary medical care with low-activity rates across the following categories: referrals to specialists, initial prescribing for long-term medications, repeat visits, patient oversight, and screening and risk management (McGrail et al., 2015 [Chapter 15]).

**mandatory private social expenditure:** Social support stipulated by legislation but operated through the private sector, e.g., direct sickness payments by employers to their absent employees as legislated by public authorities, or benefits accruing from mandatory contributions to private insurance funds.

**marginal food insecurity:** Circumstance in which people worry about running out of food and/or limit food selection because of lack of money for food.

**means-tested benefit:** Benefit, such as social assistance, for which eligibility is determined by an examination of the applicant's assets, savings, income, and expenses.

**meritocracy:** A system that rewards all talented, hard-working individuals with status and financial success. Wealth and success are determined solely by one's ability and work ethic, not by class or privilege.

**Métis:** One of Canada's three constitutionally defined "aboriginal peoples"; historically identified as the descendants of mixed-race marriages between European fur traders and Indigenous women with a focus on the culture that emerged along the Red River in southern Manitoba. Contemporary definitions, for political and land claim reasons, have emphasized Indigenous–European marriages irrespective of their geographical setting, such as the Inuit-Métis of Labrador.

**mixed economy of welfare:** The various forms in which welfare needs are met in nation-states today. This usually includes a non-profit or charitable sector, a co-operative sector, a fee-for-service/commercial sector, and a state/public sector. Determining the balance between these sectors at any point in time is a matter of political discourse and debate.

**moderate food insecurity:** A situation in which households compromise in quality and/or quantity of food due to a lack of money for food.

**moral panic:** A situation whereby the public becomes alarmed, fearful, angry because of a specific issue involving a subaltern group (e.g., Muslims in North America after 9/11; immigrants/refugees from war-torn or crime-ridden countries) or deviant behaviour (e.g., crime; reefer madness), often arising out of disproportionate (and exaggerated) attention given to a group or activity by politicians and/or by news and social media.

**mutual aid:** Those sharing a common bond working together to help one another in good times and bad.

**nationalism:** An ideology that places the needs and formation of the nation-state above all else.

**neo-conservatism:** A variant of traditional conservatism that began in the 1970s and that emphasizes political individualism and free markets, and was a label given to the governments of Margaret Thatcher in the UK (1979–90), Ronald Reagan in the US (1981–9), and Brian Mulroney in Canada (1984–93). Neo-conservatives argue social programs are too generous, create dependency, reduce individual initiative, and make the state rather than the individual responsible for welfare. They also typically take a conservative position on "moral" issues such as same-sex marriage and abortion.

**neo-liberal/neo-liberalism:** A political ideology that focuses on free markets and economic growth, with policies that emphasize deregulation, privatization, state reform (downsizing), and the creation of an outward-oriented (export) economy; linked to globalization.

**non-status Indians:** Indians who are not registered under the Indian Act. Indian women and their children typically lost their status under the Indian Act as a result of marriage.

**occupational welfare:** Non-wage benefits provided by an employer to enhance the work environment and maintain good employee relations.

**OECD (Organization for Economic Co-operation and Development):** A multilateral organization of 35 mostly developed countries, chiefly from Western Europe and other industrialized countries such as Canada, the US, and Japan, that seeks to co-ordinate social and economic policy.

**othering:** The reliance on a binary of "us" versus "them" to define power relationships and hierarchies of superiority and inferiority among groups of people.

**Paleopathology:** Science that studies the afflictions and ailments that affected the health and personal integrity of ancient peoples.

**parens patriae:** Latin term meaning "the state as parent of the nation," the underlying principle of the Juvenile Delinquents Act (1908) that prioritized guidance over punishment of young people or the protection of society.

**per capita funding:** Providing an average amount of money per person.

**positionality:** Our location in a community, which might include class, nationality, citizenship, gender, religion, level of education, and employment status.

**potlatch:** A ceremonial giveaway practice among Northwest Coast Indigenous groups to celebrate or mourn particular events, especially in relation to the host, normally a chief, who would distribute gifts—blankets, boxes, canoes, copper plates, food, utensils—in a display of generosity and wealth.

**precarious employment:** Unstable jobs with low pay and poor working conditions that are not protected by union agreements. Women are heavily over-represented in precarious work.

**priming:** The process by which news media influence and determine the criteria the public use to evaluate matters of social policy. Thus, certain aspects of a policy issue are covered (e.g., the cost of daycare) while others (e.g., no-cost universal daycare) are not. See *agenda-setting*.

**progressively redistributive taxation:** Tax system whereby those with lower incomes are taxed proportionally less than those with higher incomes.

**property taxes:** Taxes on individual or business property, such as a house or a factory, determined by the property's assessed value.

**queer:** An umbrella term to capture diverse sexualities, gender identities, and expressions, and the fluidity therein; also used as a politicized term to indicate pride in being different based on one's sexual orientation and/or gender identity and expression.

**questioning:** People who are unsure of their sexual orientation and/or gender identity and expression and who are exploring.

**race:** The visually observable physical differences among people and groups, such as skin colour, hair, and facial features. While physical traits may distinguish us from each other, social theorists now understand that the meaning-making process behind these physical traits is more significant than any real biological or physical difference.

**racialization:** The social and discursive practice that denotes some people as "different" or "inferior" because of their physical appearance as members of an identifiable group and that marks them for unequal treatment based on perceived biological, physiological, intellectual, or moral differences.

**red Tories:** "[C]onservatives who believe that government has a responsibility to act as an agent for the collective good, and that this responsibility goes far beyond maintaining law and order" (Brooks, 2012, p. 68 [Chapter 3]) to include an obligation towards the poor and less privileged through welfare state programs. While essentially paternalistic, the role of the state is to bind society together, to support the national culture, and to protect the poor.

**"regime of truth":** A Foucauldian concept that refers to how dominant understandings of "truth" are created. "Truth" is not necessarily accurate, but is subjectively and socially constructed through power relations.

**Regina v. Drybones:** Landmark case of 1969 in which the Supreme Court ruled that section 94 of the Indian Act (1951) banning Indians from being intoxicated off reserve had to be repealed. The impact of this decision was profound as it was the first sign of a more activist Court in regard to the limited 1960 Canadian Bill of Rights and signalled an initial step in Canadian jurisprudence towards the Charter.

**regressive taxation:** A tax system where lower-income individuals are taxed at the same rate as those with higher incomes or at a higher proportional rate than those with higher incomes.

**sales tax:** "Tax imposed as a percentage of the price of goods (and sometimes services). The tax is generally paid by the buyer but the seller is responsible for collecting and remitting the tax to the tax authorities" (OECD, 2017c [Chapter 5]).

**scattered site housing**: An option for more independent living for those in need of housing, such as the homeless, that provides placement in private apartments with varied levels of ongoing support by community organizations and provincial agencies. See *congregate housing*.

**scientific racism:** The scientific study of supposed biological or constitutional racial differences that aimed to classify racial superiority and inferiority.

**scripts:** A specific set of behaviours ascribed to a certain type of actors that appear in the news. In *Language and Power*, Fairclough (1989, pp. 158–9 [Chapter 2]) writes that scripts "typify the ways in which specific classes of subjects behave in social activities, and how members of specific classes of subjects behave towards each other—how they conduct relationships." There are strict social expectations about how these actors must behave in a range of situations.

**securitization:** The process of transforming a policy area into the realm of security, as happened in 2018 when President Trump imposed steel and aluminum tariffs on Canada and EU countries based on the bogus rationale that this was for national security reasons.

**severe food insecurity:** When access to food is so limited that people have to miss meals, reduce meals, or go days without food.

**sex:** Biological differences between men and women. The assumption used to be that this was fixed at birth, but variants within this constructed dichotomy are possible and common.

**single-room occupancy (SRO) unit:** A form of housing consisting of a single room that is typically targeted to low-income populations. Kitchen facilities and bathrooms are often shared with other residents.

**Sixties Scoop:** The aggressive adoption practices of provincial child welfare agencies during the 1960s and 1970s, when approximately 15,000 children were placed in white middle-class homes in Canada and the United States.

**social capital**: "[T]he power within society that the individual derives from attachment to social networks, such as work, church groups, community associations, clubs, and the like" (Brooks, 2012, p. 563 [Chapter 3]).

**social conservatism:** The promotion of non-fiscal conservative values in political life such as heterosexual lifelong marriage, a traditional role for women in the family, and opposition to divorce, abortion, LGBTQ rights, and same-sex marriage (Conservapedia, 2017 [Chapter 3]). These views are commonly found in Canada among members of

the Roman Catholic and evangelical Christian churches, and among the more conservative wings of Conservative parties at the federal and provincial levels.

**social democracy:** The gradual movement towards socialism achieved through social reform in a parliamentary democracy. There is a favourable attitude towards state intervention to achieve greater equality in society, to fairly distribute economic rewards, and to manage capitalism's economic cycles. Social democrats generally favour a mixed and full employment economy, some nationalization of key industries, and an active role for government to ensure stable economic growth.

**social determinants of health:** The socio-economic conditions that influence the health of communities and individuals, such as income, conditions of childhood, the quality and availability of food, housing, education, employment, and social and health services.

**social insurance:** Programs defined through legislation and operated by government. Participants make contributions and, in return, receive benefits. Employment Insurance and the Q/CPP are examples of social insurance programs.

**social investment strategy:** Welfare state strategy, now common in the EU, to ensure maximum returns on social expenditures through active labour force employment and social participation, in effect, to change from being a "handout" state to a "hand-up" state by encouraging full employment for all those able to work.

**social policy:** Broadly, a regulatory force that constructs, maintains, and challenges social welfare and the state. It is inextricably linked to economic policy, and constructed through political processes within a context of interconnected systems and structures of power. In Canada, an examination of social policy reveals the social divisions of society and the unequal distribution of wealth and power in an increasingly neo-liberal environment.

**social provisioning**: Caring work (usually unpaid) such as rearing children and caring for those who are sick, disabled, elderly, or dying.

**social reproduction**: The range of unpaid work—social, physical, emotional, and material—involved in caring for children and families that reproduces the workforce daily and over generations.

**social security contributions:** Payments (for salaried employees, payroll deductions) made to government through the tax system by employees, employers, self-employed persons, and others subject to income tax to cover the cost of social security payments they will receive in later years.

**status Indian:** Someone registered as an Indian under the Indian Act. Bill C-31 in 1985 restored Indian status to some women and their children who lost it through marriage.

**stereotyping:** When specific labels are attached to entire groups or classes of individuals (e.g., Indigenous people, LGBTQ persons, or single mothers), whole patterns of behaviour and constellations of personality traits are ascribed to individuals.

**subjectivities:** How identities are made possible within a given discourse. In order to be socially recognized, individuals are asked, or required, to occupy certain subject positions.

**sweat lodges:** Structures constructed of willow branches and covered with tarps to create secular and ritual space. When constructed for secular, hygienic purposes, the sweat lodge is a rudimentary sauna. Hot rocks are placed in a small pit dug in the centre and water is poured on the rocks to produce steam. Building one for ceremony follows the same construction but emphasizes the ritual nature of the space.

**systemic racism:** The disenfranchisement of racialized groups at a structural level. Unlike individual racism or micro-aggressions that operate on a person-to-person level, these are macro societal structures that disadvantage racialized people.

**systems of representation:** Recurring dominant discourses that provide readily understandable ways of interpreting events, histories, and people.

**targeted or selective benefits and programs:** Benefits and programs available to some but not others, and that require applicants to meet a range of specific criteria that include need, program participation (e.g., EI), condition (e.g., disability) or income level.

**tax burden:** In public finance, "the total tax payments for a particular fiscal year as a fraction or percentage of the gross national product (GNP) or national income for that year" (OECD, 2017c [Chapter 5]).

**tax expenditure:** The policy decision to leave a certain amount of money with the taxpayer to compensate for expenses in a defined area. In effect, it is a decision by government to *not* collect taxes.

**text:** In discourse analysis, all acts of communication including written words, spoken words, body movements, gestures, clothing, accents, smells, codes, and conventions.

**transgender:** People who identify with a gender that is not necessarily congruent with the biological sex they were assigned at birth.

**transsexuals:** People who have undergone sex-reassignment surgery to transition from the biological sex assignment at birth to the opposite sex.

**tutelary complex:** State agents who apply the new knowledge claims, educative techniques, and social practices of psychiatry, psychology, and criminology to the poor and working class (Donzelot, 1997 [Chapter 3]).

**two-spirit:** An Indigenous term that recognizes people with both a male and female spirit.

**unilinear evolutionism:** The European belief that all cultures traversed or are traversing the same evolutionary route from "savagery" to European-style civilization.

**universal policy:** A policy that provides a benefit or program that is equally available to every person within a specific category (e.g., children 0 to 17).

**user fees:** Fees charged by governments, often local, only to those who use a particular service or facility, such as parks, public swimming pools, rinks, or garbage tags for garbage pickup.

**visible minorities:** Term used by Statistics Canada and the federal Employment Equity Act to define categories of racialized people, in contrast to those of European ancestry and to Indigenous people, who are not considered visible minorities.

**welfare state:** A system in which the government accepts some basic responsibility for protecting the well-being and health of its citizens—especially those in need—through various universal programs and targeted allowances and payments.

**welfare state regimes:** Those welfare systems where government recognizes the complex ties between the economy and the state.

**White Man's burden:** The Eurocentric belief that Europeans had a duty to help the non-white peoples of the world who were stalled in their inferior cultures, most famously reflected in the 1899 Rudyard Kipling poem of the same name in which he calls upon American imperialists to fulfill their duty to civilize the natives of the Philippines: "Your new-caught sullen peoples,/Half-devil and half-child."

**white privilege:** The unconscious bias white people have where they accept their experience as the normative, and therefore, superior experience.

**white settler society:** A society constructed through European colonial settler processes and policies.

**Workplace Attendant Policy**: Policy established between Nova Scotia and the federal government whereby (dis)Abled workers can be provided with an attendant to assist in basic workplace tasks.

**World Trade Organization (WTO)**: A supranational institution and set of international trade agreements that play a major role in regulating international trade, including international agriculture trade, domestic agriculture policy, and, by extension, world food security.

*Zeitgeist*: A German concept that refers to the spirit of the times.

# Index